# Quaker Records of Baltimore and Harford Counties Maryland

Births, Deaths, Marriages, Removals,
and Abstracts from the Monthly Minutes

## 1801-1825

Henry C. Peden, Jr., M.A.

HERITAGE BOOKS
2008

# HERITAGE BOOKS
*AN IMPRINT OF HERITAGE BOOKS, INC.*

**Books, CDs, and more—Worldwide**

For our listing of thousands of titles see our website
at
www.HeritageBooks.com

Published 2008 by
HERITAGE BOOKS, INC.
Publishing Division
100 Railroad Ave. #104
Westminster, Maryland 21157

Copyright © 2000 Henry C. Peden, Jr., M.A.

All rights reserved. No part of this book may be reproduced or transmitted in any form or by any means, electronic or mechanical, including photocopying, recording or by any information storage and retrieval system without written permission from the author, except for the inclusion of brief quotations in a review.

International Standard Book Numbers
Paperbound: 978-1-58549-604-4
Clothbound: 978-0-7884-7506-1

# CONTENTS

Introduction .................................................... v
Map of Quaker Meetings ........................................ vii

Gunpowder Monthly Meeting, Births and Deaths .................. 1
Gunpowder Monthly Meeting, Abstracts from the Minutes ......... 14
Little Falls Monthly Meeting, Births and Deaths ................ 58
Little Falls Monthly Meeting, Marriage Certificates ............ 73
Little Falls Monthly Meeting, Certificates of Removal .......... 77
Little Falls Monthly Meeting, Abstracts from the Minutes ....... 81
Deer Creek Monthly Meeting, Birth and Deaths .................. 94
Deer Creek Monthly Meeting, Marriage Certificates ............. 95
Deer Creek Monthly Meeting, Certificates of Removal ........... 106
Deer Creek Monthly Meeting, Minutes ........................... 114
Deer Creek Monthly Meeting, Orthodox, Members Births .......... 144
Deer Creek Monthly Meeting, Orthodox, Minutes ................. 144
Baltimore Monthly Meeting Births and Deaths ................... 156
Baltimore Monthly Meeting, Western District, Marriages ........ 169
Baltimore Monthly Meeting, Eastern District, Marriages ........ 194
Baltimore Monthly Meeting, Western District, Removals ......... 211
Baltimore Monthly Meeting, Western District, Members Births ... 240
Baltimore Monthly Meeting, Eastern District, Removals ......... 242
Baltimore Monthly Meeting, Eastern District, Births & Deaths .. 251
Baltimore Monthly Meeting, Eastern District, Minutes .......... 266

Index ......................................................... 275

Dedicated to the memory of

PHEBE ROBINSON JACOBSEN

d. April 19, 2000, aged 78

INTRODUCTION

Quakers, or Society of Friends, first settled in Maryland in 1658, primarily in southern Maryland. Their records through 1800 have been abstracted by the author in *Quaker Records of Southern Maryland: Births, Deaths, Marriages, and Abstracts from the Minutes, 1658-1800.*

On Maryland's Eastern Shore, the first Monthly Meetings were established between 1672 and 1698. Abstracts of the Eastern Shore Quaker records are included in the series *Maryland Eastern Shore Vital Records* (5 volumes) by F. Edward Wright. They are also contained in Kenneth Carroll's *Quakerism on the Eastern Shore.*

The Quaker records through 1800 in northern Maryland have been abstracted by the author in *Quaker Records of Northern Maryland: Births, Deaths, Marriages, and Abstracts from the Minutes, 1716-1800.* These records begin in 1716 for the most part, although there are references within the records as early as 1674. One should also consult *A Record of Interments at the Friends Burial Ground, Baltimore, Maryland (Est. 1681)*, by E. Erick Hoopes (1995), and *The Little Falls Meeting of Friends, 1738-1988*, by Hunter C. Sutherland (1988), for information on burials in those Quaker cemeteries.

This latest volume of Quaker records encompasses Baltimore City, Baltimore County, and Harford County from 1801 through 1825 and includes abstracts of births, deaths, marriages, burials, certificates of removal, and minutes of monthly meetings held in those areas. For more information about Quaker meetings and their records at the Maryland State Archives, one should consult Phebe R. Jacobsen's *Quaker Records in Maryland* (1966).

Briefly, however, for the purposes of this book, it should be noted that Baltimore Monthly Meeting separated from Gunpowder Monthly Meeting in 1792 and eventually led to the formation of monthly meetings circa 1800 in the Eastern and Western Districts of Baltimore City. In eastern Baltimore County the Gunpowder Monthly Meeting records begin in 1716 and include Patapsco and early Elk Ridge Meetings. In the Darlington area of northeastern Harford County the records of Deer Creek Monthly Meeting begin in 1761 and the Deer Creek Orthodox Monthly Meeting records begin circa 1819. In the Fallston area of southwestern Harford County the Little Falls Monthly Meeting records begin in 1738, but there are no minutes for that meeting until 1815.

This book is based on records at the Maryland State Archives for the five aforementioned monthly meetings from 1801 through 1825 (and in some cases beyond if the children's dates of birth started prior to 1825 and ended thereafter), as follows, with the microfilm numbers shown:

Gunpowder Monthly Meeting, Register (M626)
Gunpowder Monthly Meeting, Minutes (M628)
Gunpowder Monthly Meeting, Register (M629)
Gunpowder Monthly Meeting, Removals (M629)
Baltimore Monthly Meeting, Register (M593)
Baltimore Monthly Meeting, Minutes (M593)
Baltimore Monthly Meeting, Marriages (M577)
Baltimore Monthly Meeting, Removals (M577)
Baltimore Monthly Meeting, Western Dist., Marriages (M577)
Baltimore Monthly Meeting, Eastern Dist., Register (M593)
Baltimore Monthly Meeting, Orthodox, Minutes (M788)
Little Falls Monthly Meeting, Register (M645)
Little Falls Monthly Meeting, Minutes (M647)
Little Falls Monthly Meeting, Marriages (M645)
Little Falls Monthly Meeting, Removals (M645)
Deer Creek Monthly Meeting, Register (M609)
Deer Creek Monthly Meeting, Minutes (M608)
Deer Creek Monthly Meeting, Marriages (M609)
Deer Creek Monthly Meeting, Removals (M610)
Deer Creek Monthly Meeting, Orthodox, Register (M799)
Deer Creek Monthly Meeting, Orthodox, Minutes (M799)

It should be noted that this book contains abstracts from the above cited Quaker records that are of genealogical importance to researchers. [Notes and comments within brackets are those of the author]. One should always consult the original records for accuracy, details, and additional information.

Henry C. Peden, Jr.
Bel Air, Maryland
May 1, 2000

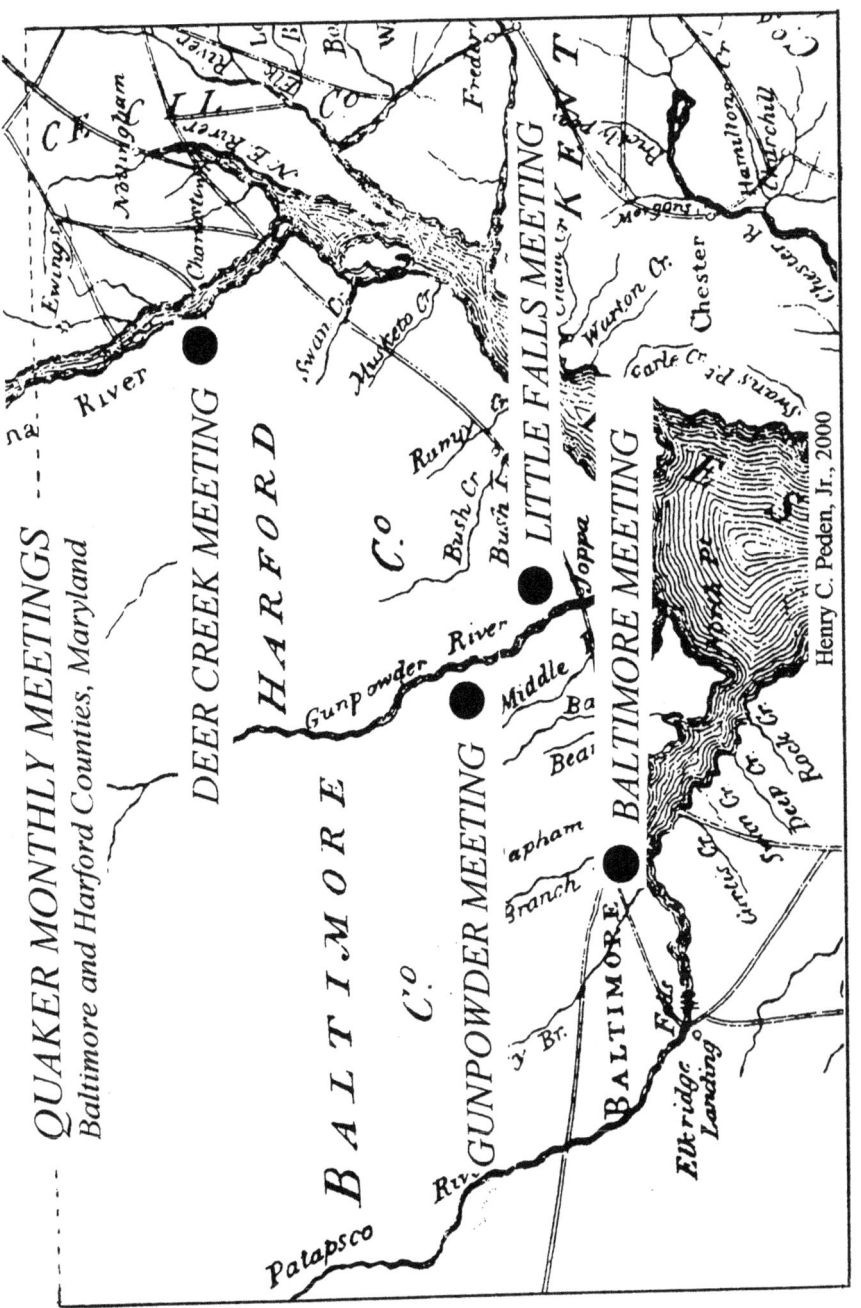

# QUAKER RECORDS OF BALTIMORE AND HARFORD COUNTIES, MARYLAND 1801-1825

## GUNPOWDER MONTHLY MEETING, BALTIMORE COUNTY
### REGISTER OF BIRTHS AND DEATHS, 1801-1825

Susannah Parrish, dau. of William, d. 24th of 1st mo., 1820 in her 71st year.

Rachel Griffith, d. 25th of 1st mo., 1821, aged 68 years and 4 mos.

John Dutton, d. 17th of 8th mo., 1805, and interred the day following in Friends Burying Ground at Little Falls Meeting House.

Elizabeth Scott, an elder, d. 12th of 10th mo., 1808 in her 71st year and interred in Friends Burying Ground at Gunpowder Meeting House the next day.

Abraham Scott, d. 29th of 3rd mo., 1804 in his 73rd year and interred in Friends Burying Ground at Gunpowder Meeting House next day.

James Hicks, d. 19th of 11th mo., 1808.

Rachel Price, dau. of Walter Moore and Ann, d. 6th of 5th mo., 1822, aged about 81 years, and buried in family burying ground.

Samuel Price, Sr., consort of Ann Price (deceased), d. in his 86th year on 16th of 4th mo., 1825.

Hannah Benson, wife of Benjamin Benson, d. 26th of 8th mo., 1805, and buried at Little Falls Meeting House Friends Burying Ground.

Benjamin Benson, d. 5th of 9th mo., 1812, aged 63 years and 7 days and was interred in Friends Burying Ground, Little Falls.

Moses Dillon, d. 23rd of 2nd mo., 180-[?].

Aaron Hollingsworth, son of Nathaniel and Abigal, d. 14th of 8th mo., 1806 and interred the day following in Friends Burying Ground at Little Falls Meeting House.

Edith Price, dau. of Daniel and Betty, b. 9th of 5th mo., 1801.

Joel Price, her brother, b. 26th of 7th mo., 1803.

Nathan Price, their brother, b. 26th of 9th mo., 1794, d. in his 11th year.

Elizabeth Scott, dau. of Thomas and Elizabeth, b. 1st of 6th mo., 1801[?].

Rachel and Eliza Scott, twins, b. 14th of 7th mo., 1807.

Elizabeth Scott, their sister, d. 16th of 7th mo., 1807, aged 5 years, 1 mo., 12 days and buried in Friends Burial Ground at Gunpowder Meeting House.

Rachel Scott, their sister, d. 11th of 8th mo., 1807, aged 1 mo. and 8 days and was buried at same place.

Mary Parsons, dau. of Daniel and Betty Price, d. 16th of 7th mo. 1823 in her 33rd year.

Jesse Price, son of Daniel and Betty Price, d. 28th of 5th mo., 1824, in his 38th year.

Rachel Price, dau. of Mordecai and Tabitha, d. 11th of 7th mo., 1808[?], aged 27 years, -?- mos., 26 days.

Joshua Price, her sister, d. 23rd of 2nd mo., 1802[?], aged 27 years, 7 mos., 21 days.

Mordecai Price, an elder and father of above named children, d. 5th of 9th mo., 1807, aged 76 years, 6 mos., 6 days, and was buried the next day in Friends Burying Ground at Gunpowder Meeting House.

Daniel Tredway, d. 25th of 5th mo., 1810, in his 86th year.

Rachel Preston, dau. of David and Judith, n. 12th of 5th mo., 1807.

Mielmer Harrison Brown, dau. of Thomas and Elizabeth, b. 8th of 9th mo., 1812.

Rachel Lancaster, wife of Benjamin Preston (deceased), d. 5th of 3rd mo., 1813, aged 85.

John Lancaster, d. 27th of 9th mo., 1803 and was buried in Friends Burying Ground, Munsey, Pennsylvania.

Mary Lancaster, dau. of Jesse and Elizabeth, his second wife, b. 30th of 7th mo., 1800.

Esther Lancaster, her sister, b. 2nd of 6th mo., 1802.

John Lancaster, her brother, b. 28th of 6th mo., 1804.

Julia Lancaster, his sister, b. 14th of 2nd mo., 1807.

James Price, d. 10th of 12th mo., 1802 and was buried at Gunpowder Meeting House.

David Harry, our esteemed friend, d. 11th of 8th mo., 1800, aged 50 yrs., 8 mos., 4 days.

Rachel Matthews, our beloved friend, wife of Thomas Matthews (deceased), d. 21st of 4th mo., 1813, in her 83rd year.

John Lukens, son of Jacob and Tace, b. 20th of 6th mo., 1802.

Rebecca Lukens, his sister, b. 3rd of 7th mo., 1804.

Merriken Lukens, her sister, b. 8th of 3rd mo., 1806.

Ruth Lukens, his sister, 12th of 1st mo., 1808.

Alice Lukens, her sister, b. 11th of 4th mo., 1810.

Jonathan Tyson, son of Jacob and Ann, b. 8th of 9th mo., 1802.

William Amos Tyson, his brother, b. 12th of 6th mo., 1805.

Eli West, d. 13th of 2nd mo., 1801, aged 14 yrs., 1 mo., 16 days.

Hannah Jones, d. 5th of 11th mo., 1812, aged 49 years.

Martha Matthews, dau. of John and Martha, d. 27th of 6th mo., 1802 and was interred the 28th of the same in the afternoon in Friends Burying Ground at Gunpowder Meeting House.

John Matthews m. Alice Kinsey on 7th of 9th mo., 1805, being his third wife.

Abel Kinsey Matthews, son of John and Alice, b. 28th of 1st mo., 1807, d. 24th of 2nd mo. and interred the 25th of same in Friends Burying Ground at Gunpowder Meeting House.

Phebe Matthews, his sister, b. 4th of 4th mo., 1808.

Martha Matthews, her sister, b. 10th of 6th mo., 1810.

Owen Matthews, her sister, b. 2nd of 6th mo., 1812.

Isaac Moore Matthews, his brother, b. 1st of 9th mo., 1814 and d. in 12th mo., 1835, aged 21 years and 3 months.

Mary Jane Matthews, his sister, b. 1st of 1st mo., 1819.

Ezra Price, son of John (of Samuel) and Mary, b. 26th of 12th mo., 1804.

Miriam Price, his sister, b. 12th of 11th mo., 1806 and d. 10th of 8th mo., 1829, aged 23.

Warrick Price, her brother, b. 17th of 8th mo., 1808.

Oliver Price, his brother, b. 13th of 5th mo., 1810 and d. 8th of 11th mo., 1810.

William Matthews Price, his brother, b. 6th of 11th mo., 1811.

Edward Price, his brother, b. 26th of 11th mo., 1813.

Samuel Price, his brother, b. 6th of 12th mo., 1815.

Elizabeth Ann Price, his sister, b. 2nd of 3rd mo., 1818.

Edward Price, d. 26th of 9th mo., 1817.

Oliver Matthews Price, b. 24th of 1st mo., 1822.

Thomas Harding, son of Charles and Elizabeth, b. 27th of 7th mo., 1801 and d. 28th of 8th mo., 1821, aged 20 years and 5 days *[sic]*.

George Harding, his brother, b. 6th of 10th mo., 1804 and d. 6th of 10th mo., 1819, aged 15 years.

Lydia W. Harding, his sister, b. 14th of 9th mo., 1807 and d. 5th of 3rd mo., 1815, aged about 7 years.

Sarah Matthews, dau. of Eli and Mary, b. 8th of 2nd mo., 1801.

Jarret Matthews, her brother, b. 25th of 10th mo., 1802 and d. 14th of 10th mo., 1803 and was interred the 15th of the same in Friends Burying Ground at Gunpowder Meeting House.

Joel Matthews, his brother, b. 8th of 2nd mo., 1805.

Elias Matthews, his brother, b. 13th of 3rd mo., 1807.

Esther Matthews, his sister, b. 13th of 6th mo., 1810.

Eli Matthews, their brother, b. 11th of 9th mo., 1812 and d. 9th of 7th mo., 1820.

Mary Matthews, their sister, b. 5th of 4th mo., 1815.

Aquilla and Precilla Matthews (twins), their brother and sister, b. 31st of 8th mo., 1817.

Margaret Matthews, their sister, b. 15th of 5th mo., 1820.

Rachel Matthews, dau. of Jesse and Milcah, b. 1st of 5th mo., 1802 about 20 minutes after 3 o'clock in the morning.

Milcah Matthews, her sister, b. 9th of 8th mo., 1798, d. 4th of 8th mo., 1803 and buried the next day in Friends Burying Ground at Gunpowder Meeting House.

Richard Matthews, their brother, b. 26th of 10th mo., 1804 about 15 minutes after 2 o'clock in the morning.

Benjamin Matthews, his brother, b. 18th of 12th mo., 1806 about half after 10 o'clock at night.

Rachel Matthews, dau. of Mordecai and Ruth, b. 22nd of 8th mo., 1802.

Edward Matthews, her brother, b. 20th of 11th mo., 1804[?].

Rachel Matthews, dau. of Thomas and Ann, b. 20th of 11th mo., 1802.

Ann Matthews, her sister, b. 10th of 2nd mo., 1804.

Elizabeth Matthews, her sister, b. 17th of 5th mo., 1805.

Thomas Matthews, her brother, b. 10th day of 2nd mo., 1807.

Rebecca Matthews, his sister, b. 26th of 10th mo., 1809.

Rhoda Matthews, her sister, b. 31st of 1st mo., 1811.

George Matthews, her brother, b. 10th of 6th mo., 1812.

Hannah Matthews, his sister, b. 14th of 5th mo., 1808, "omitted being recorded in due order."

Ariana Matthews, her sister, b. 20th of 5th mo., 1813[?].

Joshua Matthews, her brother, b. 5th of 1st mo., 1814.

Elizabeth Scott, dau. of Jessee and Rebekah, b. 19th of 12th mo., 1792 and d. 28th of 6th mo., 1801.

Rebekah Scott, her sister, b. 29th of 7th mo., 1803.

---- Scott, a sister, b. 3rd of 3rd mo., 1807 and d. same day.

Timothy Kirk, son of Timothy and Sarah, d. 8th of 1st mo., 1811.

Elihu Brown, d. 26th of 12 mo., 1810.

Eliza Price, dau. of Elijah and Sarah, b. 17th of 10th mo., 1805.

Amon Price, her brother, b. 19th of 7th mo., 1807 and d. 17th of 7th mo., 1809.

Rachel Price, his sister, b. 19th of 4th mo., 1809.

Mordecai Price, her brother, b. 5th of 5th mo., 1811.

John K. Price, his brother, b. 12th of 2nd mo., 1813.

Isaac Price, his brother, b. 25th of 3rd[?] mo., 1815.

Sarah Price, his sister, b. 29th of 12th mo., 1816.

Margaret Price, her sister, b. 1st of 2nd mo., 1819.

Mary Ann Price, ---- [blank].

Isaiah Price, son of Mordecai and Mary, b. 21st of 4th mo., 1803.

Rebecca Price, his sister, b. 14th of 2nd mo., 1805.

Elizabeth Price, her sister, b. 27th of 4th mo., 1807.

Ann Price, her sister, b. 15th of 3rd mo., 1809.

Hannah Price, her sister, b. 4th of 7th mo., 1811.

Mary Price, her sister, b. 15th of 8th mo., 1813.

Martha Price, her sister, b. 31st of 12th mo., 1817.

Moses Dillon Price, b. 15th of 3rd mo., 1820.

Mordecai D. Price, b. -?- of 5th mo., 1822.

Deborah Price, b. 2nd of 3rd mo., 1824.

James Price, son of Beal and Mary, b. 3rd of 9th mo., 1806.

Benjamin Price, his brother, b. 1st of 4th mo., 1808.

Matilda Price, his sister, b. 10th of 12th mo., 1810 and d. 15th of 5th mo., 1819, aged about 8 years and 5 months.

Thomas Price, his brother, b. 29th of 1st mo., 1815. [*Ed. Note:* In another handwriting someone inserted the initial "R" between Thomas and Price].

William R. Price, his brother, b. 19th of 11th mo., 1816 and d. 6th of 11th mo., 1837, aged 21 years old wanting 12 days.

---- Price, a son, b. 11th of 10th mo., 1815 and d. 15th of same without a name.

Maranda Price, a sister, b. 25th of 9th mo., 1820.

Benjamin Matthews, son of William and Rebecca, b. 16th of 12th mo., 1800.

Elizabeth Matthews, his sister, b. 19th of 7th mo., 1802.

Thomas Matthews, her brother, b. 24th of 12th mo., 1804 and d. 23dr of 8th mo., 1806.

Evan Matthews, their brother, b. 20th of 1st mo., 1807.

Rachel Matthews, their sister, b. 22nd of 4th mo., 1809.

Oliver Hough Amoss, son of James and Hannah, b. 18th of 8th mo., 1801.

Elisha Pearson, son of Enock and Susanna, b. 1st of 5th mo., 1807.

Deborah Reed, dau. of Samuel and Elizabeth, b. 11th of 3rd mo., 1802.

William Reed, her brother, b. 22nd of 7th mo., 1804.

Anna Reed, his sister, b. 13th of 4th mo., 1806.

Harriett Reed, her sister, b. 10th of 4th mo., 1808.

John Wilson Reed, her brother, b. 11th of 4th mo., 1810.

John West, son of Enos and Rebecca, b. 1st of 10th mo., 1801.

Thomas West, his brother, b. 10th of 12th mo., 1802.

John West, d. 23rd of 4th mo., 1803.

Emila West, their sister, b. 26th of 8th mo., 1806.

Ellwood West, their brother, b. 23rd of 3rd mo., 1808.

David West, his brother, b. 9th of 6th mo., 1809.

William Spencer, son of Mahlon and Eleanor, b. 21st of 5th mo., 1802 and d. the 8th month following.

William Lee Spencer, his brother, b. 13th of 9th mo., 1803.

Mahala Spencer, their brother [sic], b. 23rd of 10th mo., 1805.

Enoch Lucas Spencer, their brother, b. 15th of 1st mo., 1808.

Elizabeth Spencer, their sister, b. 9th of 2nd mo., 1810.

Mahlon Atkinson Spencer, their brother, b. 1st of 2nd mo., 1812.

David Branson, d. 25th of 8th mo., 1807 and "enterd" the day following in Friends Burying Ground at Little Falls Meeting house.

Sarah Hooker England, dau. of George and Catharine, b. 3rd of 10th mo., 1800.

Thomas Hooker England, her brother, b. 5th of 1st mo., 1803.

Elizabeth Dutton England, his sister, b. 16th of 4th mo., 1805.

Mary McConnell, dau. of Samuel and Francess, b. 24th of 1st mo., 1799.

James Orr McConnell, her brother, b. 14th of 10th mo., 1801.

Eliza E. Branson, dau. of Owen and Hannah, b. 31st of 1st mo., 1806.

Benjamin Branson, her brother, b. 30th of 3rd mo., 1808.

David Branson, his brother, b. 11th of 3rd mo., 1811.

Susanna S.[P.?] Benson, dau. of Amos and Margaret, b. 6th of 1st mo., 1807.

Rachel Benson, her sister, b. 26th of 2nd mo., 1808.

Margaret Benson, their sister, b. 2nd of 5th[?] mo., 1809.

Elihu Benson, her brother, b. 5th of 11th mo., 1811.

Hannah Benson, dau. of Levi and Mary, b. 1st of 9th mo., 1807.

Mary Ann Benson, her sister, b. 9th of 11th mo., 1810[?].

Eli Price, son of Mordecai Jr. and Charity, b. 3rd of 10th mo., 1801 and d. 21st of 11th mo., 1805.

Rachel Price, his sister, b. 9th of 10th mo., 1803.

Ann Price, their sister, b. 25th of 4th mo., 1806.

Mary Price, her sister, b. 18th of 11th mo., 1808 and d. in 7th mo., 1810.

Joshua C. Price, their brother, b. 26th of 8th mo., 1811.

Mordecai C. Price, his brother, b. 27th of 3rd mo., 1814 and d. 6th of 10th mo., 1820.

Rebecca Moore, d. 28th of 11th mo., 1811, aged 73.

David Price, son of Samuel Jr. and Frances, b. 9th of 7th mo., 1803.

Frances Price, mother of above, d. 14th of 7th mo., 1803 and was "entered" in Friends Burying Ground at Gunpowder Meeting House the next day.

Frances Price, dau. of Samuel Jr. and Ann, b. 13th of 8th mo., 1809.

Thomas Price, her brother, b. 18th of 6th mo., 1811.

Ellen Price, his sister, b. 30th of 6th mo., 1813.

Catharine Price, her sister, b. 9th of 5th mo., 1815.

Esther Price, her sister, b. 7th of 4th mo., 1817.

Samuel C. Price, her brother, b. 26th of 5th mo., 1819.

Priscila Price, his sister, b. 3rd of 4th mo., 1822.

Edward Price, her brother, b. 22nd of 6th mo., 1824.

John Hair, husband of Elizabeth and father of Elizabeth, Rachel, Mary, Elizabeth, Sarah, Hannah, Elenner, Phebe, Rebeckah, and Tamar [children born between 1770 and 1791], d. 11th of 11th mo., 1815.

Cassandra Thornburgh, wife of Joseph, d. 24th of 3rd mo., 1812 and was interred in Friends Burying Ground on 26th of same at Gunpowder.

Sarah Morris, wife of Israel, d. 29th of 12th mo., 1811.

Rachel Spicer, d. 12th of 6th mo., 1812.

Joseph Thornburgh, d. 2nd of 2nd mo., 1820 in his -?- year [age illegible; could be either 57 or 67?] and was interred in Friends Burying Ground near Baltimore.

Mary Naylor, dau. of Samuel and Rebekah, b. 10th of 10th mo., 1806.

Benjamin Benson, son of James and Elizabeth, b. 25th of 10th mo., 1801.

John Benson, his brother, b. 27th of 9th mo., 1802.

William Benson, her [sic] brother, b. 28th of 11th mo., 1803.

James Benson, his brother, b. 29th of 10th mo., 1807.

Elizabeth Benson, b. 11th of 11th mo., 1809.

Mordecai Benson, b. 26th of 4th mo., 1812.

Sarah Ann Benson, b. 10th of 7th mo., 1814.

Amos Benson, b. 13th of 10th mo., 1817 and d. 30th of 10th mo., 1818, aged 1 year, 17 days.

John Parrish, son of Mordecai, d. 3rd of 9th mo., 1806.

James Smith, d. 13th of 12th mo., 1820, aged about 37 years, and buried in Friends Burying Ground at Forrest Meeting in Harford County.

Hannah Tudor, dau. of William and Martha, b. 7th of 9th mo., 1801.

Ruth Tudor, her sister, b. 5th of 10th mo., 1803 and d. 5th of 8th mo., 1805.

Susanna Morthland Tudor, dau. of John and Phebe, b. 5th of 2nd mo., 1810.

Elisha Reynolds, son of Joshua and Rachel, b. 8th of 3rd mo., 1808 about the 8th hour at night.

Elizabeth Reynolds, his sister, b. 8th of 6th mo., 1811 about 8th hour.

John Price Jr., b. 2nd of 3rd mo., 1728 and d. 14th of 4th mo., 1809.

Urith Price, his wife, d. 2nd of 10th mo., 1811, aged 83.

Susanna Morthland, d. 24th of 4th mo., 1817, aged about 69.

George Mason, d. 31st of 7th mo., 1823, aged about 74, and was interred 1st of 8th mo. at the new meeting house at Gunpowder.

Hannah Lancaster, dau. of Jessee and Elizabeth, b. 22nd of 7th mo., 1810.

Sarah Lamborn, dau. of Daniel and Elizabeth, b. 3rd of 2nd mo., 1810.

Meriah Lamborn, her sister, b. 18th of 3rd mo., 1812.

Jacob Vore, son of Isaac and Ruth, b. 5th of 10th mo., 1808.

Mary Vore, his sister, b. 3rd of 5th mo., 1811.

Rebecca Smith, dau. of Amos and Rebecca, b. 23rd of 2nd mo., 1810.

James Smith, her brother, b. 7th of 3rd mo., 1812.

Sarah Andrew Evans, dau. of Edmund and Elizabeth, b. 10th of 8th mo., 1811.

John Price Wainwright, son of Samuel and Matilda, b. 20th of 3rd mo., 1811.

James Berry Wainwright, his brother, b. 14th of 12th mo., 1812.

Samuel Wainwright, d. 28th of 2nd mo., 1814, in his 31st year, and was buried at Gunpowder Meeting House.

Hannah Ely, dau. of Hugh and ---- [blank] his wife, b. 16th of 11th mo., 1806.

Elizabeth Ely, her sister, b. 16th of 2nd mo., 1809.

Sarah Ely, their sister, b. 2nd of 9th mo., 1811.

Caleb Harlan, son of John and Hannah, b. 20th of 8th mo., 1809[?].

Susanna Harlan, his sister, b. 1st of 8th mo., 1811.

Eli M. Price, son of Jehu and Susanna, b. 18th of 8th mo., 1818.

Mary Ann Price, his sister, b. 12th of 12th mo., 1819, and d. 19th of 2nd mo., 1820.

Frances Ann Price, b. 22nd of 4th mo., 1821.

Emily Price, a sister, b. 16th of 4th mo., 1823.

Mary Ann Price, dau. of James[?] and Sarrah[?] M. Price, b. 22nd of 3rd mo., 1822.

Mary Hollingsworth, dau. of Robert and Elizabeth, residence at Little Falls, b. 8th of 9th mo., 1810.

Hannah W. Hollingsworth, b. 9th of 8th mo., 1812.

Elijah M. Price, son of Elijah and Sarah, residence at Gunpowder, b. 22nd of 1st mo., 1821.

Sophia Price, dau. of Elijah and Sarah, b. 5th of 6th mo., 1823.

Mary Ann Price, dau. of Elijah and Sarah, b. 6th of 10th mo., 1825 or 1826 [year unclear].

Mariam R. Griffith, dau. of Thomas and Rachel, residence at Gunpowder, b. 19th of 5th mo., 1816, and d. 7th of 10th mo., 1818.

Mary G. Griffith, dau. of Thomas and Rachel, b. 21st of 9th mo., 1818, and d. 11th of 9th mo., 1826.

Ann S. Griffith, dau. of Thomas and Rachel, b. 4th of 8th mo., 1820, and d. 10th of 9th mo., 1821.

Oliver Matthews, d. 17th of 1st mo., 1824, aged 102 yrs., 1 mo., 19 days, and buried at Gunpowder Old Meeting House; resided near the meeting house 1 3/4 miles, where he lived for about 60 years.

Elizabeth Matthews, d. 1st of 3rd mo., 1825, aged about 63; buried at Gunpowder New Meeting House on 3rd of 3rd mo.; resided near the meeting house 1 3/4 miles, where she had lived 19 years with her husband William Matthews (of Oliver).

Jared M. Price, d. 19th of 10th mo., 1825, aged 25 years, 8 mos.; buried at Gunpowder New Meeting House; lived near meeting house.

Sophia Price, d. 19th of 3rd mo., 1824, age not given; lived on her farther's [sic] farm, Elijah Price, at Gunpowder.

Mary Ann Branson, dau. of Levi and Mary, residence at Little Falls, b. 19th of 10th mo., 1811.

Ann Eliza Griffith, dau. of Thomas and Rachel, residence at Gunpowder, b. 24th of 12 mo., 1821.

Thomas T. Griffith, son of Thomas and Rachel, residence at Gunpowder, b. 10th of 5th mo., 1823.

Joseph Bartlett, son of Joseph and Rhoda M., b. 26th of 5th mo., 1810; lived at Gunpowder, "the place of her residence after her husband's death."

William K. Plummer, son of Elisha and Mary, residence at Gunpowder, b. 20th of 8th mo., 1823.

## GUNPOWDER MONTHLY MEETING, BALTIMORE COUNTY ABSTRACTS FROM THE MINUTES, 1801-1825

[It should be noted that Men's and Women's Monthly Meetings kept separate minutes, but they have been combined into one in the following abstracts. However, the dates in parenthesis are for the women's meetings when they are different from the men's meetings, as it appears they did not always meet on the same day of the month.]

1801, 31st of 1st mo. - Little Falls Preparative Meeting informs that Mary Harry requested to be taken into membership.

1801, 28th of 2nd mo. - Jonathan Wright requested to be released from his station as overseer. Caleb Bracken appointed to serve in his stead.

1801, 27th of 3rd mo. - Nathan Hunt reported about his religious visit to Guilford County, North Carolina. Elizabeth Cole attended this meeting from Deer Creek Monthly Meeting, accompanied by Elizabeth Amos. Mary Harry was received into membership.

1801, 25th of 4th mo. - Sarah Morthland attended the women's meeting with certificate from Baltimore Monthly Meeting recommending her a member of our Society.

1801, 25th of 5th mo. - Joseph Naylor reported to have been married by a hireling preacher. Joseph Rees [also spelled Reese] requested a certificate to Baltimore Monthly Meeting for himself, wife Mary, and their children John, Sarah, William, Eleanor, Aquilla, and Morris. Amos Smith and Rebeckah West declared their intention to marry. Jesse Lankaster reportedly hath been drinking spirituous liquors to excess. Eleanor Hollen [also written as Elener Hollin and Elener Holland and Elinor Holand in other minutes], formerly Williams, reportedly married a man not in membership with Friends and, at this time, she was not found to be in a suitable disposition to condemn her misconduct.

1801, 27th of 6th mo. - Mary Hair, a birthright Quaker, reportedly went so far as to be a libertine and guilty of fornication, for which reproachful conduct we would disown her, but her father recommends we seek suitable satisfaction for the same. William Tudor requests to be taken into membership.

1801, 25th of 7th mo. - Jacob Lukens [also spelled Luking and Lukings in other minutes] and Tace Parsons [also spelled Tacy] reported to have been married in an orderly manner. Moses Dillion hath given way so far to passion as to strike a man, Samuel McConnel. Amos Smith and Rebecca West declared their intention to marry, the young man having produced a certificate.

1801, 29th of 8th mo. - Certificate presented for Ann Griffith, approved and forwarded. Amos Smith and Rebeckah West had been married in an orderly manner and the certificate was produced. Moses Dillion had met with a degree of satisfaction since he had condemned his misconduct. Thomas Scott presented a certificate from York Monthly Meeting for himself and his children, John, Esther, William and Rachel; however, women's meeting stated Amos Scot [sic] presented a certificate from York Monthly Meeting for himself and his four minor children, Levi, Ester, William and Rachel. Mary Matthews requested a certificate to Westland Monthly Meeting [Washington County, Pennsylvania]. Jacob Tyson requested to be released from the service of recorder. Little Falls Preparative Meeting appointed Ann Tyson in the station of an elder. Rebecca Smith requested a certificate to Baltimore Monthly Meeting.

1801, 25th of 9th mo. - After having laboured with her without the desired effect, it was recommended that Elener Holland be disowned. John Matthews was appointed as recorder. Enos West was reported to have been married by the assistance of a hireling.

1801, 26th (31st) of 10th mo. - Moses Dillion apologized for his actions and requested that his membership be continued. Sarah Shaw attended the meeting with a certificate from Philadelphia Monthly Meeting, Northern District. Mary Ely, now

Weeks [spelled later as Winks], was reported to have had her marriage accomplished by the assistance of a hireling teacher to a man not of our society. Martha Matthews, daughter of Daniel, who was in her minority when she left us, requested a certificate to Fairfax Monthly Meeting [Loudoun County], Virginia.

1801, 28th of 11th mo. - Elizabeth Wheeler requested that her three minor children, Honor [also spelled Onner], Aquilla [also spelled Aquillar], and Moses, be taken into membership with Friends with which her husband unites. Little Falls Preparative Meeting informs that Martha Amos requested a certificate to Baltimore Monthly Meeting.

1801, 26th of 12th mo. - Sarah Hussey attended the meeting with a certificate from York Monthly Meeting. Hannah Brady [also spelled Bradie and Braidy in other minutes] and her husband [no name given] reported to have removed to some parts of Virginia. Mary Weeks was not in a suitable disposition to condemn her misconduct, so she was disowned. The three children of Elizabeth Wheeler named above were accepted into membership.

1802, 30th of 1st mo. - Enos West apologized for having been married by a hireling teacher and requested that his membership be continued. Samuel Reed presented a certificate from Baltimore Monthly Meeting for himself, wife Elizabeth, and two minor children, Matilda and Eveline. Sarah Barcroft [also spelled Baracraft] attended the meeting with a certificate from Wrightstown Monthly Meeting [Bucks County], Pennsylvania. Sarah Shaw requested a certificate to Richland Monthly Meeting in Pennsylvania. Little Falls Preparative Meeting informs that Enoch Williams had his marriage accomplished by a hireling teacher.

1802, 27th of 2nd mo. - Little Falls Preparative Meeting informs that John Parsons, Jr. has almost entirely neglected attendance at our meetings and hath been guilty of drinking spirituous liquors to excess. Phoebe [also spelled Phebe] Price requested a certificate to Baltimore Monthly Meeting. Hester Tipton hath long neglected attendance at our meetings and hath been guilty of unseemly keeping company with a man not in membership with us. Ester Pendon, formerly Tipton, had her marriage accomplished by the assistance of a hireling teacher to a man not of our Society.

1802, 27th of 3rd mo. - Isaac Naylor had finally been met with, but he was not in a suitable disposition to condemn his outgoing. Enoch Williams did not condemn his prior misconduct, so he was disowned. Esther [also spelled Hester and Ester] Tipton was also disowned. Little Falls Preparative Meeting informs that David Lee, Jr. hath almost entirely neglected attendance at our meetings and hath made too free use of spirituous liquors.

1802, 24th of 4th mo. - Mordecai Price and Mary Dillion declared their intention of marriage, with the consent of their parents.

1802, 29th of 5th mo. - Isaac Naylor was met with, but was not found in a suitable disposition to condemn his outgoing, so he was disowned. Elener [also spelled Elinor] Bull requested a certificate to Baltimore Monthly Meeting.

1802, 26th of 6th mo. - Mordecai Price and Mary Dillon [also spelled Dillion] had been married in an orderly manner.

1802, 31st of 7th mo. - The report of a committee stated that they had "visited a number of families and individuals endeavouring according to ability given to stir up the pure mind in each other to a more diligent attending of meetings and also to the school education of the black people and as to the situation of schools amongst us there appears to be in some places a considerable straitness in the minds of some Friends for the want of right means of education their children." Jesse Lankaster apologized and condemned his previous misconduct. Mary Maulsby requested a certificate to Deer Creek Monthly Meeting.

1802, 28th of 8th mo. - Certificate requested for Luke Tipton, a minor, to Deer Creek Monthly Meeting. Certificate requested for Rebeckah [also spelled Rebecca] Tipton to Deer Creek Monthly Meeting. Little Falls Preparative Meeting informs that Elizabeth Cullum [also spelled Cullun and Cullim], formerly England, had her marriage accomplished by a hireling minister with a man not of our Society. Sarah Johnson [also spelled Jonson] had her marriage accomplished in like manner to a man not in membership with us. John Parsons gave no suitable disposition to condemn his misconduct.

1802, 30th of 8th mo. - Esther Griffith and Hannah Field, our esteemed friends, made a religious visit to Purchase Monthly Meeting in the State of New York and in company with Theodore S. Underhill also visited Amawalk Monthly Meeting. Jesse Tyson complained that Lemuel Howard neglected the payment of his just debt. Merriken Bond requested to be joined in membership.

1802, 30th of 10th mo. - Our beloved Friends Esther Griffin and Hannah Field attended this meeting with a certificate from Purchase Monthly Meeting in the State of New York.

1802, 27th of 11th mo. - Mary Jones charged with misconduct. Little Falls Preparative Meeting informs that Isaac Hollingsworth hath almost entirely neglected attendance at religious meetings, made use of unbecoming language, and attended places of diversion.

1802, 25th of 12th mo. - Daniel Price requested certificates for his two sons, Samuel and Jessee, to Baltimore Monthly Meeting, the former being placed with Rositer Scott and the latter on application to Samuel Price. Little Falls meeting informed that Morris Maulsby hath had his marriage accomplished by the assistance of a hireling. Mary Maulsby, formerly Lee, hath had her marriage accomplished by a hireling to a man in membership with Friends [later entry shows this Morris Maulsby and Mary Maulsby were husband and wife].

1803, 29th of 1st mo. - Gunpowder Monthly Meeting was held at Little Falls. Elizabeth Cullum appeared and condemned her outgoing in marriage and requested to remain in membership. Rebeckah West requested to be joined in membership.

1803, 26th of 2nd mo. - Gunpowder Preparative Meeting informs that Matilda Brackin Miller requested to be taken into membership as she had been for some time under care of Gunpowder Preparative Meeting, and was received. Betty Price was released from the station of overseer (by her request) and was replaced by Rachel Mason.

1803, 26th of 3rd mo. - David Lee, having a birthright among the people called Quakers, appeared and condemned his disorderly misconduct; John Parsons did likewise. Sarah Barcroft requested a certificate to Baltimore Monthly Meeting.

1803, 30th of 4th mo. - Matilda Brackin Miller requested a certificate to Falls Monthly Meeting in Buck County, Pennsylvania. Catherine Rees requested a certificate to Baltimore Monthly Meeting. Isaac Griffith hath frequently neglected attendance of our religious meetings, hath frequented games and other places of diversion, hath been concerned with horse racing and made use of unbecoming language, has removed within the verge of Fairfax Monthly Meeting [Loudoun County, Virginia]. Enos West requested that his minor son Thomas be taken into membership, and he was received.

1803, 28th of 5th mo. - Mary Jones appeared and condemned her misconduct by attending a marriage consummated contrary to the good order used among Friends, and also attending a dance, for which she apologized and asked to remain in membership. Ezra Brown and wife Hannah attended this meeting with a certificate from Nottingham Monthly Meeting. Sarah Johnson appeared and condemned her outgoing in marriage to a man not of our society, and requested to continue in membership. Sarah Jewel [also spelled Juel], formerly Whitsen [also spelled Whison], was reported to have married a man not of our society by a hireling teacher.

1803, 25th of 6th mo. - John Kittlewell attended our meeting from Warrington Monthly Meeting [York County, Pennsylvania] with a certificate for himself, wife Margaret, and their five children, Isaac, Thomas, Samuel, John, and Mary Kittlewell. Mary Jones requested a certificate to Deer Creek Monthly Meeting. Caleb Brackin requested to be released from the station of overseer. Eli Matthews will serve in his stead.

1803, 30th of 7th mo. - Sarah Johnson [also spelled Jonson] requested a certificate to Baltimore Monthly Meeting.

1803, 27th of 8th mo. - Joseph Shaw attended the meeting with a paper of acknowledgment from a number of Friends of Richland Monthly Meeting in Pennsylvania, and his request for reinstatement was accepted. Joseph Thornburgh produced a certificate from Baltimore Monthly Meeting to this meeting for himself, his wife Cassandra, and two minor children, Margaret and Sarah. Charles Kittlewell produced a certificate from Warrington Monthly Meeting [York County, Pennsylvania] recommending him as a member, and he was received. Isaac Kinsey, Mary Kinsey, and Sarah Hopkins attended this meeting with certificates from Baltimore Monthly Meeting. Sarah Kittlewell produced a certificate from Warrington Monthly Meeting [York County, Pennsylvania]. Sarah Jewel did not appear in a suitable disposition to make satisfaction for her misconduct, so she is disowned. Morris Maulsby and wife Mary requested a certificate to Deer Creek Monthly Meeting. Little Falls Preparative Meeting informs that Sarah Maulsby requested a certificate to Deer Creek Monthly Meeting. John Harlan and Hannah Amos declared their intention to marry, with parents consent being obtained, and pending the young woman's clearness.

1803, 24th (28th) of 9th mo. - Isaac Hollingsworth appeared and apologized for his many acts of misconduct and condemning same. Certificate was received from Mary Matthews who attended this meeting from Westland Monthly Meeting [Washington County, Pennsylvania].

1803, 29th of 10th mo. - The marriage of John Harlan and Hannah Amos had been accomplished in an orderly manner. John Price and Mary Matthews declared their intention to marry, with parents consent being obtained, pending the young woman's clearness from all others. Thomas Matthews and Sarah Hopkins declared their intention to marry, with parents consent being obtained, and pending the young woman's clearness from others. Deborah Thornburgh attended this meeting with a certificate from Baltimore Monthly Meeting.

1803, 26th of 11th mo. - Certificate produced by Benjamin [also spelled Bengamine] Benson for himself, wife Hannah, and their four minor children, Levi,

Benjamin, Hannah, and Jesse, from York Monthly Meeting. Isaac Griffith had been located and charges were presented against him in Fairfax Monthly Meeting [Loudoun County, Virginia]. Moses Dillon requested a certificate for his son Moses Jr. to Baltimore Monthly Meeting. Little Falls meeting informed that Jacob Lukens requested to be released from the station of overseer; Samuel McConnel to serve in his stead.

1803, 31st of 12th mo. - John Price and Mary Matthews had been married in an orderly manner, as was the marriage of Thomas Matthews and Sarah Hopkins. Certificate was produced to this meeting by Elizabeth Webster from Baltimore Monthly Meeting. Little Falls Preparative Meeting informs that Hannah Harlan [also spelled Harling and Harland] requested a certificate to Baltimore Monthly Meeting.

1804, 28th of 1st mo. - Sarah Matthews [also spelled Mathues and Matheus] requested a certificate to Baltimore Monthly Meeting. Isaac Griffith, a birthright Quaker, gave written testimony and apologized for his misconduct.

1804, 26th of 2nd mo. - Gunpowder Preparative Meeting informs that Hannah Dillon requested to be released from the station of overseer.

1804, 31st of 3rd mo. - Isaac Kinsey and Elizabeth Mason [also spelled Mayson] declared their intention to marry, pending parents approval and the young woman's clearness from all others. Ruth Matthews was proposed to serve in the station of an elder [and was subsequently appointed].

1804, 28th of 4th mo. - In consideration of the situation of Catherine Rees [later entry spelled it as Reece], it was agreed to raise a sum of money [8 pence per quarter?] for her support.

1804, 26th of 5th mo. - Isaac Kinsey and Elizabeth Mason had been married in an orderly manner. David Branson attended the meeting with a certificate for himself, wife Elizabeth, and six children, Aron, Joshua, Prissilla [also spelled Prisella], Ann, James and Elizabeth, from Goshen Monthly Meeting in Chester County, Pennsylvania. Owen Branson also attended with a certificate from Goshen Monthly Meeting [Chester County, Pennsylvania]. David Read attended with a certificate for himself and wife Hannah from Nottingham Monthly Meeting. George Mason (of John) requested a certificate to Baltimore Monthly Meeting.

1804, 30th of 6th mo. - Elihu Brown attended this meeting with a certificate for himself, wife Margaret, and seven children, Hannah, Stephen, Joel, Lydia, Elihu, Rachel, and Joshua, from Nottingham Monthly Meeting. Timothy Kirk attended this meeting with a certificate for himself, wife Mary, and two minor children, Mahlon and Mary, from York Monthly Meeting. Leaven Hopkins attended the meeting with a certificate from Baltimore Monthly Meeting. Gunpowder Preparative Meeting informs that Elizabeth Wright requested a certificate to Indian Spring Monthly Meeting.

1804, 28th (24th) of 7th mo. - Amos Benson attended this meeting with a certificate from York Monthly Meeting. Little Falls Preparative Meeting proposed Benjamin Benson to the station of overseer in the place of Samuel McConnel. Margaret and Amy Brown produced a certificate from York Monthly Meeting in Pennsylvania. Rachel Kirk also attended this meeting with a certificate from York Monthly Meeting.

1804, 25th of 8th mo. - Our esteemed Friends Hugh Judge and Susanna his wife attended the meeting with a certificate for themselves and two children, Phebe and Rebeccah, from New York Monthly Meeting, he being a minister recommended and it being mentioned in the certificate of Susanna as being in the station of an elder, she was accepted as a Friend qualified for that service. Since Samuel Morthland Jr. did not find it in his disposition to condemn his misconduct, the committee think it best to return his certificate to Warrington Monthly Meeting [York County, Pennsylvania]. Gunpowder Preparative Meeting informs that Rachel Hooker has neglected attendance at our meetings for several years [and was also charged later with attending places of diversion and dancing].

1804, 29th of 9th mo. - Elija [also spelled Elijah] Price and Sarah Kittlewell [also spelled Kettlewell] declared their intention to marry, with parents consent being obtained, and pending the young woman's clearness from all other marriage engagements. Susan Judge, Jr. attended the women's meeting with a certificate from New York Monthly Meeting.

1804, 27th of 10th mo. - Gunpowder Preparative Meeting informs that Carlton and Aquilla Belt have removed a considerable distance from us without certificates and settled amongst Friends and hath their marriage accomplished contrary to good order.

1804, 24th of 11th mo. - Elijah Price and Sarah Kittlewell had been married in an orderly manner. Samuel Fisher attended the meeting with a certificate for himself, wife Susanna, and their minor children, Betty, Ruth, Lydia, Elisha, Joel and Seth, from York Monthly Meeting. Stacy West attended with a certificate from Baltimore Monthly Meeting.

1804, 29th of 12th mo. - Elliner Hollin requested to be reinstated into membership again with Friends and the clerk was directed to forward a copy of her outgoing to the Friends at Munsey Monthly Meeting. Keturah Parrish attended and produced a certificate from Pipe Creek Monthly Meeting [Frederick County, Maryland]. A letter was received from Short Creek Monthly Meeting in Jefferson County, Pennsylvania [sic], expressing the desire of Amos Lasy [later spelled Lacey] to be reinstated with Friends.

1805, 26th of 1st mo. - Recommendation of Mary Kirk to be an elder was reviewed and approved. Amos Lacey [also spelled Lasy] stated in a signed letter that he was a Friend by birth and education, but through inattention in early life he deviated and married a woman of a different profession with the assistance of a hireling, for which he was justly disowned. He sincerely condemned his misconduct and requested reinstatement again in membership at Short Creek Monthly Meeting in Jefferson County, Ohio (dated 11th of 5th mo., 1804). Gunpowder Monthly Meeting approved and forwarded a certificate to him. Susanna Judge, Jr. requested a certificate to Baltimore Monthly Meeting.

1805, 23rd of 2nd mo. - William Kirk attended this meeting with a certificate from York Monthly Meeting. Rachel Hooker, a birthright amongst us, charged with attending places of diversion, dancing, and neglecting attendance at meetings, is disowned and no longer a member until she condemns her actions. Certificate received for Rachel Judge, a minor daughter of Hugh Judge, from New York Monthly Meeting. Owen Branson and Hannah Benson declared their intention to marry, having consent of parents, and pending the young woman's clearness from all others. Elloner Hair [also spelled Elaner Hare] requested a certificate to Baltimore Monthly Meeting. Mary Hix attended meeting with a certificate for herself and her husband from Baltimore Monthly Meeting.

1805, 30th of 3rd mo. - Certificate produced for James Hicks [also spelled Hick and Hix], his wife Mary, and their daughter Bathsheba, from Baltimore Monthly Meeting. Gunpowder Preparative Meeting informs that Sophiah Griffith [also spelled Griffeth], now Deaver, has gone out in marriage with a man not of our membership.

1805, 27th (29th) of 4th mo. - Little Falls Preparative Meeting informs that David Wood requested a certificate for himself, wife Hannah, and their minor daughter Elizabeth, to Little Britten [also spelled Britain] Monthly Meeting. Certificate produced for Charles Harding from Baltimore Monthly Meeting, and one for his wife Elizabeth and three minor children, David, Mary, and Thomas. Hannah Brown requested a certificate to Little Brittian [also spelled Britain] Monthly Meeting.

1805, 25th of 5th mo. - Owen Branson and Hannah Benson had been married in an orderly manner. Sophiah Griffith being removed a great distance, they had no opportunity to meet with her. Mary Maulsby [also spelled Malsby] produced a certificate from Deer Creek Monthly Meeting. Little Falls Preparative Meeting informs that Ralph Lee had his marriage accomplished by a hireling teacher, and Stacy West [later entries spelled the name Stasy West and Staca West] had also been married by a hireling teacher. Sophia Deaver is reported to have removed far distant from us [later minutes indicate Pipe Creek Monthly Meeting in Frederick County, Maryland].

1805, 26th of 6th mo. - Ralph Lee "seams to be in a tender disposition and desirious to make satisfaction" for outgoing in marriage. Stacy West "appeared tender, manifested a friendly disposition, yet did not apprehend him to be in a suitable disposition to condemn his outgoing." Gunpowder Preparative Meeting informs that Joseph Price had his marriage accomplished by a hireling teacher; likewise for Beal Price.

1805, 24th of 7th mo. - Margaret Judge, daughter of Hugh Judge, attended the meeting with a certificate from New York Monthly Meeting. Priscilla Morgan [also spelled Prissilla Morgin] produced a certificate from Baltimore Monthly Meeting. Joseph Price was not in a suitable state of mind to condemn his outgoing, but Beal Price was agreeable and asked for reconciliation with Friends. John Matthews requested a certificate to Little Britian Monthly Meeting in Pennsylvania in order to accomplish his marriage to Alice Kinsey. Ruth Matthews requested to be released from serving as clerk of the women's meeting.

1805, 25th of 9th mo. - Little Falls Preparative Meeting informs that Ruth Whitaker [also spelled Whitiker] requested to be taken into membership. John Matthews requested to be released from being overseer; Jessee Scott appointed in his stead. Elizabeth Scott appointed clerk of women's meeting in place of Ruth Matthews.

1805, 28th of 8th mo. - Sophia Deaver, formerly Griffith, gave written testimony about her outgoing in marriage, requested forgiveness for her deviation from the good order and to continue in membership [signed 8th of 5th mo., 1805]. Jonathan Wright [later entry referred to him as "Jnr."] and wife Susanna requested a certificate for themselves and three minor children, Joel, Susanna, and Rebecca, to Miami [also spelled Miammi] Monthly Meeting in the State of Ohio. Mary Wright also requested a certificate to Miammi Monthly Meeting.

1805, 23rd of 10th mo. - Our esteemed friend Bordin Stanton attended this meeting on his return from the yearly meeting and produced a minuit [minute] from Concord Monthly Meeting in the State of Ohio. Our beloved friend Nathan Hunt attended this meeting and produced a certificate from Springfield Monthly Meeting in North Carolina and endorsed at New Garden Quarterly Meeting held at Deep River Meeting House in Guilford County, North Carolina. Our esteemed friend Thomas Thornburgh attended this meeting with a certificate from Back Creek Monthly Meeting. Our beloved friend Elisha Dawson attended this meeting with a certificate from North West Fork Monthly Meeting. Gunpowder Preparative Meeting informs that Phebe Matthews requests to be released from this place of an overseer.

1805, 27th of 11th mo. - Stacy West gave testimony stating he had a birthright amongst Quakers, but by not having his mind properly influenced by their principles, went so far astray as to have his marriage accomplished contrary to their discipline. He condemned his misconduct and requested to be continued in membership. Oliver Matthews, son of William, requested a certificate for himself, his wife Phebe, and their three minor children, Joel, William, and Ann, to Miami [also spelled Miammi] Monthly Meeting in the State of Ohio. Sarah Allen [also spelled Alan], formerly Howard, hath gone out in marriage with a man not in membership with us. Sophia Deaver requested a certificate to Fairfax Monthly Meeting [Loudoun County], Virginia. Elizabeth Prosser [also spelled Proser] requested a certificate to Center Monthly Meeting in Center County, Pennsylvania. Samuel Fisher requested a certificate for himself, wife Susanna, and four minor children, Lydia, Elisha, Joel, and Seth, to Baltimore Monthly Meeting.

1805, 14th of 12th mo. - Beal Price presented written testimony in which he stated he had a right of membership with the people called Quakers, but deviated therefrom. He condemned his outgoing in marriage by the assistance of a hireling teacher and requested to continue in membership (signed 14th of 12th mo., 1805). It was decided it might be best to discontinue the membership of Sarah Allen with Friends.

1806, 22nd of 1st mo. - Testimony in the case of Sarah Allen, formerly Howard, revealed that she had a right of membership, yet she "had her marriage accomplished contrary to the good order established amongst us in a short time after the death of her former husband which conduct we do condemn and discontinue her from being any longer a member of our society until she condemns the same to the satisfaction of this meeting which is our desire." Alice Matthews produced a certificate from Little Britian [also spelled Britain] Monthly Meeting in Pennsylvania. Gunpowder Preparative Meeting informs that Sarah Hussey requested a certificate to New Garden Monthly Meeting in North Carolina.

1806, 19th of 2nd mo. - Little Falls Preparative Meeting informs that Hugh Eli [later spelled Ely] had his marriage accomplished by a hireling. Amos Benson and

Margaret Brown declared their intention to marry, pending the young woman's clearness from all others. Betty Fisher requested a certificate to Baltimore Monthly Meeting. Ruth Fisher requested a certificate to Deer Creek Monthly Meeting. Jane Hannaway, formerly Naylor, had her marriage accomplished by a hireling teacher with a man not in our membership.

1806, 26th (29th) of 3rd mo. - Ralph Lee [signed his name "Ralph Sackett Lee"] gave written testimony that he had an education among the people called Quakers, but for want of strictly adhering to the principles of truth in my own heart have so far deviated therefrom as to have my marriage accomplished contrary to the good order. Testimony by Joseph Price stated he [Price] had a birthright and education amongst Friends, but deviated from it and had been married by a hireling. Jane Hannaway hath removed a great distance and is discontinued in membership until she condemns her actions. Jonathan Marsh and Levina [also spelled Lavinia] Naylor declared their intention to marry, parents consent being obtained, and pending the young woman's clearness from all others. Charles Kittlewell requested a certificate to Warrington Monthly Meeting [York County, Pennsylvania]. John Tuder [later spelled Tewder] requested a certificate to Baltimore Monthly Meeting. Rebeccah Bracken requested a certificate for herself and five minor children, Rachel, Solomon, Elisha, Sarah, and Caleb, to Westland Monthly Meeting in Washington County, Pennsylvania. Mary Price, wife of Beal, requested to be joined in membership. Letter received from Munsey Monthly Meeting in Pennsylvania that Elloner Hollin [signed her name "Ellenner Holland"] had a birthright amongst Friends and has condemned her misconduct, expressing her unity with Friends. She also requested a certificate of removal, which was subsequently approved and forwarded.

1806, 23rd of 4th mo. - Amos Benson and Margaret Brown had been married in an orderly manner. Mary Price was accepted into membership. John Kittlewell requested a certificate for himself, his wife Margaret, and five minor children, Isaac, Thomas, Samuel, John, and Mary, to Warrington Monthly Meeting [York County], Pennsylvania. Jehosheba Brown requested to be taken into membership at the women's meeting.

1806, 28th (22nd) of 5th mo. - Jonathan Marsh and Levinia Naylor had been married in an orderly manner. David Preston attended this meeting with a certificate for himself, wife Judith, and their three minor children, Isaac Hollingsworth Preston, Hannah Preston, and Sylvestor Bills Preston, from New Garden Monthly Meeting in Chester County, Pennsylvania. Rebecah Pitts [also spelled Pits], now Price, hath had her marriage accomplished contrary to good order to a man not in membership with Friends. Deborah Thornburgh, now Denison [also spelled Dennison], had her marriage accomplished in like manner.

1806, 25th of 6th mo. - Jehosheba Brown was received into membership. Rebecca Price, formerly Pitts, "appeared desirious to retain her right in Society, but we do not apprehend her to be in a situation prophetably to make satisfaction for her deviation at this time." Deborah Dennison, formerly Thornburgh, "appeared tender and desirous to retain her right" and her case was continued.

1806, 28th (23rd) of 7th mo. - Hugh Ely gave signed testimony that he had deviated and married contrary to the good order, he condemned his misconduct and asked to be continued in membership. Rebecca Price, having a right of membership amongst us, deviated and had her marriage accomplished by a hireling, and she is discontinued from being any longer a member until she condemns her outgoing.

1806, 27th of 8th mo. - Deborah Dennison [also spelled Denison] did not appear to be in a suitable disposition to condemn her outgoing in marriage, so her right in membership was discontinued. Rachel Rush, formerly Bull, hath gone out in marriage with a man not in membership with us.

1806, 24th of 9th mo. - Josiah Brown attended this meeting with a certificate from Nottingham Monthly Meeting. Nathaniel Hollingsworth attended with a certificate for himself, wife Abigail, and their seven minor children, Aaron [also spelled Aron], Thomas, Eli, Jesse, Abigail, Nathaniel, and John, from Goshen Monthly Meeting [Chester County], Pennsylvania. Robert Hollingsworth and Hannah Hollingsworth (daughter of Nathaniel and Abigail) also presented certificates from Goshen Monthly Meeting. Gunpowder Preparative Meeting informs that Isaac Kinsey requested a certificate for himself, wife Elizabeth, and for their minor daughter Rachel, to Baltimore Monthly Meeting. Little Falls Preparative Meeting purposed Elihu Brown for the station of overseer and this meeting appoints him accordingly.

1806, 22nd of 10th mo. - Gidion Hughs [also spelled Gidian Hews] and Rebecca Dillon declared their intention to marry, parents consent being obtained, and pending the young woman's clearness from all others. Levi [also spelled Levy] Benson and Mary Maulsby [also spelled Molsbey] declared their intention to marry, pending parents consent and the young woman's clearness from all others. Hannah Brady, formerly Hair, with a birth right amongst us the people called Quakers, hath so far erred as to have her marriage accomplished by the assistance of a hireling. We disown her from being any longer a member of our society until she condemns the same. William Morris has neglected our meetings and hath purchased a lad which he holds in the state of slavery. Our beloved friend Susannah Judge feeling her mind engaged to accompany our beloved friend Elizabeth Cogshal [also spelled Cogshell] in a religious visit to the meeting constituting our quarterly.

1806, 26th of 11th mo. - Gedion Huse [also spelled Gidion Hughs and Gidian Hews] and Rebecca Dillon are cleared to marry "with parents consent obtained and nothing appearing to obstruct they going to settle a considerable distance the winter approaching." Enoch [also spelled Enock] Pearson attended with a certificate for himself, wife Susannah, and their six minor children, Deborah, William, Enoch, Rachel, Phebe, and Samuel, from Uwchland Monthly Meeting in Chester County, Pennsylvania.

1806, 24th of 12th mo. - Joshua Reynells [later spelled Reynolds] attended and produced a certificate for himself, his wife Rachel, and their three minor children, Rachel, Sarah, and Mary, from Baltimore Monthly Meeting. Gidion Huse [also spelled Hughs[ and Rebecca [also spelled Rebacca] Dillon had been married in an orderly manner, as was the marriage of Levi Benson and Mary Maulsby. Little Falls Preparative Meeting informs that Mary West requested a certificate of Baltimore Monthly Meeting. Women's minutes were abstracted by Rebecca Procter, clerk.

1807, 28th (8th) of 1st mo. - Rachel Rush was disowned until she condemned her outgoing. William Morris reportedly holds steadfast in his opinion in respect to holding a lad in bondage beyond the age of twenty-one. Melchisedeck Johnson hath joined the Methodist Society. Little Falls Preparative Meeting informs that Lyddia Ferdun [also later spelled as Lidia Ferdun, Lida Fordone, Lida Fordane, Lydia Furdun] requested to be taken into membership with Friends.

1807, 25th of 2nd mo. - William Morris was disowned until he condemns his actions [noted above]. Melchisedeck Johnson was disowned until he condemns his actions [noted above]. Rebecca Hughs [also spelled Rebecca Hugh, Rebeccah Hews, and Rebecca Hues] requested a certificate to Middletown Monthly Meeting in the State of Ohio.

1807, 25th (29th) of 3rd mo. - John Harling [also spelled Harlin] produced a certificate for himself, wife Hannah, and their two minor children, Joseph and William, from Baltimore Monthly Meeting. Regarding Lida Fordone (previously spelled Lyddia Ferdun, etc.) it was reported that the time is not yet come for her reception into membership. Samuel Price, Jr. had a child laid to his charge in an unmarried state. Matilda Brackin Miller has removed within the verge of Horsham Monthly Meeting in the State of Pennsylvania.

1807, 22nd of 4th mo. - Eli Matthews and Jessee Scott were proposed as overseers for Gunpowder Preparative Meeting, and Elihu Brown and Nathaniel Hollingsworth for Little Falls Preparative Meeting. John Tewder [also spelled Tuder and Tooder] and Phebe Morthland declared their intention to marry, with the consent of parents, pending the young woman's clearness from all others. Mary Kinsey requested a certificate to Baltimore Monthly Meeting.

1807, 27th of 5th mo. - Edward Brinton attended with a certificate from Concord Monthly Meeting in Delaware County, Pennsylvania. William Matthews attended with a certificate for himself, wife Elizabeth, and their three minor children, Samuel Hanway Matthews, George Matthews, and Susanna Matthews, from Baltimore Monthly Meeting. Samuel Price, Jr. admitted he had a child in an unmarried state, but refused to condemn his actions, and was disowned. Jacob Tyson was appointed clerk and Mordecai Price (of Samuel) as assistant clerk. Benjamin Parish [later spelled Parrish] had his marriage accomplished by a hireling teacher and was later disowned until he condemned his outgoing. Ruth Matthews was appointed clerk and Mary Kirk, Jr. as assistant clerk for the women's meeting. Cassandra Thornburg and Rachel Mason were appointed as overseers for Gunpowder Preparative Meeting, and Abigail Hollingsworth and Ann Tyson for Little Falls Preparative Meeting.

1807, 24th of 6th mo. - John Tuder and Phebe Morthland had been married in an orderly manner. Robert Morthland had his marriage accomplished by a hireling teacher. John Tipton hath accepted the office of constable and taken an oath for that purpose. [He was later disowned until he condemned his outgoings]. Little Falls reports Elihu Brown requested a certificate for his son Joel Brown, a minor, to Baltimore Monthly Meeting. Certificate for Mary Mallanee from Baltimore Monthly Meeting was received. Certificate for Elizabeth Yarnell to Third Haven Monthly Meeting on the Eastern Shore of Maryland was requested.

1807, 22nd of 7th mo. - Certificate for John Brinton from Concord Monthly Meeting in Delaware County, Pennsylvania, was received. Meriken Bond (at Little Falls) has neglected meetings, departed from plainness in dress and address, subscribed himself a scholar at a dancing school, and had gone out in marriage accomplished by a hireling teacher.

1807, 26th of 8th mo. - Certificate produced from Baltimore Monthly Meeting, Eastern District, for Samuel Naylor, wife Rebecca, and five minor children, Ann, John, Joseph, Charles, and Mary. The Warrington Monthly Meeting [York County, Pennsylvania] will be sent a letter requesting them to treat with Robert Morthland on our behalf. Certificate requested for Phebe Tuder to Baltimore Monthly Meeting, Eastern District. Meriken Bond was disowned until he condemned his outgoings. Certificate requested some time past for John Kittlewell, Margarett his wife, and their four minor children, Thomas, Samuel, John, and Mary, was approved and forwarded. Martha Blass [also spelled Blasson], formerly Hill, hath been guilty of fornication, had her marriage accomplished by the assistance of a hireling teacher, and joined in church membership with her husband. She was disowned until she condemned her outgoing. Warrington Monthly Meeting [York County, Pennsylvania] reported that Isaac Kittlewell hath paid a muster fine. William Price (son of Mordecai) hath neglected meetings, purchased and holds a fellow creature in a state of slavery, and so far given way to passion as to strike a man. He was subsequently disowned until he condemned his outgoings.

1807, 28th of 10th mo. - Elizabeth Lawson requested reinstatement into membership, having been a considerable time disowned by York Monthly Meeting [as noted in women's meeting on 26th of 8th mo., 1807]. Elener Warner, formerly Holland, received a certificate to Munsey Monthly Meeting which was returned with information that she has been guilty of unseemly company keeping defamation and hath also gone out in marriage before said certificate came into the hands of that meeting. She was disowned until she condemned her disorderly conduct.

1807, 28th (25th) of 11th mo. - Certificate produced for Lewis Harlan from Baltimore Monthly Meeting, Western District. Certificate produced for Francis Meekin [also spelled Mecham] and wife Neomi [also spelled Naimo] and their five minor children, John, Lydia, Richard, Isaac, and George, from Uwchland Monthly Meeting. York Monthly Meeting will be contacted in writing regarding Elizabeth Lawson's request for reinstatement.

1808, 27th of 1st mo. - Certificate requested for Reubin [also spelled Reuben] Griffith, wife Elizabeth, and their five minor children, Ann Moore, Rebecca, Elizabeth, Mary, and Keturah [also spelled Kitturah] to Salem Monthly Meeting in Columbia County, State of Ohio.

1808, 24th of 2nd mo. - Certificate received for Margaret Judge recommending her to Indian Spring Monthly Meeting was approved and forwarded. Edith [also spelled Edif and Ediff] Parrish reported by women's meeting to have neglected meetings and attended a marriage of members not of our society. Reported that William Gaw removed several years to the State of Ohio without a certificate and has been in the practice of drinking spirituous liquors to excess. Mary Price, wife of Mordecai, appointed overseer by women's meeting.

1808, 23rd of 3rd mo. - Edward Churchman produced a certificate for himself, his wife Rebecca and their six minor children, Micajah, Hannah, Robert, Mary, Rebecca, and Margaret, from Concord Monthly Meeting in Delaware County, Pennsylvania; likewise their dau. Anna Churchman produced one from the same meeting. "Edif [also spelled Edith] Parrish, with her birth amongst us but for want of attending to the dictates of truth in her own breast, hath so far deviated from the rules of our discipline as to neglect the attendance of our religious meetings for a long time and attended marriages of members of our society who had their marriages consummated contrary to our discipline which conduct we testify against and disown her from being a member of our religious society until she return to the satisfaction of Friends which that she may is our desire." Certificate received for Hannah Lewis from York Monthly Meeting [York County, Pennsylvania]. James Benson hath purchased a black boy which was manumitted to be free at the age of 30 years or thereabouts which he inclines to hold to that time.

1808, 27th of 4th mo. - James Smith produced a certificate from Goose Creek Monthly Meeting in Loudoun County, Virginia. Rebecca Matthews presented a certificate from Baltimore Monthly Meeting. Elizabeth Lawson was received into membership with no objection from York Monthly Meeting. Josiah Benson was charged with the act of adultery. Little Falls Preparative Meeting informs that Hugh Judge, wife Susanna, and their minor daughter Rebecca, requested a certificate to Baltimore Monthly Meeting. Thomas Amos requested a certificate to Baltimore Monthly Meeting, Eastern District.

1808, 25th of 5th mo. - David Tucker produced a certificate for himself, his wife Elizabeth, and their six minor children, James, Hannah, Elizabeth, David, Samuel, and Ann, from Sadsbury Monthly Meeting. William Gaw, having been remotely removed for several years, disorderly walking, and drinking spirituous liquors to excess, is therefore disowned until he condemns his misconduct. Little Falls informs that Samuel Hugs hath removed and resides within the limits of Concord Monthly Meeting [Delaware County, Pennsylvania]. Ruth Matthews was appointed clerk and Judith Preston as assistant clerk in women's meetings.

1808, 22nd of 6th mo. - Isaac Kittlewell was send a copy of the minute of his disownment. Little Falls Preparative Meeting informs that Deborah Whitacre [also spelled Whittaker], formerly Pearson, hath had her marriage accomplished by the assistance of a magistrate to a man not in membership with us. Isaac Vore produced a certificate for himself and wife Ruth from Deer Creek Monthly Meeting. Little Falls Preparative Meeting informs that John Brinton hath removed from amongst us to Concord Monthly Meeting [Delaware County], Pennsylvania, and since had his marriage accomplished contrary to good order.

1808, 27th of 7th mo. - Deborah Whitacre is not in a suitable condition to condemn her outgoing in marriage and is disowned.

1808, 24th of 8th mo. - William Marsh presented a certificate for himself, his wife Ann, and four minor children, John, Margaret, William, and Susanna Morthland Marsh, from Baltimore Monthly Meeting, Western District. Josiah Brown gave written testimony that "through the temptation of Satin, gave way to the lust of the flesh" and committed adultery. He condemned his sinful misconduct and was later reinstated into membership. Lavina Marsh's certificate to Baltimore Monthly Meeting, Western District, was approved. Amos Scott has been in the practice of drinking spirituous liquors to excess. John Mason, Jr. has neglected meetings, gone out in marriage, been concerned in a lottery, and joined the militia.

1808, 21st of 9th mo. - Certificate for William Squibb, Jr. from Warrington Monthly Meeting [York County, Pennsylvania] was accepted. Edward Churchman, proposed to serve in the station of overseer at Little Falls, was appointed. Reese Cadwallader and Hannah Dillon declared their intention to marry, "he being of Redstone Monthly Meeting [Fayette County, Pennsylvania] is requested to produce a certificate of his clearness of others; also consent of parents."

1808, 26th of 10th mo. - Reese Cadwallader produced a certificate from Redstone Monthly Meeting [Fayette County, Pennsylvania] for clearness of marriage, he having no parents, is left at liberty to proceed. Kitturah Parrish requested that her minor daughter Hannah be received into membership. John England produced a certificate from Westland Monthly Meeting [Washington County, Pennsylvania]. Informed by Concord Monthly Meeting [Delaware County, Pennsylvania] that John Brinton is believed not qualified to condemn his deviation at this time and is disowned until he does. Joshua Mott and Rachel Mason declared their intention to marry, he being a member of Baltimore Monthly Meeting, requested to produce a certificate of clearness of others and also consent of parents. Josiah Brown and wife Jehosheba [also spelled Jahoshaba] requested a certificate to Baltimore Monthly Meeting, Eastern District. Little Falls informs that Jessee Parsons, a minor, is placed within the verge of Warrington Monthly Meeting [York County, Pennsylvania]. Mary Gilbert, a minister, attended women's meeting with a certificate from Abington Monthly Meeting [Montgomery County, Pennsylvania].

1808, 23rd of 11th mo. - James Benson "still refused to secure the freedom of the lad" [a slave] and is therefore disowned. John Morgan requested reinstatement into membership. Reese Cadwallader and Hannah Dillon had been married in an orderly manner. Joshua Mott produced a certificate from Baltimore Monthly Meeting that he was clear to marry with his parents had consented. George Langstroth produced a certificate from Gwinedd Monthly Meeting in Pennsylvania. Certificate produced from Amos Smith, wife Rebecca, and their three minor children, Eliza, Rachel, and Mary, from Baltimore Monthly Meeting, Eastern District. Gunpowder Preparative Meeting informs that Ann Blackiston, formerly Price, hath had her marriage accomplished by a hireling teacher with a man not in membership with us.

1808, 28th (29th) of 12th mo. - Joshua Mott and Rachel Mason had been married in an orderly manner. Rachel Mott requested a certificate to Baltimore Monthly Meeting, Eastern District. Cassandra Thornburgh and Mary D. Price requested to be released from the station of overseers in the women's meeting.

1809, 25th of 1st mo. - A testimonial on the life and conversation with John Morgan will be prepared and sent to Nottingham Monthly Meeting. Ann Blackstone, formerly Price, has gone out in marriage. Clarissa Whitacre requested to be received into membership. Certificate for Rachel Mott to Baltimore Monthly Meeting, Eastern District, was signed and forwarded. Little Falls informs that Amos Ely had been guilty of attending diversions at a tavern, gaming for strong drinks, using unsavory language, attending with the militia at their military exercises, and going out in marriage. Nathaniel Hollingsworth "has so far failed in the support of our testimony against slavery as to employ a slave which he is willing to condemn." He stated he had hired the "labour of a slave for two months and notwithstanding his master allowed him one half earnings it being cause of uneasiness to my mind." William Amos, Jr. also had a slave employed in his business, and John Harlin had employed two slaves in his business. John England requested a certificate to Westland Monthly Meeting [Washington County, Pennsylvania]. Elizabeth Scott and Mary M. Price were appointed overseers in women's meeting.

1809, 22nd of 2nd mo. - John Mason acknowledged he was guilty of fornication and the committee believed he was not in a suitable disposition to condemn his misconduct at this time. William Amos, Jr. and John Harlin both appeared to be willing to condemn their respective deviations. Ann Blackstone [also spelled Blackiston] was found not to be in a suitable disposition to condemn her outgoing and was disowned. John Brinton was served with a copy of his disownment by Concord Monthly Meeting [Delaware County, Pennsylvania] and he does not incline to appeal. Certificate for Hannah D. Cadwallader to Redstone Monthly Meeting [Fayette County], Pennsylvania, was signed, recorded, and forwarded.

1809, 22nd of 3rd mo. - Certificate for Rachel Judge to Indian Spring Monthly Meeting was signed and forwarded. Edward Churchman was appointed as the clerk for this meeting. Thomas West requested to be released from the station of an elder. Clarissa Whitacre [also spelled Whittacer] was received into membership. Gunpowder Preparative Meeting informs that Elizabeth Naylor has become the mother of an illegitimate child.

1809, 26th of 4th mo. - Amos Ely refused to condemn his previous misconduct. Elizabeth Naylor has been found guilty of fornication. John Mason, in Baltimore, did not condemn his misconduct and was disowned. Little Falls informs that Enos

West "for sake of a reward has given information to a slave houlder concerning a slave who had left him, by which means it appears the man was again brought into bondage, that he kept from the owner a considerable part of a sum of money that was in a pocket book that he took up in the road (most of which the owner recovered by applying to the law)." Thomas West also had spoken falsely with some information concerning a slave who had left his master and which appears he was again brought into bondage. Isaac Atkinson, after previous caution, has had his marriage accomplished by a hireling teacher.

1809, 24th of 5th mo. - Certificates were produced for Stacy West from Baltimore Monthly Meeting, Eastern District, and John Morgan and John Brown from Nottingham Monthly Meeting. Deer Creek Monthly Meeting inquired about the readmission of Abram Huff who was disowned some years since. Amos Ely, having a birthright amongst Friends, but not adhering to our principles, hath had his marriage accomplished contrary to our order, attended at a muster, gamed for strong drink, and used unsavory language. His membership was discontinued. Isaac Atkinson was disowned for outgoing in marriage. Certificate requested for James Branson, a minor, to Nottingham Monthly Meeting. Certificate for Elizabeth Branson and her two minor daughters, Ann and Elizabeth, to Concord Monthly Meeting [Delaware County, Pennsylvania] was signed, recorded, and forwarded. Joseph Bartlett [also spelled Bartlet] and Rhoda Matthews declared their intention to marry, following their clearness and consent of their parents.

1809, 21st of 6th mo. - Certificate produced for Thomas Matthews, a minor, from Third Haven Monthly Meeting. No objection has appeared to Deer Creek Monthly Meeting receiving him as a member, he was united with by this meeting. Ann Price requested to be joined into membership, having been under the care of the Gunpowder Preparative Meeting for some time. Eli Matthews was proposed to be an elder [and was subsequently appointed]. Joseph Bartlett was cleared by Third Haven Monthly Meeting for marriage to Rhoda Matthews. Gunpowder Preparative Meeting proposed Joshua Reynolds [earlier spelled Reynells] for the station of overseer in stead of Eli Matthews who requested to be released.

1809, 26th of 7th mo. - John Harlin [also spelled Harlen] gave written testimony and condemned his misconduct in the encouragement of slavery. Certificate received for Abner Jones, wife Hannah, and their three minor children, Yearsly [also spelled Yearlsey] and Aquila [also spelled Aquilla] from Uwchland Monthly Meeting in Pennsylvania. Susanna [also spelled Susannah] Jones, daughter of Abner and Hannah Jones, also produced a certificate from that meeting. Joseph Bartlett and Rhoda Matthews had been married in an orderly manner. Priscilla Brinton, late Branson, who resides within the verge of Concord Monthly Meeting [Delaware County], Pennsylvania, has her marriage accomplished contrary to our discipline with a man in membership with us and is disowned until she condemns her outgoing. Levin Hopkins has been guilty of fornication. Communication received from Warrington Monthly Meeting [York County, Pennsylvania] regarding an acknowledgement of Robert Morthland for his outgoing. Acknowledgement was received from Samuel Price, Jr. who had been disowned by our meeting some time ago. John Mason, Jr. was also disowned [see statement of misconduct in 1808 minutes].

1809, 23rd of 8th mo. - Report received that Thomas Moore on behalf of the committee on the request of Indian Spring Monthly Meeting is about to build a meeting house in the City of Washington; monetary assistance was requested; William Kenworthy, clerk [the amount of 69.75 (sic) was subsequently subscribed]. Amos Scott was disowned for his continuous excessive use of strong drink. John Matthews requested to be released from recording births and burials.

1809, 27th of 9th mo. - Robert Hollingsworth and Elizabeth West, Jr. declared their intention to marry, with consent of parents being obtained, and pending the young woman's clearness from all others. Mary Jones, late Naylor, had her marriage accomplished contrary to our order. Gunpowder Preparative Meeting informs that Peter Parrish and Mordecai Parrish, Jr. hath neglected our meetings and joined the militia.

1809, 25th of 10th mo. - Samuel Price, Jr., having a birthright amongst Friends, condemned his misconduct and was received back into membership. William Matthews (of Oliver) agreed to record minutes and also births and burials. Ann Baker, late Tudor, hath long neglected attendance at meetings and has recently married her first cousin [prior to 27th of 9th mo., 1809 meeting]. Mary Jones was disowned until she condemned her misconduct to the satisfaction of Friends. Gunpowder Preparative Meeting complained against John Matthews for not abiding by an award given by arbitrators chosen by himself and another member in a case of difference between them. Certificates were produced for Susanna Buffington Jones to Baltimore Monthly Meeting, Western District, and Mary Matthews, Sr. to Plymouth Monthly Meeting in the State of Ohio. John Naylor, Jr. also requested a certificate to Plymouth Monthly Meeting.

1809, 22nd of 11th mo. - Robert Hollingsworth and Elizabeth West had been married in an orderly manner. Gunpowder Preparative Meeting informs that Rhoda M. Bartlet requested a certificate to Third Haven Monthly Meeting.

1809, 27th of 12th mo. - Gunpowder Preparative Meeting reports that Urith Parrish has neglected attendance at meetings and had her marriage accomplished by the assistance of a hireling minister.

1810, 24th of 1st mo. - Edmund Evans produced a certificate from the monthly meeting of Friends for the Western Division of Devonshire held at Plymouth, Great Britain, dated 13th of 9th mo. last, with an endorsement by the monthly meeting of Philadelphia for the Northern District dated 26th of last month.

1810, 21st of 2nd mo. - Peter Parrish and Mordecai Parrish, Jr., having a birthright amongst us but so far deviating from our principles as to neglect meetings and join the militia, were disowned from any longer being members. Certificate produced for Ann Churchman to Philadelphia Monthly Meeting. Little Falls informed that Elihu Brown and Nathaniel Hollingsworth requested to be released from serving as overseers.

1810, 28th of 3rd mo. - Thomas West gave written testimony in which he condemned his misconduct in the hiring of a black man and being his master. Enos West also condemned his own actions in having a man brought into bondage and also having "detained more money for finding a pocketbook than was right." Nathaniel Yet[?] was proposed to serve in the station of overseer. Certificate produced for Mary Hay, wife of William Hay, from Chesterfield Monthly Meeting in the State of New Jersey. Reported that Caleb Price had his marriage accomplished by the assistance of a hireling, and by this marriage obtained a black man which he intends to hold in bondage to the age of 30 years. William Marsh and wife Ann requested a certificate to Plymouth Monthly Meeting in the State of Ohio for themselves and their four minor children, John, Margaret, William, and Susanna Morthland Marsh. Isaac Dillon, a minor, having resided some time within the verge of Baltimore Monthly Meeting, Western District, a certificate was ordered to be prepared for him. Joshua Branson requested a certificate to Mount Holly Monthly Meeting in the State of New Jersey.

1810, 25th of 4th mo. - Robert Morthland gave written testimony condemning his outgoing in marriage accomplished by the assistance of a hireling teacher, and requested continuance in membership. Amos Benson was proposed for the station of overseer [and was subsequently appointed]. Testimony against the misconduct of Urith Parrish, now Stubbins, was forwarded to women's meeting. Caleb Price was disowned. Elizabeth Amos requested that her granddaughter [no name given] be received into membership. Little Falls reports Jesse Lancaster has taken strong drink to excess. Jesse Scott requested to be released from the station of overseer and appointed Joshua Reynolds in his stead. Mordecai Price requested to be released from being assistant clerk. Samuel Wainwright and Matilda Matthews declared their intention to marry, he having before this meeting produced a certificate of clearness of others from Third Haven Monthly Meeting and also consent of his parents, and she (a young woman) to obtain clearness of other marriage engagements and her parents consent. Rhoda M. Bartlet, being left a widow and again returned to reside within the verge of this meeting, produced a certificate from Third Haven Monthly Meeting.

1810, 23rd of 5th mo. - Certificate produced for Mary Hicks [also spelled Hix] to Baltimore Monthly Meeting, Western District, signed, recorded, and forwarded. Elizabeth Sims Trimble, the minor granddaughter of Elizabeth Amos, and both being present, was accepted into membership at her grandmother's request and with her father's consent. Robert Morthland requested a certificate to Warrington Monthly Meeting [York County], Pennsylvania.

1810, 27th of 6th mo. - Samuel Wainwright and Matilda Matthews had been married in an orderly manner. Certificate was produced for John Tuder, his wife Phebe, and their two children, Samuel and Martha, from Baltimore Monthly Meeting, Western District. Little Falls Preparative Meeting informs that David Maulsby [also spelled Malsby] requested a certificate for himself, his wife Sarah, and their minor daughter Frances, to Baltimore Monthly Meeting, Western District. Certificates also received from women's meeting for Pamelia Maulsby [also listed as Permelia Malsby] and Sarah Maulsby [also listed Sarah Malsby, Jr.] to Baltimore Monthly Meeting, Western District, which were recorded and forwarded. Little Falls Preparative Meeting informs that Aaron Branson is removed within the verge of Concord Monthly Meeting [Delaware County], Pennsylvania. They also reported that Israel Morris has been instrumental in detaining in service two black people named Aquila and Milcha a considerable time after they were justly entitled to freedom. He has also been charged by a man with fraud and in answer to these charges he has given way to a refractory disposition against some of those who were authorized to treat with him. Little Falls Preparative Meeting informs that Mary Kirk, Jr. requested a certificate to Philadelphia Monthly Meeting.

1810, 25th of 7th mo. - Caleb Price was disowned for outgoing in marriage and holding a black man in bondage. Certificate requested for Samuel Naylor, wife Rebecca, and six minor children, Ann, John, Joseph, Charles, Mary, and Rebecca, to Plymouth Monthly Meeting in the State of Ohio. Also reported that William Naylor had removed and settled with the limits of Plymouth Monthly Meeting and had been married contrary to our good order. Little Falls Preparative Meeting informs that a certificate has been requested by John Morgan and wife Priscilla to Baltimore Monthly Meeting, Western District.

1810, 22nd of 8th mo. - Certificate produced for William Glover, wife Mary, and their five minor children, George, Michel *[sic]*, Sarah, Ann, Thomas, and Hannah, from London Grove Monthly Meeting [Chester County, Pennsylvania]. Little Falls Preparative Meeting reports misconduct by Israel Morris; committee to investigate. Thomas H. Dawson and Edith Matthews declared their intention to marry, and he is to produce a certificate from Third Haven Monthly Meeting for his clearness of others, and with the consent of his surviving parent. She is a young woman and will produce a certificate of clearness from all other engagements, her parents consent being obtained. Certificate requested for Edmund Evans to Baltimore Monthly Meeting, Eastern District, to enable his marriage to Elizabeth Husband, a member of that meeting.

1810, 26th (20th) of 9th mo. - Elizabeth Pitts, formerly Price, had gone out in marriage and not having condemned her misconduct, she is disowned. Thomas Hammersley Dawson and Edith Matthews were cleared for marriage [It was later accomplished in an orderly manner].

1810, 24th of 10th mo. - Levin Hopkins had a birthright amongst us, but hath so far erred as to commit fornication and not willing to condemn his misconduct, he is disowned. Complaint received that James Smith hath so far given way to passion as to kick a woman.

1810, 21st of 11th mo. - James Smith gave written testimony for his misconduct, which he condemned, and was sorry for having kicked a woman. Certificate produced for Daniel Lamborn [also spelled Lamborne], his wife Elizabeth, and six minor children, John, Jane, Daniel, William, Eliza, and Sarah, from Nottingham Monthly Meeting. Certificate for Hannah Lewis to Robinson Monthly Meeting in Pennsylvania was signed, recorded, and a copy handed to her; also one for Matilda Wainwright to Third Haven Monthly Meeting was signed, recorded, and directed to be forwarded; one for Elizabeth Branson from Concord Monthly Meeting [Delaware County], Pennsylvania, was received and endorsed, as she is about to return there. Gunpowder Preparative Meeting informs that Rachal Mott (formerly Griffith) has had her marriage accomplished contrary to our discipline.

1810, 20th of 12th mo. - Information received from Plymouth Monthly Meeting stating William Naylor has returned to this neighborhood.

1811, 23rd of 1st mo. - Martha Dillon, now Marple, hath had her marriage accomplished contrary to the our good order and having previously removed to the western country remote from any of our Society, she is discontinued as a member. Certificate produced for Edith Dawson to Third Haven Monthly Meeting. Complaint received that John Tudor has a slave in his employ for some time past. Certificate received for Elizabeth Evans from Baltimore Monthly Meeting, Eastern District.

1811, 27th of 3rd mo. - Israel Morris charged with manifesting an irritable disposition which caused him to make use of unbecoming language and conduct towards Friends, but with respect to his age and great infirmity, no further action will be taken in his case. Signed by: John McKim, Thomas Moore, Joshua Husband, Roger Brooke, William Husband, Ely Balderston, John Jewet, Isaac Tyson, Thomas Ellicott, and Silas Warner. William Naylor is not in a suitable disposition to condemn his outgoing, so he will be disowned. Amos Smith was appointed clerk and David Preston as assistant clerk. Rachel Mott, formerly Griffith, gave written testimony that she had a birthright and education amongst Friends, but for want of due watchfulness hath suffered herself to be prevailed upon to have her marriage accomplished contrary to this discipline for which transgression she has felt much sorrow, and she hopes she will be continued in membership. Signed: Rachel Moat. Certificate requested for Luke Tipton to Deer Creek Monthly Meeting. Little Falls reports that Edward Churchman requested to be released from the station of overseer. Abner Jones requested a certificate of removal for his son Yearsley Jones, a minor, to Uwchland Monthly Meeting in Pennsylvania. Complaint against Stacey West for taking strong drink so as to be disguised or overcome thereby for which he had been several times admonished. Samuel Reed (in writing) requested a certificate of removal for himself, wife Elizabeth, and their seven minor children, Matilda, Eveline [listed as Ebelina in women's meeting], Deborah [listed as Elenora in women's meeting], William, Anne [listed as Anna in women's meeting], Harriet [listed as Harriot in women's meeting], and John Wilson Reed [listed only as John in women's meeting], to Baltimore Monthly Meeting, Eastern District. Certificate produced from Tottenham [also spelled Totingham] Monthly Meeting in Great Britain for our beloved friend Susanna Horne [also spelled Horn], dated 3rd mo., 1810, with an endorsement by the Quarterly Meeting of London and Middlesex held in London 27th of 3rd mo., 1810, both expressed unity with her in a religious visit to this country, and also a certificate from the Meeting of Ministers and Elders held in London on 1st of 6th mo., 1810. Certificate produced for Mary Allison [also spelled Allenson], companion of Susanna Horne, from Burlington Monthly Meeting [Burlington County, New Jersey], dated 1st of 10th mo. last. Also a minute for Caleb Shreeve from Philadelphia Monthly Meeting, Northern District, was received, stating he was to accompany Susanna Horne in part of her visit in this country.

1811, 24th of 4th mo. - William Naylor, having had a birthright amongst Friends, but for want of attending has had his marriage accomplished by the assistance of a magistrate, is disowned until he condemns his misconduct to our satisfaction. Reported that John Tudor had been charged with fighting and removed within the verge of Huntington Monthly Meeting in Pennsylvania, preventing our opportunity to meet with him. Samuel Price, Jr. and wife Ann requested that their minor daughter Frances be received into membership. Certificate produced for Rachal Mott to Baltimore Monthly Meeting, Eastern District. John Needles and Eliza Matthews declared their intention to marry. The young man was requested to produce a certificate of clearness and right of membership from his own monthly meeting, and the young woman to obtain clearness from similar engagements, parents consent being obtained. Thomas Parsons and Mary Price declared their intention to marry. The young man was requested to produce a certificate of clearness and right of membership from his own monthly meeting, and the young woman to obtain clearness from all other similar engagements, parents consent being obtained.

1811, 22nd of 5th mo. - Stacey West gave written testimony that he had a right in membership with Friends but through unwatchfulness he had taken too freely of intoxicating liquors for which he is sincerely sorry. Letter received from Monallen Monthly Meeting [Adams County], Pennsylvania, regarding the misconduct of John Tudor, a member of that meeting, and requested the Gunpowder Monthly Meeting to treat with him on their behalf in the handling of charges (employing a slave and fighting) brought against him. Little Falls reported that William Kirk requested a certificate to York Monthly Meeting. Complaint brought against Enoch Pearson for drinking too freely of strong drink, using unbecoming language, and giving way to passion so far as to take a man by the collar. These certificates were produced and accepted: William Trego and wife Rebecca from Wrightstown Monthly Meeting in Bucks County, Pennsylvania; Thomas Trego, wife Sarah, and their eight minor children, William, Harriet, Francenia, Albert, David, Sarah, Hannah, and James Duffel [Dussel?] Trego, from the same meeting; Mary Trego, from same meeting; Mary Maulsby, wife of Morris Maulsby [also spelled Malsby], and their minor child David Lee Maulsby from Deer Creek Monthly Meeting; and, one for Anna Churchman from Philadelphia Monthly Meeting.

1811, 26th of 6th mo. - John Needles and Eliza Matthews had been married in an orderly manner. Thomas Parsons and Mary Price had been married in an orderly manner. Yearsley Jones returned from Uwchland Monthly Meeting and the certificate issued previously was detained. Jesse Scott, Jacob Tyson, Amos Smith, and Daniel Price were appointed to examine our records of birth and burials. Bathsheba Johnson, formerly Hicks [also spelled Hix], had her marriage accomplished contrary to our rules. Catharine Watkins, formerly Maulsby [also spelled Malsby], has been guilty of fornication with a man she had since married contrary to our discipline.

1811, 24th of 7th mo. - Catharine Watkins, late Maulsby, had her birth and education among Friends, but refused to condemn her misconduct (fornication and marriage); she was disowned. Isaac Smith produced a certificate from Little Britton Monthly Meeting. Certificate for Eliza Needles to Baltimore Monthly Meeting, Western District, was read, recorded, and forwarded.

1811, 28th of 8th mo. - Certificate for Mary Parsons to Third Haven Monthly Meeting was approved, signed, and forwarded.

1811, 25th of 9th mo. - Enoch Pearson gave written testimony that he had been overtaken with too much strong drink and in a passion took a man by the collar, for which he was sorry and requested to continue in membership. Levi Benson replaced Jacob Tyson on the committee on birth and burials. On account of Timothy Kirk's death, David Preston was added to the standing committee for the relief of the poor. Little Falls informed that Edward Brinton had married by the assistance of a methodist teacher. Mahlon West charged with outgoing in marriage with his first cousin, a member. Nathaniel Hollingsworth requested to be released from the station of overseer. Susanna Thomas (formerly Jones) has had her marriage performed contrary to Friends discipline.

1811, 23rd of 10th mo. - Complaint of the disorderly marriage of Mahlon West to Mary West (formerly Trego) was investigated further and found that she had been married by a magistrate to her first cousin. Little Falls Preparative Meeting informs that Isaac Smith requested a certificate to enable him to accomplish his marriage with Margaret Cole, a member of Deer Creek Monthly Meeting. Edmund [also spelled Edmond] Evans and Elizabeth Evans, in writing, requested a certificate of removal to Indian Spring Monthly Meeting.

1811, 27th of 11th mo. - Jesse Lancaster gave written testimony and condemned his misconduct in making too free use of spirituous liquors and promised to be more careful, with divine help, in the future. Susanna Thomas (late Jones) was charged with outgoing in marriage. An application was about to be made to the General Assembly of this State to pass a law to stop a road leading to Gunpowder Meeting House. William Matthews (of Oliver), Thomas Scott, Thomas Price, Jacob Tyson, and Amos Smith were appointed to take such steps in the case as the nature of it should require.

1811, 25th of 12th mo. - Mahlon and Mary West, having joined in marriage, they being first cousins, have agreeably to our discipline, forfeited their right of membership. Certificate produced for Sarah Bond to Baltimore Monthly Meeting, Eastern District, was recorded and forwarded.

1812, 22nd of 1st mo. - Edward Brinton gave written testimony that he had his marriage accomplished contrary to the order of Friends for which he was sorry and requested to continue to membership. Certificate received for William B. Kirk from Nottingham Monthly Meeting. David Preston was appointed to the station of overseer and Nathaniel Hollingsworth was released.

41

1812, 26th of 2nd mo. - Certificate received for Samuel Wainwright, wife Matilda, and their minor son John Price Wainwright from Third Haven Monthly Meeting. William Squib had reportedly removed within the limits of Warrington Monthly Meeting [York County, Pennsylvania] without requesting a certificate. Charles Harding requested a certificate for his son Davis, a minor, to Baltimore Monthly Meeting, Eastern District. John Naylor requested a certificate for himself, wife Mary, and son Abraham, a minor, to Plymouth Monthly Meeting in the State of Ohio. Jesse Scott, William Matthews (of Oliver), and Edward Churchman are directed to unite with a committee of women Friends in visiting the families of such of our members as have "coulerd people" under their care. Joshua Reynolds requested to be released from serving as overseer and Amos Smith requested to be released from serving as clerk.

1812, 25th of 3rd mo. - Certificate received for Thomas Brown and his wife Betty Way Brown from Nottingham Monthly Meeting [Cecil County, Maryland]; also one for Townsend and Carpenter Jefferis from Goshen Monthly Meeting [Chester County, Pennsylvania]. Thomas Price was appointed overseer in room of Joshua Reynolds (since deceased). Certificate produced for Mary Kirk, Jr. from Philadelphia Monthly Meeting. Mahlon Kirk, by Little Falls, requested a certificate of removal to Baltimore Monthly Meeting, Western District.

1812, 22nd of 4th mo. - Certificates for Mary Kirk, Sr., Rachal Kirk, and Mary Kirk, Jr. to Baltimore Monthly Meeting, Western District, were approved, signed and forwarded. Certificate produced for Margaret Smith, wife of Isaac, from Deer Creek Monthly Meeting. Certificate for Ann Sanderson, a minor, from Baltimore Monthly Meeting, Eastern District, was read and accepted. William Matthews (of O.) also requested a certificate for his son Samuel Hanway Matthews to Baltimore Monthly Meeting, Western District. Edward Jones, a ministering friend from Warrington Monthly Meeting [York County, Pennsylvania], attended this meeting. Gunpowder Preparative Meeting reports that one of their overseers [no name given] had recently been removed by death.

1812, 27th of 5th mo. - Susanna Thomas gave written testimony to condemn her outgoing in marriage by the assistance of a methodist teacher and requested to continue as a member. Jacob and Tacey Lukins [also spelled Tacy Lukens] requested a certificate for themselves and their five minor children, John, Rebecca, Merrikan [also spelled Merican], Ruth, and Alice [also spelled Allice], to Plymouth Monthly Meeting in the State of Ohio. Certificate requested for Margaret Smith and her husband [name not given] to Indian Spring Monthly Meeting.

1812, 24th of 6th mo. - John Tuder, having had a right amongst Friends but so far deviated as to have a slave in his employ for some time, and also been guilty of fighting, is disowned until he comes to a light and sense of his errors. Lewis Horlen [Harlen?] requested a certificate to Warrington Monthly Meeting [York County, Pennsylvania]. Certificate for William Squib was returned from Warrington Monthly Meeting [York County, Pennsylvania] as not being accepted.

1812, 22nd of 7th mo. - Certificate for William Squib was read, approved, and forwarded, and the former to be erased. Complaint received that Samuel Hugs had taken an oath and joined the military service. Elizabeth Lea attended women's meeting with a certificate from Baltimore Monthly Meeting, Western District.

1812, 27th of 8th mo. - Rhoda M. Bartlet was appointed clerk of the women's meeting. [No men's meeting minutes were found in book for 8th and 9th months, 1812].

1812, 28th of 10th mo. - James Tucker was charged with outgoing in marriage, and also Benjamin Benson "on the like occasion." Rachel Reynolds requested a certificate to Nottingham Monthly Meeting for herself and her four minor children, Sarah, Mary, Elisha Brown, and Elizabeth. Rachel Reynolds, Jr. requested a certificate to Baltimore Monthly Meeting, Eastern District. Phebe Tuder being for some time within the verge of Huntington Monthly Meeting we think right to send her a certificate.

1812, 25th of 11th mo. - Certificate produced for George Davis from Concord Monthly Meeting [Delaware County, Pennsylvania]. Certificates produced for: Rachel Reynolds, Jr. to Baltimore Monthly Meeting, Western District; Phebe Tudor and her three minor children [no names given] to Monallen Monthly Meeting [Adams County, Pennsylvania]; and, Susanna Thomas to Deer Creek Monthly Meeting. Gunpowder Preparative Meeting informs that Isaac Vore requested a joint certificate with his wife Ruth and their two minor children, Jacob and Mary, to Deer Creek Monthly Meeting.

1812, 23rd of 12th mo. - James Tucker, having been tenderly treated with in order to impress his mind with a just sense of his deviation from the good order, but not in suitable disposition to condemn his procedure, we disown him from being a member. Gunpowder Preparative Meeting informs that Jesse Scott requested to be released from the station of overseer.

1813, 27th of 1st mo. - Benjamin Benson gave written testimony that he had deviated so far as to be married by the assistance of a baptist teacher, and condemned his misconduct. Elizabeth Spencer requested her three minor children, Hannah, Sarah, and Hugh, to be received into membership with Friends. Certificate produced for Elizabeth Brown, wife of David, from Nottingham Monthly Meeting.

Certificate produced for Esther Garrett [also spelled Garret], wife of Jonah, and her three minor children, Eliza, Jessee, and Abigail, from Goshen Monthly Meeting [Chester County, Pennsylvania]. Gunpowder Select Preparative Meeting proposed Mary D. Price for the station of minister.

1813, 24th of 2nd mo. - Mordecai Price (of Samuel) was appointed to the station of overseer.

1813, 24th of 3rd mo. - Elizabeth Lee requested to be taken into membership. Seth Smith and Anne Churchman declared their intention to marry; he was directed to obtain a certificate of clearness from the meeting he belongs and the consent of parents. Certificate for Susanna B. Jones produced from Baltimore Monthly Meeting, Western District. Certificate for Rachel Parrish to Plymouth Monthly Meeting in the State of Ohio was approved, recorded, and forwarded [no date indicated].

1813, 21st of 4th mo. - Women's Meeting: Israel Clerck and Amy his wife produced a certificate for themselves and their four minor children, Elizabeth, Deborah, Phebe, and Ruth, from Salsbury Monthly Meeting; also, Rachel and Mary Clerck, their daughters, produced certificates from the same meeting.

1813, 26th of 5th mo. - Women's Meeting: William Glover requested a certificate for himself and wife Mary and their six minor children, George, Michel, Sarah, Ann, Thomas, Hannah, and Eliza, to Baltimore Monthly Meeting, Eastern District. Anne Smith requested a certificate to Goose Creek Monthly Meeting in Louden County, Virginia.

1813, 23rd of 6th mo. - Women's Meeting: Bartholomew Fussell and Rebecca his wife produced a certificate for themselves and their two minor children, Bartholomew and Rebecca, likewise for their daughter Esther Fussell, from Gwynedd Monthly Meeting in Pennsylvania. Moses Dillion [also spelled Dillon] requested a certificate for himself and his wife Hannah to Stillwater Monthly Meeting in the State of Ohio.

1813, 28th of 7th mo. - Women's Meeting: Judith Preston and Sarah Trego were appointed to the station of overseers.

1813, 23rd of 8th mo. - Women's Meeting: Agreement proposed and signed by the following Friends to hold a meeting in Abraham Huff's house for worship twice a week except the time of our meeting for discipline and to be excused from attending at our usual meeting place with the same exceptions. Signed: (first column) Elizabeth West, Ruth Whitaker, Fraces [sic] McConnell, Mercy Huff,

Rebecca Smith, Elizabeth Tucker; (second column) Thomas West, Samuel McConnell, Abraham Huff, John White, Amos Smith, David Tucker.

1813, 22nd of 9th mo. - Women's Meeting: Abraham Huff and Mercy his wife produced a certificate for themselves and their five minor children, Martha, John, Elizabeth, Samuel, and Mary Ann, from Deer Creek Monthly Meeting. Susanna Parsons requested a certificate to Plymouth Monthly Meeting in the State of Ohio. Meeting previously proposed at Abraham Huff's house was approved. Mariah Curtis, having been some time under the care of Little Falls Preparative Meeting, requests to be taken into membership. Aquilla Starr and Abigail his wife produced a certificate for themselves and their six minor children, Sidney, Engle, James, Mary, Joseph, and Sally Ann, from Goshen Monthly Meeting in Chester County, Pennsylvania. Plymouth Monthly Meeting in the State of Ohio informs that Ann Blackson [also spelled Blackiston] hath applied to them for readmission into membership.

1813, 27th of 10th mo. - Women's Meeting: Friends who have removed without certificates should be sent one, namely Mary Lee at Short Creek Monthly Meeting in the State of Ohio, and Mary Hay at Crosswich Monthly Meeting. Copy of a certificate for Margaret Pearsons, now Edy [also spelled Eddy] from New Garden Monthly Meeting was handed to this meeting, dated 8th of 10th mo., 1812, which she never produced, but she since accomplished her marriage with a man not in membership with us; the same meeting hath now requested we deal with her on their behalf. Margaret Smith joined with her husband [not named] to request a certificate to Deer Creek Monthly Meeting.

1813, 24th of 11th mo. - Women's Meeting: Rhoda M. Bartlett requested to be released from the station of clerk.

1814, 26th of 1st mo. - Women's Meeting: Rebecca Beans produced a certificate from Buckenham Monthly Meeting. Sarah Procter, a minister in good esteem, attended this meeting from Baltimore Monthly Meeting, Eastern District, and Judith Preston will accompany in her religious visit with Friends of Gunpowder Monthly Meeting, particularly those of Little Falls. Abner Jones and Maria Curtis declared their intention to marry, and the young woman to obtain clearness from other engagements, parents consent being obtained.

1814, 23rd of 3rd mo. - Women's Meeting: Little Falls Preparative Meeting informs that Mahlon and Mary West request reinstatement in membership. Achsah Brown produced a certificate from Deer Creek Monthly Meeting. "Esther Scott requests a certificate to Plymouth Monthly Meeting, State of Ohio; Amos Scott one for his minor daughter Rachel." David Maulsby produced a certificate for himself and Mary his wife from Baltimore Monthly Meeting, Western District.

1814, 27th of 4th mo. - Women's Meeting: Gunpowder Preparative Meeting informs that Phebe Haire [also spelled Hair] had an illegitimate child. John Underwood and Mary Clark [also spelled Clerck] and Oliver Kinsey and Sarah Griffith, declared their intentions to marry, and the young women to obtain clearness from other like engagements, consent of parents obtained.

1814, 25th of 5th mo. - Women's Meeting: Gunpowder Preparative Meeting informs that Kiturah Bond, formerly Price, daughter of Mordecai Price, had recently accomplished her marriage contrary to our discipline. Little Fawls [sic] Preparative Meeting informs that Mary Caldwell, formerly Amos, has accomplished her marriage with a man not in membership with Friends.

1814, 22nd of 6th mo. - Women's Meeting: John Underwood and Mary Clerck [also spelled Clark] had been married in an orderly manner, as were Oliver Kinsey and Sarah Griffith.

1814, 27th of 7th mo. - Women's Meeting: Mary Underwood requested a certificate to Deer Creek Monthly Meeting. Rebecca James produced a certificate from Chester Monthly Meeting. John Hutten and Sarah his wife produced a certificate from Goshen Monthly Meeting [Chester County, Pennsylvania]. Mary D. Price, a minister in good esteem, in a weighty manner mentioned a prospect that had for some time past accompanied her mind to attend the yearly meeting in the State of Ohio, which she is left at liberty to pursue. Susanna Pearson requested a certificate joint with her husband [name not given] and their four minor children, Rachel, Phebe, Samuel, and Elisha, to Deer Creek Monthly Meeting.

1814, 24th of 8th mo. - Women's Meeting: Sarah Kinsey requested a certificate to New Garden Monthly Meeting [Chester County, Pennsylvania]. Mary M. Price requested to be released from the station of overseer. Jonathan Wright and Susannah Buffiting Jones declared their intention to marry, pending proper clearness of the young woman from all others [which was subsequently accomplished].

1814, 21st of 9th mo. - Women's Meeting: Certificate received for Fracis [sic] Maulsby from Baltimore Monthly Meeting, Western District; also one for Sarah Bond from Baltimore Monthly Meeting, Eastern District. Jacob Hare and Elizabeth Clark declared their intention to marry, pending needful inquiry of the young woman.

1814, 20th of 10th mo. - Women's Meeting: Jonathan Wright and Susannah B. Jones had been married in an orderly manner. Susannah B. Wright requested a certificate to Miammi Monthly Meeting in the State of Ohio. Certificate produced for John Mott, wife Rachel, and their minor son Abraham G. Mott, from Baltimore Monthly Meeting, Eastern District. Jacob Fussell and Clarissa Whittiker declared their intention to marry, pending the needful inquiry respecting the young woman [for which she was subsequently cleared and with her mother's consent].

1814, 23rd of 11th mo. - Women's Meeting: Elizabeth Vore requested a certificate to Deer Creek Monthly Meeting.

1814, 31st of 12th mo. - Women's Meeting: Jacob Fussell and Clarissa Whittiker had been married in an orderly manner. Hannah Jones requested a certificate to Miammi Monthly Meeting in the State of Ohio. Elizabeth Brown requested a certificate to East Nottingham Monthly Meeting. Mary D. Price returned her minute with an endorsement from the Ohio Yearly Meeting "expressive of her exceptable service therein."

1815, 25th of 1st mo. - Women's Meeting: Martha Forwood requested to be united to our Society, having been disowned at Deer Creek Monthly Meeting.

1815, 22nd of 3rd mo. - Women's Meeting: Certificate for Mary Hays was returned with an endorsement from Philadelphia Monthly Meeting, Northern District.

1815, 26th of 4th mo. - Women's Meeting: Rachel Tucker requested to become a member of our Society. William Tuder and wife Martha requested a certificate for themselves and four minor children, William, Abraham, Martha, and Hannah, to Plainfield Monthly Meeting in the State of Ohio; also their daughter Elizabeth requested one to the same meeting. Rachel Mott requested a certificate joint with her husband and minor son, Abraham Griffeth Mott, to Baltimore Monthly Meeting, Eastern District. Mary Kittlewell produced a certificate from Warrington Monthly Meeting [York County, Pennsylvania]. Owen Branson requested a certificate form himself, wife Hannah, and four minor children, Eliza E., Benjamin, David, and Mary Ann, to Baltimore Monthly Meeting, Eastern District. Thomas T. Griffeth and Rachel Matthews declared their intention to marry.

1815, 27th of 5th mo. - Women's Meeting: Little Fawls [Falls] Preparative Meeting informs that Sarah Jones, formerly Spencer, had accomplished her marriage contrary to the order of our Society with a man not in membership.

1815, 21st of 6th mo. - Women's Meeting: Kiturah Bond attended this meeting and condemned her deviation in marrying a man not in membership with Friends.

Thomas T. Griffeth and Rachel Matthews had been married in an orderly manner. Virgil Eaches and wife Mary requested to be again united to the Society of Friends. Lydia Barcroft requested a certificate to Baltimore Monthly Meeting, Eastern District. Thomas Brown, wife Betty Way Brown, and their minor son John Brown have removed without a certificate within the compass of Nottingham Monthly Meeting. Jacob Fussell and wife Clarissa requested a certificate to Baltimore Monthly Meeting, Western District.

1815, 26th of 7th mo. - Women's Meeting: Certificate was produced for Mary Dawes and Friends objected to the reception of it on account of her "none attendance of meeting." Jacob Vore and wife Elizabeth produced a certificate from Deer Creek Monthly Meeting. Samuel Reed produced a certificate for himself and six minor children, Deborah, William, Harriot, John Wilson, Elizabeth, and Samuel D. Reed, from Baltimore Monthly Meeting, Eastern District; also a certificate for Matilda Reed was received from the same meeting. Jonathan Warner, wife Sarah, and their two minor children, Hannah and Brinton, produced a certificate from Goshen Monthly Meeting [Chester County, Pennsylvania]. Certificate received for Margarum Pearson from New Garden Monthly Meeting [Chester County, Pennsylvania]. Margarum Eddy requested a certificate to Deer Creek Monthly Meeting. Maria Jones requested a certificate jointly with her husband and minor daughter Hannah to Deer Creek Monthly Meeting.

1815, 25th of 10th mo. - Women's Meeting: Rachel Parrish requested a certificate to Plymouth Monthly Meeting in the State of Ohio.

1815, 27th of 12th mo. - Communication received from Chester Monthly Meeting in Pennsylvania (dated 27th of 11th mo., 1815) respecting Virgil Eaches and wife [no name given] in uniting them in membership, they living in the verge of Little Falls Monthly Meeting. Certificate received for David and Hannah Smith from Fallowfield Monthly Meeting in the State of Pennsylvania, they living within the verge of Little Falls Monthly Meeting. [No minutes recorded between 1st mo., 1815 and 1st mo., 1816].

1816, 24th of 1st mo. - Memorial of our beloved friend William Amos to be forwarded to the Quarterly Meeting.

1816, 21st of 2nd mo. - Matilda Wainwright, now Chilcoat, had her marriage accomplished by the assistance of a hireling teacher to a man not in membership with us.

1816, 27th of 3rd mo. - Caleb Hunt and Rhoda M. Bartlett declared their intention to marry and he is to obtain a certificate of clearness from the meeting he belongs, and consent of parents. Erastus U. Kirk and Maria Matthews declared their intention to marry and he is to obtain a certificate of clearness from the meeting he belongs, and consent of parents. Rachel Carrol, formerly Clark, has had her marriage accomplished by a hireling teacher to a man not in membership with us.

1816, 24th of 4th mo. - Certificate received from Redstone Monthly Meeting [Fayette County, Pennsylvania] clearing Caleb Hunt for marriage, with the consent of his surviving parent. Certificate received from York Monthly Meeting clearing Erastus M. Kirk for marriage, with the consent of his parents. Mordecai Price (of Samuel) and Mary M. Price were appointed to the station of elders.

1816, 22nd of 5th mo. - Caleb Hunt and Rhoda M. Bartlett had been married in an orderly manner. Erastus Kirk and Maria Matthews had been married in an orderly manner. Matilda Chilcoat gave written testimony that she has a birthright amongst us but for want of a strict adherence had her marriage accomplished by a hireling teacher; she condemned her misconduct and asked to continue in membership. Oliver Matthews requested to be released of having care of the graveyard and also the deed which is granted. Thomas Scott and Samuel Price were appointed to take charge of the graveyard and the title papers. Elizabeth Scott was appointed clerk and Rebecca Matthews as assistant clerk for the women's meeting. Rachel Mason requested to be released from the station of overseer.

1816, 26th of 6th mo. - Gunpowder Preparative Meeting informs that Aquilla Wheeler, a minor, has removed within the verge of Cincinnati Monthly Meeting in Ohio, and Friends think it best that he should have a certificate to join him thereto. Rhoda M. Hunt requested a certificate for herself and minor son Joseph Bartlett to Redstone Monthly Meeting [Fayette County, Pennsylvania].

1816, 24th of 7th mo. - Our beloved friend Charles Osborn attended this meeting. It was also reported "We, the committee appointed to make inquiry concerning those of the African race in Friends families respecting their school education, have paid considerable attention to the service and find that those who have them have paid some attention thereto. Signed: Daniel Price, Thomas Price, George Mason, William Matthews." Certificate was received for Martha Powel from Philadelphia Monthly Meeting, Southern District.

1816, 28th of 8th mo. - Certificate of Martha Powel was endorsed and forwarded to Little Falls Monthly Meeting.

1816, 23rd of 10th mo. - Rachel Carrol, having her birth and education amongst Friends, gave written testimony that she had gone out in marriage to a man not in membership, for which she is sorry and asks to continue as a member. Our esteemed friend Sarah Scull and her companion Rebecca Hubbs attended this meeting with their certificates from Piles Grove Monthly Meeting in New Jersey. Certificate for Maria M. Kirk to York Monthly Meeting in Pennsylvania was approved, signed and forwarded.

1816, 4th of 12th mo. - Thomas Scott and Eli Matthews are appointed to open subscriptions for the use of contemplated school and report on their progress at next meeting.

1817, 8th of 1st mo. - Joseph Price and Thomas Scott requested to be released from serving as clerk and assistant clerk.

1817, 5th of 2nd mo. - Our esteemed friend Huldah Hoag attended this meeting with a minute from Ferrisburgh Monthly Meeting in the State of Vermont, with her companion Elizabeth Tabor. Amy Clark requested to be released from the station of overseer.

1817, 5th of 3rd mo. - Thomas Scott was proposed and appointed as clerk and Elijah Price to assist him. Mordecai Price (of Mordecai) requested a certificate for his minor son Amos to Baltimore Monthly Meeting, Western District.

1817, 9th of 4th mo. - Rachel Carrol requested a certificate to Little Falls Monthly Meeting.

1817, 9th of 7th mo. - Certificate received for Jehu Price from Hopewell Monthly Meeting [Frederick County, Virginia].

1817, 6th of 8th mo. - Our friend Isaac Hammer attended this meeting with a certificate from New Hope Monthly Meeting in Green County, Tennessee, with his companion James Johnson.

1817, 3rd of 9th mo. - Mary Matthews requested to be released from the station of overseer.

1817, 8th (9th) of 10th mo. - Gunpowder Preparative Meeting informs that Israel Clark and wife Amy requested a certificate for themselves and their minor daughter Ruth to White Water Monthly Meeting in the State of Indiana; a certificate for Deborah Clark to the same meeting was requested. Jehu Price and Susanna Matthews declared their intention to marry, with consent of parents being obtained.

1817, 5th of 11th mo. - Gunpowder Preparative Meeting informs that Samuel Morthland Tudor requested a certificate to Menallen Monthly Meeting [Adams County], Pennsylvania.

1817, 3rd of 12th mo. - Jehu Price and Susanna Matthews had been married in an orderly manner. Certificate for Sarah Morthland to Monallen Monthly Meeting [Adams County], Pennsylvania, was recorded and forwarded [although the women's meeting last month indicated Huntington Monthly Meeting]. Elizabeth Scott requested to be released from the station of clerk and Rebecca Matthews from being assistant clerk.

1818, 4th of 2nd mo. - Certificate produced for Phebe Clark to Deer Creek Monthly Meeting was recorded and forwarded.

1818, 4th of 3rd mo. - Communication received from Menallen Monthly Meeting [Adams County, Pennsylvania] that John Tudor requested to be received into membership.

1818, 8th of 4th mo. - Certificate produced for Elizabeth Hair to Baltimore Monthly Meeting, Eastern District, was recorded and forwarded.

1818, 3rd of 6th mo. - Communication received from Westland Monthly Meeting [Washington County, Pennsylvania] informing that John Smith requests to be received into membership and he being formerly disowned, inquire as to any objection. A few lines were subsequently prepared that no objection appeared.

1818, 8th of 7th mo. - Certificate produced by women's meeting for Tamer Hair to Baltimore Monthly Meeting, Western District; also one for Jemmiah [also spelled Jemimah] Sulavin to the same meeting.

1818, 6th of 8th mo. - William Gawthrop and Mary Griffith declared their intention to marry, with consent of parents being obtained, and he is to produce a certificate of clearness from the meeting he belongs.

1818, 9th of 9th mo. - Certificate produced for William Gawthrop from Kennet Monthly Meeting [Chester County], Pennsylvania, to enable him to proceed in marriage with Mary Griffith. Jessee Scott, Thomas Price, and John Matthews were appointed to examine the records of birth and burials of this meeting.

1818, 7th of 10th mo. - William Gawthrop and Mary Griffith had been married in an orderly manner. Certificate produced for Elizabeth Webster to Baltimore Monthly Meeting, Eastern District.

1818, 4th of 11th mo. - Gunpowder Preparative Meeting informs that Thomas Scott and Mordecai Price request to be released from serving as overseers.

1819, 6th of 1st mo. - Thomas Matthews was appointed as an overseer and Mordecai Price was continued in that service.

1819, 3rd of 2nd mo. - Certificate produced for Mary Gawthrop to Kennet Monthly Meeting [Chester County], Pennsylvania, was signed, recorded and forwarded.

1819, 7th of 4th mo. - Robert Morthland requested that his 5 minor children, Susanna, Edward H., Samuel, Mary, and Robert, be taken into membership.

1819, 7th of 7th mo. - Thomas Scott was appointed clerk and Elijah Price to assist him. Complaint received that James Mason has been in the practice of drinking spirituous liquors to excess.

1819, 6th of 10th mo. - Mordecai Price (of Samuel) offered one acre of land in fee simple on the ridge between Caleb Bosley and Joseph Price as a suitable place to build a meeting house.

1819, 3rd of 11th mo. - Our friend Mildred Ratclif [also spelled Radcliff] attended this meeting with a certificate from Short Creek in Ohio, with an endorsement from Short Creek Quarterly Meeting in Jefferson County, Ohio. Her companion Mary Slater produced a minute from Concord Monthly Meeting in Belmont County, Ohio. John Lloyd also attended with a minute from that same meeting.

1819, 8th of 12th mo. - James Mason gave written testimony condemning his misconduct in drinking to excess, which has given cause of uneasiness to Friends, and asked to continue in membership with us.

1820, 9th of 2nd mo. - Our beloved friend Hinchman Haines attended this meeting with a minute from Eversham Monthly Meeting in New Jersey. Reuben Benson has had his marriage accomplished by the assistance of a hireling to a woman not of our society.

1820, 3rd of 5th mo. - Rebecca Matthews asked to be released as clerk of women's meeting.

1820, 7th of 6th mo. - Reuben Benson was disowned for outgoing in marriage. Committee on the new meeting house proposed the plan, viz., build it on the lot offered by Mordecai Price (of Samuel); the house will be 56 feet long by 32 feet wide, one story high, with 4 doors, 8 windows, 24 lights each 8 by 10 glass, and built of stone, and when neatly finished for a meeting house will cost $1350 of which $1750 is subscribed. The following Friends are to secure the lot of ground, continue the subscription, collect money, purchase materials, and receive proposals for building the house as soon as practible or convenient, Thomas Scott, Eli Matthews, John Price, Jessee Scott and Mordecai Price (of Samuel). Rachel Benson (now Price) had her marriage accomplished to a man not in membership with us.

1820, 5th of 7th mo. - Thomas Scott requested to be released as clerk and Elijah Price as assistant clerk. Certificates for Margaret Thornburgh and Sarah Thornburgh to Baltimore Monthly Meeting, Western District, were signed, recorded and forwarded. Jesse Scott appointed as clerk and Mordecai Price (of Samuel) as assistant.

1820, 9th of 8th mo. - Rachel Price, formerly Benson, hath gone out in marriage. Certificate produced for Elizabeth McKinsey who attended from Little Britton [also spelled Britain] Monthly Meeting.

1820, 6th of 9th mo. - Certificates produced for David Harding and William B. Price from Baltimore Monthly Meeting, Western District. Ann Price and Betty Price requested to be released from serving as overseers for the women's meeting.

1820, 4th of 10th mo. - Our esteemed friend William Foster, Jr. visited this meeting with a certificate from the Shaftsbury and Sherborne Monthly Meeting in Great Britton. Joseph M. Jessop produced his certificate from York Monthly Meeting.

1820, 8th of 11th mo. - Amos Griffith and Edith Price declared their intention to marry, consent of parents being obtained, the young man having produced a certificate of clearness from Westland Monthly Meeting [Washington County, Pennsylvania]. Samuel Scott and Elizabeth McKinsey declared their intention to marry, the young man to produce a certificate of clearness from the meeting he belongs.

1820, 6th of 12th mo. - Samuel Scott produced a certificate of clearness to marry from Baltimore Monthly Meeting, Western District.

1821, 3rd of 1st mo. - Amos Griffith and Edith Price had been married in an orderly manner. Samuel Scott and Elizabeth McKinsey had been married in an orderly manner. Certificate produced for Amos Price from Baltimore Monthly Meeting, Western District.

1821, 7th of 2nd mo. - Committee appointed to open subscriptions for Fair Hill Boarding School reported they had opened them, but no money subscribed nor collected. Signed: Thomas Scott, Eli Matthews. Certificate for Edith Griffith to Westland Monthly Meeting [Washington County], Pennsylvania, was signed, recorded and forwarded.

1821, 7th of 3rd mo. - New meeting house now finished and the whole amount of cost is $1396; balance of $122 yet to be paid. Thomas Scott and Thomas Price were appointed to take care of the old meeting house and graveyard.

1821, 4th of 4th mo. - Jared M. Price and Sarah Matthews declared their intention to marry, consent of parents being obtained.

1821, 9th of 5th mo. - Elisha Plummer produced a certificate from Pipe Creek Monthly Meeting [Frederick County, Maryland]. Certificate for Elizabeth M. Scott to Baltimore Monthly Meeting, Western District, was signed, recorded and forwarded.

1821, 1st (6th) of 6th mo. - Jared M. Price and Sarah Matthews had been married in an orderly manner. Gunpowder Preparative Meeting informs that Elijah Benson had his marriage accomplished contrary to the order of our Society. James Cockburn attended this meeting with a certificate from Nottingham Monthly Meeting, accompanied by Joshua Husband from Deer Creek Monthly Meeting, who also produced a certificate, and stated they are visiting Friends belonging to the Baltimore Yearly Meeting.

1821, 4th of 7th mo. - Thomas Matthews was proposed to serve in the station of an elder. The women's meeting proposed Elizabeth Scott.

1821, 8th of 8th mo. - Elijah Benson, visited by a committee, stated he had no desire to be continued a member of our Society.

1821, 6th of 9th mo. - Elijah Benson, having a birthright amongst us, but deviated so far as to marry a woman not of our Society, is disowned. Jessee Scott requested to be released as clerk and Mordecai Price as assistant.

1821, 3rd of 10th mo. - Thomas Scott appointed clerk and Jared M. Price as assistant clerk.

1822, 9th of 1st mo. - Certificate produced for George Mason, Jr. from Baltimore Monthly Meeting, Western District.

1822, 6th of 2nd mo. - Communication received from Baltimore Monthly Meeting to treat with George Mason, Jr. for drinking spirituous liquors to excess.

Gunpowder Preparative Meeting informs that Elisha Plummer has had his marriage accomplished by a hireling to a woman in membership with us. Samuel Price, Jr. requested a certificate for his son David to Baltimore Monthly Meeting, Western District.

1822, 6th of 3rd mo. - The men's and women's committee jointly, comprised of Daniel Price, Thomas Matthews, Ruth Matthews, Elizabeth Scott, and Mary M. Price, have met with Elisha Plummer and Mary his wife, who appeared tender and desired to make satisfaction to Friends. Gunpowder Preparative Meeting informs that Mordecai Price and Thomas Matthews request to be released from serving as overseers. A minute from Quarterly Meeting reported that the price of board and tuition at Fairhill Boarding School had been reduced to $80 per annum.

1822, 8th of 5th mo. - Gunpowder Preparative Meeting informs that Abraham Benson has removed to the west of the mountains without a certificate and a great distance from Friends. Jesse Scott at the request of the overseers hath taken an opportunity with him and informs that he don't desire one as he has joined another Society as a member; therefore, we disown him from being a member of our Society.

1822, 3rd of 7th mo. - Elisha Plummer gave written testimony that he had a birthright and education amongst the people called Quakers, but deviated so far as to be married contrary to the good order, for which he was sorry, and requested to continue in membership. Mary K. Plummer also condemned her own outgoing.

1822, 7th of 8th mo. - Our esteemed friend Priscilla Hunt attended this meeting with a certificate from Blue River Monthly Meeting in Washington County, State of Indiana. Her companion Rachel Johnson also attended this meeting with a certificate from Lick (or Licken) Creek in Orange County, State of Indiana. They were accompanied by Burnard [Barnard?] Taylor with a minute from Goose Creek Monthly Meeting in Louden County, Virginia. The Preparative Meeting of Ministers and Elders proposed Mary Matthews to be considered as a minister, with which this meeting united.

1822, 4th of 12th mo. - William T. Heston attended this meeting with a certificate from Alexandria Monthly Meeting. Samuel Price, Sr. and Thomas Scott requested to be released from the care of interments at the old meeting house.

1823, 8th of 1st mo. - Minute received from Smithfield Monthly Meeting in Ohio asking the concurrence of this meeting in receiving Amos Parsons into membership who was disowned by this meeting.

1823, 5th of 2nd mo. - Thomas Scott appointed clerk and Jared M. Price as assistant clerk.

1823, 4th of 6th mo. - Gunpowder Preparative Meeting informed that Joseph M. Jessop has been in the practice of drinking spirituous liquors to excess.

1823, 9th of 7th mo. - Certificate received for Amos Read, a minor, from Baltimore Monthly Meeting; he being removed within the limits of Indian Spring Monthly Meeting, it was endorsed and forwarded to that meeting.

1823, 6th of 8th mo. - Jehu Price and wife Susanna M. requested a certificate for themselves and their three minor children, Eli, Frances Ann, and Emily [also spelled Emely], to Indian Spring Monthly Meeting.

1823, 8rd of 10th mo. - Certificate produced for George Price to Indian Spring Monthly Meeting.

1823, 3rd of 9th mo. - Rebecca Matthews asked to be released as clerk of women's meeting.

1823, 5th of 11th mo. - Mary D. Price laid a concern before this meeting she had of visiting Friends in Zanesville, Ohio, and to attend meetings within the verge of Baltimore Yearly Meeting; she being a minister amongst us was left at liberty to pursue her prospect as truth may open the way. Mordecai Price, husband of Mary D. Price, he being an elder amongst us, will accompany her.

1823, 3rd of 12th mo. - Elisha Plummer and wife Mary requested a certificate for themselves and their minor son William K. Plummer to Pipe Creek Monthly Meeting [Frederick County, Maryland]. Gunpowder Preparative Meeting informs that James Mason has been guilty of drinking spirituous liquors to excess, which misconduct he does not deny.

1824, 7th of 1st mo. - Daniel Price appointed clerk and Samuel H. Matthews as assistant clerk. Gunpowder Preparative Meeting informs that Eli Matthews (of Thomas) has had his marriage accomplished by a hireling minister to a woman not in membership with us.

1824, 4th of 2nd mo. - Certificate of removal produced for Rebecca Matthews to New Garden Monthly Meeting, State of Ohio, was signed, recorded and forwarded. Mordecai Price (of Samuel) and Mary his wife had completed their religious visit to Ohio with satisfaction. Certificate was produced for Mary Prevail to Baltimore

Monthly Meeting, Western District. Mary Matthews, an approved minister amongst us, was left at liberty to visit York Monthly Meeting in Pennsylvania.

1824, 3rd of 3rd mo. - Joseph M. Jessop gave testimony (through Eli Matthews) that he had deviated in making use of spirituous liquors for which he was sorry and he condemned his misconduct "hoping you will pass it by York 2 mo. 19, 1824." Eli Matthews, Jr. had been met with, but not ready to make a full report.

1824, 7th of 4th mo. - James Mason reported as not being in a suitable disposition to condemn his misconduct. Thomas Matthews, an elder amongst us, was left at liberty to accompany Margaret Judge, a member of Indian Spring Monthly Meeting, in a religious visit to some of the southern states. Certificate was produced for Eleanor Blanchard from Sandy Spring Monthly Meeting held at Augusta, State of Ohio. Thomas Matthews requested and was released from the station of overseer.

1824, 5th of 5th mo. - James Mason was disowned for refusing to condemn his misconduct in drinking to excess.

1824, 9th of 6th mo. - William Matthews (of Thomas) was appointed to serve in the station of overseer. Certificates were produced from Baltimore Monthly Meeting for Israel Price, his wife Jane, their minor son Richard, and their daughters Elizabeth and Frances. Certificate produced from Little Falls Monthly Meeting for William Parsons, his wife Ann, and their four minor children, Ann, Elizabeth, William, and James. Joseph M. Jessop requested a certificate to York Monthly Meeting.

1824, 8th of 9th mo. - Gunpowder Preparative Meeting informs that William Heston has neglected meetings for some time and had engaged in dealing in spirituous liquors.

1824, 6th of 10th mo. - Eli Matthews, Jr. gave written testimony that he had right of membership amongst Friends but deviated so far as to be married to a woman not in membership with the help of a hireling teacher, for which he condemned his misconduct and hoped Friends would continue him in membership.

1825, 5th of 1st mo. - William Huston has a right of membership amongst us the people called Quakers but so far deviated that he dealt in spirituous liquors and neglected meetings, for which he will not condemn himself, and is disowned until he does.

1825, 9th of 3rd mo. - Certificate received for Rebecca Matthews from New Garden Monthly Meeting in the State of Ohio. Women's Meeting listed her name as "Rebecca Matthews, Junior."

1825, 1st of 5th month - Elenor Blanchard requested a certificate to Sandy Spring Monthly Meeting at Augusta in Columbiana County, State of Ohio.

1825, 8th of 6th mo. - Gunpowder Preparative Meeting informs that George Matthews has had an illegitimate child laid to his charge.

1825, 6th of 7th mo. - Committee reported that George Matthews has removed a considerable distance from any meeting of Friends and is desirous of being disunited therefrom.

1825, 3rd of 8th mo. - A suitable minute of disownment was prepared for George Matthews, who had a birthright amongst us, but deviated so far as to have an illegitimate child. Isaac Tudor requested a certificate to Monallen Monthly Meeting [Adams County], Pennsylvania. Gunpowder Preparative Meeting informs that Mary Shaw, formerly Harden [also spelled Harding], has had her marriage accomplished to a man not in membership with us, and also had a child too soon after marriage.

1825, 7th of 9th mo. - Gunpowder Preparative Meeting informs that Thomas Matthews requested our certificate for his minor son Thomas to Indian Spring Monthly Meeting. Abraham Scott and Rachel [also spelled Rachal] Matthews declared their intention to marry, after inquiry of clearness and parents consent were obtained.

1825, 5th of 10th mo. - John Price requested to be released from the station of overseer. Mary Shaw, formerly Harden, not being in a suitable disposition to condemn her outgoing, is disowned until she condemns the same (disownment recorded 9th of 11th mo., 1825).

1825, 9th of 11th mo. - Abraham Scott and Rachel P. Matthews had been married in an orderly manner. Ann Price, having attended the women's meetings for some time, requested to be taken into membership, which was approved and she was united and received.

1825, 9th of 12th mo. - Rebecca Griffith, formerly Scott, gave written testimony that she had so far deviated from the principles of the Society of Friends as to have her marriage accomplished by a hireling minister, and to a man not in membership with us, for which she condemns her misconduct and requested to be continued under the care of Friends.

## LITTLE FALLS MONTHLY MEETING, HARFORD COUNTY REGISTER OF BIRTHS AND DEATHS, 1801-1825

[It should be noted that Little Falls Monthly Meeting was established in 1815 and the following names and ages are of its members who were born between 1801 and 1825 as subsequently recorded in their register. Some births that follow herein may be later than 1825 so as to complete the list of the children born to any one particular family; however, the lists will be incomplete for those born prior to 1801 since they were published in 1993 in Henry C. Peden, Jr.'s *Quaker Records of Northern Maryland, 1716-1800.*]

Oliver Huff Amos, son of James and Hannah, b. 18th of 9th mo., 1801.

William Brown, son of Stephen and Achsah, b. 8th of 11th mo., 1814.

Children of Amos and Margaret Benson:
    Susanna J. Benson, b. 6th of 1st mo., 1807.
    Rachel Benson, b. 26th of 2nd mo., 1808.
    Margaret Benson, b. 2nd of 5th mo., 1808.
    Elihu Benson, b. 5th of 11th mo., 1811.
    Elihu Benson, d. 18th of 7th mo., 1825.
    Elihu Benson, bur. Little Falls Burying Ground.
    Hannah Benson, b. 20th of 6th mo., 1814.
    Hannah Benson, d. 24th of 7th mo., 1825.
    Hannah Benson, bur. Little Falls Burying Ground.
    Lydia Benson, b. 14th of 6th mo., 1816.
    Lydia Benson, d. 21st of 7th mo., 1825.
    Lydia Benson, bur. Little Falls Burying Ground.
    Amy Benson, b. 24th of 6th mo., 1820.
    Amos Benson, b. 7th of 2nd mo., 1823.
    Mary Benson, b. 17th of 5th mo., 1825.

Children of Levi and Mary Benson:
    Hannah Benson, b. 1st of 9th mo., 1807.
    Sarah Benson, b. 30th of 9th mo., 1809.
    Maryann Benson, b. 19th of 10th mo., 1811.
    Pamala Benson, b. 20th of 2nd mo., 1814.

Children of Isaac and Hannah Beans:
    William Trego Beans, b. 4th of 10th mo., 1804.
    Charles Beans, b. 15th of 9th mo., 1806.
    Sarah Beans, b. 18th of 10th mo., 1810.
    Wilson Beans, b. 8th of 5th mo., 1813.
    Mary Beans, b. 21st of 2nd mo., 1817.

"The following transcript of Joel Carter's memorandum of the births and deaths of his family is made from an apprehension that it is not recorded at the meeting from whence they came."

Children of Joel and Margaret Carter:
    Hannah Carter, b. 23rd of 9th mo., 1799.
    Isabel Carter, b. 23rd of 11th mo., 1800.
    Sarah Carter, b. 28th of 6th mo., 1802.
    John Carter, b. 1st of 8th mo., 1803.
    Samuel Carter, b. 14th of 4th mo., 1805.
    Joel Carter, b. 31st of 12th mo., 1806.
    Edith Carter, b. 25th of 9th mo., 1808.
    Enos P. Carter, b. 24th of 4th mo., 1810.
    Ellis Carter, b. 28th of 12th mo., 1811.
    Ellis Carter, d. 30th of 11th mo., 1813.
    Mercy Carter, b. 5th of 7th mo., 1813.
    Mercy Carter, d. 2nd of 11th mo., 1813.
    Levi Carter, b. 25th of 8th mo., 1814.
    Margaret A. Carter, b. 10th of 6th mo., 1816.
    James Carter, b. 12th of 3rd mo., 1819.
    Margaret Carter, d. 22nd of 11th mo., 1820.

Abigail Ann Carter, dau. of Joel and Hannah, b. 1st of 9th mo., 1825.

William Dillwyn, b. 20th of 3rd mo., 1809.

Children of George and Catharine England:
    Sarah Hooker England, b. 3rd of 10th mo., 1800.
    Thomas Hooker England, b. 5th of 1st mo., 1803.
    Elizabeth Dutton England, b. 16th of 4th mo., 1805.

Children of Virgil and Mary Eachus:
    Mahalah Eachus, b. 5th of 11th mo., 1802.
    Abner Eachus, b. 21st of 10th mo., 1804.
    Preston Eachus, b. 3rd of 2nd mo., 1807.

Vanleer Eachus, b. 27th of 6th mo., 1808.
Bathsheba Eachus, b. 17th of 12th mo., 1809.
Minshall Eachus, b. 1st of 6th mo., 1811.
Sarah Eachus, b. 10th of 2nd mo., 1813.
Virgil Eachus, b. 12th of 7th mo., 1815.
Virgil Eachus, d. 3rd of 8th mo., 1818.
Virgil Eachus, bur. Little Falls Burying Ground.
Rebecca Ann Eachus, b. 14th of 7th mo., 1817.
Virgil Trego Eachus, b. 23rd of 10th mo., 1820.

Children of Joseph and Elizabeth Fussell:
Henry Bartholowmew Fussell, b. 15th of 3rd mo., 1815.
Rebecca Bond Fussell, b. 14th of 7th mo., 1816.
Priscilla Fussell, b. 14th of 5th mo., 1818.
Priscilla Fussell, d. 11th of 9th mo., 1818.
Priscill Fussell, bur. Little Falls Burying Ground.
Samuel Fussell, b. 31st of 7th mo., 1819.
Mary Jane Fussell, b. 24th of 11th mo., 1821.
Solomon Fussell, b. 4th of 6th mo., 1823.
Solomon Fussell, d. 26th of 8th mo., 1824.
Solomon Fussell, bur. Little Falls Burying Ground.
Solomon Fussell 2nd, d. 25th of 6th mo., 1825.
Solomon Fussell 2nd, bur. Little Falls Burying Ground.

Children of Nathaniel and Abigail Hollingsworth:
Nathaniel Hollingsworth, b. 20th of 2nd mo., 1801.
John Hollingsworth, b. 11th of 1st mo., 1805.

Children of Robert and Elizabeth Hollingsworth:
Mary Hollingsworth, b. 8th of 9th mo., 1810.
Isaiah Hollingsworth, b. 29th of 11th mo., 1814.
Mahlon Hollingsworth, b. 7th of 2nd mo., 1817.
Amos Hollingsworth, b. 31st of 8th mo., 1819.
Elizabeth Hollingsworth, b. 26th of 8th mo., 1821.
Jane S. Hollingsworth, b. 30th of 11th mo., 1823.
Henry Hollingsworth, b. 8th of 3rd mo., 1829.
Rebecca Hollingsworth, b. 2nd of 5th mo., 1831.

Children of John and Hannah Harlan:
Joseph Harlan, b. 3rd of 7th mo., 1804.
William Harlan, b. 16th of 2nd mo., 1806.
Caleb Harlan, b. 20th of 20th of 8th mo., 1808.

Susannah Harlan, b. 1st of 8th mo., 1811.
Elizabeth Harlan, b. 8th of 11th mo., 1813.
Hannah Ann Harlan, b. 26th of 6th mo., 1816.
John L. Harlan, b. 27th of 2nd mo., 1820.

Children of Abraham and Mercy Huff:
    Martha Huff, b. 10th of 9th mo., 1805.
    John Huff, b. 8th of 3rd mo., 1807.
    Elizabeth Huff, b. 19th of 8th mo., 1808.
    Samuel Huff, b. 18th of 6th mo., 1810.
    Mary Ann Huff, b. 12th of 4th mo., 1812.
    Richard Huff, b. 22nd of 1st mo., 1815.
    Abraham Huff, b. ---- [blank].
    George N. Huff, b. 29th of 12th mo., 1819.
    Joseph B. Huff, b. 21st of 10th mo., 1821.

Hannah Jones, dau. of Abner and Maria, b. 5th of 12th mo., 1814.

Children of Jesse and Elizabeth Lancaster:
    Esther Lancaster, b. 2nd of 5th mo., 1802.
    John Lancaster, b. 28th of 6th mo., 1804.
    Julia Lancaster, b. 14th of 2nd mo., 1807.
    Hannah Lancaster, b. 22nd of 3rd mo., 1810.

James McConnell, son of Samuel and Frances M., b. 14th of 10th mo., 1801.

Children of Francis and Naomi Mechem:
    George Mechem, b. 4th of 3rd mo., 1804.
    William Mechem, b. 8th of 6th mo., 1807.

Children of James and Sarah McComass:
    Cassandra McComass, b. 24th of 3rd mo., 1808.
    James Howard McComass, b. 22nd of 3rd mo., 1811.

Children of David and Judith Preston:
    Hannah Preston, b. 3rd of 11th mo., 1801.
    Silvester Bills Preston, b. 23rd of 8th mo., 1804.
    Rachel Preston, b. 12th of 5th mo., 1807.
    Edmond Preston, b. 25th of 9th mo., 1814.
    Deborah Preston, b. 4th of 11th mo., 1817.

Children of Samuel Reed and ---- [blank]:

Deborah Reed, b. 11th of 3rd mo., 1802.
Deborah Reed, d. 28th of 8th mo., 1821.
Deborah Reed, bur. in Alexandria, Virginia.
William Reed, b. 22nd of 7th mo., 1804.
Harriet Reed, b. 10th of 4th mo., 1808.
John Wilson Reed, b. 11th of 4th mo., 1810.
Elizabeth Reed, b. 25th of 4th mo., 1812.
Samuel D. Reed, b. 28th of 8th mo., 1814.

George Reese, b. 15th of 1st mo., 1808.

Rebecca A. Reese, b. 14th of 7th mo., 1817.

Children of Amos and Rebecca Smith:
    Elizabeth Smith, b. 10th of 8th mo., 1802.
    Rachel C. Smith, b. 21st of 8th mo., 1804.
    Mary Smith, b. 18th of 10th mo., 1807.
    Rebecca Smith, b. 23rd of 2nd mo., 1810.
    James W. Smith, b. 7th of 3rd mo., 1812.
    James W. Smith, d. 15th of 12th mo., 1819.
    James W. Smith, bur. Little Falls Burying Ground.
    Amanda Smith, b. 3rd of 6th mo., 1814.
    Lavinia Smith, b. 16th of 8th mo., 1816.
    Lavinia Smith, d. 19th of 10th mo., 1817.
    Lavinia Smith, bur. in Forrest Burying Ground.
    Lavinia Smith, b. 21st of 8th mo., 1818.
    James West Smith 2nd, b. 14th of 3rd mo., 1821.
    James West Smith 2nd, b. at Morning Shade, Harford Co.
    James West Smith 2nd, d. 29th of 4th mo., 1825.
    James West Smith 2nd, bur. in Forest Burying Ground.
    Susan W. Smith, b. 25th of 10th mo., 1824.

Children of Aquila and Abigail Starr:
    Molly Starr, b. 29th of 9th mo., 1803.
    Joseph Starr, b. 23rd of 12th mo., 1807.
    Sally Ann Starr, b. 13th of 5th mo., 1811.
    George Starr, b. 22nd of 8th mo., 1818, Baltimore Co.

Abigail Starr, d. 20th of 8th mo., 1823, age -- [blank].

Children of Mahlon and Elenor (Eleanor) Spencer:
    Ann Spencer, b. 11th of 5th mo., 1800.

William Lee Spencer, b. 13th of 9th mo., 1803.
Mahalah Spencer, b. 23rd of 10th mo., 1805.
Enoch Spencer, b. 15th of 1st mo., 1808.
Elizabeth Spencer, b. 9th of 9th mo., 1810.
Mahlon Spencer, b. 1st of 2nd mo., 1812.
Hannah Spencer [twin], b. 29th of 7th mo., 1814.
Eloiza Spencer [twin], b. 29th of 7th mo., 1814.
John Mott Spencer, b. 19th of 4th mo., 1817.
Harriet Ann Spencer, b. 19th of 9th mo., 1819.
Thomas Ellwood Spencer, b. 13th of 5th mo., 1822.
Mahlon A. Spencer, d. 31st of 8th mo., 1825.
Mahlon A. Spencer, bur. Little Falls Burying Ground.

Sarah Spencer, b. 4th of 3rd mo., 1802.

Hugh Ely Spencer, b. 31st of 5th mo., 1805.

Children of Thomas and Sarah Trego:
    Albert David Trego, b. 16th of 4th mo., 1802.
    Sarah Trego, b. 7th of 8th mo., 1805.
    Hannah Trego, b. 6th of 5th mo., 1807.
    James D. Trego, b. 9th of 12th mo., 1810.

Children of David and Elizabeth Tucker:
    Samuel Tucker, b. -- of 9th mo., 1802.
    Ann Tucker, b. -- of 11th mo., 1804.

Thomas Brogden Trimble, son of John, b. 31st of 1st mo., 1806.

Children of Enos and Rebecca West:
    Thomas West, b. 10th of 12th mo., 1802.
    Emily West, b. 26th of 8th mo., 1806.
    Elwood West, b. 23rd of 3rd mo., 1808.
    David West, b. 9th of 6th mo., 1810.
    Rebecca West, b. 31st of 5th mo., 1812.
    Rebecca West, d. --- of 9th mo., 1821.
    Rebecca West, bur. Little Falls Burying Ground.

Children of Mahlon H. and Mary West:
    William T. West, b. 20th of 3rd mo., 1812.
    Jesse H. West, b. 6th of 7th mo., 1814.
    Elizabeth West, b. 8th of 1st mo., 1817.

Elizabeth West, d. 17th of 12th mo., 1817.
Elizabeth West, bur. in Forrest Burying Ground.
Rebecca Trego West, b. 4th of 11th mo., 1818.
Granville S. West, b. 24th of 9th mo., 1823.
Amos Smith West, b. 10th of 4th mo., 1826.
Amos Smith West, d. 3rd of 2nd mo., 1827.
Amos Smith West, bur. in Forest Burying Ground.
Mary West, b. 2nd of 8th mo., 1830.

Children of Daniel and Elizabeth Lamborn:
John Smith Lamborn, b. 2nd of 2nd mo., 1801.
Jane Lamborn, b. 31st of 7th mo., 1802.
Daniel Lamborn, b. 26th of 4th mo., 1804.
William Lamborn, b. 26th of 3rd mo., 1806.
Elizabeth Lamborn, b. 2nd of 4th mo., 1808.
Sarah Lamborn, b. 4th of 2nd mo., 1810.
Maria Lamborn, b. 18th of 3rd mo., 1812.
Susanna Lamborn, b. 19th of 12th mo., 1814.
George Washington Lamborn, b. 3rd of 5th mo., 1817.
Julian Lamborn [twin], b. 3rd of 5th mo., 1817.
Lydia Lamborn, b. 2nd of 3rd mo., 1820.

Children of Jonathan and Esther Pugh:
Lydia Pugh, b. 3rd of 2nd mo., 1801.
Hannah Pugh, b. 2nd of 10th mo., 1802.
Job Pugh, b. 13th of 5th mo., 1805.
Jonathan Pugh, b. 28th of 1st mo., 1809.
Stephen Pugh, b. 8th of 10th mo., 1810.
Levi Pugh, b. 14th of 11th mo., 1812.
Lewis D. Pugh, b. 16th of 3rd mo., 1816.

Children of James and Rachel Tucker:
Ely Tucker, b. 26th of 3rd mo., 1815.
Aaron Harkins Tucker, b. 14th of 1st mo., 1817.

Children of Jonathan and Sarah Warner:
Mary Ann Warner, b. 19th of 9th mo., 1818.
William Warner, b. 11th of 7th mo., 1820.
John Warner, b. 25th of 4th mo., 1823.
Brinton Warner, d. 4th of 9th mo., 1827.
Brinton Warner, bur. Little Falls Burying Ground.

Jesse Benson, d. 5th of 3rd mo., 1817, aged 26 yrs., 7 mos., 25 days; bur. in Little Falls Burying Ground.

Rachel Lancaster, widow of Benjamin, d. 5th of 3rd mo., 1813, aged 85 yrs. and 2 days; bur. in Little Falls Burying Ground.

Joanna Dyer, widow of Joseph, d. 26th of 3rd mo., 1815, aged 83 yrs., 11 mos., 21 days; bur. in Little Falls Burying Ground.

Mary Lancaster, d. 16th of 9th mo., 1816, aged 15 yrs., 1 mo., 16 days; bur. in Little Falls Burying Ground.

Mary Benson, d. 12th of 4th mo., 1817, aged 35 yrs., 9 mos., 21 days; bur. in Little Falls Burying Ground.

David Lee, d. 15th of 12th mo., 1815, aged 75 yrs.; bur. in Little Falls Burying Ground.

Sarah Hutton, d. 19th of 4th mo., 1818, aged 45 yrs., 6 mos., 3 days; bur. in Little Falls Burying Ground.

Israel Morris, d. 3rd of 4th mo., 1818, aged 79 yrs., 9 mos., 17 days; bur. at his own house.

Thomas Hollingsworth, d. 7th of 9th mo., 1820, aged 29 yrs., 1 mo.; bur. in Little Falls Burying Ground.

John Hutton, d. 3rd of 10th mo., 1820, aged 59 yrs., 9 mos.; bur. in Little Falls Burying Ground.

Children of Jacob and Clarissa Fussell, of Baltimore County:
    William Fussell, b. 5th of 10th mo., 1815.
    Joshua Fussell, b. 26th of 10th mo., 1817.
    Jacob Fussell, b. 24th of 2nd mo., 1819.
    Ruth Anna Fussell, b. 21st of 1st mo., 1821.

Children of Joseph and Ann Trimble:
    Phebe Trimble, b. 13th of 2nd mo., 1823.
    Rachel Trimble, b. 4th of 1st mo., 1825.
    Elizabeth Trimble, b. 21st of 3rd mo., 1827.

Jonah Garrett, d. 23rd of 7th mo., 1823, age -- [blank]; bur. in Little Falls Burying Ground.

Elizabeth Hoskins, d. 3rd of 1st mo., 1825, aged 40 yrs., 10 mos., 6 days; bur. in Little Falls Burying Ground.

Mary Ann Claiborne, d. 18th of 3rd mo., 1831, aged 19 yrs., 5 mos., 1 day; residence in Baltimore; bur. in Little Falls Burying Ground; "This was the dau. of L. & M. Benson."

Sarah Spencer, d. 27th of 5th mo., 1819, age -- [blank]; bur. "supposed" in Little Falls Burying Ground.

Children of John and Hannah Mechem:
    Joshua Mechem, b. 19th of 1st mo., 1820.
    Elisha G. Mechem, b. 20th of 2nd mo., 1821.
    Oliver H. Mechem, b. 19th of 9th mo., 1822.
    David T. Mechem, b. 16th of 1st mo., 1824.
    Jonathan Mechem, b. 13th of 2nd mo., 1826.
    Lydia Ann Mechem, b. 11th of 6th mo., 1828.

Children of Levi and Rachel Benson:
    Emily Benson, b. 2nd of 3rd mo., 1822.
    Jesse Benson, b. 22nd of 10th mo., 1823.
    Julia Benson, b. 23rd of 7th mo., 1825.

Children of David and Abigail Ely:
    Alice Ely, b. 10th of 2nd mo., 1822.
    Jonathan T. Ely, b. 11th of 9th mo., 1823.

Children of William Lee and Abigail Amoss:
    Elias E. Amoss, b. 28th of 10th mo., 1822.
    Garrett Amoss, b. 8th of 9th mo., 1824.
    Esther Amoss, b. 23rd of 6th mo., 1828.

Hannah Mechem, d. 21st of 6th mo., 1830, aged 3 yrs., 4 mos., 14 days; bur. "supposed" in Little Falls Burying Ground.

Lydia Ann Mechem, d. 9th of 3rd mo., 1821, aged about 2 yrs., 9 mos.; bur. "supposed" in Little Falls Burying Ground.

John Harlan, d. 9th of 4th mo., 1821, aged 44 yrs.; bur. in Little Falls Burying Ground; "A pattern[?] to his children."

Esther Atkinson, wife of Israel, d. 17th of 4th mo., 1830, in her 29th year; bur. in Little Falls Burying Ground.

Joseph T. Hoskins, son of Nathaniel and Elizabeth, b. 30th of 6th mo., 1822.

Sidney S. Way, d. 13th of 1st mo., 1843, in her 25th year; residence in Forest; bur. in Little Falls Burying Ground, "a meek, goodly woman."

[It should be noted that the following information was gleaned from a microfilm copy of an original book entitled "A List of the Members of Little Falls Monthly Meeting in the State of Maryland, 1846." However, regardless of the title, dates in the book range from the late 1700's to the late 1800's and many people are listed without any dates.]

Sarah Amoss m. Thomas Morgan [no date given] in Baltimore; buried at Old Town, Baltimore, 1824.

Children of Amos and Margaret Benson:
    Susannah J. Benson, b. 6th of 1st mo., 1807.
    Rachel Benson, b. 26th of 2nd mo., 1808.
    Margaret Benson, b. 2nd of 5th mo., 1809.
    Elihu Benson, b. 5th of 11th mo., 1811.
    Hannah Benson, b. 20th of 6th mo., 1814.

William Brown, son of Elihu and Margaret Brown, b. 8th of 11th mo., 1814.

Children of Nathaniel and Elizabeth Hoskins:
    Cheyney Hoskins, b. 13th of 9th mo., 1805.
    Joseph C. Hoskins, b. 22nd of 2nd mo., 1807.
    Joseph C. Hoskins, d. 17th of 3rd mo., 1807.
    Elizabeth W. Hoskins, b. 1st of 5th mo., 1808.
    Jesse Hoskins, b. 5th of 2nd mo., 1810.
    Hiram Hoskins, b. 21st of 9th mo., 1811.
    Edith Hoskins, b. 15th of 9th mo., 1813.
    Martha J. Hoskins, b. 18th of 10th mo., 1816.
    William C. Hoskins, b. 18th of 1st mo., 1818.
    Sarah Ann Hoskins, b. 27th of 12th mo., 1819.
    Phebe H. Hoskins, b. 13th of 1st mo., 1821.
    Joseph T. Hoskins, b. 30th of 6th mo., 1822.

Elizabeth Hoskins (mother), d. 3rd of 1st mo., 1825.

Abigail Amoss, b. 9th of 4th mo., 1803.

Garrett Amoss, b. 8th of 9th mo., 1824.

Jonathan Ambler, b. 25th of 11th mo., 1817.

Rachel Ambler, b. 3rd of 6th mo., 1820.

Beulah E. Amoss (formerly Twining), b. 15th of 12th mo., 1811.

Amy Benson, b. 24th of 6th mo., 1820.

Amos S. Benson, b. 7th of 2nd mo., 1823.

Edward Beans, b, 15th of 6th mo., 1818.

Margaret L. Beans, b. 13th of 3rd mo., 1816.

Elias H. Beans, b. 7th of 1st mo., 1825.

Thomas Blakey, b. 23rd of 4th mo., 1810.

Lydia W. Blakey, b. 7th of 4th mo., 1810.

Elizabeth S. Blackwell, b. 4th of 8th mo., 1819.

Abigail Ann Carter, b. 1st of 9th mo., 1825.

Levi Carter, b. 25th of 8th mo., 1814.

Susan W. Cock, wife of George D. Cock and dau. of Amos Smith, b. 25th of 10th mo., 1824.

Jane R. Cornthwait, wife of William H. Cornthwait, b. 31st of 10th mo., 1824.

Isaac F. Dixon, b. 22nd of 3rd mo., 1806.

Elizabeth S. Dixon, b. 9th of 2nd mo., 1810.

Hannah B. Forwood, b. 8th of 6th mo., 1811.

Mary Ann Hanway, b. 19th of 9th mo., 1818.

Amos Hollingsworth, b. 31st of 8th mo., 1819.

Lois Hollingsworth, b. 21st of 11th mo., 1822.

John L. Harlan, b. 27th of 2nd mo., 1820.

Elizabeth A. Harlan, b. 1st of 12th mo., 1821.

Susanna Harlan, b. 1st of 8th mo., 1811.

Elizabeth Harlan, b. 8th of 11th mo., 1813.

Hannah Ann Harlan, b. 26th of 6th mo., 1816.

Joseph Harlan, b. 3rd of 7th mo., 1804.

Abigail Ann Harlan, b. 1st of 9th mo., 1825.

William A. Harlan, b. 16th of 2nd mo., 1806.

Sarah Harlan, b. 30th of 9th mo., 1809.

Hiram Hoskins, b. 21st of 9th mo., 1811.

William C. Hoskins, b. 18th of 1st mo., 1818.

Joseph T. Hoskins, b. 30th of 6th mo., 1822.

Sarah Ann Hoskins, b. 27th of 12th mo., 1819.

Isaiah B. Hollingsworth, b. 29th of 11th mo., 1814.

Martha J. (Hoskins) Hollingsworth, b. 18th of 10th mo., 1816.

Elizabeth Mildred Hollingsworth, b. 26th of 8th mo., 1821.

Mahlon W. Hollingsworth, b. 7th of 2nd mo., 1817.

William C. Hoskins, b. 18th of 1st mo., 1818.

Amy Hoskins, b. 24th of 6th mo., 1824.

Edith Hollingsworth, b. 25th of 9th mo., 1808.

Nathaniel Hollingsworth, b. 20th of 2nd mo., 1801.

Mary Hollingsworth, b. 1803.

John Hollingsworth, b. 11th of 1st mo., 1805.

Rachel Hollingsworth, b. 26th of 2nd mo., 1808.

Albert Hoopes, b. 7th of 10th mo., 1818.

Elizabeth Hoskins, b. 1st of 5th mo., 1808.

Abel A. Hull, b. 9th of 10th mo., 1808.

Almira Ann Hull, b. 15th of 11th mo., 1813.

Darlington Hoopes, b. 11th of 5th mo., 1820.

Rachel T. Hoopes, b. 4th of 1st mo., 1825.

Edmund Hoopes, b. 31st of 1st mo., 1822.

Phebe T. Hoopes, b. 13th of 2nd mo., 1823.

Caroline P. Haviland, b. 27th of 1st mo., 1821.

Charles C. Haviland, b. 26th of 8th mo., 1823.

Bartlett Haviland, b. 25th of 3rd mo., 1816.

Susan M. Haviland, b. 20th of 2nd mo., 1822.

Susan H. James, b. 9th of 1st mo., 1811.

Thomas Kemp, b. 8th of 1st mo., 1802.

Elizabeth T. Kemp, b. 11th of 5th mo., 1811.

John Lancaster, b. 28th of 6th mo., 1804.

Mary Ann Lancaster, wife of John, b. 2nd of 9th mo., 1808.

Walter F. Leggett, b. 27th of 1st mo., 1817.

Rosanna Leggett, b. 18th of 11th mo., 1819.

Joseph H. Lewis, b. 3rd of 4th mo., 1811.

Hannah Lewis, b. 29th of 7th mo., 1814.

Priscilla Livezey, b. 10th of 12th mo., 1809.

Mary G. Moore, b. 7th of 11th mo., 1806.

Robert Moore, b. 21st of 3rd mo., 1825.

Isaac Mechem, b. 8th of 4th mo., 1801.

William Mechem, b. 8th of 6th mo., 1807.

David L. Mechem, b. 16th of 1st mo., 1824.

Thomas A. Morgan, b. 31st of 8th mo., 1815.

Cynthia Mabbitt [Maffitt?], b. 1st of 7th mo., 1814.

Lloyd Norris, b. 29th of 11th mo., 1800.

Sarah E. Norris, b. 10th of 9th mo., 1804.

Deborah Preston, b. 4th of 11th mo., 1817.

Edmund Preston, b. 25th of 9th mo., 1814.

Phebe H. Preston, b. 13th of 1st mo., 1821.

Caroline P. Price (formerly Haviland, now wife of Edward C. Price), b. 27th of 1st mo., 1821.

John F. Price, b. 21st of 4th mo., 1821.

Edward Painter, b. 29th of 11th mo., 1812.

Louisa G. Painter, wife of Edward, b. 11th of 12th mo., 1814.

George Reese, b. 15th of 1st mo., 1808.

Rebecca Reese, b. 14th of 7th mo., 1817.

Ann L. Rutledge, b. 3rd of 11th mo., 1804.

William H. Roberts, b. 11th of 8th mo., 1802.

Jane P. Roberts, wife of William H., b. 24th of 3rd mo., 1806.

James Remington, b. 25th of 4th mo., 1806.

Lucilla B. Remington, b. 18th of 10th mo., 1810.

Amanda Smith, b. 3rd of 6th mo., 1814.

Isaac Twining, b. 16th of 8th mo., 1802.

Ann H. Twining, b. 19th of 3rd mo., 1803.

Isabella Tyson, b. 17th of 4th mo., 1823.

Anna Tyson, b. 26th of 2nd mo., 1825.

Ann Trimble, b. 14th of 3rd mo., 1802.

Phebe Trimble, b. 13th of 2nd mo., 1823.

Margaret Trimble, b. 4th of 7th mo., 1809.

John C. Underhill, b. 10th of 10th mo., 1824.

Sarah R. Underhill, wife of John C., b. 27th of 4th mo., 1818.

Thomas West, b. 10th of 12th mo., 1802.

Ellwood West, b. 23rd of 3rd mo., 1808.

Clarkson West, b. 17th of 8th mo., 1816.

William Warner, b. 11th of 7th mo., 1820.

J. Edward Warner, b. 25th of 4th mo., 1823.

Samuel B. Walton, b. 11th of 12th mo., 1822.

Mifflin Way, b. 3rd of 11th mo., 1825.

Granville S. West, b. 24th of 9th mo., 1823.

James Walton, b. 10th of 9th mo., 1817.

Hannah C. Walton, b. 12th of 10th mo., 1819.

Ellen N. Watson, b. 4th of 2nd mo., 1806.

Francis Way, b. 14th of 11th mo., 1822.

Ann Eliza Way, wife of Francis, b. 2nd of 10th mo., 1823.

Jesse C. Young, b. 1st of 9th mo., 1822.

## LITTLE FALLS MONTHLY MEETING, HARFORD COUNTY MARRIAGE CERTIFICATES, 1818-1825

**John Lewis**, of Vincent Township, Chester County, Pennsylvania, son of John Lewis of same place and Grace his wife, and **Esther Fussell**, dau. of Bartholomew Fussell of Baltimore County and Rebecca his wife, married at Little Falls in Harford County on 10th of 9th mo., 1818.
Witnesses: 1st column - William Lee Amoss, Isaac H. Preston. 2nd column - Hannah Trego, Rebecca Malsby, Susanna Benson, Elizabeth Norris, Rachel Benson, Rachel Lancaster, Hannah Preston, Susan Amoss, William Trego. 3rd column - Eloiza Day, Mary Starr, Temperance Benson, Eliza M. Hughes, Cassandra Day, Esther Lancaster, Julia Lancaster, Amy Brown, Frances Ann Malsby, Levi Benson. 4th column - John Hutton, Jesse Lancaster, Elizabeth Lancaster, Nathaniel Hollingsworth, Amos Benson, Hannah Lancaster, Francenia Trego, Elizabeth Tucker, Harriet Trego, Sidney Starr. 5th column - Bartholomew Fussell, Rebecca Fussell, Rebecca Fussell Jacobs, William Fussell, Jr., David Preston, Judith Preston, Thomas Trego, Sarah Trego, Samuel McConnell. 6th

column - Bartholomew Fussell, Rebecca Fussell, William Fussell, James R. Fussell, Thomas Jacobs, Sarah Jacobs, Joseph Fussell, Elizabeth M. Fussell, Jacob Fussell, Clarissa Fussell, Henry B. Fussell.

**John Mechem**, of Harford County, son of Francis Mechem of same place and Naomi his wife, and **Hannah Tucker**, dau. of David Tucker of same place and wife Elizabeth, married at Little Falls in Harford County on 1st of 10th mo., 1818.
Witnesses: 1st column - Samuel Rigdon, Mary Smith. 2nd column - Mahlon H. West, Isaac Beans, William Trego, Jr., Thomas Barton, Harmon Pyle, Isaac Stubbs. 3rd column - Rebecca Fussell, Hannah Hollingsworth, Rebecca Beans, Elizabeth Hollingsworth, Rebecca Smith, Harriet Trego. 4th column - Amos Smith, Abraham Huff, Bartholomew Fussell, Samuel McConnel, Frances McConnel, Mercy Huff, Kesiah Ashton. 5th column - Samuel Tucker, Ann L. Tucker, Lucretia Moore, Rebecca West, Isabella Street, Elizabeth Welch, Samuel Reed, Thomas Martin. 6th column - Francis Mechem, David Tucker, Naomi Mechem, Elizabeth Tucker, James Tucker, Elizabeth Tucker, Lydia Mechem, David Tucker.

**Levi Benson**, of Harford County, son of Benjamin Benson, of same place and Hannah his wife, both deceased, and **Rachel Lancaster**, dau. of Jesse Lancaster of same place and Mary his deceased wife, married at Little Falls in Harford County on 16th of 9th mo., 1819.
Witnesses: 1st column - Bartholomew Fussell, Nathaniel Hollingsworth, John Watson, Engle Starr, James Starr, Sidney Starr, Mary Starr, Rebecca West, Thomas Trego, Sarah Trego, Richard Parsons. 2nd column - John Harland, David Hanway, David Peyton, Jonathan Pugh, Richard Harkins, Hester Bush, Elizabeth M. Dobbin, Jonathan Warner, Thomas Murphy, Elizabeth Trimble, Rebecca Fussell. 3rd column - Lydia Pugh, Hannah Pugh, Abigail Pugh, Jane Bush, Matilda Reed, Hannah Preston, Elizabeth Amos, Deborah Reed, William Amos, Maria Harry, Elizabeth Amos, Judith Preston. 4th column - Sarah Warner, Sophia Hendon, Elizabeth Harry, David Ely, Isaac H. Preston, David Atkinson, James Hendon, George R. Lynch, Samuel B. Hugo, Rebecca Beans. 5th column - William Lee Amos, Bartholomew Fussell, Susanna Amos, Alice Pugh, Thomas B. Trimble, John Scott, Eliza E. Branson, Eanos West, Ann Mason, Franceonia Trego. 6th column - Jesse Lancaster, Eliza Lancaster, Amos Benson, Benjamin Benson, Temperance Benson, Hannah Benson, Margarett Benson, Sarah Benson, Mary Benson, Esther Lancaster, Julia Lancaster, Joseph Lancaster, John Lancaster.

**Thomas Hollingsworth**, of Harford County, son of Nathaniel Hollingsworth of same place and Abigail his wife, and **Eliza Garrett**, dau. of Jonah Garrett of Baltimore County and Esther his wife, married at Little Falls in Harford County on 21st of 10th mo., 1819.

Witnesses: 1st column - Bartholomew Fussell, Virgil Eachus, Mary Eachus, John Hutton, James D. Trego, Saisan Norris of William, Levy Benson, Elizabeth Amos. 2nd column - Elizabeth Lancaster, William Amos, Rachel Benson, Rebecca James, Ann Parsons, Nathaniel Hollingsworth, Jonathan Warner, David Preson [sic], Thomas Trego. 3rd column - Sarah Trego, Martha Gwinn, Jesse Lancaster, Ann Mason, Ishmael Day, Hannah Preston, Ralph Lee, Cassandra Day. 4th column - Hannah Williamson, Susanna Dawson, Rebbecca Dimmitt, John King, Rebbecca Lee, Franceonia Trego, Jacob Dimmitt. 5th column - Samuel Lee Moores, John R. Keech, Adam Z. Williamson, William Sinclair, Anthony Baker, William Dimmitt, Charlottee Lud. 6th column - Nathaniel Hollingsworth, Esther Garrett, Hannah Hollingsworth, Abigail Hollingsworth, Abigail Garrett, Jesse Garrett, Eliza Hibberd.

**David Ely**, of Harford County, son of Thomas Ely of same place and Hannah his deceased wife, and **Abigail Pugh**, dau. of Jonathan Pugh of same place and Esther his wife, married at Little Falls on 11th of 11th mo., 1819.
Witnesses: 1st column - Bartholomew Fussell, David Preston, Mildred Ratcliff, Virgil Eachus, Engle Starr, James Starr, Sidney Starr, Mary Starr. 2nd column - William Jones, Joseph Lancaster, Sarah Warner, Levi Benson, Rachel Benson, Susanna Amoss, Elizabeth Amoss, Elizabeth Trimble, Elizabeth Lancaster. 3rd column - Elizabeth Morgan, Mary Harry, Ann Mason, Sophia Hendon, Elizabeth Amoss, Francenia Trego, Sarah Spencer, Jonathan Pugh, Jr., Stephen Pugh. 4th column - Jonathan Warner, Jesse Lancaster, John Hutton, William Lee Amoss, Joel Potts, Joseph Parsons, Ann Parsons. 5th column - Hannah Lancaster, Julia Lancaster, Ann Ely, Hannah Spencer. 6th column - Jonathan Pugh, Esther Pugh, Hannah Ely, Hugh Ely, Thomas Ely, Ann Ely, Elizabeth Spencer, Eli Pugh, Jane Pugh, Alice Pugh, Lydia Pugh, Hannah Pugh.

**John Hutton**, of Harford County, son of Thomas Hutton and Katherine his wife, both deceased, and **Sarah Johnson** of the same place, widow and relict of James Johnson, deceased, and dau. of John Mason and Ann his wife, at Little Falls in Harford County on 17th of 8th mo., 1820.
Witnesses: 1st column - Henry C. Morgan; 2nd column - Isaac H, Reston, Joseph Harlan, William Harlan, Caleb Harlan, Susan A. Morgan, Elizabeth Amoss, Jr., B. Amos Cunningham; 3rd column - Elizabeth Lancaster, Nathaniel Hollingsworth, Abigail Hollingsworth, Levi Benson, Rachel Benson, John Harlan, William Lee Amoss, Worth H. Cunningham; 4th column - David Preston, Mary Eachus, Maria Jones, Ann Spencer, Rebecca Fussell, Susan Brenton, Mary Harry, Sarah D. Lee, Judith Preston; 5th column - George Johnson, Hannah Harlan, Susanna Harlan, Elizabeth Harlan, Hannah Ann Harlan, John Lewis Harlan, Bartholomew Fussell, Jesse Lancaster; 6th column - Ann Mason, Howard Mason, William Amoss,

Elizabeth Amoss, Susanna Amoss, Martha Amoss, Juliett McComas, John Johnson, James Johnson.

**William Lee Amoss**, of Harford County, son of James Amoss and Hannah his wife, of the same place, and **Abigail Garrett**, dau. of Jonah Garrett and Esther his wife, of Baltimore County, married at Little Falls in Harford County on 14th of 2nd mo., 1822.
Witnesses: 1st column - David Preston, Juliett McComas, Sarah Trego, Rebecca West, Abigail Hollingsworth, Daniel M. Cunningham, Enoch Clap, Hannah Preston, Elizabeth Amoss, Elizabeth Ann Norris; 2nd column - Caroline S. Calwell, Martha Huff, Mary Ann Bond, Emely West, Elizabeth Amoss, Temperance Benson, Rachel Preston, Margaret Benson, Hannah Lancaster, Rebecca Norris; 3rd column - Amos Lake, John Enlows, Engle Starr, Aaron Lancaster, Arnold Williams, John Herbert, Susanna Brenton, Levin Benson; Ann Parsons; 4th column - Joseph G. Johnson, Mary Harry, Joshua Wilson, Thomas T. Bond, John Watson, David Harry, Mary Eachus, Albert Trego; 5th column - Jesse Lancaster, Elizabeth Lancaster, Virgil Eachus, Thomas Trego, Bartholomew Fussell, Jonathan Warner, Edward Brenton, Ann Mason; 6th column - James Amoss, Esther Garrett, Jessee Garrett, Mary Calwell, Eliza Hollingsworth, Rebecca Lee, Lloyd Norris, William Amoss.

**Jacob Ely**, of Harford County, son of William and Martha Ely of the same place, and **Elizabeth Cooper**, dau. of Nicholas and Sarah Cooper, of the same place, married at Little Falls in Harford County on 12th of 6th mo., 1822.
Witnesses: 1st column - no names listed; 2nd column - Hannah Beans, Joseph Trimble, Amos Smith, Mahlon H. West, Mary West, Amer Stubbs, James Moores; 3rd column - Anna W. West, Rebecca Smith, Jr., Mary Smith, Esther Cheyney, Robert Martin, Joel Carter, Joel Harry, Isaac Beans; 4th column - Samuel McConnal, Frances McConnal, Elizabeth Warner, John C. Boyd, Emely West, Isaac Stubbs, Henry G. Walters, Eliza H. Smith; 5th column - Eliza R. Barcly, Abraham Streett, Nicholas Jones, Rebecca Smith, Amanda Smith, James McConnal, David Tucker, Elizabeth Tucker; 6th column - Nicholas Cooper, Martha Ely, Isaiah Cooper, Martha Ely, Jr., Anna Cooper, William Ely, Nicholas Cooper, Jr., Priscilla Jones.

**Joel Carter**, of Harford County, son of Samuel and Sarah Carter, the latter deceased, and **Hannah Hollingsworth**, dau. of Nathaniel and Abigail, of the same place, married at Little Falls in Harford County on 16th of 1st month, 1823.
Witnesses: 1st column - Rhesa Norris, Hannah Preston, Elizabeth Ann Norris, Jessee Garrett, Isaac W. Preston, David Lee Norris, Nicholas Cooper, Levi Benson; 2nd column - Rachel Smith, Mary Smith, Hannah Trego, Sarah Trego, Joseph G. Johnson, Abigail I. Amoss, Nathaniel Hoskins, William Harlan; 3rd column -

David Harry, Thomas T. Bond, Amer Stubbs, Francenia Trego, Joshua B. Bond, Benjamin R. Bond, Jonathan Warner, Emely West; 4th column - Edith Carter, Silvester B. Preston, David Preston, Jessee Lancaster, Elizabeth Lancaster, William Amoss, Mary Calwell; 5th column - John Carter, Robert Hollingsworth, Samuel Carter, Mary Harry, Rachel Benson, Elizabeth Hollingsworth, Susanna Amoss, Mary Hollingsworth; 6th column - Nathaniel Hollingsworth, Abigail Hollingworth, Eli Hollingsworth, Nathaniel Hollingsworth, Jr., John Hollinsgworth, Amor Carter, Abigail Hollingsworth, Jr., Eliza Hollingsworth.

## LITTLE FALLS MONTHLY MEETING, HARFORD COUNTY CERTIFICATES OF REMOVAL, 1815-1825

1815, 19th of 10th mo. - Edward Churchman, wife Rebecca, and minor children Robert, Mary, Rebecca and Margaret, requested a certificate of removal to Concord Monthly Meeting [Delaware County], Pennsylvania. Hannah James Churchman requested a certificate of removal to Concord Monthly Meeting in Pennsylvania. Jacob and Ann Tyson and their four minor children, George, Ann, Jonathan, and William Amos Tyson, requested a certificate of removal to Baltimore Monthly Meeting, Western District. Margaret and Sarah Tyson requested a certificate of removal to Baltimore Monthly Meeting, Western District.

1815, 16th of 11th mo. - Solomon Fussell requested a certificate of removal to Gwynnedd Monthly Meeting in Pennsylvania.

1816, 18th of 4th mo. - Jacob Vore and wife Elizabeth requested a certificate of removal to Deer Creek Monthly Meeting. Jonathan and Sarah Warner and their two minor children, Hannah and Brinton, requested a certificate of removal to Baltimore Monthly Meeting, Western District.

1816, 16th of 5th mo. - Stephen Brown, wife Achsah, and their infant son William requested a certificate of removal to Deer Creek Monthly Meeting. Joseph Eachus requested a certificate of removal to Baltimore Monthly Meeting, Western District.

1816, 20th of 6th mo. - Rebecca Beans requested a certificate of removal to Baltimore Monthly Meeting, Western District.

1816, 18th of 7th mo. - Horatio Townsend Jefferis requested a certificate of removal to West Chester Monthly Meeting. William H. Amoss requested a certificate of removal to Baltimore Monthly Meeting, Eastern District.

1816, 19th of 9th mo. - Carpenter Jefferis requested a certificate of removal to West Chester Monthly Meeting in Pennsylvania.

1816, 24th of 10th mo. --Elizabeth D. Parsons requested a certificate of removal to Deer Creek Monthly Meeting.

1816, 21st of 11th mo. - Joseph D. Parsons requested a certificate of removal to Deer Creek Monthly Meeting. Yearsly Jones requested a certificate of removal to Baltimore Monthly Meeting, Eastern District.

1816, 3rd of 12th mo. - Abner Jones, wife Maria and infant dau. Hannah requested a certificate of removal to Baltimore Monthly Meeting, Eastern District.

1817, 4th of 2nd mo. - Jonathan Vanhorn requested a certificate of removal to Baltimore Monthly Meeting, Western District.

1817, 8th of 4th mo. - Samuel Trego requested a certificate of removal to Baltimore Monthly Meeting, Western District.

1817, 2nd of 12th mo. - Elias Ellicott Amos, a minor, requested a certificate of removal to Baltimore Monthly Meeting, Western District.

1818, 5th of 5th mo. - Obed Eachus some time ago requested a certificate of removal to Goshen Monthly Meeting [Chester County, Pennsylvania]. David Smith and wife Hannah requested a certificate of removal to Fallowfield Monthly Meeting in Pennsylvania.

1818, 2nd of 6th mo. - John White and family [unnamed] requested a certificate of removal to White Water Monthly Meeting in Indiana.

1818, 7th of 7th mo. - George Langstroth several years ago requested a certificate of removal to Fallowfield Monthly Meeting in Pennsylvania.

1818, 4th of 8th mo. - Susannah H. Hurdle requested a certificate of removal to Alexandria Monthly Meeting.

1818, 8th of 9th mo. - Rachel Carroll requested a certificate of removal to White Water Monthly Meeting in Indiana.

1818, 6th of 10th mo. - Matilda Reed requested a certificate of removal to Baltimore Monthly Meeting, Eastern District.

1818, 3rd of 11th mo. - Thomas West and wife Cassandra and family [unnamed] requested a certificate of removal to Baltimore Monthly Meeting, Eastern District. Esther Lewis and husband [unnamed] requested a certificate of removal to Uwchland Monthly Meeting.

1819, 6th of 7th mo. - Harriet Trego requested a certificate of removal to Nottingham Monthly Meeting. William Trego requested a certificate of removal to Nottingham Monthly Meeting.

1820, 4th of 1st mo. - Sarah McComas and her two minor children, Cassandra and James Howard McComas, requested a certificate of removal to Deer Creek Monthly Meeting.

1820, 2nd of 5th mo. - Thomas and Sarah Trego and their five minor children, Albert, David, Sarah, Hannah, and James Duffel Trego, requested a certificate of removal to Nottingham Monthly Meeting. Francenia Trego and her parents [unnamed] requested a certificate of removal to Nottingham Monthly Meeting.

1820, 4th of 7th mo. - Rebecca Beans requested a certificate of removal to Wrightstown Monthly Meeting in Bucks County, Pennsylvania.

1820, 8th of 8th mo. - Elizabeth Reynolds and her husband [unnamed] requested a certificate of removal to Nottingham Monthly Meeting. Samuel Tucker, a minor, requested a certificate of removal to Nottingham Monthly Meeting.

1821, 3rd of 4th mo. - Sarah Hutton and her four minor children, George, Howard, Ann, and Lemuel Stansbury Johnson, requested a certificate of removal to Deer Creek Monthly Meeting.

1821, 8th of 5th mo. - Jonathan and Esther Pugh and their four minor children, Job, Jonathan, Stephen, and Levi, requested a certificate of removal to Gwynnedd Monthly Meeting in Pennsylvania. Eli Pugh requested a certificate of removal to Gwynnedd Monthly Meeting. Rachel, Alice, Lydia, and Hannah Pugh and their parents [unnamed] requested a certificate of removal to Gwynnedd Monthly Meeting.

1821, 7th of 8th mo. - Mary Maulsby requested a certificate of removal to Deer Creek Monthly Meeting.

1821, 6th of 11th mo. - Jane Pugh requested a certificate of removal to Gwynnedd Monthly Meeting in Pennsylvania.

1822, 7th of 5th mo. - Daniel M. Reese, a minor, requested a certificate of removal to Baltimore Monthly Meeting, Western District.

1822, 2nd of 7th mo. - Abraham and Mary Huff and their eight minor children, John, Elizabeth, Samuel, Mary Ann, Richard, Abraham, George Norbray, and Joseph, requested a certificate of removal to Deer Creek Monthly Meeting. Martha Huff and her parents [unnamed] requested a certificate of removal to Deer Creek Monthly Meeting. Abner Eachus, a minor, requested a certificate of removal to Chester Monthly Meeting in Pennsylvania.

1822, 6th of 8th mo. - William Dillen, a minor, requested a certificate of removal to Abington Monthly Meeting [Montgomery County], Pennsylvania.

1822, 3rd of 9th mo. - Mary Carpenter requested a certificate of removal to Concord Monthly Meeting [Delaware County], Pennsylvania.

1822, 5th of 11th mo. - Edward Brinton, wife Susanna, and their son Thomas Ellwood Brinton, requested a certificate of removal to Birmingham Monthly Meeting in Pennsylvania.

1823, 3rd of 6th mo. - Isaac and Hannah Beans and their six minor children, William T., Charles, Sarah, Wilson, Mary, and Thomas, requested a certificate of removal to Wrightstown Monthly Meeting [Bucks County], Pennsylvania. William Trego requested a certificate of removal to Wrightstown Monthly Meeting [Bucks County], Pennsylvania.

1823, 5th of 8th mo. - Hannah Stump requested a certificate of removal to Deer Creek Monthly Meeting.

1823, 2nd of 9th mo. - Jemima Parsons requested a certificate of removal to Chester Monthly Meeting in Pennsylvania.

1824, 6th of 4th mo. - Mahala Spencer requested a certificate of removal to Baltimore Monthly Meeting, Western District.

1824, 4th of 5th mo. - Sidney and Molly Starr requested a certificate of removal to Baltimore Monthly Meeting, Western District. Mahala Eachus requested a certificate of removal to Chester Monthly Meeting in Pennsylvania. William Parsons, wife Ann, and their four minor children, Ann, Elizabeth, William, and James, requested a certificate of removal to Gunpowder Monthly Meeting.

1824, 8th of 6th mo. - Bartholomew Fussell requested a certificate of removal to Nottingham Monthly Meeting.

1824, 3rd of 8th mo. - Israel Coates requested a certificate of removal to Baltimore Monthly Meeting, Western District.

1824, 2nd of 11th mo. - Powel Carpenter, a minor, requested a certificate of removal to Goshen Monthly Meeting [Chester County], Pennsylvania.

1824, 7th of 12th mo. - Acquila Starr and his three minor children, Joseph, Sally Ann, and George, requested a certificate of removal to Baltimore Monthly Meeting, Western District. Jacob and Clarissa Fussell and their six minor children, William, Joshua, Jacob, Ruth Anna, Hannah, and Bartholomew, requested a certificate of removal to Baltimore Monthly Meeting, Western District.

1825, 4th of 1st mo. - Ann Parsons and her husband [unnamed] and two minor children, Edmund and Maria, requested a certificate of removal to Baltimore Monthly Meeting, Western District.

1825, 3rd of 5th mo. - Virgil Eachus, wife Mary, and six minor children, Reston, Vanleer, Bathsheba, Minshall, Sarah, and Virgil, requested a certificate of removal to Goshen Monthly Meeting [Chester County], Pennsylvania.

1825, 7th of 6th mo. - David Ely, wife Abigail, and their three minor children, Emmaline, Alice, and Jonathan Thomas Ely, requested a certificate of removal to Gwynnedd Monthly Meeting in Pennsylvania.

1825, 4th of 10th mo. - William Reed requested a certificate of removal to York Monthly Meeting in Pennsylvania.

## LITTLE FALLS MONTHLY MEETING, HARFORD COUNTY
## ABSTRACTS FROM THE MINUTES, 1815-1825

[Little Falls became a monthly meeting around the 9th mo., 1815 and copies of minutes of Gunpowder Monthly Meeting were received and directed to be entered into their minutes. They have been abstracted as follows for the 5th and 8th months, and the actual Little Falls Monthly Meeting minutes begin with the 10th month below, with men's and women's meetings as indicated.]

1815, 5th mo. - Aquila Jones accomplished his marriage contrary to the order of our society with a woman in membership with Friends.

1815, 8th mo. - William H. Amoss requested to be reinstated into membership with Friends. Certificate forwarded from Baltimore Monthly Meeting, Eastern District, for Mary Dawes. Certificate requested for Abner Jones, wife Maria, and their infant dau. Hannah Jones, to Deer Creek Monthly Meeting. Little Falls Preparative Meeting informs that Jacob Tyson and wife Ann requested a certificate for themselves and their four minor children, George, Ann, Jonathan, and William Amoss Tyson, to Baltimore Monthly Meeting, Western District. Edward Churchman and wife Rebecca requested a certificate for themselves and their four minor children, Robert, Mary, Rebecca, and Margaret Churchman, to Concord Monthly Meeting [Delaware County], Pennsylvania.

1815, 19th of 10th mo. - Women's Meeting: Certificate requested by Maria Jones for herself, her husband [not named], and minor dau. Hannah, to Deer Creek Monthly Meeting. Sarah Jones, formerly Spencer, had her marriage accomplished contrary to established order with a man not in membership with Friends. Certificate received from May Dawes from Baltimore Monthly Meeting, Eastern District. Edward and Rebecca Churchman requested a certificate to Concord Monthly Meeting [Delaware County], Pennsylvania, for themselves and their four minor children, Robert, Mary, Rebecca, and Margaret Churchman. Hannah James Churchman also requested a certificate to that same place. Jacob and Ann Tyson requested a certificate to Baltimore Monthly Meeting, Western District, for themselves and their four minor children, George, Ann, Jonathan, and William Amos Tyson. Margaret Tyson and Sarah Tyson also requested certificates to that same place. Aquila and Sarah Jones were reported to not be in a disposition to condemn their deviation from our good order. Men's Meeting: Solomon Fussell requested a certificate to Gwynnedd Monthly Meeting, Pennsylvania.

1815, 10th of 11th mo. - Men's Meeting: Little Falls Preparative Meeting informs that Jonathan Vanhorn requested to be received into membership. John Harlan, Levi Benson, Samuel McConnell, William Amoss, and Amos Smith were appointed to the care of our burying grounds, to grant liberty of interment, and dig graves, and David Preston, Jesse Lancaster, John White, and Amos Smith to attend the funerals of those who may be interred therein to see that good order and becoming solemnity are observed.

1815, 21st of 12th mo. - Women's Meeting: Rebecca Smith, Elizabeth Tucker, Mercy Huff, and Mary West were appointed to oversee the Forest School. Judith Preston requested to be released from oversight of the poor and Elizabeth Amos was appointed for that service. Men's Meeting: William H. Amoss was reinstated into membership.

1816, 15th of 2nd mo. - Women's Meeting: Certificate received from Fallowfield Monthly Meeting, endorsed by Gunpowder Monthly Meeting, for David Smith and wife Hannah. Virgil Eachus and wife Mary, having some time since made a request to Gunpowder Monthly Meeting to be reunited in membership with Friends, with their five minor children, Vanleer, Bathsheba, Minshall, Sarah, and Virgil Eachus, and that meeting finding no obstruction wrote to Chester Monthly Meeting (by which they were disowned) for its approbation, and they having moved their residence within the verge of this meeting, were received into membership. Sarah Trego will inform them thereof. Men's Meeting: Little Falls Preparative Meeting informs that Lemuel H. Amoss has been guilty of fornication with a woman whom he has since married. Communication received from Little Britain Monthly Meeting requesting our assistance in treating with Thomas Wilkinson, a member of that meeting who now resides within our limits, for accomplishing his marriage by the assistance of a justice of the peace.

1816, 21st of 3rd mo. - Women's Meeting: Jonathan Warner and wife Sarah requested a certificate for themselves and their two minor children, Hannah and Brinton Warner, to Baltimore Monthly Meeting, Western District. Jacob Vore and wife Elizabeth requested a certificate to Deer Creek Monthly Meeting.

1816, 18th of 4th mo. - Women's Meeting: Stephen Brown and wife Achsah requested a certificate for themselves and their infant son William Brown to Deer Creek Monthly Meeting. Men's Meeting: Joseph Eachus requested a certificate to Baltimore Monthly Meeting, Western District.

1816, 16th of 5th mo. - Women's Meeting: Rebecca Beans requested a certificate to Baltimore Monthly Meeting, Eastern District. Men's Meeting: William H. Amoss requested a certificate to Baltimore Monthly Meeting, Eastern District.

1816, 20th of 6th mo. - Men's Meeting: Horatio Townsend requested a certificate to West Chester Monthly Meeting.

1816, 18th of 7th mo. - Men's Meeting: Enos West has been so unguarded as to take strong drink so as to be intoxicated and that he was also chargeable with unseemly behaviour towards a young woman.

1816, 15th of 8th mo. - Women's Meeting: Elizabeth Parsons reported to have removed and settled within the compass of Deer Creek Monthly Meeting without having requested a certificate. Certificate received from Philadelphia Monthly Meeting, Southern District, endorsed by Gunpowder Monthly Meeting, for Martha Powell. Men's Meeting: Mahlon Spencer gave written testimony in which he condemned his drinking of spirituous liquors to excess and "hoping I may keep on my guard in future" and continue on in membership with Friend. Carpenter Jefferis requested a certificate to West Chester Monthly Meeting.

1816, 19th of 9th mo. - Men's Meeting: Little Falls Preparative Meeting informs that Joseph Parsons had removed and settled within the limits of Deer Creek Monthly Meeting without requesting a certificate.

1816, 24th of 10th mo. - Women's Meeting: Certificate produced for Elizabeth D. Parsons. Sarah McComas [who had been disowned by Gunpowder Monthly Meeting] requested to be reinstated into membership with Friends. Esther Fussell and Elizabeth Hollingsworth requested to be released from serving as clerks. Men's Meeting: Little Falls Preparative Meeting informs that Yearsley Jones requested a certificate to Baltimore Monthly Meeting, Eastern District. James Tucker requested that his infant son Eli Tucker be received into membership.

1816, 21st of 11th mo. - Women's Meeting: Abner Jones requested a certificate for himself, his wife [not named], and minor daughter Hannah, to Baltimore Monthly Meeting, Eastern District. Men's Meeting: Certificate received for Martha Powell from Philadelphia Monthly Meeting, Southern District, endorsed by Gunpowder Monthly Meeting. Little Falls Preparative Meeting informs that Samuel Trego was chargeable with making an engagement of marriage and afterwards breaking it.

1817, 7th of 1st mo. - Men's Meeting: Jonathan Vanhorn, by a friend, requested a certificate to Baltimore Monthly Meeting, Western District.

1817, 4th of 2nd mo. - Men's Meeting: Little Falls Preparative Meeting informed that Daniel Lamborn held in his service a black child [later stated it was black girl] whose freedom was not secured at the age prescribed by our discipline.

1817, 4th of 3rd mo. - Men's Meeting: Samuel Trego requested a certificate to Baltimore Monthly Meeting, Western District.

1817, 8th of 4th mo. - Women's Meeting: Little Falls Preparative Meeting informed that Elizabeth Timmons [also spelled Tymmons], formerly Lee, had accomplished her marriage with a man not in membership with Friends by the assistance of a Methodist minister.

1817, 6th of 5th mo. - Women's Meeting: Certificate received for Jonathan Warner, wife Sarah, and their two minor children, Hannah and Brinton, from Baltimore Monthly Meeting, Western District. Men's Meeting: Little Falls Preparative Meeting informed that Abraham Parsons some time ago went away and took from his brother [not named] a sum of money in a clandestine way and he has since returned and made his brother satisfaction. Abraham was later referred to as Abraham Parsons, of Abner, when he formally apologized for his misbehavior.

1817, 8th of 7th mo. - Women's Meeting: Certificate received for Rebecca Beans from Baltimore Monthly Meeting, Eastern District. Certificate received for Joseph Fussell, wife Elizabeth, and their two minor children, Henry Bartholomew Fussell and Rebecca Bond Fussell, from Sadsbury Monthly Meeting, Pennsylvania.

1817, 5th of 8th mo. - Women's Meeting: Certificate received for Rachel Carroll from Gunpowder Monthly Meeting.

1817, 2nd of 9th mo. - Women's Meeting: Little Falls Preparative Meeting informed that Susanna Hurdle, formerly Mason, had accomplished her marriage with a man not in membership with Friends.

1817, 7th of 10th mo. - Men's Meeting: Certificate that was granted to Samuel Trego for Baltimore Monthly Meeting, Western District, was returned with information that he had accomplished his marriage contrary to the order of our society.

1817, 4th of 11th mo. - Women's Meeting: Certificate produced for Mary Carpenter, a minor, from Goshen Monthly Meeting [Chester County], Pennsylvania. Men's Meeting: Certificate produced for Daniel M. Reese, a minor, from Baltimore Monthly Meeting, Western District. David Preston requested to be released from the station of overseer. James Amoss requested a certificate for his son Elias Ellicott Amoss to Baltimore Monthly Meeting, Western District.

1817, 2nd of 12th mo. - Men's Meeting: Samuel Trego was disowned for his outgoing in marriage. Thomas West requested a certificate to Baltimore Monthly Meeting, Western District, to enable him to accomplish his marriage with Cassandra McCoy, a member of that meeting.

1818, 3rd of 3rd mo. - Women's Meeting: Certificate will be forwarded for David Smith, wife Hannah, and their minor dau. Asenath, to Fallowfield Monthly Meeting, Pennsylvania.

1818, 7th of 4th mo. - Men's Meeting: Little Falls Preparative Meeting informs that William Whitson had his marriage accomplished contrary to the order of our society with a woman not in membership. Obed Eachus, through the medium of his father [not named], requested a certificate to Goshen Monthly Meeting [Chester County], Pennsylvania. John White, by letter, requested a certificate to White Water Monthly Meeting, Indiana.

1818, 5th of 5th mo. - Men's and Women's Meetings: Certificates received: for Cassandra West from Baltimore Monthly Meeting, Western District; for Jonathan Pugh, wife Esther, and their seven minor children, Lydia, Hannah, Job, Jonathan, Stephen, Levi, and Lewis Pugh, from Gwinedh [Gwynedd] Monthly Meeting, Pennsylvania; for Jane, Rachel, Abigail, and Alice Pugh, from that same place; and, for Isaac Beans, wife Hannah, and their five minor children, William T., Charles, Sarah, Wilson, and Mary Beans, from Buckingham Monthly Meeting [Bucks County], Pennsylvania. Information received from Alexandria Monthly Meeting that Susanna H. Hurdle had acknowledged her breach of our discipline and requested her membership be continued.

1818, 2nd of 6th mo. - Women's Meeting: Little Falls Preparative Meeting informed that Elizabeth Smithson, formerly Lee, had her marriage accomplished contrary to the good order of Friends, with a man not in membership, by the assistance of a Methodist minister. Mary Hay, having removed and settled within the compass of Baltimore Monthly Meeting, Western District, requested a certificate. Men's Meeting: Informed that George Langstroth a member who several years ago left us and could not be found, was lately living within the limits of Fallowfield Monthly Meeting, Pennsylvania.

1818, 7th of 7th mo. - Men's and Women's Meetings: Committee reported that Elizabeth Smithson was not in a state of mind that qualified her to condemn her deviation and she was subsequently disowned. Ann Parsons attended this meeting with a certificate for herself and her two minor children, Edmond and Maria, from Chester Monthly Meeting, Pennsylvania; also one for William Parsons, wife Ann, and their five minor children, Jamima, Ann P., Elizabeth, William P., and Margaret J. Parsons, from that same place.

1818, 4th of 8th mo. - Women's Meeting: Little Falls Preparative Meeting informed that Mary Whitaker, formerly McConnell, had accomplished her marriage contrary to our order with a man not in membership with Friends by the assistance of a magistrate. Certificate requested for Rachel Carroll to White Water Monthly Meeting, Indiana. John Lewis and Esther Fussell declared their intentions of marriage.

1818, 8th of 9th mo. - Women's Meeting: Matilda Reed requested a certificate to Baltimore Monthly Meeting, Eastern District. John Michem [also spelled Mechem] and Hannah Tucker declared their intentions of marriage. Men's Meeting: John Lewis produced the certificate required from Uwchland Monthly Meeting and was left at liberty to accomplish his marriage.

1818, 6th of 10th mo. - Men's and Women's Meeting: Mary Whitaker [also spelled Marry Whitiker], late McConnell, had accomplished her marriage contrary to our order and with a man not of our society. Women's Meeting: Esther Lewis requested a certificate to Uwchland Monthly Meeting, Pennsylvania. Thomas West and wife Cassandra requested a certificate (by a friend) to Baltimore Monthly Meeting, Eastern District. Men's Meeting: Little Falls Preparative Meeting informed that Samuel Reed had so far erred as to commit fornication with a woman whom he had since married.

1819, 8th of 6th mo. - Women's Meeting: Harriott Trego requested a certificate to Nottingham Monthly Meeting. Men's Meeting: William Trego requested a certificate to Nottingham Monthly Meeting.

1819, 3rd of 8th mo. - Men's and Women's Meetings: Levi Benson and Rachel Lancaster (a young woman) declared their intentions of marriage.

1819, 7th of 9th mo. - Men's and Women's Meetings: Thomas Hollingsworth and Eliza Garrett (a young woman) declared their intentions of marriage.

1819, 5th of 10th mo. - Women's Meeting: Sarah McComas [also spelled McComus] requested that her minor dau. Cassandra McComas become a member of our society and she was "excepted" into membership. David Ely and Abigail Pugh (a young woman) declared their intentions of marriage.

1819, 7th of 12th mo. - Men's and Women's Meetings: Sarah McComas [also spelled McComass] requested a certificate for herself and two minor children, Cassandra McComas and James Howard McComas, to Deer Creek Monthly Meeting.

1820, 7th of 3rd mo. - Women's Meeting: Elizabeth Reynolds, formerly Tucker, had her marriage accomplished with a man not in membership with us by the assistance of a magistrate.

1820, 4th of 4th mo. - Women's Meeting: Mary Maulsby attended this meeting with a certificate from Deer Creek Monthly Meeting. Men's and Women's Meeting: Thomas Trego and wife Sarah requested a certificate for themselves and their five minor children, Albert, David, Sarah, Hannah, and James Duffel Trego, to Nottingham Monthly Meeting. Francenie Trego also requested a certificate to that same place.

1820, 6th of 6th mo. - Women's Meeting: Rebecca Beans requested a certificate to Wrightstown Monthly Meeting, Bucks County, Pennsylvania. Elizabeth Reynolds condemned in writing her outgoing in marriage and it was accepted.

1820, 4th of 7th mo. - Women's Meeting: Certificate received from Deer Creek Monthly Meeting for Sarah Johnson and her five minor children, James, George, Howard, Anna, and Lemuel Stansbury Johnson. Certificate received from Baltimore Monthly Meeting, Western District, for Abner Jones, wife Maria, and their two minor children, Hannah and Rebecca. Elizabeth Reynolds requested a certificate to Nottingham Monthly Meeting. John Hutton [also spelled Hutten] and Sarah Johnson declared their intentions of marriage, parents consent being expressed. Certificate produced for Sarah Morris [no details given]. Men's Meeting: Certificate requested for Samuel Tucker, a minor, to Nottingham Monthly Meeting.

1820, 7th of 11th mo. - Men's and Women's Meetings: Ann Parsons acknowledged her deviation in writing, stating "for want of giving heed to the dictates of truth in my own breast have so far deviated as to act in a clandestine manner, whereby I have brought trouble on myself and Society for which I am sincerely sorry..." and it was accepted.

1820, 5th of 12th mo. - Women's Meeting: Little Falls Preparative Meeting informs that Susanna Brinton requests to be joined in membership with Friends.

1821, 2nd of 1st mo. - Men's and Women's Meetings: Certificate received for Jacob Fussell, wife Clarissa, and their three minor children, William, Joshua, and Jacob Fussell, from Baltimore Monthly Meeting, Western District.

1821, 3rd of 4th mo. - Men's and Women's Meetings: Certificate produced for Sarah Hutton and children [not named] to Deer Creek Monthly Meeting. Jonathan Pugh and wife Esther requested a certificate for themselves and their four minor children, Job, Jonathan, Stephen, and Levi Pugh, to Gwyned Monthly Meeting, Pennsylvania. Rachel, Alice, Lydia, and Hannah Pugh also requested certificates to that same place.

1821, 8th of 5th mo. - Women's Meeting: Certificate received for Elizabeth Moore from Centre Monthly Meeting [Centre County], Pennsylvania. Little Falls Preparative Meeting informs that Sarah Atkinson, late Spencer, has kept company in order for marriage with a man not in membership with Friends and accomplished the same by the assistance of a Methodist minister.

1821, 5th of 6th mo. - Women's Meeting: Certificate received for Sarah Carter from Deer Creek Monthly Meeting. Men's Meeting: James Cockburn, of

Nottingham Monthly Meeting, and Joshua Husband, of Deer Creek Monthly Meeting, attended our meeting on a religious visit. David Preston was appointed as recorder of marriage certificates at Little Falls Monthly Meeting.

1821, 3rd of 7th mo. - Men's and Women's Meetings: Certificate received for Joel Carter and his eight minor children, John, Samuel, Joel, Edith, Enos, Levi, Margaret, and James Carter, from Deer Creek; also a certificate for Hannah Carter from that same meeting. Women's Meeting: Mary Maulsby requested a certificate to Deer Creek Monthly Meeting. Mary Harry requested to be released from her station as overseer.

1821, 7th of 8th mo. - Women's Meeting: Mary West requested to be released from serving the meeting as clerk and Susanna Amoss from assistant clerk. Men's Meeting: Certificate produced for Isaiah Quinby from Little Britain Monthly Meeting.

1821, 2nd of 10th mo. - Women's Meeting: Jane Pugh requested a certificate to Gwynnedd Monthly Meeting.

1821, 6th of 11th mo. - Men's Meeting: Certificate produced for Powel Carpenter, a minor, from Goshen Monthly Meeting [Chester County, Pennsylvania].

1822, 8th of 1st mo. - Men's and Women's Meetings: William Lee Amos [also spelled Amoss] and Abigail Garrett (a young woman) declared their intentions of marriage.

1822, 5th of 3rd mo. - Men's Meeting: Jesse Hollingsworth reported to be sensible of his deviations, but not in a right disposition to condemn them [no details given].

1822, 2nd of 4th mo. - Men's Meeting: Certificate requested for Daniel M. Reese, a minor, to Baltimore Monthly Meeting, Western District.

1822, 7th of 5th mo. - Men's and Women's Meetings: Certificate received from Deer Creek Monthly Meeting for Nicholas Cooper and wife [not named] and their six minor children, Nicholas, Priscilla, Esther, Ely B., Margaret, and Gulielma Cooper. Certificate also received from that same meeting for Elizabeth, Martha, Anna, and Sarah Cooper. Jacob Ely and Elizabeth Cooper declared their intentions of marriage.

1822, 4th of 6th mo. - Men's and Women's Meetings: Abraham Huff and wife Mercy requested a certificate for themselves and their eight minor children, John, Elizabeth, Samuel, Mary Ann, Richard, Abraham, George, and Joseph Huff, to

Deer Creek Monthly Meeting. Martha Huff (their eldest dau.) also requested a certificate to that same place. Men's Meeting: Certificate requested for William Dillon, a minor, to Abington Monthly Meeting [Montgomery County], Pennsylvania. Virgil Eachus requested a certificate for his son Abner Eachus, a minor, to Chester Monthly Meeting, Pennsylvania.

1822, 2nd of 7th mo. - Women's Meeting: Mary Carpenter requested a certificate to Concord Monthly Meeting [Delaware County], Pennsylvania. Men's Meeting: Reported that Engle Starr was so ignorant of the discipline of our society as not to know that lotteries are totally opposed thereto.

1822, 6th of 8th mo. - Women's Meeting: Certificate received for Nathanial Hoskins and wife Elizabeth from Baltimore Monthly Meeting, Western District.

1822, 3rd of 9th mo. - Women's Meeting: Certificate produced for Joseph Trimble and wife Ann from Baltimore Monthly Meeting, Western District. Certificate for Hannah D. Morrison was handed to this meeting, but she was not present. Our affectionate and well esteemed sister Priscilla Hunt from Blue River Monthly Meeting, Washington County, Indiana, attended our meeting accompanied by Rachel Johnson from Lick Creek Monthly Meeting, Orange County, Indiana. David Tucker and Sarah Carter (a young woman) declared their intentions of marriage.

1822, 8th of 10th mo. - Men's and Women's Meetings: Certificate received for Hannah D. Morrison from Concord Monthly Meeting [Delaware County], Pennsylvania. Edward Brinton and wife Susanna requested a certificate for themselves and their infant child [also referred to as their minor son] Thomas Elwood Brinton to Birmingham Monthly Meeting, Pennsylvania.

1822, 3rd of 12th mo. - Men's and Women's Meetings: Joel Carter and Hannah Hollingsworth declared their intentions of marriage.

1823, 7th of 1st mo. - Men's and Women's Meetings: Certificate received for Sarah Trego and her five minor children, Albert, David, Sarah, Hannah, and James D. Trego, from Nottingham Monthly Meeting; also one for Harriet and Francenia Trego from the same meeting. Men's Meeting: Joseph Lancaster reported to have so far deviated as to take strong drink so as to be intoxicated, and has taken some property in a fraudulent manner, but not being in a suitable disposition to condemn his deviation, we disown him from membership.

1823, 4th of 2d mo. - Men's Meeting: Certificate produced for William Coale from Wilmington Monthly Meeting, Delaware, directed to and endorsed by Deer Creek Monthly Meeting.

1823, 8th of 4th mo. - Women's Meeting: Elizabeth Moore some time ago removed from this meeting without a certificate [place not stated]. Little Falls Preparative Meeting informs that Hannah Stump, formerly Carter, had her marriage accomplished by the assistance of a Methodist minister with a man not in membership with Friends. Little Falls Preparative Meeting informs that Sarah Tucker, formerly Carter, had committed fornication with a man whom she has since married by the assistance of a magistrate.

1823, 6th of 5th mo. - Men's and Women's Meetings: Isaac Beans and wife Hannah requested a certificate for themselves and their six minor children, William T., Charles, Sarah, Wilson, Mary, and Thomas Beans, to Wrightstown Monthly Meeting, Bucks County, Pennsylvania. Men's Meeting: Little Falls Preparative Meeting informed that David Tucker, Jr. had been guilty of fornication with a woman whom he has since married.

1823, 3rd of 6th mo. - Women's Meeting: Temperance Benson, wife of Benjamin, requested to be received into membership with Friends. Men's Meeting: Informed by Women's Meeting that Sarah Tucker, late Carter, had been guilty of fornication with a man whom she has since married.

1823, 8th of 7th mo. - Women's Meeting: Hannah Stump requested a certificate to Deer Creek Monthly Meeting.

1823, 5th of 8th mo. - Women's Meeting: William Parsons requested a certificate for his dau. Jamima Parsons to Chester Monthly Meeting, Pennsylvania.

1823, 7th of 10th mo. - Men's Meeting: Certificate produced for Joel Brown from Baltimore Monthly Meeting, Western District.

1823, 2nd of 12th mo. - Women's Meeting: Little Falls Preparative Meeting informs that Ann Garrison [later spelled Garretson], formerly Spencer, has been guilty of fornication with the man she has since married. Men's and Women's Meeting: Communication received from Gwinedd Monthly Meeting, Montgomery County, Pennsylvania, that Alice Hendon, formerly Pugh, a member of our meeting, has had her marriage accomplished by the assistance of a hireling minister, and desire Friends to treat with her, she being within the compass of this meeting.

1824, 3rd of 2nd mo. - Men's and Women's Meetings: Alice Glendon charged with deviation so far as to have her marriage accomplished by the assistance of a hireling minister.

1824, 2nd of 3rd mo. - Women's Meeting: Mahala Spencer requested a certificate to Baltimore Monthly Meeting.

1824, 6th of 4th mo. - Women's Meeting: Certificate requested by William and Ann Parsons for themselves and four minor children, Ann, Elizabeth, William, and James Parsons, to Gunpowder Monthly Meeting; for Mahala Eachus to Chester Monthly Meeting, Pennsylvania; and, for Sidney and Molly Star to Baltimore Monthly Meeting.

1824, 8th of 6th mo. - Men's and Women's Meetings: Little Falls Preparative Meeting informs that Isaiah Quimby [later spelled Quinby] and Elizabeth Moore had their marriage accomplished contrary to the good order amongst us and have removed within the limits of Center Monthly Meeting, Pennsylvania. Men's Meeting: Aquila Starr was charged with the evil tendency of the practice of vending spirituous liquors. He was visited, subsequently refused to cease, and was disowned.

1824, 12th of 10th mo. - Men's Meeting: Certificate requested for Powell Carpenter, a minor, to Goshen Monthly Meeting [Chester County], Pennsylvania.

1824, 2nd of 11th mo. - Men's and Women's Meetings: Certificate received for John Lewin, his wife [not named], and their five minor children, William, Ann, Amos, Mary, and Lydia Lewin, from Deer Creek Monthly Meeting. Aquila Star [also spelled Aquila Starr] requested a certificate for his three minor children, Joseph, Sally Ann, and George Star, to Baltimore Monthly Meeting, Western District. Jacob Fussell and wife Clarissa requested a certificate for themselves and their six minor children, William, Joshua, Jacob, Ruth Ann [also spelled Ruth Anna], Hannah, and Bartholomew Fussell, to Baltimore Monthly Meeting, Western District.

1824, 7th of 12th mo. - Men's and Women's Meetings: Ann Parsons requested a certificate for herself and two minor children, Edward [also listed as Edmund] and Maria, to Baltimore Monthly Meeting, Western District.

1825, 4th of 1st mo. - Men's and Women's Meetings: Nathaniel and Elizabeth Hopkins requested that their seven minor children, Jesse, Hiram, Edith, Martha Jane, William Curtiss, Sarah Ann, and Phebe Hannah Hopkins, be received into membership and they were accepted. Eliza Hoskins [also listed as Elizabeth W.

Hoskins] requested to be received into membership and was subsequently accepted. Men's Meeting: Cheyney Hoskins requested to be received into membership and was subsequently accepted.

1825, 8th of 2nd mo. - Men's and Women's Meetings: Virgil and Mary Eachus requested a certificate for themselves and their six minor children, Preston, Vanleer, Bathsheba, Minshall, Sarah, and Virgil Trego Eachus, to Goshen Monthly Meeting [Chester County], Pennsylvania. Men's Meeting: Benjamin and Temperance Benson requested that their two minor children, Joshua Price Benson and Benjamin Benson, be received into membership and they were accepted.

1825, 8th of 3rd mo. - Women's Meeting: Meeting informed that Emily West has been so unguarded as to commit fornication [and she was subsequently disowned]. Men's Meeting: Little Falls Preparative Meeting informs that Mahlon H. West had taken strong drink so as to be intoxicated. Thomas West requested to be received into membership.

1825, 3rd of 5th mo. - Men's and Women's Meetings: David and Abigail Ely requested a certificate for themselves and their three minor children, Emaline, Alice, and Jonathan Thomas Ely, to Guinard [Gwynned] Monthly Meeting, Pennsylvania. Men's Meeting: Communication received from Baltimore Monthly Meeting that Aquila Jones requested reinstatement into membership. Answer to a communication from Centre Monthly Meeting [Centre County], Pennsylvania, about Isaiah and Elizabeth Quinby is that they should be disowned for their outgoing in marriage. Certificate received for John Lewin, Jr. from Deer Creek Monthly Meeting.

1825, 7th of 6th mo. - Men's Meeting: Little Falls Preparative Meeting informs that Thomas England has wholly neglected the attendance of our religious meetings.

1825, 2nd of 8th mo. - Women's Meeting: Certificate received from Guyned Monthly Meeting, Pennsylvania, for Alice Hendon. Little Falls Preparative Meeting informs that Catherine England and Mary Malsby have wholly neglected the attendance of our religious meetings. Men's Meeting: Little Falls Preparative Meeting informs that Francis Metcham [also spelled Mechem] and Hugh Ely have wholly neglected the attendance of our religious meetings.

1825, 6th of 12th mo. - Women's Meeting: Catherine England does not manifest any disposition to attend out meetings and will therefore be disowned. Elizabeth Tucker, Esther Garrett, and Sarah Warner were appointed women's representatives to the Quarterly Meeting. Men's Meeting: Jonathan Warner, Nathaniel

Hollingsworth, Jr., David Tucker, and Harmon Pyle were appointed men's representatives to the Quarterly Meeting.

## DEER CREEK MONTHLY MEETING, HARFORD COUNTY
## RECORD OF BIRTHS AND DEATHS, 1801-1823

[These records of births begin as early as 1761 and, with a few exceptions, only those born or deceased on or after 1801 have been abstracted herein. For earlier records, consult *Quaker Records of Northern Maryland, 1716-1800*, by Henry C. Peden, Jr., 1993].

Children of William and Jane Scotten:
    Matilda Scotten, b. 18th of 1st mo., 1802.
    Joshua Scotten, b. 13th of 2nd mo., 1805.

Children of Aquila and Anna Massey:
    Sarah Bolton Massey, d. 6th of 9th mo., 1801, age 3.
    Isaac Massey, b. 9th of 10th mo., 1801.
    Aquila Bolton Massey, b. 11th of 2nd mo., 1804.
    Rigbie Massey, b. 15th of 2nd mo., 1807.
    William Massey, b. 27th of 4th mo., 1809.

Children of Silas and Sarah Warner:
    Ruth Warner, b. 24th of 10th mo., 1808.
    Joseph Warner, b. 19th of 6th mo., 1810.

Children of Samuel and Lydia Coale:
    Ellis P. Coale, b. 1st of 5th mo., 1802.
    Joshua Coale, d. 12th of 7th mo., 1802, age 20.
    Samuel Coale, d. 31st of 8th mo., 1804, age 21.

Children of Joshua and Margaret Husbands:
    John Jewett Husband, b. 10th of 3rd mo., 1803.
    Joshua Husband, b. 16th of 11th mo., 1807.
    Margaret Husband, b. 12th of 9th mo., 1810.

Children pf Samuel and Rachel Hopkins:
    John Hopkins, b. 4th of 4th mo., 1799.
    Priscilla Hopkins, b. 9th of 7th mo., 1801.
    Joseph Hopkins, b. 18th of 1st mo., 1803.
    Joseph Hopkins, d. 17th of 9th mo., 1803.

Joseph Hopkins, b. 13th of 11th mo., 1804.
Henry Hopkins, b. 4th of 2nd mo., 1807.
Eliza Hopkins, b. 15th of 4th mo., 1809.
Elenor Hopkins, b. 21st of 9th mo., 1811.
Samuel Hopkins, b. 24th of 4th mo., 1814.

Children of Thomas and Mary Worthington:
Joshua Worthington, b. 8th of 8th mo., 1817.
John Worthington, b. 1st of 3rd mo., 1819.
Margaret Worthington, b. 6th of 2nd mo., 1821.

Children of Silas and Hannah Bond:
Benjamin Bond, b. 30th of 10th mo., 1807.
Eli Bond, b. 24th [26th?] of 12th mo., 1808.
Silas Bond, b. 22nd of 1st mo., 1811.

Children of Mordecai and Sarah Thomas:
Amos P. Thomas, b. 29th of 9th mo., 1813.
Benjamin D. Thomas, b. 1st of 8th mo., 1816.
Elizabeth Jane Thomas, b. 3rd of 8th mo., 1818.

Children of Isaac and Hannah Stubbs:
Hannah Brown Stubbs, b. 27th of 5th mo., 1808.
Sarah Ann Stubbs, b. 31st of 8th mo., 1810.
Daniel Stubbs, b. 17th of 7th mo., 1812.
Isaac Stubbs, b. 9th of 4th mo., 1815.
Isaac Stubbs, d. 6th of 11th mo., 1823.
Joseph Stubbs, b. 2nd of 1st mo., 1818.
Slater Stubbs, b. -- of -- mo., 18-- [blank].
Deborah K. Stubbs, b. 5th of 10th mo., 1823.

## DEER CREEK MONTHLY MEETING, HARFORD COUNTY
## MARRIAGE CERTIFICATES, 1801-1825

[It should be noted that these marriage certificates begin in 1761, but only those which occurred on and after 1801 have been abstracted here. For earlier records, consult *Quaker Records of Northern Maryland, 1716-1800*, by Henry C. Peden, Jr., 1993].

**Joseph Husbands**, of Baltimore City, son of Joseph and Mary Husbands (the father being deceased), married **Sarah Brown**, of Harford County, dau. of

Freeborn and Mary Brown, at Deer Creek Monthly Meeting on 8th of 1st mo., 1801.
Witnesses: 1st column - Alisanna Wilson, Susan Hopkins, Hannah Bradford, Ann Massey, Margaret Massey, Sarah Warner, Jacob Balderston, Mary Balderston, Thomas Jeffery, Thomas Brown, William Brown, Ephrum Cox, William Cox, Jr., Isaac W. Robardson, William Coale, Jr. 2nd column - Oliver Fuller, Susan Coale, Margaret Husbands, Skipwith Coale, Jr., Elizabeth Husbands, Mary Coale, William Coale, Peter Wilson, Joseph Wigins, Ann Wigins, Joseph Jay, Joseph Ely, William Watson, Patty Jay, John Jewett. 3rd column - Freeborn Brown, Joshua Husbands, William Husbands, William Cox, Sarah Hopkins, Lydia Coale, Isaac Coale, Mary Cox, Samuel Hopkins, William Hayward, John Cornthwait.

**Joshua Brown**, of Lancaster County, Pennsylvania, son of Joshua and Hannah Brown (both deceased), married **Sarah Ely**, relict of Hugh Ely, late of Harford County, at Deer Creek Monthly Meeting on 5th of 2nd mo., 1801.
Witnesses: 1st column - Samuel Hopkins, Sarah Hopkins, Isaac Massey, Joseph Warner, Joseph Ford, Hugh Ely, Mary Cooper, John Pugh, John Wiggins. 2nd column - Sarah Warner, Harriot Sweeney, Peter Wilson, Samuel Coale, Jeremiah Harland, Grace J. Hopkins, John Carter, Rebecca Richardson, John Forwood, William McCoy, Thomas Wilson, Sarah Jinny, James Coale, Richard Coale, Charlotta Wilson, Elija B. Lendrum, Mary Stump, Easther Harland, Hugh Morgain, John Hill, Joseph Husbands. 3rd column - Isaiah Brown, Joshua Brown, Jacob Balderson, Mary Balderson, Aron Qumbey, Lydia Brown, Hannah Brown, Mary King, Jr., Joseph Wiggins, Anna Wiggins, William Brown, James King, Elisha Brown, Jr., William Cooper, Elizabeth Norton, Ann Warner, Sarah Norton, Mary Ely.

**William Watson**, son of Joseph Watson and Sarah his wife, late of Cumberland County, Old England (both deceased), married **Martha Jay**, dau. of Stephen Jay and Hannah his wife, late of Harford County (both deceased), at Deer Creek Monthly Meeting on 5th of 3rd mo., 1801.
Witnesses: 1st column - Joseph Wiggins, Anna Wiggins, Sarah Hopkins, Margaret Massey, Comberland Wilson. 2nd column - Thomas Wilson, Mary Coale, Jacob Balderston, Mary Balderston, Martha Wilson, Thomas Jinney, Thomas Wilson, Richard Dallam, Christopher Hall, Ann Massey, Joshua Husbands, Samuel Hopkins of Joseph, Samuel Hopkins, Isaac Coale, Joseph Ely, Stephen Norton, William McCoy. 3rd column - Peter Wilson, Samuel Jay, Eliza Barton, Hannah Thompson, Phillip A. Barton, Joseph Wilson, Joseph Jay, Sarah Jay, Thomas Jay, James Thompson, Christopher Wilson, Susanna Hopkins, John Dallam, Henry Stump, Jr., Samuel Coale, Lidia Coale, Anna Wilson, Alexanna Wilson, Margret Wilson.

**Isaac Wright**, of Frederick County, Maryland, son of Isaac Wright and Eleanor his wife (both deceased), married **Elizabeth Cox**, of Harford County, dau. of William Cox and Racheal his wife, at Deer Creek on 31st of 12th mo., 1801.
Witnesses: 1st column - Ephraim Hopkins, Cristopher *[sic]* Wilson, Joseph Johnson, Jacob Balderston, Joshua Husbands, Lydia Coale, Samuel Hopkins, Rachel Hopkins, Elizabeth Coale, William Coale, Hannah Richardson, Isaac Massey, Nicholas Cooper, Ann Massey, Sarah Jinny. 2nd column - Ephreal Cox, William P. Farquhar, R. W. Hall, William W. Hall, William Miller, Priscilla Miller, Mary Cox, Lydia Pusy, Sarah Cox of William, John Forwood, William Watson, Francis T. Wheeler, William Watson, Margreat Massey, Margreat Husband. 3rd column - William Cox, Racheal Cox, John Hopkins, Ellenor Hopkins, John Cox, Guta. Cox, Baines Cox, Samuel Cox, George Cox, Joseph Prigg, Isaac Coale, William Brown, William McCoy, Aquila Massey.

**Abraham Huff**, of Harford County, son of Abraham Huff and Phebe his wife, of the same place, married **Mary Web**, dau. of Richard Web and Elizabeth his wife, of Yourk *[sic]* County, Pennsylvania (the mother being deceased), on 28th of 11th mo., 1804.
Witnesses: 1st column - Mary Thomkins, Henry Ewing, Thomas Jones, Ely Kenard, Joseph Bennett, Antony Jones, Lucy Kenard, Ann Ewing, Mary Vore, Elizabeth Jones, Sarah Tomkins, Isaac Jons *[sic]*, Mary Webb, Limrey[?] Webb at his grandfather request. 2nd column - Richard Webb, Sarah Curley, Mary Webb, Hannah Bennett, Elizabeth Walton, Susanna Thomas, Mary Walton, Mary Bond, Ruth Bond, Ann Kenard, Prescella Eaton, Racheal Underwood, Rebecah Tipton, Elizabeth Kenny, Hannah Eaton, Ann Kenard, Sarah Curley. 3rd column - Richard Webb, Mary Webb, Mikal Huff, James Webb, John Webb, Martha Huff, Samuel Carter, Jr., Mary Malsby, Martha Tomkins, Nancy Webb, John Webb, James Webb, John Webb.

**Robert Cornthwait**, of the City of Baltimore, son of John Corntwait and Mary his wife (both deceased), married **Alisanna Wilson**, dau. of John Wilson and Alisanna his wife (both deceased), of Harford County, at Deer Creek Monthly Meeting on 3rd of 10th mo., 1805.
Witnesses: 1st column - Hannah R. Bradford, Rachel Coale, Margaret Husband, Joshua Husbands, Isaac Coale, Rebekah Carter, Peggy W. Robardson, William Bromwell, Jr., John Worthington, Amos Brown, Mary Coale, Jr., Aquila Massey. 2nd columen - Rachel Hopkins, William Worthington, Ann Massey, Joseph Lancester, William Coale, Isaac Massey, Jacob Baldston *[sic]*, Mary Balderston, Samuel Hopkins of William, Nicholas Cooper, Silas Warner, William McCoy, Sally Wilson. 3rd column - John Cornthwait, Cristoper *[sic]* Wilson, Ann Peck, Nixon[?] Wilson, Thomas Wilson, John J.[?] Peck, Thomas Cornthwait, Mary Cornthwait, Peter Wilson, Elizabeth Coale, Samuel Coale, Ann Willetts.

**John Wiggins**, of Harford County, son of Joseph Wiggins and Sarah his wife (the mother being deceased), married **Sarah Norton**, dau. of Stephen Norton and Sophia his wife, all of Harford County, at Deer Creek Monthly Meeting on the 3rd of 11th mo., 1803.
Witnesses: 1st column - Samuel Hopkins of William, Peter Wilson, Alisanna Wilson, Hannah R. Bradford, Ann Peck, John Cornthwait, John Dukehart, Joshua Husband, John Spotswood Peck, Thomas Jay, William Johnston, Samuel Coal. 2nd column - Jacob Balderson, Mary Balderson, Elizabeth Coal, Joseph Ely, Lydia Coal, Hannah Richardson, Silas Warner, William Ely, Margaret Massey, Richard Ward, Grace J. Hopkins, Sarah Templin, Ann Warner, John Fossitt, Abraham Huff, Sarah Warner, Ann Nevill, Agness Warner. 3rd column - Joseph Wiggins, Anna Wiggins, Stephen Norton, Elizabeth Barton, Phillip A. Barton, Bazl. Wiggins, Margaret Wiggins, Sally Wiggins, Margery Wiggins, Elizabeth Wiggins, Thomas Norton, Nathaniel Norton.

**David Malsby**, of Harford County, son of John and Mary Malsby (the father being deceased), married **Mary Coale**, dau. of Samuel and Lydia Coale, of Harford County, on 2nd of 10th mo., 1806.
Witnesses: 1st column - Jacob Balderson, Mary Balderson, William Hayward, Samuel Hopkins of William, Joshua Husband, Isaac Coale, Sarah Jinney, George G. Presbury 3rd, Margaret Husband. 2nd column - Sarah Massey, Ann Willets, Cassandra Willets, Sarah Warner, Margaret Massey, Ann Peck, William McCoy, Margaret Ewing, David Parr, Abraham Huff, John Wible, Mercey Huff, Angeline Orr, Sarah Wilson, Sally W. Coale, Skipwith Coale, James Coale, Elizabeth Coale, Bains Cox, Sarah Coale. 3rd column - Samuel Coale, Lydia Coale, Mary Webb, Skipwith Coale, Ann Coale, Mary Malsby, Margaret Coale, William Coale, Joseph Coale, Samuel Coale, Jr.

**Silas Bond**, son of Benjamin Bond and Mary his wife, married **Hannah Kennard**, dau. of Ely Kenard and Elizabeth his wife (the mother being deceased) of Fawn Township, York County, Pennsylvania, on 4th of 2nd mo., 1806.
Witnesses: 1st column - Elenor Manifold, Richard Webb, Joseph Bennett, Jacob Vore, Mary Vore, John Miller, John Sharp, Mary Webb, Isac Jones. 2nd column - William Kennard, Thomas Kenard, Thomas Kenard [listed twice], Isaac Vore, Elizabeth Kennard, John Eweng[?], Sarah Tomkins, Mary Tomkins, Martha Tomkins, Elizabeth Jones, Anthony Kenard. 3rd column - Bengamin Bond, Ely Kenard, Mary Bond, Martha Bond, Ruth Bond, Eli[?] Bond, Joseph Strawbridge, Elizabeth Strawbridge, Ann Kenard, Joseph Kenard, Pricialla Kennard.

**Silas Warner**, of Harford County, son of Joseph Warner and Ruth his wife (the mother being deceased), married **Sarah Warnock**, dau. of Philip Warnock and

Mary his wife (the mother being deceased), of Harford County, on 3rd of 12th mo., 1807.
Witnesses: 1st column - John Brown, Agness Warner, Achsah Warner, Ann Massey, Margrett Massey, Mary Prevale, Cassandra Willitts, Sally Massey, Anna Worthington, Letitia Warner, Sally W. Coale, Margrett Coale, Isaac Massey, Elizabeth Wiggins, Rebecca Rodgers. 2nd column - Anna Rodgers, Mary Rodgers, Richard McMurry, Joseph Rodgers, William Rodgers, Samuel Hopkins of William, William Stump of Henry, William Worthington, Joshua Husbands, William McCoy, Joseph H. Coale, William M. Chew, Andrew McCay, William Coale, George Wilson. 3rd column - Philip Warnock, Isaac Warner, Jan[?] Warnock, Mary Warnock, Charity Silvers, Benjamin Silvers Jr., Ann Warner, Thomas Warner, Joseph Rodgers, Aron Warner, Sarah Warner, Charity Rodgers, Jacob Baldsanton, Samuel Coale, Lidia Coale, Mary Balderston, Mary Rodgers, Rachel Rodgers, Ruth Ann Warner, Pamala Warner.

**Isaac Pidgeon**, of Campbell County, Virginia, son of William Pidgeon and Rachel his wife, of Belmont County, Ohio, married **Sarah Warner**, dau. of Crosdal Warner and Mary his wife, late of Harford County, Maryland, deceased, on 29th of 3rd mo., 1808.
Witnesses: 1st column - John Jewet, Isaac Massey, John Coarse, Joseph Ely, Eliza Worthington, Eliza Prevail, Ann Massey, Cassey Worthin, Mary Stump, Sarah Ely. 2nd column - Jacob Balderson, Stephen Norton, Joshua Husband, Joseph Wiggins, Anna Wiggins, Richard Macelmery, Samuel Coal, Mercy Huff, Sally Webster, Rebecca D. Richardson, Sally W. Coale, Sally Massey, Sally Wilson, Mary Perval, Mary Hopkins, Anna Massey. 3rd column - Hannah Ely, Crosdal Warner, Aaron Warner, Ann Warner, Agness Warner, Achsah Warner, Elizabeth Barton, Silas Warner, Sarah Warner, Cassandra Willets, Martha Ely, Mary Husband, Eliza Coale, Jr.

**Isaac Vore**, of Fawn Township, York County, Pennsylvania, son of Jacob Vore and Mary his wife, of the same place, married **Ruth Bond**, dau. of Benjamin Bond and Mary his wife, of the same place, on 13th of 5th mo., 1807.
Witnesses: 1st column - John Webb, Mary Walton, Mary Malsby, Thomas Kennard, Richard Webb, Joseph Thomkins. 2nd column - Ely Kennard, Mary Webb, John Channall, William Kennard, John Miller, Edith Miller, Joseph Bennett, Martha Tomkins, Anthony Jones, John Thomkins, Morgan Richardson. 3rd column - Jacob Vore, Benjamin Bond, Mary Vore, Mary Bond, Jacob Vore, Silas Bond, Ely Bond, Martha Bond, Hannah Bond, Isaac Jones, Elizabeth Jones, Joseph Strawbridge, Elizabeth Strawbridge, Thomas Jones.

**Mordicai Thomas**, of Harford County, son of John Thomas and Mary his wife, married **Sarah Pyle**, dau. of Amos Pyles [sic] and Ruth his wife, all of Harford County, on 26th of 4th mo., 1812.
Witnesses: 1st column - Amos Pyle, Ruth Pyle, Moses Medcalf, Isaac Stubs, Hannah Stubs, Grace Pyle, Susan Allen, John Pyle, Jacob Vore, Mary Vore, Susan Thomas, Elizabeth Sharp, John Sharp, Benjamin B. Bond, Esai [Esau?] Jones, Ely Bond. 2nd column - Isaac Jones, Benjamin Thompkins, John Thompkins, Sarh [sic] Thomkins, Susanna Medcalf, Sarah Chanel, Mary Web, Mary Bond, Hannah Holton, Mary Thomkins, Anthony Jones, William Jones, Richard Web, Ann Stewart, Rachel Thomas, Ann Kenard, Jehu Thomas. 3rd column - Elizabeth Medcalf, Benjamin Davis, Mary Medcalf, Isac [sic] Thomas, Abram Medcalf, John Vore, Jacob Vore, Thomas Thomkins, Amos Stubbs, Elizabeth Kenard, Isaac Thomas, Anthony Kenard, Benjamin Thomas, Jacob Vore, John Vore.

**Isaac Smith**, of Little Falls, Harford County, Maryland, son of Isaac Smith and Sarah his wife, of Chester County, Pennsylvania, married **Margaret Coale**, dau. of Samuel Coale and Lydia his wife, of Deer Creek, Harford County, Maryland, on 5th of 12th mo., 1807.
Witnesses: 1st column - Sarah Ruff, James Ruff, Eliza Worthington, Sarah Worthington, Joseph Husbands, James R. Massey, Ann Churchman, Mary Husbands, Lewis Coale, Mary Coale, Sarah Massey. 2nd column - Isaac Coale, Samuel Hopkins, Sarah Coale, Eliza Coale, Rachel Smith, Hannah Coale, Lydia Massey, Sarah[?] Massey[?]. 3rd column - David Smith, Skipwith Coale of Rd.[?], Joseph Coale, Jonathan Smith, Joshua Husbands, William Coale, Jacob Balderston, Micajah Churchman, J---? C---? [obliterated name]. 4th column - Samuel Coale, Lydia Coale, Mary Malsby, David Malsby, David Wents[?], Joseph Wents[?].

**Thomas Kennard**, son of Levy Kennard and Ann his wife, of Fawn Township, York County, Pennsylvania, married **Elizabeth Medcalf**, dau. of Moses Medcalf and Susannah his wife, of Harford County, Maryland, at Deer Creek Monthly Meeting on 1st of 12th mo., 1813.
Witnesses: 1st column - James Webb, Isaac Morris, Mary Medcalf, John Sharpe, William John, Asa Jones, Thomas Sharpe, Nicholas Cooper, Jacob Vore, Mary Vore, Mary Thomkins, A. O.[?] Medcalf, Rebecca Medcalf. 2nd column - Jeney Dunca [sic], Mary Maulsby, Martha Tomkins, Elezabeth Walton, Martha Eley, Elizabeth McFadden, Margret Midshill, Mary King, Sarah Channal, Abel Channal, Nathan Pyle, Grace Pyle, Isaac Channal, Elizabeth Kennard, William Kennard, Mary Kennard, John Channal, Isaac James, James Dunkin. 3rd column - Levi Kennard, Moses Midcalf, Ann Kinnard, Susanna Midcalf, Jacob Balderston, Marry [sic] Balderston, Mary Wells[?], Joseph Kinnard, Precilla Kinnard, Elezabeth Sharpe, Thomas Kinnard, Levi Kinnard, Jacob Ely, Abraham Medcalf, Elizabeth Sharpe, Rachel Eton, Elizabeth Jones.

**Stephen Brown**, of Gunpowder, son of Elihu Brown and Margaret his wife, married **Axsah Warner**, dau. of Aron Warner and Axsah his wife, the latter deceased, all of Harford County, at Deer Creek Monthly Meeting on 2nd of 12th mo., 1813.
Witnesses: 1st column - Aquila Massey. 2nd column - Joseph Husbands, Isah [sic] Cooper, Harmon Pyle, John Husbands, Joseph Webster, Margarett Smith, Isaac Willapey, Anna Husbands, Jonathan Massey, Samuel Hopkins (of William), Nicholas Cooper, John Lewen, Margatt Husbands, Anna Richardson, Sarah Massey, Rebecca Worthington, Anna Massey, Mararett [sic] Massey, William McCoy, Richard Coale, Isaac Coale, Isaac Massey, Joseph Rodgers. 3rd column - Joseph Wiggens, Lydia Brown, David Ely, Agness C. Warner, Thomas Ely, Jr., Amy Brown, Joel Brown, Rachel Ely, Ann Wiggins, Joshua Husbands, Samuel Coale, Sarah Ely, Sarah Hopkins, Sarah Cooper, Mary C. Rodgers, Eliza Prigg, Perthenia Cooper, Amfield C. Morgan, Eliza Spensor, Mary Warnock, Samuel Norton, Thomas C. Morgan, Amos J. Ely, Isaac Ely, Lydia Coale, Nathan Norton, James Coale.

**Isaac Turner**, of Cessil Monthly Meeting, Kent County, Maryland, son of Joseph Turner and Sarah his wife (the mother being deceased), of the same place, married **Sarah Massey**, dau. of Isaac Massey and Margaret his wife, at Deer Creek Monthly Meeting on 5th of 5th mo., 1814.
Witnesses: 1st column - Joshua Husbands, Samuel Hopkins (of William), Nicholas Cooper, Skipwith H. Coale, Lidia McCay, Lidia Coale, Hannah Piyle [sic], Jonathan Massey, Anna Massey. 2nd column - Cristopher Wilson, Aquila Massey (of Isaac), Isaac W. Massey, William McCay, Priscilly McCay, John Jewett, Samuel Hopkins, Jacob Balderston, Sarah Webster, Joseph Webster. 3rd column - Isaac Massey, Margaret Massey, Sarah Turner, Aquila Massey, Eliza Caulk, Sarah Turner 3rd, Jonathan W. Mifflin, Ann Massey, Ann Peck, John S. Peck.

**Philip Price, Jr.**, of the City of Philadelphia, Pennsylvania, son of Benjamin Price and Ruth his wife, of West Township, Chester County, Pennsylvania, married **Elizabeth Coale**, dau. of Isaac Coale and Rachel his wife, of Deer Creek, Harford County, Maryland, on 31st of 8th mo., 1815.
Witnesses: 1st column - Mrs. C. Coale, Susan H. Coale, Mary Husband, William Coale, Jr., W. E. Coale, W. H. Freeman, Christopher Wilson, Jr., Eliza Quarles, Susan Bagley, Susanna Rogers, Ann Massey, Anna Massey, Margaret Massey, Sarah Orr, Eliza Jones, Mary Miflin, Jacob Balderston, Mary Balderston, Dolly Bradford. 2nd column - William Husband, Silas Warner, Margaret R. Massey, Sarah Warner, Mary Hopkins, Isaac Massey, Sarah M. Turner, Isaac Turner, Jr., Ann M. Price, Hanna Price, Cassandra Willets, Joshua Husbands, Thomas Worthington, Thomas Brown, John Jewett, D. J. Davis, James B. Price, Joseph Husbands, Jr., Samuel Coale, James Coale, Sarah Coale, Alisan Wilson, J. W.

Coale, Isaac Coale, Jr., Lydia Coale, Hannah Coale, Eliza Coale, Susanna Jewett. 3rd column - Isaac Coale, Rachel Coale, Benjamin Price, Ruth Price, Philip Price, Rachel Price.

**Thomas Jones**, son of Isaac and Elizabeth his wife, of Fawn Township, York County, Pennsylvania, married **Martha Tomkins**, of the same place, dau. of John Thomkins *[sic]* and Sarah his wife (the father being deceased), at Deer Creek Monthly Meeting on 3rd of 4th mo., 1816.
Witnesses: 1st column - Priscilla Kennard, Richard Webb, James Webb, William Akins, Rebecca Jones, Mara *[sic]* Webb, Perthenia Coopper, Frances Roe, John Heaton, Sarah Jones, Samuel Jones, Ann Ewing, Yory [Gorg?] Burges, Martha Norbury, Elizabeth Sharp, George Norbury. 2nd column - Tacy B. Norbury, Benjamin Bond, Mary Bond, Antony Jones, Mary Jones, Jr., John Sharp, John Channell, Joseph Burnett, John Pusey, Ezekiel Jones, Thomas Sharp, William John, Richard Webb, Jr., Joseph Kennard. 3rd column - Isaac Jones, Sarah Tomkins, Elizabeth Jones, Marah Tomkins, Bengamin Tomkins, Asa Jones, John Thomkins, John Jones, Mary Jones, Diborough Tomkins, Jacob Thomkins.

**Thomas Worthington**, of Harford County, son of John Worthington and Priscilla his wife, of the same place (both deceased), married **Mary Husbands**, dau. of Joshua Husbands and Margaret his wife, of the same place, on 13th of 5th mo., 1816.
Witnesses: 1st column - Martha G. Morehead, Sarah Worthington, William Worthington, Joseph H. Coale, Joseph Parker, Joseph Webster, John Jewett, G. G. Worthington, Priscilla Webster, John Archer, Cassandra Willets, Susannah Rodgers, Hannah C. Stump, Anna Peters, Anna Massey, Margaret Stump, Rubin Stump, Cristopher Wilson, Susannah Jewett. 2nd column - Isaac Coale, James Coale, Ann Dunbar, Elizabeth Coale, Samuel Coale, Samuel Hopkins (of William), Cilas Warner, Isaac Massey, Joshua Hopkins, Thomas Hayward, Sophia Webster, Cassandra Worthington, Susannah O. Bagley, Racheal Coale, Priscilla McCay, Mary Vore, Jacob Balderston, Ann Massey. 3rd column - Joshua Husbands, Margaret Husbands, Mary Mifflin, William Husbands, Mary Hayward, Sarah Hopkins, Harmon Husbands, John Husbands, Anna Worthington, Joseph Husbands, Samuel Worthington, Lydia Coale, Sarah G. Husbands, Elizabeth Worthington, Elizabeth Yellott, Sarah Coale, Mary B. Coale, Margaret M. Stump, Margaret Massey, Margay *[sic]* Parker, Mary Hopkins, Cassandra M. Chew, Wilson Worthington, Joseph Husbands, Jr., Anna Husbands, Samuel Hopkins of Jo--[?].

**William Worthington**, of Harford County, son of John Worthington and Priscilla his wife, of the same place (both deceased), married **Hannah Coale**, dau. of

William Coale and Elizabeth his wife, of the same place (likewise deceased), on 12th of 6th mo., 1817.
Witnesses: 1st column - Nancy Piayas[?], Cassandra W. Breuett, Hannah C. Stump, Rachel Haviland, Sarah Warner, Samuel Hopkins (of William), Joseph C. Daddral. 2nd column - Eliza Jones, William Caarn[?], Samuel Coale, Lydia Coale, Susanna Rodgers, Cassandra Willets, Vesto Guild, Joseph H. Coale, Mary Coale, Hannah Bristor [Briston?], Nathan R. Wilson, Joseph Husbands, Jr., Ferrie Printon, Hannah Worthington, Cassandra Carn[?], Cassandra Worthington. 3rd column - Isaac Coale, Ann Massey, Joseph Coale, William Coale, Lydia F. Coale, Mary C. Coale, Sophia Webster, Susan Coale, John W. Coale, Elizabeth Coale, Sarah W. Dadral, Cassandra Worthington, Sarah Coale.

**Yearsley Jones**, of the City of Baltimore, son of Abner Jones and Hannah his wife, of the same place (the mother being deceased), married **Susanna Underwood**, dau. of Nehemiah Underwood and Mary his wife (both deceased), formerly of Fawn Township, York County, Pennsylvania, on 10th of 10th mo., 1817.
Witnesses: 1st column - Martha T. Jones, Ganar Parsons, Sarah Tomkins, Elizabeth Sharp, Mary Redman, Mary Welle [Wells?], Asa Jones, John Tomkins, Thomas Jones, Joseph Eton, Robert Allan, Elizabeth Jones, Hannah Hall, Mary Jones, Ann Madden, Sarah Jones. 2nd column - Tacy N. Norbary, Debry B. Thomkins, Joseph Strawbridge, John Channel, Isaac Jones, Susanna Allin, Mary Bond, Mary Thomkins, Rebecca Jones, Rebeca Allan, Mary Jones, Rebeca McClary, Ruth Redmond, James Webb. 3rd column - Thomas Brookes, Antony Jones, Susanna Thomas, Racheal Brookes, Mordica Underwood, Danial Pyle, Racheal Thomas, John Jones, James Allin, Benjamin Tomkins, William Willy, Edward Mansfield, Ely Bond, Nicholas Jones, Ann Ewing, Henry[?] Ewing, Eliza Watter [Walton?].

**Anthony P. Morris**, of the City of Philadelphia, Pennsylvania, son of Isaac W. Morris and Sarah his wife, of the same place, married **Anna Husbands**, dau. of Joshua Husbands and Margaret his wife, of Harford County, at Deer Creek Monthly Meeting on 14th of 9th mo., 1820.
Witnesses: 1st column - Thomas Worthington, Mary H. Worthington, Cassandra Worthington, Margaret Husband, Martha Morris, Hannah Hopkins, Elizabeth Robertson, Susannah Morris, Isaac Coale, Jr., John Husband, John Jewett, Susanna Jewett, James Jewett, Samuel Hopkins (of William), James Coale, Sarah G. Husband, Stephen Boyd. 2nd column - Rebeca Morris, Mary L. Morris, Catharine Morris, Isaac T.[?] Morris, Henry Morris, Elizabeth Morris, Samuel E. Husband, Joshua Husband, Jr., Joseph Husband, Jr., Isaac Coale, John W. Coale, Lydia Coale, Scipwith Coale, Thomas Hayward, Mary Hayward, Sary Hopkins, Mary C. Cole, Elizabeth Coale, John Parker, Jacob Balderson, Samuel Coale, Joseph Breuett, William Worthington, Ann Massey. 3rd column - Isaac W. Morris, Sarah Morris, Joshua Husband, Margaret Husband, Mary Mifflin, Catharine W. Morris,

Elizabeth G. Morris, Jacob S. Morris, Silas Warner, Sarah Warner, Elizabeth Hopkins, Cassandra M. Chew, Eliza Chase Coale, Priscilla Gover, Lydia F. Coale, Ann H. Bagley, H. Worthington, Mary B. Coale, Hannah Worthington, Cassandra Willets, Samuel Worthington, Nicholas Coopper, Aquila Massey.

**John Harmer**, of Harford County, son of Abraham Harmer and Hannah his wife (the mother being deceased), married **Pathenia Cooper**, dau. of Nicholas Cooper and Sarah his wife, of the same place, on 14th of 3rd mo., 1822.
Witnesses: 1st column - Ann Massey, Ann Harmer, Margaret R. Massey, Sarah Smith, Robert Morgan of Wm.[?], Alisan Brannan, Lydia Hopkins, Mary Hopkins, Rachel Lewen, John P. Rigdon, Sarah Lewin, Skipwith Coal [sic], Samuel Coale, Anna Massey, Sarah Coale. 2nd column - Jacob Balderston, John Boyd, Elizabeth Harmer, Ann Worthington, Margaret Massey, Casandria Willits, Thomas C. Stump, Joseph Harmer, Nicholas Cooper, Rachel T. Harland, Casandria Nevill, Juli Ann Davis, Mary T. Prigg, Susan Coale, William Brinton. 3rd column - Abraham Harmer, Nicholas Cooper, Isaiah Cooper, Yolenda D. Cooper, John Dukehard, Pathena Dukehard, Mary Harmer, Hannah Harmer, Martha Cooper, Mary C. Stump, John T. Cooper, Sarah A. Harmer, Joshua Harmer, Martha McCracken, Mary Husband, Mary Evens, Casandri Course, Sarah Evens.

**John Jones**, of Fawn Township, York County, Pennsylvania, son of Isaac and Elizabeth Jones, of the same place, married **Deborah B. Tomkins**, dau. of John and Sarah Tomkins, of the same place [one or both deceased, not clarified in record], at Deer Creek Monthly Meeting on 18th of 9th mo., 1822.
Witnesses: 1st column - Samuel Brooks, Abraham Harmer, Joseph Strawbridge, William Wibey, R. T. Hall, Elizabeth Harmer, Folger Pope, Elizabeth Braman, Nancy Manifole, Theodat Pope. 2nd column - Nelly Duncan, Jane McLaughlin, William McCoy, David S. Pope, Anthony Jones, Joseph Bennett, Mary Bond, Elizabeth Trimble, Rachel Eaten, John Tomkins. 3rd column - Martha McCoy, Anna Price, Elizabeth Sharp, Benjamin Tomkins, Tacy B. Norbury, William McCoy, Jr., Rebecca Jones, Amas Baters, Lydia M. Tomkins, Ann Tomkins.

**Oliver Caulk**, of Cecil County, Maryland, son of Isaac and Elizabeth Caulk, both deceased, married **Rachael G. Cox**, of Harford County, dau. of William and Rachael Cox (the mother being deceased), at Deer Creek on 19th of 12th mo., 1822.
Witnesses: 1st column - Susanna Jewett, Ann Massey, Samuel Coale, Lydia Coale, Jacob Balderson, Mary B. Coale, Isaac Massey, William Cox, Cassandra Hopkins, Sarah G. Husband. 2nd column - Margaret Massey, Cassandra Coarse, Mary Husband, Sarah Hopkins, Margaret Husband, Anne Worthington, Anna Husband, Julia T. Husband, William Coale, Joshua Husband. 3rd column - Anna Massey,

Jesse Hartly, William B. Stephens, Joseph Kent, J. H. Hopkins, Margaret Husband, John Jewett, George S. Cook, Elisha Cook.

**Elisha Cook**, of Deer Creek in Harford County, son of Samuel and Ruth Cook of Pennsylvania, married **Elizabeth Worthington**, dau. of John and Priscilla Worthington, of Harford County, on 29th of 5th mo., 1823.
Witnesses: 1st column - Anna Worthington, Thomas Worthington, Hannah Worthington, Samuel Hopkins, Samuel Worthington, Samuel Coale, Jacob Balderson, Lydia F. Coale. 2nd column - Anna Massey, Margaret Massey, Hannah L. Archer, Rachael F. Harlan, Thomas Wilson, Robert Parker, Mary C. Coale, Lydia Hopkins, Elizabeth Hopkins, 3rd column - Margarett R. Massey, Sarah Patterson, Sarah W. Watson, Susan Coale, Hannah Jay, John Hopkins, Joshua Husband.

**Ezra Gillingham**, of Baltimore City, son of James and Elizabeth Gillingham of Baltimore County, married **Mary C. Coale**, dau. of Isaac and Rachael Coale, of Harford County, on 28th of 8th mo., 1823.
Witnesses: 1st column - Samuel Hopkins (of William), Sarah Hopkins, Margaret Massey, Cassandra Willets, Joseph H. Coale, Louisa Cook, Hannah Worthington, Anna Massey, Margarreth R. Massey, H. L. Archer, Rachael L. Harlan, Eliza Hopkins, Martha Huff, Lydia Hopkins, Margarett Husband, Susan Corse, Rachel C. Stump, Mary C. Stump. 2nd column - John Lewin, Abraham Harman, John Jewett, William Coarse, A. B. Cleveland, Thomas Worthington, Joshua Rilus[?], John Havrace, Mary M. Brevett, Elisha Cook, Herman Husband, Anna Worthington, Cassandra Coarse, Anna Morris, Jas. C. Doddrell, Elizabeth Coale. 3rd column - James Gillingham, Rachael Coale, L. H. Coale, John Gillingham, Hannah E. Coale, Susan Coale, Ho.[?] Worthington, Elizabeth Gillingham, Lydia F. Coale, James Coale, Samuel Coale, William Coale, Eliza C. Price, Susanna Jewett.

**Eli Garretson**, of Anne Arundel County, Maryland, son of Cornelius and Hannah Garretson, of the same place, married **Anna Massey**, dau. of Isaac and Margaret Massey, of Harford County, at Deer Creek Monthly Meeting on 23rd of 9th mo., 1824.
Witnesses: 1st column - Thomas Worthington, Harmond Husbands, John J. Husbands, Samuel Worthington, Aquila B. Massey, John W. Brett, William Coale, Rigbee Massey, William Massey, Isaac Wilson, Isaac Massey, Jr., Ann Massey, Mary Hopkins, Sarah R. Webster, James W. Gillingham, Ellin Norris, Anna Husbands, Alisan Wilson, Mary Ann Norris. 2nd column - Margaret Husbands, Eliza B. Hammond, Racheal C. Stump, Susanna Coale, Agness C. Warner [name listed twice], Mary C. Stump, Sarah W. Watson, Priscilla Worthington, Eliza H. Hopkins, Robert Morgain, John C. McCay, M. Churchman, Joseph Hopkins,

Kakeman [Wakeman] B. Hopkins, George O. Cook, William Cox, Susanna Jewett, Samuel Hopkins (of William). 3rd column - Cornelius Garretson, Hannah Garretson, Isaac Massey, Margaret Massey, Sarah M. Turner, Samuel Garretson, Margaret R. Massey, Joseph Garretson, Aquila Massey, Jr., Margaret Garretson, Jesse Garretson, Racheal Garretson, John Jewett, Jacob Balderson, Samuel Coale, Joshua Husbands, John Wallis, Sarah Hopkins.

**Joshua Matthews**, of Baltimore City, son of Thomas and Ann Matthews, of Baltimore County (both deceased), married **Mary Hopkins**, dau. of Samuel and Sarah Hopkins, of Harford County, at Deer Creek Monthly Meeting on 25th of 11th mo., 1824.

Witnesses: 1st column - James Coale, John Jewett, Mary Balderston, Cassandra Matthews, Amelia Hopkins, Joshua Hopkins, Jr., Elizabeth Coale, Mary B. Coale, John O.[?] Bagley, Barthikinew Fussell, Samuel Worthington, Levin H. Hopkins, George Mason, Rachel Warner[?], Mary Bagley, David W. Brown, John W. Coale. 2nd column - Sarah Warner, Sarah Coale, Mary C. Stump, Martha Huff, Priscilla Worthington, Ann Massey, Lydia F. Coale, Jacob Balderston, Samuel Coale, Susanna Jewett, Lydia Coale, Margaret Husbands, Sarah G. Husband, Joshua Husbands, Rebecca Hayward, Thomas Hayward. 3rd column - Samuel Hopkins (of William), Thomas Matthews, Sarah Hopkins, Sarah Matthews, Jos. Husbands, Eliza H. Hopkins, Joshua Hopkins, William Hopkins, Lydia Hopkins, Hannah Hopkins, Anna Husbands, Racheal Bagley, Margaret Brown, Ann Chandley, Sarah Brown, Margaret Husband.

## DEER CREEK MONTHLY MEETING, HARFORD COUNTY, CERTIFICATES OF REMOVAL, 1810-1825

1810, 27th of 9th mo. - Thomas Worthington requested a certificate of removal to Indian Spring Monthly Meeting. Stephen Norton requested a certificate of removal to Little Britton Monthly Meeting.

1810, 22nd of 11th mo. - Mary Walton requested a certificate of removal to Philadelphia Monthly Meeting.

1811, 21st of 2nd mo. - Bains Cox requested a certificate of removal to Philadelphia Monthly Meeting.

1811, 23rd of 5th mo. - John Burges requested a certificate of removal to Baltimore Monthly Meeting, Eastern District. Joseph Burges and wife Ann requested a certificate of removal to Baltimore Monthly Meeting, Eastern District. Martha

Tompkins requested a certificate of removal to Baltimore Monthly Meeting, Western District.

1811, 29th of 8th mo. - John Cox and wife Sarah requested a certificate of removal to Baltimore Monthly Meeting, Eastern District. Isaac Morris, wife Martha, and two minor children, Nehemiah and Martha, requested a certificate of removal to Warrington Monthly Meeting [York County, Pennsylvania]. James Walton, minor son of James Walton, about to be placed in the verge of Philadelphia Monthly Meeting.

1811, 26th of 9th mo. - Sarah Hough requested a certificate of removal to Nottingham Monthly Meeting. Eli Kennard, wife Catharine, and four minor children, Joseph Kennard, Betsey Kennard, Hannah Tompson, and David Tompson, requested a certificate of removal to Short Creek Monthly Meeting in Ohio. George Cox requested a certificate of removal to Baltimore Monthly Meeting, Eastern District. Elizabeth Coale, dau. of Philip Coale who settled in the verge of Baltimore Monthly Meeting, Western District, requested a certificate of removal to same place.

1811, 24th of 10th mo. - Mary Prevale requested a certificate of removal to Baltimore Monthly Meeting, Western District.

1812, 17th of 2nd mo. - Mary McCoy requested a certificate of removal to Baltimore Monthly Meeting, Western District.

1812, 26th of 3rd mo. - Margret Smith requested a certificate of removal to Gunpowder Monthly Meeting.

1812, 23rd of 4th mo. - John Underwood requested a certificate of removal to Baltimore Monthly Meeting, Western District.

1812, 23rd of 7th mo. - Susannah Allen removed with her husband [not named] to Baltimore Monthly Meeting, Western District.

1812, 24th of 9th mo. - Ann Gover removed with her husband [not named] to Baltimore Monthly Meeting, Eastern District. Elizabeth Prevail requested a certificate of removal to Baltimore Monthly Meeting, Eastern District.

1812, 29th of 10th mo. - Skipwith Wilson, a minor, placed as an apprentice and removed within the verge of Baltimore Monthly Meeting, Eastern District.

1812, 26th of 11th mo. - Margaret Prevail requested a certificate of removal to Baltimore Monthly Meeting, Western District. Mary Ann Gover requested a certificate of removal to Baltimore Monthly Meeting, Eastern District.

1812, 24th of 12th mo. - William E. Coale requested a certificate of removal to Baltimore Monthly Meeting, Eastern District.

1813, 25th of 3rd mo. - Skipwith Coale, wife Ann, and three minor children, Sarah Smith Coale, Margaret Elgare Coale, and George Mathews Coale, requested a certificate of removal to Nottingham Monthly Meeting.

1813, 27th of 5th mo. - Peter Prine, wife Mary, and three minor children, Maulden, Ann, and Peter, to Baltimore Monthly Meeting, Eastern District.

1813, 26th of 8th mo. - Abraham Huff, wife Mercy, and five minor children, Martha, John, Elizabeth, Samuel, and Mary Ann, requested a certificate of removal to Gunpowder Monthly Meeting.

1813, 23rd of 9th mo. - Priscilla Rogers and her husband [not named] requested a certificate of removal to Westland Monthly Meeting [Washington County, Pennsylvania].

1813, 25th of 11th mo. - Ann Warner requested a certificate of removal to Hopewell Monthly Meeting [Frederick County, Virginia].

1813, 23rd of 12th mo. - Samuel Coale, Jr. requested a certificate of removal to Kennet Monthly Meeting [Chester County, Pennsylvania].

1814, 24th of 2nd mo. - Axsah Brown and her husband [not named] requested a certificate of removal to Gunpowder Monthly Meeting.

1814, 26th of 5th mo. - Susanna Gist and her husband [not named] requested a certificate of removal to Warrington Monthly Meeting [York County, Pennsylvania].

1814, 23rd of 6th mo. - Susanna Underwood, a minor, requested a certificate of removal to Warrington Monthly Meeting [York County, Pennsylvania].

1814, 28th of 7th mo. - Levi Kennard requested a certificate of removal to Short Creek Monthly Meeting in Ohio for himself, wife Ann, and minor son Levi. Thomas Kennard requested a certificate of removal to Short Creek Monthly Meeting in Ohio for himself and wife Elizabeth. Ann Kennard requested a certificate of removal to Short Creek Monthly Meeting in Ohio. Mary Kennard requested a certificate of removal to Short Creek Monthly Meeting in Ohio. Elizabeth Kennard requested a certificate of removal to Short Creek Monthly Meeting in Ohio. Isaac Smith requested a certificate of removal to Nottingham Monthly Meeting for himself, wife Margaret, and infant dau. Mary Ann.

1814, 25th of 8th mo. - Moses Midkelf [Medcalf] requested a certificate of removal to Short Creek Monthly Meeting in Ohio for himself, wife Susannah, and eight minor children, Abraham, Mary, Rebeckah, Jesse, Joseph, Rachel, Moses, and David.

1815, 23rd of 3rd mo. - David G. McCoy requested a certificate of removal to Baltimore Monthly Meeting, Western District.

1815, 27th of 4th mo. - Lewis Coale requested a certificate of removal to Pipe Creek Monthly Meeting [Frederick County, Maryland]. Hannah Walton, wife of James Walton, and four minor children, Rebecca, John, William, and Hannah, requested a certificate of removal to Fallowfield Monthly Meeting.

1815, 22nd of 6th mo. - Sarah M. Turner and her husband [not named] requested a certificate of removal to Cicel Monthly Meeting. Jacob Vore and wife Elizabeth requested a certificate of removal to Gunpowder Monthly Meeting.

1815, 27th of 7th mo. - Joseph Webster, a minor, requested a certificate of removal to Baltimore Monthly Meeting, Eastern District. Mary Whitson and her husband [not named] and two minor children, Benjamin and William, requested a certificate of removal to Sadsbury Monthly Meeting.

1815, 24th of 8th mo. - Mary Whitson, Jr. requested a certificate of removal to Sadsbury Monthly Meeting.

1815, 26th of 10th mo. - Jonathan Massey requested a certificate of removal to Baltimore Monthly Meeting, Western District.

1815, 23rd of 11th mo. - Elizabeth C. Price and her husband [not named] requested a certificate of removal to Arch Street Monthly Meeting in Philadelphia.

1816, 25th of 1st mo. - Charles Lukins and wife Sarah requested a certificate of removal to Baltimore Monthly Meeting, Western District.

1816, 22nd of 2nd mo. - Anna Whitson requested a certificate of removal to Sadsbury Monthly Meeting.

1816, 28th of 3rd mo. - Moses Whitson requested a certificate of removal to Sadsbury Monthly Meeting. Hermon Pile requested a certificate of removal to Little Falls Monthly Meeting.

1816, 25th of 5th mo. - John Quarles requested a certificate of removal to Baltimore Monthly Meeting, Eastern District.

1816, 27th of 6th mo. - Mary Dallam requested a certificate of removal to Baltimore Monthly Meeting, Eastern District. John Underwood, wife Mary, and minor dau. Anne requested a certificate of removal to Baltimore Monthly Meeting, Eastern District.

1816, 25th of 7th mo. - Thomas Coale, a minor, requested a certificate of removal to Baltimore Monthly Meeting, Eastern District.

1816, 29th of 8th mo. - Phebe Pearson, a minor, requested a certificate of removal to Baltimore Monthly Meeting, Western District.

1816, 24th of 10th mo. - John Pile, a minor, requested a certificate of removal to London Grove Monthly Meeting.

1817, 6th of 1st mo. - Reuben Valentine requested a certificate of removal to Center Monthly Meeting in Center County, Pennsylvania.

1817, 3rd of 3rd mo. - Skipwith Coale requested a certificate of removal to Baltimore Monthly Meeting, Western District. George Valentine requested a certificate of removal to Center Monthly Meeting in Center County, Pennsylvania.

1817, 2nd of 6th mo. - Susanna Brinton requested a certificate of removal to Sadsbury Monthly Meeting.

1817, 7th of 7th mo. - John Hopkins, a minor, placed as an apprentice and removed within verge of Baltimore Monthly Meeting, Western District. Lewis Coale requested a certificate of removal to Fairfax Monthly Meeting [Loudoun County], Virginia.

1817, 4th of 8th mo. - Margert Ady and her husband [not named] requested a certificate of removal to Baltimore Monthly Meeting, Western District. Mary Hopkins requested a certificate of removal to Nine Partners Monthly Meeting in the State of New York. Rebecca Hayward, a minor, also requested a certificate of removal to Nine Partners Monthly Meeting [New York State].

1818, 6th of 7th mo. - Sarah Janney and her husband [not named] requested a certificate of removal to Baltimore Monthly Meeting, Eastern District. Christopher Wilson, Jr. requested a certificate of removal to Baltimore Monthly Meeting, Eastern District.

1818, 3rd of 8th mo. - Jacob Vore, Jr. requested a certificate of removal to White Water Monthly Meeting in Indiana for himself, wife Elizabeth, and two minor children Samuel C. and Ann. Mary Vore, Jr. requested a certificate of removal to White Water Monthly Meeting in Indiana. Jacob Vore and wife Mary requested a certificate of removal to White Water Monthly Meeting in Indiana. Isaac Vore requested a certificate of removal to White Water Monthly Meeting in Indiana for himself, wife Mary, and four minor children Jacob, Mary, Eliza, and Ruth. John Vore requested a certificate of removal to White Water Monthly Meeting in Indiana. Phebe Clark requested a certificate of removal to White Water Monthly Meeting in Indiana. Susannah Allen and her husband [not named] requested a certificate of removal to Baltimore Monthly Meeting, Eastern District.

1819, 5th of 4th mo. - Ganer Parsons and her husband [not named] requested a certificate of removal to Smithfield Monthly Meeting in Jefferson County, Ohio. William Scotten, wife Jane, and their minor son Joshua, requested a certificate of removal to Little Britton Monthly Meeting.

1819, 7th of 6th mo. - Mary Malsby requested a certificate of removal to Baltimore Monthly Meeting, Western District.

1819, 5th of 7th mo. - Ellis P. Coale, placed as an apprentice, removed within the verge of Nottingham Monthly Meeting.

1819, 4th of 10th mo. - Mordica Underwood, a minor, requested a certificate of removal to Baltimore Monthly Meeting, Western District.

1820, 6th of 3rd mo. - Thomas E. Warner requested a certificate of removal to Redstone Monthly Meeting [Fayette County, Pennsylvania]. James Gillingham, wife Sarah, and three minor children, Phebe, Samuel and Charles, requested a certificate of removal to Baltimore Monthly Meeting, Western District.

1820, 3rd of 4th mo. - Mary Malsby requested a certificate of removal to Little Falls Monthly Meeting. Anna Gillingham requested a certificate of removal to Baltimore Monthly Meeting, Western District.

1820, 5th of 6th mo. - Sarah Morris requested a certificate of removal to Little Falls Monthly Meeting.

1820, 3rd of 7th mo. - Sarah Johnson and her husband [not named] and five minor children, James, George, Howard, Anna, and Lemuel Stansbury Johnson, requested a certificate of removal to Little Falls Monthly Meeting.

1820, 6th of 11th mo. - Thomas Sharp requested a certificate of removal to Sadsbury Monthly Meeting.

1821, 5th of 2nd mo. - Anna Morris and her husband [not named] requested a certificate of removal to Philadelphia Monthly Meeting, Southern District.

1821, 2nd of 4th mo. - Susanna Dutton requested a certificate of removal to Baltimore Monthly Meeting, Western District. David Jourdan requested a certificate of removal to Baltimore Monthly Meeting, Western District.

1821, 7th of 5th mo. - Joel Carter and his eight minor children, John, Samuel, Joel, Edeth, Enos, Leven, Margaret, and James, requested a certificate of removal to Little Falls Monthly Meeting. Hannah Carter also requested a certificate of removal to Little Falls Monthly Meeting. Sarah Carter also requested a certificate of removal to Little Falls Monthly Meeting. Joseph M. Downing, wife Mary Ann, and their three minor children, Sarah E., William M., and Joseph Warner Downing, requested a certificate of removal to Middle Town Monthly Meeting.

1822, 1st of 4th mo. - Nicholas Cooper, wife Sarah, and their six minor children, Nicholas, Priscilla, Esther, Ely B., Margaret, and Gulielma, requested a certificate of removal to Little Falls Monthly Meeting. Elizabeth, Martha, Anna, and Sarah Cooper [listed together] also requested a certificate of removal to Little Falls Monthly Meeting.

1822, 7th of 11th mo. - Sarah McComas and her two minor children, Cassandra McComas and James Howard McComas, requested a certificate of removal to Baltimore Monthly Meeting, Western District.

1823, 16th of 1st mo. - Luke Tipten, wife Priscilla, and their eight minor children, David, Mary, Hester, Rachel, Abijah, Elihu, John, and Hannah, requested a certificate of removal to Smithfield Monthly Meeting in Ohio.

1823, 13th of 11th mo. - William McCoy, Jr. requested a certificate of removal to Baltimore Monthly Meeting, Western District.

1824, 13th of 5th mo. - Joseph Kemp requested a certificate of removal to Fallowfield Monthly Meeting.

1824, 17th of 6th mo. - William Corse, a minor, requested a certificate of removal to Wilmington Monthly Meeting in Delaware.

1824, 15th of 7th mo. - Mary C. Gillingham and her husband [not named] requested a certificate of removal to Baltimore Monthly Meeting, Western District.

1824, 12th of 8th mo. - Isaac Stubbs, wife Hannah, and their seven minor children, Jeremiah B., Hannah Brown, Sarah Ann, Daniel, Joseph, Slater, and Deborah R., requested a certificate of removal to Little Britain Monthly Meeting. John Lewin, wife Lydia, and their five minor children, William, Ann, Amos, Mary, and Lydia, requested a certificate of removal to Little Falls Monthly Meeting.

1824, 16th of 9th mo. - Jesse Hartly, wife Mary, and their six minor children, Rachel, William, Edwin, Joseph, Jesse, and Thomas, requested a certificate of removal to Hartland Monthly Meeting in the State of New York. Rachel Chalk and her husband [not named] requested a certificate of removal to Duck Creek Monthly Meeting [Kent County, Delaware].

1824, 14th of 10th mo. - George Mason requested a certificate of removal to Nottingham Monthly Meeting.

1824, 16th of 12th mo. - Anna Garretson requested a certificate of removal to Baltimore Monthly Meeting, Western District. Elisha Pearson, a minor, requested a certificate of removal to Baltimore Monthly Meeting. Western District.

1825, 17th of 3rd mo. - John Lewin, Jr. requested a certificate of removal to Little Falls Monthly Meeting.

1825, 12th of 5th mo. - Mary H. Mathews and her husband [not named] requested a certificate of removal to Baltimore Monthly Meeting, Western District.

1825, 15th of 9th mo. - Isaac Coale requested a certificate of removal to Baltimore Monthly Meeting, Western District. Benjamin Bond and Eli Bond, minor sons of Silas Bond, requested a certificate of removal to Still Water Monthly Meeting in Ohio.

1825, 13th of 10th mo. - Thomas Watson, a minor, requested a certificate of removal to Baltimore Monthly Meeting, Western District.

1825, 17th of 11th mo. - William Rickman requested a certificate of removal to New Garden Monthly Meeting [Chester County], Pennsylvania.

## DEER CREEK MONTHLY MEETING, HARFORD COUNTY
## ABSTRACTS FROM THE MINUTES, 1810-1825

1801, 23rd of 4th mo. - Certificate received from Nottingham Monthly Meeting for Samuel Carter, a minor. Mary Davis, late Webb, has been guilty of falsehood and has also accomplished her marriage contrary to the good order established amongst us. Certificate produced for Sarah Brown, signed and forwarded [place not stated]. Certificate requested for John Prevail, a minor, and also one for Agness Warner to Baltimore Monthly Meeting.

1801, 29th of 5th mo. - Deer Creek Preparative Meeting informs that Mary Prigg, late Cox, has gone out in marriage to a man not of our society and was married to him.

1801, 27th of 8th mo. - Certificate received from Horsham Monthly Meeting, endorsed by Baltimore Monthly Meeting, for Martha Bond; likewise for Mary Webb from Baltimore Monthly Meeting; both reside within the verge of Fawn Meeting. Deer Creek Deer Creek Preparative Meeting informs that Richard Webb requests to be joined in membership with Friends.

1801, 24th of 9th mo. - Certificate requested by Amos Evans for himself, wife [not named], and four minor children, Tace, Cadwallader, Benjamin, and John Evans, to Muncy Monthly Meeting. Certificate requested by Moses Lukins for himself, wife [not named] and five minor children, Lidia, Benjamin, Rachel, Pheby, and Hannah Lukins, to Muncy Monthly Meeting.

1801, 29th of 10th mo. - Susannah Hopkins, late Dellam, had her marriage accomplished contrary to our good order and was disowned. Women's Meeting informs that Elizabeth Strawbridge had her marriage accomplished with a man not of our society. Mary Webb requested a certificate for her son David Malsbee [later spelled Malsby] to Gunpowder Monthly Meeting. Isaac McCoy requested a certificate to Baltimore Monthly Meeting.

1801, 26th of 11th mo. - William Cox gave testimony condemning his deviation so far as to partake in a dance, and attending the consummation of a marriage accomplished contrary to the order established amongst Friends, for which he hopes to be more guarded in the future. Certificate produced for Ann Coale from Baltimore Monthly Meeting. Letter received from Muncy Monthly Meeting informing hat George Harris had attended [militia] musters contrary to the principles of Friends. Isaac Wright, of Pipe Creek [Frederick County, Maryland], son of Isaac and Ellenor Wright (both deceased), and Elizabeth Cox, dau. of William and Rachel Cox (parents consenting), declared their intentions of marriage. Deer Creek Preparative Meeting informs that Mary Barkly, late Stokes, has gone out in marriage and accomplished the same with the assistance of a hireling teacher. William Coale [later listed as William Coale, Jr.] requested a certificate to Pipe Creek Monthly Meeting [Frederick County, Maryland].

1801, 24th of 12th mo. - Deer Creek Preparative Meeting informs that Isaac Robertson attended a marriage consulated contrary to the order established amongst Friends.

1802, 28th of 1st mo. - Certificate received from Sadsbury Monthly Meeting for Mary Whitson, wife of Benjamin, and their minor children, Henry, Elizabeth, Moses, Thomas, Burt, Mary, Benjamin, and Anna Whitson. Certificate requested by Hugh Morgan to South River Monthly Meeting.

1802, 25th of 2nd mo. - Certificate received from Baltimore Monthly Meeting for Nicholas Kooper [also spelled Cooper], wife Sarah, and their five minor children, Pathanie, Isaiah, Elizabeth, Martha, and Ann.

1802, 25th of 3rd mo. - Certificate produced from Baltimore Monthly Meeting for Agnes Warner. Mary Barkley, late Stokes, having married a man not of our society in disregard to our good order, was disowned. Elizabeth Wright requested a certificate to Pipe Creek Monthly Meeting [Frederick County, Maryland]. Benjamin Lukins requested a certificate to Baltimore Monthly Meeting for himself and wife Alse Lukins. John Cox, a minor son of William Cox, requested a certificate to Pipe Creek Monthly Meeting [Frederick County, Maryland].

1802, 27th of 5th mo. - Women's Meeting informs that Ann Way, late Lukins, has gone out in marriage with a man not of our society by the assistance of a Baptist teacher; likewise, Alse Lukins has attended a disorderly marriage and partook in dancing.

1802, 24th of 6th mo. - Certificate produced for John Corse, Jr. from Cicle [Cecil] Monthly Meeting. Fawn Preparative Meeting informs that Isaac Jones and wife [not named] requests their five minor children [not named] be taken into membership.

1802, 29th of 7th mo. - Elizabeth Strawbridge, late Bond, having so far deviated as to let out her affections to a man not in membership with us and accomplished her marriage with the assistance of a Baptist teacher, is disowned. Deer Creek Preparative Meeting informs that John Bruce has been guilty of fornication.

1802, 20th of 8th mo. - Sarah Street, having so fare deviated as to marry a man not in membership with us, is disowned.

1802, 23rd of 9th mo. - Certificated produced from Nottingham Monthly Meeting for Moses Midcalf, wife Sarah, and their four minor children, Abraham, Elizabeth, Mary, and Rebecca Midcalf. David Stokes, having so far deviated as to let our his affections to a woman not of our society and accomplished his marriage with her by the assistance of a Baptist teacher, is disowned. William Cox [later listed as William Cox, Jr.] requests our certificate for marriage with Ann Shepherd, a member of Pipe Creek Monthly Meeting [Frederick County, Maryland].

1802, 28th of 10th mo. - Certificates requested for Ann Juett [later spelled Jewett] and Emelia [later spelled Amelia] Hopkins, a minor, to Baltimore Monthly Meeting. Certificate was handed here from Gunpowder Monthly Meeting for Luke Tipton who is received as a member of Fawn Preparative Meeting. Ephraim Hopkins, having not attended to the wholesome order established in our society by deviating so far as to be concerned in a horse race and also departing from the plainness which becomes us, is disowned. John Bruce, having deviated so far as to be guilty of fornication, is disowned.

1802, 25th of 11th mo. - Deer Creek Preparative Meeting informs that Martha Huff requests to become a member.

1802, 23rd of 12th mo. - Ann Plummer, late Wallis, having gone out in marriage to a man not of our society, is disowned. Isaac Robertson requested a certificate to Baltimore Monthly Meeting. Deer Creek Preparative Meeting informs that Abraham Huff requests to become a member.

1803, 26th of 1st mo. - John Spotswood Peck produced a certificate from Peel Monthly Meeting, London, dated 21st of 4th mo., 1802, recommending him to Baltimore Monthly Meeting, with an endorsement by that meeting to this meeting. Mary Malsby produced a certificate from Gunpowder Monthly Meeting recommending her to Deer Creek Monthly Meeting; likewise for Rebecca Tipton, who was received as a member of Fawn Meeting. Deer Creek Preparative Meeting informs that Samuel Hopkins, son of Samuel, has accomplished his marriage to a woman not of our society with the assistance of a Baptist teacher; likewise Ephraim Cox has accomplished his marriage with a woman not of our society with the assistance of a hireling minister.

1803, 24th of 2nd mo. - Women's Meeting informs that Gulielma Stansbury [also listed as Guli Elma Stanbery, Guli Elma Stanbury, and Guli Elma Stansbury], late

Cox, has gone out in marriage with a man not of our society by the assistance of a Baptist teacher.

1803, 24th of 3rd mo. - Women's Meeting informs that Ann Ewin [also spelled Ewen], late Tomkins, has gone out in marriage with a man not of our society with the assistance of a Methodist teacher. She was subsequently disowned. Deer Creek Preparative Meeting informs that Joseph Wiggins has taken strong drink to excess, and that Mary Worthington and Elizabeth Worthington [later referred to as Elizabeth Worthington, of Charles] "have attended a place of divertion where there was musick and partook in dancing." Fawn Preparative Meeting informs that William Walton refused to settle with his creditors.

1803, 28th of 4th mo. - Mary Johns produced a certificate from Westland Monthly Meeting [Washington County, Pennsylvania]. Deer Creek Preparative Meeting informs that William Worthington has been guilty of profane language and "has attended a place of divertion where there was musick and dancing." Likewise [the latter deviation] for Samuel Hopkins, of Joseph.

1803, 26th of 5th mo. - Ann Way, having so far deviated as to let our her affections to a man not in membership and accomplished her marriage by the assistance of a Baptist teacher, is disowned. Mercy Bayfield requested a certificate to Baltimore Monthly Meeting.

1803, 26th[?] of 6th mo. - Deer Creek Preparative Meeting informs that Susannah Rodgers and Elizabeth Coale (of Philip) "have attended a place of divertion where there was musick and are charged with taking part in a dance." Francis Hopkins requested a certificate to Baltimore Monthly Meeting.

1803, 28th of 7th mo. - Alice Lukins, Jr. has attended a marriage accomplished contrary to the order established amongst Friends. Deer Creek Preparative Meeting informs that Sarah Car, late Murry, has accomplished her marriage with a man not of our society by the assistance of a Methodist teacher; likewise for Elizabeth Barton, late Norton. William Watson requested a certificate for himself, wife Martha, and their child Sarah Wilson Watson, to Nottingham Monthly Meeting. Deer Creek Preparative Meeting informs that Thomas Wilson "has attended a place of divertion where there was musick and partook in dancing."

1803, 22nd of 9th mo. - John Wiggins, son of Joseph and Sarah Wiggins (the latter deceased), and Sarah Norton, dau. of Steven and Sophia Norton, declared their intentions of marriage, the young woman's father being present expressed his consent as likewise the consent of his wife. It is expected the young man will produce his father's consent.

1803, 26th of 10th mo. - Certificate produced for Mary Jones from Gunpowder Monthly Meeting. Deer Creek Preparative Meeting informs that Charles Worthington, of Charles, has consulated his marriage with a woman not of our society. William Cox, Jr. requested a certificate to Pipe Creek Monthly Meeting [Frederick County, Maryland]. Certificate produced from Baltimore Monthly Meeting for Mary Prine, wife of Peter Prine [later spelled Perine], and their son Malden Prine.

1803, 24th of 11th mo. - Deer Creek Preparative Meeting informs that Ann Fisher, late Coale, has accomplished her marriage with a man not of our society with the assistance of a Methodist teacher. Susanna Hopkins requested a certificate to Baltimore Monthly Meeting. Richard Webb requested a certificate for his son Jessy Webb to London Grove Monthly Meeting.

1803, 26th of 12th mo. - George Harris, having so far deviated as to attend the militia muster and neglects payment of his just debts, is disowned. Sarah Morris produced a certificate from Gunpowder Monthly Meeting. Peter Perine produced a certificate from Baltimore Monthly Meeting. Deer Creek Preparative Meeting informs that John Coars and Susanna Coars [later spelled Corse] late Coale, being first cousins, have intermarried. They were subsequently disowned. Joseph Dellam "has attended a place of divertion where were music and partook in dancing and has accomplished his marriage by the assistance of a Methodist teacher." John Spotswood Peck has also accomplished his marriage contrary to the order used amongst us.

1804, 26th of 1st mo. - Ann Fisher, having deviated so far as to marry a man not in membership with us, is disowned. Susanna Rodgers "has attended a place of divertion where was dancing" and is owned.

1804, 23rd of 2nd mo. - Ephraim Cox went out in marriage to a woman not in membership by the assistance of a hireling teacher and is disowned.

1804, 29th of 3rd mo. - Sarah Car had accomplished her marriage with a man not of our society by the assistance of a Methodist teacher and is disowned. Sarah Wornock requested to become a member of our society. Nathaniel Norton requested a certificate to Baltimore Monthly Meeting.

1804, 26th of 4th mo. - Deer Creek Preparative Meeting informs that Mary Rodgers, later Johns, having accomplished her marriage with a man not of our society by the assistance of a Methodist teacher, is disowned. Joseph Bennet, having gone out in marriage with a woman not of our society by the assistance of a Baptist teacher, is disowned. Joshua Bennet requested a certificate for himself, wife Mary, and their five minor children, Hannah, Joshua, Mary, Sarah, and Jessey Bennet, to Bradford Monthly Meeting [Chester County, Pennsylvania].

1804, 24th of 5th mo. - Baltimore Monthly Meeting has received a certificate for Massey Bayfield [female] from Deer Creek Monthly Meeting. William Hopkins, of Gerard, requested a certificate to Baltimore Monthly Meeting.

1804, 26th of 7th mo. - Deer Creek Preparative Meeting informs that Andrew Mecoy (McCoy) complains against Samuel Hopkins (of Joseph) for not paying him a just debt.

1804, 23rd of 8th mo. - Joseph Dellam and Mary Dellam, late Worthington, having "attended a place of diversation and partook in dancing" and having accomplished their marriage contrary to our order, are disowned. Charles Worthington, having accomplished his marriage with a woman not of our society, is disowned.

1804, 27th of 9th mo. - Skipwith Coale produced a certificate from Baltimore Monthly Meeting. Deer Creek Preparative Meeting informs that Harvy Stokes has gone out in marriage with a woman not of our society with the assistance of a hireling minister. This meeting is informed that Daniel Robertson has failed in his circumstances.

1804, 25th of 10th mo. - Abraham Huff, son of Abraham and Phebe Huff, and Massey Webb, dau. of Richard and Elizabeth Webb (the latter deceased), declared their intentions of marriage, the young woman's father being present.

1804, 22nd of 11th mo. - Priscilla Hopkins and Ann Peck produced certificates from Baltimore Monthly Meeting. Elizabeth Johnson, late Worthington, having attended a place of diversion and dancing and since having gone out in marriage with a man not of our society by the assistance of a hireling teacher, is disowned.

1804, 27th of 12th mo. - Cassandra Willits produced a certificate from Baltimore Monthly Meeting. Fawn Preparative Meeting informs that Mary Dungan, late Lukins, requests to be reinstated amongst Friends. Silas Warner and Isaac Coale are appointed to write to Muncy Monthly Meeting (where she resides) on her behalf. Certificate produced from Baltimore Monthly Meeting for Benjamin Lukins and wife Alse.

1805, 24th of 1st mo. - Deer Creek Preparative Meeting reports that Elizabeth Albert, late Stokes, has gone out in marriage with a man not of our society by the assistance of a hireling minister; likewise, Sarah and Hannah Stokes have attended their sister's marriage consulated contrary to the order of our society.

1805, 28th of 3rd mo. - Morris Malsby produced a certificate for himself and wife Mary from Gunpowder Monthly Meeting. Benjamin Bond and Mary Bond were proposed for the station of Elders at Fawn Preparative Meeting.

1805, 25th of 4th mo. - Deer Creek Preparative Meeting informs that John F. Webster complains of Joseph Burgess for not paying him a just debt. Sarah Walton requested a certificate for herself and six minor children, Lukins, Elizabeth, Alice Ann, Salem, Elisha, and Jacob Walton, to Horsham Monthly Meeting. Sarah Allen requested a certificate to Baltimore Monthly Meeting.

1805, 27th of 6th mo. - Grace Hopkins requested a certificate to Baltimore Monthly Meeting.

1805, 25th of 7th mo. - Certificate produced for Ann Willits from Baltimore Monthly Meeting.

1805, 29th of 8th mo. - Robert Cornthwait, son of John and Mary Cornthwait, of Baltimore (both deceased), and Alisannah Wilson, dau. of John and Alisannah Wilson (both deceased), declared their intentions of marriage, the young woman's (guardian) brother [not named] being present. Fawn Preparative Meeting informs that William Walton has removed and gone out of the limits of our monthly meeting and has left several creditors dissatisfied, and also has been in the practice of using profane language. Elizabeth Barton, having so far deviated as to marry a man not of our society by the assistance of a Methodist teacher, is disowned.

1805, 26th of 9th mo. - Deer Creek Preparative Meeting informs that Joseph Wiggins has taken strong drink to intoxication and denies the same. Certificate requested for Larken Cox (a minor) to Baltimore Monthly Meeting. William Dellam and Richard Dellam (minors) now reside in Baltimore and have not had certificates.

1805, 24th of 10th mo. - Certificate requested for Francis Crawford to Westland Monthly Meeting [Washington County, Pennsylvania].

1805, 17th of 12th mo. - Deer Creek Preparative Meeting informs that Richard Ward has declined the attendance of our meeting and has joined to another society [later reported to be a Methodist and was discontinued from membership with Friends]. Fawn Preparative Meeting informs that Eley Kennard requests to be released from the station of an overseer; also, Anthony Jones requests to be reinstated with Friends and his two minor children, Rebecca and Joseph Jones, to be taken under care also.

1806, 23rd of 1st mo. - Elizabeth Albert, late Stokes, having accomplished her marriage with a man not of our society by the assistance of a hireling teacher, is disowned.

1806, 20th of 2nd mo. - Andrew McCoy informs that he had purchased a right of dower in land that William McCoy is in possession of and, having not secured same, requests permission to proceed in a legal and amicable way, which this meeting accordingly grants. Deer Creek Preparative Meeting informs that Rebecca Carter requested a certificate for herself and two minor children, John and Henry Carter, to Abington Monthly Meeting [Montgomery County, Pennsylvania]; likewise, Alisanna Cornthwait requested a certificate to Baltimore Monthly Meeting. Fawn Preparative Meeting informs that Benjamin Thomas and Rebecca Tipton have accomplished their marriage by the assistance of a Baptist teacher.

1806, 27th of 3rd mo. - Joseph Wiggins, having "so far deviated as to take strong drink to excess so as to be disguised therewith" is therefore disowned. Guli Elma *[sic]* Stansbury, having gone out in marriage with a man not in membership with us by the assistance of a Baptist teacher, is disowned. Certificate requested for Thomas Worthington (a minor) for Sadsbury Monthly Meeting.

1806, 24th of 4th mo. - William Walton, having neglected attendance at our meetings, used profane language, and moved away without settling his creditors, is disowned. Fawn Preparative Meeting informs that Joseph Strawbridge requests to be received into membership.

1806, 29th of 5th mo. - Anthony Jones, having a birthright amongst Friends, condemned his misconduct in marrying a woman not in membership with us by the assistance of a Baptist teacher. Deer Creek Preparative Meeting informs that Skipwith Coale, son of Samuel, requests a certificate to Baltimore Monthly Meeting in order to marry Ann Matthews. Mary Dungan condemned her misconduct in marrying her first cousin by the assistance of a Baptist teacher "some years ago" [and made her "X" mark on the written statement dated 22nd of 1st mo., 1806]. James Walton requested a certificate for himself, wife Hannah, and their six minor children, Elizabeth, Mary, Rebecca, James, John, and William Walton.

1806, 26th of 6th mo. - John Channel presented a certificate from Little Briton Monthly Meeting for himself and his three minor children, Isaac, Able, and Sarah Channel. Elizabeth Strawbridge condemned her misconduct (in a signed statement) for marrying a man not of out society. John Miller, Jr. produced a certificate from New Garden Monthly Meeting [Chester County, Pennsylvania] for himself, wife Edith, and their two minor children, Lidia and Rachel Miller.

1806, 28th of 8th mo. - William John produced a certificate for himself and wife Mary from London Grove Monthly Meeting [Chester County, Pennsylvania], as members of Fawn Preparative Meeting; likewise for Martha Brooks from that same meeting. Women's Meeting informs that Martha Harrod, late Huff, has gone out in marriage with a man not of our society by the assistance of a Methodist teacher. David Malsby, son of John and Mary Malsby (the former deceased), and Mary Coale, dau. of Samuel and Lydia Coale, declared their intentions of marriage, their surviving parents being present.

1806, 25th of 9th mo. - Deer Creek Preparative Meeting informs that John Wiggins has given way to passion so far as to strike a man and abuse a woman. Hannah Richardson requested to be taken into membership at Deer Creek Preparative Meeting; likewise, Mary Rodgers requested to be reinstated amongst Friends.

1806, 27th of 11th mo. - Joel Carter produced a certificate from Little Briton Monthly Meeting for himself, wife Margaret, and their five minor children, Hannah, Isabel, Sarah, John, and Samuel Carter. Deer Creek Preparative Meeting informs that John S. Peck [and wife] requested a certificate to Baltimore Monthly Meeting.

1806, 25th of 12th mo. - Deer Creek Preparative Meeting informs that Peter Wilson has taken strong drink to excess. Silas Bond, son of Benjamin and Mary Bond, and Hannah Kennard, dau. of Eley and Elizabeth Kennard (the latter deceased), declared their intentions of marriage, their surviving parents being present. A certificate granted to William Hopkins some time back to Baltimore Monthly Meeting has miscarried and another applied for.

1807, 29th of 1st mo. - Jonathan Burgess wrote to this meeting condemning his outgoing in marriage and desiring reinstatement. Certificate received from Baltimore Monthly Meeting for Ann Coale.

1807, 26th of 2nd mo. - Certificate produced from Baltimore Monthly Meeting for George Mason.

1807, 26th of 3rd mo. - Fawn Preparative Meeting informs that Nehemiah Underwood has so far deviated from our principles as to strike a man in anger. Isaac Vore, son of Jacob and Mary Vore, and Ruth Bond, dau. of Benjamin and Mary Bond, declared their intentions of marriage, their parents being present. Isaac Coale requested to be released from the service of clerk.

1807, 28th of 5th mo. - Margaret Ward, late Worthington, having so far deviated as to marry her first cousin, is disowned. Certificate requested for Thomas Wilson, a minor, to Baltimore Monthly Meeting.

1807, 25th of 6th mo. - Communication received from Baltimore Monthly Meeting that Cassandra Durbin and Margaret Hill Bradford have requested reinstatement into membership. Certificate received [place of origin not stated] for Amos Pyle, wife Ruth, and their six minor children, Sarah, Daniel, John, Phebe, Joseph, and Amos Pyle. Certificate requested for Benjamin Jones, a minor, to Muncy Monthly Meeting.

1807, 29th of 10th mo. - Deer Creek Preparative Meeting informs that Robert Bruce has accomplished his marriage with a woman not of our society by the assistance of a hireling teacher. Silas Warner and Sarah Warnock declared their intentions of marriage, the written consent of their surviving parents having been received.

1807, 26th of 11th mo. - Nathan Pyle produced a certificate from Little Britain Monthly Meeting for himself, wife Grace, and their two minor children, David and Elizabeth Pyle. Certificate received from Baltimore Monthly Meeting, Western District, for Sarah Allen.

1808, 25th of 2nd mo. - Certificate received from Little Britain Monthly Meeting for Sarah Hough. Isaac Pigeon, son of William and Rachel Pigeon, of South River Monthly Meeting, Virginia, and Sarah Warner, dau. of Crosdale and Mary Warner, deceased, declared their intentions of marriage.

1808, 24th of 3rd mo. - Isaac Vore requested a certificate for himself and wife Ruth to Gunpowder Monthly Meeting. Fawn Preparative Meeting informs that Joseph Webb has accomplished his marriage contrary to our good order.

1808, 28th of 4th mo. - Certificate received from Baltimore Monthly Meeting, Eastern District, for John Worthington. Women's Meeting informs that Rachel Brooks, late Underwood, has accomplished her marriage with a man not in membership with us and has been guilty of fornication.

1808, 26th of 5th mo. - Certificate received from Duck Creek Monthly Meeting [Kent County, Delaware] for William Liston, wife Mary, and their two minor children, James Thomas Liston and Jonathan Allec Liston, who reportedly have removed within the limits of Sadsbury Monthly Meeting. Certificates received for Ann Jewett and Thomas Norton from Baltimore Monthly Meeting. Women's Meeting informs that Susanna Course requests to be reinstated into membership.

1808, 23rd of 6th mo. - Women's Meeting requested assistance in treating with Elizabeth Forsyth, late Wiggins, for her outgoing in marriage. Certificate also produced for Sarah Pigeon to South River Monthly Meeting, Virginia.

1808, 20th of 7th mo. - Certificate received from Little Britain Monthly Meeting for Isaac Stubbs, wife Hannah, and their three minor children, Amos, Jeremiah, and Daniel Stubbs. Deer Creek Preparative Meeting informs that Peter Wilson has taken strong drink to excess. Maurice Malsby has been guilty of gambling and pursued a man with firearms who had offended him. William Worthington has accomplished his marriage with a woman not in membership with us by the assistance of a hireling teacher.

1808, 25th of 8th mo. - Communication received from Baltimore Monthly Meeting, Western District, that Alice Nicholson had applied to be reinstated into membership [written in margin: "Alice Lukens, cause of disownment, 7th mo. 1803"]. John Webb requested a certificate to Hopewell Monthly Meeting [Frederick County, Virginia].

1808, 22nd of 9th mo. - Certificate requested for Skipwith Coale, of Isaac, to Philadelphia Monthly Meeting, Northern District. Certificate received from Baltimore Monthly Meeting, Eastern District, for John Jewett and wife Susanna. Letter received from Baltimore Monthly Meeting, Western District, informing that Nathaniel Norton had joined a militia company.

1808, 29th of 12th mo. - Deer Creek Preparative Meeting informs that Mordicai Warner has joined a militia company in order to learn the art of war. Certificate requested for Wilson Worthington, a minor, to Baltimore Monthly Meeting.

1809, 26th of 1st mo. - Certificate received from New Garden Monthly Meeting [Chester County, Pennsylvania] for Abraham Harmer, wife Hannah, and their five minor children, Mary, John, Joseph, Michel, Joshua, and Sarah Ann Harmer. Deer Creek Preparative Meeting informs that John Lewin requests to be joined in membership.

1809, 23rd of 2nd mo. - Deer Creek Preparative Meeting informs that Abraham Huff, who was disowned by Gunpowder Monthly Meeting, requests to be reinstated into membership. Certificate to Indian Spring Monthly Meeting for Ann Coale has miscarried; a copy will be forwarded.

1809, 23rd of 3rd mo. - Letter received from Little Britain Monthly Meeting requesting our treatment with Eldwood [also spelled Elwood] Harlin on account of his having paid an exempt tax.

1809, 27th of 4th mo. - Certificate produced for Isaac McCoy [place not stated]. John Cox requested a certificate for himself and wife Sarah Cox to Baltimore Monthly Meeting, Eastern District. Communication received that the certificate to Baltimore Monthly Meeting for Larkin Cox has miscarried and that he has joined a militia company.

1809, 25th of 5th mo. - Certificate received from Baltimore Monthly Meeting, Eastern District, for Rachel Judge. Women's Meeting produced a certificate for Elizabeth Walton to Philadelphia Monthly Meeting, Northern District.

1809, 22nd of 6th mo. - Women's Meeting produced a certificate for Mary Cox to Baltimore Monthly Meeting, Eastern District.

1809, 27th of 7th mo. - William Worthington, having married a woman not in membership with us, is disowned. Deer Creek Preparative Meeting informs that Asa Warner has been guilty of taking strong drink to excess, and Samuel Worthington has accomplished his marriage by the assistance of an hireling teacher to a woman not in membership with us.

1809, 26th of 10th mo. - Fawn Preparative Meeting informs that John Miller expects to removed out of the verge of this meeting and requests to be released from the station of overseer. Ely Kennard requested a certificate in order for marriage with Catharine Thompson, a member of New Garden Monthly Meeting [Chester County, Pennsylvania]. Certificate received from Little Brittain Monthly Meeting for Rachel Harlan and her two minor children, Hannah and John Harlan.

1809, 23rd of 11th mo. - Fawn Preparative Meeting informs that James Walton has so far deviated from our principles as to administer an oath.

1809, 28th of 12th mo. - Women's Meeting informs that Sarah Dodrel [also spelled Dodrell], late Coale, has accomplished her marriage with man not in membership with us; likewise for Sarah Forsythe. John Miller requested a certificate for himself, wife Edith, and their three minor children, Lydia, Rachel, and William John Miller, to Baltimore Monthly Meeting, Western District. Larkin Cox, having deviated so far as to joint a militia company, is disowned. Peter Wilson condemned his misconduct in writing.

1810, 22nd of 2nd mo. - Women's Meeting produced a certificate for Sarah Webster and Martha Brooks to Baltimore Monthly Meeting, Western District, and for Rachel Judge for Baltimore Monthly Meeting, Eastern District. Deer Creek Preparative Meeting informs that Thomas Jay has been guilty of fighting.

1810, 29th of 3rd mo. - Certificate received from Little Britain Monthly Meeting for William Watson, wife Martha, and their four minor children, Sarah W., Joseph D., William, and Hannah Watson. Certificate received from New Garden Monthly Meeting [Chester County, Pennsylvania] for Catharine Kennard and her two minor children, Hannah Kennard and David Thompson Kennard.

1810, 26th of 4th mo. - Communication received from Westland Monthly Meeting [Washington County, Pennsylvania] regarding Mary Rodgers [no details were given]. Women's Meeting produced a certificate for Mary Morris to Warrington Monthly Meeting [York County, Pennsylvania]. Samuel Worthington, having gone out in marriage to a woman not in membership by the assistance of a hireling teacher, is disowned. Asa Warner, having so far deviated as to take strong drink to access, is disowned.

1810, 28th of 6th mo. - Women's Meeting requested assistance in treating with Sarah Hopkins, late Wilson, on her marrying contrary to the order used amongst us. Sarah Dodrel [also spelled Doderel], having gone out in marriage, is disowned.

1810, 26th of 7th mo. - Communication received from Baltimore Monthly Meeting, Western District, informing that Robert McCoy requested reinstatement into membership. Thomas Jay, having so far deviated as to strike a man in passion and also having paid a tax in lieu of personal service in the militia, is disowned.

1810, 23rd of 8th mo. - Certificate produced for Aquilla Massey, Peter Wilson, and Nathan Wilson [place not stated]. Joseph Husband produced a certificate from Baltimore Monthly Meeting, Eastern District, for himself and wife Sarah Husband. Certificate produced for Thomas Worthing[ton] to Sadsbury Monthly Meeting did not reach that meeting, but he now resides within the verge of Indian Spring Monthly Meeting and requests another certificate. Certificate requested for Stephen Norton, a minor, to Little Brittain Monthly Meeting.

1810, 27th of 9th mo. - Certificate requested for Isaac Morris, wife Martha, and their two minor children, Nehemiah and Martha, to Warrington Monthly Meeting [York County, Pennsylvania].

1810, 22nd of 11th mo. - Communication received from Baltimore Monthly Meeting, Eastern District, that Susanna Allen and Ann Ewing have applied for reinstatement into membership. Women's Meeting produced a certificate for Mary Watson to Philadelphia Monthly Meeting. Mary Malsby [later spelled Maulsby], wife of Maurice, requested a certificate for herself and two minor children, David Lee Malsby and Sebina Malsby, to Gunpowder Monthly Meeting.

1811, 24th of 1st mo. - Certificates requested for John Worthington to Baltimore Monthly Meeting, Western District; George Mason to Baltimore Monthly Meeting, Eastern District; and, Banes Cox to Philadelphia Monthly Meeting.

1811, 21st of 2nd mo. - Certificate requested for Rachel Harlin and her children, Hannah, John, and Matilda, to New Garden Monthly Meeting [Chester County, Pennsylvania]. Deer Creek Preparative Meeting informs that James Norton has joined a militia company.

1811, 25th of 4th mo. - Certificate requested for Joseph Burges and wife Ann, and for John Burges, to Baltimore Monthly Meeting, Eastern District.

1811, 23rd of 5th mo. - Deer Creek Preparative Meeting informs that George Cox has removed to Baltimore Monthly Meeting, Eastern District, without a certificate. Women's Meeting produced a certificate for Martha Tompkins to Baltimore Monthly Meeting, Western District.

1811, 27th of 6th mo. - Certificate received from Gunpowder Monthly Meeting for Luke Tipton, who was received into Fawn Preparative Meeting.

1811, 25th of 7th mo. - Certificate received from London Grove Monthly Meeting [Chester County, Pennsylvania] for John E. Pusey, who was received into Fawn Preparative Meeting. Certificate produced from Baltimore Monthly Meeting, Eastern District, for Richard Dallam, but as from reports it appears his conduct since his return has been in several respects disorderly. Certificate received from New Garden Monthly Meeting [Chester County, Pennsylvania] for Hannah Harmer, a minor, who was received into Deer Creek Preparative Meeting. Fawn Preparative Meeting informs that Eli Kennard requests a certificate for himself, wife Catharine, and four minor children, Joseph Kennard, Betsey Kennard, Hannah Thompson, and David Thompson, to Short Creek Monthly Meeting, Ohio. James Walton requested a certificate for his son James Walton, a minor, to Philadelphia Monthly Meeting.

1811, 26th of 9th mo. - Women's Meeting informs that Susanna Stokes has attended a marriage accomplished contrary to the order established by our society. They also produced a certificate for Sarah Hough to Nottingham Monthly Meeting.

1811, 24th of 10th mo. - Women's Meeting produced certificates for Elizabeth Coale (of Philip) and Mary Perveil to Baltimore Monthly Meeting, Western District. Fawn Preparative Meeting informs that Jehu Thomas, Jr. has accomplished his marriage contrary to the order of our society. They also inform that Enoch Underwood accomplished his marriage with a woman not of our society by the assistance of a hireling teacher. Isaac Smith, son of Isaac and Sarah Smith, and Margaret Coale, dau. of Samuel and Lydia Coale, declared their intentions of marriage, their parents being present.

1811, 28th of 11th mo. - Women's Meeting informs that Ducket Stump requested to be joined in membership with Friends. Fawn Preparative Meeting informs that Silas Bond "was accused with being guilty of addultry which appeared by a woman having proved him the father of her child."

1811, 26th of 12th mo. - Certificate received from London Grove Monthly Meeting [Chester County, Pennsylvania] for Edward Brook. Deer Creek Preparative Meeting informs that Isaac Wilson, son of William, has accomplished his marriage with a woman not in membership with us.

1812, 23rd of 1st mo. - Communication received from Baltimore Monthly Meeting, Eastern District, that Sarah W. Dodrell [also spelled Doddrell] and Sarah Hopkins have requested to be reinstated into membership.

1812, 27th of 2nd mo. - Women's Meeting produced a certificate for Mary McCoy to Baltimore Monthly Meeting, Western District. They also inform that Sarah Hopkins, late Cox, has married her first cousin [no name was given].

1812, 26th of 3rd mo. - Women's Meeting produced a certificate for Margaret Smith to Gunpowder Monthly Meeting. Mordecai Thomas, son of Jehu and Sarah Thomas, and Sarah Pyle, dau. of Amos and Ruth Pyle, declared their intentions of marriage, their parents being present. Fawn Preparative Meeting informs that John Underwood requests a certificate to Baltimore Monthly Meeting, Western District.

1812, 23rd of 4th mo. - Jehu Thomas, Jr. prepared a signed, written statement condemning his misconduct in being married by a Methodist teacher and requested to be continued as a member of Friends. Susanna Stokes, having attended a marriage of a member accomplished contrary to the order established amongst us and not appearing to be in a disposition to condemn her misconduct, is disowned.

1812, 28th of 5th mo. - James Walton, having so far deviated from out testimony against swearing as to administer oaths, also having joined in marriage a couple who were members of our society and first cousins, is disowned. Enoch Underwood, having had his marriage accomplished by the assistance of an hireling teacher to a woman not in membership, is disowned.

1812, 25th of 6th mo. - Certificate received from Indian Spring Monthly Meeting for Thomas Worthington. Deer Creek Preparative Meeting informs that Thomas Wilson is guilty of using profane language.

1812, 23rd of 7th mo. - Women's Meeting informs that Lydia Lewin requests to become a member of our society. Certificates produced from Baltimore Monthly Meeting, Eastern District, for William Haward, wife Mary, and their minor children, Thomas, Rebecca, Hannah, Jacob, and Elizabeth, and also one for Joseph Haward. Certificate produced for Susanna Allen to Baltimore Monthly Meeting, Western District.

1812, 27th of 8th mo. - Certificate requested by Ann Gover for herself and her three minor children, Philip, Priscilla, and Samuel Gover, to Baltimore Monthly Meeting, Eastern District.

1812, 24th of 9th mo. - Samuel Worthington prepared a signed, written statement condemning his misconduct by being married through the aid of a hireling minister. Certificate received from Warrington Monthly Meeting [York County, Pennsylvania] for Susanna Griest. Certificate produced by Women's Meeting for Elizabeth Preveil to Baltimore Monthly Meeting, Eastern District. Deer Creek Preparative Meeting informs that Christopher Wilson requests a certificate for his son Skipwith Wilson, a minor, to Baltimore Monthly Meeting, Eastern District.

1812, 29th of 10th mo. - Deer Creek Preparative Meeting informs that Richard Coale has given so far way to passion as to strike a man. Certificate requested for William E. Coale, a minor, to Baltimore Monthly Meeting, Eastern District. Skipwith Coale is guilty of disreputable converses to a woman.

1812, 26th of 11th mo. - Women's Meeting produced a certificate for Margaret Preveil to Baltimore Monthly Meeting, Western District; also one for Mary Ann Gover to Baltimore Monthly Meeting, Eastern District. Reported that James Orr has taken strong drink to intoxication and has manifested an irritable disposition. Fawn Preparative Meeting informs that Luke Tipton appears to be guilty of fornication. A certificate was granted some time past for George Cox to Baltimore Monthly Meeting, Eastern District, which has not been received by that meeting, and he has since gone out in marriage with a woman not in membership with us.

1813, 25th of 2nd mo. - Certificate requested by Skipwith Coale, wife Ann, and their three minor children, Sarah Smith Coale, Margaret Elgan Coale, and George Mathews Coale, to Nottingham Monthly Meeting. Women's Meeting informs that Susanna Rogers and Priscella Rogers have requested to be reinstated into membership. Certificate received from Gunpowder Monthly Meeting for Isaac Vore, his wife [not named] and their two minor children, Jacob and Mary Vore.

1813, 25th of 3rd mo. - Fawn Preparative Meeting informs that Abel Channel is guilty of taking strong drink to excess and fighting. Certificate produced form Gunpowder Monthly Meeting for Susanna Thomas.

1813, 22nd of 4th mo. - Fawn Preparative Meeting informs that Anthony Kennard is guilty of rioting. He also used bad language and stripped off his clothes to fight, as did Mordecai Thomas. Certificate requested by Peter Perian [later spelled Prine] for himself, his wife Mary, and their three minor children, Mauldin, Mary, and Peter Amos Perian, to Baltimore Monthly Meeting, Eastern District.

1813, 27th of 5th mo. - Thomas Wilson was disowned for using profane language. Deer Creek Preparative Meeting informs that Hermon Pyle requested to become a member of our society.

1813, 24th of 6th mo. - George Cox was disowned for outgoing in marriage to a woman not in membership with us. Deer Creek Preparative Meeting informs that John Dallam has taken strong drink to intoxication. Women's Meeting requested assistance in dealing with Margaret Miller, late Hopkins, who has gone out in marriage with a man not in membership.

1813, 29th of 7th mo. - Priscilla Rogers, a birthright friend, gave a signed, written statement condemning her misconduct in her "departure from the simplicity incucated *[sic]* by the principles of our holy profession..." Abraham Huff requested a certificate for himself, his wife Massey, and their five minor children, Martha, John, Elizabeth, Samuel, and Mary Ann Huff, to Gunpowder Monthly Meeting. Our friend, John Forwood, deceased, in his last will and testament, bequeathed a legacy to this meeting.

1813, 26th of 8th mo. - Richard Coale, having deviated so far as to strike a man in anger, is disowned. Certificate received from Warrington Monthly Meeting [York County, Pennsylvania] for Susanna Underwood.

1813, 23rd of 9th mo. - James Orr, having taken strong drink to intoxication and manifested an irritable disposition, is disowned. Fawn Preparative Meeting informs that Nathaniel Brindle requests to be taken into membership. Women's Meeting produced a certificate for Priscilla Rogers [place not stated]. Rachel Brooks requested to be reinstated into membership.

1813, 28th of 10th mo. - Women's Meeting informs that Hannah Hall, late Stokes, has gone out in marriage. Samuel Coale requested a certificate to Kennet Monthly Meeting [Chester County, Pennsylvania]. Stephen Brown and Achsah Warner declared their intentions of marriage, their parents signified their consent. Thomas Kennard and Elizabeth Metkelf declared their intentions of marriage, their parents being present expressed their consent.

1813, 25th of 11th mo. - Women's Meeting produced a certificate for Ann Warner[?] to Hopewell Monthly Meeting [Frederick County, Virginia].

1813, 23rd of 12th mo. - Certificate produced from Gunpowder Monthly Meeting for Isaac and Margaret Smith. Margaret Miller, having had her marriage accomplished with a man not in membership, is disowned.

1814, 27th of 1st mo. - Certificate received from New York Monthly Meeting for Skipwith Coale, and one from Baltimore Monthly Meeting, Western District, for Joseph Webster. Rachel Brooks, formerly Underwood, gave a signed, written statement that she had been justly disowned and now fully convinced of her error, requested reinstatement. Abel Channel, having taken strong drink to excess and guilty of fighting, is disowned. Mordecai Thomas, having been guilty of using bad language and stripping off his clothes to fight, is disowned.

1814, 24th of 2nd mo. - Women's Meeting produced a certificate for Achsah Brown to Gunpowder Monthly Meeting.

1814, 24th of 3rd mo. - Certificates received from Bradford Monthly Meeting [Chester County, Pennsylvania] for Jacob Valentine and Reuben Valentine; for Charles Jenkins and wife Sarah from Baltimore Monthly Meeting, Western District; and, for Martha Tompkins from that same place. Isaac Turner, of Kent County [later entry indicated Cecil Monthly Meeting], Maryland, and Sarah Massey declared their intentions of marriage, the young woman's parents being present.

1814, 28th of 4th mo. - Deer Creek Preparative Meeting informs that Jonathan Vanhorn and John Quarles request to become members of our society. Women's Meeting informs that Hannah Chew, late Richardson, has accomplished her marriage with a man not in membership by the assistance of a hireling minister.

1814, 26th of 5th mo. - Communication from Baltimore Monthly Meeting, Eastern District, that George Cox has requested to be reinstated into membership. Certificate produced for Susanna Allen from Baltimore Monthly Meeting, Western District.

1814, 23rd of 6th mo. - Edward Brooks has accomplished his marriage with a woman not in membership and also has been fighting and attending the military muster. Certificates requested for Levy Kennard, his wife Ann, and their minor son Levy, and for Thomas Kennard, his wife Elizabeth, and for Moses Medcalf, his wife Susanna, and their eight minor children, Abraham, Mary, Rebecca, Jessy, Joseph, Rachel, Moses, and David, all to Short Creek Monthly Meeting, Ohio.

1814, 28th of 7th mo. - Certificate produced from Baltimore Monthly Meeting, Western District, for Margaret Hill Bradford. Women's Meeting produced certificates for Elizabeth, Mary, and Ann Kennard to Short Creek Monthly Meeting, Ohio.

1814, 25th of 8th mo. - Women's Meeting informs that Elizabeth Whitson "has been guilty of unchaste conduct which appears by her having an illegitimate child" [she was subsequently disowned]. Jacob Vore, Jr. requested a certificate in order to accomplish marriage with Elizabeth Clark, a member of Gunpowder Monthly Meeting.

1814, 27th of 10th mo. - Certificates received from Gunpowder Monthly Meeting for William Pearson, and Enoch Pearson, his wife Susanna, and their four minor children, Rachel, Phebe, Samuel, and Elisha.

1814, 29th of 12th mo. - Anthony Kennard, having been guilty of using bad language and stripping off his clothes to fight, is disowned. Certificate received from Gunpowder Monthly Meeting for Mary Underwood. Deer Creek Preparative Meeting informs that Henry Whitson has had his marriage accomplished contrary to the order established amongst us about 9 years since, and Thomas Whitson has had his marriage accomplished contrary to order about 3 years since, and that from information it appears they both reside in Lancaster County; they are therefore discontinued from being members of our society. Joseph Hopkins has also had his marriage accomplished contrary to our order. John and Lydia Lewin requested that their seven minor children, Sarah, John, William, Ann, Amoss, Mary, and Lydia, be received into membership. Susanna Corse requests her four minor children, William, Cassandra, James, and Elizabeth, be received into membership. Women's Meeting informs that Rachel Lewin, a young woman, requests to become a member amongst us.

1815, 26th of 1st mo. - Edward Brookes, having married a woman not in membership, also fighting and attending military musters, is disowned. Certificate received from Baltimore Monthly Meeting, Eastern District, for Sarah Johnson, wife of James, with her five minor children, John, George, James, Howard, and Ann.

1815, 23rd of 2nd mo. - Hannah Hall, late Stokes, having married a man not in membership with us, is disowned. Certificate received from Gunpowder Monthly Meeting for Elizabeth Vore. Deer Creek Preparative Meeting informs that David G. McCoy requests a certificate to Baltimore Monthly Meeting, Western District.

1815, 23rd of 3rd mo. - Certificate requested for Hannah Walton and her four minor children [not named here, but later listed as Rebecca, John, William, and Hannah Walton] to Fallowfield Monthly Meeting. Joseph H. Coale requested a certificate in order to marry Mary Brinton, a member of Sadsbury Monthly Meeting. Lewis Coale requested a certificate to Pipe Creek Monthly Meeting [Frederick County, Maryland].

1815, 27th of 4th mo. - Deer Creek Preparative Meeting informs that Moses Whitson has deviated so far as to joint the militia and take up arms. Certificate requested for Jacob Vore, Jr. and wife Elizabeth to Gunpowder Monthly Meeting.

1815, 25th of 5th mo. - Communication received from Gunpowder Monthly Meeting regarding whether or not Martha Forwood, who had been disowned from our meeting, could be reinstated into membership there. Deer Creek Preparative Meeting informs that William Cavender requests to become a member of our society.

1815, 22nd of 6th mo. - Women's Meeting informs that Rachel Cavender requests to become a member of our society. They also produced a certificate for Sarah Turner to Ceicil Monthly Meeting. Certificate requested for Mary Whitson and her two minor children, Benjamin and William, to Sadsbury Monthly Meeting. Joseph Webster requested a certificate to Baltimore Monthly Meeting, Eastern District.

1815, 27th of 7th mo. - Deer Creek Preparative Meeting informs that Burt Whitson has joined the militia. Philip Price, a young man from Philadelphia Monthly Meeting (with his parents' consent in writing) and Elizabeth Coale, dau. of Isaac (with her parents being present), declared their intentions of marriage.

1815, 24th of 8th mo. - Certificate received from Sadsbury Monthly Meeting for Mary B. Coale.

1815, 28th of 9th mo. - Women's Meeting informs that Mary Warnick requests to be received into membership with us. Certificate requested for Jonathan Massey to Baltimore Monthly Meeting, Western District.

1815, 26th of 10th mo. - Certificate received from Gunpowder Monthly Meeting for Margary Ady.

1815, 23rd of 11th mo. - Certificate produced by Women's Meeting for Elizabeth C. Price to Arch Street Monthly Meeting, Philadelphia.

1815, 28th of 12th mo. - Deer Creek Preparative Meeting informs that William Pearson has attended the marriage of a member accomplished contrary to our society. Also, Jacob Valentine has "so far deviated as to make a frolick, at which there was fidling and dancing and to partake of the same." Charles Lukins and wife Sarah requested a certificate to Baltimore Monthly Meeting, Western District.

1816, 22nd of 2nd mo. - Moses Whitson gave a signed, written statement condemning his deviation as far as to train in a military way, for which he was sincerely sorry and requests to remain in membership if Friends are willing. Being satisfied, a certificate of removal to Sadsbury Monthly Meeting was ordered prepared for Moses Whitson as requested. Hermon Piles requested a certificate to Little Falls Monthly Meeting. Women's Meeting produced a certificate for Anna Whitson to Sadsbury Monthly Meeting. Thomas Jones and Martha Tompkins declared their intentions of marriage, parents consenting thereto.

1816, 28th of 3rd mo. - John Quarles requested a certificate to Baltimore Monthly Meeting, Eastern District. Reported that Isaac Morris, Jr. has been concerned in a lottery and follows the distilling business. Certificate received from Monallen Monthly Meeting [Adams County, Pennsylvania] for Susanna Underwood.

1816, 25th of 4th mo. - Certificate requested for John Underwood, wife Mary, and their minor child Ann, to Baltimore Monthly Meeting, Eastern District. Certificate received from Warrington Monthly Meeting [York County, Pennsylvania] for Elisha Cook, wife Lydia, and their five minor children, George, P. William, M. Louisa, Joel, and Nathan Cook; also one from Pipe Creek Monthly Meeting [Frederick County, Maryland] for Lewis Coale. Thomas Worthington and Mary Husband declared their intentions of marriage, parents present consented thereto.

1816, 25th of 5th mo. - Certificate received from Little Falls Monthly Meeting for Jacob Vore and wife Elizabeth, and also one for Michael Harlon from New Garden Monthly Meeting [Chester County, Pennsylvania].

1816, 27th of 6th mo. - Women's Meeting produced a certificate for Mary Dallum to Baltimore Monthly Meeting, Eastern District. Deer Creek Preparative Meeting informs that Enoch Pearson has taken strong drink to intoxication. Certificate requested for Thomas Coale, a minor, to Baltimore Monthly Meeting, Eastern District.

1816, 25th of 7th mo. - Certificate received from Little Falls Monthly Meeting for Stephen Brown, wife Achsah, and their minor child William Brown. Fawn Preparative Meeting informs that Richard Webb, Jr. has gone out in marriage to a woman not in membership with us by the assistance of a Methodist minister. William Coale requested a certificate to Sadsbury Monthly Meeting in order to accomplish his marriage with Lydia Brinton, a member of that meeting.

1816, 29th of 8th mo. - Amos Piles requested a certificate for his minor son John Piles to London Grove Monthly Meeting [Chester County, Pennsylvania]. Women's Meeting produced a certificate for Phebe Pearson, a minor, to Baltimore Monthly Meeting, Western District.

1816, 28th of 9th mo. - Fawn Preparative Meeting informs that Isaac Thomas has married his first cousin [and he was subsequently disowned]. Reuben Valentine requests a certificate to Centre Monthly Meeting [Centre County], Pennsylvania.

1816, 28th of 11th mo. - Women's Meeting informs that Rachel Amos, late Pearson, has gone out in marriage and been guilty of other breaches of our discipline. Isaac Morris, Jr., having so far deviated as to have part in a lottery and practice the distillation of grain, is disowned.

1817, 6th of 1st mo. - Certificates received for David Jordan from Western Branch Monthly Meeting, Isle of Wight County, Virginia; for Joseph D, Parsons from Little Falls Monthly Meeting; and, for Elizabeth D. Parsons, from that same meeting. Certificate requested for George Valentine to Centre Monthly Meeting, Centre County, Pennsylvania, and Skipwith Coale to Baltimore Monthly Meeting, Western District.

1817, 3rd of 3rd mo. - Women's Meeting informs that Rachel Amos, late Pearson, having gone out in marriage, is disowned.

1817, 7th of 4th mo. - Communication from Plymouth Monthly Meeting, Ohio, informs that Ann Way, formerly of our meeting, has applied for reinstatement. Women's Meeting informs that Hannah Hall has also applied for reinstatement. Susanna Underwood had declined Friends and joined the Methodist society.

1817, 5th of 5th mo. - William Worthington and Hannah Coale declared their intentions of marriage.

1817, 2nd of 6th mo. - Samuel Hopkins (of Joseph) requested a certificate for his son John Hopkins to Baltimore Monthly Meeting, Western District. Lewis Coale requested a certificate to Fairfax Monthly Meeting [Loudoun County], Virginia.

Isaac Channell has accomplished his marriage with a woman not in membership with us. Women's Meeting produced a certificate for Susanna Brinton to Sadsbury Monthly Meeting.

1817, 7th of 7th mo. - Hannah Hall gave a signed, written statement condemning her misconduct for outgoing in marriage.

1817, 4th of 8th mo. - Women's Meeting produced certificates for Margary Ady to Baltimore Monthly Meeting, Western District, and for Mary Hopkins and Rebecca Hayward to Nine Partners Monthly Meeting, New York [State].

1817, 3rd of 11th mo. - Isaac Channell, having married a woman not in membership with us, is disowned.

1817, 1st of 12th mo. - Yearsley Jones produced a certificate from Baltimore Monthly Meeting, Eastern District, regarding his to proceeding to marriage to Susanna Underwood, and with his father's consent. Women's Meeting informs that Susanna Allen requests her three minor children, Sarah T., Susanna Jane, and Rachel T. Allen, be received into membership.

1818, 2nd of 2nd mo. - Women's Meeting informs that Priscilla Tipton requests to be received into membership.

1818, 2nd of 3rd mo. - Certificate received from Gunpowder Monthly Meeting for Phebe Clarke. Certificate granted to Skipwith Coale to Baltimore Monthly Meeting, Western District, was returned with information that he had married a woman not in membership by the assistance of a hireling teacher.

1818, 5th of 4th mo. - Certificate produced by women friends for Susanna Jones to Baltimore Monthly Meeting, Eastern District.

1818, 1st of 6th mo. - Women's Meeting informs that Mary Webb requests to be received into membership. Christopher Wilson, Jr. requests a certificate to Baltimore Monthly Meeting, Eastern District.

1818, 6th of 7th mo. - Isaac Hammer made a religious visit to our meeting from New Hope Monthly Meeting, Tennessee. Certificates received for James Gillingham, wife Sarah, and their five minor children, Elizabeth, Anna, Phebe, Samuel, and Charles Gillingham, from Frankford Monthly Meeting; for Joseph M. Downing, wife Mary Ann, and their two minor children, Sarah E. and William M. Downing, from Falls Monthly Meeting; for Jesse Hartley, wife Mary, and their three minor children, Rachel, William, and Edwin Hartley, from Muncy Monthly

Meeting; and, for Philip Coale from Green Street Monthly Meeting, Philadelphia. Certificates requested to White Water Monthly Meeting, Indiana, for Jacob Vore and wife Mary; for Isaac Vore, wife Ruth, and their four minor children, Jacob, Mary, Eliza, and Ruth Vore; for Jacob Vore, Jr., wife Elizabeth, and their two minor children, Israel C. and Anna Vore; and, another for John Vore. Christopher Wilson has been guilty of arming himself with firearms in order to arrest a man and of using profane language. Women's Meeting produced a certificate for Sarah Jenny to Baltimore Monthly Meeting, Eastern District.

1818, 7th of 12th mo. - Women's Meeting informs that Elizabeth Parsons has been guilty of a breach of chastity which appears by her becoming a mother in an unmarried state. Jane Warnock requests to become a member of our society.

1819, 1st of 2nd mo. - Certificate requested for William Scotten, wife Jane, and their minor son Joshua, to Little Britain Monthly Meeting. Richard Webb, Jr. and wife Mary request their two minor children, Tace and John Webb, be received into membership.

1819, 1st of 3rd mo. - Deer Creek Preparative Meeting informs that Isaiah Cooper has accomplished his marriage with a woman not in membership by the assistance of a hireling teacher.

1819, 5th of 4th mo. - Women's Meeting produced a certificate for Ganer Parsons to Smithfield Monthly Meeting, Jefferson County, Ohio. Certificate granted to Mary Hopkins for Nine Partners Monthly Meeting, New York [State], was returned with information that it was not their practice to accept certificates for those who enter the boarding school.

1819, 7th of 6th mo. - Luke Tipton and wife [not named] requested their five minor children, David, Mary, Esther, Rachel, and Abigail Tipton, be received into membership. Women's Meeting produced a certificate for Mary Malsby to Baltimore Monthly Meeting, Western District. Certificate requested for Ellis P. Coale, a minor, to Nottingham Monthly Meeting.

1819, 5th of 7th mo. - Women's Meeting informs that Ann Pearson, late Jay, has accomplished her marriage contrary to our good order. Fawn Preparative Meeting informs that Thomas Jones has paid a fine for not attending military service when drafted.

1819, 2nd of 8th mo. - Women's Meeting informs that Susanna Dutton requests to be joined in membership.

1819, 6th of 9th mo. - Hugh Dever requested to become a member of our society. Certificate requested for Mordecai Underwood, a minor, to Baltimore Monthly Meeting, Western District.

1819, 1st of 11th mo. - Women's Meeting informs that Isabella Stephenson, late Carter, has been guilty of inchastity.

1819, 4th of 12th mo. - Certificate received from Baltimore Monthly Meeting, Western District, for Aquilla Massey. Information received that John Tompkins has voted for a militia officer and attended places of diversion.

1820, 3rd of 1st mo. - Certificate granted some time past for Mary Malsby to Baltimore Monthly Meeting, Western District, was returned, she having removed within the limits of another meeting. Women's Meeting informs that Matilda Coil, late Scotten, has gone out in marriage to a man not in membership and for which they recommend disownment. Deer Creek Preparative Meeting informs that Enoch Pearson had his marriage accomplished contrary to our good order and has also been guilty of quarreling and fighting.

1820, 7th of 2nd mo. - Thomas E. Warner requested a certificate to Redstone Monthly Meeting [Fayette County], Pennsylvania.

1820, 6th of 3rd mo. - Women's Meeting produced a certificate for Mary Malsby to Little Falls Monthly Meeting. Mary E. Rogers requests to be joined in membership with Friends.

1820, 3rd of 4th mo. - Certificate received from Baltimore Monthly Meeting, Western District, recommending Mary Mifflin as a member and minister, and she was received. Women's Meeting informs that Susan Wilson had married a man not in membership with us. Certificate received from Little Falls Monthly Meeting for Sarah McComas and her two minor children, Cassandra and James Howard McComas.

1820, 1st of 5th mo. - Communication received from Sadsbury Monthly Meeting that they had visited William Pearson and he did not appear in a capacity to condemn his misconduct. Women's Meeting informs that William and Hannah Worthington requested for their four minor children, Hannah, Priscilla, Susanna, and Anna, be received into membership. Daniel Piles appears to be guilty of fornication by a woman charging him with being the father of an illegitimate child.

1820, 5th of 6th mo. - Certificate produced for Sarah Morris to Little Falls Monthly Meeting. Sarah John requested a certificate for herself and five minor children, James, George, Howard, Ann, and Lemuel, to Little Falls Monthly Meeting.

1820, 3rd of 7th mo. - Information received that David [Daniel?] Piles resides within the verge of London Grove Monthly Meeting [Chester County, Pennsylvania]. [Note: Later minutes state the case of Daniel Piles was continued while other entries state the case of David Piles was continued. His first name appears to have been confused by the clerk at various meetings. The name appears to be Daniel, rather than David, Piles].

1820, 7th of 8th mo. - Fawn Preparative Meeting informs that Rice J. Hall requests to be received into membership. Communication received from Uchland Monthly Meeting requesting us to treat with Enoch Pearson on their behalf. Anthony P. Morriss, son of Isaac and Sarah Morriss, and Ann Husband, dau. of Joshua and Margaret Husband, declared their intentions of marriage, the parents being present consented.

1820, 2nd of 10th mo. - Certificate received from Little Britain Monthly Meeting for Joseph Kent. Certificate requested for Thomas Sharp to Sadsbury Monthly Meeting. Communication received from Sadsbury Monthly Meeting that they not think that Mary Hinsel [also spelled Hensil] did not make satisfaction for her outgoing in marriage. Certificate requested by Thomas Sharp for Sadsbury Monthly Meeting.

1820, 6th of 11th mo. - Communication received from Concord Monthly Meeting [Belmont County, Ohio] that Isaiah Ely had married his first cousin.

1820, 4th of 12th mo. - Certificate received from Bolton Monthly Meeting, Massachusetts for Theodate Pope.

1821, 5th of 2nd mo. - Women's Meeting produced a certificate for Anna Morris to Philadelphia Monthly Meeting, Southern District. Rachel Thomas has so far deviated as to become a mother in an unmarried state.

1821, 5th of 3rd mo. - David Jorden requested a certificate to Baltimore Monthly Meeting, Western District. Fawn Preparative Meeting informs that Nathaniel Brindly has married his first cousin and is therefore no longer member.

1821, 2nd of 4th mo. - Joseph Hayward has been guilty of fornication. Certificate requested for Joseph M. Downing, wife Mary Ann, and their three minor children, Sarah E., William M., and Joseph Warner Downing, to Middle Town Monthly

Meeting, Pennsylvania. Joel Carter requested a certificate for himself and eight minor children, John, Samuel, Joel, Edith, Enos, Levi, Margaret, and James Carter, to Little Falls Monthly Meeting. William and Rachel Cavender requested their five minor children, Abram Widner, Mary, Margaret, Rachel, and Leah, be received into membership.

1821, 6th of 8th mo. - Certificate received from Little Britain Monthly Meeting for William Scotten and wife Jane.

1821, 3rd of 8th mo. - Samuel Worthington requested that his five minor children, Elizabeth, Thomas, Henry, Priscilla, and William, be received into membership.

1821, 1st of 10th mo. - Certificate received from Little Falls Monthly Meeting for Mary Malsby. Samuel Cox requested a certificate to Duck Creek Monthly Meeting [Kent County, Delaware] in order to marry Elizabeth Carroll, a member of that meeting.

1822, 7th of 1st mo. - Certificate received from Baltimore Monthly Meeting, Western District, for Susanna Allen.

1822, 4th of 2nd mo. - John Harmer, son of Abraham and Hannah Harmer (the latter deceased), and Catherine Cooper, dau. of Nicholas and Sarah Cooper, declared their intentions of marriage, parents being present consented.

1822, 4th of 3rd mo. - Nicholas Cooper and wife Sarah requested a certificate for themselves and their six minor children, Nicholas, Priscilla, Esther, Ely B., Margaret, and Gulielma Cooper, to Little Falls Monthly Meeting.

1822, 1st of 4th mo. - Women's Meeting produced a certificate for Elizabeth, Martha Anna, and Sarah Cooper to Little Falls Monthly Meeting.

1822, 6th of 5th mo. - Certificate requested for Jacob Ely to Little Falls Monthly Meeting in order to marry Elizabeth Cooper, a member of that meeting.

1822, 3rd of 6th mo. - Sarah McComas requested a certificate for herself and two minor children, Cassandra and James Howard McComas, to Little Falls Monthly Meeting.

1822, 11th of 7th mo. - Certificate received from Little Falls Monthly Meeting for Abram Hugg, wife Mary, and their eight minor children [not named]; also one for Martha Huff from that same meeting. Certificate received from Cecil Monthly Meeting [Kent County, Maryland] for Elizabeth Cox.

1822, 15th of 8th mo. - A proposal of marriage by John Jones, son of Isac and Elizabeth Jones, and Deborah Tompkins, dau. of John and Sarah Tompkins, was offered to this meeting for its approbation. It was orderly accomplished and reported to the subsequent meeting.

1822, 12th of 12th mo. - Women's Meeting informs that there is no obstruction to Rachel Cox proceeding in marriage with Oliver Caulk. Luke Tipton requested a certificate for himself, wife Priscilla, and their eight minor children, David, Mary, Esther, Rachel, Abijah, Elihu, John, and Hannah, to Smithfield Monthly Meeting, Ohio. Fawn Preparative Meeting informs that Benjamin Tompkins has gone out in marriage with a woman not in membership with us. Certificate received from Wilmington Monthly Meeting for William Corse recommending him to our meeting, but he lives in the limits of Little Falls Monthly Meeting.

1823, 15th of 1st mo. - Women's Meeting informs that Anna ---- [illegible], late Coal, had her marriage accomplished with a man not of our society. [Later entry gives her name as Anna Brunnon]. Certificate produced for Mary John to Carmel Monthly Meeting, Columbiana County, Ohio.

1823, 13th of 2nd mo. - Fawn Preparative Meeting informs that Jonathan Atkins requests to be received into membership. Isaac Stubbs is complained of for not complying with a contract.

1823, 13th of 3rd mo. - Certificate requested for Enoch Gray, a minor, to New Garden Monthly Meeting [Chester County, Pennsylvania].

1823, 17th of 4th mo. - Certificates requested for Joseph Pyle, a minor, to Little Britain Monthly Meeting, and for Amos Pyle, a minor, to London Grove Monthly Meeting [Chester County, Pennsylvania]. A proposal of marriage by Elisha Cook and Elizabeth Worthington was presented to this meeting for its approbation. They were subsequently married before the next meeting. Women's Meeting informs that Mary Jones has been guilty of unchastity.

1823, 12th of 6th mo. - Certificate received from Baltimore Monthly Meeting, Western District, for George Mason.

1823, 14th of 8th mo. - Women's Meeting produced a certificate from Little Falls Monthly Meeting for Hannah Stump.

1823, 16th of 9th mo. - Committee reported that the marriage of Ezra Gillingham and Mary C. Coale had been orderly accomplished. Women's Meeting informs that Mary Atkinson *[sic]*, wife of Jonathan Atkins *[sic]*, requests to be received into membership. Certificates received from women's meeting for Oppu[?] Pyles *[sic]* to London Grove Monthly Meeting [Chester County, Pennsylvania], and Ruth Ann Pyle *[sic]* to Nottingham Monthly Meeting [Cecil County, Maryland], and Phebe Pyle to Little Britain Monthly Meeting [Lancaster County, Pennsylvania].

1823, 16th of 10th mo. - Certificate received from Baltimore Monthly Meeting, Western District, for Sarah W. Dodrell.

1823, 13th of 11th mo. - Jonathan and Mary Atkins requested their two minor children, Joseph and Elizabeth, be received into membership. Certificate received from Baltimore Monthly Meeting, Western District, for Folger Pope, wife Ann, and their five minor children, Franklin F., Joseph D., Sarah R., Theodate, and William R. Pope.

1824, 12th of 2nd mo. - Certificate received from Baltimore Monthly Meeting, Western District, for James C. Doddrell. Certificate requested by Asa Jones to Baltimore Monthly Meeting, Western District, in order to marry with Hannah Riley, a member of that meeting.

1824, 11th of 3rd mo. - Joseph Kent requested a certificate to Warrington Monthly Meeting in order to marry with Maria J. Cook, a member of that meeting.

1824, 15th of 4th mo. - Joseph Kent requested a certificate of removal to Fallowfield Monthly Meeting, Pennsylvania.

1824, 13th of 5th mo. - Certificate requested for William Coars, a minor, to Wilmington Monthly Meeting. Women's Meeting informs that Rachel Harland requested to become a member of our society.

1824, 17th of 6th mo. - Certificate received from Nottingham Monthly Meeting for William Rickman. Certificate requested for John Lewin, wife [not named], and minor children, William, Ann, Amos, Mary, and Lydia Lewin, to Little Falls Monthly Meeting.

1824, 15th of 7th mo. - Women's Meeting produced a certificate for Mary C. Gillingham to Baltimore Monthly Meeting, Western District.

1824, 12th of 8th mo. - Folger Pope, who has been disunited from membership by the monthly meeting of friends at Bolton in State of Massachusetts and County of Worcester, requests to be reinstated. Jesse Hartly and wife Mary requested a certificate for themselves and six minor children, Rachel, William, Edwin, Joseph, Jesse, and Thomas Hartly, to Hartland Monthly Meeting, Niagara County, New

York. Certificate received from Baltimore Monthly Meeting, Western District, for Hanna Jones. Ely Garretson, son of Cornelius and Hannah Garretson, and Anna Massey, dau. of Isaac and Margaret Massey, declared their intentions of marriage.

1824, 16th of 9th mo. - Ely Garretson received a certificate from Baltimore Monthly Meeting, Western District, that no obstruction appears to his marriage with Ann Massy. Women's Meeting produced a certificate to Duck Creek Monthly Meeting [Kent County, Delaware] for Rachel Caulk. Certificate requested by George Mason for Nottingham Monthly Meeting.

1824, 14th of 10th mo. - Deer Creek Preparative Meeting informs that John Wilson has accomplished his marriage contrary to our order. Joshua Matthews, son of Thomas and Ann Matthews, and Mary Hopkins, dau. of Samuel and Sarah Hopkins, declared their intentions of marriage.

1824, 11th of 11th mo. - Ely Bond, having deviated from the path of rectitude as to be guilty of fornication, is disowned. Certificate requested for Elisha Pearson, a minor, to Baltimore Monthly Meeting, Western District. Baltimore Monthly Meeting requests this meeting to treat with Christopher Wilson, Jr. on account of his outgoing in marriage.

1824, 12th of 12th mo. - Women's Meeting informs that Elizabeth Hayley should be disunited for outgoing in marriage. They also produced a certificate for Anna Garitson to Baltimore Monthly Meeting.

1825, 17th of 2nd mo. - John Wilson, having married a woman not in membership with us, is disowned. John Lewin, Jr. requested a certificate to removed his membership to Little Falls Monthly Meeting.

1825, 12th of 5th mo. - Folger Pope, Sr. was shown the communication from Bolton Monthly Meeting about him [see minutes on 12th of 8th mo., 1824].

1825, 16th of 6th mo. - Samuel Worthington proposed for clerk and Folger Pope for assistant clerk.

1825, 14th of 7th mo. - Certificate requested for Ele *[sic]* Bond, a minor, to Stillwater Monthly Meeting, Ohio. Elizabeth Hayley [also spelled Haley], late Warner, having accomplished her marriage contrary to our good order, is disowned. Women's Meeting informs that Sarah G. Husband has in her possession coloured people whose freedom is not secured and she is remiss in the attendance of meetings.

1825, 13th of 10th mo. - William Rickman requested a certificate to New Garden Monthly Meeting [Chester County], Pennsylvania.

## DEER CREEK MONTHLY MEETING (ORTHODOX), DARLINGTON HARFORD COUNTY, BIRTHS OF MEMBERS, 1801-1825

[It should be noted that the following information about members who were born between 1801 and 1825 was gleaned from the membership rosters as they were recorded in subsequent years.]

Joseph Edge, son of George and Sarah Edge, b. 15th of 5th mo., 1814.

Mary S. Edge (neé Smith), dau. of John D. and Elizabeth Smith, b. 15th of 12th mo., 1819.

Children of Samuel and Rachel Hopkins:
    Priscilla W. Hopkins, b. 9th of 7th mo., 1801.
    Joseph Hopkins, b. 13th of 11th mo., 1804.
    Henry W. Hopkins, b. 4th of 2nd mo., 1807.
    Eliza Hopkins, b. 12th of 4th mo., 1809.
    Charles W. Hopkins, b. 21st of 6th mo., 1811.
    Wilson W. Hopkins, b. 17th of 9th mo., 1818.
    Anna W. Hopkins, b. ---- [blank], 1822.

Thomas King, son of Joseph and Tacy King, b. 19th of 8th mo., 1820 in Baltimore, Maryland.

Rebecca Worthington, b. 13th of 1st mo., 1818.

## DEER CREEK MONTHLY MEETING (ORTHODOX) DARLINGTON, MARYLAND AND FAWN GROVE, PENNSYLVANIA ABSTRACTS FROM THE MINUTES, 1819-1825

1819, 1st of 3rd mo. - Meeting held at Fawn Grove. Certificate produced for William Scotten, his wife Jane, and their son Joshua. Request by Richard Webb, Jr. and wife [unnamed] for their two minor children, Tace and John, to be received in membership. Deer Creek Preparative Meeting informs that Isaiah Cooper accomplished his marriage to a woman not in membership with the assistance of a hireling teacher.

145

1819, 5th of 4th mo. - Christopher Wilson's case, in which he was charged with arming himself with firearms, was continued. Women Friends produced a certificate for Ganor Parsons to Smithfield Monthly Meeting in Jefferson County, Ohio. Certificate granted for Mary Hopkins dated 4th of 8th mo., 1817 to Nine Partners Monthly Meeting, State of New York, was returned endorsed by the Superintendent of Nine Partners School with information that it was not the practice of said meeting to accept certificates for those who enter the boarding school.

1819, 3rd of 5th mo. - Christopher Wilson made use of profane language and provided himself with firearms in order to arrest a man, and since he is not willing to make satisfaction, is disowned [recorded in the minutes on 2nd of 8th mo., 1819].

1819, 7th of 6th mo. - Meeting held at Fawn Grove. Luke Tipton and wife [unnamed] requested their five minor children, David, Mary, Esther, Rachel and Abijah, be received into membership. Certificate produced for Mary Malsby to Baltimore Monthly Meeting for the Western District. Certificate requested for Ellis Pusey Coale, a minor, to Nottingham Monthly Meeting.

1819, 5th of 7th mo. - Women Friends report that Ann Pearson (late Jay) accomplished her marriage contrary to our good order and on treating with her she manifested an inclination to make satisfaction. Fawn Preparative Meeting reported that Thomas Jones paid a fine for not attending military service when draughted. Susanna Jewitt was given permission to visit families of Friends constituting Fawn Preparative Meeting, with Samuel Coale and Joshua Husband to accompany her.

1819, 2nd of 8th mo. - William Cavender, John Jewitt, Joseph Strawbridge, and Thomas Worthington were appointed representatives to the Quarterly Meeting. Susanna Dutton requested to be joined in membership. Abraham Hebberd produced a certificate from Goshen Monthly Meeting in Chester County, Pennsylvania, endorsed by Concord Quarterly Meeting. Isaiah Cooper, earlier disowned for outgoing in marriage, was now recorded in the minutes.

1819, 6th of 9th mo. - Hugh Dever requested to become a member. Certificate requested for Mordecai Underwood, a minor, to Baltimore Monthly Meeting for the Western District.

1819, 4th of 10th mo. - Thomas Jones apologized for paying a draught fine and promised to live more circumspectly in the future. Certificate granted to Rebecca Hayward, a minor, to Nine Partners Monthly Meeting [New York State] was returned as it was not their practice to receive certificates for those entering boarding school.

1819, 1st of 11th mo. - Women Friends requested help from men Friends in the case of Isabella Stevenson (late Carter) who has been guilty of inchastity. Sadsbury Monthly Meeting reported that William Pearson, a member of this meeting, had resided for some time within their limits and has lately gone out in marriage with a woman not in membership with Friends. William Ely, Samuel Coale, Samuel Worthington, and Asa Jones were appointed representatives to the Quarterly Meeting.

1819, 6th of 12th mo. - Meeting held at Fawn Grove. Four dollars due Jeremiah Brown for a book for recording the minutes of our Quarterly Meeting. Certificate received from Baltimore Monthly Meeting for Aquila Massey. Information received that John Tomkins has voted for a militia officer and attended places of diversion.

1820, 3rd of 1st mo. - Certificate granted some time past for Mary Malsby to Baltimore Monthly Meeting was returned as she has removed within the verge of another meeting [name was not stated at the time, but it was later indicated to be Little Falls Monthly Meeting]. Women Friends report that Matilda Coil (late Scotten) had gone out in marriage with a person not a member, and they recommend she be disowned. Deer Creek Preparative Meeting informs that Enock Pearson has accomplished his marriage contrary to the good order and has also been guilty of quarrelling and fighting; on inquiry, it appears he is a member of Uwchlan Monthly Meeting [Chester County, Pennsylvania].

1820, 7th of 2nd mo. - Isaac Coale, Elisha Cooke, Asa Jones, and David Malsby were appointed representatives to the Quarterly Meeting. Friends appointed to visit Silas Bond and judge his sincerity and capacity to make satisfaction [nature of case was not stated]. Women Friends report that Mary C. Stump and Elizabeth Stump requested to be received into membership. James Gillingham requested a certificate for himself, his wife Sarah, and their three minor children, Phebe, Samuel, and Charles [destination was not stated at the time, but later indicated to be Baltimore Monthly Meeting]. Thomas W. Warner having removed within the verge of Redstone Monthly Meeting [Fayette County], Pennsylvania, requested a certificate to become a member thereof.

1820, 6th of 3rd mo. - Meeting held at Fawn Grove. Women Friends inform that Mary C. Rogers requested to be joined in membership.

1820, 3rd of 4th mo. - Women Friends produced a certificate to Baltimore Monthly Meeting for the Western District for Anna Gillingham. Certificate received from Baltimore Monthly Meeting for the Western District for Mary Mifflin recommending her a minister in good esteem and she was received a member of our meeting. Women Friends inform that Susan Wilson had accomplished her marriage with a man not in membership. Certificate received from Little Falls Monthly Meeting for Sarah McComas and her two minor children, Cassandra and James Howard McComas.

1820, 1st of 5th mo. - Mary Hensil (late Norton) has gone out in her marriage to a man not in membership and is now residing in Lancaster; Sadsbury Monthly Meeting will be contacted in this matter. Women Friends report that William and Hannah Worthington have requested their four minor children, Hannah, Priscilla, Susannah, and Anna, be received into membership. Certificate received from Baltimore Monthly Meeting for the Western District for Mary Cooper. Daniel Piles appears to have been guilty of fornication from a woman charging him to be the father of her illegitimate child. Ann Pearson was disowned for having accomplished her marriage contrary to the good order.

1820, 5th of 6th mo. - Meeting held at Fawn Grove. Deer Creek Monthly Meeting sent a letter to Sadsbury Monthly Meeting informing them that William Pearson had deviated from our principles so far as to marriage a woman not in membership and he was therefore disowned. Women Friends produced a certificate for Sarah Morris to Little Falls Monthly Meeting. Sarah Johnson requested a certificate for herself and five minor children, James, George, Howard, Ann, and Lemuel, to Little Falls Monthly Meeting.

1820, 7th of 8th mo. - William Ely, Samuel Worthington, John Lewin, and John Sharp were appointed representatives to the Quarterly Meeting. Fawn Preparative Meeting informs that Rice Johnson Hall requested to be taken into membership. Anthony P. Morris, son of Isaac W. Morris and Sarah his wife, and Anna Husband, daughter of Joshua and Margaret Husband, declared their intention to marry, he having produced a certificate from the Philadelphia Monthly Meeting for the Southern District.

1820, 4th of 9th mo. - Meeting held at Fawn Grove. Women Friends inform that Sarah Worthington requested to be received into membership.

1820, 2nd of 10th mo. - The marriage of Anthony P. Morris and Anna Husband had been orderly accomplished. Thomas Worthington was appointed clerk and James Coale assistant clerk. Certificate was received from Little Britain Monthly Meeting recommending Joseph Kent a member. Certificate was requested by

Thomas Sharp to Sadsbury Monthly Meeting. Our beloved friend William Forster attended our meeting and produced a certificate from the monthly meeting at Shaftsbury and Sherborne dated 12th of 4th mo., 1819, and endorsed by the Quarterly Meeting at Dorset and Hanys in Great Britain, and one from the Yearly Meeting of Ministers and Elders held in London by adjournments on the 17th, 19th, and 29th of 5th mo., 1819.

1820, 6th of 11th mo. - Meeting held at Deer Creek. Informed by Concord Monthly Meeting [Belmont County], Ohio, that Isaiah Ely had accomplished his marriage with Elizabeth Kennard, a first cousin. Certificate received from New Garden Monthly Meeting [Chester County, Pennsylvania] recommending Enock Sewell Gray, a member in his minority, to the care of Deer Creek Monthly Meeting.

1820, 4th of 12th mo. - Meeting held at Fawn Grove. Certificate received from Bolton Monthly Meeting in Massachusetts recommending Theodate Pope as a member of Deer Creek Monthly Meeting. Informed by Fawn Preparative Meeting that John Tompkins has been guilty of striking a man in anger and of profane swearing.

1821, 1st of 1st mo. - Isaiah Ely was disowned for outgoing in marriage to his first cousin [not named].

1821, 5th of 2nd mo. - Certificate produced for Anna Morris to the Philadelphia Monthly Meeting, Southern District. Informed by women's meeting that Rachel Thomas has so far deviated from what is right as to become a mother in an unmarried state.

1821, 5th of 3rd mo. - Rachel Thomas was disowned for having an illegitimate child. Certificate requested by David Jourdan to be joined to Baltimore Monthly Meeting, Western District. Fawn Preparative Meeting informs that Nathaniel Brindley has married his first cousin and is therefore no longer considered a member. Certificate produced for Susanna Dutton to Baltimore Monthly Meeting, Western District. Matilda Coil (late Scotten) has gone out in marriage with a man not of our society and accomplished by the assistance of a magistrate contrary to the good order and is therefore disowned. Susanna Wilson has gone out in marriage with a man not in membership and is disowned.

1821, 2nd of 4th mo. - Joseph Hayward has been found guilty of fornication. Certificate requested for Joseph M. and Mary Ann Downing and their 3 minor children, Sarah E., William E., and Joseph Warner Downing, to Middletown Monthly Meeting in Pennsylvania. Certificate requested for Joel Carter and 8 minor children, John, Samuel, Joel, Edith, Enos, Levi, Margaret, and James, to Little Falls

Monthly Meeting. William and Rachel Cavender requested their 5 minor children, Abram Widner, Mary, Margaret, Rachel, and Leah, be received into membership.

1821, 7th of 5th mo. - Certificate received from Little Falls Monthly Meeting for Sarah Hutton and her 4 minor children [unnamed]. Certificates were handed in by women Friends for Sarah and Hannah Carter. Joseph Husband, an esteemed elder, proposed accompanying James Coburn, a minister of Nottingham Monthly Meeting, in a religious visit to the different meeting constituting the Yearly Meeting of Baltimore, which was approved.

1821, 4th of 6th mo. - Informed that Daniel Piles has taken up residence within the compass of London Grove Monthly Meeting [Chester County, Pennsylvania]. Subsequent minutes state he was charged with being guilty of fornication from a woman who named him as the father of her illegitimate child. He was found not to be in a state of mind suitably to condemn it.

1821, 6th of 8th mo. - Certificate received from Little Brittian Monthly Meeting for William Scotten and wife Jane.

1821, 3rd of 9th mo. - John Tompkins was disowned for striking a man in anger and using profane swearing. Joseph Hayward was disowned for fornication. Samuel Worthington requested that his 5 minor children, Elizabeth, Thomas, Henry, Priscilla, and William, be taken into membership.

1821, 1st of 10th mo. - Daniel Piles was disowned for fornication. Certificate received from Little Falls Monthly Meeting recommending Mary Malsby as a member of Fawn Preparative Meeting. Samuel Cox requested a certificate to Duck Creek Monthly Meeting [Kent County, Delaware] in order to marry Elizabeth Cork [also spelled Caulk].

1821, 5th of 11th mo. - Sarah Warner had been recommended as a minister and, after a time of solid deliberation, it was united with.

1822, 7th of 1st mo. - Reported that relief has been granted to Sarah Hutton and children [unnamed] in the amount of $9.60, plus payment to the schoolmaster for her children's schooling in the amount of $11.53, and she stands in need of further assistance. Certificate received from Baltimore Monthly Meeting, Western District, for Susanna Allen and was accepted. Request from Friends on south side of Deer Creek for the indulgence of a meeting for the winter season to be held at Green Spring School House on the 1st and 4th days of the week, was granted.

1822, 4th of 2nd mo. - John Harmor, son of Abram and Hannah Harmor, the latter deceased, and P---- [blank] Cooper, dau. of Nicholas and Sarah Cooper, declared their intention to marry, the consent of their parents being obtained.

1822, 4th of 3rd mo. - Nicholas Cooper and wife Sarah requested certificates for themselves and their 6 minor children, Nicholas, Priscilla, Esther, Ely B., Margaret, and Gulielma, to Little Falls Monthly Meeting.

1822, 1st of 4th mo. - The marriage of John Harmor and Parthenia Cooper was reported accomplished orderly. Women Friends produced a certificate for Elizabeth, Martha, Anna, and Sarah Cooper to Little Falls Monthly Meeting.

1822, 6th of 5th mo. - Certificate requested for Jacob Ely to Little Falls Monthly Meeting in order to marry Elizabeth Cooper.

1822, 3rd of 6th mo. - Sarah McComas requested a certificate for herself and 2 minor children, Cassandra and James Howard McComas, to ----- [not stated].

1822, 11th of 7th mo. - Certificate received from Little Falls Monthly Meeting recommending Abraham Huff and wife and 8 minor children [unnamed] be considered members. Certificates received for Martha Huff from Little Falls Monthly Meeting and Elizabeth Cox from Cecil Monthly Meeting [Kent County, Maryland].

1822, 15th of 8th mo. - Proposal of marriage by John Jones, son of Isaac and Elizabeth Jones, and Deborah Tomkins, dau. of John and Sarah Tomkins, received by this meeting and pending clearness from other engagements.

1822, 12th of 9th mo. - Parents of John Jones and Deborah Tomkins gave their consent to their marriage.

1822, 17th of 10th mo. - Reported that the marriage of John Jones and Deborah Tomkins had been orderly accomplished. The certificate granted to Reuben Valentine some time age had miscarried and the recorder was directed to forward a copy of the certificate [place not stated].

1822, 14th of 11th mo. - Elizabeth Coale was recommended as a minister, which was united with. Stephen Brown, William Coale, Asa Jones, and Asaph Warner were appointed as representatives to attend the ensuing quarterly meeting. Oliver Caulk, son of Isaac and Elizabeth Caulk, and Rachel Cox, dau. of William and Rachel Cox, declared their intentions of marriage. He being present produced a certificate from Duck Creek Monthly Meeting [Kent County, Delaware] of which he is a member, with their concurrence, and the consent of parents living will be expected.

1822, 12th of 12th mo. - Joseph Husband, Jr. appointed clerk. Luke Tipten [Tipton] requested a certificate for himself and his wife Priscilla and eight minor children, David, Mary, Esther, Rachel, Abijah, Elihu, John, and Hannah, to Smithfield Monthly Meeting in Ohio. Fawn Preparative Meeting informs that Benjamin Tomkins has accomplished his marriage to a woman of another society. Certificate received from Wilmington Monthly Meeting for William Coale recommending him to our care, as he is now living within the verge of Little Falls Monthly Meeting.

1823, 16th of 1st mo. - Women's meeting informs that Ann Brannon (late Coale) has had her marriage accomplished with a man not of our society. Certificate produced for Mary John to Cannel Monthly Meeting in Columbiana County, Ohio. The marriage of Oliver Caulk and Rachel Cox had been accomplished in good order.

1823, 13th of 2nd mo. - Elisha Cooke, Samuel Hopkins (of William), David Malsby, and Joseph Strawbridge were appointed representatives to attend the quarterly meeting. John Jewitt reported on behalf of the Quarterly Meeting of Ministers and Elders that Elizabeth Coale had been approved as a minister. Fawn Preparative Meeting informs that Jonathan Atkins requested to be received into membership, and Isaac Stubbs has been complained of for not complying with a contract.

1823, 13th of 3rd mo. - Certificate requested for Enoch Gray, a minor, to New Garden Monthly Meeting [Chester County, Pennsylvania].

1823, 7th of 4th mo. - Certificates requested for Joseph Pyle, a minor son of Amos Pyle, to Little Britain Monthly Meeting [Lancaster County, Pennsylvania], and Amos Pyle, also a minor son of Amos Pyle, to London Grove Monthly Meeting [Chester County, Pennsylvania]. Elisha Cooke, son of Samuel and Ruth Cooke, deceased, and Elizabeth Worthington, dau. of John and Priscilla Worthington, also deceased, declared their intention to marry. Reported that Mary Jones has been guilty of unchastity and not capable of condemning her conduct.

1823, 12th of 6th mo. - Benjamin Tompkins apologized for outgoing in marriage, "for which I am sincerely sorry." William Worthington was appointed treasurer. Elisha Cook and Elizabeth Worthington had their marriage accomplished in good order.

1823, 17th of 7th mo. - Ezra Gillingham, son of James and Elizabeth Gillingham, and Mary C. Coale, dau. of Isaac and Rachel Coale, declared their intention to marry. Certificate received for George Mason from Baltimore Monthly Meeting, Western District, "recommending him to our notice and care."

1823, 14th of 8th mo. - James Coale, Samuel Worthington, John Sharp, and John Lewin were appointed representatives to the quarterly meeting. Women Friends produced a certificate for Hannah Stump from Little Falls Monthly Meeting. Our much esteemed friend Micaijah Collins attended this meeting from Salem Monthly Meeting in Massachusetts.

1823, 16th of 9th mo. - Ezra Gillingham and Mary Coale had been married in an orderly manner. Women Friends inform that Mary Atkins, wife of Jonathan Atkins, requests to become a member of our society and was received. Ely Bond has been guilty of fornication. Certificate produced for Orpha Pyle [also spelled Pyles] to London Grove Monthly Meeting [Chester County, Pennsylvania], for Ruth Ann Pyle to Nottingham Monthly Meeting, and for Phebe Pyle to Little Britain Monthly Meeting [Lancaster County, Pennsylvania].

1823, 16th of 10th mo. - Certificate produced from Baltimore Monthly Meeting, Western District, for Sarah W. Doddrell. William McCoy, Jr. requested a certificate to Baltimore Monthly Meeting, Western District.

1823, 13th of 11th mo. - Sarah Warner expressed a concern which she felt to visit a few families to the northwest of the meeting house, which was united with, and John Jewitt appointed to accompany her. Susanna Jewitt expressed that she felt her mind drawn to attend the southern quarterly meeting, which was united with, and Elizabeth Coale, a minister in good esteem, will accompany her. John Jewitt, Thomas Worthington, and Samuel Hopkins (of William) were appointed to take into consideration the state of Friends title to the meeting house land at Deer Creek and if necessary to draft a petition to the Legislature of the state and produce it to the next meeting, praying for a special law to enable Friends to hold it and perpetuate the trust agreeable to the original title. Jeremiah Low requested to be taken into membership.

1823, 11th of 12th mo. - Isaac Stubbs has removed the complaint entered against him by John Channel by making satisfaction for the debt due him. Memorial for Mary Mifflin, deceased, was produced and read. Jonathan and Mary Atkins requested their 2 minor children, Joseph and Elizabeth, be taken into membership. Certificate received from Baltimore Monthly Meeting, Western District, recommending Folger Pope, his wife Ann, and their 5 minor children, Franklin F.,

Joseph D., Sarah R., Theodate, and William R. Pope, for membership with Fawn Preparative Meeting.

1824, 15th of 1st mo. - Deer Creek Preparative Meeting informs that William Cavender, Jr. requests to be taken into membership.

1824, 12th of 2nd mo. - Certificate produced from Baltimore Monthly Meeting for James C. Dodderell recommending him as a member. Asa Jones requested a certificate to Baltimore Monthly Meeting, Western District, in order to marry Hannah Riley.

1824, 11th of 3rd mo. - Jeremiah Low was received into membership. Joseph Kent requested a certificate to Warrington Monthly Meeting [York County, Pennsylvania] in order to marry Maria J. Cook.

1824, 15th of 4th mo. - Joshua Husband, Elisha Cook, James Coale, Aquila Massey, Jacob Balderston, and William Ely were proposed to have charge of interments, and William Worthington, Samuel Hopkins (of Joseph), and Joshua Hopkins were proposed to have charge of the graveyard at Deer Creek. Joseph Kent requested a certificate to Fallowfield Monthly Meeting. Samuel Worthington appointed clerk. Susanna Jewett, an esteemed minister, was approved to attend the yearly meeting at Philadelphia, accompanied by Sarah Hopkins.

1824, 13th of 5th mo. - Certificate requested for William Corse, a minor, to Wilmington Monthly Meeting. Rachel Harlan requested to become a member of our society.

1824, 17th of 6th mo. - Certificate received from Nottingham Monthly Meeting for William Rickman recommending him as a member. Isaac Stubbs [also spelled Stubs] and wife Hannah requested a certificate for themselves and their 7 minor children, Jeremiah B., Hannah Brown, Sarah Ann, Daniel, Joseph, Slater, and Deborah K. Stubbs, to Little Britain Monthly Meeting. Certificate requested for John Lewin, his wife [not named, but later identified in the minutes as Lydia] and their 5 minor children, William, Ann, Amos, Mary, and Lydia, to Little Falls Monthly Meeting.

1824, 15th of 7th mo. - A memorial to the Legislature on behalf of the property attached to the Deer Creek meeting house, was recorded as follows: "An Act for the benefit of Deer Creek Monthly Meeting of the people called Quakers in Harford County: Whereas a certain James Rigby, late of Harford County, did by his deed of conveyance bearing date on the twenty-fifth day of May in the year of our Lord seventeen hundred and eighty nine, convey and make over a parcel of a

tract of land called "Philips Purchase" being in said county and containing three acres and a half, unto Joseph Warner, Hugh Ely, Jacob Balderson, and Isaiah Balderson to be held in trust for the use of the Deer Creek Monthly Meeting called Friends, and whereas three of the above named trustees have since deceased and the survivor is advanced in years, and the said meeting having found it necessary to enlarge their burial ground, therefore be it enacted by the General Assembly of Maryland that is shall and may be lawful for Joshua Husbands, James Coale, William McCoy, and Aquilla Massey of the Deer Creek meeting of Friends, they conforming to the rules and regulations of said Society, to hold any tracts or parcel of land, that the said meeting may by deed of bargain and sale, deed of gift, or by devise acquire, not exceeding twenty acres, solely for the use of the said meeting, and the said trustees and their successors, shall have an estate in fee simply in all such lands no exceeding twenty acres as aforesaid, And be it enacted that the said meeting shall from time to time fill up vacancies that may happen in the said board of trustees, by death, resignation, or otherwise, so as to keep up the number four."
It was noted that Joseph Husband, who paid for recording the deed lately obtained of Isaac Massey for land attached to the meeting house, is authorized to call on the treasurer for this meeting for reimbursement. Certificate produced for Mary C. Gillingham to Baltimore Monthly Meeting, Western District.

1824, 12th of 8th mo. - Folger Pope, who has been disunited from membership by Bolton Monthly Meeting in Massachusetts, County of Worcester, requests to be reinstated. Jesse Hartly and his wife Mary requested certificates for themselves and their six minor children, Rachel, William, Edwin, Joseph, Jesse, and Thomas, to Hartland Monthly Meeting in Niagara County, New York. Certificate received from Baltimore Monthly Meeting, Western District, for Hannah Jones to join Friends at Fawn Preparative Meeting. Ely Garretson, son of Cornelius and Hannah Garretson, and Anna Massey, dau. of Isaac and Margaret Massey, declared their intention to marry and he is to produce a certificate from the monthly meeting of which he is a member.

1824, 16th of 9th mo. - Ely Garretson produced a certificate from Baltimore Monthly Meeting, Western District, with his parents consent, and Anna Massey's parents appeared and gave their consent to the marriage. Certificate produced for Rachel Caulk to Duck Creek Monthly Meeting [Kent County, Delaware]. George Mason requested a certificate to Nottingham Monthly Meeting.

1824, 14th of 10th mo. - Ely Garretson and Anna Massey had been married in an orderly manner. Deer Creek Preparative Meeting informs that John Wilson has accomplished his marriage contrary to the good order. Joshua Matthews, son of Thomas and Ann Matthews, and Mary Hopkins, dau. of Samuel and Sarah Hopkins, declared their intention to marry.

1824, 11th of 11th mo. - Ely Bond, having so far deviated from the path of rectitude as to be guilty of fornication, is disowned. Joshua Matthews requested a certificate to Baltimore Monthly Meeting in order to marry Mary Hopkins. Deer Creek Preparative Meeting informs that a certificate has been requested for Elisha Pearson, a minor, to Baltimore Monthly Meeting, Western District. Communication from Baltimore Monthly Meeting requests that this meeting should treat with Christopher Wilson, Jr. on account of his outgoing in marriage.

1824, 16th of 12th mo. - Folger Pope, Sr. was reinstated into membership. Joshua Matthews and Mary Hopkins had been married in an orderly manner. Women's Meeting informs that Elizabeth Haley [late Warner, as noted in minutes on 17th of 3rd mo., 1825, and 14th of 7th mo., 1825] has gone out in marriage and is not in a suitable frame of mind to condemn the same. Certificate produced for Anna Garretson to Baltimore Monthly Meeting, Western District.

1825, 17th of 2nd mo. - John Wilson had married a woman not in membership and was disowned. John Lewin, Jr. requested a certificate to Little Falls Monthly Meeting.

1825, 14th of 4th mo. - James Lovegrove was paid fifty cents for the amount of portage on the letter sent to Bolton Monthly Meeting in Massachusetts.

1825, 12th of 5th mo. - Samuel Worthington was appointed overseer in the place of Samuel Hopkins, and Folger Pope, Jr. in the place of John Sharp. Certificate produced for Mary H. Matthews to Baltimore Monthly Meeting, Western District.

1825, 16th of 6th mo. - Samuel Worthington proposed for clerk and Folger Pope, Jr. for assistant clerk; both were appointed.

1825, 14th of 7th mo. - Certificates requested for Benjamin Bond and Eli [also spelled Ely] Bond, both minors, to Stillwater Monthly Meeting in Ohio. Isaac Coale requested a certificate to Baltimore Monthly Meeting, Western District. Elizabeth Haley (late Warner) accomplished her marriage contrary to the good order and not appearing sensible of her deviation was disowned. Women's Meeting informs that Sarah G. Husbands has colored people in her possession whose freedom is not secure and she is remiss in the attendance of our meetings; a committee will visit her in this matter.

1825, 15th of 9th mo. - Certificate requested for Thomas Watson, a minor, to Baltimore Monthly Meeting, Western District.

1825, 13th of 10th mo. - William Rickman requested a certificate to New Garden Monthly Meeting [Chester County], Pennsylvania.

1825, 17th of 11th mo. - William Worthington, Jeremiah Low, and David Maulsby were appointed representatives to the quarterly meeting. The following lines were recorded in the minutes of 12th of 1st mo., 1826, for matters that occurred in late 1825: Deer Creek Preparative Meeting informs that William Ely, Jr. has accomplished his marriage with the assistance of a hireling minister. Silas Warner has accepted the office of captain of a militia company and Joseph Warner has joined a militia company and mustered. Certificate for John Quarles was received from Baltimore Monthly Meeting, Western District. Sarah Hutton has removed within the verge of Little Falls Monthly Meeting with her 4 minor children, Howard Johnson, Ann Johnson, Lemuel Johnson, and Thomas Hutton.

## BALTIMORE MONTHLY MEETING
## BIRTHS AND DEATHS, 1801-1825

[It should be noted that the following births and deaths between 1801 and 1825 were gleaned from membership rolls as the information was recorded in subsequent years.]

Henry Armstrong, b. 24th of 2nd mo., 1819.

Children of Hugh and Margaret Balderston:
    Isaiah Balderston, b. ---- [blank].
    John Peck Balderston, b. ---- [blank].
    Jacob Balderston, b. 26th of 10th mo., 1810.
    William Handy Balderston, b. 14th of 7th mo., 1815.
    Martha Ann Balderston, b. 2nd of 9th mo., 1817.

Eliza Ann Bailey, dau. of Vincent and Susannah, b. 8th of 10th mo., 1814.

Elizabeth Brooks, dau. of William and Sophia, b. 20th of 12th mo., 1817.

Children of Joseph and Cassandra Brevett:
    Cassandra A. Brevett, b. ---- [blank].
    Elizabeth Boraston Brevett, b. ---- [blank].
    James M. Brevett, b. ---- [blank].
    Ellen Isolobo Brevett, b. 11th of 4th mo., 1818.
    Joseph Plummer Brevett, b. 15th of 11th mo., 1820.

Children of David and Ann B. Brown:
    Mary D. Brown, b. ---- [blank].
    Rebecca Brown, b. ---- [blank].
    Elizabeth Brown, b. 6th of 8th mo., 1820.
    William Truth Brown, b. ---- [blank].

Children of William E. and Mary Bartlett:
    Rebecca Bartlett, b. 30th of 12th mo., 1817.
    James M. Bartlett, b. 15th of 9th mo., 1820.
    William E. Bartlett, b. 31st of 5th mo., 1823.
    Mary Bartlett, b. 26th of 12th mo., 1825.

Children of William and Sophia Brooks:
    Samuel Brooks, b. 15th of 11th mo., 1819.
    Hannah Brooks, b. 6th of 7th mo., 1822.
    Hannah Brooks, d. 14th of 8th mo., 1823.
    Ann Brooks, b. 23rd of 7th mo., 1824.
    Ann Brooks, d. 23rd of 5th mo., 1826.
    William Brooks, b. 1st of 9th mo., 1826.

Children of Vincent and Susanna Baily:
    Samuel Painter Baily, b. 1st of 1st mo., 1804.
    Jeremiah Baily, b. 5th of 9th mo., 1805.
    Joseph Clemson Baily, b. 23rd of 8th mo., 1808.
    Isaac Baily, b. 25th of 2nd mo., 1810.
    Bernard Baily, b. 26th of 3rd mo., 1812.
    Lydia Baily, b. 3rd of 4th mo., 1817.
    Matilda Baily, b. 21st of 1st mo., 1821.
    Louisa Baily, b. 22nd of 5th mo., 1825.

James Carey, son of John E. and Ann J., b. 19th of 1st mo., 1821.

Children of Daniel and Ruth Cobb:
    Anna Almy Cobb, b. ---- [blank].
    William Almy Cobb, b. 25th of 5th mo., 1823.
    Elizabeth Cobb, b. 4th of 9th mo., 1824.
    Edward D. Cobb, b. 17th of 3rd mo., 1826.
    Henry Samson Cobb, b. 24th of 9th mo., 1827.
    Susan Almy Cobb, b. 12th of 8th mo., 1829.

Children of William and Ann Cornthwait:
    Johanna H. Cornthwait, b. 9th of 2nd mo., 1817.

John Cornthwait, b. 17th of 8th mo., 1819.

David Wilson Cornthwait, son of John and ---- [blank], b. 11th of 10th mo., 1817.

Mary Elizabeth Chandlee, dau. of Benjamin and ---- [blank], b. 4th of 2nd mo., 1819.

Lydia Dukehart, b. 17th of 6th mo., 1818.

Children of John and Ann Dukehart:
    John Peck Dukehart, b. 31st of 7th mo., 1824.
    Margaret Ann Dukehart, b. 29th of 6th mo., 1826.

Children of John and Parthenia Dukehart:
    Martha Dukehart, b. ---- [blank].
    John Dukehart, b. ---- [blank].
    William Dukehart, b. ---- [blank].
    Sarah Dukehart, b. ---- [blank].
    Edward Dukehart, b. ---- [blank].
    Robert Dukehart, b. ---- [blank].
    Catherine Dukehart, b. ---- [blank].
    Parthenia Dukehart, b. ---- [blank].
    Balderston Dukehart, b. ---- [blank].
    Isaiah Dukehart, b. 13th of 9th mo., 1820.
    Isaiah Dukehart, d. 13th of 1st mo., 1822.
    Margaret Dukehart, b. ---- [blank].

Children of William and Ann Dawson:
    Ann Dawson, b. ---- [blank].
    John Dawson, b. ---- [blank].
    Jane Dawson, b. ---- [blank].
    William Dawson, Jr., b. ---- [blank].
    Elizabeth Robertson Dawson, b. ---- [blank].
    Joseph Dawson, b. 10th of 9th mo., 1818.
    Joseph Dawson, d. 24th of 9th mo., 1819.
    Mary Miflin Dawson, b. 30th of 10th mo., 1820.

Children of William and Sarah Dallam:
    John Dallam, b. ---- [blank].
    Henry Dallam, b. ---- [blank].
    Thomas Barber Dallam, b. ---- [blank].
    William Dallam, b. 2nd of 4th mo., 1822.

Mary Dallam, b. 15th of 11th mo., 1824.

Margaret Dukehart, mother of John Dukehart, d. 2nd of 3rd mo., 1824, aged 81 years.

Children of Thomas and Mary M. Ellicott:
    William M. Ellicott, b. ---- [blank].
    Sarah Ann Ellicott, b. 21st of 1st mo., 1808.
    Hannah Ellicott, b. 21st of 8th mo., 1810.
    Lydia Ellicott, b. 4th of 2nd mo., 1812.
    Mary T. Ellicott, b. 10th of 9th mo., 1813.
    Esther Ellicott, b. 12th of 11th mo., 1814.
    Rebecca Ellicott, b. 6th of 3rd mo., 1816.
    Catherine Ellicott, b. 12th of 11th mo., 1817.
    Elizabeth Ellicott, b. 1st of 1st mo., 1822.

Maria Ellicott, b. 26th of 12th mo., 1816.

Eliza Edmondson, b. 3rd of 8th mo., 1810.

Children of Edmond and Elizabeth Evens:
    Sarah Andrew Evens, b. ---- [blank].
    Mary Mifflin Evens, b. ---- [blank].
    Anna Evens, b. ---- [blank].
    Susanna Evens, b. ---- [blank].
    John Evens, b. ---- [blank].
    Lydia Evens, b. ---- [blank].
    Elizabeth Evens, b. 15th of 5th mo., 1821.

Children of Jacob and Clarissa Fussell:
    William Fussell, b. ---- [blank] c.1815.
    William d. 28th of 11th mo., 1834 in 19th year
    Joshua Fussell, b. ---- [blank].
    Jacob Fussell, b. ---- [blank].
    Ruth Fussell, b. 20th of 1st mo., 1821.
    Hannah Fussell, b. 6th of 4th mo., 1822.
    Bartholomew Fussell, b. 16th of 12th mo., 1823.
    Joseph Brevett Fussell, b. 15th of 1st mo., 1826.

Children of John and Mary Gillingham:
    Hannah Gillingham, b. ---- [blank].
    Mary Gillingham, b. 15th of 8th mo., 1825.

Children of George and Merian Gillingham:
    Amos Gillingham, b. ---- [blank].
    Elizabeth Gillingham, b. ---- [blank].
    Edward Gillingham, b. ---- [blank].
    Ezra Gillingham, b. 21st of 6th mo., 1818.
    Rachel Gillingham, b. 2nd of 1st mo., 1820.
    Ann Gillingham, b. 13th of 11th mo., 1821.
    Lucy Gillingham, b. 23rd of 6th mo., 1823.
    Susanna Gillingham, b. 22nd of 6th mo., 1820 *[sic]*.

Children of William E. and Sarah E. George:
    Elizabeth George, b. ---- [blank].
    Philip Thomas George, b. ---- [blank].
    Ann George, b. 23rd of 10th mo., 1817.
    Jonathan E. George, b. 18th of 8th mo., 1819.
    Robert George, b. 12th of 5th mo., 1822.
    Sarah Harvey George, b. 6th of 12th mo., 1823.
    Frances George, b. 21st of 9th mo., 1825.

Children of Elijah and Mary Mott Goldsmith:
    Edw. W. Goldsmith [twin], b. 6th of 7th mo., 1822.
    William Henry Goldsmith, b. 6th of 7th mo., 1822.
    Isaac Procter Goldsmith, b. 3rd of 4th mo., 1824.
    Elizabeth Goldsmith, b. 6th of 6th mo., 1828.

Eliza Garretson, b. 3rd of 9th mo., 1814.

Thomas Garretson, b. 18th of 9th mo., 1818.

John Garretson, b. 25th of 6th mo., 1820.

Cornelius Garretson, b. 19th of 3rd mo., 1819.

William Garretson, b. 23rd of 7th mo., 1820.

Anna Garretson, b. 18th of 7th mo., 1822.

Children of Samuel and ---- [blank] Garretson:
    Samuel Garretson, b. 4th of 12th mo., 1823.
    Eli Garretson, b. 5th of 5th mo., 1825.

Children of Ephraim and Mary Gardner:

Sarah P. Gardner, b. ---- [blank].
James Gardner, b. ---- [blank].
Mary Jane Gardner, b. ---- [blank].
Mary Jane Gardner, d. 20th of 4th mo., 1821.
Aldred S. Gardner, b. 2nd of 2nd mo., 1822.
Ann Eliza Gardner, b. 3rd of 12th mo., 1823.
Martha S. Gardner, b. 15th of 4th mo., 1826.

Children of William and Jane Gillingham:
    James Gillingham, b. ---- [blank].
    Isaac Gillingham, b. ---- [blank].
    Eliza Gillingham, b. ---- [blank].
    Catharine Gillingham, b. 29th of 1st mo., 1820.
    Esther Gillingham, b. ---- [blank].

Children of Gerard and Dorothy Hopkins:
    Deborah Hopkins, b. ---- [blank].
    Deborah Hopkins, d. 13th of 11th mo., 1830, age 29.
    Elizabeth Hopkins, b. ---- [blank].
    Sarah Hopkins, b. ---- [blank].
    Thomas Hopkins, b. 19th of 5th mo., 1811.
    William Hopkins, b. 5th of 7th mo., 1813.
    Gerard Hopkins, b. 5th of 10th mo., 1815.
    Margaret Hopkins, b. ---- [blank].
    Rachel Hopkins, b. 9th of 5th mo., 1822.

Children of Isaac and Elizabeth Hayward:
    William Brown Hayward, b. 25th of 5th mo., 1818.
    Ely Balderston Hayward, b. 8th of 1st mo., 1820.
    Frances W. Hayward, b. 7th of 9th mo., 1822.
    Frances W. Hayward, d. 14th of 9th mo., 1823.
    Marcellus B. Hayward, b. 12th of 9th mo., 1824.
    Marcellus B. Hayward, d. 23rd of 8th mo., 1825.
    Elizabeth Hayward, b. 29th of 12th mo., 1826.

Children of William W. and Elizabeth Handy:
    Jesse Tyson Handy, b. ---- [blank].
    Jane Winder Handy, b. 19th of 9th mo., 1819.
    Henry Handy, b. 14th of 12th mo., 1821.
    Elizabeth Ann Handy, b. 23rd of 7th mo., 1823.
    William Winder Handy, b. 28th of 3rd mo., 1825.

Thomas Poultney Handy, son of William W. Handy and Mary Ann, b. 19th of 12th mo., 1843. [Elizabeth Handy, first wife of William W. Handy, d. 1st of 8th mo., 1840, in her 50th year].

Children of Charles and Sarah Halwadt:
    Elizabeth Halwadt, b. 23rd of -- [blank] mo., 1812.
    Sarah Halwadt [twin], b. 25th of 2nd mo., 1818.
    Rebecca Halwadt [twin], b. 25th of 2nd mo., 1818.

Children of Samuel and Lavinia Hartly:
    Samuel Hartly, b. ---- [blank].
    Lavinia Hartly, b. 8th of 6th mo., 1817.
    Samuel E. Hartly, b. 25th of 9th mo., 1818.

Catharine P. Hartly, b. 13th of 11th mo., 1819.

Elizabeth Paxson Hartly, b. 23rd of 4th mo., 1821.

Charles L. Hartly, b. 30th of 6th mo., 1820.

William S. Hough, b. 2nd of 9th mo., 1818.

Marietta Hough, b. 11th of 10th mo., 1811.

Charles Alexander Hough, b. 22nd of 5th mo., 1816.

Children of John and Rebecca Hopkins:
    Able James Hopkins, b. 23rd of 5th mo., 1822.
    John George Hopkins, b. 11th of 4th mo., 1824.
    Samuel Wilson Hopkins, b. 7th of 3rd mo., 1826.

Pheniah Hartly, b. 14th of 9th mo., 1824.

Children of Thomas and Harriet Hull:
    William Hull, b. 9th of 3rd mo., 1822.
    Frances Ann Hull, b. 19th of 5th mo., 1824.

William B. Hartly, son of William and ---- [blank], b. 25th of 12th mo., 1823.

Mary H. Jones, dau. of Aquila and Ann, d. 25th of 6th mo., 1825.

Children of Joseph and Tacy King:

Francis Thompson King, b. ---- [blank].
Thomas King, b. ---- [blank].
Mary Ellicott King, b. 2nd of 9th mo., 1823.
Joseph King, b. 17th of 7th mo., 1825.
Elias Ellicott King, b. 28th of 2nd mo., 1828.

Children of Daniel and Anne Larrabee:
    Ephraim Larrabee, b. ---- [blank].
    Hannah Larrabee, b. ---- [blank].
    Elizabeth Larrabee, b. ---- [blank].
    William Larrabee, b. 23rd of 2nd mo., 1811.
    Joseph W. Larrabee, b. 21st of 7th mo., 1816.
    Edward W. Larrabee, b. ---- [blank].
    Mary Larrabee, b. 13th of 12th mo., 1818.
    Almira Larrabee, b. 6th of 6th mo., 1821.

Children of James and Lydia Lovegrove:
    Jane Lovegrove, b. ---- [blank].
    Folger Lovegrove, b. ---- [blank].
    Hannah Lovegrove, b. 5th of 7th mo., 1816.
    Lydia Lovegrove, b. 2nd of 2nd mo., 1818.
    Thomas Judge Lovegrove, b. 13th of 1st mo., 1819.
    James Lovegrove, b. 14th of 12th mo., 1821.
    William Riley Lovegrove, b. 7th of 4th mo., 1823.
    Theodate Lovegrove, b. 20th of 4th mo., 1825.

Children of Daniel, Jr. and Mary Lamb:
    Rebecca Lamb, b. ---- [blank].
    George M. Lamb, b. 16th of 9th mo., 1815 *[sic]*.
    Thomas Alexander Lamb, b. 10th of 10th mo., 1826.

Mary Lytle, dau. of William and Elizabeth, b. 29th of 3rd mo., 1823.

Children of Jacob and Phebe Lafettra:
    Mary Lafettra, b. ---- [blank].
    Sarah Lafettra, b. ---- [blank].
    Thomas H. Lafettra, b. ---- [blank].
    Lydia Lafettra, b. ---- [blank].
    Jane B. Lafettra, b. ---- [blank].
    Phebe Lafettra, b. 3rd of 12th mo., 1819.

Isaac McCoy, son of David G. and Elizabeth, b. 24th of 8th mo., 1824.

Children of Thomas and Tacy Mackinzie:
    George Norbury Mackinzie, b. 11th of 2nd mo., 1824.
    Sarah Mackall Mackinzie, b. 27th of 7th mo., 1827.
    Cosmo Taylor Mckinzie, b. 23rd of 6th mo., 1829.
    Calin Burgess McKinzie, b. 3rd of 4th mo., 1831.
    Martha Norbury Mackinzie, b. 2nd of 7th mo., 1833.

Children of Samuel T. and Hannah Matlack:
    Susanna S. Matlack, b. 12th of 10th mo., 1808.
    Ann Maria Matlack, b. 6th of 2nd mo., 1810.
    Emily Matlack, b. 2nd of 7th mo., 1818.
    Elizabeth S. Matlack, b. 4th of 8th mo., 1819.
    Mary W. Matlack, b. 25th of 9th mo., 1821.
    Armistead Matlack, b. 4th of 5th mo., 1823.

Children of Benjamin P. and Mary Moore:
    Gerard Hopkins Moore, b. ---- [blank].
    Rebecca Moore, b. ---- [blank].
    William Wilson Moore, b. 1st of 1st mo., 1824.
    Robert Moore, b. 21st of 3rd mo., 1825.
    Elizabeth Hopkins Moore, b. 11th of 8th mo., 1826.
    Deborah Hopkins Moore, b. 10th of 9th mo., 1830.
    Benjamin P. Moore, b. 24th of 9th mo., 1831.
    John W. Moore, b. 17th of 3rd mo., 1833.

Children of Thomas and Sarah Matthews:
    Joseph Matthews, b. ---- [blank].
    Cassandra Matthews, b. ---- [blank].
    Ann Matthews, b. ---- [blank].
    Thomas Matthews, b. ---- [blank].
    John Matthews, b. 7th of 11th mo., 1819.

William Medcalf, b. 17th of 10th mo., 1822.

Sarah Moore Medcalf, b. 5th of 7th mo., 1820.

Lydia Medcalf, dau. of Abraham and Mary, b. 18th of 8th mo., 1824.

Sarah Elizabeth Mott, dau. of John and Rachell, b. 18th of 8th mo., 1819.

Thomas Moore, b. 9th of 9th mo., 1824.

John Morgan, son of ---- [blank] and Sarah, d. 23rd of 7th mo., 1822.

John Medcalf, son of A. and Mary, d. 2nd of 10th mo., 1822.

Children of Robert and Mary Norris:
    Thomas Morgan Norris, b. 8th of 1st mo., 1819.
    Sarah Ann Norris, b. 29th of 1st mo., 1821.
    Matilda D. Norris, b. -- [blank] of 8th mo., 1823.

Children of John and Eliza Needles:
    Mary Lamb Needles, b. 1st of 5th mo., 1812.
    Ruth Ann Needles, b. 24th of 3rd mo., 1815.
    Edith Needles, b. 30th of 9th mo., 1817.
    Ann Maria Needles, b. 22nd of 7th mo., 1819.
    Edward M. Needles, b. 26th of 4th mo., 1823.
    Elijah Marsh Needles, b. 18th of 4th mo., 1826.
    Elizabeth Needles [twin], b. 18th of 4th mo., 1826.
    John Amos Needles, b. -- [blank] of 10th mo., 1828.
    Sarah Needles, b. 19th of 5th mo., 1831.

Children of David and Jane Newlin:
    Ann Eliza Newlin, b. ---- [blank].
    Rebecca Newlin, b. 31st of 1st mo., 1811.
    David N. Dawson Newlin, b. ---- [blank].

Children of William and Ann Procter:
    Deborah W. Procter, b. ---- [blank].
    Wilson Procter, b. ---- [blank].
    Edward Procter, b. ---- [blank].
    Isaac Procter, b. ---- [blank].
    Elizabeth Robson Procter, b. 20th of 4th mo., 1823.
    Rebecca Procter, b. 20th of 7th mo., 1825.
    Sarah Procter, b. ---- [blank].

John C. Powell, d. 2nd of 6th mo., 1824.

Children of Charles and ---- [blank] Read:
    Robert Read, b. ---- [blank].
    Charles Read, b. ---- [blank].
    Betty Read, b. ---- [blank].
    Joseph Read, b. ---- [blank].
    Thomas Read, b. ---- [blank].

Samuel Read, b. ---- [blank].
Elizabeth Read, b. 20th of 8th mo., 1817.

Children of Samuel and Elizabeth Regester:
Mary Ann Regester, b. ---- [blank].
Elizabeth Jane Regester, b. --- [blank].
John Regester, b. 25th of 3rd mo., 1824.

Children of Amos and Grace Read:
Jane Read, b. 31st of 10th mo., 1821.
Amos James Read, b. 3rd of 2nd mo., 1824.
Anna Braithwait Read, b. 22nd of 7th mo., 1826.

Charles Reese, b. 16th of 6th mo., 1823.

Edward Reese, b. 16th of 6th mo., 1825.

Mary B. Reese, dau. of Thomas S. and Mary, d. 27th of 1st mo., 1822.

Joseph Starr, b. 29th of 11th mo., 1815.

Thomas Starr, b. 1st of 4th mo., 1823.

Benjamin Starr, b. 23rd of 5th mo., 1819.

Children of Samuel and Elizabeth Scott:
Sarah Ann Scott, b. 9th of 9th mo., 1821.
Caroline Scott, b. 25th of 11th mo., 1823.

Children of Matthew and Catharine M. Smith:
Thomas M. Smith, b. ---- [blank].
Robert M. Smith, b. ---- [blank].
Elizabeth Ann Smith, b. 7th of 5th mo., 1816.
John Marsh Smith, b. 20th of 8th mo., 1818.
Anthony Marsh Smith, b. ---- [blank].
Hannah Ann Smith, b. 18th of 4th mo., 1821.
Mary Marsh Smith, b. 14th of 10th mo., 1823.

Children of Townsend and Edith B. Scott:
Edith Ann Scott, b. 22nd of 3rd mo., 1825.
Rossetter Stockton Scott, b. 24th of 10th mo., 1826.

Children of John and Eliza Smith:
    Charlotte Lawrence Smith, b. 21st of 12th mo., 1823.
    Lindley Murray Smith, b. 3rd of 2nd mo., 1824.

Children of William and Elizabeth Tyson:
    Jonathan Tyson, b. ---- [blank].
    William A. Tyson, b. ---- [blank].
    Samuel Tyson, b. 16th of 11th mo., 1809.
    Mary Tyson, b. 19th of 9th mo., 1811.
    Elizabeth Tyson, b. 12th of 2nd mo., 1813.
    Francis Tyson, b. 20th of 8th mo., 1815.
    Jane Tyson, b. 1st of 7th mo., 1817.
    Edward Tyson, b. 28th of 12th mo., 1818.
    Charles S. Tyson, b. 22nd of 4th mo., 1820.
    Martha Ann Tyson, b. 2nd of 6th mo., 1822.
    Letitia E. Tyson, b. 16th of 2nd mo., 1825.
    Nathaniel E. Tyson, b. 4th of 5th mo., 1826.

Children of Elisha, Jr. and Sarah Morris Tyson:
    Margaret Tyson, b. ---- [blank].
    Mary M. Tyson, b. 2nd of 10th mo., 1820.
    Marshall Tyson, b. 21st of 7th mo., 1822.
    Sarah S. Tyson, b. 4th of 2nd mo., 1826.

Children of Isaac, Jr. and Hannah Ann Tyson:
    Richard Wood Tyson, b. 20th of 9th mo., 1824.
    Jesse Tyson, b. 22nd of 8th mo., 1826.

Children of Nathan and Martha E. Tyson:
    James Ellicott Tyson, b. 21st of 8th mo., 1816.
    Elizabeth Brook Tyson, b. 3rd of 3rd mo., 1818.
    Isabella Tyson, b. 17th of 3rd mo., 1823.
    Ann Tyson, b. 26th of 2nd mo., 1825.

Children of Philip E. and Elizabeth Thomas:
    Rachel Thomas, b. ---- [blank].
    Evan Ph. Thomas, b. ---- [blank].
    William George Thomas, b. ---- [blank].
    Mary Thomas, b. ---- [blank].
    Elizabeth Thomas, b. 22nd of 1st mo., 1817.
    Harriet Thomas, b. 25th of 10th mo., 1820.
    Sarah G. Thomas, b. ---- [blank].

Children of Joseph, Jr. and Rebecca Turner:
    Elizabeth Turner, b. 25th of 9th mo., 1815.
    Hannah Turner, b. ---- [blank].
    Richard Townsend Turner, b. 22nd of 8th mo., 1819.
    Sally Ann Turner, b. 27th of 9th mo., 1821.
    Rebecca Turner, b. 25th of 10th mo., 1825.

Children of William and Maria Trimble:
    George Fox Trimble, b. 13th of 3rd mo., 1823.
    Hannah Maria Trimble, b. 23rd of 3rd mo., 1826.

Children of Nicholas and Elizabeth Taylor:
    Isabella Taylor, b. 6th of 3rd mo., 1819.
    Thomas Taylor, b. 27th of 3rd mo., 1821.
    Jane Taylor, b. 29th of 11th mo., 1822.
    Sarah Taylor, b. 13th of 9th mo., 1824.

Julian Wooderson Townsend, son of Joseph and Esther, d. 18th of 6th mo., 1825.

Children of Cornelius and Catherine Vansant:
    James Edward Vansant, b. 9th of 8th mo., 1821.
    Mary Elizabeth Vansant, b. 9th of 9th mo., 1823.
    Joseph Townsend Vansant, b. 14th of 4th mo., 1825.

Benjamin H. Vansant, b. 13th of 2nd mo., 1817.

Tacy Ann Vansant, b. 6th of 10th mo., 1819.

Morris Jackson Valentine, b. 18th of 3rd mo., 1823.

Children of Ennion and ---- [blank] Williams:
    Hannah Williams, b. 22nd of 9th mo., 1820.
    Rebecca Williams, b. ---- [blank].
    Lydia Williams, b. ---- [blank].

Children of John and ---- [blank] Wilson:
    Mary Ann Wilson, b. ---- [blank].
    Margaret Wilson, b. ---- [blank].
    Elizabeth Wilson, b. ---- [blank].
    Elisha T. Wilson, b. ---- [blank].
    Alisanna Wilson, b. 5th of 7th mo., 1816.

Children of Lewin and Elizabeth Wethered:
Peregrin Wethered, b. ---- [blank].
Charles Elias Wethered, b. ---- [blank].
John Wethered, b. ---- [blank].
Samuel Wethered, b. 22nd of 2nd mo., 1811.
Mary Wethered, b. ---- [blank].
Ann Poultney Wethered, b. 26th of 11th mo., 1814.
Elizabeth Wethered, b. 2nd of 2nd mo., 1822.
James Sykes Wethered, b. 24th of 3rd mo., 1824.

Edward Waters, son of Edwin and Sarah, b. 3rd of 6th mo., 1819.

Children of Amos and Elizabeth West:
Ely West, b. ---- [blank].
Jane West, b. ---- [blank], m. ---- Tilton.
Elizabeth West, Jr., b. ---- [blank].
Grace A. West, b. ---- [blank], m. ---- Francis.
Susanna West, b. ---- [blank].
Sarah West, b. ---- [blank].
Charles West, b. 27th of 9th mo., 1817.
Adeline West, b. 2nd of 3rd mo., 1820.

## BALTIMORE MONTHLY MEETING, WESTERN DISTRICT MARRIAGE CERTIFICATES, 1807-1825

**Edward Stabler Hough**, of Baltimore County, son of Samuel and Ann Hough, of Louden County, Virginia, married **Sarah Atkinson**, dau. of Joseph and Rachel Atkinson, of Anne Arundel County, Maryland, in Baltimore on 16th of 12 mo., 1807.
Witnesses: 1st column - Elizabeth Thomas, Ann Poultney, Elizabeth Tyson, Martin Lowns, Ruth Buckman, Sarah Ellicott, Elizabeth Ellicott, George Ellicott, Hannah Smith, Benjamin Parmer, Thomas Poultney. 2nd column - Evan Thomas, Andrew Ellicott, Jonathan Ellicott, David Buckman, Isaac McPherson, Nicholas Popeline, Phineas Buckman, Samuel Kanby [Canby], Joseph Lowns, Samuel Richmond, Jr., J. Black, Bethula Lowns, Grace Buckman, Peter Buckman. 3rd column - Joseph Atkinson, Rachel Atkinson, Abbigal Atkinson, Rachel Atkinson, Jr., Ruth Atkinson, Isaac Atkinson, Joseph Atkinson, Jr., Mary Kinsey, Oliver Kinsey.

**Abraham Barker**, of New York City, son of Robert and Sarah Barker, late of Kennebeck, Massachusetts (the father being deceased), married **Priscilla Hopkins**,

dau. of Gerrard and Rachel Hopkins, late of Baltimore (deceased), in Baltimore on 17th of 5th mo., 1809.
Witnesses: 1st column - Lawson Alexander, Rachel Mason, Mary Tyson, Amos A. Williams, Susan Hopkins, Rebecca Cope, Margaret Carey, Tacey Ellicott, Priscilla Lee, Richea Carey, Hannah Carey, John Worthington, Joel Hopkins, R. E. Thomas, Peggy Wilson, Priscilla Dare, Richard Hopkins, Andrew Ellicott, Jr., William Gillingham, Ennion Williams, George Mason, Benjamin Ellicott, Jr., Eliza Yellott, Tacy Mitchell, Rebecca Procter, Mary Waybill, Frances R. Bowley, Sarah Adson, Martha Burrows Stump, John Cornthwait, Jr., John Comegys. 2nd column - Hannah Williams, William Hayward, James Gillingham, Mary Tyson, Jr., William Tyson, Isaac Scott, Rachel T. Ellicott, Ann Mifflin, Jr., Mary Janney, Martha Carey, Elizabeth Cornthwait, John Cornthwait, Joseph Rolet, Elizabeth Howell, Elizabeth Hopkins, Isaac Tyson, Charles W. Smith, Samuel H. Harris, R. Sterrett, William Riley, John Nicholson, George Williams, Mary Ellicott, Jr., Sarah Tyson, Sarah Procter, Francis Hazelhurst, Ann Peters, Eliza Gilmyer, Mariam James, William Jones. 3rd column - Mary Barker, Gideon Gardner, Gerrard Wilson, John W. Stump, Samuel Harris, Sarah Mathews, Rachel Thomas, Mary Ellicott, Ann Poultney, Elias Ellicott, James Carey, James Ellicott, John Ellicott, Thomas Ellicott, Mary M. Ellicott, Nathan Tyson, Jr., Charles Worthington, Eliza Worthington.

**Jonathan Janney**, of Loudoun County, Virginia, son of Israel and Anna Janney, of same place, married **Elizabeth McPherson**, dau. of Isaac and Elizabeth McPherson, of Baltimore City, in Baltimore on 16th of 5th mo., 1810.
Witnesses: 1st column - Isaac McPherson, Tacy McPherson, Jane Janney, Jane McPherson, Nathaniel Ellicott, Ann McPherson, Daniel Janney, Israel Janney, Daniel M. Moor, Mary M. Ellicott, Hannah Henderson, Eliza Wethered, Ann Poultney, Dorothy Hopkins, Elizabeth Y.Tyson, William Tyson, Andrew Ellicott, Jr., Hannah Marsh, Jr., Hannah McPherson, Martha McPherson, Nicholas Popplein, Grace Knox, Elizabeth Hayward, Mary Ann Davis, Mary Tyson, Susan Hopkins, Elizabeth Gillingham, Hannah Robertson. 2nd column - Rachel Hough, Rachel Mason, Sarah Sinclair, Martha Carey, Thomas Poultney, James Carey, James Gillingham, Mary Hopkins, Mary James, Deborah Hopkins, Elizabeth Hopkins, John Nicholson, Elizabeth Louden (by request), Gerard T. Hopkins, Hannah Marsh, Rebecca Procter, John Marsh, Mary Marsh, Sarah A. Henderson, Izak Procter, Edmund Prior Procter, Rebecca Lindenberger, Susan Legg, William Riley, John Gillingham.

**Enoch Gray**, of New Garden Township, Chester County, Pennsylvania, married **Mary Hicks**, of Baltimore City (widow of James Hicks of Harford County, Maryland, deceased), in Baltimore at the meeting house on Lombard Street on 17th of 4th mo., 1811 [Enoch signed his name and Mary made her mark].

Witnesses: 1st column - Isaac Underwood, George Harris, Jr., Jesse Cook, Mary Cook, Joseph Stapler, Jacob Mendenhall, Hannah Stapler, John Mitchel, Rebecca Webster, Izak Procter, Thomas Ellicott, James Gillingham, John Marsh, Gerard T. Hopkins, Hugh Balderston, William Gillingham, George Gillingham, John Nicholson, Andrew McCoy, Samuel Byrnes. 2nd column - Hicks Harris, Daniel Sitler, Robert Johnson, Ann McCoy, Joseph McCoy, Tamar Sitler, Beulah Harris, James Underwood, Sarah Webster, Eliza Marsh, Mary Hopkins, Ann Waterhouse, Martha McCoy, Elizabeth Swain, Isaac McCoy, Thomas Butler, Grace Knox, Mary M. Ellicott, Deborah Hopkins. 3rd column - George Harris, Enoch Gray, Jr., Enoch Underwood, Mary Tyson, Susanna Harris, Mary Harris, Henry James, Meriah Cook, Tacy Mitchel, Priscilla Bull, Ruthy Byrnes, Elizabeth Comfort, Mary McCoy, Hannah Byrnes, William Hayward, Nathan Sheppard, Hannah Marsh, Rachel Thomas, Elizabeth Bidgood, Elizabeth Robertson, Sr.

**James Hambleton**, of Baltimore County, son of William and Mary Hambleton, of Belmont County, Ohio, married **Mary Brooks**, of Baltimore City, dau. of Thomas and Mary Brooks, late of Chester County, Pennsylvania (the father being deceased), in Baltimore on 12th of 6th mo., 1811.
Witnesses: 1st column - Gerard T. Hopkins, Isaac Tyson, John Marsh, John Livingston, William Gillingham, Ezra Gillingham, John Gillingham, Joseph Tomkins, Samuel Canby, John Nicholson, George Norbury, Martha Norbury, Ann Ewing, Henry Ewing, Jonathan Roberts, Margaret Bailey, Hannah Kenny. 2nd column - Elizabeth Thomas, Martha Carey, Sarah Tyson, Tacy Mitchel, Ann Poultney, Esther Buckman, Sarah Webster, Miriam James, Eliza Gillingham, Hannah Marsh, Eliza Marsh, Mary Marsh, Martha Tomkins, Rebecca Procter, Elizabeth Loudon, Elizabeth Bailey, Phebe Kenny. 3rd column - Mary John, Charles Hambleton, Thomas Brookes, Rachel Hambleton, Joseph Hambleton, Benjamin Hambleton, Thomas Kenny, Betty Kenny, John Underwood, Thomas McCormick, William M. Townsend, Joseph Townsend, Jr., Samuel Harlan, Izak Procter, Daniel Kenny, Eleanor Kenny, Anne Larrable.

**George Gillingham**, of Baltimore City, son of James and Elizabeth Gillingham, of the same place, married **Miriam James**, dau. of Amos and Ann James, of Baltimore City (the mother being deceased), in Baltimore on 18th of 9th mo., 1811.
Witnesses: 1st column - William Hopkins, Susan B. Jones, Nathan Tyson, Jr., Isaac Tyson, Jr., Charles Harlan, Joel Hopkins, John Comegys, John Baker, John Thomas, Joseph Bruff, Samuel Myers, R. Kilgour, William Riley, Ennion Williams, Gerard T. Hopkins, William Hayward, E. Loudon, William K. Gwinn. 2nd column - William E. George, Elizabeth Tyson, Hannah Carey, Mary Tyson, Priscilla James, Joseph Turner, Jr., William Dallam, Jesse Tyson, Mary Jones, Izak Procter, Hannah Williams, John Hayward, Samuel Carey, James Hambleton, Joseph Tomkins, John Nicholson, Samuel G. Jones, John G. Worthington. 3rd

column - Mary C. James, Elizabeth Gillingham, James Gillingham, Amos James, William Gillingham, Elizabeth Gillingham, Mary Tyson, Samuel Jefferis, Lydia Jefferis. Mary James, Eliza Jones, Elizabeth James, Rachel Updegraff, Tacy Mitchell, Ezra Gillingham, Ann James, Susan Hopkins.

**Charles Halwadt**, of Baltimore City, son of Christopher and Elizabeth Halwadt, of Exter in the County of Flatho and Principality of Menden in Prussia (both deceased), married **Sarah Frazier**, dau. of William and Rosey Frazier, of Northeast in Cecil County, Maryland, in Baltimore on 9th of 10th mo., 1811.
Witnesses: 1st column - John Gillingham, John Livingston, Samuel Carey, John Gillingham, William Gillingham, John Needles, Isaac Starr, Catherine Starr, Samuel G. Jones, Charles Lukens, David Rukefuss, Mary H. Marsh. 2nd column - William Hayward, Hannah Litle, Elizabeth Gillingham, Hannah Marsh, Jr., Miriam Gillingham, Amos James, Margaret Carey, Eliza Marsh, John Marsh, John Nicholson, Nicholas Popplein, Ennion William, William Riley. 3rd column - Martha Carey, Rebecca Procter, Hannah Marsh, Elizabeth Thomas, Susan Hopkins, Hannah Carey, Mary Jones, Rachel Mason, Rebecca Sinclair, William Tyson, Jesse Tyson, Isaac Tyson, Mary Harris.

**William W. Handy**, of Baltimore City, son of Henry and Jane Handy, of Somerset County, Maryland (both deceased), married **Elizabeth Tyson**, dau. of Jesse and Margaret Tyson, of Baltimore City (the mother being deceased), in Baltimore on 27th of 11th mo., 1811.
Witnesses: 1st column - Sabina Crownover, Anna Tyson, Sarah R. Webster, Maria Aitken, Enoch Clap, Robn. Johnston, Sarah W. Hudson, Rebecca Warfield, Eliza Sinclair, Israel Hanney, Hugh Balderston, Rebecca Procter, Mary Robertson, Samuel H. Smith, C. D. Gwinn, Jane McPherson, Catharine M. Smith, Hannah Carey, Hannah Marsh, Jr., Prudence Gough, Rebecca Sinclair, Araminta Harrison, Ann H. Griffith. 2nd column - Thomas Tyson, Isaac Tyson Jr., Margaret Tyson, William B. Hebbard, J. G. Worthington, John Thomas Brooke, Maria Dorsey, Juliana Knight, Margaret Carey, Evan Poultney, Mary James, Ezra Gillingham, John C. Clay, Alfred H. Dashiell, William Gillingham, John Nicholson, Elizabeth L. Davis, Margaret Balderston, Ann McCoy, Dorothy Webster, Caroline Hammond, Mary Ann Davis, Hannah James. 3rd column - Jesse Tyson, Sarah Tyson, Rachel Hough, William W. Polk, Elizabeth Dashiell, Mary Tyson, Lucretia Wilson, Mary Amos, Anna Norris, John Gillingham, Ruthy Byrnes, John W. Wilson, F. Hopkins, Henrietta M. Sappington, Hannah Tyson, Nathan Tyson, Jr., Gerard T. Hopkins, Amos James, Tacy Mitchell, Rezin Hopkins, Hannah Marsh, Richard Hopkins, M.D., Izak Procter.

**John Hewes**, of Baltimore City, son of Edward and Mary Hewes, of the Town of Wilmington, Delaware, married **Rachel Thomas Ellicott**, dau. of Elias and Mary

Ellicott, of Baltimore City (the mother being deceased), in Baltimore on 15th of 1st mo., 1812.
Witnesses: 1st column - Hannah Talbott, Jesse Talbott, John Litle, Lucy R. Griffith, Matilda L. Ridgely, Maria Dorsey, Mary James, William Martin, Jr., Elizabeth James, William E. George, William Hopkins, William Gillingham, Jonathan Harvey, Jonathan Balderston, Elizabeth C. Davis, Gerard T. Hopkins, John Nicholson, Elizabeth Lowden, William Riley, Samuel G. Jones, Mary Jones, Margaret Carey, Esther McPherson, Sarah Riley, James Carey, Martha Carey. 2nd column - Rachel Poultney, Rachel Dorsey, Deborah Hopkins, Mary Ann Davis, Elizabeth Tyson, Jesse Tyson, Enoch Clap, Hannah James, Mary Hopkins, William Hayward, Joseph Bruff, James Gillingham, Hannah Carey, George Carey, Jane McPherson, Sarah Ellicott, Mary Tyson, Nathan Tyson, Jr., H. U. Cope, Thomas Ellicott, Samuel Ellicott, Andrew Ellicott, Jr., James Ellicott (of Elias), Samuel Cary, Izak Procter, Rebecca Procter. 3rd column - E. Ellicott, Evan Thomas, Rachel Thomas, Eliza Wethered, Bena. Ellicott, Tacy Ellicott, James Ellicott, Lewin Wethered, Ann Hewes, Rachel Hough, Ann Poultney, Nathaniel Ellicott, Evan Thomas Ellicott, James Ellicott, Jr., Thomas Ellicott, Jr., William Ellicott, Evan Poultney, Rebecca Norris, Susan Hopkins, Ann Pope, Rachel Mason, Mary Waybill, Mary James, Eliza Riggs, Rebecca Sinclair, Eliza Sinclair.

**William Gillingham**, of Baltimore City, son of James and Elizabeth Gillingham, of the same place, married **Jane McPherson**, dau. of Isaac and Elizabeth McPherson (deceased), of Baltimore City, on 18th of 3rd mo., 1812.
Witnesses: 1st column - George Gillingham, Miriam Gillingham, John Gillingham, Izak Procter. James Carey, Hannah Marsh, Hannah Marsh, Jr., Ann Waterhouse, Thomas Ellicott, Jr., Eliza Marsh, Grace Knox, William Riley, Ennion Williams, Samuel Canby, Joseph Turner, Jr., Valerius Dukehart, Samuel H. Matthews, Andrew Ellicott, Jr., Daniel Kenny, Tacy Ellicott, P. E. Thomas, Nicholas Taylor, Eliza Procter. 2nd column - Elizabeth Hayward, Esther McPherson, Ezra Gillingham, Jonathan Janney, Elizabeth M. Janney, Elizabeth Lowden, Isaac Hayward, Ann Coates, Mary McPherson, Ann McPherson, Israel Janney, Andrew Ellicott, E. Ellicott, James Ellicott, Jr., William R. Gwinn, Enoch Clap, John G. Worthington, William Husband, George J. Knight, William Tyson, Samuel T. Matlack, John Hayward, John Marsh. 3rd column - Tacey McPherson, Isaac McPherson, James Gillingham, William Hayward, Elizabeth Gillingham, Ann Poultney, Elizabeth Thomas, Mary Curle, Rebecca Sinclair, Maria S. Johnston, Margaretta E. Wilson, Jane W. Muir, Mary James, Mary Ann Davis, Mary Hartshorn, Maria Dorsey, Rachel Poultney, Deborah Tyson, Deborah Hopkins, Susannah Hopkins, Eliza S. Sinclair, Elizabeth James, Hannah Hussey.

**Samuel Heston**, of Baltimore County, son of Joseph and Phebe Heston (deceased), of the same place, and **Rebecca Lownes**, dau. of Joseph and Miriam Lownes, of

Anne Arundel County, Maryland, declared their intentions to marry in Baltimore City and were married at the meeting house on Elk Ridge in Anne Arundel County on 21st of 10th mo., 1812.

Witnesses: 1st column - William Ellicott, John Ellicott (of John), Ruth Hallifield, Beulah Mendenhall, Rachel Updegraff, Sarah Ellicott, Cornelius Garretson, Nathaniel Ellicott, Mary Canby, Sarah Dorsey, Elizabeth Ellicott, Jr., Mary Kenneard, Martha Ellicott, Frances Ellicott, Joseph Evans, Edward S. Hough. 2nd column - Samuel Smith, Hannah Smith, Samuel Canby, Asenath Hamton, James Hamton, Jesse B. Hamton, Esther Smith, Jane Smith, Jonathan Ellicott, Esther Ellicott, Caleb Dorsey (of Thomas), Mary Kirk, John Thomas, Jacob Mendenhall, Samuel Godfrey, William Brown. 3rd column - Joseph Heston, Joseph Lownes, Miriam Lownes, Ann Heston, Esther E. Lownes, Joseph Heston, Jr., Charles Lownes, Letitia Heston, Zachariah Lownes, Jane Heston, Bethula Lownes, Josiah Lownes, William Heston, Charles Heston, Phebe Heston, Joseph H. Wright.

**Joseph Turner, Jr.**, of Baltimore City, son of Joseph and Sarah Turner, of Kent County, Maryland (the mother being deceased), married **Rebecca Sinclair**, dau. of John and Elizabeth Sinclair, of Baltimore City, on 21st of 10th mo., 1812.

Witnesses: 1st column - Edmund Prior Procter, Ann Douglass, Eliza S. Sinclair, Jr., Hannah Matlack, Mary King, Sarah Sinclair, Matilda Chamberlain, Rachel Poultney, Deborah Tyson, Mary Hopkins, Sarah Webster, Miriam Gillingham, Esther Sinclair, John Gillingham, Hugh Balderston, Robert Sinclair, John Ready, Samuel T. Matlack, P. E. Thomas, Isaac Tyson, James Robinson, Elisha Tyson, Jr., Valerius Dukehart, John Nicholson, Robert Sinclair, Jr. 2nd column - Anne Churchman, Elizabeth Ready, Gerard T. Hopkins, Izak Procter, Rebecca Procter, Mary Procter, Elizabeth Procter, Rebecca C. James, Susan Hopkins, Sophia Diffenderffer, Sarah B. Thomas, Hannah James, Catherine Diffenderffer, Elizabeth James, Hannah Carey, Sarah Massey, Ann Sinclair, Alisan Wilson, Caroline McKuine, Harriet Lee, Ruthy Byrnes, Elizabeth Tyson, Elizabeth Gillingham, Margaret Carey, Susanna Dukehart. 3rd column - Joseph Turner, Sarah Turner, John Sinclair, Elizabeth Sinclair, Micajah Churchman, William Sinclair, William Dallam, Edward King, Hannah Churchman, Margaret Balderston, Hannah J. Churchman, Emma Chamberlain, Eleanor Kenny, Dorothy Hopkins, Sarah Tyson, Tacy Mitchell, John Mitchel, Ann Douglas, Thomas Wilson, Elizabeth Thomas, Rachel Thomas, Ann Poultney, Rebecca Norris, Elizabeth Handy.

**Thomas Lea, Jr.**, son of Thomas and Sarah Lea, of New Castle County, Delaware, and **Elizabeth Ellicott, Jr.**, dau. of George and Elizabeth Ellicott, of Baltimore County, declared their intentions to marry in Baltimore City and were married at the meeting house on Elk Ridge in Anne Arundel County, Maryland, on 18th of 11th mo., 1812.

Witnesses: 1st column - John Ellicott, Jr., Edward S. Hough, Tacy Mitchell, Margaret Carey, Mary Moore, Gerard T. Hopkins, John E. Carey, Nathaniel Ellicott, Jr., Nathaniel Ellicott (of Jonathan), William Ellicott, Samuel Heston, Bethula Lownes, Cornelius Garretson, Hannah Garretson, Samuel Smith, Hannah Smith, Samuel Godfrey. 2nd column - John Ellicott (of John), Martha Ellicott, Hannah E. Carey, Frances Ellicott, John Lea, Jr., Ann B. Ellicott, Joseph Ellicott, Jr., Evan Thomas Ellicott, Thomas Moore, Jonathan Ellicott, Ambrose Updegraff, Jacob Mendenhall, Samuel Garretson, Joseph Lownes, William Kenworthy, Emmor Baily, Rebecca L. Heston. 3rd column - Thomas Lea, George Ellicott, Joseph Lea, Sarah Ann Lea, Ann Bellach, Joseph Bailey, Esther McPherson, Hannah Ellicott, Tacy Ellicott, Sarah Ellicott, Jr., B. Ellicott, Jr., Jonathan Ellicott, Esther Ellicott, Ann Moore, George Ellicott, Rachel Updegraff, Sarah A. Hough.

**William Edmondson George**, of Baltimore City, son of Robert and Ann George, both late of Kent County, Maryland, deceased, married **Sarah Ellicott, Jr.**, dau. of Jonathan and Sarah Ellicott, of Baltimore County, declared their intentions to marry in Baltimore City, Western District, and were married at a public meeting of Friends held at Elk Ridge in Anne Arundel County, Maryland, on 23rd of 12th mo., 1812.
Witnesses: 1st column - Samuel Ellicott, Frances Ellicott, Nathaniel Ellicott, George Ellicott, John Ellicott, Jr., Mary T. Worthington, Beulah Mendenhall, Abigail Atkinson, Joseph Hoag, Wesson Macomber, Hiel Peck, Emmor Baily, Ann Heston, Rebecca L. Heston, Elizabeth Baily, Letitia Heston, Sarah Evans, Bethula Lownes. 2nd column - Elizabeth Tyson, William Tyson, Mary Ellicott, Jr., Esther Ellicott, Jesse Tyson, Sarah Tyson, Joseph Lownes, Joseph Heston, Rob N. Johnston, John Thomas, William Brown, Charles Lownes, Joseph Evans, N. W. P. Pierpoint, Isaac C. Atkinson, Abraham Baily, Esther Smith, Ann B. Ellicott, Rebecca Kenworthy, William Kenworthy. 3rd column - Jonathan Ellicott, Sarah Ellicott, P. E. Thomas, Elizabeth Thomas, Evan Thomas, William Ellicott, Joseph Ellicott, Jr., Letitia Ellicott, John Ellicott (of John), Ann Thomas, Rachel Thomas, Mary Ann Ellicott, Hannah E. Carey, Tacy Ellicott, Sarah E. Tyson, Joseph G. Thomkins, Samuel Smith, Hannah Smith, Thomas Poultney.

**William Dallam**, of Baltimore City, son of John and Mary Dallam, of Harford County, married **Sarah Webster**, dau. of Isaac and Sarah Wesbter, of the same place, in Baltimore on 24th of 3rd mo., 1813.
Witnesses: 1st column - Sarah Savage, Rachel Poultney, Elizabeth Procter, Hannah Riley, Mary Ann Poultney, John Sinclair, Samuel Canby, Ann Watts, Elizabeth Hopkins, Joseph Turner, Jr., Gerard T. Hopkins, William Riley, John Marsh, Samuel G. Jones, Izak Procter, Rebecca Procter, Edmund Prior Procter, John Platts, Charles Hambleton. 2nd column - Sarah Riley, John Gillingham, John D. Toy, Margaret Fowler, Susanna Dukehart, Elizabeth Gillingham, Sarah W. Doddrell,

Thomas Wilson, Henry W. Webster, Elizabeth James, Deborah Hopkins, Ann Sinclair, Hugh Balderston, Samuel Jefferis, Ezra Gillingham, Thomas Dear, Elisha Tyson, Jr., N. W. Townsend. 3rd column - John Dallam, Sarah Webster, Sr., Wilson Worthington, Margaret Welmore, Frances Toy, Susanna Hopkins, Hannah Worthington, Ann B. Winstandly, Ann Peck, Priscilla James, John S. Peck, Sarah Webster, Rebecca Turner, Hannah E. Carey, Maria Dorsey, Margaret Carey, Elizabeth Hopkins, Eliza S. Sinclair.

**Thomas L. Reese**, of Baltimore City, son of John E. (deceased) and Ann Reese, married **Mary Moore, Jr.**, dau. of Thomas and Mary Moore, of Baltimore County, declared their intentions to marry in Baltimore City and were married at a public meeting of Friends at Elk Ridge in Anne Arundel County, Maryland, on 24th of 11th mo., 1813.
Witnesses: 1st column - William Brown, Ezra Gillingham, William Tyson, Nathaniel Ellicott, William Ellicott, Charles Lownes, Samuel Garretson, Ambrose Updegraff, Isaac Garretson, John Ellicott (of John), Ja. Hollingsworth, Henry Baily, Charles E. Baldwin, Joseph Garretson, Isaac C. Atkinson, Jonathan Ellicott, Jr., William Hopkins. 2nd column - Rebecca L. Heston, Frances Ellicott, Mary Kirk, Leaticia Ellicott, Rachel Ellicott, Esther Smith, Elizabeth Baily, Bethula Lownes, Abraham Baily, Ezra Baily, George Ellicott, John Hillen, George Ellicott, Jr., Sarah Ellicott, Isaac Tyson, Jr., Jonathan Ellicott, Joseph Lownes, Phinehas Buckman, Samuel Smith. 3rd column - Thomas Moore, Mary Moore, Ann McCormick, Dorothy Hopkins, Esther Reese, Mary Brown, Mary Hopkins, Mary Ellicott, Ann Moore, Gerard T. Hopkins, Isaac Briggs, Sarah B. Thomas, Caleb Moore, Margaret Bailey, Mary G. Ellicott, Hannah Smith, Rachel Updegraff, Hannah Smith, Elizabeth Tyson.

**John Ellicott**, of Baltimore County, son of John and Leah Ellicott, of the same place (deceased), and **Mary Kirk**, dau. of Timothy and Mary Kirk, of Baltimore County, declared their intentions to marry in Baltimore City and were married at the meeting house on Elk Ridge in Anne Arundel County, Maryland, on 19th of 1st mo., 1813.
Witnesses: 1st column - Josiah Lownes, Eli Garretson, Leaticia Ellicott, Mary Ann Ellicott, William Ellicott, Samuel Ellicott, Evan T. Ellicott, Samuel Godfrey, Samuel Smith, John E. Carey, John Ellicott, Jr., Alfred P. Gilpin, William Brown, George Ellicott, Jr., Mary Ellicott, Nathaniel Ellicott, Samuel Jefferis, Jonathan Ellicott, John Marsh, Cornelius Garretson. 2nd column - Bena. Ellicott, George Ellicott, Sarah Ellicott, Timothy Kirk, Arthur Pue, Edward S. Hough, Joseph Lownes, Richard Cassy, Isaac Garretson, Thomas Moore, John Thomas, Edward Pue, Rebecca L. Heston, Samuel Heston, Esther E. Lownes, Bethula Lownes, Rebecca Procter, Hannah Garretson, Mary Updegraff, Lydia Jefferis, Rachel Mason. 3rd column - Martha Carey, Rachel Kirk, Mahlon Kirk, Jonathan Ellicott,

Jr., Edith Kirk, Margaret Carey, Tacey Ellicott, Esther McPherson, Hannah Carey, Frances Ellicott, Hannah Ellicott, Hannah Price, Hetty Few, Esther Smith, Rachel Ellicott, Martha Ellicott, Emmor Baily, Samuel Garretson, Elizabeth Baily, Jr., N. W. P.[R.?] Pierpoint, Hannah Marsh, Sr.

**Nathan Tyson, Jr.**, of Baltimore City, son of Elisha and Mary Tyson (the mother being deceased), of Baltimore County, married **Martha Ellicott**, dau. of George and Elizabeth Ellicott, of Baltimore County, declared their intention to marry in Baltimore City and were married at the meeting house on Elk Ridge in Anne Arundel County, Maryland, on 27th of 9th mo., 1815.
Witnesses: 1st column - Margaret Prine, Mary Ann Wilson, Jonathan Ellicott, Jr., John Sinclair, Robert Turner, Charles E. Baldwin, N. W. P. Pierpoint, Samuel Heston, Thomas Moore, Gerard T. Hopkins, Cornelius Garretson, Hannah Garretson, Samuel Smith, Hannah Smith. 2nd column - Elisha Tyson, William Ellicott, Esther McPherson, Tacy Ellicott, Elisha Tyson, Jr., B. Ellicott, Mary McPherson, Deborah Tyson, Rachel Updegraff, Margaret Moore, Mary K. Ellicott, Eliza Sinclair, John Ellicott, Samuel Ellicott, Evan T. Ellicott. 3rd column - George Ellicott, Margaret Tyson, Mary Clap, Sa.[?] B. Ellicott, Nathaniel Ellicott, Nathaniel Ellicott, Jr., William Tyson, Ann B. Ellicott, Esther Smith, Sarah Knight, J. W. Wilson, Isaac Tyson, Elizabeth Tyson, Patience Tyson, Enoch Clap.

**Micajah Churchman**, of Baltimore County, son of Edward and Rebecca Churchman, of Delaware County, Pennsylvania, married **Eliza Sinclair**, dau. of John and Elizabeth Sinclair, of Baltimore City, in Baltimore on 20th of 12th mo., 1815.
Witnesses: 1st column - Rebecca Turner, Mary J. Ellicott, Eleanor Kenny, Susanna Needles, Amos James, Mary C. James, Rebecca Procter, Martha E. Tyson, Rebecca Beans, Hannah E. Carey, Rachel Mason, Hannah Stapler, Matilda Chamberlain, Deborah W. Starr, Emma Chamberlain, Betty Loudon, Susanna James, Mary Ann Sheppard, Deborah James, Mary Procter. 2nd column - Izak Procter, Philip E. Thomas, William R. Gwinn, Mary James, Joseph King, Jr., William E. George, Elisha Tyson, Jr., Ann Thomas, Priscilla James, Samuel R. Turner, William H. Sinclair, Sarah Poultney, Hannah Ellicott, Benjamin Palmer, Mary Palmer, Bethula Lownes, Samuel Trego, Charles Canby, Andrew Ellicott. 3rd column - John Sinclair, Elizabeth Sinclair, Caleb Churchman, Hannah James Churchman, Owen Churchman, William Painter, Phebe Painter, Mahlon Chandlee, Ann Sinclair, Deborah Hopkins, Elizabeth James, Margaret Carey, Sally B. Thomas, Mary Hopkins, Ann M. Sanderson, Elizabeth Gillingham, Rachel Thomas, Mary Ann Poultney, Rachel Thomas.

**William Hartley**, of Baltimore County, son of Samuel and Lavinia Hartley, of the same place, and **Tacy Buckman**, dau. of Phineas and Susanna Buckman (the

mother being deceased), of Anne Arundel County, Maryland, declared their intentions to marry in Baltimore City and were married at the meeting house on Elk Ridge in Anne Arundel County on 20th of 12th mo., 1815.
Witnesses: 1st column - William Ellicott, Isaac C. Atkinson, Joseph Hollingsworth, John Ellicott, Jonathan Ellicott, Jr., Josiah Lownes, Joseph Garretson, Israel Atkinson, Thomas Moore, George Ellicott, Cornelius Garretson, Hannah Garretson, Noah Worthington. 2nd column - Mary K. Ellicott, Rachel Updegraff, Rachel Buckman, Ruth Brown, Isaac Garretson, Margaret Garretson, Ann Elizabeth Watkins, Mary Fox, Mary Walters, Abigail Atkinson, Jonathan Ellicott, Samuel Smith, Joseph Lownes, Nathaniel Ellicott, Jr. 3rd column - Samuel Hartley, Leavinia Hartley, Phineas Buckman, C. Buckman, Abner Buckman, Levi Hartley, Samuel Buckman, Ruth Hartley, Thomas Hartley, Grace Buckman, Sarah Ellicott, Mary McCormick, Ann Moore, Esther Smith.

**Samuel Baily**, of Baltimore City, son of Joseph and Elizabeth Baily, of the Borough of Wilmington, Delaware (the mother being deceased), married **Hannah James**, dau. of Joseph and Mary James, in Baltimore on 17th of 1st mo., 1816.
Witnesses: 1st column - Mary M. Ellicott, Patience Tyson, Deborah Tyson, Elisha Tyson, Jr., Mary Ann Hayward, Thomas Tyson, Samuel Carey, John J. Ellicott, John Hughes, Isaac Hayward, James Gillingham, Gerard T. Hopkins, Rachel Hough, Samuel Byrnes, Susanna Needles, Ann W. Sanderson, Elizabeth Robertson, Elizabeth Baily. 2nd column - Elizabeth Hopkins, Hannah Litle, Rebecca Procter, John C. Norris, William Gillingham, Israel Janney, John Litle, Rod. William McKinnon, William Litle, John. C. Worrall, Thomas Duer, John Needles, Jr., Ann Waterhouse, Izak Procter, Grace Knox, Elizabeth Gillingham, Elizabeth K. West, Sarah Sinclair, Elizabeth Hayward, Hannah Ellicott. 3rd column - Joseph James, Mary James, George Baily, Rebecca C. James, Sarah Savage, Ruthy Byrnes, Sarah James, James Baily, W. B. Atterbury, William Hopkins, John G. Worthington, Mary J. Ellicott, Mary Clap, Margaret Carey, Hannah E. Carey, Eleanor Kenny, Mary D. Snyder, Hannah Riley, Deborah Hopkins, Mary L. James.

**John Litle**, of Baltimore City, son of John and Hannah Litle of the City of Washington (the father being deceased), married **Sarah Sinclair**, dau. of Robert and Esther Sinclair, of Baltimore County, in Baltimore City at the meeting of Friends on Lombard Street on 19th of 6th mo., 1816.
Witnesses: 1st column - Hannah Litle, Mary C. James, Margaret Balderston, Mary Hopkins, William E. Bartlett, Sarah Brown, Eliza Brown, Caleb Pancoast, Elizabeth Sinclair, Ann W. Sanderson, Susan Hopkins, Elizabeth Lawelen (per order), Hannah J. Baily, Rachel Updegraff, Ann Scott, Mary Hartshorn, Mary Procter, Sarah Hopkins, John Sinclair, Izak Procter, Elizabeth Sinclair, Jr. 2nd column - Esther Sinclair, Ann Poultney, Deborah Hopkins, Elizabeth Louden (per proxy), Mary J. Ellicott, Sarah Savage, Sarah R. Webster, Margaretta E. Wilson,

Hannah E. Carey, Eliza Hastings, Mary Ann Jones, Sarah E. Byrnes, John Ruckle, David Brown, Samuel Baily, Isaac Tyson, Jr., John C. Norris, John L. Hayward, Jacob T. Bunting, George J. Knight, Ann Sinclair. 3rd column - Robert Sinclair, Jesse Talbott, Hannah Talbott, Elizabeth Litle, Charles Litle, W. Litle, R. Litle, S. T. Gilpen, Esther Sinclair, Jr., David Saunders, Joseph Turner, Jr., Rebecca Turner, Mary Ann Davis, Ann James, Mary L. James, Elizabeth Thomas, Rachel Thomas, Eliza Churchman, Mary M. Ellicott, Rachel Mason, Ruthy Byrnes.

**Isaac Garretson**, of Elkridge, Annarundle County, Maryland, son of Cornelius and Hannah Garretson, of the same place, and **Rachel Ely**, dau. of Mahlon (deceased) and Mary Ely, of Baltimore County, declared their intentions to marry in Baltimore City and were married at the meeting house at Elkridge on 25th of 9th mo., 1816. Witnesses: 1st column - Hannah Smith, Samuel Godfrey, John Ellicott, R. Bond, James Harvey, Charles Canby, Jonathan Ellicott, Jr., Nathaniel Ellicott, Jr., Joseph Lownes. 2nd column - Jesse Garretson, Rachel Updegraff, Rachel Kirk, Bethula Lownes, Asher Ely, Eli Garretson, Joseph Ely, Elizabeth E. Lea, George Ellicott, Samuel Smith. 3rd column - Cornelius Garretson, Hannah Garretson, Rachel Garretson, Jr., Margaret Garretson, Rachel John, Jonathan Ellicott, Samuel Garretson, Ann Garretson, Hugh Ely, Joseph Garretson.

**William E. Bartlett**, of Baltimore City, son of Richard and Rebecca Bartlett, of Talbot County, Maryland (both deceased), married **Mary James**, dau. of Amos and Mary James, of Baltimore City (the mother being deceased), in Baltimore on 20th of 11th mo., 1816.
Witnesses: 1st column - Eliza Jones, Ann James, Edward Stabler, Jr., Elias B. Smith, Elizabeth Norris, Elizabeth Gillingham, Elizabeth N. Scott, Rachel Mathews, Mary Tunis, Susan Hopkins, Elizabeth Lowden, Amos Gillingham, Patience Tyson, Sarah Savage, Ann W. Sanderson, Jane Harvey, Martha E. Tyson, Rebecca C. James, Eleanor Kenny, Elizabeth Tyson, Mary M. Ellicott, Hannah Ellicott, Polly Ellicott, Ann B. Ellicott, Rebecca Procter. 2nd column - William E. George, Elisha Tyson, Jr., T. R. Mathews, Deborah James, Mary Grier Cope, Dorothy Hopkins, Rachel Hough, Gerard T. Hopkins, Andrew Ellicott, George Baily, Hannah Carey, Deborah Hopkins, William R. Gwinn, Margaret Carey, Mary Hopkins, Ann Sinclair, Benjamin P. Moore, Elizabeth Baily, Ann S. White. Rebecca Turner, Esther Sinclair, Sarah S. Litle, Rachel Mason, Mary J. Ellicott, Maria Kenly. 3rd column - Amos James, Mary C. James, Hannah Bartlett, Ann James, William L. James, Priscilla Morgan, Elizabeth James, George Gillingham, Herman Cope, Miriam Gillingham, Priscilla James, Susan James, Samuel Carey, James C. Hough, Jonathan Harvey, Isaac Tyson, Jr., John Thomas Moon, John M. Howland, Israel Janney, John C. Norris, John Gillingham, George H. Kearl, John Thomas Brooke, John Needles, Jr., William Litle.

**James Large**, of the City of Philadelphia, son of Ebenezer Large (deceased) and his wife Dorothea Large, of the same place, married **Elizabeth Poultney**, dau. of Thomas and Ann Poultney, of Baltimore City, in Baltimore on 15th of 1st mo., 1817.
Witnesses: 1st column - James Carey, Sarah Riley, Evan Thomas (of Philip), Ben Ellicott, Jr., Rachel Mason, Margaretta E. Wilson, Maria C. Tate, Juliana Hughes, Frances Sappington, Rebecca Turner, Fanny Van Wyck, Martha Carey. Elisha Tyson, Jr., Sarah Matilda McCoy, Achsah Gwinn, Nancy Mactier, Rachel Dorsey, John C. Moale, William Hopkins, Izak Procter, Rebecca Procter, Eliza Procter. 2nd column - Sarah Poultney, James B. Thompson, Evan T. Ellicott, Evan Thomas, Jr., Philip E. Thomas, William G. Thomas, Rebecca Hudson, Mary Harlan, Sarah M. A. Betts, Tacy Ellicott, J. R. Tunis, Pim *[sic]* Nevins, Jr., Mary M. Ellicott, Caroline H. Walker, Francina A. Cheston, Anna W. Thomas, Elizabeth C. Tilghman, Susanna Warfield, Mary Griffith, Mary Sheppard, Mary Betts, Elizabeth Scott, Margaret Carey. 3rd column - Thomas Poultney, Ann Poultney, Evan Thomas, Rachel Thomas, John Large, Thomas Mifflin, Evan Poultney, Samuel Poultney, Deborah Tyson, Ann Thomas, Philip Poultney, Rachel Poultney, Mary Ann Poultney, Rebecca C. James, Hannah Proud, Fanny Glasauy[?], Maria V. Renaudet, Rachel Ellicott, Sarah Hopkins, Rachel Thomas, Jr., Ann B. Ellicott, James Hough, Hannah Carey.

**Abijah Janney**, of Alexandria in the District of Columbia, son of Israel and Pleasant Janney, of Loudoun County, Virginia (the mother being deceased), married **Mary Ellicott**, of Baltimore City, dau. of John Mitchel *[sic]* and wife Tacy (the mother being deceased), in Baltimore on 16th of 4th mo., 1817.
Witnesses: 1st column - Mary Hopkins, Elizabeth Robertson, Mary Ann Norris, Sarah B. Hopkins, H. E. Carey, Martha Balderston, Isaiah Balderston, Sarah R. Webster, Rachel Hough, Rachel Mason, Hannah Litle, Sabina Crownover, R. G. Etting, Izak Procter, Andrew McCoy, Thomas Harris (Virginia), Samuel Heston, George J. Knight, Moses Sheppard, Stephen Procter, Edward Farquhar. 2nd column - Mary Waterhouse, Jane Knight, Ann Ellicott, Maria Tyson, Hannah Stapler, Sarah Comfort, Jr., Margaret Carey, Ann James, Elizabeth Gillingham, Susanna Needles, Ann W. Sanderson, Susanna Hopkins, Abel Knight, Elizabeth Knight, Thomas S. Sheppard, Rebecca Procter, Elizabeth Procter, Ezra Gillingham, John Marsh, Nicholas Popplein, Jonathan Harvey, Joseph C. Worral, James Hough. 3rd column - John Mitchel, Ann Waterhouse, Phineas Janney, Ann B. Ellicott, Andrew Ellicott, Jonathan Janney, Mary M. Ellicott, Sarah S. Janney, Dorothy Webster, Rachel Ellicott, Eleanor Tyson, Mary Ann Sheppard, Catharine Etting, A. C. Clapham, Elizabeth Scott, Mary J. Bartlett, R. Updegraff, Miriam Gillingham, Ann Norris, Gerard T. Hopkins, Hannah Pope, Theodate Pope, Dorothy Hopkins.

**Benjamin P. Moore**, of Talbot County, Maryland, son of Robert Moore, of Easton, Talbot County, and wife Mary (deceased), married **Mary Hopkins**, dau. of Gerard T. Hopkins, of Baltimore City, and wife Dorothy, in Baltimore on 21st of 5th mo., 1817.
Witnesses: 1st column - Hannah J. Baily, Mary M. Ellicott, Jane Harvey, Rebecca Turner, Esther Sinclair, Miriam Gillingham, Rebecca H. Gillingham, Ann Norris, Ann James, William E. Bartlett, Samuel T. Kennard, Thomas R. Matthews, Andrew Ellicott, Deborah James, Susan James, Martha Penfold, Mary Cope, Samuel Hough, Robert Hough, H. M. Bond, Izak Procter, Elizabeth Procter, Stephen Procter, Edward A. Farquhar. 2nd column - Margarett Carey, H. E. Carey, Mary Ellicott, Hannah Ellicott, Rachel Matthews, Mary J. Bartlett, Martha E. Tyson, Grace Knox, Priscilla James, James Gillingham, William Riley, John Marsh, Ennion Williams, Robert Sinclair, Elias B. Smith, William Litle, John Thomas Moon, James C. Hough, Hannah Ellicott, Mary Ann Marshall, Tacy Ellicott, Ann Sinclair, Patience Tyson, Susanna Needles, Rachel Mason. 3rd column - Dorothy Hopkins, Gerard T. Hopkins, Robert Moore, M.D., Deborah Hopkins, Rachel Hough, Evan Thomas, Sr., Richard Hopkins, M.D., Amos James, Jesse Tyson, Frances Hopkins, Elizabeth Hopkins, Sarah B. Hopkins, Johns Hopkins, Thomas Tyson, William Hopkins, Reynolds Knox, Elizabeth Louden, Anna Tyson, Maria Norwood, Mary A. Norris, Rachel Ellicott, Ann Ellicott, Elizabeth James, Mary Hough, Margaret Tyson.

**Joseph King**, merchant, of Baltimore City, son of Thomas and Jane King, both late of Newcastle upon Tyne in the County of Northumberland, Kingdom of Great Britain, deceased, married **Tacy Ellicott**, dau. of Elias and Mary Ellicott, of Baltimore City (the mother being deceased), in Baltimore at the meeting house on Lombard Street on 17th of 12th mo., 1817.
Witnesses: 1st column - Samuel G. Jones, Esther Sinclair, Jr., Mary James, Rachel Mason, Margaretta E. Wilson, Eliza Bond, Harriet Tippe, Mary Williams, Rebecca Procter, Ruthy Byrnes, Mary B. Wilson, Dorothy Hopkins, Rebecca C. James, Elizabeth Gillingham, Frances B. Harris, Ann H. James, Ann H. Sanderson, Ann Sinclair, Rachel Ellicott, Hannah McPherson, Sarah B. Hopkins, John C. Moale, Josiah Marsh, Thomas Tyson, John Thomas Brook, Ezra Gillingham, William Hopkins. 2nd column - E. B. Smith, John Gillingham, John C. Norris, Howard Sims, Jonathan E. Tyson, Henry Ellicott, Gerard T. Hopkins, James Gillingham, Isaac Tyson, Elizabeth Louden, Ann Sheppard, Rachel Hough, George Carey, P. Poultney, Mary Tyson, Evan T. Tyson, Rachel Tyson, Henrietta E. Tyson, Margaret Carey, Hannah E. Carey, Mary McPherson, Nathaniel Ellicott, Jr., Evan Poultney, Bena. Ellicott, Jr., Rachel Poultney, Deborah Tyson. 3rd column - Elias Ellicott, Evan Thomas, Bena. Ellicott, James Ellicott, John Ellicott, Lewin Wethered, Elizabeth E. Wethered, Rachel T. Hewes, Eliza K. Updegraff, John Hewes, Evan T. Ellicott, Andrew T. Ellicott, James Ellicott, Jr., Elias Ellicott, Jr.,

Philip T. Ellicott, Mary Ellicott, Ann B. Ellicott, Ann McPherson, Ann Thomas, Hannah Ellicott, Esther McPherson, Martha Evans, Mary Ellicott, Eleanor King, Samuel Ellicott.

**Thomas West**, of Harford County, son of Nathaniel and Elizabeth West (the mother being deceased), married **Cassandra McCoy**, of Baltimore City, dau. of Philip Coale *[sic]* and wife Ann (deceased), in Baltimore on 21st of 1st mo., 1818.
Witnesses: 1st column - Rebecca Procter, Margaret Balderston, Mary Robertson, Deborah Hopkins, Hannah J. Baily, Ruthy Byrnes, Grace Knox, Sarah Riley, Hannah E. Carey, Rachel Hough, Mary Ann Jones, Elizabeth Hopkins, Mary Ann Hayward, Martha Norbury, Sarah James, Eliza Updegraff, Elizabeth Gillingham, Sarah B. Hopkins, Elizabeth McDowell, Elizabeth James. 2nd column - Ann T. Sinclair, Elizabeth G. Sinclair, Hannah L. Riley, Reynolds Knox, Isaac N. Toy, Andrew McCoy, George Norbury, Hugh Balderston, Jane West, Grace Ann West, Rebecca Beans, Thomas W. Coale, Alisann C. Foard, Eliza H. Smith, P. Taylor, John Elias Hicks, Ann Coates, Ann Poultney, Elizabeth K. West, William McCoy. 3rd column - Frances Foard, Sarah Lukens, Mahlon West, Mary West, Ann Coale, Clarissa Fussell, Ann McCoy, John C. McCoy, David G. McCoy, Amos West, Mary Dallam, Margaret Wellmore, Sarah Ruff, Elizabeth Loudon, Eli C. West, Robert McCoy, Jas. Baily[?], Sarah Janette Cohen, Marriet Foard.

**William Birdsall**, of Montgomery County, Maryland, son of Whitson and Rachel Birdsall, of Loudon County, Virginia, married **Ruth Hartly**, dau. of Samuel and Levinia Hartly, of Baltimore County, declared their intentions to marry in Baltimore and were married at the meeting house on Elk Ridge in Anne Arundel County, Maryland, on 15th of 4th mo., 1818.
Witnesses: 1st column - Andrew M. Birdsall, William Hartly, Samuel Hartly, Jr., Just.[?] Hardfield, Samuel Canby, Elizabeth Ellicott, Samuel Godfrey, Joseph Lowns, Esther Smith, Hannah Kenny, Joseph Garretson. 2nd column - Hannah Birdsall, Livi Hartly, Thomas Hartly, John Birdsall, Mary Canby, Esther E. Lownes, George Ellicott, Jonathan Ellicott, Eli Garretson, Bethula Lowns, Josiah Lownes. 3rd column - Samuel Hartly, Sr., Levania Hartly, Whitsone Birdsall, Eliza Birdsall, Miriam Lownes, Rachel Updegraff, Rachel Garretson, Sarah Moore, Elias B. Smith, Samuel Heston.

**Aquila M. Kirk**, of York County, Pennsylvania, son of Caleb and Lydia Kirk, married **Sarah Needles**, of Baltimore City, dau. of Edward and Sarah Needles (both deceased), in Baltimore on 27th of 5th mo., 1818.
Witnesses: 1st column - William Riley, Josh. Browne, Hugh Balderston, Hannah Marsh, Cathe. M. Smith (per order), Rebecca Procter, Grace Knox, Ann Pope, Sarah Riley, Maria Pope, Rebecca Turner, Ann Norris, Elizabeth Lowdon (per order), Mary James, Hannah Pope, Eleanor Kenny (by request), Margarett Carey,

Ann Ewing, Elizabeth Gillingham, Elizabeth Scott, Ann Scott, Sr. 2nd column - John C. Norris, Thomas Meconckin, Mordocai Matthews, Jr., Amos Matthews, Henry Dowell, Benjamin P. Parrott, John Meconckin (per order), John Harris (by request), Martha E. Tyson, Hannah E. Carey, Dorothy Hopkins (per order), Mary Bartlett (by request). Rachel Mason, Ann Sinclair, Elizabeth Y. Balderston, Eliza Ann Balderston, Izak Procter, Stephen Procter (per order), James Gillingham, Ennion Williams, Eleanor Kenny. 3rd column - John Needles, Elizabeth Needles, James B. Needles, Edward Needles, Jr., Susannah Needles (per order), Elmer Kirk, Josiah Kirk, Eli Kirk, John Marsh, Samuel T. Kemp, M.D., Mary Ann Norris, George Norbury, Eliza Marsh, Susan Yarnall, Mary H. Marsh, Martha Norbury, Tacy B. Norbury, Rachel P. Matthews, Hannah Marsh, Sr., Maria R. Briedenbough.

**John Hopkins**, of Baltimore County, son of John and Elizabeth Hopkins (both deceased), married **Rebecca C. James**, dau. of Joseph and Mary James, in Baltimore at the meeting house on Lombard Street on 10th of 6th mo., 1818.
Witnesses: 1st column - Rebecca Procter, Martha Carey, Hannah Ellicott, Mary M. Ellicott, Frances B. Harris, Lydia Webster, Ann G. Maxwell, Margarett Savage, H. E. Carey, Margaret Tyson, Ann B. Ellicott, Amos James, George Norbury, Martha Norbury, M. A. Jones, Susan James, Mary Hough, Deborah James. 2nd column - Eleanor Sudler, Juliana Hughes, Eliza Conkling, Priscilla Beckett, James C. Hough, Eleanor Tyson, Eleanor Kenny, Nathan Tyson, Ann W. Sanderson, Sarah Savage, Catharine Sanderson, William Mecteer, Hannah Mecteer, Hannah Proud, Rachel Hough, Elizabeth H. Tyson, Patience Tyson, Rachel Mason. 3rd column - Joseph James, Mary James, Ann H. James, Sarah James, Samuel James, Samuel Baily, Howard Sims, Alisanna Wilson, Mary Ann Hopkins, Charlotte W. Hopkins, Sophia Hopkins, Christopher Wilson, Jr., William Hopkins, Mary Hartshorne, Lurana Broud [Proud?], Frances Hopkins, Eliza Hopkins, Dorothy Hopkins.

**Isaac Wilson**, of Belmont County, Ohio, son of Samuel and Rebeckah Wilson, of Bucks County, Pennsylvania (deceased), and **Ann McCoy**, of Baltimore City, widow of Joseph McCoy and dau. of James Hicks, late of Harford County (deceased), and wife Mary, married in Baltimore on 14th of 4th mo., 1819.
Witnesses: 1st column - Grace Knox, Esther H. Townsend, Ezra Gillingham, Matilda Chamberlain, Cassandra West, Esther Sinclair, Ruthy Byrnes, David G. McCoy, John C. McCoy, Esther Sinclair, Jr., Deborah Sinclair, Hannah Riley, Eleanor Kenny, Eleanor A. Kenny, Ann Ewing, Mary Ann Sinclair, Eleanor Boyd, Elizabeth Sinclair, William Gillingham, William K. Jones, John Gillingham. 2nd column - Gerard T. Hopkins, James Gillingham, Reynolds Knox, Robert Sinclair, Ann Waterhouse, Margaret Cary, Ann W. Sanderson, Susanna Hopkins, Mary Bartlett, Susanna Needles, Ann Sinclair, Rachel Mason, Elizabeth Robertson, Mary M. Ellicott, Thomas Stapler, Hannah Stapler, Mary Ann Norris, Jacob Tyson,

Esther Ellicott (by request), Hoopes Chamberlain, Elizabeth Scott. 3rd column - George Harris, Jr., J. G. Underwood, H. Harris, William McCoy, Joseph Sitler, David Wilson, Mary Grey, Martha McCoy, Mary Malsby, John Baker, Enoch Underwood, Mary Underwood.

**Thomas Atkinson**, of Easton, Talbot County, Maryland, son of Aaron and Ann Atkinson (both deceased), married **Hannah Hussey**, of Baltimore City, dau. of George and Rachel Hussey (both deceased), in Baltimore on 15th of 12th mo., 1819.
Witnesses: 1st column - Elizabeth James (by request), Priscila James (by request), Susanna James (by request), Sarah Riley, Ann Waterhouse, William Riley, Joseph K. Neall, Daniel Troth, Sarah Riley, Jr. (by request). 2nd column - Sarah Brooks, Jr., Rachel Brooks, R. Mathewes, Elizabeth James (by request), Amos James, Edith Price, Ann B. Troth, Mary C. James, Martha M. Edmondson, Ann James (by request). 3rd column - Joseph Hussey, Ellen Hussey, Rachel Hussey, John Brooks, William E. Bartlett, Isaac Brooks, Sarah Brooks, Ennion Williams, Hannah Williams, Alice Brooks.

**Thomas J. Hull**, of Baltimore City, son of David and Phebe Hull, of Chestertown, Kent County, Maryland (both deceased), married **Harriet Foard**, dau. of Joseph and Frances Foard, of Baltimore City (the father being deceased), in Baltimore on 12th of 4th mo., 1821.
Witnesses: 1st column - William Procter, John Dukehart, Thomas Matthews, John Brooks, Richard H. Townsend, Michael Lamb, Edith Scott, Mary Perine, Mary B. Mullikin, David Holman, John M. Foulke, Maulden Perine, Jane Waite (by desire), Mary B. Waters, Susan A. Morgan, Martha Balderston, Elizabeth B. Hayward, Frances H. Hunter, Margaret Brown, Ann Reed, Mary B. Lafetra, Phebe Townsend. 2nd column - James Clark, Alexander Smith, John H. Naff, Elizabeth Yerkess (by desire), Tacy Norbury, Eliza Ann Smith, Mary Hopkins, Margaret Young, Hannah J. D. Fearson, Cassandra A. Brevitt, Esther A. Townsend, Maria E. Conn, Naomi Taylor, Sophia Hopkins, Priscilla Gover, Charlotte W. Hopkins, Ann Gover, Phebe Lafetra, Jane Brown, Rachel Mott, Alisanna Cornthwait, Mary Y. Thomas, Eliza Sylvester. 3rd column - Frances Foard, Cassandra West, Thomas West, Caaary Southcomb, Allisanna Southcomb (per order), John C. McCoy, Robert McCoy, Ann Perine (by order), Thomas Mackenzie, Ann B. Brown, Mary R. Medcalf, Elizabeth Comegys, Mary Brown, Rachel McKinsey, Abigail Medcalf, Mary Townsend, Hannah P. Townsend, Sarah Lafetra, Ann Chandlee, Elizabeth S. Trimble, Eleanor Orem, Elizabeth Jones.

**Israel Price**, of Baltimore City, son of Samuel and Ann Price, of Baltimore County (the mother being deceased), married **Jane Trimble**, dau. of Isaac and Elizabeth

Trimble, of Baltimore County (the mother being deceased), in Baltimore on 16th of 5th mo., 1821.
Witnesses: 1st column - Elizabeth Trimble, Jr., Elizabeth Price, Francis Price, Elizabeth Trimble, Jane Trimble, Isaac Trimble, Jr., David U. Brown, Rachel McKinsey, Catharine Brown, Jr., Mary D. Brown, Frances Brown, David Brown, Gerard T. Hopkins, Hugh Balderston, G. S. Townsend, M.D.; 2nd column - William Brown, Jane Brown, Joseph Trimble, James Gillingham, Philip E. Thomas, William R. Jones, William Riley, John Marsh, Hannah Marsh, Thomas Winn, Martha E. Tyson, Deborah Pleasants, Rachel Mason, Hannah E. Carey. 3rd column - Sarah W. Doddrell, Hanna P. Townsend, Mary Townsend, Sarah Lafetra, Rachel Mott, Joshua Mott, Grace Knox, Rebecca Procter, Elizabeth Scott, Sarah Knight, Mary J. Bartlett.

**Elijah Goldsmith**, of Baltimore City, son of Nathan and Elizabeth Goldsmith, of Suffolk County, New York (both deceased), married **Mary M. Procter**, dau. of Izak and Rebecca Procter, of Baltimore City (the father being deceased), in Baltimore on 13th of 6th mo., 1821.
Witnesses: 1st column - Daniel Cobb, Isaac Tyson, Rachel T. Green, Emily West, Cassandra West, Elizabeth Ellicott, Sarah Riley, Ann Peck, Susanna Walthams, Evelina Reed, Hannah Kenny, Matilda Reed, Margaret Norris, Martha E. Tyson, Ann Jones, Elizabeth McDowell, Hugh Balderston, John Gillingham, John Marsh, Reynolds Knox, Thomas Norris (of Thomas), John C. Norris, John C. McCoy, Edith Kenny, Dorothy Hopkins. 2nd column - Eliza Procter, Tacy B. Norbury, Gerard T. Hopkins, Thomas Winn, Martha Norbury, Ruth Cobb, Deborah Procter, William Kenworthy, George Carey, David U. Brown, Thomas Mackenzie, Isaac N. Hoopes, John H. Hewes, Ephraim Larrabee, Richard H, Townsend, George Norbury, John M. Foulke, William Smith, Mary Ann Norris, Jane Yates, Elizabeth Byrnes, Catharine Popplien, Daniel Pope, Ennion Williams, Martha Carey. 3rd column - Rebecca Procter, William Procter, Anna Procter, Margaret C. Clowdsley, Jane R. Way, Jane Clowdsley, Mary B. Lafetra, Hannah Marsh, Thomas M. Smith, John Smith, John Warder, Andrew Ellicott, Susan Hopkins, Lois R. Pope, Mary Allen, H. E. Carey, Ann Norris, Mary McPherson, Hannah P. Townsend, Ann W. Sanderson, Mary Bartlett, Mary H. Marsh, Rachel Brooks, Ann James, Eliza Marsh.

**William Litle**, of Baltimore City, son of John and Hannah Litle (both deceased), married **Elizabeth James**, dau. of Amos and Mary James, of Baltimore City (the mother being deceased), in Baltimore on 10th of 4th mo., 1822.
Witnesses: 1st column - Mary Ann Norris, Rachel Mason, Elizabeth Thomas, Robert Sinclair, Hannah Ann Tyson, John Sinclair, H. E. Carey, Susan Hopkins, Deborah Tyson, Ann Sewell, Martha Carey, Ruth Cobb, Rebecca Webster, Joseph Turner, Jr., Rachel H. Green, Eliza Procter, Sarah Hopkins, Mary M. Goldsmith,

Mary M. Ellicott, Mary Jefferis, Joel Brown, John H. Hewes, William L. Bull, Daniel Cobb, William Hopkins, T. M. Smith, S. S. Wood, R. M. Smith, Elizabeth Hopkins, Gerard T. Hopkins, William Riley, Hugh Balderston, Andrew Ellicott. 2nd column - John L. Talbott, John M. Foulke, Ann S. Foulke, Margaret Balderston, Grace Knox, Reynolds Knox, Eliza Churchman, Micajah Churchman, Cassandra West, John P. Sinclair, John C. McCoy, Elizabeth Pancoast, Rebecca Turner, Mary Ann Sinclair, Esther Sinclair, Deborah Hopkins, Deborah Sinclair, Ann W. Sanderson, E. C. Jefferis, Rebecca Bartlett, John Gillingham, Thomas S. Sheppard, Mary Gillingham, Rachel Hough, Isaac Tyson, Jr., Isaac Wilson, Samuel Carey, Ennion Williams, P. E. Thomas, William Tyson, William K. Rowe, John C. Norris, William H. Sinclair. 3rd column - Amos James, Mary C. James, John Litle, Hannah Talbott, Sarah S. Litle, Mary J. Bartlett, Robert Litle, Susanna Jessop, Susan James, Richard H. Litle, William E. Bartlett, Miriam Gillingham, Charles Litle, Ann James, Joseph Stretch, George Gillingham, Hannah Litle, Jesse Talbott, Thomas Mills, William A. Talbott, Priscilla James, T. R. Matthews, James Gillingham, George Carey.

**John M. Foulke**, of Baltimore City, son of William and Margaret Foulke, of Gwynedd in Montgomery County, Pennsylvania (the mother being deceased), married **Ann Sinclair**, dau. of Robert and Esther Sinclair, of Baltimore City, on 10th of 4th mo., 1822.
Witnesses: 1st column - Charles Litle, Mary J. Bartlett, Hannah Talbott, Elizabeth Litle, George Carey, William Litle, Miriam Gillingham, Elizabeth Hopkins, Joseph Stretch, Priscilla James, Susan Hopkins, Ruth Cobb, Deborah Sinclair, Elizabeth G. Sinclair, John Sinclair, Mary Ann Sinclair, Elizabeth Pancoast, Reynolds Knox, John Smith, Grace Knox, Cassandra West, Thomas West, S. A. Stansbury, S. Lukens (by request), Rachel Mason, Hannah Ann Tyson, Mary M. Ellicott, Elizabeth Thomas, Rachel H. Green, Patience Tyson, Ann Peck, Mary M. Goldsmith, Eliza Procter. 2nd column - Esther Sinclair, Jr., John P. Sinclair, Levi Foulke, E. M. Deaver, W. W. Handy, Samuel Byrnes, Ann P. Cornthwait, Rachel P. Matthews, P. E. Thomas, William Tyson, James Gillingham, Elizabeth B. Hayward, Mariam Randall, Elizabeth Price, Ennion Williams, Ann Sewell, Joseph Turner, Jr., Rebecca Turner, Eliza Churchman, Gerard T. Hopkins, William K. Rowe, Harriet M. Anderson, Isaac Tyson, Jr., William Riley, John C. Norris, John H. Hewes, William Hopkins, John E. Reese, Andrew Ellicott, E. C. Jefferis, Josiah Small, T. M. Smith, W. L. James. 3rd column - Robert Sinclair, Esther Sinclair, Sarah S. Litle, John Litle, Anna Foulke, Sarah Pancoast, Hugh Balderston, Micajah Churchman, John C. McCoy, Susan James, Sarah Hopkins, George Gillingham, Mary Jefferis, Deborah Hopkins, Ann James, Robert Litle, John L. Talbott, Thomas Mills, Richard H. Litle, William E. Bartlett, Daniel Cobb, S. S. Wood, Ann W. Sanderson, Ruthy Byrnes, William H. Sinclair, Sarah Byrnes, Sarah Turner, Jr.,

George Hughes, M.D., Joseph Branson, Caleb Byrnes, Margaret Balderston, Elizabeth Sinclair.

**Joseph Trimble**, of Baltimore County, son of Isaac and Elizabeth Trimble, of the same place (the mother being deceased), married **Ann Cheyney**, of Baltimore County, dau. of Jesse and Rachel Cheyney, of Delaware County, Pennsylvania (the mother being deceased), in Baltimore on 17th of 4th mo., 1822.
Witnesses: 1st column - Gerard T. Hopkins, John Marsh, Hugh Balderston, Thomas Norris (of Thomas), John H. Hewes, Richard H. Townsend, William Tyson, Reynolds Knox, David U. Brown, John E. Reese, Tacy Burgess, Isaac Wilson, Tacy B. Norbury, Mary Ann Norris, Sarah Langdon. 2nd column - Elizabeth Handy, Mary E. C---- [blank], Ann S. Foulke, Anna M. Foulke, Esther Sinclair, Jr., Rebecca Turner, Harriet M. Anderson, Elizabeth G. Sinclair, Hannah Riley, Catharine M. Smith, Eliza Procter, Mary Vincent Hands, Martha E. Tyson, John Knight. 3rd column - Isaac Trimble, John Trimble, Elizabeth Trimble, Jr., John Trimble, Jr., Jane Price, Nathaniel Hoskin, Esther Cheyney, Sarah B. Townsend, Hannah Kenny, Israel Price, Mira Knight, Sarah Knight, Mary Brown, Sarah Riley, John Gillingham.

**William Trimble**, of Baltimore City, son of William and Hannah Trimble, of same place (both deceased), and **Mary Brown**, dau. of Uria and Mary Brown, of Baltimore City, declared their intentions to marry in Baltimore City, Western District, and were married in Baltimore City, Eastern District, on 16th of 5th mo., 1822.
Witnesses: 1st column - David U. Brown, Ann Ewing, Mary Jons [sic], Elizabeth Evens, Ann Massey, Phebe Lafetra, Elizabeth Trimble, Sarah Matthews, Esther Sinclair, Esther Lucas (by request), John Knight, Jr., Townsend Scott, Thomas Scott, Sarah Lafetra, Jane W. Cornthwait, Mary A. Stansbury, Elizabeth Hopkins, Sarah Hopkins, Ann E. Chandlee, Susan A. Abbott, Mary Ann Carroll, Ann Matthews, Hannah Chandlee, Sophronia E. Bosley, Cassandra Matthews, Georgeana Steever, Deborah Procter, Mary A. Dorsey, Eleanor Ann Kenny, Priscilla E. Pitt, Elizabeth Bidgood. 2nd column - Martha Norbury, Susanna Norbury, Hannah Price, Hannah Leakin, Elizabeth S. Trimble, Tacy B. Norbury, Diana Brown, Elizabeth Kirk, Nicholas Taylor, Elizabeth Taylor, Abigail Medcalf, Mary Waybill, Elizabeth Cornthwait, William H. Trimble, Sarah S. Chandlee, David Brown, Ann B. Brown, Israel Price, John C. Norris, William Reaney, Jeremiah Gatchell, Richard H. Townsend, Joseph G. Hopkins, George F. Janney, William Brown, Abel Spencer, William Procter, Anna W. Procter, Joshua Mott, Rachel M. Mott, Lydia W. Kirk. 3rd column - Uria Brown, Mary Brown, Tacey Burgess, John Wilson, David Wilson, William Trimble, Deborah Wilson, George Norbury, Elizabeth Ennis, T. Reaney, Eliza Trimble, Elizabeth Morgan, Mary P. Morgan, Elizabeth Price, Jane Jacob, Sarah Brown, Mira Knight, Harriet Chandlee,

Job Trimble, Samuel Wilson, Jr., Mary Kelso, Elizabeth B. Hayward, Martha Balderston, Matilda Reed, Susanna Matthews, Jane Brown (by request), Jesse Fearson, Hannah Fearson, Rossiter Scott, Edith Scott, Elizabeth Yerkes (by request).

**John Smith**, of Baltimore City, son of John and Martha Smith, of Moneymore, County of Londonderry, Kingdom of Ireland, married **Eliza Procter**, dau. of Izak and Rebecca Procter, of Baltimore City, on 12th day of 2nd mo., 1823.
Witnesses: 1st column - Elizabeth K. West, Mary V. Cole, Elizabeth Handy, Mary Jane Niles, Mary Ann Ridgely, Arietta A. R. Wellmore, Isaac Tyson, Isaac Wilson, Hugh Balderston, Gerard T. Hopkins, John Marsh, Daniel Pope, Nicholas Popplein, John C. Norris, James Gillingham, John H. Hewes, Woodnut Byrnes, R. H. Townsend, John Gillingham, John D. Jones, Isaac N. Hoopes. 2nd column - Mary H. Marsh, Sarah Riley, Elizabeth Hopkins, Martha Carey, Mary T. Ellicott, Mary Wethered, Tacy B. Norbury, Eleanor Ann Kenny, Ann M. Matlack, Mary E. Ross, Ruth B. Wooddy, Ellen Denny, Mary B. Lafetra, Catharine Popplein, Dorothy Hopkins, Alice Brooks, R. H. Green, Hannah N. Pope, Grace Knox, Ellen Norris, Catharine Maclay. 3rd column - Rebecca Procter, Mary Smith, Catharine Alexander, William Smith, Eliza L. Smith, Mary M. Goldsmith, John E. Reese, Johns Hopkins, Sarah Byrnes, Frances Baker, Jane Smith, Ann Wilson, Lois K. Pope, Elijah Goldsmith, Chloe Ann Baker, E. G. Byrnes, Susanna J. West, Reynolds Knox, Matthew Smith, Mary H. Moore, John Kingston, Jr.

**William Ellis Coale**, of Baltimore City, son of Isaac and Rachel Coale, of Harford County, married **Hannah E. Carey**, dau. of James and Martha Carey, of Baltimore City, on 16th of 4th mo., 1823.
Witnesses: 1st column - Anna E. Sinclair, Mary P. Freeman, Matilda C. Ridgely, John P. Ellicott, Philip T. Ellicott, S. S. Wood, Elisha Tyson, Jr., Thomas Tyson, Hammond Dugan, Richard Emory, Ezra Gillingham, George W. Waring, John W. Massey, Joshua Soule, Jr., A. B. Cleveland, George Harris, Jr., John C. Norris, Paul Allen, John Marsh, Woodnutt Byrnes, Eliza Marsh, M. H. Marsh, Mary C. Norris, Eliza George, Mary Wethered, Frances F. King, Isaac Tyson, T. Moore, James Ellicott. 2nd column - John S. Tyson, Evan Poultney, James Harwood, Joseph Y. Tomkins, Chloe Ann Baker, Frances P. Baker, Rebecca Procter, Elizabeth Tyson, Hannah N. Pope, Ellen Irwin, Metta Waesche, Mary McPherson, Eliza Smith, Ann S. Foulke, Hannah Ann Tyson, Elizabeth Gillingham, Hannah Riley, Rebecca Turner, Louisa C. Martin, Jane Ellicott, Patience Tyson, Sarah S. Tyson, Rachel T. Tyson, Henrietta P. Tyson, Gerard T. Hopkins, Mary E. James, James C. Hough, Deborah Tyson, Mary Tyson, Benjamin Ellicott, Jr. 3rd column - Margaret Carey, Mary Ellicott, Martha Carey, Mary C. Coale, Samuel Carey, Susan Coale, James C. Doddrell, H. M. Ellicott, Anna Martin, William Martin, Jr., Isaac Coale, W. W. Handy, Isaac Tyson, Jr., Mary M. Ellicott, Jane Tunis, Rachel Mason, Elias

Ellicott, Rachel T. Hewes, Henry Ellicott, Elizabeth Wethered, Ann M. Price, Sarah E. Tyson, Ann McPherson, Thomas Ellicott, Esther McPherson, James Harwood, Margaret Carey, John Hewes, Evan T. Tyson.

**Thomas Mackenzie**, of Baltimore City, son of Cosmo and Sarah Mackenzie, of Calvert County, Maryland, married **Tacy B. Norbury**, dau. of George and Martha Norbury, of Baltimore City, on 14th of 5th mo., 1823.
Witnesses: 1st column - John Smith, Mary K. Marsh, Edward Needles, Jr., Justinian Bowdler, Eliza Smith, John C. Norris, Thomas Tyson, Townsend Scott, Samuel Evans, R. H. Townsend, Thomas B, Kingston, John Kingston, Jr., Samuel Whitelock, Reynolds Knox, Isaac Wilson, John Gillingham, Charles Halwadt. 2nd column - Hannah E. Coale, Mary H. Moore, Martha Carey, Ruth B. Wooddy, Hannah Marsh, Eliza Marsh, Elizabeth Halwadt, Matthew Smith, Thomas Smith, Hales E. Walker, John Livingston, John Marsh, Robert H. Smith, Elizabeth Ann Smith, Isaac Tyson, Jr., W. L. James, Ann McPherson, Catharine Popplein. 3rd column - Martha Norbury, Tacey Burges, Sarah Mackenzie, Rebecca W. Pinkerton, Susanna Norbury, Hannah Marsh, Rebecca Procter, Mary Walker, Rachel P. Matthews, Judith Hunt, R. H. Green, Ann Ewing, Anna Price, Hannah Leakins, Elizabeth L. Trimble, Ann S. Foulke, Anna E. Sinclair, Margaret Carey.

**Joshua W. Canby**, of Baltimore County, son of Samuel and Elizabeth Canby, of the same place, and **Esther E. Downes**, dau. of Joseph and Miriam Lownes, of Anne Arundel County, Maryland, declared their intentions to marry in Baltimore City and were married at the meeting house at Elkridge in Anne Arundel County on 10th of 9th mo., 1823.
Witnesses: 1st column - Thomas Hartley, Ezra Fell, Charles Gillingham, Elizabeth N. Scott, Mary Ellicott, Mary Ann Ellicott, Jane D. Smith, Ann B. Ellicott, Phebe W. Gillingham, Anna Gillingham, Letitia C. Ellicott, Esther Smith, Charles Canby, Mary Canby, Josiah Lownes, George Ellicott, Jr., Cornelius Garretson, Joseph Garretson. 2nd column - Elizabeth Ellicott, William Ellicott, Eli Garretson, Amasa Clapp, Isaac Garretson, Samuel Canby, Jr., Samuel Garretson, Jesse Garretson, Samuel Gillingham, Isaac Garretson, Jr., Mary Clapp, Hannah Fell, Elizabeth Hartley, Benjamin Palmer, Enoch Clapp, James W. Gillingham, Ezra Baily, Maxwell Kenny. 3rd column - Samuel Canby, Elizabeth Canby, Joseph Lownes, Miriam Lownes, Bethula Lownes, Thomas Y. Canby, Zachariah Lownes, James Gillingham, Beulah Canby, Hannah Smith, Sarah Ann Fell, George Ellicott, Samuel Smith, Samuel Godfrey, Samuel Hartley, Jr., Andrew Ellicott, S. B. Smith, Asa C. Hampton.

**James Moore, Jr.**, of George Town in the District of Columbia, son of James and Phebe Moore, of Waterford, Loudon County, Virginia (the mother being deceased),

married **Esther Sinclair, Jr.**, dau. of Robert and Esther Sinclair, of Baltimore City, on 15th of 10th mo., 1823.
Witnesses: 1st column - Joshua Riley, Sarah M. Hutchinson, Ann Hutchinson, Mary C. James, Dorothy Hopkins, Ann Sheppard, Thomas Wilson, Sarah Dukehart, Margaret Brown, Margaret Tyson, David U. Brown, Elizabeth B. Hayward, Maria Esling, Elizabeth Starr, Ann P. Wethered, Mary B. Lafetra, Rachel M. Betterton, Mary M. Townsend, A. Henderson, Rachel T. Tyson, H. E. Tyson, Joseph Turner, Jr., Evan P. Thomas, John P. Balderston, Benjamin Clap, William Procter, Ellen Irwin, Ann B. Ellicott, Deborah Tyson, Mary Ellicott. 2nd column - S. Wilson, Jr., John Brown, Griffith Jones, David S. Pope, Lloyd Norris, Gerard T. Hopkins, John Dukehart, Mary A. Sheppard, Mary Robertson, Mary H. Worthington, William Dukehart, Ann Peck, Alisan Cornthwait, Alisan Wilson, Mary Ann Duer, Thomas S. Sheppard, John S. Miller, Martha Kelso, Sally Ann Ellicott, Rebecca Turner, Thomas Mackenzie, John Torrance, William Willess Stratton, Nicholas Popplein, John H. Hewes, William Riley, James Gillingham, John L. Talbott. I. N. Hoopes. 3rd column - Robert Sinclair, Esther Sinclair, Sarah S. Litle, John M. Foulke, Ann S. Foulke, Elizabeth G. Sinclair, Robert Sinclair, Jr., Deborah S. Sinclair, John Sinclair, Elizabeth Sinclair, Woodnut Byrnes, Parthenia Dukehart, Martha Dukehart, Margaret Dukehart, William Gwynn Jones, Sarah Dukehart, Wilson Balderston, Mary Ann Sinclair, Isaac Tyson, Jr., P. E. Thomas, Thomas Tyson, John Marsh, Mary Cowman, Isaac Wilson, Richard H. Jones, Townsend Scott, William L. James, John C. Norris, John M. Pugh, Sarah E. Tyson, T. R. Matthews.

**John Dukehart, Jr.**, of Baltimore City, son of John and Parthenia Dukehart, of the same place, married **Ann P. Cornthwait**, dau. of Robert and Alisann Cornthwait, of Baltimore City, on 15th of 10th mo., 1823.
Witnesses: 1st column - Sarah Dukehart, William Gwynn Jones, Sidney S. Kelso, Margaret Balderston, Elizabeth Robertson, Margaret Dukehart, Martha Dukehart, Hannah Riley, Ann Ewing, Margaret Brown, Sarah A. Evens, Mary M. Evens, R. H. Green, Margaret Norris, Sarah Mecteer, Hannah Kenny, Ellen S. Denny, Rebecca Turner, Lois K. Pope, C. E. Wethered, Deborah Tyson, Mary Ellicott, Mary B. Lafetra, John P. Balderston, Joshua Riley, Martha Kelso, Maria Esling, Ann B. Ellicott, Mary Ann Sinclair. 2nd column - Hugh Balderston, Nixon Wilson, Elizabeth Cornthwait, Thomas Wilson, Sally Ann Ellicott, Elizabeth B. Hayward, Phebe S. Townsend, John C. Norris, Thomas Mackenzie, William Willess Stratton, James Gillingham, Griffith Jones, Isaac Tyson, Richard H. Jones, Mary Robertson, Rachel Hough, Jane W. Cornthwait, Wilson Balderston, Mary Ann Duer, William L. James, Ann Sheppard, J. N. Hoopes, John L. Hewes, John L. Talbott, J. P. Smith, Rachel M. Betterton, William Procter, John Hewes, Mary C. James. 3rd column - John Dukehart, Parthenia Dukehart, Alisan Cornthwait, Ann Peck, Isaiah Balderston, Mary S. Sheppard, Mary H. Worthington, Cassandra T. Ewing,

William Dukehart, Mordecai Matthews, Jr., Parthenia Dukehart, Alisan Wilson, Lydia H. Dukeheart, Isaac Tyson, Jr., Townsend Scott, David S. Pope, Rachel P. Matthews, John Brown, S. Wilson, Jr., James Moore, Jr., Esther Moore, John M. Foulke, Ann S. Foulke, John S. Miller, Sarah M. Hutchinson, Elizabeth G. Sinclair, John P. Sinclair, Sarah S. Litle, Ann Hutchinson.

**John Ferriss**, of the Borough of Wilmington, County of New Castle, Delaware, son of Zechariah and Elizabeth Ferriss, of Wilmington (both deceased), married **Mary Price**, of Baltimore City, dau. of William and Priscilla Fentham *[sic]*, of Philadelphia (deceased), in Baltimore on 22nd of 10th mo., 1823.
Witnesses: 1st column - Sally Canby, Mary Ann Marshall, Sarah S. Tyson, Isaac Tyson, Jr., Isaac Tyson, R. H. Townsend, Thomas McKenzie, Evan P. Thomas, Caleb Jones, Deborah Tyson, Mary Tyson, A. S. Norris, Rachel T. Tyson, Hester Fisher, P. E. Thomas. 2nd column - Hugh Balderston, Ennion Williams, Elizabeth Thomas, Patience Tyson, Hannah Talbott, Paul Allen, Grace Knox, Margaret Carey, Hannah E. Coale, Dorothy Hopkins, Rachel Mason, Sally Ann Ellicott, Ann McPherson, Ann Peck, Hannah Riley. 3rd column - Ann M. Price, Henry Price, Philip Price, Samuel G. Jones, Hetty Few, Benaiah Sawyer, Ann Jones, Mary G. Jones, Elizabeth H. Tyson, Rachel Updegraff, Mary M. Ellicott, Eliza Marsh, Martha Carey, Jr., Gerard T. Hopkins.

**Asa Jones**, of Fawn Township, York County, Pennsylvania, son of Isaac and Elizabeth Jones, of the same place, married **Hannah Riley**, dau. of William and Sarah Riley, of Baltimore City, on 14th of 4th mo., 1824.
Witnesses: 1st column - Sophia E. Twisler, Margaret Dukehart, Mary J. Dukehart, William Dukehart, Margaret Brown, Elizabeth Fergusson, N. Riley, Hannah Fergusson, Sarah Riley, Sarah Dukehart, Valerius Riley, Meredith Helm, Mary Bowen, John Brown, Joshua Riley, William Riley, Jr., Joseph Davenport, John Jones, P. E. Thomas, Franklin F. Pope, Mary Wethered, Gerard T. Hopkins, Mary B. Lafetra, Jane Ellicott, Sarah Evens, Elizabeth Hopkins, Samuel G. Jones. 2nd column - Martha T. Jones, Ann Pope, Deborah B. Jones, Eliza Ann Smith, Elizabeth Simmonds, John Livingston, Elizabeth Turner, Hetty Few, Elizabeth Smith, Hugh Balderston, Mary H. Moore, Reynolds Knox, Thomas Matthews, W. Willess Stratton, John Marsh, Elizabeth Thomas, Caleb Jones, Bartholew Fussell, M.D., Ann Peck, Mary McKim (by request), Ann P. Dukehart, Elizabeth Gillingham, Elizabeth Hainey, Rachel M. Betterton, Anna Price, Elizabeth S. Trimble, Lucy Poultney. 3rd column - William Riley, Sarah Riley, Thomas Jones, Mary M. Evens, Lois K. Pope, Eliza Marsh, Mary H. Marsh, Mary Thomas, John C. Norris, John H. Hewes, John Sinclair, John Gillingham, Ann Ewing, Elizabeth Thomas, Caleb Jones, James Lovegrove, David S. Pope, Hannah Mitchell, Rebecca Procter, Isaac Tyson, Jr., Thomas Mackenzie, John Dukehart, Jr., Ennion Williams, Eleanor Kenny, Asenath Harwood, Susanna Waltham, Rebecca Turner.

**Aquila Jones**, of Baltimore City, son of Abner and Hannah Jones, of Harford County (the mother being deceased), married **Ann H. Perine**, dau. of Peter and Mary Perine (the father being deceased), in Baltimore City, Eastern District, on 11th of 8th mo., 1825.
Witnesses: 1st column - Elizabeth T. Wilson, Margaret B. Wilson, Elizabeth B. Hayward, Sarah C. Updegraff, Margaret Brown, Deborah W. Procter, Catherine Langley, Hannah P. Townsend, Mary B. Jones, Ann Matthews, Abel Spencer, Mahala Spencer, Sarah Lukens, Sarah Dutton, Mary Ann Dutton, Mary Young, Susan H. Hurdle, Mary Brown, Mary Jones, Abigal Medcalf, Nicholas Taylor. 2nd column - Tacey Burges, Sarah Matthews, Ann B. Brown, Mary B. Mullikin, Elizabeth Comegys, S. A. Stansbury, William H. Amoss, John Dukehart, Joshua Mott, James Clark, Griffith Jones, Isaiah Balderston, David Brown, J. N. Hoops, Mary B. Lafetra, Eliza A. Smith, Michael Lamb, Ann Lamb, Mary Gardner, Elizabeth Pugh, Elizabeth Taylor. 3rd column - Mary Perine, Sarah McComass, Juliett McComass, Malden Perine, Susannah Perine, Susan A. Morgan, Samuel W. Stratton, Julia A. Douglas, Ann M. Jenkins, Mary M. Evans, Sarah A. Evans, Ann Evans, Susannah Evans, William Brown, Jane Brown, Jacob Tyson, Ann Tyson, John Dutton, Robert Dutton, William S. Young.

**Jeremiah Brown**, of Little Britain Township, Lancaster County, Pennsylvania, son of Joshua and Hannah Brown (deceased), married **Sarah Lukens**, of Baltimore City, dau. of Philip and Ann Coale *[sic]*, also deceased, in Baltimore at the Eastern District meeting house on 8th of 10th mo., 1825.
Witnesses: 1st column - Edith Scott, Abigal Medcalf, Rossiter Scott, Ann Matthews, Samuel Hopkins, David Brown, John Dukehart, Jacob Lafetra, Abel Spencer, A. P. Medcalf, Joseph Brevitt, William Hopkins, Uria Brown, Mary Jones (by desire), William Procter, Sarah Matthews, S. A. Stansbury, Mary Ann Duer, Jane T. Ellicott, Deborah W. Procter, Sarah Hopkins, Mary Brown, Margaret Brown. 2nd column - Margaret B. Wilson, Anna Reed, Elizabeth Morgan, Hannah P. Townsend, Eleanor A. Kenny, Mary D. Brown, Margaret Balderston, Ann Peck, Ann W. Sanderson, Elizabeth Evans, Phebe Lafetra, Esther Townsend, Susan A. Morgan, Sophia Harwood, Mary Perine, Tacey Burges, Charlotte W. Hopkins, Thomas J. Hull, Harriot Hull, Ann Coale (by request), John C. McCoy, Robert McCoy, Andrew McCoy, William Brown, Jane Brown, Deborah Jones, Frances Toy (by request), Jehosheba Brown.

**Thomas Tyson**, of Baltimore City, son of Jesse and Margaret Tyson (they being deceased), and **Mary Ellicott**, dau. of George and Elizabeth Ellicott, of Baltimore County, declared their intentions to marry in Baltimore and were married at a meeting at Elk Ridge on 19th of 10th mo., 1825.
Witnesses in 1st column - George E. Lea, Sarah Lea, James Tyson, James E. Lea, Gerard T. Hopkins, John Cowman, Enoch Clap, Samuel Godfrey, Joseph Lowns,

Miriam Lowns, Esther E. Canby, Bethula Lowns, Anna Garretson, Esther Smith, Mary Denny, Jane D. Smith, Mary A. Tyson, Ezra Fell, Ann Fell, Samuel Smith, Charles Baldwin, Joseph Garretson, Rachel Updegraff (by request), B. H. Ellicott, Josiah Lowns, Jesse Garretson, John Gillingham. "Relatives" in 2nd column - George Ellicott, Elizabeth Ellicott, Thomas Lea, Elizabeth E. Lea, Isaac Tyson, Jr., Hannah Ann Tyson, Nathan Tyson, Martha E. Tyson, William W. Handy, Elizabeth Handy, Anna Tyson, Margaret Tyson, Ann Brooke Ellicott, George Ellicott, Jr., John S. Tyson, Nath. H. Ellicott, Jonathan H. Ellicott, Benjamin P. Moore, Mary H. Moore, Rachel Mayson, Charles T. Ellicott.

**Charles Ellis**, of Philadelphia, Pennsylvania, son of William and Mercy Ellis, late of Muney Township, Lycoming County, Pennsylvania (the father being deceased), married **Deborah Tyson**, dau. of Isaac and Elizabeth Tyson (deceased), of Baltimore City, on 23rd of 11th mo., 1825.
Witnesses: 1st column - Isaac Tyson, Patience Tyson, Mercey Ellis, Philip T. Tyson, Mary Tyson, Rachel T. Tyson, Henrietta E. Tyson, Evan T. Tyson, Mary Clap, Enoch Clap, E. Ellicott, Elizabeth Tyson, Rebecca Tyson, Martha E. Tyson, Ann Thomas, Elisha Tyson, Sarah S. Tyson, Nathan Tyson, Evan Thomas, Philip E. Thomas, Evan Thomas, Jr., Mary Thomas, Elizabeth Thomas, Thomas Poultney, Ann Poultney, Philip Poultney, Thomas Poultney, Jr., Samuel Poultney, Mary Ann Poultney, Sarah Poultney, Evan Ph.[?] Thomas, Benjamin Ellicott, J. S. Ellicott, James Ellicott, Samuel P. Griffitts, Jr., George Ellicott, Margaret Tyson, Sr., Hetty B. Ellicott. 2nd column - Jonathan H. Ellicott, Thomas A. Norriss, Lloyd Norriss, Margaret Tyson, Sarah E. Tyson, Marshall Tyson, Mary M. Tyson, Jonathan E. Tyson, Evan Thomas Tyson, Frances T. King, Elizabeth Thomas, Harriet Thomas, Elizabeth Simmonds, John P. Tyson, Thomas King, Griffith Jones, Margaret Brown, Phebe S. Townsend, Eleanor A. Kinney, Hugh Balderston, John Marsh, John Gillingham, W. Worthington, John Wethered, Maria Marriott, Ann Brook Ellicott, Elizabeth T. Wilson, Margaret B. Wilson, Mary Ann Duer, Isaac P. Morris, Peter Haslett, Isaac Tyson, Jr., Isaac Wilson, Hannah Ann Tyson, Mary Robertson, Anna Tyson, Mary Bartlett (per order), Mary T. Ellicott. 3rd column - Mary McPherson, John McPherson, Martha Carey, Jr., Ann Peck, Hannah Worthington, Gerard T. Hopkins, Mary E. Tyson, Thomas Tyson, Jane T. Ellicott, Lydia Hopkins, Jacob Tyson, Richard K. Thompson, Richard G. Howland, William Ellis Coale, Hannah E. Coale, Susan Coates, Joseph T. Webster, Elizabeth Robson, Ruth Ely, Elizabeth Osborn, Jane Roberts, Lydia Poultney, Rachel Mason, George Carey, Jonathan E. George, Mary Ellicott, Harvey M. Ellicott, Joseph King, Jr., Thomas Ellicott, Mary Ellicott, Margaret Carey, Martha Carey, James C. Dodrell, Samuel Carey, Mary Ellicott, Lydia L. Ellicott, Emily Ellicott, Hannah B. Ellicott.

Lloyd Norris, of Baltimore City, son of Edward and Rebecca Norris, of Harford County, married Sarah Tyson, dau. of William and Elizabeth Tyson, of the county aforesaid, on 21st of 12th mo., 1825.
Witnesses: 1st column - William Tyson, Elizabeth Tyson, Jonathan E. Tyson, William A. Tyson, Samuel E. Tyson, Mary Tyson, Elizabeth Tyson, Jr., Frances E. Tyson (by request), Jane S. Tyson (by request), Anna Tyson, Rachel T. Tyson, Henrietta E. Tyson, Nathan Tyson, Martha E. Tyson, Henry Tyson (by request), Isaac Tyson, Jr., Mary E. Tyson, Margaret Tyson, Elisha Tyson, Thomas Tyson, Ralph S. Lee, David Lee Norris, Oliver H. Amos, William Norris, John Duer, Edward S. Norris, Elizabeth Norris, Thomas A. Norris, Charles Duer, George Ellicott, Martha Carey, Jr., Mary Jane Norris, Eliza A. Norris. 2nd column - Sarah R. Webster, William E. George, Sarah E. George, Evan Thomas, Gerard T. Hopkins, Margaret Carey, Hannah E. Coale, Ann Brook Ellicott, Rachel Mason, Elizabeth Norris, Margaret Norris, Mary Ann Duer, James Gillingham, Ann Waterhouse, Hugh Balderston, John Marsh, Lewin Wethered, Sarah Poultney, Sarah Ann Ellicott, Mary M. Ellicott, Elizabeth Morgan, S. A. Morgan, Ann Thomas, Catherine Tiernan, Lydia Poultney, Lydia L. Ellicott, Mary T. Ellicott, Hetty B. Ellicott, Hannah M. Ellicott, Eliza George, Rebecca Key, Harvey M. Ellicott, Charlotte Stricker, Ann McPherson. 3rd column - Ann P. Thomas, M. H. Worthington, Hannah McPherson, Mary Ann Sinclair, Thomas A. Fisher, Isaac McPherson, William Hopkins, Elisha T. Wilson, Thomas M. Smith, William Ellicott, B. H. Ellicott, Philip T. George, W. L. McPherson, Thomas McKensey, Isaac Wilson, Ennion Williams, John L. Talbott, Robert M. Smith, Edward Hewes (of John), Edward C. Jefferis, Henry Hewes, Ann Hewes, John Hewes, Evan Thomas, Jr., Michael Lamb.

## BALTIMORE MONTHLY MEETING, EASTERN DISTRICT MARRIAGE CERTIFICATES, 1802-1817

Amos West, of Baltimore City, son of Thomas and Elizabeth West, of Harford County, married Elizabeth Coates, dau. of Jonathan and Jane Coates (deceased), of Baltimore City, on 15th of 4th mo., 1802.
Witnesses: 1st column - John Marsh, John Wilson, Peter Pollard, William Riley, William Brown, David Wilson, Joseph England, James Hance, Thomas C. Hance, Rossiter Scott, Isaac Hayward, John Mitchel, John Ellicott. 2nd column - David Brown, James Gillingham, Martha Balderston, Ann Matthews, Cassandra Thornburgh, Mary Jones, Tacy Mitchel, Rebecca Medcalf, Hannah Marsh, Mary Brown (by desire), Margaret Dukehart, Ann Riley, Edith Scott. 3rd column - Thomas West, Jonathan Coates, Elizabeth West, Rebecca West, Jane Coates, Reynolds Knox, Grace Knox, Warrick Price, Susanna Price, Stacy West, William Hayward, Richard Price, Ann Wilson, Amos Smith.

**William Brown**, of Baltimore City, and **Jane Ellicott**, widow of Thomas Ellicott, late of Bucks County, Pennsylvania, deceased, were married in Baltimore on 19th of 8th mo., 1802.
Witnesses: 1st column - Joseph Townsend, Margaret Wilson, Ann Wilson, Sally G. Husband, Susan Husband, Lydia Husband, Mary Mitchel, Elizabeth Husband, Susan Hopkins, Sarah Procter, Mary Hussey, Mary James, Mary Jones, Abigail Medcalf, Sarah Matthews, Elizabeth Brown, Rebecca Medcalf, Hannah England, Martha Davis, Maria Reese. 2nd column - Elias Ellicott, Thomas Parvin, John Marsh, Ennion Williams, William Riley, James Gillingham, John McKim, Gerard T. Hopkins, David Brown, James Brown, David Wilson, Jane Wilson, John Wilson, Izak Procter, Rebecca Procter, William Procter, Joseph P. Plummer, Hannah Ellicott, Sarah Kenny, David Wilson, Jr. 3rd column - Andrew Ellicott, Ely Balderston, Esther Balderston, Israel Price, Hannah Price, Joseph Brown, Fanny Brown, Ann Brown, Isaac Kenny, Joseph Kenny, Mary Kenny, Hannah Kenny, Ann Reese, Mary McKim, Elizabeth Matthews, Hannah Williams, Rebecca Williams, Martha Balderston, Mary Davis.

**Hugh Balderston**, of Baltimore City, son of Isaiah and Martha Balderston, of the same place, married **Margaret Wilson**, dau. of John and Aliceanna Wilson, of Harford County (both deceased), in Baltimore on 23rd of 12th mo., 1802.
Witnesses: 1st column - John S. Webster, John Dukehart, John Cornthwait, William Husband, Gerard T. Hopkins, Isaac Tyson, John Marsh, Ennion Williams, John Parrish, James Brown, William Riley, John Trimble, James Gillingham, Isaac G. Hopkins, Isaac W. Robertson, Jacob Pugh, Thomas Matthews, Samuel Matthews, William Tyson, Elisha Tyson, John Spottiswood Peck. 2nd column - Mary Robertson, Elizabeth Husband, Susan Husband, Mary Mifflin, Rebecca Williams, Mary Jones, Hannah Marsh, Hannah Williams, Mary Brown, Mary Tyson, Ann Jewett, Elizabeth Robertson, Betsey Webster, Hannah Robertson, Mary Mitchel, Frances Brown, Sarah Hopkins, Ann M. Richards, Deborah Thornburgh, David Wilson, Jane Wilson. 3rd column - Isaiah Balderston, Martha Balderston, Christopher Wilson, Isaac Wilson, John W. Wilson, James Wilson, Nixon Wilson, Jonathan Balderston, Alisanna Wilson, Sarah Cooper, Susanna Wilson, Parthenia Dukehart, Lucretia Wilson, Esther Balderston, Elizabeth Robertson, Ely Balderston, Rachel Mason, Anna Webster, Samuel Winchester, Richard Jones, Alisanna Wilson.

**John Ellicott, Jr.**, of Baltimore City, son of Andrew and Esther Ellicott, of Baltimore County, married **Mary Mitchel**, dau. of John and Tacy Mitchel, of Baltimore City, on 20th of 1st mo., 1803.
Witnesses: 1st column - Ennion Williams, Joseph Thornburgh, James Carey, Jasper Cope, Elisha Tyson, Nathan Tyson, George Mason, Amos James, Gerard T. Hopkins, William Husband, John W. Wilson, John Marsh, William Riley, James

Gillingham, Joseph England, David Wilson, John McKim. 2nd column - Mary Mifflin, Margaret Tyson, Susanna Mason, Rebecca Cope, Sarah Hopkins, Mary Tyson, Elizabeth Husband, Sarah Robertson, Rachel Mason, Hannah Cope, Ann Waterhouse, Hannah Marsh, Mary Boyd, Tacy Crownover, Susanna Wilson, Elizabeth Tyson. 3rd column - John Mitchel, Tacy Mitchel, Esther Ellicott, George Ellicott, Jonathan Ellicott, Cassandra Thornburgh, Elizabeth Ellicott, Tacy McPherson, Sarah Ellicott, John Ellicott, Martha Carey, James Ellicott, Andrew Ellicott, Jr., Rachel T. Ellicott, Elizabeth Ellicott, Jr., Moses Sheppard, Abel Knight, Isaac Knight.

**Joseph McCoy**, of Baltimore City, son of Andrew and Mary McCoy, of Harford County (both deceased), married **Ann Hicks**, dau. of James and Mary Hicks, of Baltimore City, on 17th of 2nd mo., 1803.
Witnesses: 1st column - John Wilson, Isaac G. Hopkins, Samuel Cook, John Hughes, Daniel Keighler, William Hopkins, Samuel Hance, William Riley, Ennion Williams, Izak Procter, Rossiter Scott, John Dukehart, M. Sheppard, John Cornthwait, John W. Wilson, James Brown, Joel Hopkins, James Wainwright, Abm. Pyle Medcalf. 2nd column - Mary Mifflin, Cassandra Thornburgh, Margaret Balderston, Tacy Mitchel, Elizabeth Webster, Mary Brown, Elizabeth Matthews, Susan Husband, Lydia Husband, Jane Wilson, Hannah Matthews, Rebecca Williams, Rebecca Norris, Mary Tyson, Susanna Norris, Alisanna Wilson, Mary Jones, Elizabeth Louden. 3rd column - James Hicks, Mary Hicks, Enoch Underwood, Mary Underwood, Jane Cook, David Hicks, James Hicks, George Harris, Andrew McCoy, Isaac McCoy, Bathsheba Hicks, Martha McCoy, Hannah Scott, Mary Ellicott, Jr., Sarah Hopkins, Hannah P. Townsend, Ann Matthews, Jr., Mary Keighler.

**Thomas C. Dare**, of Calvert County, Maryland, son of Gideon and Elizabeth Dare, married **Elizabeth Snowden**, dau. of Richard and Hannah Snowden, of Prince George's County, Maryland (the father being deceased), in Baltimore City on 19th of 5th mo., 1803.
Witnesses: 1st column - David Brown, Andrew Ellicott, Jr., John W. Wilson, William Tyson, William Riley, Hugh Balderston, Amos West, William Cornthwait, William Jones, William Gillingham, John Marsh, George Mason, Samuel Hance, Robert Cornthwait, Nixon Wilson, William Hopkins, James Brown, Zebulon Whippey, James Gillingham. 2nd column - Rachel Hopkins, Miriam James, Mary Ellicott, Jr., Margaret Balderston, Priscilla Hopkins, Mary Mifflin, Hannah Marsh, Susanna Wilson, Eliza Hopkins, Susan Husband, Henrietta Hopkins, Eliza Hopkins, Amelia Hopkins, Dennis Nowland, David Brown, Jr., Thomas Wainwright, Joseph P. Plummer, Rossiter Scott, Ennion Williams. 3rd column - Edward Waters, Rachel Husband, Priscilla Dare, Rachel Mason, Harriett Hopkins, George Mason, John Hopkins, Isaac H. Hopkins, Nicholas Hopkins, William

Harris, Frances Hopkins, Isaac G. Hopkins, Susan Hopkins, Frances Hopkins, Henry Wilson, Margaret Tyson, Samuel Harris, Henrietta Snowden, William Husband, Joseph Townsend.

**William Tyson**, of Baltimore City, son of Elisha and Mary Tyson, of the same place, married **Elizabeth Ellicott**, dau. of Jonathan and Sarah Ellicott, of Baltimore County, on 26th of 10th mo., 1803.
Witnesses: 1st column - John Ellicott, Jr., James Ellicott, John Ellicott, Evan T. Ellicott, John Mitchel, Samuel Ellicott, Isaac McPherson, George Ellicott, Samuel Smith, Allen Wright, Samuel Hopkins, Richard Palmer, Thomas Poultney, William Waterhouse, Andrew Ellicott, Jr., Joel Wright, 2nd column - Tacy Ellicott, Mary Ellicott, Tacy Mitchel, Tacy McPherson, Patience McPherson, Hannah Smith, Letitia Heston, Mary Palmer, Sarah Atkinson, Margaret Prian, Phebe Wright, Ann Poultney, Mary Ellicott, Jr., Henrietta Thomas, Eliza Norris. 3rd column - Jonathan Ellicott, Sarah Ellicott, Mary Tyson, Elisha Tyson, Andrew Ellicott, Esther Ellicott, John W. Wilson, Lucretia Wilson, Nathaniel Ellicott, Sally Ellicott, William Ellicott, James Ellicott, Rachel Ellicott, Eliza Ellicott (of George), Thomas Ellicott, Isaac Tyson, Mary Tyson.

**Allen Wright**, son of Joel and Elizabeth Wright, of Frederick County, Maryland, married **Phebe Heston**, dau. of Joseph and Phebe Heston, of Anne Arundel County, Maryland (the mother being deceased), in Baltimore City on 26th of 10th mo., 1803.
Witnesses: 1st column - John W. Wilson, Isaac Tyson, John Ellicott, John Ellicott, Jr., Isaac McPherson, William Waterhouse, Oliver P. Norris, Samuel Hopkins, William Evans, Moses Wright, Alexander Walton (of Samuel), Thomas Hudson, James Gillingham, Nathaniel Ellicott, James Ellicott (of George), James N. Worthington, Samuel Carey, Sarah Atkinson, Eliza Ellicott (of George), Tacy McPherson, Eliza Norris, Thomas Poultney, James Ellicott, Thomas Ellicott, Jonathan Ellicott, Elisha Tyson, Andrew Ellicott, Jr., Isaac Wright, Samuel Canby, George Ellicott, Samuel W. Dorsey, Joseph E. Evans, Evan McKinstry, Sarah Ellicott, Mary Ann Evans, Abigail Atkinson, Elizabeth Dorsey, Rachel Atkinson, Ann Poultney, Mary Ellicott, Eliza Ellicott. 3rd column - Joel Wright, Joseph Heston, Ann Heston, Elizabeth Wright, Sr., Ann Elgar, Rachel Wright, Joseph Heston, Jr., Jonathan Wright, Hannah Smith, Mahlon Farquhar, Samuel Smith, Elizabeth Wright, Jr., Leticia Heston, William Heston, Polly Palmer, Judith Evans, Benjamin Palmer, Joseph Atkinson, Rachel Atkinson, Richard Palmer, Mary Tyson, William Tyson, Elizabeth Tyson.

**Samuel Smith**, son of Henry and Martha Smith, of Washington County, Pennsylvania, married **Ann Brown**, dau. of William and Elizabeth Brown, of Baltimore City (deceased), in Baltimore on 21st of 6th mo., 1804.

Witnesses: 1st column - David Brown, Isaac Bassett, John W. Wilson, Hugh Balderston, William Matthews (of O.), William Richardson, James Brown, John Marsh, James Gillingham, Ezra Gillingham, John McKim, George Williamson, Jr., Moses Dillon, Jr., Joshua Matthews, Samuel Wainwright, David Brown, Jr., Samuel Wilson, William Riley, Rossiter Scott, Joseph Kenny. 2nd column - Rebecca Procter, Patience Graham, Mary Mifflin, Elizabeth Matthews, Dorothy Brown, Sarah G. Whiffing, Hannah Marsh, Miriam James, Susanna Dutton, Martha Dillon, Rebecca Marsh, Margaret Hussey, Edith Scott, Mary Work, Mary Cornthwait, Rachel Mason, Thomas Matthews, William Cornthwait, James Brown, Jr., Thomas Cornthwait. 3rd column - William Brown, Jane Brown, Esther Balderston, Ann Reese, Joseph Brown, Hannah Price, Israel Price, Frances Brown, Ely Balderson, Mary Brown, Thomas Reese, Maria Reese, Hannah Ellicott, Eliza Brown, Ann Wilson, Jonathan Balderston, John Wilson, Ann Matthews, Grace Cornthwait, Deborah Wilson, Sarah Brown, Mary Cornthwait, Hannah Matthews.

**Samuel Cookson**, of Baltimore County, son of Samuel and Jane Cookson (both deceased), married **Rachel Roach**, dau. of Henry and Hannah Roach, of Baltimore City (the father being deceased), on 20th of 6th mo., 1805.
Witnesses: 1st column - William Waterhouse, Valerius Dukehart, David Wilson, Isaac Atkinson, Jessee Morgan, David Brown, George Matthews, Samuel Matthews, John Marsh, William Riley, Joseph Brevitt, William Trimble. 2nd column - Mary Mifflin, Gerard T. Hopkins, Phebe Price, Miriam James, Martha Balderston, Mary Jones, Elizabeth Diffenderfer, Cassandra W. Brevit, Mary Hussey, Lydia Husband, John W. Wilson, James Gillingham. 3rd column - Hannah Roach, Mary Underwood, Mary Cookson, Barbara Roach, Thomas Sherwood, William Underwood, Hannah Williams, Ann Matthews, Amos James, Elinor Atkinson, Ennion Williams, Jane Wilson, Rebecca Vore, Sarah Vore, John Mitchel, Elizabeth Husband, Margaret Balderston, Elizabeth Gillingham, Jr., Hannah Marsh, Jr.

**Samuel Brown**, of Winchester, Frederick County, Virginia, son of Isaac and Sarah Brown, of the same place, married **Hannah Matthews**, dau. of Thomas and Ann Matthews, of Baltimore County (the father being deceased), in Baltimore City on 12th of 12th mo., 1805.
Witnesses: 1st column - Susanna Nicoll, Mary Coulter, Susan Hopkins, Elizabeth Lowden, Amelia Hopkins, Joseph Brevitt, Eliza Robertson, Joseph Heston, Jr., P. T. Thomas, Mary Mifflin, Elizabeth Naylor, Gerard T. Hopkins, John M. Brown, John H. Henry, Joseph Neil, William Trimble, William Riley, David Brown, David Wilson, Amos Brown. 2nd column - Elizabeth Tyson, Isaac Tyson, William Tyson, Jonathan Ellicott, Andrew Ellicott, Mary Tyson, Sr., George P. Waters, John W. Wilson, Hannah Marsh, Jr., Tacey Ellicott, Elizabeth Brown, Alisanna Cornthwait, Mary Brown, Parthenia Dukehart, Robert Cornthwait, Jonathan Balderston, Samuel

Miller, Samuel Wilson, Kitty Wilson, Benjamin Chandlee, Ann Baker. 3rd column - Isaac Brown, Ann Matthews, Margaret Dukehart, Sarah Riley, Sarah Matthews, Elizabeth Wilson, George Matthews, David Brown, Jr., Margaret H. Brown, Cassandra Brown, Dorothy Brown, Valerius Dukehart, Jr., Ann Riley, Anna Wilson, Elizabeth Husband, Hannah E. Townsend, Lydia Townsend, Joshua Matthews, William Husband, John Cornthwait, Ann Matthews, Jr., Susan Husband.

**Joseph P. Plummer**, of Anne Arundel County, Maryland, son of John and Johannah Plummer (the father being deceased), married **Susanna Husband**, dau. of Joseph and Mary Husband, of Harford County (the father being deceased), in Baltimore City on 10th of 3rd mo., 1806.
Witnesses: 1st column - Margaret Balderston, Sarah Peach, Ann Matthews, Lewis Richards, William Brown, Jane Brown, John Marsh, Rachel Naylor, Sally L. Aisquith, Nancy N. Collins, William Riley, James Gillingham, David Wilson, Jane Wilson, David Brown, Jr., George Matthews, William E. George, Joel Hopkins, John Jewitt. 2nd column - Elizabeth Brown, Hanna M. Waters, Elizabeth Robinson, Elizabeth Matthews, Elizabeth Wilson, Ann Matthews, Jr., Margaret Cowman, Mary Brown, Elizabeth Lowden, Mary Brown, Ann M. Richards, William Tyson, Mary Ellicott, Jr., Grace J. Hopkins, Rachel Mason, Milcah Goodwin, Henrietta Thomas, Ann Riley, Alisanna Cornthwait. 3rd column - Mary Mifflin, Joshua Husband, Margaret Husband, Evan Thomas, Rachel Thomas, Jm. P. Plummer, William Husband, Joseph Husband, Sally G. Husband, Lydia Husband, Amelia Hopkins, Henrietta Hopkins, Mary Husband, Gerard T. Hopkins, P. E. Thomas, George Passmoore, Samuel Hopkins, Joshua Matthews, David Brown.

**Benjamin Chandlee**, of Winchester, Virginia, son of Goldsmith and Ann Chandlee (deceased), of the same place, married **Elizabeth Matthews**, dau. of Thomas (deceased) and Ann Matthews, of Baltimore County, in Baltimore City on 22nd of 5th mo., 1806.
Witnesses: 1st column - Catharine Dimmitt, Frances Brown, Eliza Norris, Susanna Norris, Elizabeth Robinson, Miriam James, Catharine Daugherty, Rebekah Williams, Hannah Trimble, Elizabeth Naylor, Elizabeth Husband, Sarah Brown, Lydia Husband, Mary Brown, Isaac Parkins, Jr., Jonathan Balderston, John M. Brown, Amos Brown, William Riley. 2nd column - Robert Cornthwait, Elizabeth Brown, Sarah D. Brown, Ann Matthews, Jr., Margaret Davenport, James Page, William Burn, Seth Smith, Samuel Matthews, James Gillingham, William Trimble, Gerard T. Hopkins, James Brown, Dorothy Brown, Rossiter Scott, Mary S. Clark, John Riley. 3rd column - Goldsmith Chandlee, Ann Matthews, Margaret Dukehart, William Matthews (of O.), David Wilson, Thomas Matthews, John Dukehart, Sarah Matthews, Ann Riley, Catharine Brown, Alisanna Cornthwait, Sarah Brown, David Brown, Elizabeth Trimble, Rebecca Ball, Joshua Matthews, David Brown, Jr.

**Ambrose Updegraff**, of York County, Pennsylvania, son of Joseph and Susanna Updegraff (deceased), married **Rachel Hayward**, of Anne Arundel County Maryland, dau. of William and Sidney Hayward, in Baltimore City on 21st of 5th mo., 1806.
Witnesses: 1st column - Ann Read, Hannah Updegraff, Samuel Canby, Elizabeth Canby, John Ellicott, Joseph Atkinson, Joseph Lownes, Isaac Atkinson, George Ellicott, George Ellicott (of George), William Gillingham, Ezra Gillingham, Andrew Ellicott, George Gillingham, Joel Updegraff, Isaac Scott. 2nd column - Mary Elms, Mary Kinsey, Rachel Atkinson, Eliza Ellicott, Sarah Ellicott, Frances Ellicott, Elizabeth Ellicott, Miriam Lownes, Abigal Atkinson, Jonathan Ellicott, Edward H. Dorsey, Samuel Smith, Emmor Bailey, Thomas Townsend, Misail Pierpoint, Mary Pierpoint, 3rd column - William Hayward, Elizabeth Gillingham, Susanna Updegraff, John Hayward, Elizabeth Gillingham, Jr., Elizabeth Hayward, Rebecca Hayward, Ann Scott, Elizabeth L. Gillingham, Jane Coates, James Gillingham, Edith Kirk, Mary Cope, Ann Pierpoint, Sarah Ellicott, Elizabeth Bailey, Ann Patrige, Latitia Brown, Sarah Atkinson.

**Skipwith Coale**, of Deer Creek, Harford County, son of Samuel and Lydia Coale, of the same place, married **Ann Matthews**, dau. of George and Sarah Matthews, of Baltimore City, on 17th of 7th mo., 1806.
Witnesses: 1st column - William Tyson, William Procter, John Marsh, John McKim, William Brown, John Jewitt, Rachel Naylor, Elizabeth Naylor, Mary Matthews, William E. George, George Baker, Ann Matthews, Sophia Matthews, Jane Trimble, Gerard T. Hopkins, Robert Cornthwait, Susanna Judge, Jr., Elizabeth Trimble, Rachel C. Wainwright, James Wainwright, Joseph James, Samuel Wilson, Sarah Rough, Cassandra Durbin, Mary James, Elizabeth Robinson, Jane Wilson. 2nd column - Jessee Lamborn, Mary Jones, Richard H. Jones, John Trimble, George Passmoore, David Brown, Samuel Matthews, Jane Catts, Sarah Smith, Bell Hutton, Susan Hopkins, Mary Worthington, Eliza Torrence, Rachel Mason, Martha Balderston, Mary Leypold, John Cornthwait, Rebecca Goodwin, Rebecca Judge, Sarah Brown, Sarah Catts, Hannah P. Townsend, Ann Jewitt, Sarah Cresson, Ellis Yarnall, Catharine Morris, 3rd column - Samuel Coale, George Matthews, Lydia Coale, Sarah Matthews, Dorothy Brown, Elizabeth Husband, Bulah Brown, Mary Coale, Lydia Husband, Eliza Matthews, Elizabeth Brown, David Brown, Jr., Elizabeth Naylor, Hannah Wollen, Hester H. Townsend, Samuel Catts, Samuel Matthews, Dorothy Hopkins, John Wilson, Frances Hopkins, Phoebe Judge, Hannah Lightler, Jr., Emilie Hopkins, Anne Wilson, Elizabeth Hopkins, William Husband, Joshua Kersey.

**Elisha Hunt**, of Fayette County, Pennsylvania, son of Joshua and Esther Hunt, of the same place (the father being deceased), married **Mary Hussey**, of Baltimore

City, dau. of Riccord and Miriam Hussey, of York County, Pennsylvania (the father being deceased), in Baltimore City on 12th of 12th mo., 1806.
Witnesses: 1st column - William E. George, David Brown, Jr., George E. Carey, Amos Brown, Peter Forney, George Popplein, William Cooper, Andreas Popplein, Thomas Mummey, Valerius Dukehart, Seth C. Smith, John Nicholson, Gerard T. Hopkins, William Waterhouse, William Husband, Nicholas Popplein, Isaac McPherson, William Procter, Rhoda Matthews, John Cornthwait, Jane McPherson, Eliza McPherson, Ann Edmundson, Reese Cadwalader, Taci Norbury. 2nd column - Elizabeth Tyson, Ann Riley, Rebecca Norris, Miriam James, Elizabeth Norris, Rachel Mason, Elizabeth Robertson, Mary Robertson, Ann Poultney, Henry Thomas, Hannah P. Townsend, Ann James, Martha Ellicott, Mary Tyson, Sr., Tacy Ellicott, Hannah Carey, Mary James, Esther H. Townsend, George Matthews, Elisha Tyson, John McKim, George S. Baker, W. Penniman, Joel Hopkins. 3rd column - John Marsh, Hannah Marsh, Mary H. Marsh, Mordecai Matthews, Ruth Matthews, Nathan Hunt, Joseph Edmundson, Eliza Marsh, John Dillon, Edith Dillon, Enoch R. Allen, Grace Allen, Dorothy Hopkins, Rebecca Procter, Izak Procter, Tacey McPherson, Grace Knox, Reynolds Knox, Martha Norbury, George Norbury, Katharine Mummey, Mary Ellicott, Jr., Ann Stouffer.

**William Cornthwait**, of Baltimore City, son of Robert and Grace Cornthwait, of the same place (the father being deceased), married **Ann Hill**, dau. of John and Ann Hill (the mother being deceased), of Baltimore City, on 18th of 12th mo., 1806.
Witnesses: 1st column - John McKim, William Dawson, George Matthews, Joseph James, William Trimble, Dorothy Brown, Ann Peck, William Husband, Mary Mifflin, Elizabeth West, Susan Price, William Brown, Jane Brown, Frances Hopkins, Joseph Brown, John M. Brown, Thomas Wilson, Thomas Amos. 2nd column - Margaret Balderston, Martha Davis, Catharine Sanderson, Hannah James, Sarah Brown, Sarah James, David Brown, Jr., Eliza Brown, Hannah Trimble, Ann Matthews, Frances Brown, David Brown, Rossiter Scott, William Jones, Joel Hopkins, Valerius Dukehart, Isaac Brooks. 3rd column - Grace Cornthwait, Thomas Cornthwait, Deborah Cornthwait, Mary Cornthwait, Miranna Cornthwait, John Cornthwait, Robert Cornthwait, John Cornthwait, Jr., John Wilson, Deborah Wilson, Samuel Wilson, Anna Wilson, Elizabeth Wilson, Jane Wilson, H. P. Townsend, Ann Price, Susan Hopkins, Elizabeth Husband.

**James Ellicott**, of Baltimore City, son of Andrew and Esther Ellicott, of Baltimore County, married **Henrietta Thomas**, dau. of Philip William Thomas, of London, and wife Elizabeth (deceased), in Baltimore City on 18th of 2nd mo., 1807.
Witnesses: 1st column - Samuel Carey, John W. Wilson, William Gwynn (of John), Gerard T. Hopkins, John Cornthwait, William E. George, Mordecai Yarnall, Peregrine Wethered, Thomas B. Baker, John Comegys, Richard D. Mullikin,

George Mason, Maria Cox, Hannah Robertson, William Waterhouse, James Gillingham, Evan Poultney, John Nicholson, Samuel Poultney, Philip Poultney, John Marsh. 2nd column - Hannah Ellicott, Jane McPherson, Rachel Mason, Jonathan Ellicott, Eliza McPherson, Mary Tyson, Elisha Poultney, Elizabeth Tyson, Hannah Marsh, Tacy Ellicott, John Ellicott Carey, Sarah Ellicott, Benjamin Ellicott, Jr., Nathaniel Ellicott, James Ellicott, Evan Thomas, Philip E. Thomas, Evan Thomas, Jr., Thomas Poultney, Isaac Tyson, Lewin Weathered, William Tyson.

"Relations Names" (in 3rd column) - Andrew Ellicott, George Ellicott, John Ellicott, Jr., Thomas Ellicott, Andrew Ellicott, Jr., Isaac McPherson, Tacy McPherson, Sarah Ellicott, Mary Ellicott, Mary M. Ellicott, Mary Ellicott, Jr., Tacy Mitchel, Benjamin Ellicott, Martha Carey, Ann Poultney, Henrietta Thomas, Rachel Thomas, Elizabeth Tyson, Elizabeth Thomas.

**Samuel Jefferis**, of Baltimore City, son of William Jefferis, of the State of Pennsylvania (deceased), and his wife Priscilla, married **Hannah Townsend**, dau. of Joseph Townsend, of Baltimore City, and his wife Mary (deceased), on 16th of 4th mo., 1807.
Witnesses: 1st column - Sarah Brown, Jane Burnet, Beulah Brown, John Cornthwait, Jr., Amos Brown, Valerius Dukehart, Thomas Macilroy, Isaac Brooks, Ennion Hussey, John Loney, Henry Bromwell, Samuel Wilson, Valerius Riley, William Loney, Thomas Mecteer, William B. Lucas, Dorothy Brown, Frances Hopkins, Mercy Mecteer, Annabella Fisher, David Brown, Jr., Eliza Matthews, Anna Wilson, Mary Matthews, Sophia Matthews (per desire), William Townsend, Emily Sharpless, Elizabeth Wilson, William Husband. 2nd column - Eliza Diffenderffer, Alissanna Cornthwait, Catharine Diffenderffer, Sophia Diffenderffer, Harriet Benson, Mary Enniss, Harriet Richardson, Provey Langworthy, Elizabeth Phenix, Matilda Inglis, Juliana Enniss, Maria Baneker, Susan Taylor, Elizabeth Morgan, Elenor Norris, Phebe H. Lafetra, Rachel Hussey, Miriam James, Mary Heley, Joseph James, Catharine Sanderson, Hannah James, Sarah James, George Dobbin, Samuel Conrad, John Duer, Mary Tyson (per desire), Elizabeth Dukehart, Margaret Conrad. 3rd column - Esther T. Townsend, Priscilla Morgan (per desire), G. M. Jefferis, Samuel Matthews, Ann Matthews, Benjamin Townsend, Granville S. Townsend, Samuel P. Matthews, John Brown, Samuel H. Matthews, Nicholas W. Townsend, Jesse Morgan, Jr., David Brown, Elizabeth Brown, Ann Matthews (by request), Amos James, James Brown, John Cornthwait, William Mecteer, John Vance, Samuel Cole, John Jefferis, Ann Jefferis, Sarah Smith, Bell Hutton, M. Hutton, S. Dukehart, John Wilson, E. Dukehart, John M. Brown, William Brown.

**Benjamin Townsend**, of the State of Ohio, son of Joseph and Lydia Townsend, of East Bradford Township, Chester County, Pennsylvania (both deceased), married

**Elizabeth Naylor**, dau. of John and Jane Naylor, of Baltimore City (both deceased), in Baltimore on 18th of 6th mo., 1807.
Witnesses: 1st column - Rebecca C. James, Susanna Cochran, Catharine Sanderson, Hannah James, Sarah S. James, Maria James, Hannah Hussey, Susanna Judge, Jr., William Husband, Robert Cornthwait, Valerius Dukehart, N. W. Townsend, Joel Hopkins, N. W. Easton, Granville Townsend, Robert Townsend, Samuel P. Matthews, Joseph James. 2nd column - George Matthews, Sarah Matthews (by request), Rebecca Williams (by request), David Brown, Mary Mifflin (by request), Dorothy Brown, Elizabeth Trimble, Hannah Jefferis, David Brown, Jr., Mary Jones (by request), Hannah Trimble, Ann Matthews (by request), Jane Wilson (by request), Margaret Dukehart, Ann Jewitt, Ruth Easton, Elizabeth Husband, Elizabeth Hopkins, Elizabeth Robertson, Susan Butler.

**John Cornthwait**, merchant, of Baltimore City, son of John and Mary Cornthwait, of the same place (both deceased), married **Elizabeth Wilson**, dau. of David and Jane Wilson, of Baltimore City, on 19th of 11th mo., 1807.
Witnesses: 1st column - Sarah Matthews, Lydia Husband, Elizabeth Trimble, Sarah Thornburgh, Ann Riley, Catharine Brown, David Brown, Elizabeth Davenport, Mary Ball, Eliza Ball, Sarah Brown, Martha Balderston, Ely Balderston, Grace Cornthwait, Mary Martin, Mary Brown, Margaret Thornburgh, Parthenia Dukehart, William Riley, Andrew Ellicott, Jr., Mordecai Yarnall, Thomas Wilson, Margaret Dukehart, James Brown. 2nd column - Fitch Hall, Jr., James Gunn, James Hanna, William E. George, Ellen Bowen, John Reese, John Sterett, N. Tyson, Jr., William Jones, Folger Pope, Amos West, Lewis M. Richards, John Loney, William Hayward, William Trimble, Hannah H. James, Catharine Sanderson, Sarah James, Maria L. Jones, Nicholas Riley, John Brown, Robert Wilkinson, Samuel P. Matthews, Samuel Matthews, Joseph James, William Husband, James Martin. "Names of Relatives" (in 3rd column) - David Wilson, Jane Wilson, Robert Cornthwait, Samuel Wilson, Jr., William Cornthwait, Isa Little, John Dukehart, John Wilson, Samuel Wilson, Anna Wilson, Mary Cornthwait, Ann Cornthwait, Deborah Wilson, Alisan Cornthwait (by request), Mary Waybill, Joshua Matthews, Ann Matthews, Susanna Martin, Elizabeth White, Ann Peck, Sarah Wilson, Rebecca Goodwin, Milcah Goodwin, Benjamin Goodhue, Nath. Saltonstall.

**Valerius Dukehart**, of Baltimore City, son of Valerius (deceased) and Margaret Dukehart, of the same place, married **Anna Jones**, dau. of Robinson (deceased) and Mary Jones, of the same place, in Baltimore City, Eastern District, on 17th of 12th mo., 1807.
Witnesses: 1st column - Betty Jones, Mary Mifflin (by request), George Matthews (by request), Elizabeth Trimble, Amelia Pervail, John Pervail, William Gillingham, Sarah Procter, Tacy Burgess (by desire), Esther Townsend, James Hanna, Campbell S. Askew, Nathan Tyson, Jr., J. Baynard, George S. Baker, Seth Smith, Joseph

James, John Loney, Henry Bromwell, Nicholas Riley, Samuel Wilson. 2nd column - Sarah Brown, Hannah Ellicott, Elizabeth Foxall, Sarah Brown, Hannah H. James, Maria L. Jones, Catharine Sanderson, Mary Ball, Elizabeth Repkey, Elizabeth Ball, Sarah James, Martha Price, David Brown, John Brown, Samuel P. Matthews, George Brown, William Hayward, John McKim, Hannah Byrns, William Trimble, Hannah Trimble, Isaac Brooks. 3rd column - Mary Jones, Margaret Dukehart, William Jones, Robinson Jones, John Dukehart, Ann Riley, Parthenia Dukehart, Catharine Brown, James Brown, Mary Brown (at her request), David Wilson, Joshua Matthews, Mary McKim, Elizabeth Hopkins, Eliza White, Dorothy Brown, Ann Matthews, Margaret McGowan, Martha McGowan, Elizabeth Kinser, Rebecca C. James, Mary Brown, Rebecca M. Headington, Harriet Bussey.

**Robert Young**, son of William and Amelia Young, of Kent County, Maryland (both deceased), married **Rebecca Hussey**, dau. of George and Rachel Hussey (the mother being deceased), in Baltimore City on 21st of 4th mo., 1808.
Witnesses: 1st column - Susannah Judge, Jr., Rebecca Procter, Sarah Procter, Hannah Trimble (per order), Tacy Burgess, Elizabeth Lowden (per order), Martha Balderston, Edith Dillon, Margaret Moore, Susanna Martin, Sally G. Husband, Mary Webster, Esther Townsend, Rachel Naylor, Mary Mifflin (by request), Frances Hopkins, Jane Wilson, Grace Cornthwait, Deborah Wilson, John Wilson, Elizabeth Trimble, John Trimble, Hannah James, Mary Ball, Deborah Jones, Rebecca M. Headington. 2nd column - Sarah Brown, Elizabeth Husband, Elizabeth Hopkins, Amelia Hopkins, Jane Jacobs, Maria McDonnell, Hannah Marsh, Elizabeth Fisher, Mary Cornthwait, Lydia Husband, Mary Mince, Joel Hopkins, Stephen Cooke, Charles Read, Mary Jones, William Jones, Elizabeth Mince, Elizabeth Mince, Jr., Ennion Williams, William Trimble, Isaac Brookes, Amos Smith, Joseph James, Valerius Dukehart, Henry Bromwell, Nicholas Riley. "Names of Relatives" (in 3rd column) - George Hussey, Grace Hussey, Mary Price, Hannah Hussey, William Hussey, Caleb Price, Joseph Hussey, John Marsh, Edward Dawes, Rachel Hussey, Isaac Hussey, John R. Price, Ennion Hussey .. [space] .. Samuel Wilson, John Brown, John Fisher, David Wilson, Joshua Mott, William Husband, William Dawson, John Cornthwait, Thomas Cornthwait, Jonathan McDermet, Jesse Price, Robert McDermit, Mary Parks, Cassander Bondfield.

**John Jewett**, of Baltimore City, son of Thaddeus and Ann Jewett, married **Susanna Judge**, dau. of Hugh and Susanna Judge, of the same place, in Baltimore City, Eastern District, on 16th of 6th mo., 1808.
Witnesses: 1st column - John Morgan, Granville S. Townsend, Nicholas Riley, John Price, John Brown, George Brown, Samuel Wilson, Valerius Dukehart, William Morgan, Clement Marshall, William Marshall, John Dawson, Hugh Balderston, John S. Peck, James Brown, Samuel Byrnes, John Mitchel, Tacy Mitchel, Isaac McPherson, John Marsh, William Husband, William Trimble, Jr.,

Robinson Jones, Joel Hopkins, Joseph James, William Procter. 2nd column - Mary James, Hannah Byrnes, Amelia Hopkins, Anna Dukehart, Susanna Martin, Rebecca Smith, Penelope E. D. Cockey, John S. Webster, Jane Wilson, Rebecca M. Headington, Sarah Brown, Mary McKim, Eda Dawes, Martha Balderston (per order), Elizabeth Lowden (per order), Rebecca C. James, Lydia Dixon, Ann Marshall, Sarah Procter, Anna Wilson, William Brown, Isaac Brookes, David Wilson, William Jones, Ely Balderston. 3rd column - Hugh Judge, Susanna Judge, Elizabeth Robertson, Joshua Husband, Eliza Robertson, Jr., Rachel Judge, Rebecca Judge, Mary Robertson, Margaret Balderston, Elizabeth Thomas, Sally G. Husband, Eliza P. Brooke, Margaret Judge, Phebe Judge, Joshua Mott, Lucretia Wilson, Ann Fisher (per order), R. Cornthwait, Hannah Trimble (per order), Tacy Burgess, Frances Hopkins, Elizabeth Husband, Elizabeth Hopkins, Joseph Husband, Rebecca Procter.

**Charles Read**, of Baltimore County, son of Jacob and Ann Read, of Anne Arundel County, Maryland, married **Betty Fisher**, dau. of Samuel and Susanna Fisher, of Baltimore City, in Baltimore, Western District, on 16th of 3rd mo., 1809.
Witnesses: 1st column - Isaac Tyson, Jr., John Reece, Samuel Wilson, Joseph W. Miller, John Needles, Valerius Dukehart, Joseph James, David Brown, mary Mifflin (per request), David Wilson, Sarah Fisher, Dorothy Brown, Frances Hopkins, Mary Ann Lynch, William Brown, Eleanor Bowen, Richard Hopkins, John Trimble. 2nd column - Esther Townsend, Amelia Hopkins, Mary Cornthwait, Anna Wilson, Rebecca C. James, William Hayward, Hannah James, Susanna Waters, Ann Peck, Sophia Bernard, Alissanna Okely, Deborah Jones, William Cornthwait, Folger Pope, James Brown, William Gillingham, George Gillingham, Mary Brown, Edith Reed (by request). 3rd column - Samuel Fisher (by order), Jacob Read, Hannah White James Fisher, Larkin Read, John Brown, Ruth Fisher, Lydia Fisher, Seth Fisher, Elisha Fisher, Joel Fisher, Ann Reed, Grace Read, Samuel Harlan, Sarah Matthews, Sarah Procter, Esther Balderston, Tacy Burgess. Abigail Medcalf, Jane Wilson, Elizabeth Husband, Elizabeth Hopkins.

**William Procter**, of Baltimore City, son of Stephen and Rebecca Procter, of the City and County of York in the Island of Great Britain (both deceased), married **Anna Wilson**, dau. of John and Deborah Wilson, of Baltimore City, in Baltimore, Eastern District, on 16th of 11th mo., 1809.
Witnesses: 1st column - William Trimble, William Dawson, William Brown, William Cornthwait, Ann Cornthwait, Joseph James, Joel Hopkins, Elizabeth Hopkins, Mary Cornthwait, Amelia Hopkins, Mary Brown, Sarah Brown, Hannah Ellicott, Elizabeth Balderston, Martha Balderston, Nancy Matthews (by desire), Ann Matthews, Thomas Cornthwait, Charles Hambleton, William Trimble, Jr., John Cadue, Eliza Cadue. 2nd column - Mary Waybill, Susan Bond, Mary James, Mary Hall, Harriet Kell, Alisanna Kell, Milcah L. Maddux, Caroline Hargrove,

Harriet Beard, Susan B. Jones, Ann Peck, Ellen Norris, Rebecca Matthews, Susannah Amos, Sarah Hopkins, Hannah Marsh, Mary Mifflin (by desire), William Husband, William Hayward, William Comegys, Valerius Dukehart. 3rd column - John Wilson, Izak Procter, Deborah Wilson, Rebecca Procter, Sarah Procter, David Wilson, Jane Wilson, Samuel Wilson, Elizabeth Reed, Thomas Wilson, David Wilson, Jr., Mary M. Procter, Eveline Reed, Ann Pope, Allisanna Cornthwait, Elizabeth Hopkins, Elizabeth Kinsey, Margaret Carey, Sarah James, Ann Sanderson, Frances Hopkins, Hannah Trimble, Sarah Day, Elizabeth Cornthwait, Deborah Reed.

**William Comegys**, of Baltimore City, son of Cornelius and Elizabeth Comegys (both deceased), married **Elizabeth Kinsey**, dau. of James Mason *[sic]* and Rachel his wife, of Baltimore County, in Baltimore on 20th of 9th mo., 1810.
Witnesses: 1st column - Benjamin Comegys, Mary Snyder, Priscilla Comegys, Elizabeth Buchanan, May *[sic]* Comegys, Rachel Mason, Edith Scott, Sophia Matthews, Rebecca C. James, Hannah James, Margareta Bassett, Joseph W. Miller, John Needles, Rossiter Scott, William F. Miller. 2nd column - Peter Snyder, Jesse Comegys, Rebecca Medcalf, Esther Townsend, Eleanor Atkison, Rachael Judge, Mary James, Mary Matthews, Ann Aitken, Ann W. Sanderson, Caroline S. Waters, Israel Price, Ann Matthews, Samuel Matthews, Mary Price. 3rd column - Rachel Mott, Joshua Mott, Amelia Hopkins, John Nupear, Benjamin Maynor, Christopher Vansant, Mary Martin, Sarah Scott, Elisha Scott, Sarah James, Valerius Dukehart, Alexander Boyd, Phebe H. Lafetra, Joseph James, Joel Hopkins. 4th column - James Mason, Mary Comegys.

**Edmund Evens**, of Baltimore County, son of John and Sarah Evens, of the County of Devon in the Island of Great Britain, married **Elizabeth Husband**, dau. of Joseph (deceased) and Mary Husband, of Harford County, in Baltimore, Eastern District, on 15th of 11th mo., 1810.
Witnesses: 1st column - Joel Hopkins, Sarah Tyson, Susanna Judge, Mary Jones, Ann Matthews, Alisanna Cornthwait, Sarah Matthews, Susanna Martin, Ann Peck, Eleanor Atkison, Ann B. Brown, John S. Peck, Sarah James, Isaac Tyson, Jr., Thomas Wilson, William Trimble, Izak Procter, Elizabeth Hopkins, 2nd column - Elizabeth Hunt, Jemima Shotwell, Sarah Riley, Mary James, Rebecca Procter, Elizabeth Louden, Sarah W. Doddrell, Alisanna Oakly, Elizabeth Trimble, John Hillen, Sarah T. Gilpin, Mary James, David Brown, William Trimble, Jr., William M. Medcalf, Joseph James, Margaret Dukehart. 3rd column - Mary Mifflin, John McKim, Mary McKim, Joshua Husband, William Husband, Joseph Husband, Lydia Husband, Susanna Plummer, Joseph Husband, Jr., Lloyd Mifflin, Amelia Hopkins, Edwin Waters, Joseph W. Miller, Joseph Townsend, Esther Townsend, Abigail Medcalf, Jane Wilson, David Wilson.

**James C. Armstrong**, of Baltimore City, son of James (deceased) and Peggy Armstrong, of the same place, married **Hannah Ellicott**, dau. of Thomas (deceased) and Jane Ellicott, of Bucks County, Pennsylvania, in Baltimore City on 16th of 4th mo., 1812.
Witnesses: 1st column - Eliza Gillingham, Jane Gillingham, Miriam Gillingham, Hannah Marsh, Mary Wilson, Sarah T. Gilpin, Israel Price, Ely Balderston, Samuel S. Smith, Elizabeth Price, Mary Brown (of Joseph), William Husband, Thomas Wilson, Thomas L. Reese, Dorothy Brown, Ann Matthews, Deborah Wilson, Maria K. Reese, Edwin Waters, Mary Trimble, Elizabeth Trimble. 2nd column - Mary Mifflin, Sarah Procter, Susanna Judge, Ann Ewing, Alisanna Cornthwait, Mary Cornthwait, Elizabeth Pugh, Hannah Carey, Elizabeth Comegys, Ann Peck, Hannah James, Joel Brown, Mary Waybill, John W. Brevitt, Sarah Brown, Caroline S. Waters, Esther Reese, Deborah Jones, John Trimble, Stephen Cook, Jr., George S. Knight, William Hopkins. 3rd column - Joshua Barney, Jane Brown, Peggy McLaughlin, Benjamin Ellicott, Rachel Ellicott, Ann Smith, Henry Armstrong, Sarah W. Brown, Mary Brown, Margaret Carey, Richard Morris, E. Riggs, John Mott, John S. Peck, Bulah Brown, Frances Price, Susan H. Waters, Charlotte Watters, Eliza Ann Smith, Elizabeth Balderston, Martha Balderston, Marcelious Balderston.

**Israel Price**, of Baltimore City, son of Samuel and Anne Price, of Baltimore County, and **Martha Davies**, dau. of John and Mary Davies, formerly of the Town of Baltimore, married in Baltimore, Eastern District, on 18th of 3rd mo., 1813.
Witnesses: 1st column - Thomas Wilson, Richard Frisby, Ann Ewing, Joshua Matthews, Joseph Townsend, Eleanor Atkison, Larkin Read, Mary Brown, Esther Townsend, William Husband, Isaac Brooks, Ann Matthews. 2nd column - Sarah Procter, Elijah Stansbury, John Trimble, Ann Coates, Joshua Mott, Oliver Kinsey, Alisann Cornthwait, Sarah Brown, Edwin Waters, Mary McKim, Grace J. Hopkins, Rachel Mott, Ruthy E. Stansbury. 3rd column - Samuel Price, Daniel Price, Elizabeth Edwards, Francess Brown, Jesse Price, Frances Price, Mary Mifflin, Amelia Hopkins, Phebe Lafetra, Deborah Jones.

**William Shepherd**, of Frederick County, Maryland, son of Solomon and Susanna Shepherd, of the same place, married **Ruth Fisher**, dau. of Samuel and Susanna Fisher, of Baltimore City, in Baltimore, Eastern District, on 20th of 5th mo., 1813.
Witnesses: 1st column - Ely Balderston, John Dukehart, John Trimble, Matilda Reed, Eveline Reed, William Procter, Elizabeth Nailor (by desire), Frances Jones (by desire), Mary Brown (by desire), John McKim, William Brown, Jane Brown (by request), Dorothy Brown, Jane Wilson, Mary McKim. 2nd column - Joseph Townsend, Sarah Matthews, Anna Ewing, Abigail Medcalf, Susan H. Waters, Phebe Lafetra, Elizabeth Pugh, Amelia Hopkins, Elizabeth Gillingham, Martha Price, Rachel Atkison, Caroline S. Waters, Esther Townsend, Elizabeth Trimble,

Jr., Ann Peck. 3rd column - Samuel Fisher (by desire), Lydia Fisher, Mary Shepherd, Betty Read, James Farquhar, Joel Fisher, Elisha Fisher, Charles Read, Susanna Judge, Parthena Dukehart, Sarah Procter, John S. Peck, Joel Hopkins, William Husband.

**Edward Wilson**, of Philadelphia, Pennsylvania, merchant, son of William and Mary Wilson, of Yendon in the County of York in the Island of Great Britain (both deceased), and **Sarah Procter**, of Baltimore City, dau. of Stephen and Rebecca Procter, of the City and County of York in the Island aforesaid, married in Baltimore, Eastern District, on 15th of 9th mo., 1814.
Witnesses: 1st column - Joseph James, Grace Cornthwait, Dorothy Hopkins, Elizabeth Hopkins, Gerard T. Hopkins, John Paul, William Brown, Joel Hopkins, Tacy Burgess (by desire), Mary Cornthwait (by desire), Deborah Cornthwait (by desire), Elizabeth Long (by desire), Nathaniel Knight (by request), John Ogston, William Dawson, Ann Dawson, Jr., Joseph P. Plummer, John Hopkins, Jr., Ann Peck Cornthwait, Ann Dawson. 2nd column - Hannah Trimble, Jr., Jane Brown (by request), Martha Balderston (by request), Ely Balderston, William Riley, James Gillingham, John McKim, William Trimble, Hugh Balderston, Samuel Matthews, Thomas Matthews, Jacob Lafetra, Reynold Knox, David Brown, John S. Peck, Ann Matthews (by desire), Ann Peck, Elizabeth Trimble, Deborah Wilson. 3rd column - Izak Procter, William Procter, Rebecca Procter, Anna Procter, Mary James, Elizabeth Procter, Deborah Reed, John Pacey Platts, John Wilson, Elizabeth Amoss, Esther Townsend, Sarah W. Doddrell, Susanna Martin, Rebecca Medcalf, Eleanor Atkison, Elizabeth Pugh, David Wilson, Thomas Wilson, Theeodat Pope, Hannah Pope.

**Edwin Waters**, of Baltimore City, son of Edward and Hannah Waters, of the same place, married **Sarah W. Brown**, dau. of William and Elizabeth Brown, of the same place (the mother being deceased), in Baltimore, Eastern District, on 21st of 12th mo., 1815.
Witnesses: 1st column - Sarah Brown, Henrietta Dukehart, Elizabeth Trimble, Mary Mifflin (by desire), Martha Balderson, Ann Matthews, Lydia Husband, Mary Brown, Mary Morgan, Ann Smith, Mary Sykes, Harriet Sykes, Deborah R. Jones, Maria L. Jones, Hannah Armstrong, Sarah Matthews. 2nd column - William Procter, William Husband, Israel Price, Joshua Mott, John Nancanow[?], Samuel S. Smith, Rossiter Scott, Alisanna Okely, Jane Eliza Calder, Susanna Amoss, Martha Amoss, Rebecca James, Esther Townsend, Rachel Naylor, Albina Powell, Eliza W. Yerkes. 3rd column - William Brown, Edward Watters, Jane Brown (by request), John Wilson, Francess Brown, Caroline S. Waters, Ruth B. Atkison, Elizabeth Price, Elizabeth Balderston, Hannah Pope, Samuel Matthews, Charles Waters, J. Perry McCandless, William P. Morgan, Joseph Webster, Joshua Matthews, William K. Jones.

**George F. Janney**, of Baltimore City, son of Lewis (deceased) and Mary Janney, of the same place, married **Sarah H. John**, dau. of Reuben and Lydia John, of Uwchlan Township, Chester County, Pennsylvania (the mother being deceased), in Baltimore City, Eastern District, on 16th of 5th mo., 1816.
Witnesses: 1st column - James Lovegrove, Rachel Mott, Margaret Garretson, Hannah Kenney, N. W. Townsend, Hannah P. Townsend, Mary B. Lafetra, Sarah Lafetra, Ann Peck, Jane Sterling, Mary Hopkins, Charles Diffendaffer, Isaac Atkison, Joshua Mott, Lydia Husband, Henry W. Webster, Mary M. Townsend, Elizabeth Trimble, William Cole, James Heighe, Jr., William Procter, Anna Procter, Martha Balderston (by request), Elizabeth Townsend (by request), Elizabeth Bidgood (by request), Elizabeth Lowden (by request), William P. Sevear (by request), William Husband. 2nd column - Abner Pope, Isaac Tyson, Jr., Eliza W. Yerkes, Martha Balderston, Hannah Trimble, Tasey Burges, Ann M. Caldwell, Hannah Riley, Mary E. Silvester, Jacob Lafetra, Volerius Dukehart, John Morgan, Hester Dobbin, John Hillen, John Stricker, Ge. *[sic]* Decker, Hetty Few, Amelia Hopkins, Phebe Lafetra, Eleanor Atkison, John Glendy, John S. Peck, William K. Jones, Elizabeth Hopkins, Mary McKim, John McKim, Isaac Garretson, Joseph Davenport, John Trimble, William Trimble, 3rd column - Joseph Townsend, Mary Janney, Esther Townsend, Robert John, J. W. Townsend, James J. Sharpless, Eascheus Townsend, Phebe John, Julia A. Sharpless, Catreine *[sic]* John, Grace J. Hopkins, G. S. Townsend, H. Love, Joseph Webster, Ann Ewing, Sarah Matthews, Elizabeth Pugh, Mary Kelso, Hannah Pope, Elizabeth Balderston, Ann Pope, Hannah Houlton, Phebe S. Townsend, Deborah Jones.

**Isaac Hayward**, of Baltimore City, son of William and Keziah Hayward, of the same place, married **Elizabeth Balderston**, dau. of Ely and Esther Balderston, of the same place, on 20th of 6th mo., 1816.
Witnesses: 1st column - Ann M. Harper, Sarah W. Byrnes, Ann P. Cornthwait, John Moore, David Brown (per request), Ann B. Brown, Hepzebah Buchanan, Susan B. Buchanan, Charles A. Buchanan, Jacob T. Bunting, Isaac Atkison, Robert H. Norris, William P. Morgan, Elias Pugh, William Trimble, Samuel Matthews, Ann Matthews (by request), William Procter, Anna Procter, D. R. Wilson, Frances Woodward, Isaac Tyson, Jr., Elizabeth Hayward, W. H. Freeman. Martha Balderston, John Hayward, Margaret Dukehart, John C. Howell, Thomas Wilson. 2nd column - John S. Tyson, Phebe S. Townsend, Hannah P. Cowman, Mary M. Townsend, Mary J. Ellicott, Eliza K. West, E. S. Moore, Ellen W. Armstrong, Hannah Trimble, Tacey Burgess, Elizabeth Pugh, J. Kingston, Ann Pope, Leroy Swarmstadt, David G. McCoy, W. G. Atkison, William Hamilton, Skipwith Wilson, Elizabeth Bidgood, Mary C. Silvester, Elizabeth Comegys, Rebecca Beans, Susanna Amoss, J. Wilson, Esther Townsend, Ann Ewing, A. M. Caldwell, Isabella Freeman, John M. Kelso, Andrew Hemphill, Louis R. Techtey[?], William Comegys, Eliza W. Yerkes, Mary Y. Thomas. 3rd column - Ely Balderston,

William Hayward, Esther Balderston, Josiah Balderston, Martha Balderston, William Brown, Jane Brown, Margaret Balderston, Francess Brown, Ann Smith, Samuel Smith, James Sykes, Mary Sykes, Mary Brown, Francess Price, Eliza A. Smith, Rachel Updegraff, John Dukehart, Hugh Balderston, Elizabeth Price, Joseph Townsend, John S. Peck, Ann Peck, Dorothy Brown, Ann Scott (per order), Elizabeth Gillingham, Reynold Knox, Grace Knox, Harriot Sykes, Mary Scott, Catharine Howell, Mary Ann Hayward, Sarah B. Waters, Ann Hatson[?], Elizabeth Cooper, Thomas Tyson, Thomas M. Langstroth, George J. Knight.

**Thomas Amoss**, of Baltimore City, son of William and Susanna Amoss, of Harford County (the mother being deceased), married **Caroline Waters**, dau. of Edward and Hannah Waters, of Baltimore City, on 21st of 11th mo., 1816.
Witnesses: 1st column - Alisan Cornthwait, Ann Gover, Elizabeth Comegys, Eliza Trimble, Mary Brown, Eliza W. Yerkes, Mary Y. Thomas, David Watson, John S. Peck, William G. Atkison, Samuel Matthews, William Gorten, William Husband, John T. Plummer, Joseph P. Plummer, Mary Hopkins. 2nd column - Phebe Lafetra, Sarah Roberts, Esther Dobbin, Ann Pope, Margaret Dukehart, Hannah Riley, William Brown, Jane Brown, George F. Janney, Nicholas W. Taylor, John Morgan, Abner Pope. 3rd column - William Amoss, Eliza S. Dare, Edwin Waters, Stephen S. Johns, Susan H. Johns, Susanna Amoss, Charlotte Waters, Martha Amoss, Joseph Townsend, Rachel Mott, Sarah Morgan, Eleanor Atkison, Mary Morgan, Robert H. Norris, William Morgan, Rossiter Scott.

**Samuel Regester**, of Baltimore City, son of John and Esther Regester, of Talbot County, Maryland (both deceased), married **Elizabeth Amoss**, dau. of Robert Cornthwait *[sic]* and wife Grace, of Baltimore City (the father being deceased), in Baltimore, Eastern District, on 23rd of 10th mo., 1817.
Witnesses: 1st column - Mary Brown, Susanna Waltham, Esther Stokersly, Sarah James, Mary Richards, Hannah Mendenhall, Elizabeth Comegys, Elizabeth B. Hayward, Tacy Burges, Mary Brown, Harriott R. Cobb, Esther Townsend, T. R. Wilson, Mary B. Lafetra, Susanna Yarnall, Amelia Hopkins, Ann Dawson, John Dukehart, William Brown, Thomas Amoss, William R. Morgan, Sarah Morgan, Ann Smith (by desire), Mary Hewes, Daniel Perrigo, Ann Matthews, Elizabeth Yerkes, Abner Pope, Ann B. Brown, John Cornthwait, Ann Procter, James Edmondson, Sophia Perrigo. 2nd column - Ann Peck, John S. Peck, Henry Smith, Elizabeth Bidgood, Rebecca Medcalf, Hannah Pope, Elleanor Atkinson, Deborah Stabler, Elizabeth Pugh, Eliza W. Yerkes, Juliann C. Barnes, Sarah L. Barnes, Eliza Ann Smith, William A. Gorton, Elizabeth Hopkins, Grace J. Hopkins, Charlotte Dawson, William Trimble, Abel Spencer, John Harlan, Robert H. Norris, Samuel S. Smith, John Hewes, Ann Dawson, Mary Mifflin (by request), Mary McKim, Nicholas Taylor, David Brown, Jane Brown (by request), Thomas Morgan, Ann Cornthwait, Margaret Dukehart. 3rd column - Rachel Nock, John Wilson, Grace

Cornthwait, Thomas Cornthwait, Eliza Cornthwait, Robert Cornthwait, Mary Cornthwait, William Cornthwait, Alisanna Cornthwait, Eliza Ann Cornthwait, Grace R. Cornthwait, Mary Ann Regester, Eliza Regester, Jane Wilson Cornthwait, Deborah Cornthwait, Samuel Wilson, William Dawson, William Procter, Susanna Amoss, Mary Morgan, Deborah Wilson, Elizabeth Amoss, Eveline Read, Ann Read, Ann P. Cornthwait. Recorded by William Husband.

**Robert H. Norris**, of Baltimore City, son of Thomas and Ann Norris, of the same place, married **Mary Morgan**, dau. of Thomas and Sarah Morgan, of the same place, in Baltimore, Eastern District, on 13th of 11th mo., 1817. Witnesses: 1st column - Susanna Martin, Mary Jones, Ann Jones, Tacy Burges, Elleanor Atkison, Elizabeth B. Hayward, Michael Diffendaffer, M.D., Martha Balderston, Sarah Brown, Eveline Reed, Mary B. Lafetra, Hannah Townsend, Hannah Riley, Mary R. Lamb, John S. Peck, Eliza W. Yerkes, Rachel Young, Margaret Young, Abner Pope, William Brown, Samuel Regester, Ann Peck, David Yerkes, Grace Cornthwait, Susanna Duer. 2nd column - Rebecca Medcalf, Mary G. Allen, Elizabeth Comegys, Alisanna Cornthwait, Ellen Rich, Margaret Dukehart, Daniel Pope, Ann P. Cornthwait, Sarah Riley, Eliza Ann Smith, Sarah Lafetra, Phebe S. Townsend, Esther H. Townsend, William Procter, Eliza N. Scott, Mary Cornthwait, Ann Caldwell, John E. Reese, Abigal Medcalf, Mary Perine, Elizabeth Regester, Elizabeth Yerkes, W. M. Gover, Mary L. Jones, Elizabeth McComas. 3rd column - Thomas Norris (of Thomas), Thomas Morgan, Ann Norris, Sarah Morgan, John C. Norris, William R. Morgan, Thomas Morgan, Jr., John Morgan, Priscilla Morgan, Mary Ann Norris, Susan A. Morgan, Elizabeth Amoss, Margaret Norris, Ellen Norris, Eliza Morgan, B. A. Cunningham, William H. Amoss, Martha H. Amoss, Elizabeth Page, Charles Dawson, Susanna Amoss, Susan Yarnall, Ann H. Perine, Phebe Lafetra, Eliza Norris. Recorded by William Husband.

## BALTIMORE MONTHLY MEETING, WESTERN DISTRICT
## CERTIFICATES OF REMOVAL, 1801-1825

[It should be noted that the extant certificates of removal for Baltimore Monthly Meeting are contained in a book entitled *Records of Baltimore Monthly Meeting Certificates of Removal, ---- to 1807. Eastern District, 1807 to 1819.* A note written on the cover states "This book, after having been lost for many years, was recovered in 1877 and re-bound -- the first twenty pages are missing." Signed by Edwin Blackburn.]

1801, 12th of 2nd mo. - Sarah Townsend requested a certificate of removal to Duck Creek Monthly Meeting [Kent County, Delaware], having already moved there.

Sarah Morthland requested a certificate of removal to Gunpowder Monthly Meeting, having already moved there. James Neale requested a certificate of removal to Third Haven Monthly Meeting, having returned to settle within the limits of that meeting. Edward Wilson requested a certificate of removal to Philadelphia Monthly Meeting, having led an orderly life during his short residence amongst us.

1801, 12th of 3rd mo. - Benjamin Wilson, a minor, requested a certificate of removal, having been placed within the verge of that meeting [but no name was indicated]. Richard Carter requested a certificate of removal to Westland Monthly Meeting [Washington County], Pennsylvania, having already moved there.

1801, 9th of 4th mo. - Isaiah Lancaster requested a certificate of removal to Gunpowder Monthly Meeting, having for some time past removed from amongst us.

1801, 14th of 5th mo. - Our beloved friend Nathan Hunt attended our last monthly meeting on a religious visit with a certificate from Springfield Monthly Meeting in Guilford County, North Carolina, dated in 12th mo., 1799. Joseph Hewes requested a certificate of removal to Nottingham Monthly Meeting, having already moved there. Ezekiel Harlan requested a certificate of removal to Hopewell Monthly Meeting [Frederick County, Virginia], having removed within the compass of that meeting.

1801, 11th of 6th mo. - Israel French requested a certificate of removal to Indian Spring Monthly Meeting, having already moved there. Mercy Webb requested a certificate of removal to Deer Creek Monthly Meeting. Oliver Fuller requested a certificate to Salem Monthly Meeting in Massachusetts in order to accomplish his marriage with Rebecca Chase, a member of that meeting.

1801, 9th of 7th mo. - Amos Smith requested a certificate to Gunpowder Monthly Meeting in order to accomplish his marriage with Rebecca West, a member of that meeting.

1801, 13th of 8th mo. - John Ransom requested a certificate of removal to Amawalk Monthly Meeting in the State of New York for himself, wife Elizabeth, and minor dau. Elizabeth. Samuel Reed requested a certificate of removal to Gunpowder Monthly Meeting for himself, wife Elizabeth, and their two minor children, Matilda and Eveline Reed, having already moved there.

1801, 10th of 9th mo. - Ann Coale requested a certificate of removal to Deer Creek Monthly Meeting.

1801, 8th of 10th mo. - Israel Cope requested a certificate to Philadelphia Monthly Meeting in order for marriage with Margaret Cooper, a member of that meeting. Hannah Morgan requested a certificate of removal to Westland Monthly Meeting [Washington County], Pennsylvania, having already removed with her husband [not named] within the compass of that meeting.

1801, 10th of 12th mo. - Benjamin Fell requested a certificate of removal to New Garden Monthly Meeting [Chester County], Pennsylvania, for himself, wife Jane, and their two minor children, Mary and Leah Fell, having frequently attended our meetings during their short residence amongst us.

1802, 14th of 1st mo. - William Morgan requested a certificate of removal to Westland Monthly Meeting [Washington County], Pennsylvania, having already moved there.

1802, 11th of 2nd mo. - Nicholas Cooper, requested a certificate of removal to Deer Creek Monthly Meeting for himself, wife Sarah, and their five minor children, Pathenia, Isaiah, Elizabeth, Martha, and Ann Cooper, having returned to reside within the verge of that meeting. Agness Warner requested a certificate of removal to Deer Creek Monthly Meeting.

1802, 11th of 3rd mo. - Joseph Hibbard requested a certificate of removal to Fairfax Monthly Meeting [Loudoun County], Virginia, having already moved there.

1802, 13th of 5th mo. - Jacob Harry requested a certificate of removal to Kennett Monthly Meeting [Chester County], Pennsylvania, having returned to reside within the verge of that meeting after a short stay amongst us as an apprentice. John Morgan requested a certificate of removal to Westland Monthly Meeting [Washington County, Pennsylvania] for himself, wife Ann, and their two minor children, Mary and Hannah Morgan, having already moved there. Beulah Canby requested a certificate of removal to Buckingham Monthly Meeting in Bucks County, Pennsylvania.

1802, 10th of 6th mo. - Thomas Brown requested a certificate of removal to Indian Spring Monthly Meeting, having already moved there.

1802, 12th of 8th mo. - Elizabeth Matthews and Miriam Matthews (a minor) requested a certificate of removal to Westland Monthly Meeting [Washington County], Pennsylvania, having already moved there.

1802, 9th of 9th mo. - Certificate received from Nantucket Monthly Meeting, North District, dated 31st of 3rd mo., 1802, for Hephsibah Shearman, being about to remove with her family [not named] to within the verge of Baltimore Monthly Meeting, and she having returned since our last meeting to Nantucket Monthly Meeting.

1802, 11th of 11th mo. - Certificate received from Peel Monthly Meeting in London, dated 21st of 4th mo., 1802, for John Spottiswood Peck who had expressed his interest to embark for America and to take up his residence in or near Baltimore City. Endorsed by John Warner, Stephen Matthews, Jacob Post, Benjamin Betts, William Grimshaw, Robert Fossick, John Fleet, John Hodgkin, Halsey Janson, John Eliot, Jr., George Stacy, John Pinn, John Eliot, Robert Howard, John Bevans, John Withers, John Firth, John Beavens, Jr., Benjamin Webb, John Mayne, John Fisher, and John Bruett. It was reported that John Spottiswood Peck had settled within the compass of Deer Creek Monthly Meeting and a certificate was forwarded this date.

1802, 9th of 12th mo. - Our beloved friend Esther Griffin made a religious visit to our meeting in the 10th mo. with a certificate dated 7th mo. last from Purchase Monthly Meeting in the State of New York. Certificate received from Nantucket Monthly Meeting dated 2nd of 7th mo., 1801, for Charles Spencer Lawrence and Mary Lawrence, children of George Lawrence, Jr., deceased, being about to removed with their grandfather George Lawrence to settle within the verge of Baltimore Monthly Meeting.

1803, 13th of 1st mo. - The Lawrence children named above had already settled within the verge of Alexandria Monthly Meeting and a certificate was forwarded to them.

1803, 10th of 2nd mo. - Mary Perine, wife of Peter Perine, and their minor son Malden Perine had removed within the verge of Deer Creek Monthly Meeting and a certificate of removal was requested and forwarded. Samuel Heston requested a certificate of removal to Alexandria Monthly Meeting, having already moved there.

1803, 10th of 3rd mo. - Lydia Green requested a certificate of removal to Alexandria Monthly Meeting, having already moved there.

1803, 14th of 4th mo. - Sarah Brown requested a certificate of removal to New Garden Monthly Meeting [Chester County], Pennsylvania, having already moved there.

1803, 14th of 7th mo. - Joseph Thornburgh requested a certificate of removal to Gunpowder Monthly Meeting for himself, wife Cassandra, and their two minor children, Margaret and Sarah Thornburgh, having already moved there. Deborah Thornburgh, having removed with her parents [not named], requested a certificate of removal to Gunpowder Monthly Meeting. Sarah Hopkins requested a certificate of removal to Gunpowder Monthly Meeting, having already moved there. Isaac Kinsey requested a certificate of removal to Gunpowder Monthly Meeting, having already moved there. Mary Kinsey requested a certificate of removal to Gunpowder Monthly Meeting, having already moved there. Jacob Janney requested a certificate of removal to Alexandria Monthly Meeting, having already moved there. Moses Kinsey requested a certificate of removal to Alexandria Monthly Meeting, having already moved there. Sarah Kinsey requested a certificate of removal to New Garden Monthly Meeting [Chester County], Pennsylvania, having already moved there. Oliver Fuller requested a certificate of removal to Salem Monthly Meeting in Massachusetts, having already moved there.

1803, 11th of 8th mo. - Joseph England requested a certificate of removal to Nottingham Monthly Meeting for himself and wife Hannah, having already moved there.

1803, 8th of 9th mo. - Benjamin Hance requested a certificate of removal to Farmington Monthly Meeting in Ontario County, New York, for his son Thomas C. Hance, a minor and lad of orderly life and conversation, he being removed within the compass of that meeting.

1803, 20th of 10th mo. - Peter Perine requested a certificate of removal to Deer Creek Monthly Meeting, having some time past removed and settled within the compass of that meeting. Ann Haines requested a certificate of removal to Goshen Monthly Meeting [Chester County], Pennsylvania, she having removed and settled within the compass of that meeting and hath had her marriage accomplished contrary to the good order used among Friends for which we have received her acknowledgement and think it unnecessary to say more concerning her than to recommend her to the care of that meeting. Ann Griffith requested a certificate of removal to Concord Monthly Meeting [Belmont County], Ohio, having already moved there.

1803, 10th of 11th mo. - Certificate of removal requested for Benjamin, Rachel, Joseph, William, and Isaac Hambleton, minor children of William Hambleton, they having removed with their parents within the verge of Nottingham Monthly Meeting.

1803, 8th of 12th mo. - Israel Cope requested a certificate of removal to Philadelphia Monthly Meeting for himself, wife Margaret, and their minor dau. Mary Ann Cope. Elizabeth Webster requested a certificate of removal to Gunpowder Monthly Meeting, having already moved there.

1804, 9th of 2nd mo. - Hannah Brown requested a certificate of removal to New Garden Monthly Meeting [Chester County], Pennsylvania. Mary Hill requested a certificate of removal to Philadelphia Monthly Meeting, having already moved there. Samuel Hance requested a certificate of removal to Indian Spring Monthly Meeting for himself, wife Sarah, and their two minor children, William and Rachel Hance, having already moved there.

1804, 8th of 3rd mo. - Elizabeth Harding, wife of Charles, requested a certificate of removal to Gunpowder Monthly Meeting for herself and her three children, David, Mary, and Thomas Harding. Levin Hopkins requested a certificate of removal to Gunpowder Monthly Meeting, having already moved there.

1804, 10th of 5th mo. - Joel Wright requested a certificate of removal to Pipe Creek Monthly Meeting [Frederick County, Maryland] for himself, his wife [not named], and two minor children, Israel and Elizabeth Wright, having returned to reside with the limits of that meeting. Sarah Rich requested a certificate of removal to Buckingham Monthly Meeting [Bucks County], Pennsylvania, for herself and her four minor children, Ann, John, Sarah, and Benjamin Rich, as it appears she hath been of a sober deportment, frequently attended religious meetings, and settled her affairs to satisfaction as a member. Phinehas Pickering, a young man some time ago recommended by certificate from Buckingham Monthly Meeting [Bucks County], Pennsylvania, has requested to become again a member of that meeting.

1804, 14th of 6th mo. - Skipwith Cole requested a certificate of removal to Deer Creek Monthly Meeting, having already moved there. Hannah Kinsey requested a certificate of removal to Indian Spring Monthly Meeting, having already moved there. Isaac Bowman, a young man convinced of Friends' principles and who was received into membership about two years ago at Hardshaw Monthly Meeting, requested a certificate of removal to Philadelphia Monthly Meeting on 25th of 8th mo., 1803. Endorsed by John Bludwick, Abraham Binms *[sic]*, Joseph Atkinson, James Still, William Oddie, Samuel Blain, James Bolton, William Farrier, John Field, Roger Merrick, William Flounders, James Newill, Joseph Farver, James Hall, William Leicester, John Goodier, John Harrison, James Cropper, Joseph Hadwen, John Davies, Nicholas Waterhouse. On 30th of 3rd mo., 1804, said Isaac Bowman requested a certificate of removal to Baltimore Monthly Meeting from Philadelphia Monthly Meeting, having resided a short time with them. On 14th of 6th mo., 1804, said Isaac Bowman requested a certificate of removal to Middleton

Monthly Meeting in Ohio from Baltimore Monthly Meeting, having resided a short time with them as well. Rachel Wright requested a certificate of removal to Pipe Creek Monthly Meeting [Frederick County, Maryland].

1804, 12th of 7th mo. - Priscilla Hopkins requested a certificate of removal to Deer Creek, having already moved there.

1804, 9th of 8th mo. - Stacy West requested a certificate of removal to Gunpowder Monthly Meeting.

1804, 8th of 9th mo. - Ann Peck requested a certificate of removal to Deer Creek Monthly Meeting, having already settled there with her husband [not named].

1804, 11th of 10th mo. - Rachel Paul requested a certificate of removal to Horsehem Monthly Meeting in Pennsylvania for herself and minor dau. Phebe Paul, having already removed with her husband [not named].

1804, 8th of 11th mo. - William Hambleton requested a certificate of removal to Kingwood Monthly Meeting in New Jersey for his minor dau. Mary Hambleton. Ann Willets requested a certificate of removal to Deer Creek Monthly Meeting, having already moved there. Cassandra Willets requested a certificate of removal to Deer Creek Monthly Meeting, having already moved there.

1804, 13th of 12th mo. - Joseph P. Plummer requested a certificate of removal to Indian Spring Monthly Meeting, having already moved there. Caleb Matson requested a certificate of removal to Concord Monthly Meeting [Delaware County], Pennsylvania, having already moved there.

1805, 10th of 1st mo. - Isaac Wilson requested a certificate of removal to Middleton Monthly Meeting in Ohio for himself, wife Susanna, and their three minor children, Alizanna, David, and John Webster Wilson, having already moved there. James Hicks and wife Mary requested a certificate of removal to Gunpowder Monthly Meeting, having already moved there. Bathsheba Hicks requested a certificate of removal to Gunpowder Monthly Meeting, having removed there with her parents [not named].

1805, 14th of 3rd mo. - Sarah Updagraff requested a certificate of removal to Monallin Monthly Meeting [Adams County], Pennsylvania, having already moved there after a short residence amongst us. James Hicks, Jr. requested a certificate of removal to Monallin Monthly Meeting [Adams County], Pennsylvania, having already moved there.

1805, 11th of 4th mo. - Charles Harding requested a certificate of removal to Gunpowder Monthly Meeting, having already removed there with his family [not named].

1805, 9th of 5th mo. - Thomas Wainwright requested a certificate of removal to Third Haven Monthly Meeting. Eli Plummer requested a certificate of removal to Sadsbury Monthly Meeting in Lancaster County, Pennsylvania, for himself, wife Alice, and their two minor children, James and Sarah Plummer, having already moved there. Silas Wharton requested a certificate of removal to Falls Monthly Meeting in Bucks County, Pennsylvania, for himself, wife Mary and their three minor children, Nehemiah, Mary, and James Wharton, having already moved there.

1805, 13th of 6th mo. - Sarah Procter, intending to return to her native land, requested a certificate of removal to Pickering Monthly Meeting in Yorkshire, Great Britain. Endorsed by Esther Ellicott, Mary Mifflin, Rebecca Williams, Tacy Mitchel, Frances Hopkins, Mary McKim, Mary Hussey, Hannah Marsh, Elizabeth Ellicott, Hannah Smith, Abigail Medcalf, Dorathy Brown, Sarah Day, Elizabeth Gillingham, Deborah Wilson, Ann Matthews, Jr., Elizabeth Robertson, Hannah Trimble, Mary Boyd, Elizabeth Lowden, George Ellicott, William Hayward, Isaiah Balderson, William Trimble, David Brown, William Riley, James Gillingham, E. Ellicott, John Wilson, George Matthews, John Marsh, George Brantingham, Izak Procter, William Procter, Amos James. Elisha Talbot requested a certificate of removal to Alexandria Monthly Meeting, having already moved there.

1805, 11th of 7th mo. - Priscilla Morgan, wife of John, requested a certificate of removal to Gunpowder Monthly Meeting, having already moved there with her husband. Elizabeth Hubbard requested a certificate of removal to Deep River Monthly Meeting in North Carolina.

1805, 12th of 9th mo. - Amy Wilson requested a certificate of removal to Pine Grove Monthly Meeting in New Jersey, having already moved there.

1805, 10th of 10th mo. - Ann Smith requested a certificate of removal to Philadelphia Monthly Meeting, Northern District, having already moved there with her husband [not named]. Levis Janney requested a certificate of removal to Alexandria Monthly Meeting for himself, wife Mary, and their son Benjamin Jay Janney, having already moved there.

1805, 14th of 11th mo. - Joshua Stapleton requested a certificate of removal to Westland Monthly Meeting [Washington County], Pennsylvania for himself, wife Susannah, and their minor dau. Susanna Stapleton, having already moved there.

1805, 12th of 12th mo. - Hannah Dutton requested a certificate of removal to Buckingham Monthly Meeting [Bucks County], Pennsylvania, having already moved there with her husband [not named].

1806, 9th of 1st mo. - Philip Coale requested a certificate of removal to Philadelphia Monthly Meeting, having already moved there. Evan Harry requested a certificate of removal to Indian Spring Monthly Meeting, having already moved there. Thomas Boyce requested a certificate of removal to Salem Monthly Meeting in Massachusetts, having returned to reside within the compass of that meeting. James Marsh requested a certificate of removal to Redstone Monthly Meeting [Fayette County, Pennsylvania] for himself, wife Edith, and their three minor children, Zillah, Amos, and Miriam Marsh, having already moved there.

1806, 13th of 2nd mo. - William Matthews Townsend, a minor, requested a certificate of removal to Concord Monthly Meeting [Delaware County, Pennsylvania].

1806, 13th of 3rd mo. - Jonathan Wright requested a certificate of removal to Monallin Monthly Meeting [Adams County, Pennsylvania]. Israel Price requested a certificate of removal to Short Creek Monthly Meeting in Ohio for himself, wife Hannah, and their four minor children, Elizabeth, William, Frances, and Israel Price, having already moved there. Hannah Brown requested a certificate of removal to Hopewell Monthly Meeting [Frederick County], Virginia, having already moved there with her husband [not named].

1806, 10th of 4th mo. - Stephen Wilson requested a certificate of removal to Wilmington Monthly Meeting for himself, wife Mary, and their three minor children, Isaac, Elizabeth, and Joseph Wilson, having already moved there.

1806, 8th of 5th mo. - Joseph Pleasants requested a certificate of removal to Philadelphia Monthly Meeting, having already moved there.

1806, 12th of 6th mo. - Elizabeth Janney requested a certificate of removal to Alexandria Monthly Meeting, having already moved there. Susanna Plummer requested a certificate of removal to Indian Spring Monthly Meeting, having already moved there with her husband [not named].

1806, 10th of 7th mo. - Our ancient friend Thomas Plummer and Phoebe his wife, being about to remove within the limits of Concord Monthly Meeting [Belmont County], Ohio, requested a certificate of removal. We certify they are of orderly life and conversation and, considering the infirmities of advanced age, they have been frequent attenders of our religious meetings. Eleanor Plummer requested a certificate of removal to Concord Monthly Meeting in Ohio.

1806, 14th of 8th mo. - Elizabeth Chandley requested a certificate of removal to Crooked Run Monthly Meeting in Virginia. Rachel Updegraff requested a certificate of removal to York Monthly Meeting in Pennsylvania, having removed with her husband [not named] to reside within their limits. George Pearse requested a certificate of removal to Bradford Monthly Meeting [Chester County], Pennsylvania, having already moved there.

1806, 11th of 9th mo. - Joshua Reynolds requested a certificate of removal to Gunpowder Monthly Meeting for himself, wife Rachel, and their three minor children, Rachel, Sarah, and Mary Reynolds.

1806, 13th of 11th mo. - George Mason, son of John, requested a certificate of removal to Deer Creek Monthly Meeting, having already moved there. Ann Cole requested a certificate of removal to Deer Creek Monthly Meeting, having already moved there with her husband [not named]. Israel Pleasants requested a certificate of removal to Philadelphia Monthly Meeting for himself, wife Ann, and their ten minor children, Samuel, Thomas Franklin, Mary, Elizabeth Rhodes, Ann, Sarah, Israel Pemberton, John, Walter, and Hannah Pleasants, having already moved there.

1806, 11th of 12th mo. - Samuel Thomas and Richard Thomas, minor sons of Richard S. Thomas, having some time ago been recommended to Baltimore Monthly Meeting by certificate from Cecil Monthly Meeting [Kent County, Maryland] and after a short stay with us returned with their father within the compass of Cecil Monthly Meeting. Deborah Joyce, wife of Thomas, requested a certificate of removal to Redstone Monthly Meeting [Fayette County], Pennsylvania, having already moved their to reside with her husband. Samuel Stapleton requested a certificate of removal to Westland Monthly Meeting [Washington County], Pennsylvania, having already moved there with his father [not named].

1807, 8th of 1st mo. - Mary Hunt requested a certificate of removal to Redstone Monthly Meeting [Fayette County], Pennsylvania, having already moved there with her husband [not named]. Charles Lukens requested a certificate of removal to Indian Spring Monthly Meeting, having already moved there. Gideon Hughes requested a certificate of removal to Middleton Monthly Meeting in Ohio. George Hussey requested a certificate of removal to Middleton Monthly Meeting in Ohio, having already moved there. Michael Graham requested a certificate of removal to Concord Monthly Meeting [Belmont County], Ohio, for himself, wife Patience, and their three minor children, Elizabeth Ann, Deborah, and James Graham.

1807, 12th of 2nd mo. - James Trimble requested a certificate of removal to Waynesville Monthly Meeting in Ohio, having already moved there. William Hopkins requested a certificate of removal to Alexandria Monthly Meeting, having already moved there. William Hamilton requested a certificate of removal to Short Creek Monthly Meeting in Ohio. John Harlan requested a certificate of removal to Gunpowder Monthly Meeting for himself, wife Hannah, and their two minor children, Joseph and William Harlan, having already moved there.

1807, 9th of 4th mo. - Mary Malonee requested a certificate of removal to Gunpowder Monthly Meeting, having already moved there.

1807, 14th of 5th mo. - William Matthews requested a certificate of removal to Gunpowder Monthly Meeting for himself, wife Elizabeth, and their three minor children, Samuel Hanway, George, and Susanna Matthews.

1807, 12th of 8th mo. - William Cooper requested a certificate of removal to Redstone Monthly Meeting [Fayette County, Pennsylvania], having already moved there. Lewis Harlin requested a certificate of removal to Gunpowder Monthly Meeting, having already moved there.

1807, 9th of 9th mo. - Sarah Allen requested a certificate of removal to Deer Creek Monthly Meeting with her husband [not named], having already moved there. Jonathan Marsh requested a certificate of removal to Warrington Monthly Meeting [York County], Pennsylvania, having already moved there.

1807, 9th of 12th mo. - Malen Farquhar requested a certificate of removal to Centre Monthly Meeting in Ohio, having already moved there. Edward Stabler, of Alexandria Monthly Meeting, united with Mary Mitchell, of Baltimore Monthly Meeting, in a religious visit to Friends within our verge.

1808, 11th of 5th mo. - Thomas Townsend requested a certificate of removal to Concord Monthly Meeting [Belmont County], Ohio. John Shreve[?] requested a certificate of removal to Alexandria Monthly Meeting, having already moved there. Evan Hopkins requested a certificate of removal to Indian Spring Monthly Meeting. having already moved there. Susanna Judge, Jr. requested a certificate of removal to Baltimore Monthly Meeting, Eastern District, having already moved there. Mary Jones, wife of William, requested a certificate of removal to Baltimore Monthly Meeting, Eastern District, having already moved there.

1808, 8th of 6th mo. - William Marsh requested a certificate of removal to Gunpowder Monthly Meeting for himself, wife Ann, and their four minor children, John, Margarett, William, and Susanna Morthlin Marsh.

1808, 7th of 9th mo. - Benjamin Vore requested a certificate of removal to Redstone Monthly Meeting [Fayette County], Pennsylvania, having already moved there.

1808, 19th of 10th mo. - William Embree requested a certificate of removal to Philadelphia Monthly Meeting, Northern District. having already moved there.

1808, 9th of 11th mo. - Sarah Bonsall, wife of Vincent, requested a certificate of removal to Darby Monthly Meeting for herself and her three minor children, William, Catherine, and Thomas Bonsall, having already moved there. John Cornthwait requested a certificate of removal to Baltimore Monthly Meeting, Eastern District. Stephen Cook requested a certificate of removal to Baltimore Monthly Meeting. Eastern District.

1808, 7th of 12th mo. - James Wainwright requested a certificate of removal to Third Haven Monthly Meeting for himself and wife Rachel Wainwright, having already moved there.

1809, 11th of 1st mo. - Hannah Underwood requested a certificate of removal to Redstone Monthly Meeting [Fayette County, Pennsylvania] with her husband [not named], having already moved there.

1809, 8th of 3rd mo. - Charles Read requested a certificate of removal to Baltimore Monthly Meeting, Eastern District. Hannah Linton requested a certificate of removal to Plymouth Monthly Meeting in Ohio with her husband [not named] and four minor children, Elizabeth, Esther, William, and Samuel Linton, having already removed there.

1809, 10th of 5th mo. - Christopher Reckifuss [Rickefuss] requested a certificate of removal to Horsham Monthly Meeting in Pennsylvania for himself, wife Maria, and their two minor children, Samuel and Hannah Reckifuss [Rickefuss]. James Jenkinson Wright requested a certificate of removal to Baltimore Monthly Meeting, Eastern District. Rebecca Medcalf requested a certificate of removal to Baltimore Monthly Meeting, Eastern District, for herself and two minor children, Joshua and Elijah Medcalf.

1809, 8th of 11th mo. - John Sinclair requested a certificate of removal to Indian Spring Monthly Meeting for himself, wife Rachel, and their three minor children, Abraham, Sarah, and Isaac Procter Sinclair. Jasper and Rebecca Cope requested a certificate of removal to Philadelphia Monthly Meeting for themselves and their three minor children, Charles Shoemaker Cope, Abigal Ann Cope, and Emma Cope.

1809, 13th of 12th mo. - Sarah Savage requested a certificate of removal to Baltimore Monthly Meeting, Eastern District, for herself and minor sister Ann Sanderson.

1810, 10th of 1st mo. - Samuel Cookson requested a certificate of removal to Pipe Creek Monthly Meeting [Frederick County, Maryland] for himself, wife Rachel, and minor son Joseph, having already moved there. Mary Cookson requested a certificate of removal to Pipe Creek Monthly Meeting [Frederick County, Maryland], having already moved there. Priscilla Barker, wife of Abraham, requested a certificate of removal to New York Monthly Meeting for herself and her husband [not named], having already moved there. John Tudor requested a certificate of removal to Gunpowder Monthly Meeting for himself, wife Phebe, and their two minor children, Samuel and Martha Tudor, having already moved there.

1810, 7th of 2nd mo. - Richard Kenney requested a certificate of removal to Uchland Monthly Meeting in Pennsylvania, having already moved there. Oliver Buckman requested a certificate of removal to Greenwich Monthly Meeting in West New Jersey, having been placed an apprentice within their limits.

1810, 13th of 6th mo. - Richard Palmer requested a certificate of removal to West Branch Monthly Meeting in Ohio.

1810, 11th of 7th mo. - Cornelius Vansant requested a certificate of removal to Baltimore Monthly Meeting, Eastern District, for himself, wife Catharine, and their two minor children, Sarah and Catharine Vansant, having already moved there. Joseph Brevett requested a certificate of removal to Baltimore Monthly Meeting, Eastern District, for himself, wife Cassandra, and their four minor children, John Webster Brevett, George Fox Brevett, Edwin Woodland Brevett, and Cassandra Brevett, having already moved there. George Brantingham requested a certificate of removal to Goshen Monthly Meeting [Chester County], Pennsylvania for himself, wife Phebe, and their two minor children, Joseph and Hannah Brantingham. Daniel Byrnes requested a certificate of removal to Wilmington Monthly Meeting in Delaware for himself, wife Rachel, and their two minor children Jonathan and Eleanor Byrnes, having already moved there.

1810, 8th of 8th mo. - Sarah Boulton requested a certificate of removal to Goshen Monthly Meeting [Chester County], Pennsylvania, having already moved there. Elizabeth Janney requested a certificate of removal to Goose Creek Monthly Meeting for herself and her husband [not named]. Jonathan Marsh requested a certificate of removal to Plymouth Monthly Meeting in Ohio for himself, wife Leviney, and their two minor children, Margaret and Mary, having already moved there. Isaac Bonsal requested a certificate of removal to Wilmington Monthly

Meeting in Delaware for himself and wife Mary Bonsal, having already moved there.

1810, 12th of 9th mo. - Margaret Powel requested a certificate of removal to Baltimore Monthly Meeting, Eastern District, for herself, her husband [not named], and three minor children, Hannah, Albina, and Benjamin Wayne Powel, having already moved there.

1811, 12th of 6th mo. - Henry Dickenson requested a certificate of removal to Sadsbury Monthly Meeting in Pennsylvania. Mary Gray requested a certificate of removal to New Garden Monthly Meeting [Chester County], Pennsylvania, having already moved there. Rachel Kinsey requested a certificate of removal to New Garden Monthly Meeting in Pennsylvania, having already moved there. John Trimble requested a certificate of removal to Baltimore Monthly Meeting, Eastern District, for himself, wife Elizabeth, and their five minor children, Elizabeth, Isaac, Mary, Jane, and John Trimble.

1811, 7th of 8th mo. - Robert Townsend requested a certificate of removal to Redstone Monthly Meeting [Fayette County], Pennsylvania, having already moved there.

1811, 11th of 12th mo. - Eleanor Bonsal requested a certificate of removal to Wilmington Monthly Meeting, having already moved there.

1812, 8th of 1st mo. - Samuel Embree requested a certificate of removal to Short Creek Monthly Meeting in Ohio for himself, wife Hannah, and their six minor children, Lydia, Joseph, Phebe, John, Jesse, and Israel Embree, having already moved there. James Embree requested a certificate of removal to Bradford Monthly Meeting [Chester County], Pennsylvania, having already moved there.

1812, 12th of 2nd mo. - Catherine Sanderson requested a certificate of removal to New York Monthly Meeting, having already moved there. Grace Hopkins requested a certificate of removal to Baltimore Monthly Meeting, Eastern District.

1812, 11th of 3rd mo. - Philip Dennis requested a certificate of removal to Indian Spring Monthly Meeting for himself, wife Hannah, and their nine minor children, Abraham, Benjamin, Philip, Jonathan, Elizabeth, Hannah, George, Mary and Grace Dennis, having already moved there. Joseph P. Plummer requested a certificate of removal to Baltimore Monthly Meeting, Eastern District, for himself, wife Susannah, and their three minor children, John, Mary, and Johannah Plummer.

1812, 8th of 4th mo. - William Hill requested a certificate of removal to York Monthly Meeting in Pennsylvania, having already moved there. Elizabeth Lee requested a certificate of removal to Gunpowder Monthly Meeting, having when a minor removed within the limits of their meeting.

1812, 8th of 7th mo. - James Dawson requested a certificate of removal to Cecil Monthly Meeting [Kent County, Maryland] for himself, wife Ann, and their five children, Elizabeth, Lydia, Sarah, Mary Ann, and James W. Dawson.

1812, 9th of 9th mo. - Folger Pope requested a certificate of removal to Baltimore Monthly Meeting, Eastern District, for himself, wife Ann, and their three minor children, Franklin F., William R., and Joseph Pope; and, also David S. Pope, a minor.

1812, 7th of 10th mo. - Isaac Knight requested a certificate of removal to Indian Spring Monthly Meeting, having already moved there.

1812, 9th of 12th mo. - David Rickefuss [Reckifuss], a minor, requested a certificate of removal to Philadelphia Monthly Meeting, Northern District. Samuel Harlan requested a certificate of removal to York Monthly Meeting in Pennsylvania, having already moved there. Hannah Matthews, having returned again to reside amongst Friends at York Monthly Meeting in Pennsylvania, requested a certificate of removal. Phebe May requested a certificate of removal to Sadsbury Monthly Meeting.

1813, 13th of 1st mo. - Susanna B. Jones requested a certificate of removal to Gunpowder Monthly Meeting, having already moved there.

1813, 10th of 2nd mo. - Elizabeth E. Lea requested a certificate of removal to Wilmington Monthly Meeting in Delaware for herself and her husband [not named], having already moved there. Joseph U. Kirk requested a certificate of removal to York Monthly Meeting.

1813, 7th of 4th mo. - William Kenworthy requested a certificate of removal to Alexandria Monthly Meeting for himself and wife Rebecca Kenworthy.

1813, 12th of 5th mo. - Michael M. Maslin requested a certificate of removal to Cecil Monthly Meeting [Kent County, Maryland], having already moved there. Jacob Mendenhall requested a certificate of removal to Fairfax Monthly Meeting in Loudon County, Virginia, for himself and wife Beulah Maslin.

1813, 11th of 8th mo. - Moses Dillon requested a certificate of removal to Still Water Monthly Meeting in Ohio for himself and his minor son Isaac Dillon.

1813, 8th of 9th mo. - Samuel Myers, a minister of Baltimore Monthly Meeting, Western District, requested a certificate of removal to Indian Spring Monthly Meeting in order to be joined with them.

1813, 10th of 11th mo. - Jesse Embree requested a certificate of removal to Waynesville Monthly Meeting in Ohio. Oliver Kinsey requested a certificate of removal to New Garden Monthly Meeting [Chester County], Pennsylvania, having already moved there.

1813, 8th of 12th mo. - Joseph Webster requested a certificate of removal to Deer Creek Monthly Meeting, having already moved there.

1814, 12th of 1st mo. - David Malsby, having returned to reside within the limits of Gunpowder Monthly Meeting, requested a certificate of removal for himself and wife Sarah Malsby. Richard Dawson requested a certificate of removal to Indian Spring Monthly Meeting, having already moved there. Charles Hambleton requested a certificate of removal to Middletown Monthly Meeting in Ohio, having already moved there. Benjamin Hambleton requested a certificate of removal to Middletown Monthly Meeting in Ohio, having already moved there. David Evans, having returned to reside within the limits of Philadelphia Monthly Meeting, Northern District, requested a certificate of removal for himself, wife Anne Evans, and their son Nathan Evans. Martha Tomkins requested a certificate of removal to Deer Creek Monthly Meeting, having already moved there.

1814, 9th of 2nd mo. - Mary Walton requested a certificate of removal to Indian Spring Monthly Meeting, having already moved there. Charles Lukens requested a certificate of removal to Deer Creek Monthly Meeting for himself and wife Sarah Lukens. Margaret Hill Bradford requested a certificate of removal to Deer Creek Monthly Meeting, having already moved there.

1814, 11th of 5th mo. - Jonathan Janney requested a certificate of removal to Alexandria Monthly Meeting in the District of Columbia for himself, wife Elizabeth, and their three minor children, Anna, Isaac, and Richard T. Janney, having already moved there. Sarah Dallam requested a certificate of removal to Baltimore Monthly Meeting, Eastern District, for herself and her husband [not named], having already moved there. Susannah Allen requested a certificate of removal to Deer Creek Monthly Meeting for herself and her husband [not named], having already moved there.

1814, 8th of 6th mo. - Margaret and Elizabeth Baily, being about to removed to settle with their parents [not named] with the verge of Short Creek Monthly Meeting in Ohio, requested a certificate of removal. Emmor Baily requested a certificate of removal to Short Creek Monthly Meeting in Ohio for himself, wife Elizabeth, and their ten minor children, Henry, Mary, Abraham, Jacob, Ezra, Hannah, Phebe, Emmor, Martha, and Ann Baily, having already moved there. Frances Malsby requested a certificate of removal to Gunpowder Monthly Meeting.

1814, 13th of 7th mo. - Charles Lownes requested a certificate of removal to Short Creek Monthly Meeting in Ohio, having already moved there. Samuel R. Turner requested a certificate of removal to Cecil Monthly Meeting [Kent County, Maryland].

1814, 10th of 8th mo. - Rachel Hambleton requested a certificate of removal to London Grove Monthly Meeting [Chester County], Pennsylvania, having already moved there. Joseph Clemson requested a certificate of removal to Philadelphia Monthly Meeting, Western District, for himself and wife Esther Clemson. Jane and Laticia Heston requested a certificate of removal to Alexandria Monthly Meeting. John Nicholson requested a certificate of removal to Plymouth Monthly Meeting in Ohio for himself, wife Alice, and their three minor children, William L., Eliza, and Charles L. Nicholson. William R. Wanton, a minor, requested a certificate of removal to Alexandria Monthly Meeting, having already moved there. Benjamin Ellicott and Joseph Ellicott, who some years ago removed from amongst us and settled at Batavia in the State of New York, requested a certificate of removal to Farmington Monthly Meeting.

1814, 7th of 9th mo. - Robert Young requested a certificate of removal to Baltimore Monthly Meeting, Eastern District, for himself, wife Rebecca, and their three minor children, William, George, and Joseph Young. Richard Rummells requested a certificate of removal to York Monthly Meeting in Pennsylvania, having already moved there. Joseph Heston requested a certificate of removal to Alexandria Monthly Meeting for himself, wife Ann, and their two minor children, William and Charles Heston, and his grandson Joseph H. Wright (also a minor), having already moved there.

1814, 9th of 11th mo. - Josiah Siddons, Jr. requested a certificate of removal to Philadelphia Monthly Meeting, Southern District. Mary West requested a certificate of removal to New Garden Monthly Meeting [Chester County], Pennsylvania. John Underwood requested a certificate of removal to Deer Creek Monthly Meeting, having already moved there.

1815, 11th of 1st mo. - James Hambleton requested a certificate of removal to Middleton Monthly Meeting in Ohio for himself, wife Martha, and their minor dau. Mary Hambleton.

1815, 8th of 2nd mo. - George F. Janney requested a certificate of removal to Baltimore Monthly Meeting, Eastern District, having already moved there. Mary Janney, requested a certificate of removal to Baltimore Monthly Meeting, Eastern District, having already moved there. Elizabeth Janney requested a certificate of removal to Baltimore Monthly Meeting, Eastern District, having already moved there. Rachel Johnston requested a certificate of removal to Hopewell Monthly Meeting [Frederick County], Virginia. Joshua Johnson requested a certificate of removal to Hopewell Monthly Meeting in Virginia for himself, wife Lydia, and their minor dau. Mary R. Johnson. Ann Eliza Gillingham and Mary Gillingham, minors, requested a certificate of removal to Falls Monthly Meeting in Bucks County, Pennsylvania. Samuel Canby requested a certificate of removal to Indian Spring Monthly Meeting for himself, wife Elizabeth, and their six minor children, Joshua, Mary, Thomas, Samuel, Beulah, and Joseph Canby, having already moved there. Nicholas W. Taylor requested a certificate of removal to York Monthly Meeting. George Mason, Sr. requested a certificate of removal to Gunpowder Monthly Meeting.

1815, 8th of 3rd mo. - William Woodnut requested a certificate of removal to Philadelphia Monthly Meeting, Middle District, having already moved there. Stephen Bonsal requested a certificate of removal to Wilmington Monthly Meeting in Delaware, having already moved there.

1815, 12th of 4th mo. - Joseph A. Needles requested a certificate of removal to Philadelphia Monthly Meeting, Northern District. Daniel and James Kenny, minors, being placed with Friends residing within the limits of Little Britain Monthly Meeting in Pennsylvania, requested a certificate of removal. Samuel H. Matthews requested a certificate of removal to Gunpowder Monthly Meeting. Thomas Brooke, having (for commercial purposes) a prospect of residing some time in England and chiefly within the limits of Birmingham Monthly Meeting, requested a certificate of removal.

1815, 8th of 11th mo. - Hannah Pope requested a certificate of removal to Baltimore Monthly Meeting, Eastern District, having already moved there. Elizabeth Hicks requested a certificate of removal to Baltimore Monthly Meeting, Eastern District, having already there with her husband [not named].

1816, 7th of 2nd mo. - Ann Paits requested a certificate of removal to Third Haven Monthly Meeting for herself and her two minor children, William and Joseph Paits.

Rachel Weeks requested a certificate of removal to Baltimore Monthly Meeting, Eastern District.

1816, 10th of 4th mo. - Samuel Peach requested a certificate of removal to Alexandria Monthly Meeting, having already moved there. Joel Wright, a minor, having removed within the limits of Alexandria Monthly Meeting, requested a certificate of removal. Sarah Hall requested a certificate of removal to Indian Spring Monthly Meeting for herself and her two minor children, Sarah Odle Hall and Thomas Samuel Hall. Isaiah R. Hughes requested a certificate of removal to Indian Spring Monthly Meeting, having already moved there. His certificate was subsequently returned in the 9th mo., 1816, with information that Isaiah had removed within the limits of Pipe Creek Monthly Meeting [Frederick County, Maryland].

1816, 8th of 5th mo. - Frances Ford requested a certificate of removal to Baltimore Monthly Meeting, Eastern District, for herself and her minor dau. Alisanna Ford, having already moved there. Harriot Ford, residing with her mother [not named] within the limits of Baltimore Monthly Meeting, Eastern District, requested a certificate of removal. Ann Coale requested a certificate of removal to Baltimore Monthly Meeting, Eastern District, having already moved there. Mahlon Atkinson requested a certificate of removal to Goshen Monthly Meeting [Chester County], Pennsylvania, having already moved there.

1816, 10th of 7th mo. - Theodate Pope requested a certificate of removal to Bolton Monthly Meeting in Massachusetts for herself and her husband [not named], having already moved there.

1816, 7th of 8th mo. - Mary McCormick requested a certificate of removal to Indian Spring Monthly Meeting, having already moved there. Thomas Moore requested a certificate of removal to Indian Spring Monthly Meeting for himself, wife Mary, and their two minor children, Asa and Caleb Moore. Ann Moore requested a certificate of removal to Indian Spring Monthly Meeting, having already moved there.

1816, 11th of 9th mo. - William Hill requested a certificate of removal to Baltimore Monthly Meeting, Eastern District, having already moved there. Rebeckah Metcalf requested a certificate of removal to Baltimore Monthly Meeting, Eastern District.

1816, 9th of 10th mo. - Abel Spencer requested a certificate of removal to Baltimore Monthly Meeting, Eastern District.

1816, 6th of 12th mo. - John Taylor completed his apprenticeship at Baltimore, returned to Fairfax Monthly Meeting [Loudoun County, Virginia] and requested a certificate of removal from Baltimore Monthly Meeting. Jacob Vore requested a certificate of removal to Westland Monthly Meeting [Washington County, Pennsylvania], having already moved there.

1817, 10th of 1st mo. - Enoch Clap requested a certificate of removal to Salem Monthly Meeting in Massachusetts for himself, wife Mary, and their two minor children, Elizabeth and Rebecca Clap, having already moved there.

1817, 7th of 2nd mo. - Jonathan Warner requested a certificate of removal to Little Falls Monthly Meeting for himself, wife Sarah, and their two minor children, Hannah and Brinton, having already moved there. Henry Smith and wife Martha requested a certificate of removal to Baltimore Monthly Meeting, Eastern District, having already moved there. Samuel Smith requested a certificate of removal to for himself, wife Ann, and their three minor children, Eliza Ann Smith, William Brown Smith, and Henry Smith, having already moved there.

1817, 6th of 6th mo. - Israel Janney requested a certificate of removal to Alexandria Monthly Meeting in the District of Columbia, having already moved there.

1817, 11th of 7th mo. - Mary Janney requested a certificate of removal to Alexandria Monthly Meeting, having removed to settle with her husband [not named] within their verge. Sarah Lukens requested a certificate of removal to Baltimore Monthly Meeting, Eastern District. Elizabeth Large requested a certificate of removal to Philadelphia Monthly Meeting, Western District, having removed with her husband [not named] to settle within their verge. Patience Hartshorn requested a certificate of removal to Cincinnati Monthly Meeting in Ohio, having already moved there. David Saunders requested a certificate of removal to Cincinnati Monthly Meeting in Ohio, having already moved there.

1817, 8th of 8th mo. - Daniel M. Reese, a minor, requested a certificate of removal to Little Falls Monthly Meeting. Benjamin W. Powell, a minor, requested a certificate of removal to Alexandria Monthly Meeting. John Needles, Jr. requested a certificate of removal to Philadelphia Monthly Meeting, having already moved there. Mary H. Moore requested a certificate of removal to Third Haven Monthly Meeting, having already settled there with her husband [not named].

1817, 7th of 11th mo. - James B. Needles requested a certificate of removal to Indian Spring Monthly Meeting.

1818, 6th of 2nd mo. - Hannah Way requested a certificate of removal to Kennett Monthly Meeting [Chester County], Pennsylvania, having for some time past resided within their verge.

1818, 6th of 3rd mo. - George Mason, Jr. requested a certificate of removal to Baltimore Monthly Meeting, Eastern District, having for some time resided within their limits. Joseph C. Woral requested a certificate of removal to Philadelphia Monthly Meeting, Northern District, having already moved there. Thomas Palmer requested a certificate of removal to Nottingham Monthly Meeting, having already moved there. John H. Price requested a certificate of removal to Smithfield Monthly Meeting in Ohio, having already moved there.

1818, 10th of 4th mo. - Cassandra West requested a certificate of removal to Little Falls Monthly Meeting, having removed there with her husband [not named].

1818, 8th of 5th mo. - Elisha Bull requested a certificate of removal to Baltimore Monthly Meeting, Eastern District. Daniel Larrabee requested a certificate of removal to Amawalk Monthly Meeting in New York for his minor son Edward W. Larrabee who has a birth right amongst us. William Hughes, having returned to reside within the limits of Pipe Creek Monthly Meeting [Frederick County, Maryland], requested a certificate of removal to from Baltimore Monthly Meeting, Western District. Margaret Powel requested a certificate of removal to Baltimore Monthly Meeting, Eastern District.

1818, 5th of 6th mo. - Eli Kirk requested a certificate of removal to York Monthly Meeting in Pennsylvania, having already moved there. Margaret Powell requested a certificate of removal to Baltimore Monthly Meeting, Eastern District, for her minor son John C. Powell.

1818, 10th of 7th mo. - John Love, Jr. requested a certificate of removal to York Monthly Meeting in Pennsylvania, having already moved there.

1818, 7th of 8th mo. - Phebe Carpenter requested a certificate of removal to Concord Monthly Meeting [Delaware County], Pennsylvania.

1818, 11th of 9th mo. - Thomas L. Reese requested a certificate of removal to Indian Spring Monthly Meeting for himself, wife Mary, and their two minor children, Mary Brooke Reese and Ann Reese, having already moved there. Rebecca C. Hopkins requested a certificate of removal to Baltimore Monthly Meeting, Eastern District, having removed to reside with her husband [not named].

1818, 6th of 11th mo. - Jane Bowmans requested a certificate of removal to Third Haven Monthly Meeting, having already moved there. Samuel Baily requested a certificate of removal to Wilmington Monthly Meeting in Delaware for himself, wife Hannah, and their minor son Samuel T. Baily, having already moved there. John Litle requested a certificate of removal to Alexandria Monthly Meeting for himself, wife Sarah, and their minor son Robert Sinclair Litle.

1818, 11th of 12th mo. - Sarah Kirk requested a certificate of removal to York Monthly Meeting in Pennsylvania, having removed to settle there with her husband [not named]. Joseph Hollingsworth requested a certificate of removal to Little Miami Monthly Meeting in Ohio.

1819, 8th of 1st mo. - Joshua Riley requested a certificate of removal to Alexandria Monthly Meeting, having already moved there.

1819, 5th of 3rd mo. - James Baily requested a certificate of removal to London Grove Monthly Meeting [Chester County], Pennsylvania, having already moved there.

1819, 9th of 4th mo. - Edward Needles, Jr. requested a certificate of removal to York Monthly Meeting in Pennsylvania.

1819, 7th of 5th mo. - Robert Bond requested a certificate of removal to Hopewell Monthly Meeting [Frederick County], Virginia.

1819, 11th of 6th mo. - Ann Hull requested a certificate of removal to Still Water Monthly Meeting in Ohio, having already moved there.

1819, 9th of 7th mo. - Amos Bullock requested a certificate of removal to Burlington Monthly Meeting [Burlington County], New Jersey, for himself, wife Elizabeth S. Bullock, and their infant son Charles Peck Bullock, having already moved there. William Wood, Jr. requested a certificate of removal to Smithfield Monthly Meeting in Ohio.

1819, 6th of 8th mo. - Edith Updegraff requested a certificate of removal to Pipe Creek Monthly Meeting [Frederick County, Maryland].

1819, 5th of 11th mo. - Aquila Massey requested a certificate of removal to Deer Creek Monthly Meeting, having already moved there. Herman U. Cope requested a certificate of removal to Philadelphia Monthly Meeting, Western District, having already moved there.

1819, 10th of 12th mo. - Jane Cook requested a certificate of removal to Warrington Monthly Meeting [York County, Pennsylvania] for herself and five minor children, Jesse W., Maria Jane, Mary Ann, Samuel H., and George W. Cook, having already moved there with her husband [not named]. Euphenia Shanahan requested a certificate of removal to Third Haven Monthly Meeting, having already moved there.

1820, 7th of 1st mo. - Mary Hartshorn requested a certificate of removal to Cincinnati Monthly Meeting in Ohio, having already moved there with her husband [not named]. Jane Vore requested a certificate of removal to Redstone Monthly Meeting [Fayette County, Pennsylvania], having already moved there. Thomas Gilpin requested a certificate of removal to Alexandria Monthly Meeting, having already moved there.

1820, 11th of 2nd mo. - Mary Miflen [Mifflin], our ancient friend and a minister much esteemed by us, requested a certificate of removal to Deer Creek Monthly Meeting, having already moved there. Mary McCoy requested a certificate of removal to Deer Creek Monthly Meeting. Hannah Atkinson requested a certificate of removal to Third Haven Monthly Meeting, having already moved there with her husband [not named].

1820, 7th of 4th mo. - Richard Dawson requested a certificate of removal to Indian Spring Monthly Meeting for himself, wife Eliza, and their minor son John Dawson, having already moved there.

1820, 5th of 5th mo. - Certificate of removal requested for John T., Mary M., Johannah, and Sarah C. Plummer (all minors) who had moved to Cincinnati Monthly Meeting in Ohio to reside with their father Joseph P. Plummer.

1820, 9th of 6th mo. - Edward Stabler, Jr. requested a certificate of removal to Indian Spring Monthly Meeting, having already moved there. Abner Jones requested a certificate of removal to Little Falls Monthly Meeting for himself, wife Maria, and their two minor children, Hannah and Rebecca Stabler, having already moved there.

1820, 7th of 7th mo. - Samuel James, a minor, requested a certificate of removal to Wilmington Monthly Meeting in Delaware, having already moved there. Joseph James requested a certificate of removal to Gwynedd Monthly Meeting in Pennsylvania for himself, wife Mary, and their two minor children, Joseph James and Able James. Sarah James and Ann James also requested a certificate of removal to Gwynedd Monthly Meeting in Pennsylvania.

1820, 11th of 8th mo. - William B. Price, a minor, requested a certificate of removal to Gunpowder Monthly Meeting. David Harding requested a certificate of removal to Gunpowder Monthly Meeting. Joseph Brevett requested a certificate of removal to Miami Monthly Meeting in Ohio.

1820, 8th of 9th mo. - Daniel Troth requested a certificate of removal to Third Haven Monthly Meeting, having already moved there.

1820, 6th of 10th mo. - Henrietta M. Thomas requested a certificate of removal to Nottingham Monthly Meeting, having already moved there. John Chew Thomas requested a certificate of removal to Nottingham Monthly Meeting for himself, wife Mary, and their four minor children, John Chew Thomas, Richard Henry Thomas, Samuel Evan Thomas, and Julia Thomas.

1820, 10th of 11th mo. - Amos Price requested a certificate of removal to Gunpowder Monthly Meeting, having already moved there. Jacob Fussell requested a certificate of removal to Little Falls Monthly Meeting for himself, wife Clarissa, and their three minor children, William, Joshua, and Jacob Fussell, having already removed within the compass of that meeting. Hannah Stapler requested a certificate of removal to Wilmington Monthly Meeting.

1821, 9th of 2nd mo. - Joseph Brown requested a certificate of removal to Philadelphia Monthly Meeting, having already moved there. Samuel R. Turner, having returned to reside within the limits of Cecil Monthly Meeting [Kent County, Maryland], requested a certificate of removal from Baltimore Monthly Meeting, Western District. George S. Knight requested a certificate of removal to LeRay Monthly Meeting in the State of New York. Abel Knight requested a certificate of removal to Philadelphia Monthly Meeting for himself, wife Elizabeth, and their seven minor children, Jane D., Sarah, Margaret S., Jarel, Isaac D., Tacy M., and Charles D. Knight. Susan Y. Kemp, having removed with her husband [not named], requested a certificate of removal to Third Haven Monthly Meeting. Susanna Needles requested a certificate of removal to Third Haven Monthly Meeting.

1821, 9th of 3rd mo. - Owen Branson requested a certificate of removal to West Grove Monthly Meeting in Indiana for himself, wife Hannah, and their six minor children, Eliza E., Benjamin, David, Mary Ann, Hannah S., and Susanna Branson.

1821, 6th of 7th mo. - Jefferson Hough requested a certificate of removal to Fairfax Monthly Meeting [Loudoun County, Virginia], having already moved there.

1821, 9th of 11th mo. - Joseph G. Hopkins requested a certificate of removal to Third Haven Monthly Meeting, having already moved there. George Mason, Jr. requested a certificate of removal to Gunpowder Monthly Meeting. His certificate was subsequently returned and one was granted to Deer Creek Monthly Meeting.

1821, 7th of 12th mo. - Jane Knock, a minor, requested a certificate of removal to Duck Creek Monthly Meeting [Kent County, Delaware]. Elizabeth H. Tyson requested a certificate of removal to Philadelphia Monthly Meeting, Western District, having returned to reside within the verge of that meeting. Thomas Underwood requested a certificate of removal to York Monthly Meeting, having already moved there. Edward Andrew Farquhar, a minor, requested a certificate of removal to Cannel Monthly Meeting in Ohio, having already moved there. Abner Pope requested a certificate of removal to Alexandria Monthly Meeting for himself, wife Maria, and their two minor children, Edward Pope and Mary Ann Pope, having already moved there. Charles Litle requested a certificate of removal to Hopewell Monthly Meeting [Frederick County, Virginia], having already moved there. Susanna Allen, wife of James, requested a certificate of removal to Deer Creek Monthly Meeting, having returned to reside within the limits of that meeting.

1822, 11th of 1st mo. - Rachel Matthews requested a certificate of removal to Third Haven Monthly Meeting, having already moved there. Elizabeth Howell, wife of John, requested a certificate of removal to Philadelphia Monthly Meeting for herself and their eight minor children, Phebe B., John, Arthur, George, Zepher[?] Carpenter, Adelia, Ann, Charles, William, and Darius Carpenter Howell, having already moved there.

1822, 8th of 3rd [2nd?] mo. - Elizabeth Janney and Mary P. Janney requested a certificate of removal to Green Street Monthly Meeting in Philadelphia, having already moved there.

1822, 15th of 3rd mo. - James Clark, having returned to his native land, requested a certificate of removal to Brighthelmstone Monthly Meeting in England. John W. Niles, a minor, requested a certificate of removal to Philadelphia Monthly Meeting, Southern District.

1822, 5th of 4th mo. - George Tyson requested a certificate of removal to Salem Monthly Meeting in Massachusetts, having already moved there. Rachel Kirk requested a certificate of removal to Indian Spring Monthly Meeting, having already moved there.

1822, 10th of 5th mo. - Dutro[?] B. Aldrich requested a certificate of removal to Smithfield Monthly Meeting in Rhode Island. Jesse Price and wife Eleanor requested a certificate of removal to Pipe Creek Monthly Meeting [Frederick County, Maryland].

1822, 7th of 6th mo. - Thomas Kinsey requested a certificate of removal to Nottingham Monthly Meeting in Maryland, having already moved there. Nathaniel Hoskins and wife Elizabeth requested a certificate of removal to Little Falls Monthly Meeting. Enos Trahern requested a certificate of removal to Goose Creek in Virginia, having already moved there [another entry in the register states 7th of 5th mo., 1822].

1822, 5th of 7th mo. - Thomas A. Worrall requested a certificate of removal to Philadelphia Monthly Meeting, Northern District, having already moved there. Isaac Scott requested a certificate of removal to Indian Spring Monthly Meeting for himself, wife Elizabeth, and their three minor children, Wilson, Martha Ann, and Ezra Scott, having already moved there. Sarah Moore requested a certificate of removal to Pelham Monthly Meeting in Upper Canada, having already moved there with her husband [not named] and their six minor children, Thomas, Andrew, Benjamin, Elizabeth, Whitsen, and Nathaniel Moore.

1822, 9th of 8th mo. - Joseph Trimble and wife Ann requested a certificate of removal to Little Falls Monthly Meeting.

1822, 11th of 10th mo. - Isaac Brayden[?] requested a certificate of removal to Nantucket Monthly Meeting, Southern District. William Gillingham requested a certificate of removal to Alexandria Monthly Meeting for himself, wife Jane, and their four minor children, Isaac, Jehu, Elizabeth, and Catharine Gillingham.

1822, 8th of 11th mo. - Mary Ann Moore requested a certificate of removal to Third Haven Monthly Meeting, having already moved there.

1823, 10th of 1st mo. - William L. Aldrich requested a certificate of removal to Smithfield Monthly Meeting in Rhode Island, having already moved there. William Reckman requested a certificate of removal to Nottingham Monthly Meeting, having already moved there.

1823, 7th of 3rd mo. - George Mason, Jr., for some time since removed from amongst us, requested a certificate of removal to Deer Creek Monthly Meeting. Samuel Fisher requested a certificate of removal to Pipe Creek Monthly Meeting [Frederick County, Maryland], having already moved there.

1823, 11th of 4th mo. - David Jordan requested a certificate of removal to Western Branch Monthly Meeting in Isle of Wight County, Virginia, having already moved there.

1823, 9th of 5th mo. - Yearsley Jones requested a certificate of removal to Goose Creek Monthly Meeting in Virginia for himself, wife Susanna, and their three minor children, Aquilla, Yearsley, and Lydia Ann Jones.

1823, 6th of 6th mo. - Amos Read, a minor, who was placed an apprentice within the limits of Gunpowder Monthly Meeting, requested a certificate of removal to that meeting.

1823, 11th of 7th mo. - Sarah W. Doddrell requested a certificate of removal to Deer Creek Monthly Meeting. Joseph Evans, having removed with his family to settle within the limits of the Monthly Meeting of Friends in New York, requested a certificate of removal for himself, wife Alice Evans, and their six minor children, William, Ellen, Samuel, Wilson, Joshua, and Robert Evans.

1823, 8th of 8th mo. - Maria C. Worrall, having removed with her husband [not named] to Chester Monthly Meeting in Pennsylvania, requested a certificate of removal for herself and their two minor children, Elwood Worrall and Anna Maria Worrall. [Written in another hand above her name are the words "Sent by Thos. A. Worrall"].

1823, 5th of 9th mo. - Joel Brown requested a certificate of removal to Little Falls Monthly Meeting, having already moved there.

1823, 7th of 11th mo. - Mary Prevail requested a certificate of removal to Gunpowder Monthly Meeting, having already moved there. Micajah Churchman requested a certificate of removal to Darby Monthly Meeting for himself, wife Eliza, and their four minor children, Sinclair, William H., Emily, and Edward Churchman, having already moved there.

1823, 5th of 12th mo. - Mary Ferris requested a certificate of removal to Wilmington Monthly Meeting, having moved there to reside with her husband [not named]. Folger Pope requested a certificate of removal to Deer Creek Monthly Meeting for himself, wife Ann, and their five minor children, Franklin F., Joseph D., Sarah R., Theodate, and William R. Pope.

1824, 9th of 1st mo. - George Harris, Jr. requested a certificate of removal to Fairfax Monthly Meeting [Loudoun County, Virginia]. William Amos Tyson, a minor, requested a certificate of removal to Salem Monthly Meeting in

Massachusetts, having already moved there. James C. Doddrell requested a certificate of removal to Deer Creek Monthly Meeting, having already moved there with his family [not named].

1824, 6th of 2nd mo. - Joel Wright, a minor, requested a certificate of removal to Alexandria Monthly Meeting, having already moved there. Esther Moore requested a certificate of removal to Alexandria Monthly Meeting, having already moved there with her husband [not named].

1824, 5th of 3rd mo. - Sarah Townsend requested a certificate of removal to Duck Creek Monthly Meeting [Kent County], Delaware, having already moved there.

1824, 7th of 5th mo. - Israel Price requested a certificate of removal to Gunpowder Monthly Meeting for himself, wife Jane, and their minor son Richard Price. Frances Price and Elizabeth Price requested a certificate of removal to Gunpowder Monthly Meeting.

1824, 11th of 6th mo. - Hannah Jones requested a certificate of removal to Deer Creek Monthly Meeting, having already moved there with her husband [not named]. Samuel McPherson requested a certificate of removal to Hopewell Monthly Meeting [Frederick County], Virginia, having already moved there.

1824, 9th of 7th mo. - William R. Wanton requested a certificate of removal to Cincinnati Monthly Meeting in Ohio, having already moved there. Micajah Alley requested a certificate of removal to New York Monthly Meeting, having already moved there. Catharine Leek requested a certificate of removal to Indian Spring Monthly Meeting for herself and minor son Richard Leek. Sarah Barker requested a certificate of removal to New York Monthly Meeting, having returned to reside within the limits of that meeting.

1824, 10th of 9th mo. - Rachel Ellicott and Ann Ellicott requested a certificate of removal to Alexandria Monthly Meeting.

1824, 8th of 10th mo. - John C. Norris requested a certificate of removal to Cecil Monthly Meeting [Kent County, Maryland] for himself and wife Mary Ann L. Norris, having already moved there.

1824, 5th of 11th mo. - Sarah H. Janney requested a certificate of removal to Birmingham Monthly Meeting for herself and her two minor daus. Mary Ann and Georgeanna Janney, having already moved there.

1824, 10th of 12th mo. - John Sinclair requested a certificate of removal to New York Monthly Meeting for himself, wife Elizabeth, and their six minor children, Anna, John, Emma, Joseph, Susan, and Margaret T. Sinclair. Mary Ann Sinclair requested a certificate of removal to New York Monthly Meeting, having already moved there and living with her parents [not named].

1825, 7th of 1st mo. - Robert W. Young requested a certificate of removal to New York Monthly Meeting for himself, wife Rebecca, and their six minor children, William, George, Joseph, Rachel, Elizabeth, and Robert Young, having already moved there. William Knock requested a certificate of removal to Duck Creek Monthly Meeting [Kent County], Delaware, having returned there to reside within the limits of that meeting. Ann Cole requested a certificate of removal to Westland Monthly Meeting [Washington County], Pennsylvania, having already moved there.

1825, 6th of 5th mo. - Isaac Dixon requested a certificate of removal to Wilmington Monthly Meeting for himself, wife Margaret, and their six minor children, Edwin S., John H., Mary, Isaac, Lucretia, and Sarah Elizabeth Dixon, having already moved there.

1825, 10th of 6th mo. - Samuel Canby requested a certificate of removal to Alexandria Monthly Meeting in the District of Columbia for himself, wife Elizabeth, and their seven minor children, Thomas, Samuel, Bulah, Joseph, Yardley, Elizabeth, and William Canby. Mary Canby also requested a certificate of removal to Alexandria Monthly Meeting, having removed with her parents to settle within the limits of that meeting.

1825, 8th of 7th mo. - Micajah Ally was granted a certificate of removal to Salem Monthly Meeting in Massachusetts "although he has left his affairs in an unsettled state, yet upon inquiry we find no objection made to his having a certificate."

1825, 9th of 9th mo. - James Gillingham requested a certificate of removal to Philadelphia Monthly Meeting for himself, wife Sarah, and their two minor children, Charles and Samuel Gillingham. James W. Gillingham also requested a certificate of removal to Philadelphia Monthly Meeting. Anna W. Gillingham requested a certificate of removal to Philadelphia Monthly Meeting, having removed with her parents [not named] to settle within the limits of that meeting. Phebe W. Gillingham also requested a certificate of removal to Philadelphia Monthly Meeting, having removed with her parents [not named] to settle within the limits of that meeting.

1825, 7th of 10th mo. - Mary C. Gillingham requested a certificate of removal to Deer Creek Monthly Meeting.

1825, 11th of 11th mo. - John Quarles requested a certificate of removal to Deer Creek Monthly Meeting, having already moved there.

1825, 9th of 12th mo. - Sarah Brown requested a certificate of removal to Little Britain Monthly Meeting, having removed there to reside with her husband [not named]. Bennaiah Sawyer requested a certificate of removal to New York Monthly Meeting, having already moved there. Joseph Bromwell requested a certificate of removal to Nottingham Monthly Meeting. Deborah Bromwell also requested a certificate of removal to Nottingham Monthly Meeting.

## BALTIMORE MONTHLY MEETING, WESTERN DISTRICT BIRTHS, 1803-1825 (GLEANED FROM MEMBERSHIP ROLLS)

Francis S. Corkran, b. 12th of 11th mo., 1814, son of Samuel Corkran and Elizabeth Withgott.

John R. Cox, b. 17th of 10th mo., 1817, son of George Cox and Sarah Roberts.

Alfred S. Gardner, b. 3rd of 2nd mo., 1822, son of Ephraim Gardner and Mary Swain.

Joseph Bernard Gilpin, b. 25th of 9th mo., 1825, son of Samuel Gilpin and Rachel Gover.

Children of William Hartley and Tacy Buckman:
    Lavinia B. Hartley, b. 8th of 6th mo., 1817.
    Samuel E. Hartley, b. 25th of 9th mo., 1818.
    Charles L. Hartley, b. 30th of 6th mo., 1820.

Children of Thomas Hartley and Elizabeth Paxon:
    Elias P. Hartley, b. 23rd of 4th mo., 1821.
    Phineas Hartley, b. 14th of 9th mo., 1824.

William Hull, b. 9th of 3rd mo., 1822, son of Thomas J. Hull and Harriet Ford.

Marietta Hough, b. 11th of 10th mo., 1811, dau. of Edward S. Hough and Sarah Atkinson.

Caroline M. Peck, b. 4th of 11th mo., 1824, dau. of George Peck and Sarah Ritter, m. John Jones [no date given].

Charles E. Kemp, b. 10th of 8th mo., 1822, son of Samuel T. Kemp and Susanna Yarnall.

Children of Daniel Larrabee and Anne (Anna) Wheeler:
    Hannah Larrabee, b. 7th of 11th mo., 1799.
    Joseph Larrabee, b. 16th of 9th mo., 1801.
    Ephraim Larrabee, b. 21st of 11th mo., 1803.
    Edward Larrabee, b. 10th of 5th mo., 1806.
    William Larrabee, b. 23rd of 2nd mo., 1811.

Children of James Lovegrove ad Lydia Pope:
    Hannah P. Lovegrove, b. 5th of 7th mo., 1816.
    Parthenia D. Lovegrove, b. ---- [blank].

John Emerson Lamb, b. 20th of 7th mo., 1803, son of Isaac Lamb and Rachel Emerson.

Children of Eli Matthews and Mary Cooper:
    Esther Matthews, b. 13th of 6th mo., 1810.
    Esther Matthews, m. John Emerson Lamb [no date].
    Aquilla Matthews [twin], b. 31st of 8th mo., 1817.
    Priscilla Matthews [twin], b. 31st of 8th mo., 1817.
    Margaret Matthews, b. 15th of 5th mo., 1820.

Joseph W. Offley, b. 30th of 9th mo., 1825, son of Michael Offley and Lydia West.

John Regester, b. 25th of 3rd mo., 1824, son of Samuel Regester and Elizabeth W. Cornthwaite.

Sarah Janney, b. 3rd of 10th mo., 1820, dau. of David Janney and Elizabeth Moore, m. Gerard H. Reese [no date given].

Children of Thomas L. Reese and Mary B. Moore:
    Thomas M. Reese, b. 18th of 7th mo., 1820.
    Edward Reese, b. 16th of 6th mo., 1825.

Children of Matthew Smith and Catherine Marsh:
    John M. Smith, b. 20th of 8th mo., 1818.
    Mary M. Smith, b. 14th of 10th mo., 1823.

Samuel Townsend, b. 13th of 9th mo., 1808, son of Joseph Townsend and Elizabeth Clark.

George W. Trimble, b. 13th of 3rd mo., 1823, son of William Trimble and Mary Brown.

Isabella Tyson, b. 17th of 3rd mo., 1823, dau. of Nathan Tyson and Martha Ellicott.

Children of Philip Thomas and Elizabeth George:
    Mary Thomas, b. 11th of 10th mo., 1813.
    Mary Thomas, m. John Wethered [no date given]
    Elizabeth Thomas, b. 22nd of 1st mo., 1817.

John Wethered, b. 8th of 5th mo., 1809, son of Lewin Wethered and Elizabeth Ellicott.

## BALTIMORE MONTHLY MEETING, EASTERN DISTRICT
## CERTIFICATES OF REMOVAL, 1807-1819

1807, 11th of 6th mo. - Samuel Naylor requested a certificate of removal to Gunpowder Monthly Meeting for himself, wife Rebecah, and their five minor children, Ann, John, Joseph, Charles, and Mary Naylor. Martha Powell requested a certificate of removal to Concord Monthly Meeting [Delaware County], Pennsylvania, having already moved there.

1807, 13th of 8th mo. - Elizabeth Townsend requested a certificate of removal to Concord Monthly Meeting [Belmont County], Ohio, having already moved there with her husband [not named].

1807, 12th of 11th mo. - Lydia Lafetra, having returned to reside within the verge of Shrewsbury Monthly Meeting, requested and was granted a certificate of removal.

1808, 11th of 2nd mo. - Thomas Sherwood requested a certificate of removal to Miama Monthly Meeting in Ohio, having already moved there.

1808, 10th of 3rd mo. - Elizabeth O. Dare [O'Dare?] requested a certificate of removal to Indian Spring Monthly Meeting, having already moved there with her husband [not named].

1808, 14th of 4th mo. - Rebecca Matthews requested a certificate of removal to Gunpowder Monthly Meeting, having resided there a considerable time. Catherine and Ann Sanderson, minors, requested a certificate of removal to Baltimore Monthly Meeting, Western District, having already moved there. John Worthington requested a certificate of removal to Deer Creek Monthly Meeting, having moved there some time ago. Isaac G. Hopkins requested a certificate of removal to Indian Spring Monthly Meeting, having moved there some time past.

1808, 12th of 5th mo. - Thomas Norton requested a certificate of removal to Deer Creek Monthly Meeting, having already moved there. Ann Jewett requested a certificate of removal to Deer Creek Monthly Meeting, having already moved there.

1808, 14th of 7th mo. - Seth Smith requested a certificate of removal to Goose Creek in Louden County, Virginia. Amos Alley requested a certificate of removal to New York Monthly Meeting.

1808, 11th of 8th mo. - John Jewett and wife Susanna requested a certificate of removal to Deer Creek Monthly Meeting, having already moved there. Elizabeth Lowden requested a certificate of removal to Baltimore Monthly Meeting, Western District.

1808, 10th of 11th mo. - Amos Smith requested a certificate of removal to Gunpowder Monthly Meeting for himself, wife Rebecca, and their three minor children, Eliza, Rachel, and Mary Smith, having already moved there.

1809, 12th of 1st mo. - Rebecca Medcalf, wife of Abraham, requested a certificate of removal to Baltimore Monthly Meeting, Western District, for herself and her two minor children, Joshua and Elijah Medcalf.

1809, 9th of 2nd mo. - Stacy West requested a certificate of removal to Gunpowder Monthly Meeting, having already moved there.

1809, 9th of 3rd mo. - Certificate of removal requested for Benjamin Jay Jennings who was placed by his father [not named] within limits of the Philadelphia Monthly Meeting, Southern District, as a student in the Pennsylvania Hospital. William and Isaac Brayton requested a certificate of removal to Nantucket Monthly Meeting, having already moved there.

1809, 13th of 4th mo. - Rachel Judge requested a certificate of removal to Deer Creek Monthly Meeting, having already moved there.

1809, 8th of 6th mo. - Oliver Wilson requested a certificate of removal to Alexandria Monthly Meeting.

1809, 13th of 7th mo. - Mary Underwood, wife of Enock, requested a certificate of removal to Warrington Monthly Meeting [York County, Pennsylvania], having moved there with her husband some time ago.

1809, 10th of 8th mo. - Margaret Croft, wife of John, requested a certificate of removal to Plainfield Monthly Meeting in Ohio, having already moved there with her husband and their two minor children, William and Stacy Croft. Hepzibah Sheerman, wife of Nathaniel, having returned to reside within the compass of Nantucket Monthly Meeting, requested and was granted a certificate of removal.

1809, 9th of 11th mo. - Moses Hutton requested a certificate of removal to Chester Monthly Meeting in Pennsylvania.

1810, 8th of 3rd mo. - Joseph Husband and wife Sarah requested a certificate of removal to Deer Creek Monthly Meeting, having already moved there.

1810, 12th of 4th mo. - Mary Kinsey requested a certificate of removal to Buckingham Monthly Meeting in Bucks County, Pennsylvania, having already moved there.

1810, 14th of 6th mo. - John Needles requested a certificate of removal to Baltimore Monthly Meeting, Western District, having already moved there.

1810, 9th of 8th mo. - Levis Janney and wife Mary requested a certificate of removal to Chester Monthly Meeting in Providence, Pennsylvania. Richard Hopkins, a minor, requested a certificate of removal to New York Monthly Meeting, having already moved there.

1810, 11th of 10th mo. - John Trimble requested a certificate of removal to Baltimore Monthly Meeting, Western District, for himself, wife Elizabeth, and their five minor children, Elizabeth, Isaac, Mary, Jane, and John Trimble. Samuel Smith requested a certificate of removal to Baltimore Monthly Meeting, Western District, for himself, wife Ann, and their two minor children, Elizabeth Ann Smith and William Brown Smith. Henry Smith and wife Martha requested a certificate of removal to Baltimore Monthly Meeting, Western District.

1810, 8th of 11th mo. - John Miller requested a certificate of removal to Short Creek Monthly Meeting in Ohio for himself, wife Edith, and their three minor children, Lydia, Rachel, and William Miller.

245

1810, 13th of 12th mo. - Mahetibal Morris requested a certificate of removal to South Monthly Meeting Nantucket, having already moved there.

1811, 10th of 1st mo. - Elizabeth Evans, wife of Edmond, requested a certificate of removal to Gunpowder Monthly Meeting, having already moved there.

1811, 11th of 4th mo. - Susanna Miller requested a certificate of removal to Deer Creek Monthly Meeting, having moved there with her husband [not named]. Thomas Bland, Jr., produced a certificate from Balby Monthly Meeting in Yorkshire, Great Britain, dated 9th of 8th mo., 1804, and shortly after left this place [Baltimore], it appearing from information received that he had returned to your parts [Great Britain].

1811, 11th of 7th mo. - Richard Dallam requested a certificate of removal to Deer Creek Monthly Meeting, having already moved there. Thomas Mecteer and wife Mary requested a certificate of removal to New Garden Monthly Meeting [Chester County], Pennsylvania, having already moved there.

1811, 12th of 9th mo. - John Burges requested a certificate of removal to Baltimore Monthly Meeting, Eastern District, from Deer Creek Monthly Meeting on 23rd of 5th mo., 1811, and after residing in Baltimore a short time requested a certificate of removal to Plymouth Monthly Meeting in Ohio. The same requests were noted for Joseph Burges and wife Ann who also removed to Plymouth Monthly Meeting in Ohio.

1811, 10th of 10th mo. - Warrick Price requested a certificate of removal to Plymouth Monthly Meeting in Ohio for himself, wife Susanna, and their four minor children, William, Ann, Isaac, and Susanna Price. Elizabeth Janney requested a certificate of removal to Philadelphia Monthly Meeting, having already moved there.

1811, 12th of 12th mo. - Ann Armstrong, wife of John, requested a certificate of removal to New Garden Monthly Meeting [Chester County], Pennsylvania, having already moved there. Rebecca Young requested a certificate of removal to Baltimore Monthly Meeting, Western District, having already moved there with her husband [not named].

1812, 9th of 1st mo. - James Dawson requested a certificate of removal to Baltimore Monthly Meeting, Western District, for himself, wife Ann, and their six children, Elizabeth, Lydia, Sarah, Mary, Ann, and James Dawson, having been received at Baltimore Monthly Meeting, Eastern District, by certificate in the 7th mo. last, since which time they removed to Baltimore Monthly Meeting, Eastern District.

1812, 13th of 2nd mo. - Joseph James requested a certificate of removal to Baltimore Monthly Meeting, Western District, for himself, wife Mary, and their six children, Hannah, Sarah, Anna, Samuel, Joseph, and Abel James. Rebecca C. James requested a certificate of removal to Baltimore Monthly Meeting, Western District, having moved there with her parents [not named]. Sarah Savage requested a certificate of removal to Baltimore Monthly Meeting, Western District, having already moved there. Elizabeth Duncan requested a certificate of removal to Deer Creek Monthly Meeting, having moved there with her husband [not named]. Martha Woolston requested a certificate of removal to Deer Creek Monthly Meeting, having already moved there.

1812, 12th of 3rd mo. - Ann Sanderson, a minor, requested a certificate of removal to Gunpowder Monthly Meeting, having already moved there.

1812, 9th of 4th mo. - Benjamin Ninde requested a certificate of removal to Indian Spring Monthly Meeting.

1812, 11th of 6th mo. - William Hayward requested a certificate of removal to Deer Creek Monthly Meeting for himself, wife Mary, and their five minor children, Thomas, Rebecca, Hannah, Jacob, and Elizabeth Hayward, having some time since removed with his family within the limits of that meeting. Joseph Hayward requested a certificate of removal to Deer Creek Monthly Meeting, having already moved there.

1812, 12th of 11th mo. - Rachel Judge requested a certificate of removal to Alexandria Monthly Meeting, having already moved there.

1813, 11th of 2nd mo. - Richard Dawson requested a certificate of removal to Baltimore Monthly Meeting, Western District, having already moved there.

1813, 11th of 3rd mo. - Hannah Gwinn requested a certificate of removal to Baltimore Monthly Meeting, Western District, having moved there with her husband [not named].

1813, 13th of 5th mo. - Margaret Naylor, a minor dau. of James Naylor, having removed with her father, requested a certificate of removal to Plymouth Monthly Meeting in Ohio.

1813, 8th of 7th mo. - William Matthews Townsend requested a certificate of removal to Concord Monthly Meeting [Delaware County], Pennsylvania.

1813, 9th of 9th mo. - Margaret Powell, having removed with her three children, Albina Powell, Benjamin Wayne Powell, and John Carpenter Powell, requested a certificate of removal to Concord Monthly Meeting [Delaware County], Pennsylvania.

1814, 10th of 2nd mo. - William Glover requested a certificate of removal to Haddonfield Monthly Meeting for himself, wife Mary, and their minor children, George Mickle, Sarah, Ann, Thomas, Hannah, and Eliza., having already moved there.

1814, 14th of 4th mo. - Hugh Judge and wife Susanna requested a certificate of removal to Indian Spring Monthly Meeting, having already moved there. Rebecca Judge, having removed with her parents [not named], requested a certificate of removal to Indian Spring Monthly Meeting.

1814, 9th of 6th mo. - Enion Hussey requested a certificate of removal to York Monthly Meeting in Pennsylvania, having already moved there.

1814, 14th of 7th mo. - Sarah Bond requested a certificate of removal to Gunpowder Monthly Meeting, having already moved there. Mary Dickenson attended Baltimore Monthly Meeting, Eastern District, last month on a religious visit from Sadsbury Monthly Meeting, accompanied by Anne Pusey.

1814, 11th of 8th mo. - Ann Armstrong requested a certificate of removal to Wilmington Monthly Meeting, having already moved there.

1814, 8th of 9th mo. - Seth Fisher, a minor placed as an apprentice to William Sheppard, requested a certificate of removal to Pipe Creek Monthly Meeting [Frederick County, Maryland]. George Cox and wife Eliza requested a certificate of removal to Pipe Creek Monthly Meeting [Frederick County, Maryland]. Ruth Sheppard, wife of William, requested a certificate of removal to Pipe Creek Monthly Meeting [Frederick County, Maryland], having settled there with her husband. John Mott requested a certificate of removal to Gunpowder Monthly Meeting for himself, wife Rachel, and their minor son Abraham G. Mott, having already moved there.

1814, 20th of 10th mo. - Sarah Johnson, wife of James, requested a certificate of removal to Deer Creek Monthly Meeting for herself and her five minor children, John, George, James, Howard, and Ann Johnson, having already moved there.

1814, 10th of 11th mo. - Sarah Wilson, a minister in good esteem and wife of Edward Wilson, requested a certificate of removal to Philadelphia Monthly Meeting, Southern District, having already moved there with her husband. Nicholas W. Townsend requested a certificate of removal to Concord Monthly Meeting [Delaware County], Pennsylvania. Phebe Judge requested a certificate of removal to Indian Spring Monthly Meeting, having already moved there.

1815, 8th of 6th mo. - Mary Dawes requested a certificate of removal to Gunpowder Monthly Meeting, having some time since removed within their verge. Samuel Reed requested a certificate of removal to Gunpowder Monthly Meeting for himself and his six minor children, Deborah, William, Harriott, John Wilson, Elizabeth, and Samuel D. Reed, having already moved there. Matilda Reed requested a certificate of removal to Gunpowder Monthly Meeting. Rebecca Medcalf requested a certificate of removal to Baltimore Monthly Meeting, Western District, for herself and son Elijah Medcalf.

1815, 13th of 7th mo. - David H. Wilson, a minor, requested a certificate of removal to Indian Spring Monthly Meeting.

1815, 9th of 11th mo. - William H. Trimble, who is placed within the limits of Baltimore Monthly Meeting, Western District, requested a certificate of removal. David Pollard and Lydia Pollard, being placed within the limits of Baltimore Monthly Meeting, Western District, requested a certificate of removal. Sarah Barcroft requested a certificate of removal to Baltimore Monthly Meeting, Western District, having already moved there.

1816, 11th of 1st mo. - Jesse Morgan requested a certificate of removal to Baltimore Monthly Meeting, Western District, having already moved there.

1816, 8th of 2nd mo. - Alisanna Okley requested a certificate of removal to Indian Spring Monthly Meeting, having already moved there. Albina Powell requested a certificate of removal to Baltimore Monthly Meeting, Western District. Margarett Powell requested a certificate of removal to Baltimore Monthly Meeting, Western District, having already moved there with her minor children, Benjamin W. Powell and John C. Powell.

1816, 9th of 5th mo. - William Pollard, a minor, requested a certificate of removal to Pipe Creek Monthly Meeting [Frederick County, Maryland], having already moved there. Susanna Harlen requested a certificate of removal to Baltimore Monthly Meeting, Western District, having already moved there.

1816, 13th of 6th mo. - Job White requested a certificate of removal to Little Britton Monthly Meeting for himself, wife Phebe, and their two minor children, John Kinsey White and Elizabeth Moore White, having already moved there.

1816, 10th of 10th mo. - Elizabeth Hayward, wife of Isaac, requested a certificate of removal to Baltimore Monthly Meeting, Western District, having already moved there.

1817, 6th of 2nd mo. - Sarah Day, a widow, requested a certificate of removal to Philadelphia Monthly Meeting, Southern District, having already moved there.

1817, 8th of 5th mo. - Thomas Ravis requested a certificate of removal to Devonshire House Monthly Meeting in London, having already moved there.

1817, 5th of 6th mo. - Lydia Barecroft requested a certificate of removal to Plymouth Monthly Meeting in Ohio, having already moved there. Rebecca Beans requested a certificate of removal to Little Falls Monthly Meeting, having returned to reside within their limits.

1817, 10th of 7th mo. - Folger Pope requested a certificate of removal to Baltimore Monthly Meeting, Western District, for himself, wife Ann, and their three minor children, Franklin F., Joseph D., and Sarah R. Pope. David S. Pope, a minor, requested a certificate of removal to Baltimore Monthly Meeting, Western District, having already moved there. Hannah Price, wife of Jarrett, requested a certificate of removal to Wilmington Monthly Meeting for herself and her six minor children, Maria, Eliza, Evan, Caroline, Julia, and Rhoda Price, having already moved there.

1817, 7th of 8th mo. - Lydia Husband requested a certificate of removal to Nine Partners Monthly Meeting in the State of New York, having moved to reside some time within their limits.

1817, 9th of 10th mo. - Certificate of removal requested for Thomas Plummer, Mary Mifflin Plummer, and Joanna Plummer, minor children of Joseph P. Plummer, who are placed at school within the limits of Nine Partners Monthly Meeting in the State of New York. Certificate requested to the same place, for the same reason, for Mary, David, and Susanna Metcalf, minor children of Abraham Metcalf.

1817, 6th of 11th mo. - Hannah Pope requested a certificate of removal to Alexandria Monthly Meeting, having already moved there. John Underwood requested a certificate of removal to White Water Monthly Meeting in Indiana for himself, wife Mary, and their two minor children, Amy and Barclay Underwood, having already moved there.

1818, 8th of 1st mo. - Joel Fisher requested a certificate of removal to Pipe Creek Monthly Meeting [Frederick County, Maryland], having already moved there.

1818, 5th of 3rd mo. - Sarah Lukens requested a certificate of removal to Baltimore Monthly Meeting, Western District, having already moved there.

1818, 9th of 4th mo. - Ann Coale requested a certificate of removal to Baltimore Monthly Meeting, Western District, having already moved there. Mary Norris requested a certificate of removal to Baltimore Monthly Meeting, Western District, having already moved their with her husband [not named].

1818, 4th of 6th mo. - Skipwith Wilson requested a certificate of removal to Baltimore Monthly Meeting, Western District, having already moved there.

1818, 9th of 7th mo. - Thomas Amoss and wife Caroline requested a certificate of removal to Wayne Oak Monthly Meeting in Virginia, having already moved there. Abner Pope requested a certificate of removal to Baltimore Monthly Meeting, Western District, having already moved there.

1818, 6th of 8th mo. - Benjamin Thomas requested a certificate of removal to Plainfield Monthly Meeting in Ohio.

1818, 10th of 9th mo. - John Morgan and wife Priscilla requested a certificate of removal to Baltimore Monthly Meeting, Western District.

1818, 8th of 10th mo. - Mary Jones requested a certificate of removal to Radnor Monthly Meeting in Pennsylvania, having already moved there. William E. Coale requested a certificate of removal to Baltimore Monthly Meeting, Western District.

1818, 5th of 11th mo. - John H. Hewes requested a certificate of removal to Baltimore Monthly Meeting, Western District, for himself, wife Mary, and their two minor children, Elizabeth M. Hewes and Esther Hewes. They also requested one for William and Jane Knock, minors, who are members of our Society.

1819, 7th of 1st mo. - Elizabeth K. West, a minor, requested a certificate of removal to Baltimore Monthly Meeting, Western District, having already moved there.

1819, 4th of 2nd mo. - Elizabeth Kirk requested a certificate of removal to Indian Spring Monthly Meeting, having already moved there with her husband [not named]. Amos Bullock requested a certificate of removal to Baltimore Monthly Meeting, Western District, for himself, wife Elizabeth, and their son Charles Leck Bullock.

1819, 4th of 3rd mo. - Sarah Barker requested a certificate of removal to Baltimore Monthly Meeting, Western District, having already moved there.

## BALTIMORE MONTHLY MEETING, EASTERN DISTRICT BIRTHS, DEATHS, AND SOME MARRIAGES, 1801-1825

James Brown, son of John and Mary, b. 1776, d. 31st of 1st mo., 1811.

Elizabeth Brown, dau. of William and Elizabeth, b. 1788, d. 21st of 8th mo., 1807.

George Matthews, b. 19th of 9th mo., 1729, d. 7th of 2nd mo., 1811, interred next day.

Sarah[?] Matthews, wife of George, b. 1st of 6th mo., 1743, d. 6th of 1st mo., 1812[?].

David Brown, b. 1751, d. 3rd of 11th mo., 1807.

George Brown, son of David and Elizabeth, b. 1785, d. 30th of 3rd mo., 1802.

Rebecca Williams, b. 1737, d. 18th of 4th mo., 1810.

Rachel Hopkins, wife of Gerrard, b. 1751, d. 9th of 1st mo., 1807 at Deer Creek.

Gerrard Hopkins, son of Gerrard and Rachel, b. 1786, d. 6th of 8th mo., 1807.

Jonathan Coates, b. 1728, d. 27th of 5th mo., 1807.

Jesse Brown, b. 1765, d. 12th of 9th mo., 1802, interred next day.

Elizabeth Hopkins, wife of John, b. 1747, d. 25th of 9th mo., 1806.

Sarah Scott, a single woman, b. 1744, d. 1805.

Frances Martin, m. Robert Hough [no date given], d. 15th of 10th mo., 1801.

Jacob Pugh, a young man, d. 1805.

James Love, a minor, d. 30th of 10th mo., 1810, interred 31st in Patapsico [sic] Grave Yard.

Hannah Yoach[?], wife of Henry, d. 18th of 4th mo., 1809.

Susanna Mason, wife of George, d. 13th[?] of 10th mo., 1805, interred next day.

Catharine Wilson, dau. of John and Deborah, d. 23rd of 10th mo., 1801.

Margaret Sanderson, wife of Thomas, d. 20th of 2nd mo., 1809.

Frances Hopkins (widow), d. 25th of 9th mo., 1811.

Deborah Tyson, dau. of Elisha and Mary, d. 12th of 5th mo., 1801.

Children of William and Elizabeth Matthews:
    Sarah Matthews, d. 3rd of 12th mo., 1801.
    Lydia Matthews, d. 25th of 10th mo., 1803.
    [Both interred the next day after they died].

Mary Hussey, a young woman, m. Elisha Hunt [no date given] and removed to Redstone Monthly Meeting [Fayette County], Pennsylvania, 1806.

Joseph Spencer, son of Abel and Rebecca, d. 27th of 6th mo., 1801.

Elizabeth Naylor, a young woman, m. Benjamin Townsend on 18th of 6th mo., 1807 and removed with him to Short Creek Monthly Meeting, Ohio, 13th of 8th mo., 1807.

Isaac Vore, d. 4th of 10th mo., 1801.

John Dillon, a young man, disowned, 12th of 11th mo., 1801.

Isaac Kinsey, d. 27th of 7th mo., 1802.

Rachel Kinsey, wife of Isaac, d. 1801.

Joseph Kinsey, son of Isaac and Rachel, d. 1805.

Sidney Hayward, wife of William, d. 31st of 10th mo., 1802.

Rebecca Hayward, dau. of William and Sidney, d. 9th of 10th mo., 1806.

John Pierpoint, d. 13th of 11th mo., 1802.

Deborah Pierpoint, dau. of John and Ann, d. 3rd of 9th mo., 1802.

Benjamin Rich, b. 1760, d. 25th of 9th mo., 1803.

George Smith, son of Samuel and Hannah, b. 1797, d. 16th of 12th mo., 1803.

Mary Gillingham, dau. of James and Elizabeth, b. 10th of 5th mo., 1801, d. 8th mo., 1803.

Mary Brown, dau. of Ann Read (wife of Jacob Read), d. 13th of 5th mo., 1811.

Joseph Pierpoint, d. 1806.

Amos Gillingham, d. 1801.

Mary Jewell, wife of George, d. 15th of 10th mo., 1802.

John Brown, son of James and Cassandra, b. 30th of 12th mo., 1802.

Betsey Byrnes, dau. of Samuel and Hannah, d. 6th of 3rd mo., 1802.

Jacob Norbary, d. 25th of 3rd mo., 1803, aged 75 yrs., 9 mo., 26 days.

Thomas Jewett, a young man, d. 10th of 8th mo., 1802.

Phebe Carr, d. 16th of 12th mo., 1801.

Olive Cookson, wife of Samuel, d. 5th of 3rd mo., 1803.

Joseph Hopkins, a minor, d. 8th of 7th mo., 1802.

Mary Helm[?], widow, d. 14th of 12th mo., 1801.

William Matthews, son of William and Elizabeth, d. 25th of 10th mo., 1803, interred next day.

Kezia Sinclair, dau. of ---- [name not given] and Rachel, removed from Monallin Monthly Meeting [Adams County, Pennsylvania] with her mother on 8th of 1st mo., 1801, d. 22nd of 3rd mo., 1802.

Anna Wilson, dau. of Isaac and Susanna, m. John Spotswood Peck and removed to Deer Creek Monthly Meeting, 9th of 8th mo., 1804.

Beulah Brown, dau. of Jesse and Dorothy, b. 30th of 1st mo., 1801.

Children of Benjamin and Sarah Rich:
 Sarah Rich, b. 6th of 4th mo., 1801.
 Benjamin Rich, b. 28th of 12th mo., 1803.

Charles Heston, son of Joseph and Ann, b. 28th of 10th mo., 1801.

Elias Pugh, son of Jacob and Elizabeth, b. 30th of 12th mo., 1801.

Josiah Brown Reynolds, son of Joshua and Rachel, b. 10th of 6th mo., 1801, d. 22nd of 7th mo., 1804.

Benjamin Amoss, son of Benjamin and Elizabeth, b. 2nd of 4th mo., 1801, d. 29th of 5th mo., 1802.

Children of John and Elizabeth Trimble:
 Mary Trimble, b. 1799, d. 27th of 7th mo., 1804.
 Elizabeth Trimble, b. 7th of 3rd mo., 1801.
 Isaac Trimble, b. 2nd of 12th mo., 1802.
 Mary Trimble, b. 20th of 9th mo., 1804.

Children of Enoch and Mary Underwood:
 Isaac Griest Underwood, b. 26th of 3rd mo., 1801.
 Alexander Underwood, b. 13th of 10th mo., 1802.
 Alexander Underwood, d. ---- [blank].

William B. Price, son of Israel and Hannah, b. 16th of 12th mo., 1801.

Joseph Hough, son of Robert and Frances, b. 7th of 8th mo., 1801, d. 1st of 9th mo., 1801.

Rachel Sanderson, dau. of Mayes[?], d. 1st of 5th mo., 1805.

Rachel Snowden, m. S. Husband, disowned 8th of 4th mo., 1802.

Elenor Griffith, m. J. Atkinson, disowned 12th of 11th mo., 1804[?].

Letitia Buckman, d. 10th of 2nd mo., 1805.

James Kinsey, d. 9th of 8th mo., 1802.

Ann Hill, d. 29th of 4th mo., 1804.

Children of John and Lucretia Wilson:
    Elisha T. Wilson, b. 14th of 3rd mo., 1801.
    Elisha T. Wilson, d. 1st of 9th mo., 1804.
    Isaac Wilson, b. 2nd of 7th mo., 1802.
    Isaac Wilson, d. ---- [blank].

Thomas Bonsall, son of Vincent and Sarah, b. 8th of 6th mo., 1801.

Children of Izac (Izak) and Rebecca Procter (Proctor):
    Mary Procter, b. 18th of 4th mo., 1801.
    Elizabeth Procter, b. 6th of 12th mo., 1802.
    Edmond Prior Proctor, b. 20th of 12th mo., 1804.
    Edmond Prior Proctor, d. 13th of 11th mo., 1806.

Children of John and Hannah Marsh:
    Mary Marsh, b. 4th of 11th mo., 1801.
    Rebecca Marsh, b. 1790, d. 4th of 3rd mo., 1805.

Cyrus Marsh, son of James and Elizabeth, b. 29th of 10th mo., 1801.

Thomas Harding, son of Charles and Elizabeth, b. 23rd of 7th mo., 1801.

Hicks Harris, son of George and Susanna, b. 3rd of 1st mo., 1802.

Children of Philip and Hannah Dennis:
    Samuel Dennis, d. 7th mo., 1801.
    Elizabeth Dennis, b. 28th of 1st mo., 1802.
    Hannah Dennis, b. 22nd of 8th mo., 1806.

Children of Rossiter and Edith Scott:
    Granville Scott, d. 8th of 5th mo., 1802.
    Susanna Scott [twin], b. 6th of 2nd mo., 1802.
    Townsend Scott [twin], b. 6th of 2nd mo., 1802.
    Susanna Scott, d. 20th of 11th mo., 1805.

Thomas Scott, b. 30th of 5th mo., 1805.
Rossiter Scott, b. 30th of 8th mo., 1808.

Maurice Reese, son of Joseph and Mary, d. 23rd of 3rd mo., 1802.

Children of Eli (Ely) and Esther Balderston:
   Isaiah Balderston, b. 27th of 5th mo., 1802.
   Isaiah Balderston, d. 27th of 9th mo., 1802.
   Marcellius Balderston, b. 5th of 11th mo., 1803.
   William Balderston, b. 10th of 7th mo., 1807.
   Ann Balderston, b. 2nd of 7th mo., 1809.
   Ann Balderston, d. 19th of 7th mo., 1809.
   Samuel Fothergill Balderston, b. 22nd of 11th mo., 1810.

Hannah Ellicott, dau. of Jane, m. James C. Armstrong [no date given, but prior to 1812].

Joseph Brooks, son of Isaac and Sarah, b. 4th of 7th mo., 1802.

Children of Jesse and Margaret Tyson:
   Margaret Tyson, b. 4th of 7th mo., 1802.
   Anna Tyson, b. 10th of 5th mo., 1804.

Margaret Tyson, wife of Jesse, d. 20th of 6th mo., 1804.

James Graham, son of Michael and Patience, b. 28th of 7th mo., 1802, d. 25th of 8th mo., 1802.

Isaac Price, son of Warrick and Susanna, b. 18th of 10th mo., 1802.

Children of Amos and Rebecca Smith:
   Eliza Smith, b. 10th of 8th mo., 1802.
   Rachel Smith, b. 21st of 8th mo., 1804.
   Mary Smith, b. 18th of 10th mo., 1807.

Children of Amos and Mary James:
   Priscilla James, b. 5th of 3rd mo., 1802.
   Amos James, b. 13th of 9th mo., 1804.
   Amos James, d. 14th of 11th mo., 1804.
   Susana James, b. 14th of 10th mo., 1805.

Children of William and Sarah Riley:

Hannah Riley, b. 19th of 1st mo., 1802.
Samuel Riley, d. 28th of 7th mo., 1803.
Sarah Riley, b. 15th of 10th mo., 1804.
William Riley, b. 17th of 2nd mo., 1807.

Jessee Reynolds, son of Joshua and Rachel, b. 7th of 7th mo., 1803, d. 12th of 7th mo., 1804.

Eli West, son of Amos and Elizabeth, b. 22nd of 1st mo., 1803.

William Hayward, son of William and Kezia, b. 25th of 1st mo., 1803, d. 6th of 5th mo., 1806.

Children of Thomas and Sarah Morgan:
    William Morgan, b. 10th of 7th mo., 1796.
    Mary Morgan, b. 17th of 4th mo., 1798.
    Thomas Morgan, b. 3rd of 7th mo., 1800.
    Susanna Morgan, b. 15th of 3rd mo., 1803.
    Evan Jones Morgan, b. 19th of 2nd mo., 1809.
    John A. Morgan, b. 10th of 3rd mo., 1811.

Children of Philip E. and Elizabeth Thomas:
    Ann Thomas, b. 17th of 2nd mo., 1803.
    Rachel Thomas, b. 1st of 2nd mo., 1805.
    Evan Thomas, b. 19th of 11th mo., 1806.

Wilson Balderston, son of Hugh and Margaret, b. 28th of 9th mo., 1803.

Joseph McCoy Underwood, son of Enoch and Mary, b. 2nd of 2nd mo., 1805, d. ---- [blank].

Children of Jacob and Elizabeth:
    John Morgan Pugh, b. 8th of 4th mo., 1803.
    Joshua Pugh, b. 12th of 10th mo., 1804.

Catharine Brown, dau. of James and Catharine, b. 8th of 12th mo., 1803.

Alice Brooks, dau. of Isaac and Sarah, b. 3rd of 5th mo., 1804.

Children of William and Mary:
    Rebecca Hayward, d. 29th of 3rd mo., 1802.
    Hannah Hayward, b. 19th of 6th mo., 1804.

Elizabeth Hayward, b. 14th of 3rd mo., 1808.
William Hayward, b. 6th of 3rd mo., 1810.
William Hayward, d. 19th of 10th mo., 1811 at Bush.

Children of Samuel and Rebecca Naylor:
    Ann Naylor, b. 17th of 2nd mo., 1796.
    Elizabeth Naylor, b. 8th of 8th mo., 1798.
    Elizabeth Naylor, d. 9th of 5th mo., 1800.
    John Naylor, b. 19th of 3rd mo., 1800.
    Joseph Naylor, b. 3rd of 10th mo., 1802.
    Charles Naylor, b. 12th of 9th mo., 1804.

Margaret Naylor, dau. of James and Margaret, b. 26th of 2nd mo., 1802.

Frances Price, dau. of Israel and Hannah, b. 12th of 9th mo., 1803.

George Matthews, son of William and Elizabeth, b. 3rd of 1st mo., 1803.

Mary Ann Wilson, dau. of John W. and Lucretia, b. 6th of 12th mo., 1803.

James Wharton, son of Silas and Mary, b. 3rd of 1st mo., 1805.

Children of John and Rebecca Sinclair:
    Abraham Sinclair [twin], b. 23rd of 2nd mo., 1802.
    Kezia Sinclair [twin], b. 23rd of 2nd mo., 1802.
    Kezia Sinclair, d. 23rd of 3rd mo., 1802.
    Sarah Sinclair, b. 11th of 1st mo., 1804.

Rachel Ellicott, dau. of John and Mary, b. 6th of 4th mo., 1804.

Sarah E. Tyson, dau. of William and Elizabeth, b. 10th of 9th mo., 1804.

Sarah Plummer, dau. of Eli and Alice, b. 1804. [A later entry indicated that Einah[?] Plummer, dau. of Eli and Alice, b. 25th of 9th mo., 1804].

Sarah Woodnut Byrnes, dau. of Samuel and Hannah, b. 18th of 3rd mo., 1804.

Mary Ann Cope, dau. of Israel and Margaret, b. 11th of 1st mo., 1803.

Children of William and Ann Marsh:
    John Marsh, b. 21st of 1st mo., 1801.
    Margaret Marsh, b. 20th of 8th mo., 1803.

William Marsh, b. 2nd of 10th mo., 1806.

Children of Jasper and Rebecca Cope:
    Charles S. Cope, b. 14th of 10th mo., 1802.
    Abigail Ann Cope, b. 28th of 9th mo., 1804.

Children of Israel and Ann P. Pleasants:
    Samuel Pleasants, b. ---- [blank].
    Thomas Franklin Pleasants, b --- [blank].
    Sarah Pleasants, b. ---- [blank].
    Mary Pleasants, b. ---- [blank].
    Elizabeth Pleasants, b. ---- [blank].
    Ann Pleasants, b. ---- [blank].
    John Pleasants, b. 24th of 9th mo., 1801.
    Walter Franklin Pleasants, b. 11th of 4th mo., 1803.
    Hannah Pleasants, b. 24th of 12th mo., 1804.
    Israel Pemberton Pleasants, b. ---- [blank].
    [This large family received from Philadelphia in 1800 and returned to Philadelphia in 1806].

Children of Elias and Mary Ellicott:
    Thomas Ellicott, b. 11th of 12th mo., 1799.
    Andrew T. Ellicott, b. 12th of 12th mo., 1801.
    James Ellicott, b. 3rd of 1st mo., 1804.
    John Ellicott, b. 18th of 1st mo., 1805.
    Samuel Ellicott, b. 11th of 8th mo., 1806.

Children of Samuel and Elizabeth Canby:
    Joshua Canby, b. 4th of 4th mo., 1801.
    Mary Canby, b. 11th of 7th mo., 1803.
    Thomas Canby, b. 7th of 6th mo., 1806.

Children of George and Elizabeth Ellicott:
    Ann Ellicott [twin], b. 14th of 5th mo., 1801.
    Mary Ellicott [twin], b. 14th of 5th mo., 1801.
    Sarah Ellicott, b. 13th of 11th mo., 1803.
    Sarah Ellicott, d. 31st of 8th mo., 1803.

Children of Samuel and Hannah Smith:
    James Smith, b. 25th of 11th mo., 1801.
    Jane Smith, b. 12th of 2nd mo., 1804.

Joseph H. Wright, son of Allen and Phebe, b. 12th of 8th mo., 1804.

Children of Jonathan and Sarah Ellicott:
    Jonathan Ellicott, b. 20th of 1st mo., 1801.
    Sibella[?] Ellicott, b. 27th of 7th mo., 1803.

Mary Reynolds, dau. of Joshua and Rachel, b. 21st of 8th mo., 1805.

Henrietta Thomas, received by request on 8th of 9th mo., 1803, m. James Ellicott [no date given], and removed to Baltimore Monthly Meeting, Western District [no date given].

Hiram Hague, received from Fairfax Monthly Meeting [Loudoun County, Virginia] on 8th of 9th mo., 1803.

Moses Dillen, Jr., received from Gunpowder Monthly Meeting on 12th of 1st mo., 1804, d. in the West Indies in 1805 [exact date not given].

Mary Houlton and dau. Jamima Houlton, received from Nottingham Monthly Meeting on 10th of 5th mo., 1804; Mary d. 1804 [exact date not given].

Leah Atkinson, received from Mount Holly Monthly Meeting on 12th of 7th mo., 1804, d. 28th of 12th mo., 1808.

Daniel Robertson and wife Elizabeth, received from Deer Creek Monthly Meeting on 14th of 3rd mo., 1805; Daniel d. 1805 [exact date not given].

Eleanor Hare, received from Gunpowder Monthly Meeting on 13th of 6th mo., 1805, m. ---- Cathcart [no first name or date given] and disowned on 14th of 7th mo., 1806.

Israel Price, son of Israel and Hannah, b. 12th of 8th mo., 1805.

Joseph Wright, received from Concord Monthly Meeting [Belmont County], Ohio, on 13th of 3rd mo., 1806, and drowned in the Chesapeake Bay on 16th of 1st mo., 1808.

Betty Fisher, received from Gunpowder Monthly Meeting on 10th of 4th mo., 1806, m. Charles Read on 16th of 3rd mo., 1809.

---- James [first name illegible], child of Joseph and Mary, d. 8th of 4th mo., 1808, interred the 9th.

John C. Powell, son of Joshua and Margaret, b. 12th of 2nd mo., 1804.

Children of John and Parthenia Dukehart:
    John Dukehart, b. ---- [blank].
    William Dukehart, b. ---- [blank].
    Sarah Dukehart, b. 23rd of 3rd mo., 1805.
    Edward Dukehart, b. 25th of 1st mo., 1807.
    Robert Dukehart, b. 8th of 9th mo., 1809.
    Catherine Dukehart, b. 8th of 9th mo., 1811.

Children of William and Ann Waterhouse:
    William Waterhouse, b. 7th of 5th mo., 1803.
    William Waterhouse, d. 22nd of 8th mo., 1804.
    Mary Waterhouse, b. 11th of 10th mo., 1805.

Mary Ann Ellicott, dau. of Jonathan and Sarah, b. 10th of 2nd mo., 1806.

Samuel B. Smith, son of Samuel and Hannah, b. 8th of 3rd mo., 1806.

Children of Joshua and Rachel Atkinson:
    Israel Atkinson, b. 11th of 1st mo., 1801.
    Amos Atkinson, b. 27th of 4th mo., 1806.

Children of Joseph and Miriam Lownes:
    Esther Lownes, b. 12th of 7th mo., 1803.
    Zachariah B. Lownes, b. 12th of 12th mo., 1805.

George Brown Meeter, son of Thomas and Mercey, b. 24th of 8th mo., 1805.

Children of Amos and Elizabeth West:
    Jane West, b. 5th of 3rd mo., 1805.
    Elizabeth West, b. 30th of 7th mo., 1807.

Children of Robert and Aliceana Cornthwait:
    Ann Peck Cornthwait, b. 26th of 7th mo., 1806.
    Mary Cornthwait, b. 12th of 12th mo., 1807.
    Mary Cornthwait, d. 27th of 8th mo., 1809.

Jacob Hayward, son of William and Mary, b. 25th of 4th mo., 1806.

Children of Jacob and Phebe Lafetra:
    Sarah Lafetra, d. 18th of 6th mo., 1805.

Mary Lafetra, b. 9th of 6th mo., 1806.
Sarah Lafetra, b. 1st of 4th mo., 1808.
Thomas H. Lafetra, 21st of 10th mo., 1810.
Lydia Lafetra, b. 28th of 11th mo., 1811.

Sarah Laffattra, dau. of Jacob and Phebe, received from Plainfield Monthly Meeting on 14th of 2nd mo., 1805, d. 18th of 6th mo., 1805.

Lydia Pollard, dau. of Peter and Elizabeth, b. 13th of 12th mo., 1802.

Isaiah Balderston, son of Hugh and Margaret, b. 20th of 8th mo., 1805.

George Fox Brevett, son of Joseph and Casandra, b. 18th of 5th mo., 1806.

Martha Carey, dau. of James and Martha, b. 12th of 5th mo., 1805.

Children of Joseph and Elizabeth Edmondson:
    James Edmondson, b. 8th of 8th mo., 1803.
    Eli Edmondson, b. 5th of 7th mo., 1806.

Children of Isaac and Tace McPherson:
    Martha McPherson, b. 19th of 12th mo., 1802.
    Hannah McPherson, b. 22nd of 4th mo., 1805.

Children of Thomas and Ann Poultney:
    Mary Ann Poultney, b. 6th mo., 1804.
    Sarah Cresson Poultney, b. 6th mo., 1806.

Ann Ellicott, dau. of John and Mary, b. 16th of 10th mo., 1805.

Children of William and Kezia Hayward:
    Hannah Hayward, b. 9th of 3rd mo., 1801.
    George Hayward, b. 18th of 5th mo., 1806.

Children of Joseph and Mary Reese:
    Elizabeth Reese, b. 23rd of 6th mo., 1803.
    Daniel M. Reese, b. 12th of 10th mo., 1805.

Children of John and Rachel Sinclair:
    Abraham Sinclair, b. 23rd of 2nd mo., 1802.
    Sarah Sinclair, b. 11th of 1st mo., 1804.

Children of Isaac and Elizabeth Tyson:
    Deborah Tyson, b. 12th of 4th mo., 1801.
    Mary Tyson, b. 8th of 8th mo., 1803.
    Sarah Tyson, b. 10th of 9th mo., 1804.
    Evan T. Tyson, b. 8th of 10th mo., 1805.
    Jonathan Tyson, b. 4th of 5th mo., 1806.

William Wilson, son of John and Lucretia, b. 9th of 4th mo., 1805.

Children of John and Hannah Harlan:
    Joseph Harlan, b. 3rd of 7th mo., 1804.
    William Harlan, b. 16th of 2nd mo., 1806.

Elizabeth Sinclair, dau. of Robert and Hester, b. 1st of 8th mo., 1805.

Mary Jones, dau. of Samuel G. and Mary, b. 7th of 10th mo., 1806.

Mary Atkinson, d. 14th of 1st mo., 1812.

Gerard Hopkins Sinclair, son of John and Elizabeth, b. 18th of 11th mo., 1806.

Susanna Matthews, dau. of William and Elizabeth, b. 2nd of 6th mo., 1805.

Children of John and Elizabeth Trimble:
    Jane Trimble, b. 25th of 3rd mo., 1807.
    John Trimble, b. 24th of 3rd mo., 1809.

Nathan Chance, formerly of Third Haven Monthly Meeting, d. 1812 [exact date not given] "on the Eastern Shore of Maryland at his father's."

Sarah Procter, a young man, received from Pickering Monthly Meeting, Yorkshire, England, on 12th of 11th mo., 1807, m. Edward Wilson on 15th of 9th mo., 1814, and removed [place not stated] on 10th of 11th mo., 1814.

Rebecca Young, late Hussey, m. Robert Young on 21st of 4th mo., 1808.

Susanna Young, a young woman, m. John Jewett [no date given] and removed with her husband to Deer Creek Monthly Meeting on 11th of 8th mo., 1808.

Thomas C. James, son of Joseph and Mary, b. 6th[?] of 2nd mo., 1807, d. 7th of 5th mo., 1809.

Mary Naylor, dau. of Samuel and Rebecca, b. 10th of 10th mo., 1806.

Children of Isaac and Sarah Brookes:
    Hannah Brookes, b. 1st of 8th mo., 1806.
    Hannah Brookes, d. 18th of 7th mo., 1807.
    Sarah Brookes, b. 26th of 7th mo., 1808.
    Rachel Brookes, b. 20th of 1st mo., 1811.

Margaret Brown, dau. of James and Catherine, b. 6th of 6th mo., 1808.

Children of William and Ann Cornthwait:
    Eiza[?] Ann Cornthwait, b. 13th of 10th mo., 1807.
    Grace Cornthwait, b. 5th of 6th mo., 1809.

Children of Isaac and Elizabeth Kinsey:
    James Kinsey, b. 25th of 2nd mo., 1807.
    James Kinsey, d. 14th of 4th mo., 1808.
    Mary Kinsey, b. 27th of 1st mo., 1809.

Children of Thomas and Sarah Matthews:
    Joseph Matthews, b. 20th of 12th mo., 1804.
    Oliver Matthews, b. 28th of 4th mo., 1807.
    Oliver Matthews, d. 1st of 7th mo., 1809.
    Cassandra Matthews, b. 23rd of 10th mo., 1809.
    Ann H. Matthews, b. 21st of 12th mo., 1811.

Children of Valerius and Ann Dukehart:
    Mary Dukehart, b. 17th of 10th mo., 1808.
    Joseph Dukehart, b. 22nd of 10th mo., 1810.

Warwick Price, son of Warwick and Susanna, b. 27th of 10th mo., 1807, d. 7th of 8th mo., 1808.

Children of Larkin and ---- [blank] Read:
    Charles Read, b. 12th of 11th mo., 1808.
    Benjamin Read, b. 16th of 8th mo., 1811.

Children of Charles and Betty Read:
    Joseph Read, b. 24th of 11th mo., 1809.
    Thomas Read, b. 21st of 1st mo., 1811.

Children of Joseph and Esther Townsend:

Richard Hallett Townsend, b. 4th of 6th mo., 1804.
Julian Wooderson Townsend, b. 1st of 9th mo., 1805.
Julian Wooderson Townsend, d. 2nd of 10th mo., 1806.
Phebe Shotwell Townsend, b. 14th of 3rd mo., 1807.
Hannah Painter Townsend, b. 14th of 10th mo., 1808.
Mary Matthews Townsend, b. 11th of 2nd mo., 1810.
Esther Fox Townsend, b. 21st of 7th mo., 1811.
Esther Fox Townsend, d. 19th of 9th mo., 1812.

Jacob Brown, son of Uriah and Mary Brown, b. 25th of 7th mo., 1807, d. 26th of 10th mo., 1807.

Ruth Fisher, a young woman, received from Pipe Creek Monthly Meeting [Frederick County, Maryland] on 17th of 6th mo., 1809, m. William Shepherd on 20th of 5th mo., 1813, and removed 8th of 9th mo., 1814 [place not stated].

Joshua Medcalf, son of ---- [not stated] and Rebecca Medcalf, d. 26th of 9th mo., 1813.

Joseph W. Miller, received by request on 9th of 14th mo., 1809, d. at Deer Creek on 23rd of 2nd, 181-? [illegible].

Eliza Reed, wife of Samuel, d. 31st of 12th mo., 1814.

Elizabeth Grey, received from Rahway Plainfield Monthly Meeting on 17th of 4th mo., 1811, d. 2nd of 8th mo., 1814.

Children of Joshua and Rachel Mott:
    James Mott, b. 18th of 10th mo., 1809.
    Elizabeth Mott, b. 21st of 3rd mo., 1811.

George Mason, son of John, received from Deer Creek Monthly Meeting on 21st of 2nd mo., 1811, d. 1814 [exact date not given].

Children of Gerard T. and Dorothy Hopkins:
    Elizabeth Hopkins, b. 31st of 3rd mo., 1802.
    Sarah Hopkins, b. 8th of 12th mo., 1805.

Children of Joseph P. and Susanna Plummer:
    John Plummer, b. ---- [no date].
    Mary Plummer, b. ---- [no date].
    Joanna Plummer, b. ---- [no date].

Sarah Cresson Plummer, b. 9th of 12th mo., 1813.

Susanna Plummer, wife of Joseph P., b. 29th of 9th mo., 1783, d. 10th of 7th mo., 1814, about 2 o'clock p.m., aged 30 years, 9 months, and 11 days.

Children of John and Elizabeth Cornthwait:
    Jane Wilson Cornthwait, b. 10th of 12th mo., 1809.
    John Oliver Cornthwait, b. 25th of 2nd mo., 1811.

Joseph S. Atkinson, son of Isaac and Elinor, b. 27th of 6th mo., 1811, d. 12th of 7th mo., 1812.

Elizabeth Reed, dau. of Samuel and Elizabeth, b. 25th of 4th mo., 1812.

Robert Cornthwait, son of William and Ann, b. 8th of 7th mo., 1810.

Children of Abraham P. and Jamima Medcalf (Midkiff):
    Mary Midkiff, b. 6th of 12th mo., 1805.
    David Medcalf, b. 28th of 8th mo., 1808.
    Susanna Medcalf, b. 8th of 9th mo., 1810.
    George Medcalf, b. 5th of 2nd mo., 1812.

Deborah W. Procter, dau. of William and Ann, b. 22nd of 10th mo., 1810.

Augusta Comegys, child of William and Elizabeth, b. 18th of 12th mo., 1811.

Cornelius Vansant, son of Cornelius and Catharine, b. 20th of 12th mo., 1810.

## BALTIMORE MONTHLY MEETING, EASTERN DISTRICT ABSTRACTS FROM WOMEN'S MINUTES, 1813-1819

1813, 14th of 1st mo. - Ann Dawson requested to be received into membership.

1813, 11th of 2nd mo. - Certificate produced for Phebe White joined with her husband [not named] from Little Brittain in Lancaster County, Pennsylvania.

1813, 11th of 3rd mo. - Alisanna Okley requested reinstatement, she having been disowned by Middletown Monthly Meeting, Ohio. Martha Davis cleared for marriage [future husband not named].

1813, 8th of 4th mo. - Sarah Procter approved as a minister by the select quarterly meeting. Rachel Shields has been accepted by the Third Haven Monthly Meeting (Eastern Shore). Certificate requested for Margaret Naylor, a minor to Plymouth Monthly Meeting, Ohio. Ruth Fisher and William Shepherd declared their intentions of marriage, they having consent of parents.

1813, 10th of 6th mo. - Certificate received from Mary Prine from Deer Creek Monthly Meeting, joined with her husband [not named] and their minor children, Malden, Ann, and Peter Amos Prine.

1813, 8th of 7th mo. - Ann Dawson and husband [not named] requested their four minor children, William, Ann, Charlotte, and John, be joined in membership.

1813, 12th of 8th mo. - Elizabeth Hopkins, formerly Prevail, had her marriage accomplished contrary to the rules of our discipline. Certificates received for Rachel Shields from Third Haven Monthly Meeting and Ann Armstrong from New Garden Monthly Meeting [Chester County], Pennsylvania. Margaret Powel requested a certificate for herself and three minor children, Albina, Benjamin Wayne, and John Carpenter Powel, to Concord Monthly Meeting [Delaware County], Pennsylvania.

1813, 9th of 9th mo. - Frances Jones requested reinstatement. Certificate received from Gunpowder Monthly Meeting for William Glover and wife Mary with their six minor children, George Mickle, Sarah, Ann, Thomas, Hannah, and Eliza.

1813, 21st of 10th mo. - Elizabeth Barker produced a certificate from Nantucket Monthly Meeting.

1813, 9th of 12th mo. - Sarah H. John produced a certificate from Concord Monthly Meeting [Delaware County], Pennsylvania.

1814, 13th of 1st mo. - William Glover and wife Mary requested a certificate for themselves and their six minor children, George, Mickle [George Mickle?], Sarah, Ann, Thomas, Hannah, and Eliza, to Hadenfield Monthly Meeting [see above].

1814, 10th of 3rd mo. - Susannah Judge requested a certificate jointly with her husband [not named], and also one for their dau. Rebecca Judge, to Indian Spring Monthly Meeting.

1814, 14th of 4th mo. - Priscilla Cooper and Eliza Cox requested to be received into membership.

1814, 12th of 5th mo. - Susanna Johns, formerly Watts, had her marriage accomplished contrary to the rules of Friends. Certificate received from Nantucket Monthly Meeting, Northern District, for Ephraim Gardener and wife Mary.

1814, 9th of 6th mo. - Mary Dickenson and Anne Pusey made a religious visit from Sadsbury Monthly Meeting. Certificates were requested for Sarah Bond to Gunpowder Monthly Meeting, James Johnson and wife [not named] to Deer Creek Monthly Meeting, and Sarah Dallam to Baltimore Monthly Meeting, Western District.

1814, 14th of 7th mo. - Ann Armstrong requested a certificate to Wilmington Monthly Meeting. Esther Townsend requested to be released from serving as clerk.

1814, 11th of 8th mo. - Certificates were requested for Ruth Shepherd to Pipe Creek Monthly Meeting [Frederick County, Maryland], also Eliza Cox with her husband [not named], and Rachel Mott with her husband [not named] and their minor son Abraham Griffith Mott to Gunpowder Monthly Meeting. Edward Wilson and Sarah Proctor declared their intentions of marriage.

1814, 20th of 10th mo. - Certificate produced for Sarah Johnson (wife of James) and their five children, John, George, James, Howard, and Ann, to Deer Creek Monthly Meeting. Certificates requested for Sarah Wilson to Philadelphia Monthly Meeting, Southern District, and Phebe Judge to Indian Spring Monthly Meeting. Baltimore Preparative Meeting informed that Christian Hance has omitted the attendance of our meetings for some years past, so she will be visited.

1814, 8th of 12th mo. - Certificate produced for Robert Young and Rebecca his wife, with their three children, William, George, and Joseph, from Baltimore Monthly Meeting.

1815, 9th of 2nd mo. - Certificate produced for Mary Burnet and her dau. Jane from Flushing Monthly Meeting, the latter being removed by death prior to the receipt thereof, Mary was accepted.

1815, 13th of 4th mo. - Certificates were requested for Rebecca Medcalf and her minor son Elijah to Baltimore Monthly Meeting, Western District, and for Samuel Reed and his six minor children, Deborah, William, Harriot, John Wilson, Elizabeth, and Samuel D. Reed, to Gunpowder Monthly Meeting.

1815, 11th of 5th mo. - Certificate received from Margaret Powel with her two minor children, Benjamin W. and John C., from Concord Monthly Meeting [Delaware County], Pennsylvania. Certificate requested for Mary Daws to

Gunpowder Monthly Meeting. Elizabeth Cornthwait requested to be released from the station of assistant clerk.

1815, 8th of 6th mo. - Ann Peck appointed assistant clerk. Certificate produced for Albina Powel from Concord Monthly Meeting [Delaware County], Pennsylvania. Ann Niles requested to be received into membership. Ann Matthews requested to be released from the station of overseer.

1815, 13th of 7th mo. - Certificates produced from Gunpowder Monthly Meeting for John Mott, wife Rachel, and their son Abraham Griffith Mott, and also for Owen Branson, wife Hannah, and their four minor children, Eliza E., Benjamin, David, and Mary Ann Branson.

1815, 10th of 8th mo. - Certificate produced for Lydia Barcroft from Gunpowder Monthly Meeting.

1815, 11th of 9th mo. - Phebe Lafetra requested to be released from the station of clerk.

1815, 12th of 10th mo. - Certificates requested for Lydia Pollard, a minor, and also for Sarah Barcroft, to Baltimore Monthly Meeting, Western District.

1815, 9th of 11th mo. - Certificates produced for Elizabeth Hicks and Hannah Pope from Baltimore Monthly Meeting, Western District, and for Tabitha Wilson from Motherkiln Monthly Meeting. Edwin Waters and Sarah Brown declared their intentions of marriage. Baltimore Preparative Meeting informed that Rachel Brown, formerly Reynolds, has removed within their verge and had her marriage accomplished contrary to good order.

1815, 14th of 12th mo. - Elizabeth Amoss appointed assistant clerk.

1816, 11th of 1st mo. - Alisan Okely requested a certificate to Indian Spring Monthly Meeting. Hannah Price, wife of Jarred, requested to be reinstated into membership. Margaret Powel requested a certificate for herself and two minor children, Benjamin W. and John C., to Baltimore Monthly Meeting, Western District. Albina Powel also requested a certificate to that same meeting.

1816, 11th of 4th mo. - Certificate produced for Rachel Weaks from Baltimore Monthly Meeting, Western District. Baltimore Preparative Meeting informed that Sarah Gary, formerly Jewel, has removed out of the verge of this meeting and had her marriage accomplished contrary to the order established amongst us. Sarah Stansbury, formerly Scott, and Mary Sykes, formerly Brown, also had their marriages accomplished contrary to our order as well. George F. Janney and Sarah H. John declared their intentions of marriage. Certificate to be produced for Susanna Harlen to Baltimore Monthly Meeting, Western District.

1816, 9th of 5th mo. - Certificates produced from Baltimore Monthly Meeting, Western District, for Frances Foard and her dau. Alisan, and also for Harriot Foard. Mary Sweat made a religious visit from Haddonfield Monthly Meeting. Baltimore Preparative Meeting requested a certificate for Phebe White and her husband [not named] and their two minor children, John Kinsey White and Elizabeth White, to Little Britain Monthly Meeting. Hannah Price requested her six minor children, Maria, Eliza, Evan, Caroline, Juliann, and Rhoda, be taken into membership. Isaac Hayward and Elizabeth Balderson declared their intentions of marriage, their parents consenting.

1816, 10th of 6th mo. - Certificate produced for Job White and wife and children [not named]. Elizabeth Townsend produced a certificate from New Garden Monthly Meeting in Ohio.

1816, 11th of 7th mo. - Elizabeth Sylvester requested her four minor children, Mary Elizabeth Sylvester, Samuel Bidgood Sylvester, Julianna Martin Sylvester, and Eleanor Susan Sylvester, be taken into membership. John Mott and wife Rachel requested their minor dau. Mary Griffith Mott be taken into membership.

1816, [?] of 8th mo. - Certificate produced for John Underwood, wife Mary, and their minor dau. Amy, from Deer Creek Monthly Meeting.

1816, 12th of 9th mo. - Thomas Amos and Caroline Waters declared their intentions of marriage. Anna Niles requested her four minor children, John Warner Niles, Mary Jane Niles, Robert Duer Niles, and Benjamin Franklin Niles, be taken into membership. Certificates produced for Elizabeth S. Bullock from Chester Monthly Meeting, New Jersey, and for Rebecca Beans from Little Falls Monthly Meeting. Mary Sinners, formerly Pollard, had her marriage accomplished contrary to the order of Friends. Certificate requested for Elizabeth Hayward to Baltimore Monthly Meeting, Western District.

1816, 10th of 10th mo. - Certificate produced from ---- (illegible) for Mary Dallam. Ann Peck appointed to take charge of the records of this meeting in place of Jane Wilson, deceased.

1816, 14th of 11th mo. - Certificate produced for Rebecca Medcalf from Baltimore Monthly Meeting, Western District.

1816, 5th of 12th mo. - Jane Brown requested to be released from the station of overseer. Elizabeth Walker, a beloved friend and minister, made a religious visit from Purchase Monthly Meeting, New York, and was accompanied by Ruth Mealy, a minister and member of Ferrisburg Monthly Meeting, Vermont.

1817, 9th of 1st mo. - Ann Peck appointed clerk, Elizabeth Amoss as assistant clerk, and Elizabeth Townsend as overseer. Sarah Fisher requested to be taken into membership. Sarah Day requested a certificate to Philadelphia Monthly Meeting, Southern District.

1817, 6th of 2nd mo. - Certificate produced for Maria Jones with her husband [not named] and infant dau. Hannah Jones, from Little Falls Monthly Meeting. Elizabeth Roberts, formerly Deavenport, had her marriage accomplished contrary to the good order established amongst us.

1817, 6th of 3rd mo. - Lydia Fisher, now Hussey, has had a child in an unmarried state. Certificates produced for Henry Smith and wife Martha, and Samuel Smith and wife Ann with their three minor children, Eliza Ann Smith, William Brown Smith, and Henry Smith, from Baltimore Monthly Meeting, Western District.

1817, 10th of 4th mo. - Certificate produced for Deborah Jones from Redstone Monthly Meeting [Fayette County], Pennsylvania. Elizabeth Trimble was released from the oversight of the poor and Ann Brown was appointed in her place.

1817, 8th of 5th mo. - Sophia Brooks, late Matthews, has had her marriage accomplished contrary to the good order used among Friends. Lydia Barcroft requested a certificate to Plymouth Monthly Meeting, Ohio, and Rebecca Beans requested one to Little Falls Monthly Meeting.

1817, 5th of 6th mo. - Hannah Price requested a certificate for herself and six minor children, Eliza, Evan, Caroline, Juliann, and Rhoda Price, to Wilmington Monthly Meeting. Certificate requested for Folger Pope, wife Ann, and their three minor children, Franklin F., Joseph D., and Sarah R. Pope, to Baltimore Monthly Meeting, Western District. Dorothy Brown requested to be released from the care of those that require aid and Elizabeth Amoss was appointed in her place.

1817, 10th of 7th mo. - Jane Brown was appointed an elder and was released from the oversight of those that require aid. Jehosheba Brown was appointed in her place. Certificate produced for Susan Yarnall from Tredhaven Monthly Meeting. Lydia Husband requested a certificate to Nine Partners Monthly Meeting [New York State]. Mary Hughes produced a certificate joined with her husband [not named] and two minor children, Elizabeth M. Hughes and Esther Hughes, from Concord Monthly Meeting [Delaware County, Pennsylvania].

1817, 7th of 8th mo. - Certificate received for Sarah Lukens from Baltimore Monthly Meeting, Western District.

1817, 4th of 9th mo. - Sophia Brooks condemned her outgoing in marriage. Elizabeth Kirk, late Brown, has had her marriage accomplished contrary to the rules of Friends. Samuel Regester and Elizabeth Amoss declared their intentions of marriage. Joseph P. Plummer requested a certificate for his minor children, John Thomas Plummer, Mary Mifflin Plummer, and Johanna Plummer, to Nine Partners Monthly Meeting [New York State], as did Abraham P. Medcalf for his minor children, Mary, David, and Susanna Medcalf, to the same meeting. Margaret Dukehart requested to be released from the oversight of those that require aid and Phebe Lafetra was appointed in her place.

1817, 9th of 10th mo. - Robert H. Norris and Mary Morgan declared their intentions of marriage, with parents consenting. Certificates requested by Hannah Pope to Alexandria Monthly Meeting, and John Underwood for himself, wife Mary, and their two minor children, Amy and Barcley, to White Water Monthly Meeting, Indiana. The committee in Sarah Garey's case report that they went to Pittsburgh in order to pay her a visit and received information from the minutes of Redstone Monthly Meeting [Fayette County, Pennsylvania] that she had removed to Nashville, Tennessee.

1817, 6th of 11th mo. - Elizabeth Kirk has expressed a desire to condemn her outgoing in marriage. Rachel M. Mott appointed clerk and Ann Proctor assistant clerk. Isaac and Sarah Brook requested a certificate for their minor dau. Alice Brook to Nine Partners Monthly Meeting [New York State], and William Trimble requested one for his minor granddau. Hannah Trimble to the same meeting.

1817, 4th of 12th mo. - Elizabeth Kirk signed an offering in writing to Friends, stating "For want of attending to right direction I have had my marriage accomplished contrary to the good order established amongst Friends, for which I can in sincerity say I am sorry." Hannah Green requested to be reinstated into membership.

1818, 5th of 2nd mo. - Jehosheba Brown requested her granddau. Lydia Wells Kirk be received into membership. Sarah Lukens requested a certificate to Baltimore Monthly Meeting, Western District. William Williams attended on a religious visit from White Water Monthly Meeting. Certificate received for Jane Nock, a minor, from Duck Creek Monthly Meeting [Kent County, Delaware].

1818, 5th of 3rd mo. - Mary Ann Hopkins, late Gover, has had her marriage accomplished contrary to the good order of our society. Mary Norris and Ann Coal requested certificates to Baltimore Monthly Meeting, Western District.

1818, 4th of 6th mo. - Certificate requested for Thomas Amos and wife Caroline to Warnock Monthly Meeting, Virginia. Certificate received from Baltimore Monthly Meeting, Western District, for Margaret Powell.

1818, 9th of 7th mo. - Certificates received for Susanna Jones from Deer Creek Monthly Meeting and for Albina Kirk from Baltimore Monthly Meeting, Western District. Samuel and Elizabeth Regester requested their minor children, Mary Ann and Eliza Jane, be taken into membership. Mary Jones requested a certificate to Radnor Monthly Meeting, Pennsylvania.

1818, 6th of 8th mo. - Certificate requested for John Morgan and wife Priscilla to Baltimore Monthly Meeting, Western District.

1818, 10th of 9th mo. - Elizabeth Taylor produced a certificate from New Garden Monthly Meeting [Chester County, Pennsylvania] and Sarah Jenny produced one from Deer Creek Monthly Meeting.

1818, 8th of 10th mo. - Alisanna Southcombe, late Ford, had her marriage accomplished contrary to the order of our society. Certificate produced for Sarah Parker from New York Monthly Meeting and endorsed by Baltimore Monthly Meeting, Western District. Certificate produced for A.J.[?] Hall[?] from Wilmington Monthly Meeting who has removed within the limits of Baltimore Monthly Meeting, Western District. Certificate received for Rebecca C. Hopkins from Baltimore Monthly Meeting, Western District. John H. Hewes and wife Mary requested a certificate for themselves and their two minor children Elizabeth M. and Esther Hewes, to Baltimore Monthly Meeting, Western District; also one for William and Jane Knock, minors, to the same meeting. William Rickman attended this meeting on a religious visit from Rochester Monthly Meeting in Kent, England.

1818, 9th of 12th mo. - Mary Waters, late Brown, has had her marriage accomplished contrary to the order of Friends.

1819, 7th of 1st mo. - Certificate requested for Elizabeth Kirk to Indian Spring Monthly Meeting. Certificate received for Elizabeth Howell and her seven minor children, Phebe P., Adelia Ann, John A., George, Zopher[?] C., Charles, and William Howell, from Coeyman[?] Monthly Meeting. Amos Bullock requested a certificate for himself, wife Elizabeth S., and their minor son Charles Peck Bullock, for Baltimore Monthly Meeting, Western District.

1819, 4th of 3rd mo. - Sarah Parker requested a certificate to Baltimore Monthly Meeting, Western District. Grace Reed requested to be taken into membership. Mary Jones requested to be released from the station of overseer.

1819, 8th of 4th mo. - Mary Jones offered a signed statement condemning her outgoing in marriage with the assistance of a hireling teacher.

1819, 6th of 5th mo. - Ann Ferris attended this meeting with a minute from Wilmington Monthly Meeting. Sarah Escavill, formerly Pollard, has had her marriage accomplished contrary to the rules of our society. Certificate was produced for Susanna Allen from Deer Creek Monthly Meeting.

1819, 10th of 6th mo. - Certificate received from Indian Spring Monthly Meeting for Elizabeth Evens joined with her husband [not named] and five minor children, Sarah Andrews Evens, Mary Mifflin Evens, Anna Evens, Susanna Evens, and John Evens.

1819, 8th of 7th mo. - Mercy Brown attended this meeting with a minute from Little Britain Monthly Meeting [Lancaster County, Pennsylvania].

# INDEX

## A

ABBOTT: Susan A., 187
ADSON: Sarah, 170
ADY: Margary, 133, 136; Margert, 110
AISQUITH: Sally L., 199
AITKEN: Maria, 172
ALAN: Sarah, 24
ALBERT: Elizabeth, 119, 121
ALDRICH: Dutro B., 235; William L., 236
ALEXANDER: Catharine, 188; Lawson, 170
ALLAN: Rebeca, 103; Robert, 103
ALLEN: Enoch R., 201; Grace, 201; Mary, 185; Mary G., 211; Paul, 188, 191; Rachel T., 136; Sarah, 24, 120, 123, 221; Sarah T., 136; Susan, 100; Susanna, 126, 129, 131, 136, 140, 149, 235, 274; Susanna Jane, 136; Susannah, 107, 111, 226
ALLEY: Amos, 243; Micajah, 238
ALLIN: James, 103; Susanna, 103
ALLISON: Mary, 38
ALLY: Micajah, 239
AMBLER: Jonathan, 68; Rachel, 68
AMOS: Caroline, 273; Elias Ellicott, 78; Elizabeth, 14, 35, 36, 74, 75, 82; Hannah, 19, 58; James, 58; Martha, 16; Mary, 45, 172; Oliver H., 194; Oliver Huff, 58; Rachel, 135; Susanna, 74; Susannah, 206; Thomas, 30, 201, 270, 273; William, 3, 32, 47, 74, 75
AMOSS: Abigail, 66, 68; Abigail I., 76; Benjamin, 254; Beulah E., 68; Caroline, 250; Elias E., 66; Elias Ellicott, 85; Elizabeth, 75, 76, 208, 210, 211, 254, 269, 271, 272; Esther, 66; Garrett, 66, 68; Hannah, 8, 76; James, 8, 76, 85; Lemuel H., 83; Martha, 76, 208, 210; Martha H., 211; Oliver Hough, 8; Sarah, 67; Susan, 73; Susanna, 75, 76, 77, 89, 208, 209, 210, 211; Thomas, 210, 250; William, 75, 76, 77, 82, 210; William H., 77, 82, 83, 192, 211; William Lee, 8, 63, 66, 73, 74, 75, 76, 89
ANDERSON: Harriet M., 186, 187
ARCHER: H. L., 105; Hannah L., 105; John, 102
ARMSTRONG, 208; Ann, 245, 247, 267, 268; Ellen W., 209; Henry, 156, 207; James, 207; James C., 207, 256; John, 245; Peggy, 207
ASHTON: Kesiah, 74
ASKEW: Campbell S., 203
ATKINS: Elizabeth, 142; Jonathan, 141, 142, 151, 152; Joseph, 142; Mary, 142, 152; William, 102
ATKINSON: Aaron, 184; Abbigal, 169; Abigail, 141, 175, 176, 178, 184, 197, 198, 200, 210; Amos, 261; David, 74; Elinor, 266; Esther, 67; Hannah, 233; Isaac, 33, 169, 198, 200, 209, 266; Israel, 67, 261; J., 255; Joseph, 169, 197, 200, 216; Joseph S., 266; Joshua, 261; Leah, 260; Mahlon, 9, 229; Mary, 263; Rachel, 169, 197, 200, 261; Ruth, 169; Sarah, 88, 169, 197, 200, 240
ATKISON: Eleanor, 206, 207, 208, 209, 210; Elleanor, 211; Isaac, 209; Rachel, 207; Rith B., 208;

W. G., 209; William G., 210
ATTERBURY: W. B., 178

B

BAGLEY: Ann H., 104; John O., 106; Mary, 106; Racheal, 106; Susan, 101; Susannah O., 102
BAILEY: Eliza Ann, 156; Elizabeth, 171, 200; Emmor, 200; Joseph, 175; Margaret, 171, 176; Susannah, 156; Vincent, 156
BAILY: Abraham, 175, 176, 227; Ann, 227; Bernard, 157; Elizabeth, 175, 176, 177, 178, 179, 227; Emmor, 175, 177, 227; Ezra, 176, 189, 227; George, 178, 179; Hannah, 227, 232; Hannah J., 178, 181, 182; Henry, 176, 227; Isaac, 157; Jacob, 227; James, 178, 232; Jas., 182; Jeremiah, 157; Joseph, 178; Joseph Clemson, 157; Louisa, 157; Lydia, 157; Margaret, 227; Martha, 227; Mary, 227; Matilda, 157; Phebe, 227; Samuel, 178, 179, 183, 232; Samuel Painter, 157; Samuel T., 232; Susanna, 157; Vincent, 157
BAKER: Ann, 34, 188, 199; Anthony, 75; Frances, 188; Frances P., 188; George, 200; George S., 201, 203; John, 171, 184; Thomas B., 201
BALDERSON, 208; Elizabeth, 270; Isaiah, 154, 218; Jacob, 96, 98, 99, 103, 104, 105, 106, 154; Mary, 96, 98
BALDERSTON: Ann, 256; Eli, 256; Eliza Ann, 183; Elizabeth, 205, 207, 208, 209; Elizabeth Y., 183; Ely, 38, 161, 195, 198,
203, 205, 207, 208, 209, 256; Esther, 195, 198, 205, 209, 210, 256; Hugh, 156, 171, 172, 174, 176, 182, 185, 186, 187, 188, 190, 191, 193, 194, 195, 196, 198, 204, 208, 210, 257, 262; Isaiah, 156, 180, 190, 192, 195, 256, 262; Jacob, 96, 97, 100, 101, 102, 104, 106, 153, 156; John P., 190; John Peck, 156; Jonathan, 173, 195, 198, 199; Josiah, 210; Marcelious, 207; Marcellius, 256; Margaret, 156, 172, 174, 178, 182, 186, 187, 190, 192, 196, 198, 199, 201, 205, 210, 257, 262; Marry, 100; Martha, 180, 184, 188, 194, 195, 198, 200, 203, 204, 205, 207, 208, 209, 210, 211; Martha Ann, 156; Mary, 96, 97, 99, 101, 106; Samuel Fothergill, 256; William, 256; William Handy, 156; Wilson, 190, 257
BALDSANTON: Jacob, 99
BALDSTON: Jacob, 97
BALDWIN: Charles E., 176, 177; Chester, 193
BALL: Eliza, 203; Elizabeth, 204; Mary, 203, 204; Rebecca, 199
BANEKER: Maria, 202
BARACRAFT: Sarah, 16
BARCLY: Eliza R., 76
BARCROFT: Lydia, 269, 271; Sarah, 16, 18, 248, 269
BARECROFT: Lydia, 249
BARKER: Abraham, 169, 223; Elizabeth, 267; Mary, 170; Priscilla, 223; Robert, 169; Sarah, 169, 238, 251
BARKLEY: Mary, 115
BARKLY: Mary, 115
BARLETT: Mary, 183, 185, 193
BARNES: Juliann C., 210; Sarah

L., 210
BARNEY: Joshua, 207
BARTLET: Rhoda M., 34, 35, 42
BARTLETT: Hannah, 179; James M., 157; Joseph, 14, 33, 48; Mary, 157; Mary J., 180, 181, 185, 186; Rebecca, 157, 179, 186; Rhoda M., 14, 44, 47, 48; Richard, 179; William E., 157, 178, 179, 181, 184, 186
BARTON: Eliza, 96; Elizabeth, 98, 99, 117, 120; Phillip A., 96, 98; Thomas, 74
BASSETT: Isaac, 198; Margareta, 206
BATERS: Amas, 104
BAYFIELD: Massey, 119; Mercy, 117
BAYNARD: J., 203
BEANS: Charles, 59, 80, 86, 91; Edward, 68; Elias H., 68; Hannah, 59, 76, 80, 86, 91; Isaac, 59, 74, 76, 80, 86, 91; Margaret L., 68; Mary, 59, 80, 86, 91; Rebecca, 44, 74, 77, 79, 83, 85, 88, 177, 182, 209, 249, 270, 271; Sarah, 59, 80, 86, 91; Thomas, 91; Thomas, 80; William T., 80, 86, 91; William Trego, 59; Wilson, 59, 80, 86, 91
BEARD: Harriet, 206
BEAVENS: John, Jr., 214
BECKETT: Priscilla, 183
BELLACH: Ann, 175
BELT: Aquilla, 21; Carlton, 21
BENNET: Hannah, 119; Jessey, 119; Joseph, 118; Joshua, 118, 119; Mary, 119; Sarah, 119
BENNETT: Hannah, 97; Joseph, 97, 98, 99, 104
BENSON: Abraham, 54; Amos, 9, 11, 21, 24, 25, 35, 58, 67, 73, 74; Amos S., 68; Amy, 58, 68; Bengamine, 19; Benjamin, 1, 11, 19, 20, 21, 42, 74, 91, 93; Elihu, 9, 58, 67; Elijah, 53; Elizabeth, 11; Emily, 66; Hannah, 1, 9, 19, 20, 22, 23, 58, 67, 74; Harriet, 202; James, 11, 30, 31; Jesse, 20, 65, 66; John, 11; Joshua Price, 93; Josiah, 30; Julia, 66; Levi, 9, 19, 26, 27, 40, 58, 66, 73, 74, 75, 76, 82, 87; Levin, 76; Levy, 26, 75; Lydia, 58; Margaret, 9, 58, 67, 76; Margarett, 74; Mary, 9, 58, 65, 74; Mary Ann, 9; Maryann, 58; Mordecai, 11; Pamala, 58; Rachel, 9, 52, 58, 66, 67, 73, 75, 77; Reuben, 51; Sarah, 58, 74; Sarah Ann, 11; Susanna, 73; Susanna J., 58; Susanna S. P., 9; Susannah J., 67; Temperance, 73, 74, 76, 91, 93; William, 11
BERNARD: Sophia, 205
BETTERTON: Rachel M., 190, 191
BETTS: Benjamin, 214; Mary, 180; Sarah M. A., 180
BEVANS: John, 214
BIDGOOD: Elizabeth, 171, 187, 209, 210
BINMS: Abraham, 216
BIRDSALL: Andrew M., 182; Eliza, 182; John, 182; Rachel, 182; Whitson, 182; Whitsone, 182; William, 182
BIRDSHALL: Hannah, 182
BLACK: J., 169
BLACKISTON: Ann, 31
BLACKSON: Ann, 44
BLACKSTONE: Ann, 32
BLACKWELL: Elizabeth S., 68
BLAIN: Samuel, 216
BLAKEY: Lydia W., 68; Thomas,

68
BLANCHARD: Eleanor, 56; Elenor, 57
BLAND: Thomas, Jr., 245
BLASS: Martha, 28
BLASSON: Martha, 28
BLUDWICK: John, 216
BOLTON: James, 216
BOND: Benjamin, 95, 98, 99, 102, 113, 120, 122, 155; Benjamin B., 100; Benjamin R., 77; Ele, 143; Eli, 95, 98, 113; Eliza, 181; Elizabeth, 115; Ely, 99, 100, 103, 143, 152, 155; H. M., 181; Hannah, 95, 99; Joshua B., 77; Kiturah, 45, 46; Martha, 98, 99, 114; Mary, 97, 98, 99, 100, 102, 103, 104, 120, 122; Mary Ann, 76; Meriken, 28; Merriken, 17; R., 179; Robert, 232; Ruth, 97, 98, 99, 122; Sarah, 40, 45, 247, 268; Silas, 95, 98, 99, 113, 122, 128, 146; Susan, 205; Thomas T., 76, 77
BONDFIELD: Cassander, 204
BONSAL: Eleanor, 224; Isaac, 223; Mary, 224; Stephen, 228
BONSALL: Catherine, 222; Sarah, 222, 255; Thomas, 222, 255; Vincent, 222, 255; William, 222
BOSLEY: Caleb, 51; Sophronia E., 187
BOULTON: Sarah, 223
BOWDLER: Justinian, 189
BOWEN: Eleanor, 205; Ellen, 203; Mary, 191
BOWLEY: Frances R., 170
BOWMAN: Isaac, 216
BOWMANS: Jane, 232
BOYCE: Thomas, 219
BOYD: Eleanor, 183; John, 104; John C., 76; Mary, 196, 218; Stephen, 103

BRACKEN: Caleb, 14, 25; Elisha, 25; Rachel, 25; Rebeccah, 25; Sarah, 25; Solomon, 25
BRACKIN: Caleb, 19
BRADFORD: Dolly, 101; Hannah, 96; Hannah R., 97, 98; Margaret Hill, 123, 132, 226
BRADIE: Hannah, 16
BRADY: Hannah, 16, 26
BRAIDY: Hannah, 16
BRAMAN: Elizabeth, 104
BRANNAN: Alisan, 104
BRANSON: Aaron, 36; Ann, 20, 33; Aron, 20; Bejamin, 46; Benjamin, 9, 234, 269; David, 9, 20, 46, 234, 269; Eliza E., 9, 46, 74, 234, 269; Elizabeth, 20; Elziabeth, 33, 37; Hannah, 9, 46, 234, 269; Hannah S., 234; James, 20, 33; Joseph, 187; Joshua, 20, 35; Levi, 14; Mary, 14, 234; Mary Ann, 14, 46, 269; Owen, 9, 20, 22, 23, 46, 234, 269; Priscilla, 33; Prisella, 20; Prissilla, 20; Susanna, 234
BRANTINGHAM: George, 218, 223; Hannah, 223; Joseph, 223; Phebe, 223
BRAYDEN: Isaac, 236
BRAYTON: Isaac, 243; William, 243
BRENTON: Edward, 76; Susan, 75; Susanna, 76
BRETT: John W., 105
BREUETT: Cassandra W., 103; Joseph, 103
BREVETT: Casandra, 262; Cassandra, 156, 223; Cassandra A., 156; Edwin Woodland, 223; Elizabeth Boraston, 156; Ellen Isolobo, 156; George Fox, 223, 262; James M., 156; John Webster, 223; Joseph, 156, 159,

223, 234, 262; Joseph Plummer, 156; Mary M., 105
BREVIT: Cassandra W., 198
BREVITT: Cassandra A., 184; John W., 207; Joseph, 192, 198
BRIEDENBOUH: Maria R., 183
BRIGGS: Isaac, 176
BRINDLE: Nathaniel, 130
BRINDLEY: Nathaniel, 148
BRINDLY: Nathaniel, 139
BRINTON: Edward, 28, 40, 80, 90; John, 28, 30, 31, 32; Lydia, 135; Mary, 133; Priscilla, 33; Susanna, 80, 88, 90, 110, 136; Thomas Ellwood, 80; Thomas Elwood, 90; William, 104
BRISTOR: Hannah, 103
BROMWELL: Deborah, 240; Henry, 202, 204; Joseph, 240; William, Jr., 97
BROOK: Alice, 272; Edward, 128; Isaac, 272; John Thomas, 181; Sarah, 272
BROOKE: Eliza P., 205; John Thomas, 172, 179; Roger, 38
BROOKES: Edward, 132; Hannah, 264; Isaac, 204, 205, 264; Racheal, 103; Rachel, 264; Sarah, 264; Thomas, 103, 171
BROOKS: Alice, 184, 188, 257; Ann, 157; Edward, 132; Elizabeth, 156; Hannah, 157; Isaac, 184, 201, 202, 204, 207, 256, 257; John, 184; Joseph, 256; Martha, 122, 125; Mary, 171; Rachel, 123, 130, 131, 184, 185; Samuel, 104, 157; Sarah, 184, 256, 257; Sarah, Jr., 184; Sophia, 156, 157, 271, 272; Thomas, 171; William, 156, 157
BROUD: Lurana, 183
BROWN: Achsah, 44, 58, 77, 83, 131; Amos, 97, 198, 199, 201, 202; Amy, 21, 73, 101; Ann, 195, 197, 271; Ann B., 157, 184, 187, 192, 206, 209, 210; Betty Way, 41, 47; Beulah, 202, 254; Bulah, 200, 207; Cassandra, 199, 253; Catharine, 185, 199, 203, 204, 257; Catharine, Jr., 185; Catherine, 264; David, 42, 157, 179, 185, 187, 192, 194, 195, 196, 198, 199, 200, 201, 202, 203, 204, 205, 206, 208, 209, 210, 218, 251; David U., 185, 187, 190; David W., 106; Diana, 187; Dorothy, 218; Dorothy, 198, 199, 200, 201, 202, 203, 204, 205, 207, 210, 254, 271; Elihu, 6, 20, 26, 27, 28, 35, 67, 101; Elisha, Jr., 96; Eliza, 178, 198, 201; Elizabeth, 2, 42, 46, 157, 195, 197, 198, 199, 200, 202, 208, 251, 272; Ezra, 18; Fanny, 195; Frances, 185, 195, 198, 199, 201, 210; Francess, 207, 208; Freeborn, 96; George, 204, 251, 261; Hannah, 18, 20, 22, 95, 96, 153, 192, 216, 219; Isaac, 198, 199; Isaiah, 96; Jacob, 265; James, 195, 196, 198, 199, 202, 203, 204, 205, 251, 253, 257, 264; Jane, 184, 185, 188, 192, 198, 199, 201, 207, 208, 210, 271; Jehosheba, 25, 26, 31, 192, 271, 272; Jeremiah, 146, 192; Jesse, 251, 254; Joel, 20, 28, 91, 101, 186, 207, 237; John, 33, 47, 99, 190, 191, 202, 203, 204, 205, 251, 253; John M., 198, 199, 201, 202; Joseph, 195, 198, 201, 207, 234; Joshua, 20, 96, 192; Josiah, 26, 30, 31, 254; Latitia, 200; Lydia, 20, 96, 101; Margaret,

20, 21, 25, 67, 101, 106, 184, 190, 191, 192, 193, 264; Margaret H., 199; Mary, 96, 176, 184, 187, 192, 194, 195, 196, 198, 199, 203, 204, 205, 207, 208, 210, 242, 251, 253, 265, 269, 273; Mary D., 157, 185, 192; Mercy, 274; Mielmer Harrison, 2; Rachel, 20, 269; Rebecca, 157; Ruth, 178; Samuel, 198; Sarah, 95, 106, 114, 178, 187, 198, 199, 200, 201, 202, 203, 204, 205, 207, 208, 211, 214, 240, 269; Sarah D., 199; Sarah W., 207, 208; Stephen, 20, 58, 77, 83, 101, 131, 135, 150; Thomas, 2, 41, 47, 96, 101, 213; Uria, 187, 192; Uriah, 265; William, 58, 67, 77, 83, 96, 97, 135, 174, 175, 176, 185, 187, 192, 194, 195, 197, 198, 199, 200, 201, 202, 205, 207, 208, 210, 211, 251, 271; William Truth, 157
BROWNE: Josh., 182
BRROKE: Thomas, 228
BRUCE: John, 115, 116; Robert, 123
BRUETT: John, 214
BRUFF: Joseph, 171, 173
BRUNNON: Anna, 141
BUCHANAN: Charles A., 209; Elizabeth, 206; Hepzebah, 209; Susan B., 209
BUCKMAN: Abner, 178; C., 178; David, 169; Esther, 171; Grace, 169, 178; Letitia, 255; Oliver, 223; Peter, 169; Phineas, 169, 177, 178; Phinehas, 176; Rachel, 178; Ruth, 169; Samuel, 178; Susanna, 177; Tacy, 177, 240
BULL: Elener, 17; Elinor, 17; Elisha, 231; Priscilla, 171;

Rachel, 26; William L., 186
BULLOCK: Amos, 232, 251, 273; Charles Leck, 251; Charles Peck, 232, 274; Elizabeth, 251; Elizabeth S., 232, 270, 274
BUNTING: Jacob T., 179, 209
BURGES: Ann, 106, 127, 245; John, 106, 127, 245; Joseph, 106, 127, 245; Tacey, 189, 192; Tacy, 210, 211; Tasey, 209; Yory, 102
BURGESS: Jonathan, 122; Joseph, 120; Tacey, 187, 209; Tacy, 187, 203, 204, 205, 208
BURN: William, 199
BURNET: Jane, 202, 268; Mary, 268
BURNETT: Joseph, 102
BUSH: Hester, 74; Jane, 74
BUTLER: Susan, 203; Thomas, 171
BYRNES: Betsey, 253; Caleb, 187; Daniel, 223; E. G., 188; Eleanor, 223; Elizabeth, 185; Hannah, 171, 205, 253, 258; Jonathan, 223; Rachel, 223; Ruthy, 171, 172, 174, 178, 179, 181, 182, 183, 186; Samuel, 171, 178, 186, 204, 253, 258; Sarah, 186, 188; Sarah E., 179; Sarah W., 209; Sarah Woodnut, 258; Woodnut, 188, 190; Woodnutt, 188
BYRNS: Hannah, 204

C

C----: Mary E., 187
CAAM: William, 103
CADUE: Eliza, 205; John, 205
CADWALADER: Reese, 201
CADWALLADER: Hannah D., 32; Reese, 31
CALDER: Jane Eliza, 208

CALDWELL: A. M., 209; Ann M., 209; Mary, 45
CALWELL: Caroline S., 76; Mary, 76, 77
CANBY: Beulah, 189, 213, 228; Bulah, 239; Charles, 177, 179, 189; Elizabeth, 189, 200, 228, 239, 259; Esther E., 193; Joseph, 228, 239; Joshua, 228, 259; Joshua W., 189; Mary, 174, 182, 189, 228, 239, 259; Sally, 191; Samuel, 171, 173, 174, 175, 182, 189, 197, 200, 228, 239, 259; Thomas, 228, 239, 259; Thomas Y., 189; William, 239; Yardley, 239
CAR: Sarah, 117, 118
CAREY: Ann J., 157; George, 173, 181, 185, 186, 193; George E., 201; H. E., 180, 181, 183, 185; Hannah, 170, 171, 172, 173, 174, 177, 179, 180, 201, 207; Hannah E., 175, 176, 177, 178, 179, 181, 182, 183, 185, 188; James, 157, 170, 173, 180, 188, 195, 262; John E., 157, 175, 176; John Ellicott, 202; Margaret, 170, 172, 173, 174, 175, 176, 177, 178, 179, 180, 181, 188, 189, 191, 193, 194, 206, 207; Margarett, 181, 182; Martha, 170, 171, 172, 173, 176, 180, 183, 185, 188, 189, 191, 193, 194, 196, 202, 262; Richea, 170; Samuel, 171, 172, 178, 179, 186, 188, 193, 197, 201
CARN: Cassandra, 103
CARPENTAR: Powell, 92
CARPENTER: Mary, 80, 85, 90; Phebe, 231; Powel, 81, 89
CARR: Phebe, 253
CARROL: Rachel, 48, 49
CARROLL: Elizabeth, 140; Mary Ann, 187; Rachel, 78, 85, 86
CARTEr: Joel, 140
CARTER: Abigail Ann, 59, 68; Amor, 77; Edith, 59, 77, 89, 140, 148; Edwth, 112; Ellis, 59; Enos, 89, 112, 140, 148; Enos P., 59; Hannah, 59, 89, 91, 112, 122, 149; Henry, 121; Isabel, 59, 122; Isabella, 138, 146; James, 59, 89, 112, 140, 148; Joel, 59, 76, 89, 90, 112, 122, 140, 148; John, 59, 77, 89, 96, 112, 121, 122, 140, 148; Leven, 112; Levi, 59, 68, 89, 140, 148; Margaret, 59, 89, 112, 122, 140, 148; Margaret A., 59; Mercy, 59; Rebecca, 121; Rebekah, 97; Richard, 212; Samuel, 59, 76, 77, 89, 97, 112, 114, 122, 140, 148; Sarah, 59, 76, 88, 90, 91, 112, 122
CARY: Margaret, 183; Samuel, 173
CASSY: Richard, 176
CATHCART
CATTS: Jane, 200; Samuel, 200; Sarah, 200
CAULK: Eliza, 101; Elizabeth, 104, 149, 150; Isaac, 104, 150; Oliver, 104, 141, 150, 151; Rachel, 143, 154
CAVENDER: Abram Widner, 140, 149; Leah, 140, 149; Margaret, 140, 149; Mary, 140, 149; Rachel, 133, 140, 149; William, 133, 140, 145, 149, 153
CHALK: Rachel, 113
CHAMBERLAIN: Emma, 174, 177; Hoopes, 184; Matilda, 174, 177, 183
CHANCE: Nathan, 263
CHANDLEE: Ann, 184, 199; Ann

E., 187; Benjamin, 158, 199; Goldsmith, 199; Hannah, 187; Harriet, 187; Mahlon, 177; Mary Elizabeth, 158; Sarah S., 187
CHANDLEY: Ann, 106; Elizabeth, 220
CHANEL: Sarah, 100
CHANNAL: Abel, 100; Isaac, 100; John, 100; Sarah, 100
CHANNALL: John, 99
CHANNEL: Abel, 130, 131; Able, 121; Isaac, 121; John, 103, 121, 152; Sarah, 121
CHANNELL: Isaac, 136; John, 102
CHASE: Rebecca, 212
CHESTON: Francina A., 180
CHEW: Cassandra M., 102, 104; Hannah, 131; William M., 99
CHEYNEY: Ann, 187; Esther, 76, 187; Jesse, 187; Rachel, 187
CHILCOAT: Matilda, 47, 48
CHURCHMAN: Ann, 35, 100; Anna, 29, 39; Anne, 43, 174; Caleb, 177; Edward, 29, 31, 32, 38, 41, 77, 82, 177, 237; Eliza, 179, 186, 237; Emily, 237; Hannah, 29, 174; Hannah J., 174; Hannah James, 77, 82, 177; M., 105; Margaret, 29, 77, 82; Mary, 29, 77, 82; Micajah, 29, 100, 174, 177, 186, 237; Owen, 177; Rebecca, 29, 77, 82, 177; Robert, 29, 77, 82; Sinclair, 237; William H., 237
CLAIBORNE: Mary Ann, 66
CLAP: Benjamin, 190; Elizabeth, 230; Enoch, 76, 172, 173, 177, 192, 193, 230; Mary, 177, 178, 193, 230; Rebecca, 230
CLAPHAM: A. C., 180
CLAPP: Amasa, 189; Enoch, 189; Mary, 189
CLARK: Amy, 49; Deborah, 49; Elizabeth, 45, 132, 242; Israel, 49; James, 184, 192, 235; Mary, 45; Mary S., 199; Phebe, 50, 111; Rachel, 48; Ruth, 49
CLAY: John C., 172
CLEMSON: Esther, 227; Joseph, 157, 227
CLERCK: Amy, 43; Deborah, 43; Elizabeth, 43; Israel, 43; Mary, 43, 45; Phebe, 43; Rachel, 43; Ruth, 43
CLEVELAND: A. B., 105, 188
CLOWDSLEY: Jane, 185; Margaret C., 185
COAL: Ann, 273; Anna, 141; Elizabeth, 98; Lydia, 98; Samuel, 98, 99; Skipwith, 104
COALE: Ann, 98, 108, 114, 118, 122, 124, 129, 182, 192, 212, 229, 250; Eliza, 99, 100, 102; Eliza Chase, 104; Elizabeth, 97, 98, 101, 102, 103, 105, 106, 107, 117, 127, 133, 150, 151, 152; Ellis P., 94, 111, 137; Ellis Pusey, 145; George Mathews, 108, 129; Hannah, 100, 102, 135; Hannah E., 105, 189, 191, 193, 194; Isaac, 96, 97, 98, 100, 101, 102, 103, 105, 113, 119, 122, 133, 146, 155, 188; Isaac, Jr., 102; J. W., 101; James, 96, 98, 101, 102, 103, 105, 106, 147, 152, 153, 154; John W., 103, 106; Joseph, 98, 100, 103; Joseph H., 99, 102, 103, 105, 133; Joshua, 94; L. H., 105; Lewis, 100, 109, 110, 133, 134, 135; Lidia, 96, 99, 101; Lydia, 94, 96, 97, 98, 100, 101, 102, 103, 104, 106, 122, 128, 200; Lydia F., 103, 104, 105, 106; Margaret, 98, 100, 128; Margaret Elgan, 129; Margaret

Elgare, 108; Margrett, 99; Mary, 96, 97, 98, 100, 103, 122, 152, 200; Mary B., 106; Mary C., 103, 105, 141, 152, 188; Mary D., 102, 104, 133; Mrs. C., 101; Philip, 107, 117, 127, 137, 182, 192, 219; Rachael, 105; Racheal, 102; Rachel, 97, 101, 102, 152, 188; Rd., 100; Richard, 96, 101, 129, 130; Sally W., 98, 99; Samuel, 94, 96, 97, 98, 99, 100, 101, 102, 103, 104, 105, 106, 108, 121, 122, 128, 131, 145, 146, 200; Sarah, 98, 100, 101, 102, 103, 104, 106, 125; Sarah Smith, 108, 129; Scipwith, 103; Skipwith, 96, 98, 100, 108, 110, 119, 121, 124, 129, 131, 135, 136, 200; Skipwith H., 101; Skipwith, Jr., 96; Susan, 96, 103, 104, 105, 188; Susan H., 101; Susanna, 105; Thomas, 110, 134; Thomas W., 182; W. E., 101; William, 91, 96, 97, 98, 99, 100, 101, 103, 104, 105, 115, 135, 150, 151; William E., 108, 129, 250; William Ellis, 188, 193; William, Jr., 96
COARS: John, 118; Susanna, 118; William, 142
COARSE: Cassandra, 104, 105; John, 99; William, 105
COATES: Ann, 173, 182, 207; Elizabeth, 194; Israel, 81; Jane, 194, 200; Jonathan, 194, 251; Susan, 193
COBB: Anna Almy, 157; Daniel, 157, 185, 186; Edward D., 157; Elizabeth, 157; Harriott R., 210; Henry Samson, 157; Ruth, 157, 185, 186; Susan Almy, 157; William Almy, 157

COBURN: James, 149
COCHRAN: Susanna, 203
COCK: George D., 68; Susan W., 68
COCKBURN: James, 53, 88
COCKEY: Penelope E. D., 205
COGSHAL: Elizabeth, 26
COGSHELL: Elizabeth, 26
COHEN: Sarah Janette, 182
COIL: Matilda, 138, 146, 148
COLE: Ann, 220, 239; Elizabeth, 14; Margaret, 40; Mary C., 103; Mary V., 188; Samuel, 202; Skipwith, 216; William, 209
COLLINS: Nancy N., 199
COMEGYS: Augusta, 266; Bejamin, 206; Cornelius, 206; Elizabeth, 266; Elziabeth, 184, 192, 206, 207, 209, 210, 211; Jesse, 206; John, 170, 171, 201; May, 206; Priscilla, 206; William, 206, 209, 266
COMFORT: Elizabeth, 171; Sarah, Jr., 180
CONKLING: Eliza, 183
CONN: Maria E., 184
CONRAD: Margaret, 202; Samuel, 202
COOK: Elisha, 105, 134, 141, 151, 153; George, 134; George O., 106; George S., 105; George W., 233; Jane, 196, 233; Jesse, 171; Jesse W., 233; Joel, 134; Louisa, 105; Lydia, 134; M. Louisa, 134; Maria J., 142, 153; Maria Jane, 233; Mary, 171; Mary Ann, 233; Meriah, 171; Nathan, 134; P. William, 134; Ruth, 105; Samuel, 105, 196; Samuel H., 233; Stephen, 207, 222
COOKE: Elisha, 146, 151; Stephen, 204

COOKSON: Jane, 198; Joseph, 223; Mary, 198, 223; Olive, 253; Rachel, 223; Samuel, 198, 223, 253
COOPEr: Ely B., 140; Martha Anna, 140; Nicholas, 140; Priscilla, 112, 140; Sarah, 112
COOPER: Ann, 213; Anna, 76, 89, 112, 150; Catherine, 140; Elizabeth, 76, 89, 112, 140, 150, 210; Ely B., 89, 112, 150; Elziabeth, 213; Esther, 89, 112, 140, 150; Gulielma, 89, 112, 140, 150; Isah, 101; Isaiah, 76, 104, 137, 144, 145, 213; John T., 104; Margaret, 89, 112, 140, 150, 213; Martha, 89, 104, 112, 150, 213; Mary, 96, 147, 241; Nicholas, 76, 89, 97, 100, 101, 104, 112, 140, 150, 213; P----, 150; Parthenia, 150; Pathenia, 104, 213; Perthenia, 101; Priscilla, 89, 150, 267; Sarah, 76, 89, 101, 104, 112, 140, 150, 195, 213; William, 96, 201, 221; Yolenda D., 104
COOPPER: Nicholas, 104; Perthenia, 102
COPE: Abigail Ann, 259; Abigal Ann, 222; Charles S., 259; Charles Shoemaker, 222; Emma, 222; H. U., 173; Hannah, 196; Herman, 179; Herman U., 232; Israel, 213, 216, 258; Jasper, 195, 222, 259; Margaret, 216, 258; Mary, 181, 200; Mary Ann, 216, 258; Mary Grier, 179; Rebecca, 170, 196, 222, 259
CORK: Elizabeth, 149
CORKRAN: Francis S., 240; Samuel, 240
CORNTHWAIT: Aliceana, 261; Alisan, 190, 203, 210; Alisann, 190, 207; Alisanna, 121, 184, 198, 199, 206, 207, 211; Allisanna, 206; Ann, 157, 203, 205, 210, 211, 264; Ann P., 186, 190, 209, 211; Ann Peck, 208, 261; David Wilson, 158; Eiza Ann, 264; Eliza, 211; Elizabeth, 170, 187, 190, 206, 266, 269; Grace, 198, 201, 203, 204, 208, 210, 211, 264; Grace R., 211; Jane R., 68; Jane W., 187, 190; Jane Wilson, 211, 266; Johanna H., 157; John, 96, 97, 98, 120, 158, 170, 195, 196, 199, 200, 201, 202, 203, 204, 210, 222, 266; John Oliver, 266; Mary, 97; Miranna, 201; R., 205; Robert, 97, 120, 190, 196, 198, 199, 200, 201, 203, 210, 211, 261, 266; Thomas, 97, 198, 201, 204, 205, 211; William, 157, 196, 198, 201, 203, 205, 211, 264, 266; William H., 68
CORNTHWAITE: Elizabeth W., 241
CORNWAIT: Mary, 97, 120, 198, 201, 203, 204, 205, 207, 208, 211, 261
CORNWAITE: Ann, 266
CORSE: Cassandra, 132; Elizabeth, 132; James, 132; John, Jr., 115; Susan, 105; Susanna, 132; William, 113, 132, 141
CORTHWAIT: Alissanna, 202; Deborah, 201, 208, 211
COULTER: Mary, 198
COURSE: Cassandri, 104; Susanna, 123
COWMAN: Hannah P., 209; John, 192; Margaret, 199; Mary, 190
COX: Baines, 97; Bains, 98, 106; Banes, 127; Eliza, 247, 267, 268; Elizabeth, 97, 114, 140,

150; Ephraim, 116, 118;
Ephreal, 97; Ephrum, 96;
George, 97, 107, 127, 129, 130,
131, 240, 247; Guta., 97; John,
97, 107, 115, 125; John R., 240;
Larken, 120; Larkin, 125; Maria,
202; Mary, 96, 97, 114, 125;
Racheal, 97; Rachel, 104, 114,
141, 150, 151; Rachel G., 104;
Samuel, 97, 140, 149; Sarah, 97,
107, 125, 128; William, 96, 97,
104, 106, 114, 115, 116, 118,
150; William, Jr., 96, 116, 118
CRAWFORD: Francis, 120
CRESSON: Sarah, 200, 262, 266
CROFT: John, 244; Margaret, 244;
Stacy, 244; William, 244
CROPPER: James, 216
CROWNOVER: Sabina, 172, 180;
Tacy, 196
CULLIM: Elizabeth, 17
CULLUM: Elizabeth, 17, 18
CULLUN: Elizabeth, 17
CUNNINGHAM: B. A., 211; B.
Amos, 75; Daniel M., 76; Worth
H., 75
CURLE: Mary, 173
CURLEY: Sarah, 97
CURTIS: Maria, 44; Mariah, 44

# D

DADDRAL: Joseph C., 103
DADRAL: Sarah W., 103
DALLAM: Henry, 158; John, 96,
130, 158, 175, 176; Mary, 110,
159, 175, 182, 270; Richard, 96,
127, 245; Sarah, 158, 226, 268;
Thomas Barber, 158; William,
158, 171, 174, 175
DALLUM: Mary, 134
DARE: Eliza S., 210; Elizabeth O.,
242; Gideon, 196; Priscilla, 170,
196; Thomas C., 196

DASHIELL: Alfred H., 172;
Elizabeth, 172
DAUGHERTY: Catharine, 199
DAVENPORT: Elizabeth, 203;
Joseph, 191, 209; Margaret, 199
DAVIES: John, 207, 216; Martha,
207; Mary, 207
DAVIS: Benjamin, 100; D. J., 101;
Elizabeth C., 173; Elizabeth L.,
172; George, 42; Juli Ann, 104;
Martha, 195, 201, 266; Mary,
114, 195; Mary Ann, 170, 172,
173, 179
DAWES: Eda, 205; Edward, 204;
Mary, 47, 82, 248; May, 82
DAWSON: Ann, 158, 208, 210,
225, 245, 266, 267; Charles,
211; Charlotte, 210, 267; Edith,
37; Elisha, 24; Eliza, 233;
Elizabeth, 225, 245; Elizabeth
Robertson, 158; James, 225,
245; James W., 225; Jane, 158;
John, 158, 204, 233, 267;
Joseph, 158; Lydia, 225, 245;
Mary, 245; Mary Ann, 225;
Mary Miflin, 158; Richard, 226,
233, 246; Sarah, 225, 245;
Susanna, 75; Thomas H., 36;
Thomas Hammersley, 37;
William, 158, 201, 204, 205,
208, 211, 267; William, Jr., 158
DAY: Cassandra, 73, 75; Eloiza,
73; Ishmael, 75; Sarah, 206,
218, 249, 271
DEAR: Thomas, 176
DEAVENPORT: Elizabeth, 271
DEAVER: E. M., 186; Sophia, 23,
24; Sophiah, 22
DECKER: Ge., 209
DELLAM: Joseph, 118, 119;
Richard, 120; Susannah, 114;
William, 120
DENISON: Deborah, 25, 26

DENNIS: Abraham, 224;
Benjamin, 224; Elizabeth, 224,
255; George, 224; Grace, 224;
Hannah, 224, 255; Jonathan,
224; Mary, 224; Philip, 224,
255; Samuel, 255
DENNISON: Deborah, 25, 26
DENNY: Ellen, 188; Ellen S., 190;
Mary, 193
DEVER: Hugh, 138, 145
DICKENSON: Henry, 224; Mary,
247, 268
DIFFENDAFFER: Charles, 209;
Michael, M.D., 211
DIFFENDERFER: Elizabeth, 198
DIFFENDERFFER: Catharine, 202;
Catherine, 174; Eliza, 202;
Sophia, 174, 202
DILLEN: Moses, Jr., 260; William,
80
DILLION: Hannah, 43; Mary, 17;
Moses, 43
DILLON: Edith, 201, 204; Hannah,
20, 31; Isaac, 35, 226; John,
201, 252; Martha, 37, 198;
Mary, 17; Moses, 1, 7, 15, 20,
198, 226; Moses, Jr., 20;
Rebacca, 27; Rebecca, 26, 27;
William, 90
DILLWYN: William, 59
DIMMITT: Catharine, 199; Jacob,
75; Rebbecca, 75; William, 75
DIXON: Edwin S., 239; Elizabeth
S., 68; Isaac, 239; Isaac F., 68;
John H., 239; Lucretia, 239;
Lydia, 205; Margaret, 239;
Mary, 239; Sarah Elizabeth, 239
DOBBIN: Elizabeth M., 74; Esther,
210; George, 202; Hester, 209
DODDRELL: James C., 142, 188,
238; Jas. C., 105; Sarah W.,
152, 175, 185, 206, 208, 237
DODREL: Sarah, 125, 126

DODRELL: James C., 193; Sarah
W., 128, 142
DORSEY: Caleb, 174; Edward H.,
200; Elizabeth, 197; Maria, 172,
173, 176; Mary A., 187; Rachel,
173, 180; Samuel W., 197;
Sarah, 174; Thomas, 174
DOUGLAS: Ann, 174; Julia A.,
192
DOUGLASS: Ann, 174
DOWELL: Henry, 183
DOWNES: Esther E., 189
DOWNING: Joseph M., 112, 136,
139, 148; Joseph Warner, 112,
148; Mary Ann, 112, 136, 139,
148; Sarah E., 112, 136, 139,
148; William E., 139, 148;
William M., 112, 136, 139
DUER: Charles, 194; John, 194,
202; Mary Ann, 190, 192, 193,
194; Susanna, 211; Thomas, 178
DUGAN: Hammond, 188
DUKEHARD: John, 104; Pathena,
104
DUKEHART: Ann, 158, 264; Ann
P., 191; Anna, 205; Balderston,
158; Catherine, 158, 261; E.,
202; Edward, 158, 261;
Elizabeth, 202; Henrietta, 208;
Isaiah, 158; John, 98, 158, 159,
184, 190, 191, 192, 195, 196,
199, 203, 204, 207, 210, 261;
John Peck, 158; Joseph, 264;
Lydia, 158; Lydia H., 191;
Margaret, 158, 159, 190, 191,
194, 199, 203, 204, 206, 209,
210, 211, 272; Margaret Ann,
158; Martha, 158, 190; Mary,
264; Mary J., 191; Parthenia,
158, 190, 191, 195, 198, 203,
204, 208, 261; Robert, 158, 261;
S., 202; Sarah, 158, 190, 191,
261; Susanna, 174, 175;

Valerius, 173, 174, 198, 199, 201, 202, 203, 204, 205, 206, 264; Volerius, 209; William, 158, 190, 191, 261
DUNBAR: Ann, 102
DUNCA: Jeney, 100
DUNCAN: Elizabeth, 246; Nelly, 104
DUNGAN: Mary, 119, 121
DUNKIN: James, 100
DURBIN: Cassandra, 123, 200
DURKEHART: John, 158
DUTTON: Hannah, 219; John, 1, 192; Mary Ann, 192; Robert, 192; Sarah, 192; Susanna, 112, 137, 145, 148, 198
DYER: Joanna, 65; Joseph, 65

E

EACHES: Mary, 47; Virgil, 47
EACHUS: Abner, 59, 80, 90; Bathsheba, 60, 81, 83, 93; Joseph, 77, 83; Mahala, 80, 92; Mahalah, 59; Mary, 59, 75, 76, 81, 93; Minshall, 60, 81, 83, 93; Obed, 78, 85; Preston, 59, 93; Rebecca Ann, 60; Reston, 81; Sarah, 60, 81, 83, 93; Vanleer, 60, 81, 83, 93; Virgil, 59, 60, 75, 76, 81, 83, 90, 93; Virgil Trego, 60, 93
EASTON: N. W., 203; Ruth, 203
EATEN: Rachel, 104
EATON: Hannah, 97; Prescella, 97
EDDY: Margarum, 47
EDGE: George, 144; Joseph, 144; Mary S., 144; Sarah, 144
EDMONDSON: Eli, 262; Eliza, 159; Elizabeth, 262; James, 210, 262; Joseph, 262; Martha M., 184
EDMUNDSON: Ann, 201; Joseph, 201

EDWARDS: Elizabeth, 207
EDY: Margaret, 44
ELEY: Martha, 100
ELGAR: Ann, 197
ELI: Hugh, 24
ELIOT: John, 214; John, Jr., 214
ELLICOTT: Andrew, 169, 170, 173, 177, 179, 180, 181, 185, 186, 189, 195, 196, 197, 198, 200, 201, 202, 203; Andrew T., 181, 259; Ann, 175, 176, 180, 181, 189, 190, 191, 238, 259, 262; Ann B., 175, 177, 179, 180, 182, 183, 189, 190; Ann Brook, 193, 194; Ann Brooke, 193; B., 177; B. H., 193, 194; B., Jr., 175; Ben, Jr., 180; Bena., 173, 176, 181; Benjamin, 170, 188, 193, 202, 207, 227; Catherine, 159; Charles T., 193; E., 173, 193, 218; Elias, 5, 66, 68, 78, 85, 163, 169, 170, 172, 173, 179, 181, 182, 189, 195, 240, 254, 259; Eliza, 197, 200; Elizabeth, 159, 169, 174, 177, 182, 185, 189, 192, 193, 196, 197, 200, 218, 242, 259; Emily, 193; Esther, 159, 174, 175, 184, 195, 196, 197, 201, 218; Evan T., 176, 177, 180, 181, 197; Evan Thomas, 173, 175; Frances, 174, 175, 176, 177, 200; George, 169, 174, 175, 176, 177, 178, 179, 182, 189, 192, 193, 194, 196, 197, 200, 202, 218, 259; H. M., 188; Hannah, 159, 175, 177, 178, 179, 181, 182, 183, 195, 198, 202, 204, 205, 207, 256; Hannah B., 193; Hannah M., 194; Harvey M., 193, 194; Henry, 181, 189; Hetty B., 193, 194; J. S., 193; James, 167, 170, 173,

181, 188, 193, 196, 197, 201, 202, 259, 260; Jane, 188, 191, 195, 207, 256; Jane T., 192, 193; John, 170, 174, 175, 176, 177, 178, 179, 181, 194, 195, 196, 197, 200, 202, 258, 259, 262; John J., 178; John P., 188; Jonathan, 169, 174, 175, 176, 177, 178, 179, 182, 196, 197, 198, 200, 202, 260, 261; Jonathan H., 193; Joseph, 175, 227; Leah, 176; Leaticia, 176; Letitia, 175; Letitia C., 189; Lydia, 159; Lydia L., 193, 194; Maria, 159; Martha, 174, 175, 177, 201, 242; Mary, 163, 170, 173, 175, 176, 180, 181, 182, 188, 189, 190, 192, 193, 196, 197, 199, 201, 202, 258, 259, 262; Mary Ann, 261; Mary G., 176; Mary J., 177, 178, 179, 209; Mary K., 177, 178; Mary M., 159, 170, 171, 178, 179, 180, 181, 183, 186, 188, 191, 194, 202; Mary T., 159, 188, 193, 194; Nath. H., 193; Nathaniel, 170, 173, 174, 175, 176, 177, 178, 179, 181, 197, 202; Philip T., 182, 188; Polly, 179; Rachel, 176, 177, 180, 181, 197, 207, 238, 258; Rachel T., 170, 196; Rachel Thomas, 172; Rebecca, 159; Sa. B., 177; Sally, 197; Samuel, 173, 175, 176, 177, 182, 197, 259; Sarah, 169, 173, 174, 175, 176, 178, 196, 197, 200, 202, 259, 260, 261; Sarah Ann, 159, 194; Sibella, 260; Tacey, 170, 177, 198; Tacy, 173, 175, 177, 180, 181, 197, 201, 202; Thomas, 38, 159, 170, 171, 173, 189, 193, 195, 197, 202, 207, 259; William, 173, 174, 175, 176, 177, 178, 189, 194, 197; William M., 159
ELLIS: Charles, 193; Mercey, 193; Mercy, 193; William, 193
ELMS: Mary, 200
ELY: Abigail, 66, 81, 93; Alice, 66, 81, 93; Amos, 32, 33; Amos J., 101; Ann, 75; Asher, 179; David, 66, 74, 75, 81, 87, 93, 101; Elizabeth, 12; Emaline, 93; Emmaline, 81; Hannah, 12, 75, 99; Hugh, 12, 24, 26, 63, 75, 93, 96, 154, 179; Isaac, 101; Isaiah, 139, 148; Jacob, 76, 89, 100, 140, 150; Jonathan, 93; Jonathan T., 66; Jonathan Thomas, 81; Joseph, 96, 98, 99, 179; Mahlon, 179; Martha, 76, 99; Mary, 15, 96, 179; Rachel, 101, 179; Ruth, 193; Sarah, 12, 96, 99, 101; Thomas, 75, 93, 101; William, 76, 98, 146, 147, 153, 156
EMBREE: Hannah, 224; Israel, 224; James, 224; Jesse, 224, 226; John, 224; Joseph, 224; Lydia, 224; Phebe, 224; Samuel, 224; William, 222
EMERSON: Rachel, 241
EMORY: Richard, 188
ENGLAND: Catharine, 9, 59; Catherine, 93; Elizabeth Dutton, 9, 59; George, 9, 59; Hannah, 195; John, 31, 32; Joseph, 194, 196, 215; Sarah Hooker, 9, 59; Thomas, 93; Thomas Hooker, 9, 59
ENLOWS: John, 76
ENNIS: Elizabeth, 187
ENNISS: Juliana, 202; Mary, 202
ESCAVILL: Sarah, 274
ESLING: Maria, 190
ETON: Joseph, 103; Rachel, 100
ETTING: Catherine, 180; R. G.,

180
EVANS: Alice, 237; Amos, 114; Ann, 192, 197; Anne, 226; Bejamin, 114; Cadwallader, 114; David, 226; Edmond, 245; Edmund, 12, 35, 37, 40; Elizabeth, 12, 37, 40, 192, 245; Ellen, 237; John, 114; Joseph, 174, 175, 237; Joseph E., 197; Joshua, 237; Judith, 197; Martha, 182; Mary M., 192; Robert, 237; Samuel, 189, 237; Sarah, 175; Sarah A., 192; Sarah Andrew, 12; Susannah, 192; Tace, 114; William, 197, 237; Wilson, 237
EVENS: Anna, 159, 274; Edmond, 159; Edmund, 206; Elizabeth, 159, 187, 274; John, 159, 206, 274; Lydia, 159; Mary, 104; Mary M., 190, 191; Mary Mifflin, 159, 274; Sarah, 104, 191, 206; Sarah A., 190; Sarah Andrew, 159; Sarah Andrews, 274; Susanna, 159, 274
EWENG: John, 98
EWIN: Ann, 117
EWING: Ann, 97, 102, 103, 126, 171, 183, 187, 189, 190, 191, 207, 209; Anna, 207; Henry, 97, 103, 171; Margaret, 98

F

FARQUHAR: Edward, 180; Edward A., 181; Edward Andrew, 235; James, 208; Mahlon, 197; Malen, 221; William P., 97
FARRIER: William, 216
FARVER: Joseph, 216
FEARSON: Hannah, 188; Hannah J. D., 184; Jesse, 188
FELL: Ann, 189, 193; Benjamin, 213; Ezra, 189, 193; Hannah, 189; Jane, 213; Leah, 213; Mary, 213
FENTHAM: Priscilla, 191; William, 191
FERDUN: Lidia, 27; Lyddia, 27
FERGUSSON: Elizabeth, 191; Hannah, 191
FERRIS: Ann, 274; Mary, 237
FERRISS: Elizabeth, 191; John, 191; Zechariah, 191
FEW: Hetty, 177, 191, 209
FIELD: Hannah, 17; John, 216
FIRTH: John, 214
FISHER: Ann, 118, 205; Annabella, 202; Betty, 21, 25, 205, 260; Elisha, 21, 24, 205, 208; Elizabeth, 204; Hester, 191; James, 205; Joel, 21, 24, 205, 208, 250; John, 204, 214; Lydia, 21, 24, 205, 208, 271; Ruth, 21, 25, 205, 207, 265, 267; Samuel, 21, 24, 205, 207, 208, 236; Sarah, 205, 271; Seth, 21, 24, 205, 247; Susanna, 21, 24, 205, 207; Thomas A., 194
FLEET: John, 214
FLOUNDERS: William, 216
FOARD: Alisan, 270; Alisann C., 182; Frances, 182, 184, 270; Harriet, 184; Harriot, 270; Joseph, 184; Marriet, 182
FORD: Alisanna, 229, 273; Frances, 229; Harriet, 240; Harriot, 229; Joseph, 96
FORDANE: Lida, 27
FORDONE: Lida, 27
FORNEY: Peter, 201
FORSTER: William, 148
FORSYTH: Elizabeth, 124
FORSYTHE: Sarah, 125
FORWOOD: Hannah B., 68; John, 96, 97, 130; Martha, 46, 133

FOSSICK: Robert, 214
FOSSITT: John, 98
FOSTER: William, Jr., 52
FOULKE: Ann S., 186, 187, 188, 189, 190, 191; Anna, 186; Anna M., 187; John M., 184, 185, 186, 190, 191; Levi, 186; Margaret, 186; William, 186
FOWLER: Margaret, 175
FOX: Mary, 178
FOXALL: Elizabeth, 204
FRAZIER: Rosey, 172; Sarah, 172; William, 172
FREEMAN: Isabella, 209; Mary P., 188; W. H., 101, 209
FRENCH: Israel, 212
FRISBY: Richard, 207
FULLER: Oliver, 96, 212, 215
FURDUN: Lydia, 27
FUSSELL: Barthikinew, 106; Bartholew, M.D., 191; Bartholomew, 43, 73, 74, 75, 76, 81, 85, 92, 159; Clarissa, 47, 65, 74, 81, 88, 92, 159, 182, 234; Elizabeth, 60, 85; Elizabeth M., 74; Esther, 43, 73, 84, 86; Hannah, 81, 92, 159; Henry B., 74; Henry Bartholowmew, 60; Jacob, 46, 47, 65, 74, 81, 88, 92, 159, 234; Joseph, 60, 74, 85; Joseph Brevett, 159; Joshua, 65, 81, 88, 92, 159, 234; Mary Jane, 60; Priscilla, 60; Rebecca, 43, 73, 74, 75; Rebecca Bond, 60, 85; Ruth, 159; Ruth Ann, 92; Ruth Anna, 65, 81, 92; Samuel, 60; Solomon, 60, 77, 82; William, 65, 74, 81, 88, 92, 159, 234; William, Jr., 73

# G

GARDENER: Mary, 268
GARDNER: Aldred S., 161; Alfred S., 240; Ann Eliza, 161; Ephraim, 160, 240; Gideon, 170; James, 161; Martha S., 161; Mary, 160, 192; Mary Jane, 161; Sarah P., 161
GARENER: Ephraim, 268
GAREY: Sarah, 272
GARITSON: Anna, 143
GARRETSON: Ann, 91, 179; Anna, 113, 155, 160, 193; Cornelius, 105, 106, 143, 160, 174, 175, 176, 177, 178, 179, 189; Eli, 105, 160, 176, 179, 182, 189; Eliza, 160; Ely, 143, 154; Hannah, 105, 106, 143, 154, 175, 176, 177, 178, 179; Isaac, 176, 178, 179, 189, 209; Jesse, 106, 179, 189, 193; John, 160; Joseph, 106, 176, 178, 179, 182, 189, 193; Margaret, 106, 178, 179, 209; Racheal, 106; Rachel, 179, 182; Rachel, Jr., 179; Samuel, 106, 160, 175, 176, 177, 179, 189; Thomas, 160; William, 160
GARRETT: Abigail, 43, 75, 76, 89; Eliza, 43, 74, 87; Esther, 43, 75, 76, 93; Jesse, 75; Jessee, 43, 76; Jonah, 43, 66, 74, 76
GARRISON: Ann, 91
GARY: Sarah, 269
GATCHELL: Jeremiah, 187
GAW: William, 29, 30
GAWTHROP: Mary, 51; William, 50
GEORGE: Ann, 160, 175; Eliza, 188, 194; Elizabeth, 160, 242; Frances, 160; Jonathan E., 160, 193; Philip T., 194; Philip Thomas, 160; Robert, 160, 175; Sarah E., 160, 194; Sarah Harvey, 160; William E., 160, 171, 173, 177, 179, 194, 199,

200, 201, 203; William
Edmondson, 175
GILBERT: Mary, 31
GILLINGHAM: Amos, 160, 179,
253; Ann, 160; Anna, 111, 136,
147, 189; Anna W., 239;
Catharine, 161, 236; Charles,
111, 136, 146, 189, 239;
Edward, 160; Eliza, 161, 171,
207, 228; Elizabeth, 105, 136,
152, 160, 170, 171, 172, 173,
174, 175, 177, 178, 179, 180,
181, 182, 183, 188, 191, 198,
200, 207, 210, 218, 236, 253;
Elizabeth L., 200; Esther, 161;
Ezra, 105, 141, 152, 160, 171,
172, 173, 176, 180, 181, 183,
188, 198, 200; George, 160,
171, 173, 179, 186, 200, 205;
Hannah, 159; Isaac, 161, 236;
James, 105, 111, 136, 146, 161,
170, 171, 172, 173, 178, 181,
183, 185, 186, 188, 189, 190,
194, 195, 196, 197, 198, 199,
200, 202, 208, 218, 239, 253;
James W., 105, 189, 239; Jane,
161, 207, 236; Jehu, 236; John,
105, 159, 170, 171, 172, 173,
174, 175, 179, 181, 183, 185,
186, 187, 188, 189, 191, 193;
Lucy, 160; Mary, 159, 186, 228,
253; Mary C., 113, 142, 154,
240; Merian, 160; Miriam, 172,
173, 174, 179, 180, 181, 186,
207; Phebe, 111, 136, 146;
Phebe W., 189, 239; Rachel,
160; Rebecca H., 181; Samuel,
111, 136, 146, 189, 239; Sarah,
111, 136, 146, 239; Susanna,
160; William, 161, 170, 171,
172, 173, 178, 183, 196, 200,
203, 205, 236
GILMYER: Eliza, 170

GILPEN: S. T., 179
GILPIN: Alfred P., 176; Joseph
Bernard, 240; Samuel, 240;
Sarah T., 206, 207; Thomas, 233
GIST: Susanna, 108
GLASAUY: Fanny, 180
GLENDON: Alice, 92
GLENDY: John, 209
GLOVEr: Michel, 36
GLOVER: Ann, 36, 43, 247, 267;
Eliza, 43, 247, 267; George, 36,
43, 267; George Mickle, 247,
267; Hannah, 36, 43, 247, 267;
Mary, 36, 43, 247, 267; Michel,
43; Mickle, 267; Sarah, 36, 43,
247, 267; Thomas, 36, 43, 247,
267; William, 36, 43, 247, 267
GODFREY: Samuel, 174, 175,
176, 179, 182, 189, 192
GOLDSMITH: Edw. W., 160;
Elijah, 160, 185, 188; Elizabeth,
160, 185; Isaac Procter, 160;
Mary M., 185, 186, 188; Mary
Mott, 160; Nathan, 185; William
Henry, 160
GOODHUE: Benjamin, 203
GOODIER: John, 216
GOODWIN: Milcah, 199, 203;
Rebecca, 200, 203
GORTEN: William, 210
GORTON: William A., 210
GOUGH: Prudence, 172
GOVER: Ann, 107, 108, 129, 184,
210; Mary Ann, 273; Philip,
129; Priscilla, 104, 129, 184;
Rachel, 240; Samuel, 129; W.
M., 211
GRAHAM: Ann, 220; Deborah,
220; Elizabeth, 220; James, 220,
256; Michael, 220, 256;
Patience, 198, 220, 256
GRAY: Enoch, 141, 151, 170, 171;
Enock Sewell, 148; Mary, 224

GREEN: Hannah, 272; Lydia, 214; R. H., 188, 189, 190; Rachel H., 185, 186; Rachel T., 185
GREY: Elizabeth, 265; Mary, 184
GRIEST: Susanna, 129
GRIFFETH: Sophiah, 22; Thomas T., 46, 47
GRIFFIN: Esther, 17, 214
GRIFFITH: Amos, 52; Ann, 15, 215; Ann Eliza, 14; Ann H., 172; Ann Moore, 29; Ann S., 13; Edith, 53; Elenor, 255; Elizabeth, 29; Esther, 17; Isaac, 18, 20; Keturah, 29; Kitturah, 29; Lucy R., 173; Mariam R., 13; Mary, 29, 50, 180, 270; Mary G., 13; Rachel, 1, 13, 14, 38; Rebecca, 29, 57; Reuben, 29; Reubin, 29; Sarah, 45; Sophia, 23; Sophiah, 22, 23; Thomas, 13, 14; Thomas T., 14
GRIFFITTS: Samuel P., Jr., 193
GRIMSHAW: William, 214
GUILD: Vesto, 103
GUNN: James, 203
GWINN: Achsah, 180; Hannah, 246; Martha, 75; William K., 171; William R., 173, 177, 179
GWINNN: C. D., 172
GWYNN: John, 201; William, 201

H

HADWEN: Joseph, 216
HAGUE: Hiram, 260
HAINES: Ann, 215; Hinchman, 51
HAINEY: Elizabeth, 191
HAIR: Elenner, 10; Elizabeth, 10, 50; Elloner, 22; Elziabeth, 10; Hannah, 10, 26; John, 10; Mary, 10, 15; Phebe, 10; Rachel, 10; Rebeckah, 10; Sarah, 10; Tamar, 10; Tamer, 50
HALL: A. J., 273; Christopher, 96; Fitch, Jr., 203; Hannah, 103, 131, 133, 135, 136; James, 216; Mary, 205; R. T., 104; R. W., 97; Rice J., 139; Rice Johnson, 147; Sarah, 229; Sarah Odle, 229; Thomas Samuel, 229; William W., 97
HALLIFIELD: Ruth, 174
HALWADT: Charles, 162, 172, 189; Christopher, 172; Elizabeth, 162, 172, 189; Rebecca, 162; Sarah, 162
HAMBLETON: Benjamin, 171, 215, 226; Charles, 171, 175, 205, 226; Isaac, 215; James, 171, 228; Joseph, 171, 215; Martha, 228; Mary, 171, 217, 228; Rachel, 171, 215, 227; William, 171, 215, 217
HAMILTON: William, 209, 221
HAMMEr: Isaac, 49, 136
HAMMOND: Caroline, 172; Eliza B., 105
HAMPTON: Asa C., 189
HAMTON: Asenath, 174; James, 174; Jesse B., 174
HANCE: Benjamin, 215; Christian, 268; James, 194; Rachel, 216; Samuel, 196, 216; Sarah, 216; Thomas C., 194, 215; William, 216
HANDS: Mary Vincent, 187
HANDY: Elizabeth, 161, 162, 174, 187, 188, 193; Elizabeth Ann, 161; Henry, 161, 172; Jane, 172; Jane Winder, 161; Jesse Tyson, 161; Mary Ann, 162; Thomas Poultney, 162; W. W., 186, 188; William W., 161, 162, 172, 193; William Winder, 161
HANNA: James, 203
HANNAWAY: Jane, 25
HANNEY: Israel, 172

HANWAY: David, 74; Mary Ann, 69
HARDEN: Mary, 57
HARDFIELD: Just., 182
HARDING: Charles, 4, 22, 41, 216, 218, 255; David, 22, 52, 216, 234; Davis, 41; Elizabeth, 4, 22, 216, 255; George, 4; Lydia W., 5; Mary, 22, 57, 216; Thomas, 4, 22, 216, 255
HARE: Elaner, 22; Eleanor, 260; Jacob, 45
HARGROVE: Caroline, 205
HARKINS: Richard, 74
HARLAN: Abigail Ann, 69; Caleb, 12, 60, 75; Charles, 171; Elizabeth, 61, 69, 75; Elizabeth A., 69; Ezekiel, 212; Hannah, 12, 20, 60, 75, 125, 221, 263; Hannah Ann, 61, 69, 75; John, 12, 19, 60, 67, 75, 82, 125, 210, 221, 263; John L., 61, 69; John Lewis, 75; Joseph, 60, 69, 75, 221, 263; Lewis, 29; Mary, 180; Rachael L., 105; Rachel, 125, 153; Rachel F., 105; Samuel, 171, 205, 225; Sarah, 69; Susanna, 12, 69, 75; Susannah, 61; William, 60, 75, 76, 221, 263; William A., 69
HARLAND: Easther, 96; Hannah, 20; Jeremiah, 96; John, 74; Rachel, 142; Rachel T., 104
HARLEN: Susanna, 248, 270
HARLIN: Eldwood, 124; Hannah, 27, 127; John, 27, 32, 33, 127; Joseph, 27; Lewis, 221; Matilda, 127; Rachel, 127; William, 27
HARLING: Hannah, 20, 27; John, 27; Joseph, 27; William, 27
HARLON: Michael, 134
HARMAN: Abraham, 105
HARMEr: Mary, 124

HARMER: Abraham, 104, 124, 140; Ann, 104, 124; Elizabeth, 104; Hannah, 104, 124, 127, 140; John, 104, 124, 140; Joseph, 104, 124; Joshua, 104, 124; Mary, 104; Michel, 124; Sarah A., 104
HARMOR: Abram, 150; Hannah, 150; John, 150
HARPER: Ann M., 209
HARRI: George, Jr., 171, 184, 188, 237
HARRIS: Beulah, 171; Frances B., 181, 183; George, 114, 118, 171, 184, 188, 196, 237, 255; H., 184; Hicks, 171, 255; John, 183; Mary, 171, 172; Samuel, 170, 197; Samuel H., 170; Susanna, 171, 255; Thomas, 180; William, 197
HARRISON: Araminta, 172; John, 216
HARROD: Martha, 122
HARRY: David, 3, 76, 77; Elizabeth, 74; Evan, 219; Jacob, 213; Joel, 76; Maria, 74; Mary, 14, 75, 76, 77, 89
HARTLEY: Charles L., 240; Edwin, 136; Elias P., 240; Elizabeth, 189; Jesse, 136; Lavinia, 177; Lavinia B., 240; Leavinia, 178; Levi, 178; Mary, 136; Phineas, 240; Rachel, 136; Ruth, 178; Samuel, 177, 178, 189; Samuel E., 240; Thomas, 178, 189, 240; William, 136, 177, 240
HARTLY: Catharine P., 162; Charles L., 162; Edwin, 113, 142; Elizabeth Paxson, 162; Jesse, 105, 113, 142, 154; Joseph, 113, 142; Lavinia, 162; Levania, 182; Levinia, 182; Livi,

182; Mary, 113, 142; Pheniah, 162; Rachel, 113, 142; Ruth, 182; Samuel, 162, 182; Samuel E., 162; Thomas, 113, 142, 182; William, 113, 142, 162, 182; William B., 162
HARTSHORN: Mary, 173, 178, 233; Patience, 230
HARTSHORNE: Mary, 183
HARVEY: James, 179; Jane, 179, 181; Jonathan, 173, 179, 180
HARWOOD: Asenath, 191; James, 188, 189; Sophia, 192
HASLETT: Peter, 193
HASTINGS: Eliza, 179
HATSON: Ann, 210
HAVILAND: Bartlett, 70; Caroline P., 70, 71; Charles C., 70; Rachel, 103; Susan M., 70
HAVRACE: John, 105
HAWARD: Elizabeth, 129; Hannah, 129; Jacob, 129; Joseph, 129; Mary, 102, 103, 129; Rebecca, 129; Thomas, 129; William, 129
HAY: Mary, 35, 44, 86; William, 35
HAYLEY: Elizabeth, 143
HAYS: Mary, 46
HAYWARD: Elizabeth, 161, 170, 173, 178, 200, 209, 246, 249, 258, 270; Elizabeth B., 184, 186, 188, 190, 192, 210, 211; Ely Balderston, 161; Frances W., 161; George, 262; Hannah, 246, 257, 262; Isaac, 161, 173, 178, 194, 209, 270; Jacob, 246, 261; John, 171, 173, 200, 209; John L., 179; Joseph, 139, 148, 149, 246; Kezia, 257, 262; Keziah, 209; Marcellus B., 161; Mary, 246, 257, 261; Mary Ann, 178, 182, 210; Rachel, 200; Rebecca, 106, 110, 136, 145, 200, 246, 253, 257; Sidney, 200, 252, 253; Thomas, 102, 103, 106, 246; William, 96, 98, 170, 171, 172, 173, 194, 200, 203, 204, 205, 206, 209, 210, 218, 246, 252, 253, 257, 258, 261, 262; William Brown, 161
HAZELHURST: Francis, 170
HEADINGTON: Rebecca M., 204, 205
HEATON: John, 102
HEBBARD: William B., 172
HEBBERD: Abraham, 145
HEIGHE: James, Jr., 209
HELEY: Mary, 202
HELM: Mary, 253; Meredith, 191
HEMPHILL: Andrew, 209
HENDERSON: A., 190; Hannah, 170; Sarah A., 170
HENDON: Alice, 91, 93; James, 74; Sophia, 74, 75
HENRY: John H., 198
HENSIL: Mary, 147
HERBERT: John, 76
HESTON: Ann, 174, 175, 197, 227, 254; Charles, 174, 227, 254; Jane, 174, 227; Joseph, 173, 174, 175, 197, 198, 227, 254; Laticia, 227; Leticia, 197; Letitia, 174, 175, 197; Phebe, 173, 174, 197; Rebecca L., 175, 176; Samuel, 173, 175, 176, 177, 180, 182, 214; William, 56, 174, 197, 227; William T., 54
HEWES: Ann, 173, 194; Edward, 172, 194; Elizabeth M., 250, 273; Esther, 250, 273; Henry, 194; John, 172, 181, 189, 190, 194, 210; John H., 185, 188, 190, 191, 250, 273; John L., 190; Joseph, 212; Mary, 172, 210, 250, 273; Rachel T., 181,

189
HEWS: Gidian, 26, 27; Rebeccah, 27
HIBBARD: Joseph, 213
HIBBERD: Eliza, 75
HICK: James, 22
HICKS: Ann, 196; Bathsheba, 22, 39, 196, 217; David, 196; Elizabeth, 228, 269; James, 1, 22, 170, 183, 196, 217; James, Jr., 217; John Elias, 182; Mary, 22, 36, 170, 196, 217
HILL: Ann, 201, 255; John, 96, 201; Martha, 28; Mary, 216; William, 225, 229
HILLEN: John, 176, 206, 209
HINSEL: Mary, 139
HIX: James, 22; Mary, 22
HOAG: Huldah, 49; Joseph, 175
HODGKIN: John, 214
HOLAND: Elinor, 15
HOLLAND: Eleanor, 15; Elener, 15, 29; Ellenner, 25
HOLLEN: Eleanor, 15
HOLLIN: Elener, 15; Elliner, 22; Eloner, 25
HOLLINGSWORTH: Aaron, 1, 26; Abigail, 26, 28, 60, 74, 75, 76, 77; Abigal, 1; Amos, 60, 69; Aron, 26; Edith, 70; Eli, 26, 77; Eliza, 76, 77; Elizabeth, 13, 60, 74, 77, 84; Elizabeth Mildred, 69; Hannah, 26, 74, 75, 76, 90; Hannah W., 13; Henry, 60; Isaac, 17, 19; Isaiah, 60; Isaiah B., 69; Ja., 176; Jane S., 60; Jesse, 26, 89; John, 26, 60, 70, 77; Joseph, 178, 232; Lois, 69; Mahlon, 60; Mahlon W., 69; Martha J. Hoskins, 69; Mary, 13, 60, 70, 77; Nathaniel, 26, 27, 32, 35, 40, 60, 70, 73, 74, 75, 76, 77; Nathaniel, Jr., 94; Rachel, 70; Rebecca, 60; Robert, 26, 34, 60, 77; Thomas, 26, 65, 74, 87
HOLLINSWORTH: Nathaniel, 1, 26; Robert, 13
HOLMAN: David, 184
HOLTON: Hannah, 100
HOOKER: Rachel, 21, 22
HOOPES: Albert, 70; Darlington, 70; Edmund, 70; I. N., 190; Isaac N., 185, 188; J. N., 190; Phebe T., 70; Rachel T., 70
HOOPS: J. N., 192
HOPKINS: Able James, 162; Amelia, 106, 196, 198, 199, 204, 205, 206, 207, 209, 210; Anna W., 144; Cassandra, 104; Charles W., 144; Charlotte W., 183, 184, 192; Deborah, 161, 170, 171, 173, 176, 177, 178, 179, 181, 182, 186; Deborah Hopkins, 164; Dorothy, 161, 170, 174, 176, 179, 180, 181, 183, 185, 188, 190, 191, 200, 201, 208, 265; Edith, 92; Elenor, 95; Eliza, 95, 105, 144, 183, 196; Eliza H., 105, 106; Elizabeth, 92, 104, 105, 161, 170, 175, 176, 178, 181, 182, 183, 186, 187, 188, 191, 200, 203, 204, 205, 206, 208, 209, 210, 251, 265, 267; Ellenor, 97; Emelia, 116; Emilie, 200; Ephraim, 97, 116; Evan, 221; F., 172; Frances, 181, 183, 197, 200, 201, 202, 204, 205, 206, 218, 252; Francis, 117; Gerard, 161, 263; Gerard T., 265; Gerrard, 170, 251; Gerrard T., 170, 171, 172, 173, 174, 175, 176, 177, 178, 179, 180, 181, 183, 185, 186, 187, 188, 190, 191, 192, 193, 194, 195, 198,

199, 200, 201, 208; Grace, 120, 224; Grace J., 96, 98, 199, 207, 209, 210; Hannah, 103, 106; Harriett, 196; Henrietta, 196, 199; Henry, 95; Henry W., 144; Hiram, 92; Isaac G., 195, 196, 197, 243; Isaac H., 196; J. H., 105; Jesse, 92; Jo, 102; Joel, 170, 171, 196, 199, 201, 203, 204, 205, 206, 208; John, 94, 97, 105, 110, 135, 162, 183, 196, 208, 251; John George, 162; Johns, 181, 188; Joseph, 94, 95, 96, 105, 117, 132, 135, 144, 253; Joseph G., 187, 235; Joshua, 102, 106, 153; Kakeman B., 106; Leaven, 21; Levin, 34, 37, 216; Levin H., 106; Lydia, 104, 105, 106, 193; Margaret, 130, 161; Martha Jane, 92; Mary, 99, 101, 102, 104, 105, 106, 110, 136, 137, 143, 145, 154, 155, 170, 171, 173, 174, 176, 177, 178, 179, 180, 181, 184, 209, 210; Mary Ann, 183, 273; Nathaniel, 92; Nicholas, 196; Phebe Hannah, 92; Priscilla, 94, 119, 169, 196, 217; Priscilla W., 144; Rachel, 94, 97, 144, 161, 170, 196, 251; Rebecca, 162; Rebecca C., 231, 273; Rezin, 172; Richard, 170, 181, 205, 244; Richard, M.D., 172; Samuel, 94, 95, 96, 97, 98, 99, 100, 101, 102, 103, 105, 106, 116, 117, 119, 135, 143, 144, 151, 152, 153, 155, 192, 197, 199; Samuel Wilson, 162; Sarah, 19, 20, 96, 101, 102, 104, 105, 106, 126, 128, 143, 153, 154, 161, 178, 180, 185, 186, 187, 192, 195, 196, 206, 215, 265; Sarah Ann, 92; Sarah B.,

180, 181, 182; Sary, 103; Sophia, 183, 184; Susan, 96, 170, 172, 173, 174, 178, 179, 185, 186, 195, 197, 198, 200, 201; Susanna, 96, 118, 176, 180, 183; Susannah, 114, 173; Thomas, 161; Wakeman B., 106; William, 97, 98, 99, 101, 102, 103, 105, 106, 119, 122, 161, 171, 173, 176, 178, 180, 181, 183, 186, 192, 194, 196, 207, 221; William Curtiss, 92; Wilson W., 144
HORLEN: Lewis, 42
HORNE: Susanna, 38
HOSKIN: Nathaniel, 187
HOSKINS: Amy, 70; Cheyney, 67, 93; Edith, 67; Eliza, 92; Elizabeth, 66, 67, 68, 70, 90, 236; Elizabeth W., 67, 93; Hiram, 67, 69; Jesse, 67; Joseph C., 67; Joseph T., 67, 69; Martha J., 67, 69; Nathanial, 90; Nathaniel, 67, 76, 236; Phebe H., 67; Sarah Ann, 67, 69; William C., 67, 69
HOUGH: Ann, 169; Charles Alexander, 162; Edward S., 174, 175, 176, 240; Edward Stabler, 169; Frances, 254; James, 180; James C., 179, 181, 183, 188; Jefferson, 234; Joseph, 254; Marietta, 162, 240; Mary, 181, 183; Rachel, 170, 172, 173, 178, 179, 180, 181, 182, 183, 186, 190; Robert, 181, 251, 254; Samuel, 169, 181; Sarah, 107, 123, 127; Sarah A., 175; William S., 162
HOULTON: Hannah, 209; Jamima, 260; Mary, 260
HOWARD: Lemuel, 17; Robert, 214; Sarah, 24

HOWELL: Adelia, 235; Adelia Ann, 273; Ann, 235; Arthur, 235; Carpenter, 235; Catharine, 210; Charles, 235, 273; Darius Carpenter, 235; Elizabeth, 170, 235, 273; George, 235, 273; John, 235; John A., 273; John C., 209; Phebe B., 235; Phebe P., 273; Phebe P., 273; William, 235, 273; Zepher, 235; Zopher C., 273
HOWLAND: John M., 179
HUBBARD: Elizabeth, 218
HUBBS: Rebecca, 49
HUDSON: Rebecca, 180; Sarah W., 172; Thomas, 197
HUES: Rebecca, 27
HUFF: Abraham, 43, 44, 61, 74, 80, 89, 97, 98, 108, 116, 119, 124, 130, 150; Abram, 33; Elizabeth, 44, 61, 80, 89, 108, 130; George, 89; George N., 61; George Norbray, 80; John, 44, 61, 80, 89, 108, 130; Joseph, 80, 89; Joseph B., 61; Martha, 44, 61, 76, 80, 90, 97, 105, 106, 108, 116, 122, 130, 140, 150; Mary, 80; Mary Ann, 44, 61, 80, 89, 108, 130; Massey, 130; Mercey, 98; Mercy, 43, 44, 61, 74, 82, 89, 99, 108; Mikal, 97; Phebe, 97; Richard, 61, 80, 89; Samuel, 44, 61, 80, 89, 108, 130
HUGG: Abram, 140; Mary, 140
HUGH: Rebecca, 27
HUGHES: Eliza M., 73; Elizabeth M., 272; Esther, 272; George, M.D., 187; Gideon, 220; Isaiah R., 7, 60, 69, 76, 89, 92, 96, 144, 145, 148, 154, 156, 158, 212, 218, 229, 256, 262; John, 178, 196; Juliana, 180, 183; Mary, 271; William, 231
HUGHS: Gidion, 26, 27; Rebecca, 27
HUGO: Samuel B., 74
HUGS: Samuel, 30, 42
HULL: Abel A., 70; Almira Ann, 70; Ann, 232; David, 184; Frances Ann, 162; Harriet, 162; Harriot, 192; Phebe, 184; Thomas, 162; Thomas J., 184, 192, 240; William, 162, 240
HUNT: Caleb, 47, 48; Elisha, 200, 252; Elizabeth, 206; Esther, 200; Joshua, 200; Judith, 189; Mary, 220; Nathan, 14, 23, 201, 212; Priscilla, 54, 90; Rhoda M., 48
HUNTER: Frances H., 184
HURDLE: Susan H., 192; Susanna, 85; Susanna H., 86; Susannah, 78
HUSBAND: Ann, 139; Anna, 104, 147; Elizabeth, 195; Elziabeth, 37, 195, 196, 198, 199, 200, 201, 203, 204, 205, 206; Herman, 105; John, 103; John Jewett, 94; Joseph, 103, 126, 149, 151, 154, 199, 205, 206, 244; Joshua, 38, 53, 89, 94, 98, 99, 103, 104, 105, 139, 145, 147, 153, 199, 205, 206; Julia T., 104; Lydia, 195, 196, 198, 199, 200, 203, 204, 206, 208, 209, 249, 271; Margaret, 94, 97, 98, 103, 104, 105, 106, 139, 147, 199; Margarett, 105; Margreat, 97; Mary, 99, 101, 104, 134, 199, 206; Rachel, 196; S., 254; Sally G., 195, 199, 204, 205; Samuel E., 103; Sarah, 126, 244; Sarah G., 103, 104, 106, 143; Susan, 195, 196, 199; Susanna, 199; William, 38, 101, 173, 195, 197, 199, 200, 201, 202, 203, 204, 206, 207, 208,

209, 210, 211
HUSBANDS: Anna, 101, 102, 103, 105, 106; Elizabeth, 96; Harmon, 102; Harmond, 105; John, 101, 102; John J., 105; Jos., 106; Joseph, 95, 96, 100, 101, 102, 103; Joshua, 94, 96, 97, 99, 100, 101, 102, 103, 106, 154; Margaret, 94, 96, 102, 103, 105, 106; Margatt, 101; Mary, 95, 100, 102; Sarah G., 102, 155; William, 96, 102
HUSE: Gedion, 27; Gidion, 27
HUSSEY: Ellen, 184; Enion, 247; Ennion, 202, 204; George, 184, 204, 220; Grace, 204; Hannah, 173, 184, 203, 204; Isaac, 204; Joseph, 184, 204; Lydia, 271; Margaret, 198; Mary, 195, 198, 200, 218, 252; Miriam, 201; Rachel, 184, 202, 204; Rebecca, 204, 263; Riccord, 201; Sarah, 16, 24; William, 204
HUSTON: William, 56
HUTCHINSON: Ann, 190, 191; Sarah M., 190, 191
HUTTEN: John, 45; Sarah, 45
HUTTON: Ann, 79; Bell, 200, 202; George, 79; Howard, 79; John, 65, 73, 75, 88; Katherine, 75; M., 202; Moses, 244; Sarah, 65, 79, 88, 149, 156; Thomas, 75, 156

I

INGLIS: Matilda, 202
IRWIN: Ellen, 188, 190

J

JACOB: Jane, 187; Rebecca Fussell, 73
JACOBS: Jane, 204; Sarah, 74; Thomas, 74
JAMES: Abel, 246; Able, 162, 233; Amos, 171, 172, 177, 179, 181, 183, 184, 185, 186, 195, 198, 202, 218, 256; Ann, 171, 172, 179, 180, 181, 184, 185, 186, 201, 233; Ann H., 181, 183; Anna, 246; Deborah, 177, 179, 181, 183; Elizabeth, 172, 173, 174, 176, 177, 179, 181, 182, 184, 185; Hannah, 77, 82, 172, 173, 174, 177, 178, 201, 202, 203, 204, 205, 206, 207, 246; Hannah H., 203, 204; Henry, 171; Isaac, 100; Joseph, 178, 183, 200, 201, 202, 203, 204, 205, 206, 208, 233, 246, 260, 263; Maria, 203; Mariam, 170; Mary, 170, 172, 173, 177, 178, 179, 181, 182, 183, 185, 195, 200, 201, 205, 206, 208, 233, 246, 256, 260, 263; Mary C., 172, 177, 178, 179, 184, 186, 190; Mary E., 188; Mary L., 178, 179; Miriam, 171, 196, 198, 199, 201, 202; Priscilla, 171, 176, 177, 179, 181, 184, 186, 256; Rebecca, 45, 75, 208; Rebecca C., 174, 178, 179, 180, 181, 183, 203, 204, 205, 206, 246; Samuel, 233, 246; Sarah, 178, 182, 183, 201, 202, 203, 204, 206, 210, 233, 246; Sarah S., 203; Susan, 179, 181, 183, 186; Susan H., 70; Susana, 256; Susanna, 177, 184; Thomas C., 263; W. L., 186, 189; William L., 179, 190
JANNEY: Abijah, 180; Anna, 170, 226; Benjamin Jay, 218; Daniel, 170; David, 241; Elizabeth, 219, 223, 226, 228, 235, 245; Elizabeth M., 173; George F.,

187, 209, 210, 228, 270;
Georgeanna, 238; Isaac, 226;
Israel, 170, 173, 178, 179, 180,
230; Jacob, 215; Jane, 170;
Jonathan, 170, 173, 180, 226;
Levis, 218, 244; Lewis, 209;
Mary, 170, 209, 218, 228, 230,
244; Mary Ann, 238; Mary P.,
235; Phineas, 180; Pleasant,
180; Richard T., 226; Sarah,
111, 241; Sarah H., 238; Sarah
S., 180
JANSON: Halsey, 214
JAY: Ann, 145; Hannah, 96, 105;
Joseph, 96; Martha, 96; Patty,
96; Samuel, 96; Sarah, 96;
Stephen, 96; Thomas, 96, 98,
125, 126
JEFFERIS: Ann, 202; Carpenter,
41, 78, 84; E. C., 186; Edward
C., 194; G. M., 202; Hannah,
203; Horatio Townsend, 77;
John, 202; Lydia, 172, 176;
Mary, 186; Priscilla, 202;
Samuel, 172, 176, 202;
Townsend, 41; William, 202
JEFFERY: Thomas, 96
JENKINS: Ann M., 192; Charles,
131; Sarah, 131
JENNINGS: Benjamin Jay, 243
JENNY: Sarah, 137, 273
JESSOP: Joseph M., 52, 55, 56;
Susanna, 186
JEWEL: Sarah, 18, 19, 269
JEWELL: George, 253; Mary, 253
JEWET: John, 38, 99
JEWETT: Ann, 123, 195, 204, 243;
James, 103; John, 94, 96, 101,
102, 103, 105, 106, 124, 204,
243, 263; Susanna, 102, 103,
104, 105, 106, 124, 153, 243;
Susannah, 102; Thaddeus, 204;
Thomas, 253

JEWITT: Ann, 200, 203; John, 145,
151, 152, 199, 200; Susanna,
145, 152
JINNEY: Sarah, 98; Thomas, 96
JINNY: Sarah, 96, 97
JOHN: Ann, 139; Catreine, 209;
George, 139; Howard, 139;
James, 139; Lemuel, 139; Lydia,
209; Mary, 122, 141, 151, 171;
Phebe, 209; Rachel, 179;
Reuben, 209; Robert, 209;
Sarah, 139; Sarah H., 209, 267,
270; William, 100, 102, 122
John H. Hewes: John H., 186, 187
JOHNS: Mary, 117, 118; Stephen
S., 210; Susan H., 210; Susanna,
268
JOHNSON: Ann, 132, 147, 156,
247, 268; Anna, 88, 112;
Bathsheba, 39; George, 75, 88,
112, 132, 147, 247, 268;
Howard, 88, 112, 132, 147, 247,
268; James, 49, 75, 76, 88, 112,
132, 147, 247, 268; John, 76,
132, 247, 268; Joseph, 97;
Joseph G., 76; Joshua, 228;
Lemuel, 147; Lemuel Stansbury,
79, 88, 112; Lydia, 228; Mary
R., 228; Melchisedeck, 27;
Melchsedeck, 27; Rachel, 54,
90; Robert, 171; Sarah, 17, 18,
19, 75, 88, 112, 132, 147, 247,
268
JOHNSTON: Maria S., 173;
Rachel, 228; Rob N., 175;
Robn., 172; William, 98
JONES: Abner, 33, 38, 44, 61, 78,
82, 84, 88, 103, 192, 233; Ann,
162, 185, 191, 211; Anna, 203;
Anthony, 99, 100, 104, 120,
121; Antony, 97, 102, 103;
Aquila, 33, 81, 82, 93, 162, 192;
Aquilla, 237; Asa, 100, 102,

103, 142, 146, 150, 153, 191;
Benjamin, 123; Betty, 203;
Caleb, 191; Deborah, 192, 204,
205, 207, 209, 271; Deborah B.,
191; Deborah R., 208; Edward,
41; Eliza, 101, 103, 172, 179;
Elizabeth, 97, 98, 99, 100, 102,
103, 104, 141, 150, 184, 191;
Esai, 100; Esau, 100; Ezekiel,
102; Frances, 207, 267; Griffith,
190, 192, 193; Hanna, 143;
Hannah, 3, 33, 46, 47, 61, 78,
82, 84, 88, 103, 154, 192, 233,
238, 271; Isaac, 99, 100, 102,
103, 104, 115, 150, 191; Isac,
98, 141; John, 102, 103, 104,
141, 150, 191, 241; John D.,
188; Lydia Ann, 237; M. A.,
183; Maria, 47, 61, 75, 78, 82,
88, 233, 271; Maria L., 203,
204, 208; Martha T., 103, 191;
Mary, 17, 18, 19, 34, 102, 103,
118, 141, 151, 171, 172, 173,
192, 194, 195, 196, 198, 200,
203, 204, 206, 211, 221, 250,
263, 273, 274; Mary Ann, 179,
182; Mary B., 192; Mary G.,
191; Mary H., 162; Mary L.,
211; Nicholas, 76, 103; Priscilla,
76; Rebecca, 88, 102, 103, 104;
Rebecca Stabler, 233; Richard,
195; Richard H., 190, 200;
Robinson, 203, 204, 205;
Samuel, 102; Samuel G., 171,
172, 173, 175, 181, 191, 263;
Sarah, 46, 82, 102, 103; Susan
B., 171, 206; Susanna, 33, 40,
136, 237, 273; Susanna B., 43,
225; Susanna Buffington, 34;
Susannah B., 46; Susannah
Buffiting, 45; Thomas, 97, 99,
102, 103, 134, 137, 145, 191;
William, 75, 100, 170, 196, 201,
203, 204, 205, 221; William
Gwynn, 190; William K., 183,
208, 209; William R., 185;
Yearsley, 38, 39, 84, 103, 136,
237; Yearsly, 33, 78
JONS: Isaac, 97; Mary, 187
JONSON: Sarah, 17, 19
JORDAN: David, 135, 237
JORDEN: David, 139
JOURDAN: David, 112, 148
JOYCE: Deborah, 220; Thomas,
220
JUDGE: Hugh, 21, 22, 23, 30, 204,
205, 247; Margaret, 23, 29, 56,
205; Phebe, 21, 205, 248, 268;
Phoebe, 200; Rachel, 22, 32,
125, 205, 243, 246; Rebecca,
30, 200, 205, 247, 267;
Rebeccah, 21; Susan, Jr., 21;
Susanna, 21, 22, 30, 200, 203,
204, 205, 206, 207, 208, 221,
247; Susanna, Jr., 22, 200, 203,
221; Susannah, 26, 267;
Susannah, Jr., 204
JUEL: Sarah, 18
JUETT: Ann, 116

K

KANBY: Samuel, 169
KEARL: George H., 179
KEECH: John R., 75
KEIGHLER: Daniel, 196; Mary,
196
KELL: Alisanna, 205; Harriet, 205
KELSO: John M., 209; Martha,
190; Mary, 188, 209; Sidney S.,
190
KEMP: Charles E., 241; Elizabeth
T., 70; Joseph, 112; Samuel T.,
183, 241; Susan Y., 234;
Thomas, 70
KENARD: Ann, 97, 98, 100;
Anthony, 98, 100; Elizabeth,

100; Ely, 97, 98; Joseph, 98;
Lucy, 97; Thomas, 98
KENLY: Maria, 179
KENNARD: Ann, 100, 108, 132;
Anthony, 130, 132; Betsey, 107;
Betsy, 127; Catharine, 107, 126,
127; David Thompson, 126;
Eley, 120, 122; Eli, 107, 127;
Elizabeth, 98, 100, 109, 122,
132, 148; Ely, 99, 125; Hannah,
98, 122, 126; Joseph, 102, 107,
127; Levi, 100, 108; Levy, 100,
132; Mary, 100, 109, 132;
Pricialla, 98; Priscilla, 102;
Samuel T., 181; Thomas, 99,
100, 108, 131, 132; William, 98,
99, 100
KENNEARD: Mary, 174
KENNEY: Hannah, 209; Richard,
223
KENNY: Betty, 171; Daniel, 171,
173, 228; Edith, 185; Eleanor,
171, 174, 177, 178, 179, 182,
183, 191; Eleanor A., 183, 192;
Eleanor Ann, 187, 188;
Elizabeth, 97; Hannah, 171, 182,
185, 187, 190, 195; Isaac, 195;
James, 228; Joseph, 195, 198;
Mary, 195; Maxwell, 189;
Phebe, 171; Sarah, 195;
Thomas, 171
KENT: Joseph, 105, 139, 142, 147,
153
KENWORTHY: Rebecca, 175,
225; William, 34, 175, 185, 225
KERSEY: Joshua, 200
KETTLEWELL: Sarah, 21
KEY: Rebecca, 194
KILGOUR: R., 171
KING: Edward, 174; Eleanor, 182;
Elias Ellicott, 163; Frances F.,
188; Frances T., 193; Francis
Thompson, 163; James, 96;
Jane, 181; John, 75; Joseph,
144, 162, 163, 177, 181, 193;
Mary, 96, 100, 174; Mary
Ellicott, 163; Mary, Jr., 96;
Tacy, 144, 162; Thomas, 144,
163, 181, 193
KINGSTON: John, Jr., 188, 189;
Thomas B., 189
KINNARD: Ann, 100; Joseph, 100;
Levi, 100; Precilla, 100;
Thomas, 100
KINNEY: Eleanor A., 193
KINSER: Elizabeth, 204
KINSEY: Alice, 3, 23; Elizabeth,
26, 206, 264; Elziabeth, 206;
Hannah, 216; Isaac, 19, 20, 26,
215, 252, 264; James, 255, 264;
Joseph, 252; Mary, 19, 28, 169,
200, 215, 244, 264; Moses, 215;
Oliver, 45, 169, 207, 226;
Rachel, 26, 224, 252; Sarah, 45,
215; Thomas, 236
KIRK: Albina, 273; Aquila M.,
182; Caleb, 182; Edith, 177,
200; Eli, 183, 231; Elizabeth,
187, 251, 272, 273; Elmer, 183;
Erastus, 48; Erastus U., 48;
Joseph U., 225; Joshia, 183;
Lydia, 182; Lydia W., 187;
Lydia Wells, 272; Mahlon, 21,
41, 176; Maria M., 49; Mary,
21, 22, 28, 36, 41, 174, 176;
Mary, Jr., 28, 36, 41; Mary, Sr.,
41; Rachal, 41; Rachel, 21, 176,
179, 235; Sarah, 6, 232;
Timothy, 6, 20, 40, 176;
William, 22, 39; William B., 40
KITTLE: Sarah, 19
KITTLEWELL: Charles, 19, 25;
Isaac, 19, 25, 29, 30; John, 19,
25, 28; Margaret, 19, 25;
Margarett, 28; Mary, 19, 25, 28,
46; Samuel, 19, 25, 28; Sarah,

21; Thomas, 19, 25, 28
KNIGHT: Abel, 180, 196, 234; Charles D., 234; Elizabeth, 180, 234; George J., 173, 179, 180, 210; George S., 207, 234; Isaac, 196, 225; Isaac D., 234; Jane, 180; Jane D., 234; Jarel, 234; John, 187; Juliana, 172; Margaret S., 234; Mira, 187; Nathaniel, 208; Sarah, 177, 185, 187, 234; Tacy M., 234
KNOCK: Jane, 235, 250, 273; William, 239, 250, 273
KNOX: Grace, 170, 171, 173, 178, 181, 182, 183, 185, 186, 188, 191, 194, 201, 210; Reynold, 208, 210; Reynolds, 181, 182, 183, 185, 186, 187, 188, 189, 191, 194, 201
KOOPER: Ann, 115; Elizabeth, 115; Isaiah, 115; Martha, 115; Nicholas, 115; Pathanie, 115; Sarah, 115

**L**

LACEY: Amos, 22
LAFETRA: Jacob, 192, 208, 209, 261; Lydia, 242, 262; Mary, 262; Mary B., 184, 185, 188, 190, 191, 192, 209, 210, 211; Phebe, 184, 187, 192, 207, 209, 210, 211, 261, 269; Phebe H., 202, 206; Sarah, 184, 185, 187, 209, 211, 261, 262; Thomas H., 262
LAFETTRA: Jacob, 163; Jane B., 163; Lydia, 163; Mary, 163; Phebe, 163; Sarah, 163; Thomas H., 163
LAFFATTRA: Jacob, 262; Phebe, 262; Sarah, 262
LAFRETRA: Phebe, 272
LAKE: Amos, 76

LAMB: Ann, 192; Daniel, Jr., 163; George M., 163; Isaac, 241; John Emerson, 241; Mary, 163; Mary R., 211; Michael, 184, 192, 194; Rebecca, 163; Thomas Alexander, 163
LAMBORN: Daniel, 12, 37, 64, 84; Eliza, 37; Elizabeth, 12, 37, 64; George Washington, 64; Jane, 37, 64; Jessee, 200; John, 37; John Smith, 64; Julian, 64; Lydia, 64; Maria, 64; Meriah, 12; Sarah, 12, 37, 64; Susanna, 64; William, 37, 64
LANCASTER: Aaron, 76; Benjamin, 65; Eliza, 74; Elizabeth, 3, 12, 61, 73, 75, 76, 77; Esther, 3, 61, 73, 74; Hannah, 12, 61, 73, 75, 76; Isaiah, 212; Jesse, 3, 35, 40, 61, 73, 74, 75, 76, 82; Jessee, 12, 77; John, 2, 3, 61, 71, 74; Joseph, 74, 75, 90; Julia, 3, 61, 73, 74, 75; Mary, 3, 65, 74; Mary Ann, 71; Rachel, 2, 65, 73, 74, 87
LANCESTER: Joseph, 97
LANGDON: Sarah, 187
LANGLEY: Catherine, 192
LANGSTRORTH: Thomas M., 210
LANGSTROTH: George, 31, 78, 86
LANGWORTHY: Provey, 202
LANKASTER: Jesse, 15, 17
LARGE: Dorothea, 180; Ebenezer, 180; Elizabeth, 230; James, 180; John, 180
LARRABEE: Almira, 163; Anne, 163; Daniel, 163, 231, 241; Edward, 241; Edward W., 163, 231; Elizabeth, 163; Ephraim, 163, 185, 241; Hannah, 163, 241; Joseph, 241; Joseph W.,

163; Mary, 163; William, 163, 241
LARRABLE: Anne, 171
LASY: Amos, 22
LAWELEN: Elizabeth, 178
LAWRENCE: Charles Spencer, 214; George, 214; George, Jr., 214; Mary, 214
LAWSON: Elizabeth, 29, 30
LEA: Elizabeth, 42; Elizabeth E., 179, 193, 225; George E., 192; James E., 192; John, Jr., 175; Joseph, 175; Sarah, 174, 192; Sarah Ann, 175; Thomas, 174, 175, 193
LEAKIN: Hannah, 187
LEAKINS: Hannah, 189
LEE: David, 16, 18, 65; David, Jr., 16; Elizabeth, 43, 84, 86, 225; Harriet, 174; Mary, 18, 44; Priscilla, 170; Ralph, 23, 25, 75; Ralph S., 194; Ralph Sackett, 25; Rebbecca, 75; Rebecca, 76; Sarah D., 75
LEEK: Catharine, 238; Richard, 238
LEGG: Susan, 170
LEGGETT: Rosanna, 71; Walter F., 71
LEICESTER: William, 216
LENDRUM: Elija B., 96
LEWEN: John, 101; Rachel, 104
LEWIN: Amos, 92, 113, 142; Amoss, 132; Ann, 92, 113, 132, 142; John, 92, 93, 105, 113, 124, 132, 142, 143, 147, 152, 153, 155; Lydia, 92, 113, 129, 132, 142; mary, 132; Mary, 92, 113, 142; Rachel, 132; Sarah, 104, 132; William, 92, 113, 132, 142
LEWIS: Esther, 79, 87; Grace, 73; Hannah, 30, 37, 71; John, 73,

86; Joseph H., 71
LEYPOLD: Mary, 200
LIGHTLER: Hannah, Jr., 200
LINDENBERGER: Rebecca, 170
LINTON: Elizabeth, 222; Esther, 222; Hannah, 222; Samuel, 222; William, 222
LISTON: James Thomas, 123; Jonathan Allec, 123; Mary, 123; William, 123
LITLE: Charles, 179, 186, 235; Elizabeth, 179, 186; Hannah, 172, 178, 180, 185, 186; John, 173, 178, 185, 186, 232; R., 179; Richard H., 186; Robert, 186; Robert Sinclair, 232; Sarah, 232; Sarah S., 179, 186, 190, 191; W., 179; William, 178, 179, 181, 185, 186
LITTLE: Isa, 203
LIVEZEY: Priscilla, 71
LIVINGSTON: John, 171, 172, 189, 191
LLOYD: John, 51
LONEY: John, 202, 203, 204; William, 202
LONG: Elizabeth, 208
LOUDEN: E., 171; Elizabeth, 170, 178, 181, 196, 206
LOUDON: Betty, 177; Elizabeth, 171, 181, 182
LOVE: H., 209; James, 252; John, Jr., 231
LOVEGROVE: Folger, 163; Hannah, 163; Hannah P., 241; James, 155, 163, 191, 209, 241; Jane, 163; Lydia, 163; Parthenia D., 241; Theodate, 163; Thomas Judge, 163; William Riley, 163
LOWDEN: Elizabeth, 173, 179, 198, 199, 204, 205, 209, 218, 243
LOWDON, 182

LOWNES: Bethula, 174, 175, 176, 177, 179, 189; Charles, 174; Esther, 261; Esther E., 174, 176, 182; Joseph, 173, 174, 175, 176, 178, 179, 189, 200, 261; Josiah, 174, 176, 178, 182, 189; Miriam, 173, 174, 182, 189, 200, 261; Rebecca, 173; Zachariah, 174, 189; Zachariah B., 261
LOWNS: Bethula, 169, 182, 193; Joseph, 169, 182, 192; Josiah, 193; Martin, 169; Miriam, 193
LUCAS: Esther, 187; William B., 202
LUDD: Charlottee, 75
LUKENS: Alice, 3; Charles, 172, 220, 226; Jacob, 3, 15, 20; John, 3; Merriken, 3; Rebecca, 3; Ruth, 3; S., 186; Sarah, 182, 192, 226, 230, 250, 272; Tace, 3; Tacy, 41
LUKING: Jacob, 15
LUKINGS: Jacob, 15
LUKINS: Alice, 41; Alice, Jr., 117; Alse, 115; Ann, 115; Bejamin, 115, 119; Benjamin, 114; Charles, 109, 134; Hannah, 114; Jacob, 41; John, 41; Lidia, 114; Merrikan, 41; Moses, 114; Pheby, 114; Rachel, 114; Rebecca, 41; Ruth, 41; Sarah, 134; Tacey, 41
LWONES: Charles, 175, 176, 227
LYNCH: George R., 74; Mary Ann, 205
LYTLE: Elizabeth, 163; Mary, 163; William, 163

**M**

MABBITT: Cynthia, 71
MACELMERY: Richard, 99
MACILROY: Thomas, 202
MACKENZIE: Calin Burgess, 164; Cosmo, 189; Cosmo Taylor, 164; George Norbury, 164; Martha Norbury, 164; Sarah, 189; Sarah Mackall, 164; Tacy, 164; Thomas, 164, 184, 185, 189, 190, 191
MACLAY: Catharine, 188
MACOMBER: Wesson, 175
MACTIER: Nancy, 180
MADDEN: Ann, 103
MADDUX: Milcah L., 205
MAFFITT: Cynthia, 71
MALONEE: Mary, 221
MALSBEE: David, 114
MALSBY: David, 98, 100, 122, 146, 151, 226; David Lee, 126; Frances Ann, 73; John, 98, 122; Mary, 23, 93, 97, 98, 99, 100, 111, 116, 122, 126, 137, 138, 140, 145, 146, 149, 184; Maurice, 124, 126; Rebecca, 73; Sarah, 36, 226; Sebina, 126
MANIFOLD: Elenor, 98
MANIFOLE: Nancy, 104
MANSFIELD: Edward, 103
MARPLE: Martha, 37
MARRIOTT: Maria, 193
MARSH: Amos, 219; Ann, 30, 35, 221, 258; Catherine, 241; Cyrus, 255; Edith, 219; Eliza, 171, 172, 173, 183, 185, 188, 189, 191, 201; Elizabeth, 255; Hannah, 170, 171, 172, 173, 177, 182, 183, 185, 189, 194, 195, 196, 198, 201, 202, 204, 206, 207, 218, 255; James, 219, 255; John, 30, 35, 166, 170, 171, 172, 173, 175, 176, 180, 181, 183, 185, 187, 188, 189, 190, 191, 193, 194, 195, 196, 198, 199, 200, 201, 202, 204, 218, 221, 255, 258; Jonathan, 25, 221, 223;

Josiah, 181; Lavina, 31;
Leviney, 223; M. H., 188;
Margaret, 30, 35, 223, 258;
Margarett, 221; Mary, 166, 170,
171, 223, 255; Mary H., 172,
183, 185, 188, 191, 201; Mary
K., 189; Miriam, 219; Rebecca,
198, 255; Susanna Morthland,
30, 35; Susanna Mortlin, 221;
William, 30, 35, 221, 258, 259;
Zillah, 219
MARSHALL: Ann, 205; Clement,
204; Mary Ann, 181, 191;
William, 204
MARTIN: Anna, 188; Frances,
251; James, 203; Louisa C., 188;
Mary, 203; Robert, 76; Susanna,
203, 204, 205, 206, 208, 211;
Thomas, 74; William, Jr., 173,
188
MASLIN: Beulah, 225; Michael
M., 225
MASON: Ann, 74, 75, 76;
Elizabeth, 20; George, 12, 20,
48, 53, 106, 113, 122, 127, 141,
143, 152, 154, 170, 195, 196,
202, 220, 228, 231, 235, 236,
252, 265; George, Jr., 53, 231,
235, 236; Howard, 75; Israel,
206; James, 51, 55, 56, 206;
John, 20, 31, 32, 34, 75, 220,
265; Rachel, 18, 28, 31, 32, 48,
170, 172, 173, 176, 177, 179,
180, 181, 183, 185, 186, 188,
191, 193, 194, 195, 196, 198,
199, 200, 201, 202, 206;
Susanna, 85, 196, 252
MASSEY: Ann, 96, 97, 99, 101,
102, 103, 104, 105, 106, 187;
Anna, 94, 99, 101, 102, 104,
105, 143, 154; Aquila, 94, 97,
101, 104, 106, 146, 153, 232;
Aquila B., 105; Aquila Bolton,
94; Aquilla, 126, 138, 154;
Isaac, 94, 96, 97, 99, 101, 102,
104, 105, 106, 143, 154; Isaac
W., 101; James R., 100; John
W., 188; Jonathan, 101, 109,
133; Lydia, 100; Mararett, 101;
Margaret, 96, 98, 101, 102, 104,
105, 106, 143, 154; Margaret R.,
101, 104, 106; Margarett R.,
105; Margarreth R., 105;
Margreat, 97; Margrett, 99;
Rigbee, 105; Rigbie, 94; Sally,
99; Sarah, 98, 100, 101, 131,
174; Sarah Bolton, 94; William,
94, 105
MASSY: Ann, 143
MATHEUS: Sarah, 20
MATHEWS: Rachel, 179
MATHUES: Sarah, 20
MATLACK: Ann M., 188; Ann
Maria, 164; Armistead, 164;
Elizabeth S., 164; Emily, 164;
Hannah, 164, 174; Mary W.,
164; Samuel T., 164, 173, 174;
Susanna S., 164
MATSON: Caleb, 217
MATTHEW: Elizabeth, 195, 196,
198, 199, 213
MATTHEWES: R., 184
MATTHEWS: Abel Kinsey, 4;
Alice, 4, 24; Amos, 183; Ann, 5,
6, 24, 106, 121, 143, 154, 164,
187, 192, 194, 196, 198, 199,
200, 201, 202, 203, 204, 205,
206, 207, 208, 209, 210, 218,
269; Ann H., 264; Aquilla, 5,
241; Ariana, 6; Benjamin, 5, 8;
Cassandra, 106, 164, 187, 264;
Daniel, 16; Edith, 36, 37;
Edward, 5; Eli, 5, 19, 27, 33, 49,
52, 53, 55, 56, 241; Elias, 5;
Eliza, 38, 39, 200, 202;
Elizabeth, 6, 8, 13, 28, 221, 252,

253, 258, 263; Esther, 5, 241; Evan, 8; George, 6, 28, 57, 198, 199, 200, 201, 203, 218, 221, 251, 258; Hannah, 6, 196, 198, 225; Isaac Moore, 4; Jarret, 5; Jesse, 5; Joel, 5, 24; John, 3, 4, 15, 23, 34, 50, 164; Joseph, 164, 264; Joshua, 6, 106, 143, 154, 155, 198, 199, 203, 204, 207, 208; Lydia, 252; Margaret, 5, 241; Maria, 48; Martha, 3, 4, 16; Mary, 5, 15, 19, 20, 34, 49, 54, 56, 200, 202, 206, 265; Mary H., 113; Mary Jane, 4; Mary, Sr., 34; Matilda, 35, 36; Milcah, 5; Miriam, 213; Mordecai, 5, 191, 201; Mordecai, Jr., 191; Mordocai, Jr., 183; Nancy, 205; O., 41, 198, 199; Oliver, 4, 13, 24, 34, 40, 41, 48, 264; Owen, 4; Phebe, 4, 24; Precilla, 5; Priscilla, 241; Rachel, 3, 5, 8, 46, 47, 57, 181, 235; Rachel P., 57, 183, 186, 189, 191; Rebecca, 6, 8, 30, 48, 50, 51, 55, 57, 206, 243; Rhoda, 6, 33, 201; Richard, 5; Ruth, 5, 20, 23, 28, 30, 54, 201; Samuel, 195, 198, 199, 200, 202, 203, 206, 208, 209, 210; Samuel H., 55, 173, 202, 228; Samuel Hanway, 28, 41, 221; Samuel P., 202, 203, 204; Sarah, 5, 20, 53, 106, 164, 170, 187, 192, 195, 199, 200, 203, 205, 206, 207, 208, 209, 251, 252, 264; Sophia, 200, 202, 206, 271; Stephen, 214; Susanna, 28, 49, 50, 188, 221, 263; T. R., 179, 186, 190; Thomas, 3, 5, 6, 8, 19, 20, 33, 51, 53, 54, 55, 56, 57, 106, 143, 164, 184, 191, 195, 198, 199, 208, 264; Thomas R., 181;

William, 4, 8, 13, 24, 28, 34, 40, 41, 48, 56, 198, 199, 219, 221, 252, 253, 258, 263
MAULSBY: David, 36, 45, 156; David Lee, 39; Frances, 36; Mary, 17, 18, 19, 23, 26, 27, 39, 79, 87, 89, 100; Morris, 18, 19, 39; Pamelia, 36; Sarah, 19, 36
MAXWELL: Ann G., 183
MAY: Phebe, 225
MAYNE: John, 214
MAYSON: Elizabeth, 20; Rachel, 193
McCAY: Andrew, 99; John C., 105; Lidia, 101; Priscilla, 102; Priscilly, 101; William, 101
McCLARY: Rebeca, 103
McCOMAS: Cassandra, 79, 87, 112, 138, 140, 147, 150; Elizabeth, 211; James Howard, 79, 87, 112, 138, 140, 147, 150; Juliett, 76; Sarah, 79, 84, 87, 112, 138, 140, 147, 150
McCOMASS: Cassandra, 61; James, 61; James Howard, 61; Juliett, 192; Sarah, 61, 192
McCONNAL: Frances, 76; James, 76; Samuel, 76
McCONNEL: Frances, 74; Samuel, 15, 20, 21, 74
McCONNELL: Fraces, 43; Frances M., 61; Francess, 9; James, 61; James Orr, 9; Mary, 9, 86, 87; Samuel, 9, 44, 61, 73, 82
McCORMICK: Ann, 176; Mary, 178, 229; Thomas, 171
McCOY: Andrew, 121, 171, 180, 182, 192, 196; Ann, 171, 172, 182, 183; Cassandra, 85, 182; David G., 109, 133, 163, 182, 183, 209; Elizabeth, 163; Isaac, 114, 125, 163, 171, 196; John C., 182, 183, 184, 185, 186,

192; Joseph, 171, 183, 196, 257;
Martha, 104, 171, 184, 196;
Mary, 107, 128, 171, 196, 233;
Robert, 126, 182, 184, 192;
Sarah Matilda, 180; William, 96,
97, 98, 99, 101, 104, 112, 121,
152, 154, 182, 184
McCRAKEN: Martha, 104
McDERMET: Jonathan, 204
McDERMIT: Robert, 204
McDONNELL: Maria, 204
McDOWELL: Elziabeth, 182, 185
McFADDEN: Elezabeth, 100
McGOWAN: Margaret, 204;
Martha, 204
McKENSEY: Thomas, 194
McKENZIE: Thomas, 191
McKIM: John, 38, 195, 196, 198,
200, 201, 204, 206, 207, 208,
209; Mary, 191, 195, 204, 205,
206, 207, 209, 210, 218
McKINNON: Rod. William, 178
McKINSEY: Elziabeth, 52; Rachel,
184, 185
McKINSTRY: Evan, 197
McKUINE: Caroline, 174
McLAUGHLIN: Jane, 104; Peggy,
207
McMURRY: Richard, 99
McPHERSON: Ann, 170, 173, 182,
189, 191, 194; Eliza, 201, 202;
Elizabeth, 170, 173; Esther, 173,
175, 177, 182, 189; Hannah,
170, 181, 194, 262; Isaac, 169,
170, 173, 194, 197, 201, 202,
204, 262; Jane, 170, 172, 173,
201, 202; John, 193; Martha,
262; Mary, 173, 177, 181, 185,
188, 193; Patience, 197; Samuel,
238; Tace, 262; Tacey, 173,
201; Tacy, 170, 196, 197, 202;
W. L., 194
MEALY: Ruth, 271

MECHAM: Francis, 29
MECHEM: David L., 71; David T.,
66; Elisha G., 66; Francis, 61,
74, 93; George, 61; Hannah, 66;
Isaac, 71; James R., 74; John,
66, 74, 86; Jonathan, 66; Joshua,
66; Lydia, 74; Lydia Ann, 66;
Naomi, 61, 74; Oliver H., 66;
William, 61, 71
MECONCKIN: John, 183; Thomas,
183
MECOY: Andrew, 119
MECTEER: Hannah, 183; Mary,
245; Mercy, 202; Sarah, 190;
Thomas, 202, 245; William,
183, 202
MEDCALF: A., 165; A. O., 100; A.
P., 192; Abigail, 184, 187, 195,
205, 206, 207, 218; Abigal, 192,
211; Abm. Pyle, 196; Abraham,
100, 132, 164, 243; Abraham P.,
266, 272; Abram, 100; David,
132, 266, 272; Elijah, 222, 243,
248, 268; Elizabeth, 100;
George, 266; Jamima, 266;
Jessy, 132; John, 165; Joseph,
132; Joshua, 222, 243, 265;
Lydia, 164; Mary, 100, 132,
164, 165, 272; Mary R., 184;
Moses, 100, 132; Rachel, 132;
Rebecca, 100, 132, 194, 195,
206, 208, 210, 211, 222, 243,
248, 265, 268, 270; Sarah
Moore, 164; Susanna, 100, 132,
266, 272; William, 164; William
M., 206
MEEKIN: Francis, 29; George, 29;
Isaac, 29; John, 29; Lydia, 29;
Naimo, 29; Neomi, 29; Richard,
29
MEETER: George Brown, 261;
Mercey, 261; Thomas, 261
MENDENHALL: Beulah, 174,

175; Hannah, 210; Jacob, 171, 174, 175, 225
MERRICK: Roger, 216
METCALF: Abraham, 249; David, 249; Mary, 249; Rebeckah, 229; Susanna, 249
METCHAM: Francis, 93
METKELF: Elizabeth, 131
MICHEM: John, 86
MIDCALF: Abraham, 116; Elziabeth, 116; Mary, 116; Moses, 100, 116; Rebecca, 116; Sarah, 116; Susanna, 100
MIDKELF: Abraham, 109; David, 109; Jesse, 109; Joseph, 109; Mary, 109; Moses, 109; Rachel, 109; Rebeckah, 109; Susannah, 109
MIDKIFF: Abraham, 266; Jamima, 266; Mary, 266
MIDSHILL: Margret, 100
MIFFLIN: Ann, Jr., 170; Jonathan W., 101; Lloyd, 206; Mary, 102, 103, 138, 147, 152, 159, 195, 196, 198, 199, 201, 203, 204, 205, 206, 207, 208, 210, 218, 249, 272, 274; Thomas, 180
MIFLEN: Mary, 233
MIFLIN: Mary, 101, 158
MILLER: Edith, 99, 121, 125, 244; John, 98, 99, 121, 125, 244; John S., 190, 191; Joseph W., 205, 206, 265; Lidia, 121; Lydia, 125; Margaret, 130, 131; Matilda Brackin, 18, 27; Priscilla, 97; Rachel, 121, 125; Samuel, 199; Susanna, 245; William, 97, 244; William F., 206; William John, 125
MILLS: Thomas, 186
MINCE: Elizabeth, 204; Mary, 204
MITCHEL: John, 171, 174, 180, 194, 195, 196, 197, 198, 204; Mary, 195; Tacy, 171, 180, 194, 195, 196, 197, 202, 204, 218
MITCHELL: Hannah, 191; Mary, 221; Tacy, 170, 172, 174, 175
MOALE: John C., 180, 181
MOAT: Rachel, 38
MOLSBEY: Mary, 26
MOON: John Thomas, 179, 181
MOOR: Daniel M., 170
MOORE: Andrew, 236; Ann, 1, 175, 176, 178, 229; Asa, 229; Benjamin, 236; Benjamin P., 164, 179, 181, 193; Caleb, 176, 229; E. S., 209; Elizabeth, 88, 91, 92, 236, 241, 249; Elizabeth Hopkins, 164; Esther, 191, 238; Gerard Hopkins, 164; James, 189; James, Jr., 189, 191; John, 209; John W., 164; Lucretia, 74; Margaret, 177, 204; Mary, 164, 175, 176, 181, 229; Mary Ann, 236; Mary B., 241; Mary G., 71; Mary H., 188, 189, 191, 193, 230; Nathaniel, 236; Phebe, 189; Rebecca, 10, 164; Robert, 71, 164, 181; Sarah, 164, 182, 236; T., 188; Thomas, 34, 38, 164, 175, 176, 177, 178, 229, 236; Walter, 1; Whitsen, 236; William Wilson, 164
MOORES: James, 76; Samuel Lee, 75
MOREHEAD: Martha G., 102
MORGAIN: Hugh, 96; Robert, 105
MORGAN: Amfield C., 101; Ann, 213; Eliza, 211; Elizabeth, 75, 187, 192, 194, 202; Evan Jones, 257; Hannah, 213; Henry C., 75; Jesse, 202, 248; Jessee, 198; John, 31, 32, 33, 36, 165, 204, 209, 210, 211, 213, 218, 250, 257, 273; John A., 257; Mary, 208, 210, 211, 213, 257, 272;

Mary P., 187; Priscilla, 23, 36, 179, 202, 211, 218, 250, 273; Robert, 104; S. A., 194; Sarah, 165, 210, 211, 257; Susan A., 75, 184, 192, 211; Susanna, 257; Thomas, 67, 210, 211, 257; Thomas A., 71; Thomas C., 101; William, 204, 210, 213, 257; William P., 209; William R., 210, 211; Wm., 104
MORGIN: Prissilla, 23
MORRIS: Anna, 105, 112, 139, 148; Anthony P., 103, 147; Catharine, 103, 200; Catharine W., 103; Elizabeth, 103; Elziabeth G., 104; Henry, 103; Isaac, 100, 107, 126, 134, 135; Isaac P., 193; Isaac T., 103; Isaac W., 103, 147; Israel, 10, 36, 37, 65; Jacob S., 104; Mahetibal, 245; Martha, 103, 107, 126; Mary L., 103; Nehemiah, 107, 126; Rebeca, 103; Richard, 207; Sarah, 10, 88, 103, 111, 118, 139, 147, 167; Susannah, 103; William, 26, 27
MORRISON: Hannah D., 90
MORRISS: Anthony P., 139; Isaac, 139; Sarah, 139
MORTHLAND: Edward H., 51; Mary, 51; Phebe, 27, 28; Robert, 28, 34, 35, 36, 51; Samuel, 51; Samuel, Jr., 21; Sarah, 14, 50, 212; Susanna, 12, 51
MOTT: Abraham G., 46, 247; Abraham Griffeth, 46; Abraham Griffith, 268, 269; Elizabeth, 265; James, 265; John, 46, 63, 164, 207, 247, 269, 270; Joshua, 31, 32, 185, 187, 192, 204, 205, 206, 207, 208, 209, 265; Mary Griffith, 270; Rachal, 37, 38;

Rachel, 32, 38, 46, 184, 185, 206, 207, 209, 210, 247, 265, 268, 269, 270; Rachel M., 187, 272; Rachell, 164; Sarah Elizabeth, 164
MUIR: Jane W., 173
MULLIKIN: Mary B., 184, 192; Richard D., 201
MUMMEY: Katherine, 201; Thomas, 201
MURPHY: Thomas, 74
MURRY: Sarah, 117
MYERS: Samuel, 171, 226

N

NAFF: John H., 184
NAILOR: Elizabeth, 207
NANCANOW, 208; John, 208
NAYLOR: Abraham, 41; Ann, 28, 36, 242, 258; Charles, 28, 36, 242, 258; Elizabeth, 32, 198, 199, 200, 203, 252, 258; Isaac, 16, 17; James, 246, 258; Jane, 25, 203; John, 28, 34, 36, 41, 203, 242, 258; John, Jr., 34; Joseph, 15, 28, 36, 242, 258; Lavinia, 25; Levina, 25; Levinia, 25; Margaret, 246, 258, 267; Mary, 11, 28, 34, 36, 41, 242, 264; Rachel, 199, 200, 204, 208; Rebecah, 242; Rebecca, 28, 36, 258, 264; Rebeckah, 11; Samuel, 11, 28, 36, 242, 258, 264; William, 36, 37, 38
NEALE: James, 212
NEALL: Joseph K., 184
NEEDLES: Ann Maria, 165; Edith, 165; Edward, 182; Edward M., 165; Edward, Jr., 183, 189, 232; Elijah Marsh, 165; Eliza, 39, 165; Elizabeth, 165, 183; james B., 183, 230; John, 38, 39, 165, 172, 178, 179, 183, 205, 206,

230, 244; John Amos, 165;
Joseph A., 228; Mary Lamb,
165; Ruth Ann, 165; Sarah, 165,
182; Susanna, 177, 178, 180,
181, 183, 234; Susannah, 183
NEGRO: Aquila, 36; Milcha, 36
NEIL: Joseph, 198
NEVILL: Ann, 98; Casandria, 104
NEVINS: Pim, Jr., 180
NEWILL: James, 216
NEWLIN: Ann Eliza, 165; David, 165; David N. Dawson, 165; Jane, 165; Rebecca, 165
NICHOLSON: Alice, 124, 227; Charles L., 227; Eliza, 227; John, 170, 171, 172, 173, 174, 201, 202, 227; William L., 227
NICOLL: Susanna, 198
NILES: Ann, 269; Anna, 270; Benjamin Franklin, 270; John W., 235; John Warner, 270; Mary Jane, 188, 270; Robert Duer, 270
NINDE: Benjamin, 246
NOCK: Jane, 272; Rachel, 210
NORBARY: Jacob, 253; Tacy N., 103
NORBURY: George, 102, 164, 171, 182, 183, 185, 187, 189, 201; Martha, 102, 164, 171, 182, 183, 185, 187, 189, 201; Susanna, 187, 189; Taacy B., 102, 104, 183, 185, 187, 188; Taci, 201; Tacy, 184; Tacy B., 189
NORRIS: A. S., 191; Ann, 180, 181, 182, 185, 211; Anna, 172; David Lee, 76, 194; Edward, 194; Edward S., 194; Elenor, 202; Eliza, 197, 199, 211; Eliza A., 194; Elizabeth, 73, 179, 194, 201; Elizabeth Ann, 76; Ellen, 188, 206, 211; Ellin, 105; John C., 178, 179, 181, 183, 185, 186, 187, 188, 189, 190, 191, 211, 238; Lloyd, 71, 76, 190, 194; Margaret, 185, 190, 194, 211; Mary, 165, 250, 273; Mary A., 181; Mary Ann, 105, 180, 183, 185, 187, 211; Mary Ann L., 238; Mary C., 188; Mary Jane, 194; Matilda D., 165; Oliver P., 197; Rebecca, 76, 173, 174, 194, 196, 201; Rhesa, 76; Robert, 165; Robert H., 209, 210, 211, 272; Saisan, 75; Sarah Ann, 165; Sarah E., 71; Susanna, 196, 199; Thomas, 185, 187, 211; Thomas A., 194; Thomas Morgan, 165; William, 75, 194
NORRISS: Lloyd, 193; Thomas A., 193
NORTON: Elizabeth, 96, 117; James, 127; Mary, 147; Nathan, 101; Nathaniel, 98, 118, 124; Samuel, 101; Sarah, 96, 98, 117; Sophia, 98, 117; Stephen, 96, 98, 99, 106, 126; Steven, 117; Thomas, 98, 123, 243
NORWOOD: Maria, 181
NOWLAND: Dennis, 196

**O**

OAGE: Elizabeth, 211
OAKLY: Alisanna, 206
O'DARE: Elizabeth, 242
ODDIE: William, 216
OFFLEY: Joseph W., 241; Michael, 241
OGSTON: John, 208
OKELY: Alisan, 269; Alisanna, 208; Alissanna, 205
OKLEY: Alisanna, 248, 266
OREM: Eleanor, 184
ORR: Angeline, 98; James, 9, 129,

130; Sarah, 101
OSBORN: Charles, 48; Elizabeth, 193

P

PAGE: James, 199
PAINTER: Edward, 72; George, 72; Louisa G., 72; Phebe, 177; William, 177
PAITS: Ann, 228; Joseph, 228; William, 228
PALMER: Benjamin, 177, 189, 197; Mary, 177, 197; Polly, 197; Richard, 197, 223; Thomas, 231
PANCOAST: Caleb, 178; Elizabeth, 186; Sarah, 186
PARISH: Benjamin, 28
PARKER: John, 103; Joseph, 102; Margay, 102; Robert, 105; Sarah, 273, 274
PARKINS: Isaac, Jr., 199
PARKS: Mary, 204
PARMER: Benjamin, 169
PARR: David, 98
PARRISH: Benjamin, 28; Edith, 29; John, 11, 195; Keturah, 22; Kitturah, 31; Mordecai, Jr., 34, 35; Peter, 34, 35; Rachel, 43, 47; Susannah, 1; Urith, 34, 35; William, 1
PARROTT: Benjamin P., 183
PARSON: Elizabeth D., 78, 84, 135
PARSONS: Abner, 85; Abraham, 84, 85; Amos, 54; Ann, 56, 75, 76, 80, 81, 86, 88, 92; Ann P., 86; Edmond, 86; Edmund, 81, 92; Edward, 92; Elizabeth, 56, 80, 83, 86, 92, 137; Ganar, 103; Ganer, 111, 137; Ganor, 145; James, 56, 80, 92; Jamima, 86; Jemima, 80; Jessee, 31; John, 17, 18; John, Jr., 16; Joseph, 75, 84; Joseph D., 78, 135; Margaret J., 86; Maria, 81, 86, 92; Mary, 2, 40; Richard, 74; Susanna, 44; Tace, 15; Tacy, 15; Thomas, 39; William, 56, 80, 86, 91, 92; William P., 86
PARVIN: Thomas, 195
PASSMOORE: George, 199, 200
PATRIGE: Ann, 200
PATTERSON: Sarah, 105
PAUL: John, 208; Phebe, 217; Rachel, 217
PAXON: Elizabeth, 240
PEACH: Samuel, 229; Sarah, 199
PEARSE: George, 220
PEARSON: Ann, 137, 145, 147; Deborah, 27, 30; Elisha, 8, 45, 113, 132, 143, 155; Enoch, 27, 39, 40, 132, 134, 138, 139; Enock, 8, 27, 146; Margarum, 47; Phebe, 27, 45, 110, 132, 135; Rachel, 27, 45, 132, 135; Samuel, 27, 45, 132; Susanna, 8, 45, 132; Susannah, 27; William, 27, 132, 134, 138, 146, 147
PEARSONS: Margaret, 44
PECK: Ann, 97, 98, 101, 119, 176, 185, 186, 190, 191, 192, 193, 201, 203, 205, 206, 207, 208, 209, 210, 211, 217, 261, 269, 270, 271; Caroline M., 241; George, 241; Hiel, 175; John J., 97; John S., 101, 122, 176, 204, 206, 207, 208, 209, 210, 211; John Spotswood, 98, 116, 118, 254; John Spottiswood, 195, 214
PENDON: Ester, 16
PENFOLD: Martha, 181
PENNIMAN: W., 201
PERIAN: Mary, 130; Mauldin, 130; Peter, 130; Peter Amos, 130
PERINE: Ann, 184; Ann H., 192,

211; Malden, 192, 214; Mary, 184, 192, 211, 214; Maulden, 184; Peter, 118, 192, 214, 215; Susannah, 192
PERRIGO: Daniel, 210; Sophia, 210
PERVAIL: Amelia, 203; John, 203
PERVAL: Mary, 99
PERVEIL: Mary, 127
PETERS: Ann, 170; Anna C., 102
PEYTON: David, 74
PHENIX: Elizabeth, 202
PHERSON: Martha, 170
PIAYAS: Nancy, 103
PICKERING: Phinehas, 216
PIDGEON: Isaac, 99; Rachel, 99; William, 99
PIERPOINT: Ann, 200, 253; Deborah, 253; John, 253; Joseph, 253; Mary, 200; Misail, 200; N. W. P., 175, 177
PIGEON: Isaac, 123; Rachel, 123; Sarah, 124; William, 123
PILE: Hermon, 110; John, 110
PILES: Amos, 135; Daniel, 138, 139, 147, 149; David, 139; Hermon, 134; John, 135
PINKERTON: Rebecca W., 189
PINN: John, 214
PITS: Rebecah, 25
PITT: Priscilla E., 187
PITTS: Elziabeth, 37; Rebecah, 25; Rebecca, 26
PIYLE: Hannah, 101
PLATTS: John, 175; John Pacey, 208
PLEASANTS: Ann, 220, 259; Ann P., 259; Deborah, 185; Elizabeth, 259; Elizabeth Rhodes, 220; Hannah, 220, 259; Israel, 220, 259; Israel Pemberton, 220, 259; John, 220, 259; Joseph, 219; Mary, 220, 259; Samuel, 220, 259; Sarah, 220, 259; Thomas Franklin, 220, 259; Walter, 220; Walter Franklin, 259
PLUMMER: Alice, 218, 258; Ann, 116; Einah, 258; Eleanor, 220; Eli, 218, 258; Elisha, 14, 53, 54, 55; James, 218; Jm. P., 199; Joanna, 249, 265; Johanna, 272; Johannah, 199, 224, 233; John, 199, 224, 265; John T., 210, 233; John Thomas, 272; Joseph P., 195, 196, 199, 208, 210, 217, 224, 233, 249, 265, 266, 272; Mary, 14, 55, 224, 265; Mary K., 54; Mary M., 233; Mary Mifflin, 249, 272; Phebe, 219; Sarah, 218, 258; Sarah C., 233; Sarah Cresson, 266; Susanna, 206, 219, 265, 266; Susannah, 224; Thomas, 219, 249; William K., 14, 55
POLK: William W., 172
POLLARD: David, 248; Elizabeth, 262; Lydia, 248, 262, 269; Mary, 270; Peter, 194, 262; Sarah, 274; William, 248
POPE: Abner, 209, 210, 211, 235, 250; Ann, 142, 173, 182, 191, 206, 209, 210, 225, 237, 249, 271; Daniel, 185, 188, 211; David S., 104, 190, 191, 225, 249; Edward, 235; Folger, 104, 142, 143, 152, 154, 155, 203, 205, 225, 237, 249, 271; Franklin F., 142, 191, 225, 237, 249, 271; Hannah, 180, 182, 208, 209, 210, 228, 249, 269, 272; Hannah N., 188; Joseph, 225; Joseph D., 142, 237, 249, 271; Lois K., 188, 190, 191; Lois R., 185; Lydia, 241; Maria, 235; Mary Ann, 235; Sarah R.,

142, 237, 249, 271; Theeodat, 208; Theodat, 104; Theodate, 139, 142, 148, 180, 229, 237; William R., 142, 153, 225, 237
POPELINE: Nicholas, 169
POPPLEIN: Andreas, 201; Catharine, 188, 189; George, 201; Nicholas, 170, 172, 180, 188, 190, 201
POPPLIEN: Catharine, 185
POST: Jacob, 214
POTTS: Joel, 75
POULTNET: Thomas, 162, 169, 170, 175, 180, 193, 197, 202
POULTNEY: Ann, 169, 170, 171, 173, 174, 175, 177, 178, 180, 182, 193, 197, 201, 202, 262; Elisha, 202; Elizabeth, 180; Evan, 172, 173, 180, 181, 188, 202; Lucy, 191; Lydia, 193, 194; Mary Ann, 262; P., 181; Philip, 180, 193, 202; Rachel, 173, 174, 175, 180, 181; Samuel, 180, 193, 202; Sarah, 177, 180, 193, 194; Sarah Cresson, 262; Thomas, 180, 262
POWEL: Albina, 224, 267, 269; Benjamin W., 268, 269; Benjamin Wayne, 224, 267; Hannah, 224; John C., 268, 269; John Carpenter, 267; Margaret, 224, 231, 267, 268, 269; Martha, 48
POWELL: Albina, 208, 247, 248; Benjamin W., 230, 248; Benjamin Wayne, 247; John C., 165, 231, 248, 261; John Carpenter, 247; Joshua, 261; Margaret, 231, 247, 261, 273; Margarett, 248; Martha, 83, 84, 242
PRESBURY: George G., 98
PRESON: David, 75

PRESTON: Benjamin, 2; David, 2, 25, 38, 40, 61, 73, 75, 76, 77, 82, 85, 89; Deborah, 61, 71; Edmond, 61; Edmund, 71; Hannah, 25, 61, 73, 74, 75, 76; Isaac H., 73, 74; Isaac Hollingsworth, 25; Isaac W., 76; Judith, 2, 25, 30, 43, 44, 61, 73, 74, 75, 82; Phebe H., 71; Rachel, 2, 61, 76; Silvester B., 77; Silvester Bills, 61; Sylvestor Bills, 25
PREVAIL: Elizabeth, 107, 267; John, 114; Margaret, 108; Mary, 55, 237
PREVALE: Mary, 99, 107
PREVEIL: Elizabeth, 129; Margaret, 129
PRIAN: Margaret, 197
PRICE: Amon, 6; Amos, 49, 52, 234; Ann, 1, 7, 10, 31, 32, 33, 38, 52, 57, 184, 201, 245; Ann M., 101, 189, 191; Anna, 104, 189, 191; Anne, 207; Beal, 23, 24, 25; Benjamin, 7, 101, 102; Betty, 1, 2, 18, 52; Caleb, 35, 36, 204; Caroline, 249, 270, 271; Caroline P., 71; Catharine, 10; Charity, 9; Daniel, 1, 2, 18, 39, 48, 54, 55, 207; David, 10, 54; Deborah, 7; Edith, 1, 52, 184; Edward, 4, 10; Edward C., 71; Eleanor, 235; Eli, 9, 55; Eli M., 12; Elija, 21; Elijah, 6, 13, 14, 21, 49, 51, 52; Elijah M., 13; Eliza, 6, 249, 270, 271; Eliza C., 105; Elizabeth, 7, 37, 56, 185, 186, 187, 207, 208, 210, 219, 238; Elizabeth Ann, 4; Elizabeth C., 109, 134; Ellen, 10; Emily, 13, 55; Esther, 10; Evan, 249, 270, 271; Ezra, 4; Frances, 10, 56, 207, 219, 238, 258; Frances

Ann, 13, 55; Francess, 210; Francis, 185; George, 55; Hanna, 101; Hannah, 7, 177, 187, 195, 198, 219, 249, 254, 258, 260, 269, 270, 271; Henry, 191; Isaac, 6, 245, 256; Isaiah, 7; Israel, 56, 184, 187, 195, 198, 206, 207, 208, 219, 238, 254, 258, 260; James, 3, 7, 13; James B., 101; Jane, 56, 187, 238; Jared M., 13, 53, 55; Jarred, 269; Jarrett, 249; Jehu, 12, 49, 50, 55; Jesse, 2, 204, 207, 235; Jessee, 18; Joel, 2; John, 4, 11, 12, 19, 20, 41, 52, 57, 204; John F., 71; John H., 231; John K., 6; John R., 204; John, Jr., 11; Joseph, 23, 25, 49, 51; Joshua, 2; Joshua C., 10; Julia, 249; Juliann, 270, 271; Kiturah, 45; Maranda, 7; Margaret, 7; Maria, 249, 270; Martha, 7, 204, 207; Mary, 4, 7, 10, 25, 29, 39, 54, 55, 191, 204, 206; Mary Ann, 7, 13; Mary D., 32, 43, 45, 46, 55; Mary M., 32, 45, 48, 54; Matilda, 7; Miriam, 4; Mordecai, 2, 6, 7, 17, 28, 29, 35, 43, 45, 48, 49, 51, 52, 53, 54, 55; Mordecai C., 10; Mordecai D., 7; Mordecai, Jr., 9; Moses Dillon, 7; Nathan, 2; Oliver, 4; Oliver Matthews, 4; Phebe, 16, 198; Philip, 101, 102, 133, 191; Philip, Jr., 101; Phoebe, 16; Priscilla, 10; Rachel, 1, 2, 6, 10, 52, 102; Rebecah, 25; Rebecca, 7, 26; Rhoda, 249, 270, 271; Richard, 56, 194, 238; Ruth, 101, 102; Samuel, 1, 4, 18, 27, 28, 34, 38, 48, 51, 52, 54, 55, 184, 207; Samuel C., 10; Samuel, Jr., 10, 27, 28, 34, 38, 54; Samuel, Sr., 1; Sarah, 6, 7, 13; Sarrah M., 13; Sophia, 13, 14; Susan, 201; Susanna, 12, 194, 245, 256, 264; Susanna M., 55; Tabitha, 2; Thomas, 7, 10, 40, 41, 48, 50, 53; Urith, 12; Warrick, 4, 194, 245, 256, 264; Warwick, 264; William, 29, 219, 245; William B., 52, 234, 254; William Matthews, 4; William R., 7
PRIGG: Eliza, 101; Joseph, 97; Mary, 114; Mary T., 104
PRINE: Ann, 108, 267; Malden, 118, 267; Margaret, 177; Mary, 108, 118, 267; Maulden, 108; Peter, 108, 118; Peter Amos, 267
PRINTON: Ferrie, 103
PROCTER: Ann, 165, 210, 266; Anna, 185, 208, 209; Anna W., 187; Deborah, 185, 187; Deborah W., 165, 192, 266; Edmund Prior, 170, 174, 175; Edward, 165; Eliza, 173, 180, 185, 186, 187, 188; Elizabeth, 174, 175, 180, 181, 208, 255; Elizabeth Robson, 165; Isaac, 160, 165; Izac, 255; Izak, 170, 171, 172, 173, 174, 175, 177, 178, 180, 181, 183, 185, 188, 195, 196, 201, 206, 208, 218, 255; Mary, 174, 177, 178, 255; Mary M., 185, 206; Rebecca, 27, 165, 170, 171, 172, 173, 174, 175, 176, 177, 178, 179, 180, 181, 182, 183, 185, 188, 189, 191, 195, 198, 201, 204, 205, 206, 208, 255; Sarah, 44, 165, 170, 195, 203, 204, 205, 206, 207, 208, 218, 263, 267; Stephen, 180, 181, 183, 205, 208; William, 165, 184, 185,

187, 190, 192, 195, 200, 201, 205, 207, 208, 209, 211, 218, 266; Wilson, 165
PROCTOR: Ann, 272; Edmond Prior, 255; Sarah, 268
PROSER: Elizabeth, 24
PROSSER: Elizabeth, 24
PROUD: Hannah, 180, 183
PUE: Arthur, 176; Edward, 176
PUGH: Abigail, 74, 75, 86, 87; Alice, 74, 75, 79, 86, 88, 91; Eli, 75; Elias, 209, 254; Elisha, 79; Elizabeth, 192, 207, 208, 209, 210, 254, 257; Esther, 64, 75, 79, 86, 88; Hannah, 64, 74, 75, 79, 86, 88; Jacob, 195, 252, 254, 257; Jane, 75, 79, 86, 89; Job, 64, 79, 86, 88; John, 96; John M., 190; John Morgan, 257; Jonathan, 64, 74, 75, 79, 86, 88; Joshua, 257; Levi, 64, 79, 86, 88; Lewis, 86; Lewis D., 64; Lydia, 64, 74, 75, 79, 86, 88; Rachel, 79, 86, 88; Stephen, 64, 75, 79, 86, 88
PULES: Oppu, 142
PUSEY: Anne, 247, 268; John, 102; John E., 127
PUSY: Lydia, 97
PYLE: Amos, 100, 123, 128, 141, 151; Danial, 103; Daniel, 123; David, 123; Elizabeth, 123; Grace, 100, 123; Harmon, 74, 94, 101; Hermon, 130; John, 100, 123; Joseph, 123, 141, 151; Nathan, 100, 123; Phebe, 123, 142, 152; Ruth, 100, 123, 128; Ruth Ann, 142, 152; Sarah, 100, 123, 128
PYLES: Amos, 100; Ruth, 100

## Q

QUARLES: Eliza, 101; John, 110, 131, 134, 156, 240
QUIMBY: Isaiah, 92
QUINBY: Elizabeth, 93; Isaiah, 92, 93
QUMBY: Aron, 96

## R

RANDALL: Mariam, 186
RANSOM: Elizabeth, 212; John, 212
RATCLIF: Mildred, 51
RATCLIFF: Mildred, 75
RAVIS: Thomas, 249
READ: Amos, 55, 166, 237; Amos James, 166; Ann, 200, 205, 211, 253; Anna Braithwait, 166; Benjamin, 264; Betty, 165, 208, 264; Charles, 165, 204, 205, 208, 222, 260, 264; David, 20; Elizabeth, 166; Eveline, 211; Grace, 166, 205; Hannah, 20; Jacob, 205, 253; Jane, 166; Joseph, 165, 264; Larkin, 205, 207, 264; Robert, 165; Samuel, 166; Thomas, 165, 264
READY: Elizabeth, 174; John, 174
REANEY: T., 187; William, 187
RECKIFUSS: Christopher, 222; Hannah, 222; Maria, 222; Samuel, 222
RECKMAN: William, 236
REDMAN: Mary, 103
REDMOND: Ruth, 103
REECE: Catherine, 20; John, 205
REED: Ann, 184, 205; Anna, 8, 192; Anne, 38; Deborah, 8, 38, 47, 62, 74, 206, 208, 248, 268; Edith, 205; Eliza, 265; Elizabeth, 8, 16, 38, 47, 62, 206, 212, 248, 266, 268; Evelina, 185; Eveline, 16, 38, 206, 207, 211, 212; Grace, 274; Harriet, 38, 62; Harriett, 8; Harriot, 47,

268; Harriott, 248; John Wilson, 8, 38, 47, 62, 248, 268; Matida, 212; Matilda, 16, 38, 47, 74, 78, 86, 185, 188, 207, 248; Samuel, 8, 16, 38, 47, 61, 74, 87, 212, 248, 265, 266, 268; Samuel D., 47, 62, 248, 268; William, 8, 38, 47, 62, 81, 248, 268
REES: Aquilla, 15; Catherine, 18, 20; Eleanor, 15; John, 15; Joseph, 15; Mary, 15; Morris, 15; Sarah, 15; William, 15
REESE: Ann, 176, 195, 198, 231; Aquilla, 15; Charles, 166; Daniel M., 80, 85, 89, 230, 262; Edward, 166, 241; Eleanor, 15; Elizabeth, 262; Esther, 176, 207; George, 62, 72; Gerard H., 241; John, 15, 203; John E., 176, 186, 187, 188, 211; Joseph, 15, 256, 262; Maria, 195, 198; Maria K., 207; Mary, 15, 166, 231, 256, 262; Mary B., 166; Mary Brooke, 231; Maurice, 256; Morris, 15; Rebecca, 72; Rebecca A., 62; Sarah, 15; Thomas, 198; Thomas L., 176, 207, 231, 241; Thomas M., 241; Thomas S., 166; William, 15
REGESTER: Eliza, 211; Eliza Jane, 273; Elizabeth, 166, 211, 273; Elizabeth Jane, 166; Esther, 210; John, 166, 210, 241; Mary Ann, 166, 211, 273; Samuel, 166, 210, 211, 241, 272, 273
REMINGTON: James, 72; Lucilla B., 72
RENAUDET: Maria V., 180
REPKEY: Elizabeth, 204
RESTON: Isaac H., 75
REVAIL: Eliza, 99
REYNELLS: Joshua, 27; Mary, 27; Rachel, 27; Sarah, 27

REYNOLDS, 27; Elisha, 11; Elisha Brown, 42; Elizabeth, 11, 79, 87, 88; Jessee, 257; Joshua, 11, 33, 35, 41, 220, 254, 257, 260; Josiah Brown, 254; Mary, 27, 42, 220, 260; Rachel, 11, 27, 42, 220, 254, 257, 260, 269; Sarah, 27, 42, 220
RICH: Ann, 216; Benjamin, 216, 253, 254; John, 216; Sarah, 216, 254
RICHARDS: Ann M., 195, 199; Lewis, 199; Lewis M., 203; Mary, 210
RICHARDSON: Anna, 101; Hannah, 97, 98, 122, 131; Harriet, 202; Morgan, 99; Rebecca, 96; Rebecca D., 99; William, 198
RICHMOND: Samuel, Jr., 169
RICKEFUSS: David, 225
RICKMAN: William, 113, 142, 144, 153, 156, 273
RIDGELY: Mary Ann, 188; Matilda C., 188; Matilda L., 173
RIGDON: John P., 104; Samuel, 74
RIGGS: E., 207; Eliza, 173
RILEY: Ann, 194, 199, 201, 203, 204; Hannah, 142, 153, 175, 178, 183, 187, 188, 190, 191, 209, 210, 211, 257; Hannah L., 182; John, 199; Joshua, 190, 191, 232; N., 191; Nicholas, 203, 204; Samuel, 257; Sarah, 173, 175, 180, 182, 184, 185, 187, 188, 191, 199, 206, 211, 256, 257; Valerius, 191, 202; William, 163, 170, 171, 172, 173, 175, 181, 182, 184, 185, 186, 190, 191, 194, 195, 196, 198, 199, 203, 208, 218, 256, 257
RILUS: Joshua, 105

RITTER: Sarah, 241
ROACH: Barbara, 198; Hannah, 198; Henry, 198; Rachel, 198
ROBARDSON: Isaac W., 96; Peggy W., 97
ROBERTS: Elizabeth, 271; Jane, 193; Jane P., 72; Jonathan, 171; Sarah, 210, 240; William H., 72
ROBERTSON: Daniel, 260; Eliza, 198; Eliza, Jr., 205; Elizabeth, 103, 158, 171, 178, 180, 183, 190, 195, 201, 203, 205, 218, 260; Hannah, 170, 195, 202; Isaac, 115, 116; Isaac W., 195; Mary, 172, 182, 190, 193, 195, 201, 205; Sarah, 196
ROBINSON: Elizabeth, 199, 200; James, 174
ROBSON: Elizabeth, 165, 193
RODGERS: Anna, 99; Charity, 99; Joseph, 99, 101; Mary, 99, 118, 122, 126; Mary C., 101; Rachel, 99; Rebecca, 99; Susanna, 103, 118; Susannah, 102, 117; William, 99
ROE: Frances, 102
ROGERS: Mary C., 146; Mary E., 138; Priscilla, 108, 129, 130; Susanna, 101, 129
ROLET: Joseph, 170
ROSS: Mary E., 188
ROUGH: Sarah, 200
ROWE: William K., 186
ROWLAND: Richard G., 193
RUCKLE: John, 179
RUFF: James, 100; Sarah, 100, 182
RUKEFUSS: David, 172
RUMMELLS: Richard, 227
RUSH: Rachel, 26, 27
RUTLEDGE: Ann L., 72

S

SALTONSTALL: Nath., 203

Samuel James, 183
SANDERSON: Ann, 41, 206, 223, 243, 246; Ann H., 181; Ann M., 177; Ann W., 178, 179, 180, 183, 185, 186, 192, 206; Catharine, 183, 201, 202, 203, 204; Catherine, 224, 243; Margaret, 252; Mayes, 254; Rachel, 254; Thomas, 252
SAPPINGTON: Frances, 180; Henrietta M., 172
SARE: Elizabeth, 196
SAUNDERS: David, 179, 230
SAVAGE: Margarett, 183; Sarah, 175, 178, 179, 183, 223, 246
SAWYER: Benaiah, 191; Bennaiah, 240
SCOT: Amos, 15
SCOTT: Abraham, 1, 57; Amos, 31, 34, 44; Ann, 178, 183, 200, 210; Caroline, 166; Edith, 184, 188, 192, 194, 198, 206, 255; Edith Ann, 166; Edith B., 166; Eliza, 2; Eliza N., 211; Elizabeth, 1, 2, 6, 23, 32, 48, 50, 53, 54, 166, 180, 183, 184, 185, 236; Elizabeth M., 53; Elizabeth N., 179, 189; Ester, 15; Esther, 15, 44; Ezra, 236; Granville, 255; Hannah, 196; Isaac, 170, 200, 236; Jesse, 35, 39, 41, 42, 52, 54; Jessee, 6, 23, 27, 50, 52, 53; John, 15, 74; Levi, 15; Martha Ann, 236; Mary, 210; Rachel, 2, 15, 45; Rebecca, 57; Rebekah, 6; Rositer, 18; Rossetter Stockton, 166; Rossiter, 188, 192, 194, 196, 198, 199, 201, 206, 208, 210, 255, 256; Samuel, 52, 166; Sarah, 251, 269; Sarah Ann, 166; Susanna, 255; Thomas, 2, 15, 40, 48, 49, 51, 52, 53, 54,

55, 187, 256; Townsend, 166, 187, 189, 190, 191, 255; William, 15; Wilson, 236
SCOTTEN: Jane, 94, 111, 137, 144, 149; Joshua, 94, 111, 137, 144; Matilda, 94, 146; William, 94, 111, 137, 140, 144, 149
SCULL: Sarah, 49
SEVEAR: William P., 209
SEWELL: Ann, 185, 186
SHANAHAN: Euphenia, 233
SHARP: Elizabeth, 100, 102, 103, 104; John, 98, 100, 102, 147, 152, 155; Thomas, 102, 112, 139, 148
SHARPE: Elezabeth, 100; Elizabeth, 100; John, 100; Thomas, 100
SHARPLESS: Emily, 202; James J., 209; Julia A., 209
SHAW: Joseph, 19; Mary, 57; Sarah, 15, 16
SHEARMAN: Hephsibah, 214
SHEERMAN: Hepzibah, 244; Nathaniel, 244
SHEPHERD: Ann, 116; Mary, 208; Ruth, 268; Solomon, 207; Susanna, 207; William, 207, 265, 267
SHEPPARD: Ann, 181, 190; M., 196; Mary, 180; Mary A., 190; Mary Ann, 177, 180; Mary S., 190; Moses, 180, 196; Nathan, 171; Ruth, 247; Thomas S., 180, 186, 190; William, 247
SHERWOOD: Thomas, 198, 242
SHIELDS: Rachel, 267
SHOTWELL: Jemima, 206
SHREEVE: Caleb, 38
SHREVE: John, 221
SILVERS: Benjamin, Jr., 99; Charity, 99
SILVESTER: Mary C., 209
SILVESTOR: Mary E., 209
SIMMONDS: Elizabeth, 191, 193
SIMS: Howard, 181, 183
SINCLAIR: Abraham, 222, 258, 262; Ann, 174, 176, 177, 179, 181, 183, 186; Ann T., 182; Anna, 239; Anna E., 188, 189; Deborah, 183, 186; Deborah S., 190; Eliza, 172, 173, 177; Elizabeth, 174, 177, 178, 183, 187, 190, 239, 263; Elizabeth G., 182, 186, 187, 190, 191; Elzia S., 173, 174, 176; Emma, 239; Esther, 174, 178, 179, 181, 183, 186, 187, 190; Gerard Hopkins, 263; Hester, 263; Isaac Procter, 222; John, 174, 175, 177, 178, 185, 186, 190, 191, 222, 239, 258, 262, 263; John P., 186, 191; Joseph, 239; Kezia, 254, 258; Margaret T., 239; Mary Ann, 183, 186, 190, 194, 239; Rachel, 222, 254, 262; Rebecca, 172, 173, 174, 258; Robert, 174, 178, 179, 181, 183, 185, 186, 190, 232, 263; Sarah, 170, 174, 178, 222, 258, 262; Susan, 239; William, 75, 174; William H., 177, 186
SINNERS: Mary, 270
SITLER: Daniel, 171; Joseph, 184; Tamar, 171
SLATER: Mary, 51
SMALL: Josiah, 186
SMITh: Margaret, 41, 44, 131
SMITH: Alexander, 184; Amanda, 62, 72, 76; Amos, 12, 15, 31, 38, 39, 40, 41, 44, 62, 64, 68, 74, 76, 82, 194, 204, 212, 243, 256; Ann, 184, 207, 208, 210, 211, 218, 230, 244, 271; Anne, 43; Anthony Marsh, 166; Asenath, 85; Catharine M., 166,

172, 187; Cathe. M., 182; Charles W., 170; Charlotte Lawrence, 167; David, 47, 78, 83, 85, 100; E. B., 181; Elias B., 179, 181, 182; Eliza, 31, 167, 188, 189, 243, 256; Eliza A., 192, 210; Eliza Ann, 191, 210, 271; Eliza Brown, 230; Eliza G., 182; Eliza H., 76; Eliza L., 188; Elizabeth, 62, 144, 191; Elizabeth Ann, 166, 189, 244; Esther, 174, 175, 176, 177, 178, 182, 189, 193; George, 253; Hannah, 47, 78, 83, 85, 169, 174, 175, 176, 177, 179, 189, 197, 218, 253, 259, 261; Hannah Ann, 166; Henry, 197, 210, 230, 244, 271; Isaac, 39, 40, 41, 100, 109, 128, 131; J. P., 190; James, 11, 12, 30, 37, 259; James W., 62; James West, 62; Jane, 174, 188, 259; Jane D., 189, 193; John, 50, 64, 167, 185, 186, 188, 189; John D., 144; John M., 241; John Marsh, 166; Jonathan, 100; Lavinia, 62; Lindley Murray, 167; Margaret, 41, 109, 128; Margarett, 101; Margret, 107; Martha, 188, 197, 230, 244, 271; Mary, 31, 62, 74, 76, 144, 188, 243, 256; Mary Ann, 109; Mary M., 241; Mary Marsh, 166; Matthew, 166, 188, 189, 241; R. M., 186; Rachel, 31, 76, 100, 243, 256; Rachel C., 62; Rebecca, 12, 15, 31, 44, 62, 74, 76, 82, 205, 243, 256; Robert H., 189; Robert M., 166, 194; S. B., 189; Samuel, 174, 175, 176, 177, 178, 179, 189, 193, 197, 200, 210, 230, 244, 253, 259, 261, 271; Samuel B., 261; Samuel H., 172; Samuel S., 207, 208, 210; Sarah, 100, 104, 128, 200, 202; Seth, 43, 199, 203, 243; Seth C., 201; Susan W., 62; T. M., 186; Thomas, 189; Thomas M., 166, 185, 194; William, 185, 188; William Brown, 230, 244, 271
SMITHSON: Elizabeth, 86
SNOWDEN: Elizabeth, 196; Hannah, 196; Henrietta, 197; Rachel, 254; Richard, 196
SNYDER: Mary, 206; Mary D., 178; Peter, 206
SOULE: Joshua, Jr., 188
SOUTHCOMB: Allisanna, 184; Caaary, 184
SOUTHCOMBE: Alisanna, 273
SPENCER: Abel, 187, 192, 210, 229, 252; Ann, 62, 75, 91; Eleanor, 8, 62; Elizabeth, 9, 42, 63, 75; Eloiza, 63; Enoch, 63; Enoch Lucas, 9; Hannah, 42, 63, 75; Harriet Ann, 63; Hugh, 42; Hugh Ely, 63; John Mott, 63; Joseph, 252; Mahala, 9, 80, 92, 192; Mahalah, 63; Mahlon, 8, 62, 63, 83; Mahlon A., 63; Mahlon Atkinson, 9; Rebecca, 252; Sarah, 42, 46, 63, 66, 75, 82, 88; Thomas Ellwood, 63; William, 8; William Lee, 8, 63
SPENSOR: Eliza, 101
SPICER: Rachel, 11
SQUIB: William, 41, 42
SQUIBB: William, Jr., 31
STABLER: Edward, 179, 221, 233; Edward, Jr., 179, 233
STACY: George, 214
STANSBURY: Elijah, 207; Guli Elma, 116, 121; Gulielma, 116; Mary A., 187; Ruthy E., 207; S. A., 186, 192; Sarah, 269
STANTON: Bordin, 23

STAPLER: Hannah, 171, 177, 180, 183, 234; Joseph, 171; Thomas, 183
STAPLETON: Joshua, 218; Samuel, 220; Susanna, 218; Susannah, 218
STAR: Aquilla, 92; George, 92; Joseph, 92; Molly, 92; Sally Ann, 92; Sidney, 92
STARR: Abigail, 44, 62; Acquila, 81; Aquila, 62, 92; Aquilla, 44; Benjamin, 166; Catherine, 172; Deborah W., 177; Elizabeth, 190; Engle, 44, 74, 75, 76, 90; George, 62, 81; Isaac, 172; James, 44, 74, 75; Joseph, 44, 62, 81, 166; Mary, 44, 73, 74, 75; Molly, 62, 80; Sally Ann, 44, 62, 81; Sidney, 44, 73, 74, 75, 80; Thomas, 166
STEEVER: Georgeana, 187
STEPHENS: William B., 105
STEPHENSON: Isabella, 138
STERETT: John, 203
STERLING: Jane, 209
STERRETT: R., 170
STEVENSON: Isabella, 146
STEWART: Ann, 100
STIDDONS: Josiah, Jr., 227
STILL: James, 216
STKES: Mary, 208
STOKERSLY: Esther, 210
STOKES: David, 116; Elizabeth, 121; Hannah, 131, 133; Mary, 115; Susanna, 127, 128
STOUFFER: Ann, 201
STRATTON: Samuel W., 192; W. Willess, 191; William Willess, 190
STRAWBRIDGE: Elizabeth, 98, 99, 114, 115, 121; Joseph, 98, 99, 103, 104, 121, 145, 151
STREET: Isabella, 74; Sarah, 116

STREETT: Abraham, 76
STRETCH: Joseph, 186
STRICKER: John, 209
STRICKLER: Charlotte, 194
STUBBINS: Urith, 35
STUBBS: Amer, 76, 77; Amos, 100, 124; Daniel, 95, 113, 124; Deborah K., 95; Deborah R., 113; Hannah, 95, 113, 124; Hannah Brown, 95, 113; Isaac, 74, 76, 95, 113, 124, 141, 151, 152, 153; Jeremiah, 124; Jeremiah B., 113; Joseph, 95, 113; Sarah Ann, 95, 113; Slater, 95, 113
STUBS: Hannah, 100; Isaac, 100
STUMP: Ducket, 128; Elizabeth, 146; Hannah, 80, 91, 141, 152; Hannah C., 102, 103; Henry, 99; Henry, Jr., 96; John W., 170; Margaret, 102; Margaret M., 102; Martha Burrows, 170; Mary, 96, 99; Mary C., 104, 105, 106, 146; Racheal C., 105; Rachel C., 105; Rubin, 102; Thomas C., 104; William, 99
SUDLER: Eleanor, 183
SULAVIN: Jemmiah, 50
SWAIN: Elizabeth, 171; Mary, 240
SWARMSTADT: Leroy, 209
SWEAT: Mary, 270
SWEENEY: Harriot, 96
SYKES: Harriet, 208; Harriot, 210; James, 210; Mary, 210, 269
SYLVESTER: Eleanor Susan, 270; Eliza, 184; Elizabeth, 270; Julianna Martin, 270; Mary Elizabeth, 270; Samuel Bidgood, 270

T

TABOR: Elizabeth, 49
TALBOT: Elisha, 218

TALBOTT: Hannah, 173, 179, 186, 191; Jesse, 173, 179, 186; John L., 186, 190, 194; William A., 186
TATE: Maria C., 180
TAYLOR: Burnard, 54; Elizabeth, 168, 187, 192, 273; Isabella, 168; Jane, 168; John, 230; Naomi, 184; Nicholas, 168, 173, 187, 192, 210; Nicholas W., 210, 228; P., 182; Sarah, 168; Susan, 202; Thomas, 168
TECHTEY: Louis R., 209
TEMPLIN: Sarah, 98
TEWDER: John, 25, 27
THOMAS: Amos P., 95; Ann, 175, 177, 180, 182, 193, 194, 257; Ann P., 194; Anna W., 180; Benjamin, 100, 121, 250; Benjamin D., 95; Elizabeth, 167, 169, 171, 172, 173, 174, 175, 179, 185, 186, 191, 193, 201, 202, 205, 242, 257; Elizabeth Jane, 95; Evan, 169, 173, 175, 180, 181, 193, 194, 199, 202, 257; Evan P., 190, 191; Evan Ph., 167, 193; Harriet, 167, 193; Henrietta, 197, 199, 201, 202, 260; Henrietta M., 234; Henry, 201; Isaac, 100, 135; Isac, 100; Jehu, 100, 127, 128; John, 100, 171, 174, 175, 176, 272; John Chew, 234; Julia, 234; Mary, 100, 167, 191, 193, 234, 242; Mary Y., 184, 209, 210; Mordecai, 95, 128, 130, 131; Mordicai, 100; P. E., 173; P. T., 198; P.E., 174, 175, 186, 190, 191, 199; Philip, 180, 242; Philip E., 167, 177, 180, 185, 193, 202, 257; Philip William, 201; R. E., 170; Racheal, 103; Rachel, 100, 139, 148, 167, 170, 171, 173, 174, 175, 177, 179, 180, 199, 202, 257; Richard, 220; Richard Henry, 234; Richard S., 220; Sally B., 177; Samuel, 220; Samuel Evan, 234; Sarah, 95, 128; Sarah B., 174, 176; Sarah G., 167; Susan, 100; Susanna, 40, 41, 42, 97, 103, 130; William G., 180; William George, 167
THOMKINS: Debry B., 103; Jacob, 102; John, 99, 102; Joseph, 99; Joseph G., 175; Mary, 97, 100, 103; Sarah, 102; Sarh, 100; Thomas, 100
THOMPKINS: Benjamin, 100; John, 100
THOMPSON: Catharine, 125; David, 127; Hannah, 96, 127; James, 96; James B., 180; Richard K., 193
THORNBURG: Cassandra, 28
THORNBURGH: Cassandra, 10, 19, 32, 194, 196, 215; Deborah, 19, 25, 26, 195, 215; Joseph, 10, 11, 19, 195, 215; Margaret, 19, 52, 203, 215; Sarah, 19, 52, 203, 215; Thomas, 24
TIEMAN: Catherine, 194
TILGHMAN: Elziabeth C., 180
TILTON
TIMMONS: Elizabeth, 84
TIPPE: Harriet, 181
TIPTEN: Abijah, 112; David, 112; Elihu, 112; Hannah, 112; Hester, 112; John, 112; Luke, 112, 151; Mary, 112; Priscilla, 112, 151; Rachel, 112
TIPTON: Abigail, 137; Abijah, 141, 145; David, 137, 141, 145; Elihu, 141; Ester, 16; Esther, 16, 137, 141, 145; Hannah, 141; Hester, 16; John, 28, 141; Luke,

17, 38, 116, 127, 129, 137, 141,
145; Mary, 137, 141, 145;
Priscilla, 136, 141; Rachel, 137,
141, 145; Rebecah, 97; Rebecca,
17, 116, 121
TOMBKINS: John, 103, 104, 146
TOMKINS: Ann, 104, 117;
Behjamin, 103, 104, 151;
Bengamin, 102; Deborah, 150;
Diborough, 102; John, 104, 150;
Joseph, 171; Joseph Y., 188;
Lydia M., 104; Marah, 102;
Martha, 97, 98, 99, 100, 102,
171, 226; Mary, 98; Sarah, 97,
98, 102, 103, 104, 150
TOMPKINS: Benjamin, 141;
Deborah, 141; John, 138, 141,
148, 149; Martha, 127, 131,
134; Sarah, 141
TOMPSON: David, 107; Hannah,
107
TOODER: John, 27
TORRANCE: John, 190
TORRENCE: Eliza, 200
TOWNSEND: Benjamin, 202, 252;
Eascheus, 209; Elizabeth, 209,
242, 270, 271; Esther, 168, 192,
203, 204, 205, 206, 207, 208,
209, 210, 264, 268; Esther A.,
184; Esther Fox, 265; Esther H.,
183, 201, 211; Esther T., 202;
G. S., 209; G. S., M.D., 185;
Granville, 203; Granville S.,
202, 204; H. P., 201; Hanna P.,
185; Hannah, 202, 211; Hannah
E., 199; Hannah P., 184, 185,
192, 196, 200, 201, 209; Hannah
Painter, 265; Hester H., 200;
Horatio, 77, 83; J. W., 209;
Joseph, 168, 171, 195, 197, 202,
206, 207, 209, 210, 242, 264;
Joseph, Jr., 171; Julian
Wooderson, 168, 265; Lydia,
199, 202; Mary, 184, 185, 202;
Mary M., 190, 209; Mary
Matthews, 265; N. W., 176, 203,
209; Nicholas W., 202, 248;
Phebe, 184; Phebe S., 190, 193,
209, 211; Phebe Shotwell, 265;
R. H., 188, 189, 191; Richard
H., 185; Richard Hallett, 265;
Robert, 203, 224; Robert H.,
184, 187; Samuel, 242; Sarah,
211, 238; Sarah B., 187;
Thomas, 200, 221; William,
202; William M., 171; William
Matthews, 219, 247
TOY: Frances, 176, 192; Isaac N.,
182; John D., 175
TRAHERN: Enos, 236
TREDWAY: Daniel, 2
TREGO: Albert, 39, 76, 79, 87, 90;
Albert David, 63; David, 39, 79,
87, 90; Francenia, 39, 73, 75,
77, 79, 90; Francenie, 87;
Franceonia, 74, 75; Hannah, 39,
63, 73, 76, 79, 87, 90; Harriet,
39, 73, 74, 79, 90; James D., 63,
75, 90; James Duffel, 39, 79, 87;
Mary, 39, 40; Rebecca, 39;
Samuel, 78, 84, 85, 177; Sarah,
39, 43, 63, 73, 74, 75, 76, 79,
83, 87, 90; Thomas, 39, 63, 73,
74, 75, 76, 79, 87; William, 39,
59, 73, 79, 80, 87; William, Jr.,
74
TRIMBLE: Ann, 65, 72, 90;
Elizabeth, 65, 74, 75, 104, 185,
187, 188, 189, 199, 200, 203,
204, 206, 207, 208, 209, 210,
224, 244, 254, 263, 271;
Elizabeth S., 184, 187, 191;
Elizabeth Sims, 36; George Fox,
168; George W., 242; Hannah,
187, 199, 201, 203, 204, 205,
206, 208, 209, 218, 272; Hannah

Maria, 168; Isaac, 184, 187, 224, 244, 254; James, 221; Jane, 184, 185, 200, 224, 244, 263; John, 63, 187, 195, 200, 204, 205, 207, 209, 224, 244, 254, 263; Joseph, 65, 76, 90, 185, 187, 236; Margaret, 72; Maria, 168; Mary, 224, 244, 254; Phebe, 65, 72; Rachel, 65; Thomas B., 74; Thomas Brogden, 63; William, 168, 187, 198, 199, 201, 203, 204, 205, 206, 208, 209, 210, 218, 242, 272; William H., 187, 248
TROTH: Ann B., 184; Daniel, 184, 234
TUCKER: Aaron Harkins, 64; Ann, 30, 63; Ann L., 74; David, 30, 44, 63, 74, 76, 90, 91, 94; Eli, 84; Elizabeth, 30, 44, 63, 73, 74, 76, 82, 87, 93; Ely, 64; Hannah, 30, 74, 86; James, 30, 42, 64, 74, 84; Rachel, 46, 64; Samuel, 30, 63, 74, 79, 88; Sarah, 91
TUDER: Abraham, 46; John, 25, 27, 28, 36, 41; Martha, 36, 46; Phebe, 28, 36, 42; Samuel, 36; William, 46
TUDOR: Ann, 34; Hannah, 11, 46; Isaac, 57; John, 11, 37, 38, 39, 50, 223; Martha, 11, 223; Phebe, 11, 42, 223; Ruth, 11; Samuel, 223; Samuel Morthland, 50; Susanna Morthland, 11; William, 11, 15
TUNIS: J. R., 180; Jane, 188; Mary, 179
TURNER: Elizabeth, 168, 191; Hannah, 168; Isaac, 101, 131; Isaac, Jr., 101; Joseph, 101, 171, 173, 174, 175, 179, 185, 186, 190; Joseph, Jr., 168; Rebecca, 168, 176, 177, 179, 180, 181, 182, 186, 187, 188, 190, 191; Richard Townsend, 168; Robert, 177; Sally Ann, 168; Samuel R., 177, 227, 234; Sarah, 101, 133, 174, 186; Sarah M., 101, 106, 109
TWINING: Ann H., 72; Beulah E., 68; Isaac, 72
TWISLER: Sophia E., 191
TYSON: Ann, 3, 15, 28, 77, 82, 167, 192; Anna, 72, 172, 181, 193, 194, 256; Charles S., 167; Deborah, 173, 174, 177, 178, 180, 181, 185, 188, 190, 191, 193, 252, 263; Edward, 167; Eleanor, 180, 183; Elisha, 174, 176, 177, 178, 179, 180, 188, 193, 194, 195, 197, 201, 252; Elisha, Jr., 167; Elizabeth, 167, 169, 171, 172, 173, 174, 175, 176, 177, 179, 183, 188, 191, 193, 194, 196, 197, 198, 201, 202, 235, 258, 263; Elizabeth Brook, 167; Elizabeth Y., 170; Evan T., 181, 189, 193, 263; Evan Thomas, 193; Frances E., 194; Francis, 167; George, 77, 82, 235; H. E., 190; Hannah, 172; Hannah Ann, 167, 185, 186, 188, 193; Henrietta E., 181, 193, 194; Henrietta P., 188; Henry, 194; Isaac, 38, 170, 171, 172, 174, 176, 177, 179, 181, 185, 186, 188, 189, 190, 191, 193, 194, 195, 197, 198, 202, 205, 206, 209, 263; Isaac, Jr., 167; Isabella, 72, 167, 242; Jacob, 3, 15, 28, 39, 40, 77, 82, 183, 192, 193; James, 192; James Ellicott, 167; Jane, 167; Jane S., 194; Jesse, 17, 161, 167, 171, 172, 173, 175, 181, 192, 256; John P., 193; John S.,

188, 193, 209; Jonathan, 3, 77, 82, 167, 263; Jonathan E., 181, 193, 194; Letitia E., 167; Margaret, 77, 82, 167, 172, 177, 181, 183, 190, 192, 193, 194, 196, 197, 256; Maria, 180; Marshall, 167, 193; Martha Ann, 167; Martha E., 167, 177, 179, 181, 183, 185, 187, 193, 194; Mary, 167, 170, 171, 172, 173, 177, 181, 188, 191, 193, 194, 195, 196, 197, 198, 201, 202, 252, 263; Mary A., 193; Mary E., 193, 194; Mary M., 167, 193; N., Jr., 203; Nathan, 167, 170, 171, 172, 173, 177, 183, 193, 194, 195, 203, 242; Nathan, Jr., 170, 171, 172, 173, 177, 203; Nathaniel E., 167; Patience, 177, 178, 179, 181, 183, 186, 188, 191, 193; Philip T., 193; Rachel, 181; Rachel T., 188, 190, 191, 193, 194; Rebecca, 193; Richard Wood, 167; Samuel, 167; Samuel E., 194; Sarah, 77, 82, 170, 171, 172, 174, 175, 194, 206, 263; Sarah E., 175, 189, 190, 193, 258; Sarah Morris, 167; Sarah S., 167, 188, 191, 193; Thomas, 172, 178, 181, 188, 189, 190, 192, 193, 194, 210; William, 167, 170, 172, 173, 175, 176, 177, 186, 187, 194, 195, 196, 197, 198, 199, 200, 202, 258; William A., 167, 194; William Amos, 3, 77, 237; William Amoss, 82

## U

UNDERHILL: John C., 72; Sarah R., 72
UNDERWOOD: Alexander, 254; Amy, 250, 270, 272; Ann, 134; Anne, 110; Barclay, 250; Barcley, 272; Enoch, 127, 128, 171, 184, 196, 254, 257; Enock, 244; Hannah, 222; Isaac, 171; Isaac Griest, 254; J. G., 184; James, 171; John, 45, 107, 110, 128, 134, 171, 227, 249, 270, 272; Joseph McCoy, 257; Mary, 45, 103, 110, 132, 134, 184, 196, 198, 244, 250, 254, 257, 270, 272; Mordecai, 138, 145; Mordica, 103, 111; Nehemiah, 103, 122; Racheal, 97; Rachel, 123, 131; Susanna, 103, 108, 130, 134, 135, 136; Thomas, 235; William, 198
UNERHILL: Theodore S., 17
UPDAGRAFF: Sarah, 217
UPDEGRAFF: Edith, 232; Eliza, 182; Eliza K., 181; Hannah, 200; Joel, 200; Joseph, 200; Mary, 176; R., 180; Rachel, 172, 174, 175, 176, 177, 178, 179, 182, 191, 193, 210, 220; Sarah C., 192; Susanna, 200
UPDEGRAFT: Ambrose, 175, 176, 200

## V

VALENTINE: George, 110, 135; Jacob, 131, 134; Morris Jackson, 168; Reuben, 110, 131, 135, 150
VAN WYCK: Fanny, 180
VANCE: John, 202
VANHORN: Jonathan, 78, 82, 84, 131
VANSANT: Bejamin H., 168; Catharine, 223, 266; Catherine, 168; Cornelius, 168, 223, 266; James Edward, 168; Joseph Townsend, 168; Mary Elizabeth,

168; Sarah, 223; Tacy Ann, 168
VORE: Anna, 137; Bejamin, 222;
Eliza, 111, 137; Elizabeth, 46,
47, 77, 83, 109, 111, 133, 134,
137; Isaac, 12, 30, 42, 98, 99,
111, 122, 123, 130, 137, 252;
Israel C., 137; Jacob, 12, 42, 47,
77, 83, 98, 99, 100, 109, 111,
122, 130, 132, 133, 134, 137,
230; Jane, 233; John, 100, 111,
137; Mary, 12, 42, 97, 98, 99,
100, 102, 111, 122, 130, 137;
Rebecca, 198; Ruth, 12, 30, 42,
111, 123, 137; Samuel C., 111;
Sarah, 198

## W

WAESCHE: Metta, 188
WAINWRIGHT: James, 196, 200, 222; James Berry, 12; John Price, 12, 41; Matilda, 12, 37, 41, 47; Rachel, 222; Rachel C., 200; Samuel, 12, 35, 36, 41, 198; Thomas, 196, 218
WALKER: Caroline H., 180; Elizabeth, 271; Hales E., 189; Mary, 189
WALLIS: Ann, 116; John, 106
WALTERS: Henry G., 76; Mary, 178
WALTHAM: Susanna, 191, 210
WALTHAMS: Susanna, 185
WALTON: Alexander, 197; Alice Ann, 120; Elezabeth, 100; Elisha, 120; Elizabeth, 97, 120, 121, 125; Hannah, 109, 121, 133; Hannah C., 73; Jacob, 120; James, 73, 107, 109, 121, 125, 127, 128; John, 109, 121, 133; Lukins, 120; Mary, 97, 99, 106, 121, 226; Rebecca, 109, 121, 133; Salem, 120; Samuel, 197; Samuel B., 73; Sarah, 120;

William, 109, 117, 120, 121, 133
WANTON: William R., 227, 238
WARD: Margaret, 123; Richard, 98, 120
WARDER: John, 185
WARFIELD: Rebecca, 172; Susanna, 180
WARING: George W., 188
WARNER: Aaron, 99; Achsah, 99, 131; Agnes, 115; Agness, 98, 99, 114, 213; Agness C., 101, 105; Ann, 96, 98, 99, 108, 131; Aron, 99, 101; Asa, 125, 126; Asaph, 150; Axsah, 101, 108; Brinton, 47, 64, 77, 83, 84, 230; Cilas, 102; Crosdal, 99; Crosdale, 123; Elener, 29; Elizabeth, 76, 143; Hannah, 47, 77, 83, 84, 230; Isaac, 99; J. Edward, 73; John, 64, 214, 270; Jonathan, 47, 64, 74, 75, 76, 77, 83, 84, 93, 230; Joseph, 94, 96, 98, 139, 148, 154, 156; Letitia, 99; Mary, 99, 123; Mary Ann, 64; Mordicai, 124; Pamala, 99; Rachel, 106; Ruth, 94, 98; Sarah, 47, 64, 74, 75, 77, 83, 84, 93, 94, 96, 98, 99, 101, 103, 104, 106, 123, 149, 152, 230; Silas, 38, 94, 97, 98, 99, 101, 104, 119, 123, 156; Thomas, 99; Thomas E., 111, 138; Thomas W., 146; William, 64, 73
WARNICK: Mary, 133
WARNOCK: Jan, 99; Jane, 137; Mary, 99, 101; Philip, 98, 99; Sarah, 98, 123
WATEERS: Edwin, 206, 207, 208, 210
WATERHOUSE: Ann, 171, 173, 178, 180, 183, 184, 194, 196, 261; Mary, 180, 261; Nicholas,

216; William, 197, 198, 201, 202, 261
WATERS: Caroline, 210, 270; Cathine, 206, 207, 208; Charles, 208; Charlotte, 210; Edward, 169, 196, 208, 210; Edwin, 169, 269; George P., 198; Hanna M., 199; Hannah, 208, 210; Mary, 273; Mary B., 184; Sarah, 169; Sarah B., 210; Susan H., 207; Susanna, 205
WATKINS: Ann Elizabeth, 178; Catherine, 39
WATSON: David, 210; Ellen N., 73; Hannah, 126; John, 74, 76; Joseph, 96; Joseph D., 126; Martha, 117, 126; Mary, 126; Sarah, 96; Sarah W., 105, 126; Sarah Wilson, 117; Thomas, 113, 155; William, 96, 97, 117, 126
WATTER: Eliza, 103
WATTERS: Charlotte, 207; Edward, 208
WATTS: Ann, 175; Susanna, 268
WAY: Ann, 115, 117, 135; Ann Eliza, 73; Francis, 73; Hannah, 231; Jane R., 185; Mifflin, 73; Sidney S.. See
WAYBILL: Mary, 170, 173, 187, 203, 205, 207
WEAKS: Rachel, 269
WEATHERED: Lewin, 202
WEB: Elizabeth, 97; Mary, 97, 100; Richard, 97, 100
WEBB: Benjamin, 214; James, 97, 100, 102, 103; Jessy, 118; John, 97, 99, 124, 137, 144; Joseph, 123; Limrey, 97; Mara, 102; Mary, 97, 98, 99, 114, 136, 137; Mercy, 212; Nancy, 97; Richard, 97, 98, 99, 102, 114, 118, 135, 137, 144; Richard, Jr., 144;

Tace, 137, 144
WEBSTER: Anna, 195; Betsey, 195; Dorothy, 172, 180; Elizabeth, 20, 50, 196, 216; Henry W., 176, 209; Isaac, 175; John F., 120; John S., 195, 205; Joseph, 101, 102, 109, 131, 133, 208, 209, 226; Joseph T., 193; Lydia, 183; Mary, 204; Priscilla, 102; Rebecca, 171, 185; Sally, 99; Sarah, 101, 125, 171, 174, 175, 176; Sarah R., 105, 172, 178, 180, 194; Sophia, 102, 103
WEEKS: Mary, 16; Rachel, 229
WELCH: Elizabeth, 74
WELLE: Mary, 103
WELLMORE: Arietta A. R., 188; Margaret, 182
WELLS: Mary, 100
WELMORE: Margaret, 176
WENTS: David, 100; Joseph, 100
WESBTER: Sarah, 175
WEST: Adeline, 169; Amos, 169, 182, 194, 196, 203, 257, 261; Amos Smith, 64; Anna W., 76; Cassandra, 79, 86, 87, 183, 184, 185, 186, 231; Charles, 169; Clarkson, 73; David, 8, 63; Eanos, 74; Eli, 3, 257; Eli C., 182; Eliza K., 209; Elizabeth, 34, 43, 63, 64, 169, 182, 194, 201, 257, 261; Elizabeth K., 178, 182, 188, 250; Ellwood, 8, 72; Elwood, 63; Ely, 169; Emely, 76, 77; Emila, 8; Emily, 63, 93, 185; Enos, 8, 15, 16, 18, 33, 35, 63, 83; Grace A., 169; Grace Ann, 182; Granville S., 64, 73; Jane, 169, 182, 261; John, 8; Lydia, 241; Mahlon, 40, 44, 182; Mahlon W., 74, 76, 93; Mary, 27, 40, 44, 63, 64, 76, 82, 89, 182, 227; Nathaniel, 182;

Rebackah, 18; Rebecca, 8, 15, 63, 74, 76, 194, 212; Rebecca Trego, 64; Rebeckah, 15; Sarah, 169; Satcy, 33, 194, 217, 243; Staca, 23; Stacey, 38, 39; Stacy, 21, 23, 24; Stasy, 23; Susanna, 169; Susanna J., 188; Thomas, 8, 18, 32, 33, 35, 44, 63, 72, 79, 85, 87, 93, 182, 184, 186, 194
WETHERED: Ann P., 190; Ann Poultney, 169; C. E., 190; Charles Elias, 169; Eliza, 170, 173; Elizabeth, 169, 189; Elizabeth E., 181; James Sykes, 169; John, 169, 193, 242; Lewin, 169, 173, 181, 194, 242; Mary, 169, 188, 191; Peregrin, 169; Peregrine, 201; Samuel, 169
WHARTON: James, 218, 258; Mary, 218, 258; Nehemiah, 218; Silas, 218, 258
WHEELER: Anne (Anna), 241; Aquilla, 16, 48; Aquillar, 16; Elizabeth, 16; Francis T., 97; Honor, 16; Moses, 16; Onner, 16
WHIFFING: Sarah G., 198
WHIPPEY: Zebulon, 196
WHISON: Sarah, 18
WHITACRE: Clarissa, 32; Deborah, 30
WHITAKER: Mary, 86, 87; Ruth, 23, 43
WHITE: Ann S., 179; Eliza, 204; Elizabeth, 203, 270; Elizabeth Moore, 249; Hannah, 205; Jane, 184; Job, 249, 270; John, 44, 78, 82, 85; John Kinsey, 249, 270; Phebe, 249, 266, 270
WHITELOCK: Samuel, 189
WHITIKER: Ruth, 23
WHITSEN: Sarah, 18

WHITSON: Anna, 109, 115, 134; Bejamin, 115; Benjamin, 109, 115, 133; Burt, 115, 133; Elizabeth, 115, 132; Henry, 115, 132; Mary, 109, 115, 133; Moses, 110, 115, 133, 134; Thomas, 115, 132; William, 85, 109, 133
WHITTIKER: Clarissa, 46
WIBEY: William, 104
WIBLE: John, 98
WIGGENS: Joseph, 101
WIGGINS: Ann, 101; Anna, 96, 98, 99; Bazl., 98; Elizabeth, 98, 99; Elziabeth, 124; John, 96, 98, 117, 122; Joseph, 96, 98, 99, 117, 120, 121; Margaret, 98; Margery, 98; Sally, 98; Sarah, 98, 117
WIGINS: Ann, 96; Joseph, 96
WILKINSON: Robert, 203; Thomas, 83
WILLAPEY: Isaac, 101
WILLETS: Ann, 98, 217; Cassandra, 98, 99, 101, 102, 103, 104, 105, 217
WILLETTS: Ann, 97
WILLIAM: Ennion, 172
WILLIAMS: Amos A., 170; Arnold, 76; Eleanor, 15; Ennion, 168, 170, 171, 173, 181, 183, 184, 185, 186, 191, 194, 195, 196, 198, 204; Enoch, 16; George, 170; Hannah, 168, 170, 171, 184, 195, 198; Lydia, 168; Mary, 181; Rebecca, 168, 195, 196, 203, 218, 251; Rebekah, 199; William, 272
WILLIAMSON: Adam Z., 75; George, Jr., 198; Hannah, 75
WILLITS: Ann, 120; Casandria, 104
WILLITTS: Cassandra, 99

WILLY: William, 103
WILSON: Alexanna, 96;
Aliceanna, 195; Alisan, 101,
105, 174, 190, 191; Alisanna,
96, 97, 98, 168, 183, 195, 196;
Alisannah, 120; Alizanna, 217;
Amy, 218; Ann, 188, 194, 195,
198; Anna, 96, 199, 201, 202,
203, 205, 254; Anne, 200;
Benjamin, 212; Catharine, 252;
Charlotta, 96; Christopher, 96,
111, 129, 136, 137, 143, 145,
155, 183, 195; Christopher, Jr.,
101; Comberland, 96; Cristoper,
97; Cristopher, 97, 101, 102; D.
R., 209; David, 158, 184, 187,
194, 195, 196, 198, 199, 203,
204, 205, 206, 208, 217; David
H., 248; Deborah, 187, 198,
201, 203, 204, 205, 206, 207,
208, 211, 218, 252; Edward,
208, 212, 248, 263, 268; Elisha
T., 168, 194, 255; Elizabeth,
168, 199, 201, 202, 203, 219;
Elizabeth T., 192, 193; George,
99; Gerrard, 170; Henry, 197;
Isaac, 105, 128, 183, 186, 187,
188, 189, 190, 193, 194, 195,
217, 219, 254, 255; J., 209; J.
W., 177; James, 195; Jane, 195,
196, 198, 199, 200, 201, 203,
204, 205, 206, 207, 266, 270;
John, 8, 62, 97, 120, 143, 154,
155, 168, 187, 194, 195, 196,
198, 200, 201, 202, 203, 204,
205, 206, 208, 210, 218, 252,
255, 263; John W., 172, 195,
196, 197, 198, 201, 258; John
Webster, 217; Joseph, 96, 219;
Joshua, 76; Kitty, 199; Lucretia,
172, 195, 197, 205, 255, 258,
263; Margaret, 96, 168, 195;
Margaret B., 192, 193;
Margaretta E., 173, 178, 180,
181; Martha, 96; Mary, 207,
208, 219; Mary Ann, 168, 177,
258; Mary B., 181; Nathan, 126;
Nathan R., 103; Nixon, 97, 190,
195, 196; Oliver, 244; Peggy,
170; Peter, 96, 97, 98, 122, 124,
125, 126; Rebeckah, 183; S., Jr.,
190, 191; Sally, 97, 99; Samuel,
162, 183, 188, 198, 199, 200,
201, 202, 203, 204, 205, 206,
211; Samuel, Jr., 188, 203;
Sarah, 98, 126, 203, 248, 268;
Skipwith, 107, 129, 209, 250;
Stephen, 219; Susan, 138, 147;
Susanna, 148, 195, 196, 217,
254; T. R., 210; Tabitha, 269;
Thomas, 96, 97, 105, 117, 123,
129, 130, 174, 176, 190, 201,
203, 206, 207, 208, 209;
William, 128, 208, 263
WINCHESTER: Samuel, 195
WINKS: Mary, 16
WINN: Thomas, 185
WINSTANDLY: Ann B., 176
WITHERS: John, 214
WITHGOTT: Elizabeth, 240
WOLLEN: Hannah, 200
WOOD: David, 22; Elizabeth, 22;
Hannah, 22; S. S., 186, 188;
William, Jr., 232
WOODDY: Ruth B., 188, 189
WOODNUT: William, 228
WOODWARD: Frances, 209
WOOLSTON: Martha, 246
WORAL: Joseph C., 231
WORK: Mary, 198
WORNOCK: Sarah, 118
WORRAL: Joseph C., 180
WORRALL: Anna Maria, 237;
Elwood, 237; John C., 178;
Maria C., 237; Thomas A., 236;
Thos. A., 237

WORTHIN: Cassey, 99
WORTHINGTON: Ann, 104;
Anna, 99, 102, 105, 138, 147;
Anne, 104; Cassandra, 102, 103;
Charles, 117, 118, 119, 170;
Eliza, 99, 100, 170; Elizabeth,
102, 105, 117, 140, 141, 149,
151; G. G., 102; H., 104, 194;
Hannah, 103, 104, 105, 138,
147, 176, 193; Henry, 140, 149;
Ho., 105; J. G., 172; James N.,
197; John, 95, 97, 102, 105,
123, 127, 170, 243; John G.,
171, 173, 178; John G., 3rd,
171; Joshua, 95; Margaret, 95;
Mary, 95, 117, 123, 200; Mary
H., 103, 190; Mary T., 175;
Noah, 178; Priscilla, 102, 105,
106, 138, 140, 147, 149, 151;
Rebecca, 101, 144; Samuel, 102,
104, 105, 106, 125, 126, 129,
140, 143, 146, 147, 149, 152,
153, 155; Sarah, 100, 102, 147;
Susanna, 138; Susannah, 147;
Thomas, 95, 101, 102, 103, 105,
106, 121, 126, 129, 134, 140,
145, 147, 149, 152; W., 193;
William, 97, 99, 102, 103, 117,
124, 125, 135, 138, 140, 147,
149, 151, 153, 156; Wilson,
102, 124, 176
WRIGHT: Allen, 197, 260;
Eleanor, 97; Elizabeth, 21, 115,
197, 216; Ellenor, 114; Isaac,
97, 114, 197; Israel, 216; James
Jenkinson, 222; Jnr., 23; Joel,
23, 197, 216, 229, 238;
Jonathan, 14, 23, 45, 46, 197,
219; Joseph, 260; Joseph H.,
260; Joseph W., 174, 227; Mary,
23; Moses, 197; Phebe, 197,
260; Rachel, 197, 217; Rebecca,
23; Susanna, 23; Susannah B.,
46

## Y

YARNALL: Ellis, 200; Mordecai,
201, 203; Susan, 183, 211, 271;
Susanna, 210, 241
YARNELL: Elizabeth, 28
YATES: Jane, 185
YELLOTT: Eliza, 170; Elizabeth,
102
YERKES: David, 211; Eliza W.,
208, 209, 210, 211; Elizabeth,
188, 210, 211
YERKESS: Elizabeth, 184
YET: Nathaniel, 35
YOACH: Hannah, 252; Henry, 252
YOUNG: Amelia, 204; Elizabeth,
239; George, 227, 239, 268;
Jesse C., 73; Joseph, 227, 239,
268; Margaret, 184, 211; Mary,
192; Rachel, 211, 239; Rebecca,
227, 239, 245, 263, 268; Robert,
204, 227, 239, 263, 268; Robert
W., 239; Susanna, 263; William,
204, 227, 239, 268; William S.,
192

## Other books by the author:

*A Closer Look at St. John's Parish Registers [Baltimore County, Maryland], 1701-1801*
*A Collection of Maryland Church Records*
*A Guide to Genealogical Research in Maryland: 5th Edition, Revised and Enlarged*
*Abstracts of the Ledgers and Accounts of the Bush Store and Rock Run Store, 1759-1771*
*Abstracts of the Orphans Court Proceedings of Harford County, 1778-1800*
*Abstracts of Wills, Harford County, Maryland, 1800-1805*
*Baltimore City [Maryland] Deaths and Burials, 1834-1840*
*Baltimore County, Maryland, Overseers of Roads, 1693-1793*
*Bastardy Cases in Baltimore County, Maryland, 1673-1783*
*Bastardy Cases in Harford County, Maryland, 1774-1844*
*Bible and Family Records of Harford County, Maryland Families: Volume V*
*Children of Harford County: Indentures and Guardianships, 1801-1830*
*Colonial Delaware Soldiers and Sailors, 1638-1776*
*Colonial Families of the Eastern Shore of Maryland
Volumes 5, 6, 7, 8, 9, 11, 12, 13, 14, and 16*
*Colonial Maryland Soldiers and Sailors, 1634-1734*
*Dr. John Archer's First Medical Ledger, 1767-1769, Annotated Abstracts*
*Early Anglican Records of Cecil County*
*Early Harford Countians, Individuals Living in Harford County, Maryland in Its Formative Years
Volume 1: A to K, Volume 2: L to Z, and Volume 3: Supplement*
*Harford County Taxpayers in 1870, 1872 and 1883*
*Harford County, Maryland Divorce Cases, 1827-1912: An Annotated Index*
*Heirs and Legatees of Harford County, Maryland, 1774-1802*
*Heirs and Legatees of Harford County, Maryland, 1802-1846*
*Inhabitants of Baltimore County, Maryland, 1763-1774*
*Inhabitants of Cecil County, Maryland, 1649-1774*
*Inhabitants of Harford County, Maryland, 1791-1800*
*Inhabitants of Kent County, Maryland, 1637-1787*
*Joseph A. Pennington & Co., Havre De Grace, Maryland Funeral Home Records:
Volume II, 1877-1882, 1893-1900*
*Maryland Bible Records, Volume 1: Baltimore and Harford Counties*
*Maryland Bible Records, Volume 2: Baltimore and Harford Counties*
*Maryland Bible Records, Volume 3: Carroll County*
*Maryland Bible Records, Volume 4: Eastern Shore*
*Maryland Deponents, 1634-1799*
*Maryland Deponents: Volume 3, 1634-1776*
*Maryland Public Service Records, 1775-1783: A Compendium of Men and Women of
Maryland Who Rendered Aid in Support of the American Cause against
Great Britain during the Revolutionary War*
*Marylanders to Carolina: Migration of Marylanders to
North Carolina and South Carolina prior to 1800*

*Marylanders to Kentucky, 1775-1825*

*Methodist Records of Baltimore City, Maryland: Volume 1, 1799-1829*

*Methodist Records of Baltimore City, Maryland: Volume 2, 1830-1839*

*Methodist Records of Baltimore City, Maryland: Volume 3, 1840-1850 (East City Station)*

*More Maryland Deponents, 1716-1799*

*More Marylanders to Carolina: Migration of Marylanders to North Carolina and South Carolina prior to 1800*

*More Marylanders to Kentucky, 1778-1828*

*Outpensioners of Harford County, Maryland, 1856-1896*

*Presbyterian Records of Baltimore City, Maryland, 1765-1840*

*Quaker Records of Baltimore and Harford Counties, Maryland, 1801-1825*

*Quaker Records of Northern Maryland, 1716-1800*

*Quaker Records of Southern Maryland, 1658-1800*

*Revolutionary Patriots of Anne Arundel County, Maryland*

*Revolutionary Patriots of Baltimore Town and Baltimore County, 1775-1783*

*Revolutionary Patriots of Calvert and St. Mary's Counties, Maryland, 1775-1783*

*Revolutionary Patriots of Caroline County, Maryland, 1775-1783*

*Revolutionary Patriots of Cecil County, Maryland*

*Revolutionary Patriots of Charles County, Maryland, 1775-1783*

*Revolutionary Patriots of Delaware, 1775-1783*

*Revolutionary Patriots of Dorchester County, Maryland, 1775-1783*

*Revolutionary Patriots of Frederick County, Maryland, 1775-1783*

*Revolutionary Patriots of Harford County, Maryland, 1775-1783*

*Revolutionary Patriots of Kent and Queen Anne's Counties*

*Revolutionary Patriots of Lancaster County, Pennsylvania*

*Revolutionary Patriots of Maryland, 1775-1783: A Supplement*

*Revolutionary Patriots of Maryland, 1775-1783: Second Supplement*

*Revolutionary Patriots of Montgomery County, Maryland, 1776-1783*

*Revolutionary Patriots of Prince George's County, Maryland, 1775-1783*

*Revolutionary Patriots of Talbot County, Maryland, 1775-1783*

*Revolutionary Patriots of Worcester and Somerset Counties, Maryland, 1775-1783*

*Revolutionary Patriots of Washington County, Maryland, 1776-1783*

*St. George's (Old Spesutia) Parish, Harford County, Maryland: Church and Cemetery Records, 1820-1920*

*St. John's and St. George's Parish Registers, 1696-1851*

*Survey Field Book of David and William Clark in Harford County, Maryland, 1770-1812*

*The Crenshaws of Kentucky, 1800-1995*

*The Delaware Militia in the War of 1812*

*Union Chapel United Methodist Church Cemetery Tombstone Inscriptions, Wilna, Harford County, Maryland*

www.ingramcontent.com/pod-product-compliance
Lightning Source LLC
Chambersburg PA
CBHW051036160426
43193CB00010B/960